Microsoft®
SQL Server 2012

Pocket Consultant

William R. Stanek
Author and Series Editor

PUBLISHED BY
Microsoft Press
A Division of Microsoft Corporation
One Microsoft Way
Redmond, Washington 98052-6399

Library of Congress Control Number: 2011944612
ISBN: 978-0-7356-6376-3

Printed and bound in the United States of America.

First Printing

Microsoft Press books are available through booksellers and distributors worldwide. If you need support related to this book, email Microsoft Press Book Support at mspinput@ microsoft.com. Please tell us what you think of this book at http://www.microsoft.com/ learning/booksurvey.

Microsoft and the trademarks listed at http://www.microsoft.com/about/legal/en/us/ IntellectualProperty/Trademarks/EN-US.aspx are trademarks of the Microsoft group of companies. All other marks are property of their respective owners.

The example companies, organizations, products, domain names, email addresses, logos, people, places, and events depicted herein are fictitious. No association with any real company, organization, product, domain name, email address, logo, person, place, or event is intended or should be inferred.

This book expresses the author's views and opinions. The information contained in this book is provided without any express, statutory, or implied warranties. Neither the authors, Microsoft Corporation, nor its resellers, or distributors will be held liable for any damages caused or alleged to be caused either directly or indirectly by this book.

Acquisitions Editor: Anne Hamiliton
Developmental Editor: Karen Szall
Project Editor: Karen Szall
Editorial Production: Christian Holdener, S4Carlisle Publishing Services
Technical Reviewer: boB Taylor
Copyeditor: Susan McClung
Indexer: Jean Skipp
Cover: Twist Creative · Seattle

To my wife—for many years, through many books, many millions of words, and many thousands of pages, she's been there, providing support and encouragement and making every place we've lived a home.

To my kids—for helping me see the world in new ways, for having exceptional patience and boundless love, and for making every day an adventure.

To Karen, Martin, Lucinda, Juliana, Ben, and many others who've helped out in ways both large and small.
—WILLIAM R. STANEK

Contents at a Glance

Contents

What do you think of this book? We want to hear from you!

Microsoft is interested in hearing your feedback so we can continually improve our
books and learning resources for you. To participate in a brief online survey, please visit:

microsoft.com/learning/booksurvey

PART III   MICROSOFT SQL SERVER 2012 DATA MANAGEMENT

PART IV   MICROSOFT SQL SERVER 2012 OPTIMIZATION, MAINTENANCE, AND RECOVERY

What do you think of this book? We want to hear from you!

Microsoft is interested in hearing your feedback so we can continually improve our
books and learning resources for you. To participate in a brief online survey, please visit:

microsoft.com/learning/booksurvey

Introduction

*M*icrosoft SQL Server 2012 Pocket Consultant is designed to be a concise and compulsively usable resource for Microsoft SQL Server 2012 administrators. It covers everything you need to know to perform the core administrative tasks for SQL Server and is the readable resource guide that you'll want on your desk at all times. Because the focus is on giving you maximum value in a pocket-sized guide, you don't have to wade through hundreds of pages of extraneous information to find what you're looking for. Instead, you'll find exactly what you need to get the job done.

This book is designed to be the one resource you turn to whenever you have questions about SQL Server administration. To this end, the book zeroes in on daily administration procedures, frequently used tasks, documented examples, and options that are representative while not necessarily inclusive. One of the key goals is to keep content concise enough that the book is compact and easy to navigate, while also ensuring that the book contains as much information as possible. Instead of a 1,000-page tome or a 100-page quick reference, you get a valuable resource guide that can help you quickly and easily perform common tasks, solve problems, and implement advanced SQL Server technologies such as replication, distributed queries, and multiserver administration.

Who Is This Book For?

Microsoft SQL Server 2012 Pocket Consultant covers the Standard, Business Intelligence, Enterprise, and Developer editions of SQL Server. The book is designed to be used in the daily administration of SQL Server and is written for:

- Current SQL Server database administrators
- Accomplished users who have some administrator responsibilities
- Administrators migrating to SQL Server 2012 from previous versions
- Administrators transitioning from other database architectures

To include as much information as possible, I had to assume that you have basic networking skills and a basic understanding of SQL Server. With this in mind, I don't devote entire chapters to understanding SQL Server architecture or running simple SQL queries. But I do cover SQL Server installation, configuration, enterprise-wide server management, performance tuning, optimization, maintenance, and much more.

I also assume that you're fairly familiar with SQL commands and stored procedures as well as the standard Windows user interface. If you need help learning SQL basics, you should read other resources (many of which are available from Microsoft Press).

How Is This Book Organized?

Speed and ease of reference are essential parts of this hands-on guide. The book has an expanded table of contents and an extensive index for finding answers to problems quickly. Many other quick reference features have been added to the book as well. These features include quick step-by-step procedures, lists, tables with fast facts, and cross-references.

The content is presented in four parts:

- Part I, "Microsoft SQL Server 2012 Essentials," discusses how to manage your SQL Server and SQL Server Services and clients.
- Part II, "Microsoft SQL Server 2012 Management and Security," dives into the details of implementing and configuring your SQL Server environment.
- Part III, "Microsoft SQL Server 2012 Data Management," focuses on data and the everyday tasks and best practices for managing your data.
- Part IV, "Microsoft SQL Server 2012 Optimization, Maintenance, and Recovery," addresses some of the more advanced topics that all administrators need to know.

What Is SQL Server 2012?

By functioning as a mission-critical data platform, allowing dynamic development, providing extensive business intelligence, and going beyond relational data, SQL Server 2012 provides the bedrock foundation on which small, medium, and large organizations can build their IT infrastructure. At the core of SQL Server 2012, you'll find the following:

- **Database Engine Services** Includes the core database, notification, and replication components. The core database—also known as the Database Engine—is the heart of SQL Server. Replication increases data availability by distributing data across multiple databases, allowing you to scale out the read workload across designated database servers.
- **Analysis Services** Delivers online analytical processing (OLAP) and data-mining functionality for business intelligence applications. Analysis Services enables your organization to aggregate data from multiple data sources, such as relational databases, and work with this data in a wide variety of ways.
- **Integration Services** Provides an enterprise data transformation and integration solution for extracting and transforming data from multiple data sources and moving it to one or more destination data sources. This functionality allows you to merge data from heterogeneous data sources, load data into data warehouses and data marts, and more.
- **Reporting Services** Includes Report Manager and Report Server, which provide a complete server-based platform for creating, managing, and distributing reports. Report Server is built on standard Microsoft Internet Information Services (IIS) and Microsoft .NET Framework technology, allowing you to combine the benefits of SQL Server and IIS to host and process reports.

- **Service Broker**   Provides reliable queuing and messaging as a central part of the database. Queues can be used to stack work such as queries and other requests and perform the work as resources allow. Messaging allows database applications to communicate with each other. The Database Engine uses Service Broker to deliver notification messages.

- **Master Data Services**   Provides a framework for creating business rules that ensure the quality and accuracy of your master data. Business rules can be used to start business processes that correct validation issues and handle workflows.

- **Data Quality Services**   Provides a framework for creating a knowledge base repository of metadata that helps to improve the quality of your organization's data. Data cleansing processes can modify or remove data that is incomplete or incorrect. Data matching processes can identify and merge duplicates as appropriate.

System Requirements

Successful database server administration depends on three things: knowledgeable database administrators, strong database architecture, and appropriate hardware. The first two ingredients are covered: you're the administrator, you're smart enough to buy this book to help you through the rough spots, and you've implemented SQL Server 2012 to provide your high-performance database needs. This brings us to the issue of hardware. You should run SQL Server 2012 on a system with adequate memory, processing speed, and disk space. You also need an appropriate data and system protection plan at the hardware level.

Key guidelines for choosing hardware for SQL Server are as follows:

- **Memory**   All editions of SQL Server 2012 except for Express require a minimum of 1 gigabyte (GB) of RAM. In most cases, you want to have at least 4 GB of RAM as a minimum starting point, even for development. The primary reason for having extra memory is performance. Additional database features—such as Analysis Services, Reporting Services, and Integration Services—increase the memory requirements. Also consider the number of user connections. Each user connection consumes about 24 KB. Data requests and other SQL Server processes use memory as well, and this memory usage is in addition to all other processes and applications running on the server.

- **Processor**   The 64-bit versions run on the x64 family of processors from AMD and Intel, including AMD64 and Intel Extended Memory 64 Technology (Intel EM64T). Multicore Intel Xeon and AMD Opteron processors are recommended starting points. SQL Server 2012 supports symmetric multiprocessors and can process complex parallel queries. Parallel queries are valuable only when relatively few users are on a system and the system is processing large queries. On a dedicated system that runs only SQL Server and supports fewer than 100 simultaneous users who aren't running complex queries, a single multicore processor should suffice (although you should always test with a representative workload). If the server supports more than 100 users or doesn't run on a dedicated system, you might consider adding processors (or using a system that can support additional processors as your needs grow). Keep in mind that the size of the queries and data sets being processed affects how well SQL Server scales. As the size of jobs being processed increases, you have increased memory and processor needs.

- **Disk drives**   The amount of data storage capacity you need depends entirely on the number and size of the databases that the server supports. You need enough disk space to store all your data plus work space, indices, system files, virtual memory, and transaction logs. For log shipping and mirroring, you need space for the backup share and, in the case of a cluster, the quorum disk. I/O throughput is just as important as drive capacity. For the best I/O performance, Fibre Channel (FC) or Fibre Channel over Ethernet (FCoE) is the recommended choice for high-end storage solutions. Strongly consider solid state drives (SSDs) over spinning disks. Instead of using a single large drive, you should use several smaller drives, which allows you to configure fault tolerance with RAID. I recommend separating data and logs and placing them on separate spindles. This includes the backup share for log shipping and the quorum disk for clustering.

- **Data protection**   You should add protection against unexpected drive failure by using RAID. For data, consider RAID 0 + 1 or RAID 5 as a starting point. For logs, consider RAID 1 as a starting point. RAID 0 (disk striping without parity) offers good read/write performance, but the effect of any failed drive is that SQL Server can't continue operation on an affected database until the drive is replaced and data is restored from backup. RAID 1 (disk mirroring) creates duplicate copies of data on separate drives, and you can rebuild the RAID unit to restore full operations. RAID 5 (disk striping with parity) offers good protection against single drive failure but has poor write performance. For best performance and fault tolerance, RAID 0 + 1 is recommended. This configuration consists of disk mirroring and disk striping without parity.

- **Uninterruptible power supply (UPS)**   SQL Server is designed to maintain database integrity at all times and can recover information by using transaction logs. However, this does not protect the server hardware from sudden power loss or power spikes. Both of these events can seriously damage hardware. To prevent this, get a UPS that conditions the power. A UPS system gives you time to shut down the system properly in the event of a power outage, and it is also important in maintaining database integrity when the server uses write-back caching controllers.

If you follow these hardware guidelines, you will be well on your way to success with SQL Server 2012.

Conventions Used in This Book

I've used a variety of elements to help keep the text clear and easy to follow. You'll find code terms and listings in monospace type, except when I tell you to actually type a command. In that case, the command appears in **bold** type. When I introduce and define a new term, I put it in *italics*.

Other conventions include the following:

- **Best Practices** To examine the best technique to use when working with advanced configuration and administration concepts
- **Caution** To warn you about potential problems you should look out for
- **More Info** To provide more information on a subject
- **Note** To provide additional details on a particular point that needs emphasis
- **Real World** To provide real-world advice when discussing advanced topics
- **Security Alert** To point out important security issues
- **Tip** To offer helpful hints or additional information

I truly hope you find that *Microsoft SQL Server 2012 Pocket Consultant* provides everything you need to perform the essential administrative tasks for SQL Server as quickly and efficiently as possible. You are welcome to send your thoughts to me at *williamstanek@aol.com* or follow me at *www.twitter.com/WilliamStanek*. Thank you.

Other Resources

No single magic bullet for learning everything you'll ever need to know about SQL Server 2012 exists. While some books are offered as all-in-one guides, there's simply no way one book can do it all. With this in mind, I hope you use this book as it is intended to be used—as a concise and easy-to-use resource. It covers everything you need to perform core administration tasks for SQL Server, but it is by no means exhaustive.

Your current knowledge will largely determine your success with this or any other SQL Server resource or book. As you encounter new topics, take the time to practice what you've learned and read about. Seek out further information as necessary to get the practical hands-on know-how and knowledge you need.

I recommend that you regularly visit the SQL Server site (*www.microsoft.com/sqlserver/*) and Microsoft's support site (*www.support.microsoft.com*) to stay current with the latest changes. To help you get the most out of this book, you can visit my corresponding website at *www.williamstanek.com/sqlserver*. This site contains information about SQL Server 2012 and updates to the book.

Support and Feedback

This section provides useful information about accessing any errata for this title, reporting errors and finding support, as well as providing feedback and contacting Microsoft Press.

Errata

We've made every effort to ensure the accuracy of this book and its companion content. Any errors that have been reported since this book was published are listed on our Microsoft Press site at oreilly.com:

http://go.microsoft.com/fwlink/?LinkId=235906

If you find an error that is not already listed, you can report it to us through the same page.

If you need additional support, email Microsoft Press Book Support at *mspinput@microsoft.com*.

Please note that product support for Microsoft software is not offered through the addresses above.

We Want to Hear from You

At Microsoft Press, your satisfaction is our top priority, and your feedback our most valuable asset. Please tell us what you think of this book at:

http://www.microsoft.com/learning/booksurvey

The survey is short, and we read *every one* of your comments and ideas. Thanks in advance for your input!

Stay in Touch

Let us keep the conversation going! We are on Twitter:
http://twitter.com/MicrosoftPress

Microsoft SQL Server 2012 Essentials

Managing Your SQL Servers

M icrosoft SQL Server Management Studio is the primary tool you use to manage databases and servers. Other tools available to manage local and remote servers include SQL Server PowerShell, SQL Server Configuration Manager, Database Engine Tuning Advisor, and SQL Server Profiler. You use SQL Server Configuration Manager to manage SQL Server services, networking, and client configurations. Database Engine Tuning Advisor is available to help optimize indexes, indexed views, and partitions, and SQL Server Profiler lets you examine events generated by SQL Server, which can provide helpful details for troubleshooting. In this chapter, you will learn how to use SQL Server Management Studio. SQL Server Configuration Manager is discussed in Chapter 2, "Managing SQL Server Services and Clients." For details on tuning and tracing, see Chapter 12, "SQL Server 2012 Profiling and Monitoring."

Whenever you're working with databases and servers, keep in mind these concepts to help ensure your success:

- **Contained databases**   These databases are fully or partially isolated databases that have no configuration dependencies on the instance of the SQL Server Database Engine where they are installed. A fully contained database does not allow any objects or functions that cross the boundary between the application model and the Database Engine instance. A partially contained database allows objects or functions that cross the boundary between the application model and the Database Engine instance. Contained database users with passwords are authenticated by the database. Authorized Microsoft Windows users and group members can connect directly to the database and do not need logins in the master database.

- **FileTable** Table structures act as virtual shares by storing FILESTREAM data and directory data as rows within tables. Even though the Database Engine manages the data at all times, a FileTable appears as a Windows share for non-transactional file access, allowing you to use MOVE, XCOPY, and other standard commands to load files when you are working with the command line or a batch script. The root of the hierarchy is established when you create the FileTable. A FileTable cannot be replicated or selected into like other tables.

- **Indirect checkpoints** Checkpoints are triggered based on the targeted recovery time you specify for a database, as opposed to automatic checkpoints, which are based on the maximum number of log records that can be processed in a particular recovery interval. A database that has a targeted recovery time does not use automatic checkpoints. Although indirect check-points can reduce read/write spikes by continually writing in the background, this continuous writing increases the total write load for the server instance, which may degrade performance for online transactional workloads.

You also should be aware of changes to the way the Database Engine works. While there are many discontinued and deprecated features, remember these important changes:

- Databases must be set to at least compatibility level 90. Level 90 is for Microsoft SQL Server 2005. Any earlier database is updated automatically when you install Microsoft SQL Server 2012.

- Indexes containing *varchar(max), nvarchar(max),* and *varbinary(max)* columns can now be rebuilt as an online operation.

- Re-create triggers that have WITH APPEND clauses, as these are no longer supported. Do the same for COMPUTE and COMPUTE BY, which must be rewritten by using the ROLLUP clause.

- Replace remote servers by using linked servers, and replace aliases with user accounts and database roles as appropriate.

- Replace the usage of SQL Mail with Database Mail and use ALTER DATABASE instead of sp_dboption.

- Use two-part table names following the syntax *schema.object* with ALTER TABLE, rather than four-part names, such as *server.database.schema.table.*

Using SQL Server Management Studio

The SQL Server Management Studio graphical point-and-click interface makes server, database, and resource management easy to perform. Using SQL Server Management Studio, you can manage local and remote server instances by establishing a connection to a SQL Server instance and then administering its resources. If you have disabled remote server connections to a particular server, you can work only with the server locally (by logging in to the system at the keyboard or by establishing a remote Terminal Server session in Windows and then running the local management tools).

Getting Started with SQL Server Management Studio

When you start working with SQL Server Management Studio, you see the Object Explorer view, shown in Figure 1-1. If this view is not displayed, you can access it (and other views) from the View menu. The following descriptions explain how to use each view:

- **Object Explorer** Allows you to view and connect to instances of SQL Server, Analysis Services, Integration Services, and Reporting Services. Once you have connected to a particular server, you can view its components as an object tree and expand nodes to work your way to lower levels of the tree.

- **Registered Servers** Shows the currently registered servers. Use Registered Servers to preserve login information for servers that you access frequently. The top bar of the view allows you to switch quickly between servers of a particular type (SQL Server, Analysis Server, Integration Server, or Report Server).

- **Template Explorer** Provides quick access to the default Query Editor templates, organized by action, and any custom templates you create. You can create templates in any script language supported by SQL Server Management Studio, SQL Server, and Analysis Server.

- **Solution Explorer** Provides quick access to existing SQL Server and Analysis Server projects. A project details the connections, queries, and other functions that are performed when the project is executed.

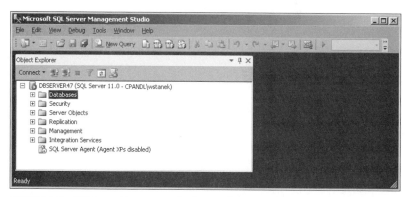

FIGURE 1-1 Use SQL Server Management Studio to perform core administration tasks.

To run SQL Server Management Studio, click Start, type **ssms.exe** in the Search box, and then press Enter. Alternatively, select the related option on the Microsoft SQL Server 2012 menu. Next, you must connect to the server you want to work with. There are several ways to do this:

- Connect using a standard login to a server instance.
- Connect using a login to a specific database.
- Connect using server groups and registered servers.

Connecting to a server instance allows you to work with that particular server and its related components. (See Figure 1-2.) Typically, you want to connect to a server's Database Engine. The Database Engine gives you access to the following components and features:

- **Databases** Manage system databases, including the *master* and *model* databases, as well as user databases and database snapshots. If you've installed Reporting Services, you also can access the *ReportServer* and *Report ServerTempDB* databases under this node.
- **Security** Manage SQL Server logins, server roles, stored credentials, cryptographic providers, and auditing.
- **Server objects** Configure backup devices, HTTP endpoints, linked servers, and server triggers.
- **Replication** Configure distribution databases, update replication passwords, and launch Replication Monitor.
- **Management** View SQL Server logs, create, view, and manage maintenance plans, Microsoft Distributed Transaction Coordinator (MSDTC), and Database Mail. Configure data collection, Resource Governor, and Policy-Based Management policies.
- **SQL Server Agent** Configure SQL Server Agent jobs, alerts, operators, proxies, and error logs.

You store server and login information by using the Registered Servers feature. Registered servers can be organized using server groups and then can be accessed quickly in the Registered Servers view. Methods to manage server groups and register servers are discussed in the "Managing SQL Server Groups" and "Managing Servers" sections later in this chapter.

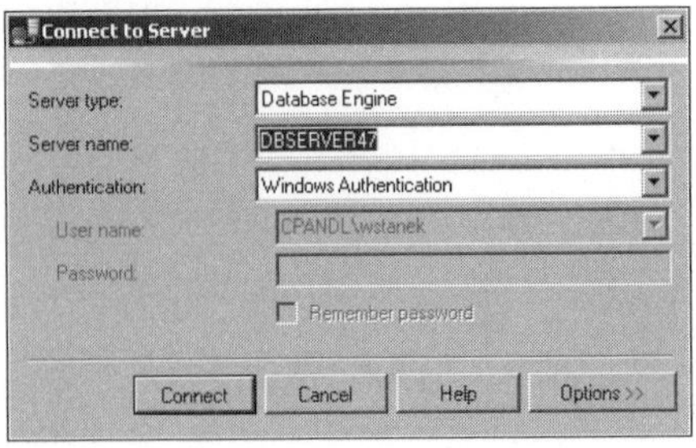

FIGURE 1-2 Use the Database Engine to access core SQL Server components and features.

Connecting to a Specific Server Instance

To connect to a specific server instance by using a standard login, follow these steps:

1. Start SQL Server Management Studio. In the Connect To Server dialog box, use the Server Type list to select the database component you want to connect to, such as Database Engine. (If you exited the Connect To Server dialog box, you can display the Connect To Server dialog box by clicking File, Connect Object Explorer in SQL Server Management Studio.)

2. In the Server Name box, type the fully qualified domain name (FQDN) or host name of the server on which SQL Server is running, such as EngDBSrv12.cpandl.com or EngDBSrv12, or select Browse For More in the related drop-down list. In the Browse For Servers dialog box, select the Local Servers or Network Servers tab as appropriate. After the instance data has been retrieved, expand the nodes provided, select the server instance, and then click OK.

   TIP The list in the Browse For Servers dialog box is populated by the SQL Server Browser service running on the database servers. There are several reasons that a SQL Server instance you want to work with might not be listed. The SQL Server Browser service might not be running on the computer running SQL Server. A firewall might be blocking User Datagram Protocol (UDP) port 1434, which is required for browsing. Or the HideInstance flag might be set on the SQL Server instance.

3. Use the Authentication list to choose the option for authentication type, which is either Windows Authentication or SQL Server Authentication (based on the authentication types selected when you installed the server). Provide a SQL Server login ID and password as necessary.

   - **Windows Authentication** Uses your current domain account and password to establish the database connection. This authentication type works only if Windows authentication is enabled and you have appropriate privileges.

   - **SQL Server Authentication** Allows you to specify a SQL Server login ID and password. To save the password so that you do not have to reenter it each time you connect, select Remember Password.

4. Click Connect. Now you can use the Object Explorer view to work with this server.

Connecting to a Specific Database

To connect to a specific database by using a standard login, follow these steps:

1. Start SQL Server Management Studio. In the Connect To Server dialog box, use the Server Type list to select the database component you want to connect to, such as Database Engine, and then, in the Server Name box, type the FQDN or host name of the server on which SQL Server is running,

such as EngDBSrv12.cpandl.com or EngDBSrv12. (If you exited the Connect To Server dialog box, you can display the Connect To Server dialog box by clicking File, Connect Object Explorer in SQL Server Management Studio.)

2. Use the Authentication list to choose the option for authentication type, which is either Windows Authentication or SQL Server Authentication (based on the authentication types selected when you installed the server). Provide a SQL Server login ID and password as necessary.

3. Click Options to display the advanced view of the Connect To Server dialog box. Select the Connection Properties tab, shown in Figure 1-3.

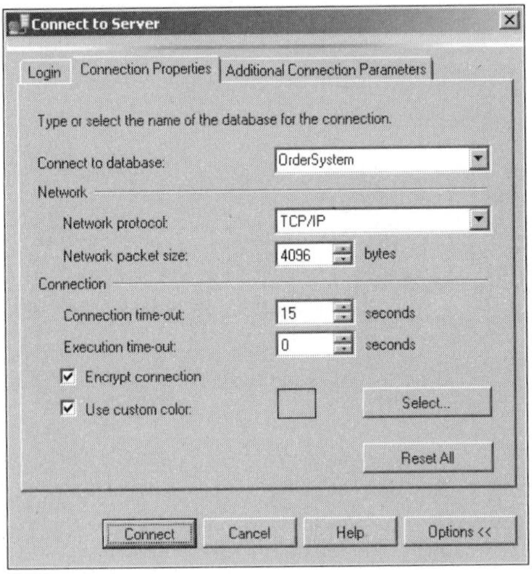

FIGURE 1-3 Connect to a specific database.

4. In the Connect To Database box, type the name of the database you want to connect to, such as Personnel, or select Browse Server in the related drop-down list. When prompted, click Yes to establish a connection to the previously designated server. In the Browse Server For Database dialog box, select the database you want to use, and then click OK.

5. Using the Network Protocol list, select the network protocol and any other connection properties if you are prompted to do so. Shared Memory is the default network protocol for local connections. TCP/IP is the default for remote connections. If you want, establish a secure connection by selecting the Encrypt Connection check box.

6. Click Connect. You are now able to work with the specified database in the Object Explorer view.

Managing SQL Server Groups

You use SQL Server groups to organize sets of computers running SQL Server. You define these server groups, and you can organize them by function, department, or any other criteria. Creating a server group is easy. You can even create subgroups within a group, and if you make a mistake, you can delete a group as well.

> **MORE INFO** Centrally managed servers also can be organized into server groups. For more information, see the "Configuring Central Management Servers" section in Chapter 3, "Implementing Policy-Based Management."

Introducing SQL Server Groups and the Registered Servers View

In SQL Server Management Studio, you use the Registered Servers view to work with server groups. To use this view, or to display it if it is hidden, press Ctrl+Alt+G.

The top-level groups are already created for you, based on the SQL Server instances. Use the Registered Servers toolbar to switch between the various top-level groups. These groups are organized by SQL Server instance as follows:

- Database Engine
- Analysis Services
- Reporting Services
- SQL Server Compact Edition
- Integration Services

Although you can add registered servers directly to the top-level groups (as explained in the "Managing Servers" section later in this chapter), in a large enterprise with many SQL Server instances, you probably want to create additional levels in the server group hierarchy. These additional levels make it easier to access and work with your servers. You can use the following types of organizational models:

- **Division or business unit model** In this model, group names reflect the divisions or business units to which the computers running SQL Server belong or in which they are located. For example, you could have server groups such as Engineering, IS, Operations, and Support.

- **Geographic location model** In this model, group names reflect the geographic location of your servers, such as North America and Europe. You could have additional levels under North America for USA, Canada, and Mexico, for example, and levels under Europe could include UK, Germany, and Spain.

Figure 1-4 shows an example of using server groups. As the figure shows, subgroups are organized under their primary group. Under Database Engine, you might have Corporate Customers, Engineering, and Enterprise Data groups. Within Engineering, you might have Dev, Test, and Core subgroups.

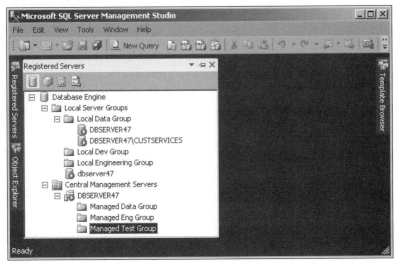

FIGURE 1-4 Use server groups to organize SQL Server deployments.

Creating a Server Group

You can create a server group or a subgroup by completing the following steps:

1. In SQL Server Management Studio, display the Registered Servers view by pressing Ctrl+Alt+G. If the view was previously hidden, this step also displays the view.

2. Use the Registered Servers toolbar to select the top-level group. For example, if you want to create a second-level or third-level group for Database Engine instances, select Database Engine.

3. As necessary, expand the top-level group node and the Local Server Groups nodes by double-clicking each in turn. You will see the names of the top-level server group and any second-level server groups that you created. You can now do the following:

   - Add a server group to one of the top-level or second-level groups by right-clicking the group name and choosing New Server Group.

   - Add a server group to a lower-level group by expanding the server group entries until the group you want to use is displayed. Right-click the group name, and then choose New Server Group.

4. In the New Server Group Properties dialog box, shown in Figure 1-5, type a name and description for the new group in the boxes provided. Click OK.

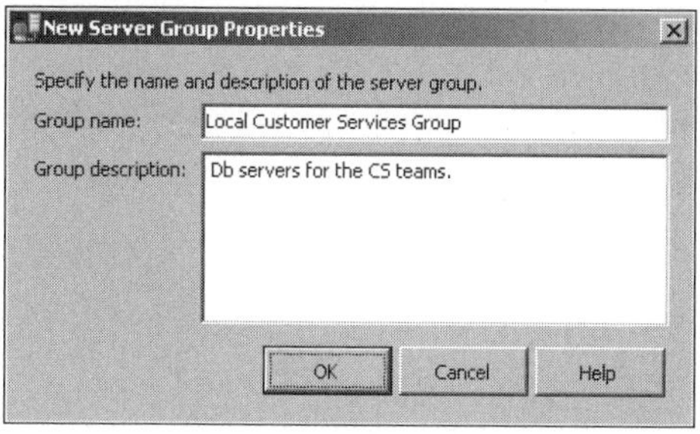

FIGURE 1-5 Enter a name and description in the New Server Group Properties dialog box.

Deleting a Server Group

You can delete a group or subgroup by completing the following steps:

1. In SQL Server Management Studio, display the Registered Servers view by pressing Ctrl+Alt+G. If the view was previously hidden, this step also displays the view.

2. Use the Registered Servers toolbar to select the top-level group in which the group you want to delete is located. For example, if you want to delete a second- or third-level group for Database Engine instances, select Database Engine.

3. Click the plus sign (+) next to the group or subgroup you want to delete. If the group has servers registered in it, move them to a different group. (The steps involved in moving servers to a new group are explained in the "Moving a Server to a New Group" section later in this chapter.)

4. Select the group or subgroup entry.

5. Press Delete. When prompted to confirm the action, click Yes.

Editing and Moving Server Groups

Server groups have several key properties that you can edit: the name, the description, and the location in the Registered Server hierarchy. To edit a group's name or description, follow these steps:

1. Right-click the group in the Registered Servers view, and then select Properties.

2. In the Edit Server Group Properties dialog box, enter the new group name and description. Click OK.

To move a group (and all its associated subgroups and servers) to a new level in the server group hierarchy, follow these steps:

1. Right-click the group in the Registered Servers view, point to Tasks, and then select Move To.

2. In the Move Server Registration dialog box, you can now do the following:
   - Move the group to the top-level group by selecting the top-level group. This makes the group a second-level group.
   - Move the group to a different level by selecting a subgroup into which you want to place the group.
3. Click OK.

Adding SQL Servers to a Group

When you register a computer running SQL Server for use with SQL Server Management Studio, you can choose the group in which you want to place the server. You can even create a new group specifically for the server. The next section covers the topic of server registration.

Managing Servers

Servers and databases are the primary resources you manage in SQL Server Management Studio. When you select a top-level group in the Registered Servers view, you can see the available server groups. If you expand the view of these groups by double-clicking the group name, you can see the subgroups or servers assigned to a particular group. Local servers are registered automatically (in most cases). If a local server is not shown, you need to update the local registration information. If the remote server you want to manage is not shown, you need to register it.

Registration saves the current connection information and assigns the server to a group for easy future access using the Registered Servers view. After you register a server, you can connect to the server to work with it and then disconnect when you have finished simply by double-clicking the server entry in the Registered Servers view. If you are not automatically connected, you can force a connection by right-clicking the server entry and then selecting New Query (if you want to create an SQL query) or Object Explorer (if you want to view and manage the server).

You can start the registration process by using either of the following techniques:

- Register a server to which you are connected in Object Explorer.
- Register a new server in the Registered Servers view.

You can manage previous registrations in a variety of ways:

- Import registration information on previously registered SQL Server 2000 servers.
- Update registration information for local servers.
- Copy registration information from one computer to another by importing and exporting the information.

Registering a Connected Server

Any server to which you have connected in Object Explorer can be registered easily. Registration saves the current connection information and assigns the server to a group for easy future access using the Registered Servers view. To register a connected server, follow these steps:

1. In Object Explorer view, right-click any server to which you are currently connected, and then choose Register to display the New Server Registration dialog box, shown in Figure 1-6.

2. On the General tab, the current values for the server name and authentication type are filled in for you. Although the Registered Server Name option is set to the same value as the server name, you can modify this name and add a description.

3. On the Connection Properties tab, you can specify the database to which you want to connect and set options for networking and connections. If you want to encrypt the connection, select the Encrypt Connection check box.

4. To test your settings before you save the registration settings, click Test. If the test is unsuccessful, verify the settings and then make changes as necessary. As discussed in Chapter 2, SQL Server doesn't allow remote connections by default, so you must change the configuration settings to allow remote connections.

5. Click Save to save the server registration.

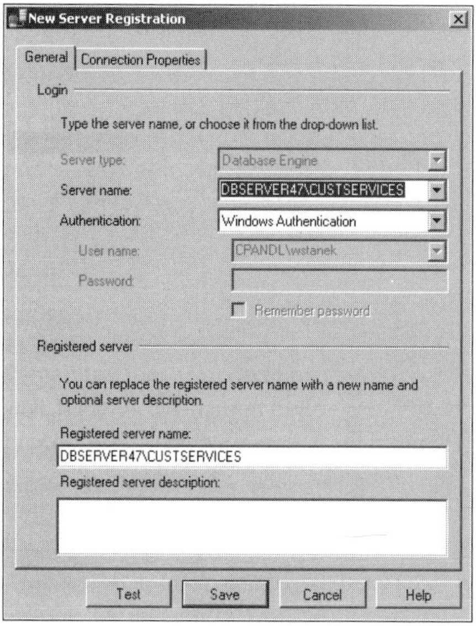

FIGURE 1-6 The New Server Registration dialog box.

By default, the server is added to the top-level group. To move the server to a new level in the server group hierarchy, follow these steps:

1. Right-click the server in the Registered Servers view, point to Tasks, and then select Move To.

2. In the Move Server Registration dialog box, you can move the server to a different level by selecting the subgroup into which you want to place the server.

3. Click OK.

Registering a New Server in the Registered Servers View

You do not have to connect to a server in Object Explorer to register the server. You can register new servers directly in the Registered Servers view by following these steps:

1. In the Registered Servers view, use the toolbar to select the type of server you want to connect to, such as Database Engine.

2. Expand the available groups as necessary. In the Registered Servers view, right-click the group into which you want to register the server, and then select New Server Registration to display the New Server Registration dialog box, shown previously in Figure 1-6.

3. In the Server Name box, type the FQDN or host name of the server on which SQL Server is running, such as EngDBSrv12.cpandl.com or EngDBSrv12.

4. Use the Authentication list to choose the option for authentication type, which is either Windows Authentication or SQL Server Authentication (based on the authentication types selected when you installed the server). Provide a SQL Server login ID and password as necessary.

   - **Windows Authentication** Uses your current domain account and password to establish the database connection. This authentication type works only if Windows authentication is enabled and you have appropriate privileges.

   - **SQL Server Authentication** Allows you to specify a SQL Server login ID and password. To save the password so that you do not have to reenter it each time you connect, select Remember Password.

5. You also can specify connection settings by using the options on the Connection Properties tab. These options allow you to connect to a specific database instance and to set the network configuration. If you want to encrypt the connection, select the Encrypt Connection check box.

6. The registered server name is filled in for you based on the previously entered server name. Change the default name only if you want SQL Server Management Studio to use an alternate display name for the server.

7. To test the settings, click Test. If you successfully connect to the server, you see a prompt confirming this. If the test fails, verify the information you provided, make changes as necessary, and then test the settings again.

8. Click Save.

Registering Previously Registered SQL Server 2000 Servers

Registration details for servers registered by SQL Server 2000 can be imported into SQL Server Management Studio. This makes it easier to work with existing SQL Server 2000 installations. If the SQL Server 2000 installations were previously registered on the computer, you can import the registration details into a specific server group by completing the following steps:

1. In the Registered Servers view, use the toolbar to select the type of server you are registering, such as Database Engine.

2. Right-click the Local Server Groups entry, point to Tasks, and then select Previously Registered Servers.

3. Available registration information for SQL Server 2000 servers will be imported. If an error prompt is displayed, you might not be logged in locally to the computer on which the servers were registered previously.

Updating Registration for Local Servers

Local servers are registered automatically (in most cases). If you have added or removed SQL Server instances on the local computer and those instances are not displayed, you need to update the local server registration. Updating the registration information ensures that all currently configured local server instances are shown in SQL Server Management Studio.

To update registration details for local servers, follow these steps:

1. In the Registered Servers view, use the toolbar to select the type of servers you are registering, such as Database Engine.

2. Right-click the Local Server Groups entry, point to Tasks, and then select Register Local Servers.

Copying Server Groups and Registration Details from One Computer to Another

After you register servers in SQL Server Management Studio and place the servers into a specific group hierarchy, you might find that you want to use the same registration information and server group structure on another computer. SQL Server Management Studio allows you to copy registration information from one computer to another by using an import/export process. You can copy the registration details with or without the user names and passwords.

To export the registration and group information to a file on one computer and then import it onto another computer, complete the following steps:

1. Start SQL Server Management Studio on the computer with the registration and group structure details that you want to copy.

2. Select the Registered Servers view by pressing Ctrl+Alt+G.

3. In the Registered Servers view, use the toolbar to select the type of servers you want to work with, such as Database Engine.

4. Right-click the Local Server Groups entry, point to Tasks, and then select Export to display the Export Registered Servers dialog box, shown in Figure 1-7.

5. Under Server Group, select the point from which the export process will begin. You can start copying registration information at any level in the group structure:

   - To copy the structure for a top-level group, all its subgroups, and all registration details for all related servers, select the Local Server Groups entry.

   - To copy the structure for a subgroup, its subgroups (if any), and all registration details for all related servers, select a subgroup.

   - To copy the registration details for a single server, select the server.

6. The server group structure and registration details are exported to a registration server file with the .regsrvr extension. By default, this file is created in the currently logged in user's Documents folder. Under Export Options, type a name for the registration server file, such as CurrentDBConfig.

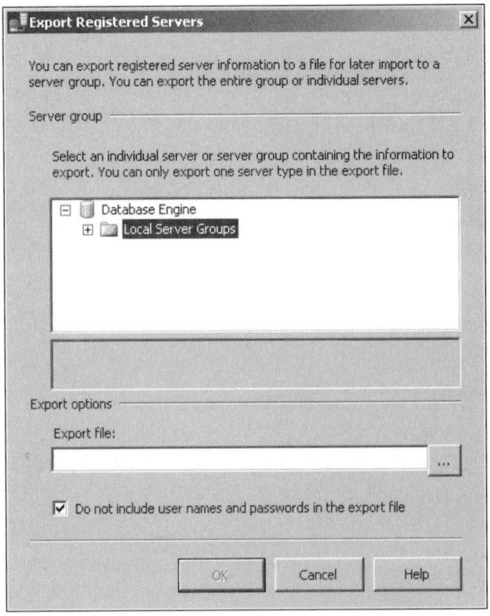

FIGURE 1-7 The Export Registered Servers dialog box.

TIP If you place the registration server file on a secure network share, you can access it on the computer to which you want to copy the registration information. Otherwise, you need to copy this file to the destination computer later.

7. By default, the current authentication details for server connections are not exported into the saved file. If you want to export user names and passwords, clear the Do Not Include User Names And Passwords In The Export File check box.

8. Click OK. If the export is successful, you see a dialog box confirming this. Click OK in the dialog box. If there is a problem, note and correct the problem.

9. Start SQL Server Management Studio on the computer to which you want to copy the server group and registration details. If you did not place the registration server file on a secure network share, you need to copy the file to this computer now.

10. Select the Registered Servers view by pressing Ctrl+Alt+G.

11. In the Registered Servers view, use the toolbar to select the type of server you want to work with, such as Database Engine.

12. Right-click the Local Server Groups entry, point to Tasks, and then select Import to display the Import Registered Servers dialog box, shown in Figure 1-8.

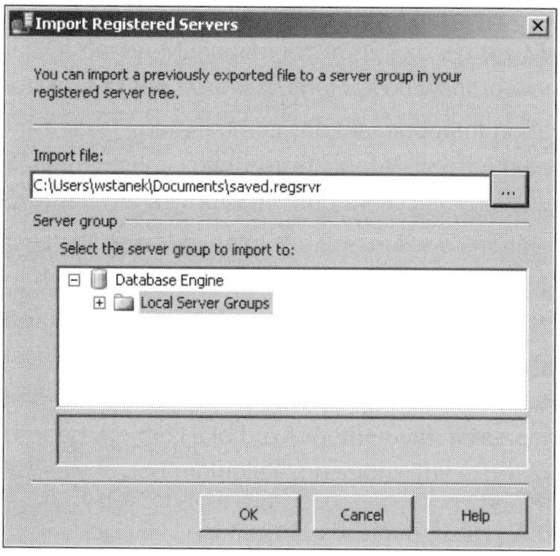

FIGURE 1-8 The Import Registered Servers dialog box.

13. In the dialog box, click the button to the right of the Import File text box, and then use the Open dialog box that appears to select the registration server file you want to import.

14. Under Server Group, select the server group under which you want the imported groups and servers to be created.

15. Click OK. If the import is successful, you see a dialog box confirming this. Click OK in the dialog box. If there is a problem, note and correct it.

Editing Registration Properties

You can change a server's registration properties at any time by right-clicking the server entry in the Registered Servers view in SQL Server Management Studio and then selecting Properties. Use the Edit Server Registration Properties dialog box to make changes. The only property you cannot change is the server type. Be sure to test the settings before saving them.

Connecting to a Server

After you register a server, connecting to it is easy. Right-click the server entry in the Registered Servers view in SQL Server Management Studio, and then select New Query (if you want to create an SQL query) or Object Explorer (if you want to view and manage the server). You also can double-click the server entry to establish a connection and then work with the server in the Object Explorer view.

> **NOTE** SQL Server Management Studio connects to other servers that are running SQL Server by using the network protocol set in the registration properties. If you have disabled the network protocol or remote access entirely for a server, you won't be able to connect to that server in SQL Server Management Studio. You need to make the appropriate changes in the registration properties or in the surface area configuration. Chapter 2 discusses surface area configuration.

Disconnecting from a Server

When you have finished working with a server, you can disconnect from it. This eliminates the back-and-forth communications to the server. To disconnect, right-click the server's entry in the Object Explorer view in SQL Server Management Studio, and then select Disconnect from the shortcut menu.

Moving a Server to a New Group

To move the server to a new group, complete the following steps:

1. Right-click the server you want to move in the Registered Servers view, point to Tasks, and then select Move To from the shortcut menu to display the Move Server Registration dialog box.

2. In the Move Server Registration dialog box, expand the Local Server Groups entry to see a list of subgroups. Expand the subgroups as necessary. You can now do the following:
   - Move the server to the top-level group by selecting the top-level group. This makes the server a member of the top-level group.
   - Move the server to a different level by selecting the subgroup into which you want to place the server.

3. Click OK.

Deleting a Server Registration

If you change a server name or remove a server, you might want to delete the server registration in SQL Server Management Studio so that SQL Server Management Studio no longer tries to connect to a server that cannot be accessed. Right-click the server entry in the Registered Servers view and then select Delete. When prompted to confirm the action, click Yes to delete the server registration details.

Using Windows PowerShell for SQL Server Management

The graphical management tools provide just about everything you need to work with SQL Server. Still, there are many times when you might want to work from the command line, such as when you are working on a Windows Server 2008 R2 Core installation. To help with all your command-line needs, SQL Server 2012 includes the SQL Server provider for Windows PowerShell (also known as "SQL Server PowerShell"). To work with SQL Server via Windows PowerShell, you must first open a Command Prompt window or Windows PowerShell prompt and then start SQL Server PowerShell by typing **sqlps** at the command line.

Windows PowerShell introduces the concept of a *cmdlet* (pronounced "commandlet"). A cmdlet is the smallest unit of functionality in Windows PowerShell. Cmdlet names are not case-sensitive. SQL Server PowerShell cmdlets include the following:

- **Backup-SQLDatabase**   Performs backup operations on SQL Server databases.

- **Convert-UrnToPath**   Converts a SQL Server Management Object Uniform Resource Name (URN) to a SQL Server provider path. The URN indicates a management object's location within the SQL Server object hierarchy. If the URN path has characters not supported by Windows PowerShell, the characters are encoded automatically.

- **Decode-SQLName**   Returns an unencoded SQL Server identifier when given an identifier that has been encoded.

- **Encode-SQLName**   Encodes special characters in SQL Server identifiers and name paths to formats that are usable in Windows PowerShell paths. The characters encoded by this cmdlet include \:/%<>*?[]|. If you don't encode these characters, you must escape them by using the single quotation mark (') character.

- **Invoke-PolicyEvaluation**   Evaluates management policies applied to SQL Server instances. By default, this cmdlet reports compliance but does not enforce compliance. To enforce compliance, set –AdHocPolicyEvaluationMode to Configure.

- **Invoke-Sqlcmd**   Runs a Transact-SQL (T-SQL) or XQuery script containing commands supported by the SQLCMD utility. By default, this cmdlet doesn't set any SQLCMD variables or return message output; only a subset of SQLCMD commands can be used.

- **Restore-SQLDatabase**   Performs restore operations on SQL Server databases.

To get detailed information about a cmdlet, type **get-help *cmdletname* –detailed,** where *cmdletname* is the name of the cmdlet you want to examine. To get detailed information about the SQL Server provider, which provides SQL Server functionality for Windows PowerShell, type **get-help sqlserver | more**.

> **REAL WORLD**   You can use the sqlps utility on any computer where you've installed SQL Server or the command-line management tools. The sqlps utility starts a Windows PowerShell session with the SQL Server PowerShell provider imported so that you can use its cmdlets and work with instances of SQL Server. When you are working with Windows PowerShell or scripts, you can import the SQLPS module to load the SQL Server provider, which automatically loads the required assemblies and initializes the environment. While you previously needed to use an initialization script, this is no longer required so long as you import the SQLPS module prior to trying to access the SQL Server instance. For best results, import the SQLPS module using the following command:

```
Import-Module "sqlps" –DisableNameChecking
```

You can work with cmdlets by executing commands directly at the shell prompt or by running commands from scripts. You can enter any command or cmdlet that you can run at the Windows PowerShell command prompt into a script by copying the related command text to a file and saving the file with the *.ps1* extension. You can then run the script in the same way that you would any other command or cmdlet. However, when you are working with Windows PowerShell, the current directory might not be part of the environment path. For this reason, you might need to use the ./ notation when you run a script in the current directory, such as the following:

```
./runtasks
```

The current execution policy for SQL Server PowerShell controls whether and how you can run scripts. Although the default configuration depends on which operating system and edition you've installed, you can quickly determine the execution policy by entering **get-executionpolicy** at the Windows PowerShell prompt.

To set the execution policy to require that all scripts have a trusted signature to execute, enter the following command:

```
set-executionpolicy allsigned
```

To set the execution policy so that scripts downloaded from the web execute only if they are signed by a trusted source, enter:

```
set-executionpolicy remotesigned
```

To set the execution policy to run scripts regardless of whether they have a digital signature and work in an unrestricted environment, you can enter the following command:

```
set-executionpolicy unrestricted
```

For administration at the Windows PowerShell prompt, you use Invoke-Sqlcmd to run T-SQL or XQuery scripts containing commands supported by the SQLCMD utility. Invoke-Sqlcmd fully supports T-SQL and the XQuery syntax supported by the Database Engine, but it does not set any scripting variables by default. Invoke-Sqlcmd also accepts the SQLCMD commands listed in Table 1-3, later in this chapter. By default, results are formatted as a table, with the first result set displayed automatically and subsequent result sets displayed only if they have the same column list as the first result set.

The basic syntax you use most often with Invoke-Sqlcmd follows:

```
Invoke-Sqlcmd [-ServerInstance ServerStringOrObject]
[-Database DatabaseName] [-EncryptConnection ]
[-Username UserName] [-Password Password] [[-Query] QueryString]
[-DedicatedAdministratorConnection]

[-InputFile FilePath] [ | Out-File -filepath FilePath]
```

The command's parameters are used as follows:

- **–Database**   Specifies the name of the database that you want to work with. If you don't use this parameter, the database that is used depends on whether the current path specifies both the SQLSERVER:\SQL folder and a database name. If both are specified, Invoke-Sqlcmd connects to the database that is specified in the path. Otherwise, Invoke-Sqlcmd connects to the default database for the current login ID.

    NOTE   Use–IgnoreProviderContext to force a connection to the database that is defined as the default for the current login ID.

- **–DedicatedAdministratorConnection**   Ensures that a dedicated administrator connection (DAC) is used to force a connection when one might not be possible otherwise.
- **–EncryptConnection**   Enables Secure Sockets Layer (SSL) encryption for the connection.
- **–InputFile**   Provides the full path to a file that should be used as the query input. The file can contain T-SQL statements, XQuery statements, SQLCMD commands, and scripting variables. Spaces are not allowed in the file path or file name.

- **–Password**   Sets the password for the SQL Server Authentication login ID that is specified in –Username.

- **–Query**   Defines one or more queries to be run. The queries can be T-SQL queries, XQuery statements, or SQLCMD commands. Separate multiple queries with semicolons.

  TIP   You do not need to use the SQLCMD GO command. Escape any double quotation marks included in the string and consider using bracketed identifiers such as [EmpTable] instead of quoted identifiers such as "EmpTable". To ensure that the message output is returned, add the –Verbose parameter. –Verbose is a parameter common to all cmdlets.

- **–ServerInstance**   Specifies the name of an instance of the Database Engine that you want to work with. For default instances, specify only the computer name, such as DbServer23. For named instances, use the format "ComputerName\InstanceName", such as DbServer23\EmployeeDb.

- **–Username**   Sets the login ID for making a SQL Server authentication connection to an instance of the Database Engine. You also must set the password for the login ID.

NOTE   By default, Invoke-Sqlcmd attempts a Windows authentication connection by using the Windows account running the Windows PowerShell session. Windows authentication connections are preferred. To use a SQL Server authentication connection instead, specify the user name and password for the SQL login ID that you want to use.

With this in mind, you could replace the following T-SQL statements:

```
USE OrderSystem;
GO
SELECT * FROM Inventory.Product
ORDER BY Name ASC
GO
```

with the following Windows PowerShell command:

```
Invoke-Sqlcmd -Query "SELECT * FROM Inventory.Product; ORDER BY Name ASC"
-ServerInstance "DbServer23\OrderSystem"
```

You also could read the commands from a script, as shown in Sample 1-1.

SAMPLE 1-1 Example SQL Command Script.

Contents of SqlCmd.sql Script.
```
SELECT * FROM Inventory.Product
ORDER BY Name ASC
```

Command to Run the Script
```
Invoke-Sqlcmd -InputFile "C:\Scripts\SqlCmd.sql"
```

When you work with Windows PowerShell, don't overlook the importance of SQL Server support being implemented through a provider. The data that providers expose appears as a drive that you can browse. One way to browse is to get or set the location with respect to the SqlServer: provider drive. The top of the hierarchy exposed is represented by the SQL folder, then there is a folder for the machine name, and finally, there is a folder for the instance name. Following this, you could navigate to the top-level folder for the default instance by entering

```
Set-Location SQLSERVER:\SQL\DbServer23\Default
```

You could then determine the available database structures by entering Get-ChildItem (or one of its aliases, such as ls or dir). To navigate logins, triggers, endpoints, databases, and any other structures, you set the location to the name of the related folder. For example, you could use Set-Location Databases and then enter **Get-ChildItem** to list available databases for the selected instance. Of course, if you know the full path you want to work with in the first place, you also can access it directly, as shown in the following example:

```
Set-Location SQLSERVER:\SQL\DbServer23\Default\Databases\OrderSystem
```

Here, you navigate to the structures for the OrderSystem database on DbServer23's default instance. If you then want to determine what tables are available for this database, you could enter:

```
Get-ChildItem Tables
```

Or you could enter:

```
Set-location Tables
Get-ChildItem
```

To manage SQL Server 2012 from a computer that isn't running SQL Server, you need to install the management tools. In the SQL Server Installation Center, select Installation, and then click the New Installation Or Add Features To An Existing Installation option. When the wizard starts, follow the prompts. On the Feature Selection page, select the Management Tools—Basic option to install Management Studio, SQLCMD, and the SQL Server provider for Windows PowerShell.

For remote management via Windows PowerShell, you need to ensure that Windows Remote Management (WinRM) and Windows PowerShell are both installed and made available by using the Add Features Wizard. You also need to enable remote commands on both your management computer and the server running SQL Server.

You can verify the availability of WinRM and configure Windows PowerShell for remoting by following these steps:

1. Click Start, All Programs, Accessories, and Windows PowerShell. Then start Windows PowerShell as an administrator by right-clicking the Windows PowerShell shortcut and selecting Run As Administrator.

2. The WinRM service is configured for manual startup by default. You must change the startup type to Automatic and start the service on each computer you want to work with. At the PowerShell prompt, you can verify that the WinRM service is running by using the following command:

```
get-service winrm
```

As shown in the following example, the value of the Status property in the output should be Running:

```
Status    Name      DisplayName
------    ----      -----------
Running   WinRM     Windows Remote Management
```

If the service is stopped, enter the following command to start the service and configure it to start automatically in the future:

```
set-service –name winrm –startuptype automatic –status running
```

3. To configure Windows PowerShell for remoting, type the following command:

```
Enable-PSRemoting –force
```

You can enable remoting only when your computer is connected to a domain or private network. If your computer is connected to a public network, you need to disconnect from the public network and connect to a domain or private network and then repeat this step. If one or more of your computer's connections has the Public connection type but you are actually connected to a domain or private network, you need to change the network connection type in the Network And Sharing Center and then repeat this step.

In many cases, you can work with remote computers in other domains. However, if the remote computer is not in a trusted domain, the remote computer might not be able to authenticate your credentials. To enable authentication, you need to add the remote computer to the list of trusted hosts for the local computer in WinRM. To do so, type the following:

```
winrm s winrm/config/client '@{TrustedHosts="RemoteComputer"}'
```

where *RemoteComputer* is the name of the remote computer, such as

```
winrm s winrm/config/client '@{TrustedHosts="DbServer23"}'
```

When you are working with computers in workgroups or homegroups, you must use HTTPS as the transport or add the remote machine to the TrustedHosts configuration settings. If you cannot connect to a remote host, you can verify that the service on the remote host is running and is accepting requests by running the following command on the remote host:

```
winrm quickconfig
```

This command analyzes and configures the WinRM service. If the WinRM service is set up correctly, you see output similar to the following:

```
WinRM already is set up to receive requests on this machine.
WinRM already is set up for remote management on this machine.
```

If the WinRM service is not set up correctly, you see errors and need to respond affirmatively to several prompts that allow you to configure remote management automatically. When this process is complete, WinRM should be set up correctly. Don't forget that you need to enable remote management on the database server as well as your management computer.

Starting, Stopping, and Configuring SQL Server Agent

SQL Server Agent runs as a service and is used to schedule jobs, alerts, and other automated tasks. After you have scheduled automated tasks, you usually want SQL Server Agent to start automatically when the system starts. This configuration ensures that the scheduled tasks are performed as expected. Using SQL Server Service Manager, you can control the related SQL Server Agent (*InstanceName*) service just as you do the SQL Server service. For details, see the "Configuring SQL Server Services" section in Chapter 2.

You use SQL Server Management Studio to configure SQL Server Agent. Chapter 10, "Automating and Maintaining SQL Server 2012," covers the agent configuration in detail, but the basic steps are as follows:

1. Connect to the Database Engine on the server you want to configure. You can do this in the Registered Servers view by double-clicking the server entry, or you can use the Object Explorer view. In the Object Explorer view, click Connect, and then select Database Engine to display the Connect To Server dialog box, which you can use to connect to the server.

2. Right-click the SQL Server Agent node, and then select Properties from the shortcut menu. You can now configure SQL Server Agent. Keep in mind that if the service is not running, you need to start it before you can manage its properties.

3. The SQL Server Agent shortcut menu also lets you manage the SQL Server Agent service. Select Start, Stop, or Restart as desired.

Starting, Stopping, and Configuring MSDTC

Microsoft Distributed Transaction Coordinator (MSDTC) is a transaction manager that makes it possible for client applications to work with multiple sources of data in one transaction.

When a distributed transaction spans two or more servers, the servers coordinate the management of the transaction by using MSDTC. When a distributed transaction spans multiple databases on a single server, SQL Server manages the transaction internally.

SQL Server applications can call MSDTC directly to start an explicit distributed transaction. Distributed transactions can also be started implicitly by using one of the following methods:

- Calling stored procedures on remote servers running SQL Server
- Updating data on multiple OLE DB data sources
- Enlisting remote servers in a transaction

If you work with transactions under any of these scenarios, you should have MSDTC running on the server, and you should set MSDTC to start automatically when the server starts. As with SQL Server itself, MSDTC runs as a service. Unlike the SQL Server service, only one instance of the MSDTC service runs on a computer, regardless of how many database server instances are available. This means that all instances of SQL Server running on a computer use the same transaction coordinator.

You can view the current state of MSDTC in SQL Server Management Studio by connecting to the server's Database Engine. In Object Explorer, expand the server and Management nodes. If the service is running, you see a green circle with a right-facing triangle in it (similar to a Play button). If the service is stopped, you see a red circle with a square in it (similar to a Stop button). You can control the MSDTC service with Computer Management. Follow these steps:

1. Start Computer Management by clicking Start, pointing to All Programs, Administrative Tools, and then selecting Computer Management.

2. By default, you are connected to the local computer. To connect to a remote computer, right-click the Computer Management node, and then select Connect To Another Computer. In the Select Computer dialog box, choose Another Computer, and then type the name of the computer. The name can be specified as a host name, such as EngDBSrv12, or as an FQDN, such as EngDBSrv12.cpandl.com.

3. Expand Services And Applications, and then select Services. Right-click Distributed Transaction Coordinator, and then choose Properties. You can now manage MSDTC.

Managing SQL Server Startup

The Database Engine has two modes of operation. It can run as a service or as a command-line application (SQLServr.exe). You normally run SQL Server as a service. Use the command-line application when you need to troubleshoot problems or modify configuration settings in single-user mode.

Enabling or Preventing Automatic SQL Server Startup

In Chapter 2, you'll see how SQL Server Configuration Manager is used to manage the SQL Server (MSSQLSERVER) service, related services for other Database Engine instances, and other SQL Server–related services. Any of these services can be configured for automatic startup or can be prevented from starting automatically. To enable or prevent automatic startup of a service, follow these steps:

1. Start SQL Server Configuration Manager by using one of the following techniques:

   - Log in to the database server through a local or remote login, and then start SQL Server Configuration Manager by clicking Start; pointing to All Programs, Microsoft SQL Server 2012, Configuration Tools; and then selecting SQL Server Configuration Manager.

   - In SQL Server Management Studio, open the Registered Servers view by pressing Ctrl+Alt+G. Use the Registered Servers toolbar to select the top-level group, and then expand the group nodes by double-clicking them. Right-click the server entry, and then select SQL Server Configuration Manager.

2. Select the SQL Server Services node. Right-click the SQL Server service that you want to start automatically, and then select Properties. You can now do the following:

   - **Enable automatic startup**   On the Service tab, set the Start Mode to Automatic. If the server state is Stopped, click Start on the Log On tab to start the service.

   - **Prevent automatic startup**   On the Service tab, set the Start Mode to Manual.

3. Click OK.

You can also use Computer Management to configure services. To configure automatic startup of a service by using Computer Management, follow these steps:

1. Click Start, point to All Programs, Administrative Tools, and then select Computer Management.

2. By default, you are connected to the local computer. To connect to a remote computer, right-click the Computer Management node and select Connect To Another Computer. In the Select Computer dialog box, select Another Computer, and then type the name of the computer. The name can be specified as a host name, such as EngDBSrv12, or as an FQDN, such as EngDBSrv12.cpandl.com.

3. Expand Services And Applications, and then select Services.

4. Right-click the SQL Server service that you want to start automatically, and then select Properties.

5. Now you can do the following:

- **Enable automatic startup** On the General tab, set the Startup Type to Automatic. If the Service Status reads Stopped, click Start.
- **Prevent automatic startup** On the General tab, set the Startup Type to Manual.

6. Click OK.

Setting Database Engine Startup Parameters

Startup parameters control how the SQL Server Database Engine starts and which options are set when it does. You can configure startup options by using SQL Server Configuration Manager or Computer Management. SQL Server Configuration Manager is the recommended tool for this task because it provides the current default settings and allows you to make modifications easily.

> **TIP** You can pass startup parameters to the command-line utility SQLServr.exe as well. Passing the –c option to this utility starts SQL Server without using a service. You must run SQLServr.exe from the Binn directory that corresponds to the instance of the SQL Server Database Engine that you want to start. For the default instance, the utility is located in MSSQL11.MSSQLSERVER\MSSQL\Binn. For named instances, the utility is located in MSSQL11.*InstanceName*\MSSQL\Binn.

Adding Startup Parameters

You can add startup parameters by completing the following steps:

1. Start SQL Server Configuration Manager by using one of the following techniques:

- Log in to the database server through a local or remote login, and then start SQL Server Configuration Manager. On the Microsoft SQL Server 2012 menu, the related option is found under Configuration Tools.
- In SQL Server Management Studio, open the Registered Servers view by pressing Ctrl+Alt+G. Use the Registered Servers toolbar to select the top-level group, and then expand the group nodes by double-clicking them. Right-click the server entry, and then select SQL Server Configuration Manager.

2. Select the SQL Server Services node. Right-click the SQL Server service that you want to modify, and then select Properties.

3. On the Advanced tab, click in the Startup Parameters box, and then press End to go to the end of the currently entered parameters. The –d, –e, and –l parameters are set by default. Be careful not to modify these or other existing parameters accidentally.

4. Each parameter is separated by a semicolon. Type a semicolon and then a hyphen followed by the letter and value of the parameter you are adding, such as ;–g512.

5. Repeat steps 3 and 4 as necessary to specify additional parameters and values.

6. Click Apply to save the changes. The parameters are applied the next time the SQL Server instance is started. To apply the parameters right away, you must stop and then start the service by clicking Restart on the Log On tab.

Removing Startup Parameters

You can remove startup parameters by completing the following steps:

1. Start SQL Server Configuration Manager by using one of the following techniques:

   ■ Log in to the database server through a local or remote login, and then start SQL Server Configuration Manager by clicking Start, pointing to All Programs, Microsoft SQL Server 2012, Configuration Tools, and then selecting SQL Server Configuration Manager.

   ■ In SQL Server Management Studio, open the Registered Servers view by pressing Ctrl+Alt+G. Use the Registered Servers toolbar to select the top-level group, and then expand the group nodes by double-clicking them. Right-click the server entry, and then select SQL Server Configuration Manager.

2. Select the SQL Server Services node. Right-click the SQL Server service that you want to modify, and then select Properties.

3. On the Advanced tab, click in the Startup Parameters box. Each parameter is specified with a hyphen, parameter letter, and parameter value. A semicolon is used to separate parameter values, as shown in the following example:

   -g512;

4. Remove the parameter by deleting its entry.

5. The change is applied the next time the SQL Server instance is started. To apply the change right away, you must stop and then start the service by clicking Restart on the Log On tab.

Common Startup Parameters

Table 1-1 shows the startup parameters in SQL Server and how they are used. The first three parameters (–d, –e, and –l) are the defaults for SQL Server. The remaining parameters allow you to configure additional settings.

TABLE 1-1 Startup Parameters for SQL Server

PARAMETER	DESCRIPTION
–d<*path*>	Sets the full path for the *master* database. If this parameter is omitted, the registry values are used. *Example:* –dC:\Program Files\Microsoft SQL Server\MSSQL11 .MSSQLSERVER\MSSQL\DATA\Master.mdf
–e<*path*>	Sets the full path for the error log. If this parameter is omitted, the registry values are used. *Example:* –eC:\Program Files\Microsoft SQL Server\MSSQL11 .MSSQLSERVER\MSSQL\LOG\ERRORLOG
–l<*path*>	Sets the full path for the *master* database transaction log. If this parameter is omitted, the registry values are used. *Example:* –lC:\Program Files\Microsoft SQL Server\MSSQL11 .MSSQLSERVER\MSSQL\DATA\Mastlog.ldf
–B	Sets a breakpoint in response to an error; used with the –y option when debugging.
–c	Prevents SQL Server from running as a service. This setting makes startup faster when you are running SQL Server from the command line.
-E	Increases the number of extents that are allocated for each file in a file group. Useful for data warehouse applications with a limited number of users.
–f	Starts SQL Server with minimal configuration. This setting is useful if a configuration value has prevented SQL Server from starting.
–g *number*	Specifies the amount of virtual address space memory in megabytes to reserve for SQL Server. This memory is outside the SQL Server memory pool and is used by the extended procedure dynamic-link libraries (DLLs), the OLE DB providers referenced in distributed queries, and the automation object referenced in T-SQL. The default value is 256. *Example:* –g256
–K	Forces regeneration of the service master key if it exists.
–k *number*	Sets the checkpoint speed in megabytes per second. Use a decimal value. *Example:* –k25

PARAMETER	DESCRIPTION
–m	Starts SQL Server in single-user mode. Only a single user can connect, and the checkpoint process is not started. Enables the sp_configure allow updates option, which is disabled by default.
–n	Tells SQL Server not to log errors in the application event log. Use with –e.
–s *instance*	Starts the named instance of SQL Server. You must be in the relevant Binn directory for the instance. *Example:* –sdevapps
–T<*tnum*>	Sets a trace flag. Trace flags set nonstandard behavior and are often used in debugging or diagnosing performance issues. *Example:* –T237
–t<*tnum*>	Sets an internal trace flag for SQL Server. Used only by SQL Server support engineers. *Example:* –t8837
–x	Disables statistics tracking for CPU time and cache-hit ratio. Allows maximum performance.
–y *number*	Sets an error number that causes SQL Server to dump the stack. *Example:* –y1803

Managing Services from the Command Line

You can start, stop, and pause SQL Server as you would any other service. On a local system, you can type the necessary command at a standard command prompt. You also can connect to a system remotely and then issue the necessary command. To manage the default database server instance, use these commands:

- **NET START MSSQLSERVER** Starts SQL Server as a service.
- **NET STOP MSSQLSERVER** Stops SQL Server when running as a service.
- **NET PAUSE MSSQLSERVER** Pauses SQL Server when running as a service.
- **NET CONTINUE MSSQLSERVER** Resumes SQL Server when it is running as a service.

To manage named instances of SQL Server, use the following commands:

- **NET START MSSQL$*instancename*** Starts SQL Server as a service; *instancename* is the actual name of the database server instance.
- **NET STOP MSSQL$*instancename*** Stops SQL Server when it is running as a service; *instancename* is the actual name of the database server instance.

- **NET PAUSE MSSQL$*instancename***   Pauses SQL Server when it is running as a service; *instancename* is the actual name of the database server instance.
- **NET CONTINUE MSSQL$*instancename***   Resumes SQL Server when it is running as a service; *instancename* is the actual name of the database server instance.

You can add startup options to the end of NET START MSSQLSERVER or NET START MSSQL$*instancename* commands. Use a slash (/) instead of a hyphen (–), as shown in these examples:

```
net start MSSQLSERVER /f /m
net start MSSQL$CUSTDATAWAREHOUS /f /m
```

> **REAL WORLD**   Instead of referencing MSSQLSERVER or MSSQL$*instancename*, you also can refer to the service by its display name. For the default instance, you use "SQL Server (MSSQLSERVER)" with NET START, NET STOP, NET PAUSE, and NET CONTINUE. For a named instance, you use net start "SQL Server (InstanceName)", where *InstanceName* is the name of the instance, such as net start "SQL Server (CUSTDATAWAREHOUS)". In both usages, the quotation marks are required as part of the command text.

Managing the SQL Server Command-Line Executable

The SQL Server command-line executable (SQLServr.exe) provides an alternative to the SQL Server service. You must run SQLServr.exe from the Binn directory that corresponds to the instance of the SQL Server Database Engine that you want to start. For the default instance, the utility is located in MSSQL11.MSSQLSERVER\MSSQL\Binn. For named instances, the utility is located in MSSQL11.*InstanceName*\MSSQL\Binn.

When SQL Server is installed on a local system, start SQL Server by changing to the directory where the instance of SQL Server you want to start is located and then typing **sqlservr** at the command line. On a remote system, connect to the system remotely, change to the appropriate directory, and then issue the startup command. Either way, SQL Server reads the default startup parameters from the registry and starts execution.

You also can enter startup parameters and switches that override the default settings. (The available parameters are summarized in Table 1-1.) You still can connect SQL Server Management Studio and SQL Server Configuration Manager to the server. However, when you do, these programs show an icon indicating that the SQL Server service is stopped because you aren't running SQL Server via the related service. You also will be unable to pause, stop, or resume the instance of SQL Server as a Windows service.

When you are running SQL Server from the command line, SQL Server runs in the security context of the user, not the security context of the account assigned to the SQL Server service. You should not minimize the command console in which SQL Server is running because doing so causes Windows to remove nearly all the resources from SQL Server.

In addition, when you are running SQL Server from the command line, you can make configuration changes that might be necessary for diagnosing and resolving problems, and you also can perform tasks that you can accomplish only when SQL Server is running in single-user mode. However, you should be careful when creating databases, changing data file locations, or making other similar types of changes. If you are logged in as an administrator and create a new database or change the location of a data file, SQL Server might not be able to access the database or data file when it runs later under the default account for the SQL Server service.

You must shut down the instance of SQL Server before logging off Windows. To stop an instance of SQL Server started from the command line, complete the following steps:

1. Press Ctrl+C to break into the execution stream.
2. When prompted, press Y to stop SQL Server.

Managing Server Activity

As a database administrator, your job is to be sure that SQL Server runs smoothly. To ensure that SQL Server is running optimally, you can actively monitor the server to do the following:

- Keep track of user connections and locks.
- View processes and commands that active users are running.
- Check the status of locks on processes and objects.
- See blocked or blocking transactions.
- Ensure that processes complete successfully, and detect errors if they do not.

When problems arise, you can terminate a process if necessary.

NOTE For more coverage of monitoring SQL Server, see Chapter 12. In that chapter, you will learn how to use Performance Monitor and SQL Server Profiler to keep track of SQL Server activity, performance, and errors.

Examining Process Information

Process information provides details about the status of processes, current user connections, and other server activity. You can view process information by completing the following steps:

1. Start SQL Server Management Studio, and then connect to a server.
2. Use the Object Explorer view to access an instance of the Database Engine.
3. Right-click the Database Engine instance and then select Activity Monitor.

In Activity Monitor, shown in Figure 1-9, you should see a graphical overview of the server activity, as well as an activity summary by processes, resource waits, data file I/O, and recent expensive queries. The overview and the summaries are provided in separate panels that you can expand to display or shrink to hide.

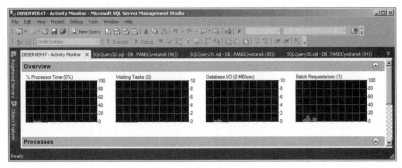

FIGURE 1-9 Activity Monitor.

The Overview panel has graphs depicting processor time, waiting tasks, database I/O, and batch requests. By default, the graphs are updated every 10 seconds. You can specify a different refresh interval by right-clicking in the panel, pointing to Refresh Interval, and then selecting an interval, such as 30 seconds.

In the Processes panel, processes are sorted by process ID by default, but you can arrange them by any of the available information categories summarized in Table 1-2. Click a category header to sort processes based on that category. Click the same category header again to perform a reverse sort on the category.

TABLE 1-2 Process Information Used in Database Administration

CATEGORY	DESCRIPTION
Session ID	Provides the session ID of the process on the server.
User Process	Flags the process as being either a user process (flag=1) or a server process (flag=0).
Login	Shows which user is running the process by SQL Server ID, service name, or domain account.
Database	Indicates the database with which the process is associated.
Task State	Shows the status of the process. A running process is active and currently performing work. A runnable process has a connection but currently has no work to perform. A sleeping process is waiting for something, such as user input or a lock. A background process is running in the background, periodically performing tasks. A suspended process has work to perform but has stopped.

CATEGORY	DESCRIPTION
Command	Displays the command being executed or the last command executed.
Application	Shows the application or SQL Server component (such as a report server) connecting to the server and running the process.
Wait Time	Indicates the elapsed wait time in milliseconds.
Wait Type	Specifies whether the process is waiting or not waiting.
Wait Resource	Displays the resource that the process is waiting for (if any).
Blocked By	Displays the process ID blocking this process.
Head Blocker	Shows 1 if the session ID is the head blocker in the blocking chain. Otherwise, it shows 0.
Memory Use	Displays the amount of memory the process is using (in kilobytes).
Host Name	Displays the host from which the connection originated.
Workload Group	Displays the name of the Resource Governor workload group for the query.

Tracking Resource Waits and Blocks

When you are diagnosing performance issues, you should look closely at the Wait Time, Wait Type, Wait Resource, and Blocked By values for each process. Most of the process information is gathered from data columns returned by various dynamic management views, including the following:

- **sys.dm_os_tasks**   Returns information about each task that is active in the instance of SQL Server.

- **sys.dm_os_waiting_tasks**   Returns information about each task that is waiting on some resource.

- **sys.dm_exec_requests**   Returns information about each request that is executing within SQL Server.

- **sys.dm_exec_sessions**   Returns information about each authentication session within SQL Server.

Although Activity Monitor provides a good overview, you might need to use these dynamic management views to get more detailed information about processes, resource waits, and resource blocks.

The Resource Waits panel provides additional information about resource waits. Each wait category combines the wait time for closely related wait types, such as buffer I/O or network I/O. Keep the following in mind:

- **Wait Time** Shows the accumulated wait time per second. Here, a rate of 3,000 ms indicates that three tasks on average were waiting with this wait category.

- **Recent Wait Time** Shows the wait average of accumulated wait time per second. This combines all the wait times over the last several minutes and averages them for this wait category.

- **Average Waiter Count** Shows the average number of waiting tasks per second for this wait category.

- **Cumulative Wait Time** Shows the total amount of wait time for this wait category since SQL Server was started or the wait statistics were reset.

TIP You can reset wait statistics using DBCC SQLPERF, as shown in this example:
DBCC SQLPERF("sys.dm_os_wait_stats",CLEAR);

To get a clearer picture of resource waits and blocks, you can use the sys.dm_tran_locks view. Table 1-3 summarizes the information returned with this view. Actual values are in parentheses, preceded by a general category name.

TABLE 1-3 Lock-Related Information Used in Database Administration

CATEGORY	TYPE	DESCRIPTION
Process ID (request_session_id)		The process ID of the related user process within SQL Server.
Object ID (resource_associated_ entity_id)		The ID of the entity with which a resource is associated.
Context (request_exec_context_id)		The ID of the thread associated with the process ID.
Batch ID (request_request_id)		The batch ID associated with the process ID.
Type (resource_type)	RID	Row identifier; used to lock a single row within a table.
	KEY	A row lock within an index; used to protect key ranges.
	PAGE	A lock on a data or index page.
	EXTENT	A lock on a contiguous group of eight data or index pages.

CATEGORY	TYPE	DESCRIPTION
	TABLE	A lock on an entire table, including all data and indexes.
	DATABASE	A lock on an entire database.
	METADATA	A lock on descriptive information about the object.
	ALLOCATION_ UNIT	A lock on allocation unit page count statistics during deferred drop operations.
	HOBT	A lock on basic access path structures for heap or index reorganization operations or heap-optimized bulk loads.
Subtype (resource_subtype)		The lock subtype, frequently used with METADATA locks to identify metadata lock activity.
Description (resource_description)		Gives optional descriptive information.
Request Mode (request_mode)	S	Shared; used for read-only operations, such as a SELECT statement.
	U	Update; used when reading/ locking an updatable resource; prevents some deadlock situations.
	X	Exclusive; allows only one session to update the data; used with the modification operations, such as INSERT, DELETE, and UPDATE.
	I	Intent; used to establish a lock hierarchy.
	Sch-S	Schema stability; used when checking a table's schema.
	Sch-M	Schema modification; used when modifying a table's schema.

CATEGORY	TYPE	DESCRIPTION
	BU	Bulk update; used when bulk copying data into a table and the TABLOCK hint is specified.
	RangeS_S	Serializable range scan; used with shared resource locks on shared ranges.
	RangeS_U	Serializable update; used for updating resource locks on shared ranges.
	RangeI_N	Insert range with a null resource lock; used to test ranges before inserting a new key into an index.
	RangeX_X	Exclusive range with an exclusive lock; used when updating a key in a range.
Request Type (request_type)		The type of object requested.
Request Status (request_status)	GRANT	The lock was obtained.
	WAIT	The lock is blocked by another process.
	CNVT	The lock is being converted— that is, it is held in one mode but waiting to acquire a stronger lock mode.
Owner Type (request_owner_type)	CURSOR	The lock owner is a cursor.
	SESSION	The lock owner is a user session.
	TRANSACTION	The lock owner is a transaction.
	SHARED_ TRANSACTION _WORKSPACE	The lock owner is the shared portion of the transaction workspace.
	EXCLUSIVE_ TRANSACTION _WORKSPACE	The lock owner is the exclusive portion of the transaction workspace.

CATEGORY	TYPE	DESCRIPTION
Owner ID (request_owner_id)		The owner ID associated with the lock.
Owner GUID (request_owner_guid)		The globally unique identifier (GUID) of the owner associated with the lock.
Database (resource_database_id)		The database containing the lock.
Object (resource_associated_ entity_id)		The name of the object being locked.

Troubleshooting Deadlocks and Blocking Connections

Two common problems you might encounter are deadlocks and blocking connections. Deadlocks and blocking connections, as described in the following list, can occur in almost any database environment, especially when many users are making connections to databases:

- Deadlocks can occur when two users have locks on separate objects and each wants a lock on the other's object. Each user waits for the other user to release the lock, but this does not happen.

- Blocking connections occur when one connection holds a lock and a second connection wants a conflicting lock type. This forces the second connection to wait or to block the first.

Both deadlocks and blocking connections can degrade server performance.

Although SQL Server can detect and correct deadlocks, you can help speed up this process by identifying potential problems and taking action when necessary. Clearing blocks is a manual step; you must kill the blocking process.

Process information can tell you when deadlocks or blocking connections occur. Examine these process information columns: Wait Time, Wait Type, Resource, Blocking, and Blocked By. When you have a deadlock or blocking situation, take a closer look at the locks on the objects that are causing problems. Refer to the "Tracking Resource Waits and Blocks" section earlier in this chapter for details. You also might want to stop the offending processes, and you can do this by following the steps described in the "Killing Server Processes" section later in this chapter.

You can also use the sys.dm_tran_locks view to obtain information about active locks. Each row in the results returned by this view represents a currently active request to the lock manager for a lock that has been granted or is waiting to be granted. The following example returns a list of locks in the Customer database:

T-SQL

```
USE customer;
GO
SELECT * FROM sys.dm_tran_locks
```

PowerShell

```
Invoke-Sqlcmd -Query "USE customer; SELECT * FROM sys.dm_tran_locks"
-ServerInstance "DbServer25"
```

In the result set, the results are organized in two main groups. Columns that begin with *resource_* describe the resource on which the lock request is being made. Columns that begin with *request_* describe the lock request itself. (Table 1-3 lists the correlation between the columns in the results and the categories listed in Activity Monitor.) While Activity Monitor returns the actual database name, the resource_database_id column returns the database_id as set in the sys.databases view. In SQL Server, database IDs are set on a per-server basis. You can determine the database name for a particular database ID on a particular server by using the following statement:

```
SELECT name, database_id FROM sys.databases
```

In the results returned by sys.dm_tran_locks, request_session_id tracks process IDs. Process IDs tracked internally by SQL Server do not correspond to process IDs tracked by the operating system. You can determine the association between the SQL Server process IDs and Windows thread IDs by using the following query:

```
SELECT ServerTasks.session_id, ServerThreads.os_thread_id
    FROM sys.dm_os_tasks AS ServerTasks
    INNER JOIN sys.dm_os_threads AS ServerThreads
        ON ServerTasks.worker_address = ServerThreads.worker_address
    WHERE ServerTasks.session_id IS NOT NULL
    ORDER BY ServerTasks.session_id;
GO
```

While you are connected to the database that contains the locking object, you get more information about the locking object and blocking information. Use the following query, where *<resource_associated_entity_id>* is the value in the related column, to get information about the locking object:

```
SELECT object_name(object_id), *
    FROM sys.partitions
    WHERE hobt_id=<resource_associated_entity_id>
```

Use the following query to get blocking information:

```
SELECT
        tr1.resource_type,
        tr1.resource_subtype,
        tr1.resource_database_id,
        tr1.resource_associated_entity_id,
        tr1.request_mode,
        tr1.request_type,
        tr1.request_status,
        tr1.request_session_id,
        tr1.request_owner_type,
        tr2.blocking_session_id
    FROM sys.dm_tran_locks as tr1
    INNER JOIN sys.dm_os_waiting_tasks as tr2
        ON tr1.lock_owner_address = tr2.resource_address;
```

Tracking Command Execution in SQL Server

Sometimes you want to track the commands that users are executing. You can do this by using Activity Monitor as follows:

1. In SQL Server Management Studio, use the Object Explorer view to access an instance of the Database Engine.

2. Right-click the Database Engine instance and then select Activity Monitor.

3. Expand the Processes panel by clicking Options. The entries in the Session ID, User Process, and Login columns can help you track user sessions and the processes they are using.

4. Right-click a process and then select Details to display the Session Details dialog box, as shown in Figure 1-10. This dialog box shows the last command batch executed by the user.

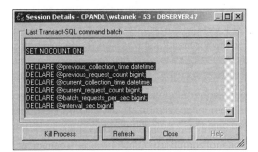

FIGURE 1-10 The Session Details dialog box displays the user's most recent command batch.

5. To track current commands being executed by the user, click Refresh periodically.

6. To end the process, click Kill Process. Then, when prompted, choose Yes.

Killing Server Processes

Sometimes you might need to stop processes that are blocking connections or using too much CPU time. To do this, complete the following steps:

1. In SQL Server Management Studio, use the Object Explorer view to access an instance of the Database Engine.

2. Right-click the Database Engine instance and then select Activity Monitor.

3. Expand the Processes panel by clicking Options.

4. Right-click the process you want to stop, and then choose Kill Process. When prompted to confirm, click Yes.

NOTE Rather than kill a process in SQL Server, you may want to stop the application that is connected to the process and restart it to check if the issue is resolved.

CHAPTER 2

Managing SQL Server Services and Clients

For controlling access to your server, few things are more important than how you configure the services, components, and networking capabilities in Microsoft SQL Server. Every SQL Server installation has a specific configuration for the services it uses, its components, and the network, and the configuration determines security levels that control access in the surface area of the server, such as:

- Who can access the server and by what means
- Where and by what means SQL Server components can connect to (or be connected from) remote resources
- What SQL Server services run automatically at startup, or manually as needed

By limiting these who, what, and where aspects of the server's configuration, you reduce the server's surface area, which improves the server's security and also can enhance overall performance because you are running only necessary services and components.

SQL Server relies on a client-server configuration. On your clients, client access to SQL Server is managed through OLE DB, ODBC, JDBC, and so on. On your servers, client access to SQL Server is managed through SQL Native Client Configuration parameters. SQL Server access to local and remote resources is determined by SQL Server services and the SQL Server network configuration. You can manage client access, SQL Server services, and the network configuration by using SQL Server Configuration Manager.

Managing SQL Server Component Feature Access

To reduce a server's surface area and improve server security, you should enable only the features needed by your clients and applications. This step limits the ways the server can be exploited by malicious users and closes avenues of potential attack. Table 2-1 details the surface area features you can manage for the SQL Server Database Engine, Analysis Services, and Reporting Services components. In SQL Server 2012, you manage these surface area features by using Policy-Based Management policies, as discussed in Chapter 3, "Implementing Policy-Based Management." By default, these features are all disabled.

TABLE 2-1 Component Features for Managing Surface Area Access

COMPONENT/FACET	DESCRIPTION/USAGE
DATABASE ENGINE	
AdHocRemoteQueriesEnabled	The OPENROWSET and OPENDATASOURCE functions can use ad hoc connections to work with remote data sources without an administrator specifically configuring linked or remote servers. If your applications or scripts use these functions, you should enable support for OPENROWSET and OPENDATASOURCE. Otherwise, this functionality should be disabled.
ClrIntegrationEnabled	With common language runtime (CLR) integration, you can write stored procedures, triggers, user-defined types, and user-defined functions using Microsoft Visual Basic, C#, and any other Microsoft .NET Framework language. If your applications or scripts use .NET Framework languages, enable this feature. Otherwise, this feature should be disabled.

COMPONENT/FACET	DESCRIPTION/USAGE
DatabaseMailEnabled	Database Mail replaces SQL Mail as the preferred technique for sending email messages from SQL Server. Database Mail uses Simple Mail Transfer Protocol (SMTP). Enable this feature if you have created a mail host database (by running the %ProgramFiles%\Microsoft SQL Server\ MSSQL.1\MSSQL\Install\Install_DBMail_ Upgrade.sql script on the server) and the necessary Database Mail profiles, and you want applications and scripts to be able to use the sp_send_dbmail stored procedure to send email messages from SQL Server. Otherwise, this feature should be disabled.
OleAutomationEnabled	OLE Automation provides the ability to use Transact-SQL (T-SQL) batches, stored procedures, and triggers to reference SQL DMO and custom OLE Automation objects. Enable this feature if you want to use OLE Automation, including the extended stored procedures sp_OACreate, sp_OADestroy, sp_OAGetErrorInfo, sp_OAGetProperty, sp_OAMethod, sp_OASetProperty, and sp_OAStop. Otherwise, this feature should be disabled.
RemoteDacEnabled	By using the SQLCMD command-line utility with the –A parameter, administrators can maintain SQL Server installations through a dedicated connection from the command line, either locally or remotely. By default, only local dedicated connections are permitted. If you want to authorize remote dedicated connections, enable this feature. Otherwise, this feature should be disabled.

COMPONENT/FACET	DESCRIPTION/USAGE
ServiceBrokerEndpointActive	Service Broker provides queuing and messaging for the Database Engine. Applications can use Service Broker to communicate across instances of SQL Server. If your applications use Service Broker and you have configured the necessary HTTP endpoints, you can configure the state of each endpoint as Started, Stopped, or Disabled.
SoapEndpointsEnabled	With native web services, you can access SQL Server over HTTP by using Simple Object Access Protocol (SOAP) messaging. SOAP messages contain text-based commands that are formatted in XML. If you plan to use SOAP for data exchange and have configured the necessary HTTP endpoints, you can configure the state of each endpoint as Started, Stopped, or Disabled. The SQL Server Reporting Services, SQL Server Service Broker, and Database Mirroring components make use of native web services, but they have separate configurations.
SqlMailEnabled	SQL Mail can be used with legacy applications for sending email messages from SQL Server using SMTP. Enable this feature if you want legacy applications and scripts to be able to use the xp_sendmail stored procedure to send email messages from SQL Server. Otherwise, this feature should be disabled.

COMPONENT/FACET	DESCRIPTION/USAGE
XPCmdShellEnabled	The xp_cmdshell stored procedure executes command strings using the operating system command shell and returns the results as rows of text. If you want applications and scripts to run operating system commands, you must enable this feature. By default, only members of the sysadmin fixed server role can execute xp_cmdshell. You can grant execution permission to other users. For sysadmin users, xp_cmdshell is executed under the security context in which the SQL Server service is running. For other users, xp_cmdshell impersonates the command-shell proxy account (as specified by using xp_cmdshell_proxy _account). If the proxy account is not available, xp_cmdshell fails.
ANALYSIS SERVICES	
AdHocDataMiningQueriesEnabled	The Data Mining Extensions OPENROWSET function establishes a connection to a data source object by using a provider name and connection string. This permits ad hoc connections to remote data sources without an administrator specifically configuring linked or remote servers. Enable this feature if your applications or scripts use OPENROWSET with Data Mining. Otherwise, this feature should be disabled to prevent applications and scripts from passing a provider name and connection string when using the OPENROWSET function.
AnonymousConnectionsEnabled	With anonymous connections, unauthenticated users can establish connections with Analysis Services. Enable this feature if your applications and scripts require unauthenticated user access. Otherwise, disable this feature.

COMPONENT/FACET	DESCRIPTION/USAGE
LinkedObjectsLinksFromOtherInstancesEnabled	With Analysis Services, you can use linked objects to link dimensions and measure groups between servers. If you want an instance to be linked from other servers, enable this feature. Otherwise, disable this feature.
LinkedObjectsLinksToOtherInstancesEnabled	With Analysis Services, you can use linked objects to link dimensions and measure groups between servers. If you want Analysis Services to link to other servers, select Enable Links To Other Instances. Otherwise, disable this feature.
ListenOnlyOnLocalConnections	Analysis Services can work with remote resources as well as local resources. When you allow Analysis Services to work with remote resources, Analysis Services listens for TCP/IP connections from both local and remote server instances, which allows connections from remote computers. When you restrict Analysis Services from working with remote resources, Analysis Services opens a TCP/IP port on the server but listens only for connections from local server instances. If you want Analysis Services to work only with local resources, enable this feature. Otherwise, disable this feature.
UserDefinedFunctionsEnabled	Analysis Services is integrated with the .NET Framework and can load assemblies containing user-defined functions. These functions can be written using the CLR or with component object model (COM) objects. CLR objects and functions have an integrated security model. COM objects do not use this model and are therefore inherently less secure. Enable this feature if your applications and scripts require user-defined COM functions. Otherwise, disable this feature to permit only CLR functions.

COMPONENT/FACET	DESCRIPTION/USAGE
REPORTING SERVICES	
ScheduledEventsAndReportDeliveryEnabled	With Reporting Services, you can use ad hoc, on-demand reports and scheduled reports. Typically, when you have installed Reporting Services, both types of reports are enabled. If you do not use scheduled reports, you can disable this aspect of report generation and delivery by disabling this feature.
WebServiceRequestsAndHTTPAccessEnabled	Reporting Services components use SOAP messaging over HTTP for communications and use HTTP for URL access requests. These features are handled by the Report Server Web Service and permit you to work with Reporting Services through Report Manager, Report Designer, and SQL Server Management Studio. Typically, if Reporting Services is installed, the server handles HTTP and Web Service requests. Enable this feature if your client applications use the Report Server Web Service or if you use Report Manager, Report Designer, or SQL Server Management Studio with this Reporting Services installation. Otherwise, disable this feature.

Managing the Network and SQL Server Native Client Configuration

SQL Server installations can be configured to allow local and remote connections. SQL Server can use several protocols, including Shared Memory, Named Pipes, and TCP/IP. These protocols all have separate server and client configurations that you manage by using SQL Server Configuration Manager.

SQL Server Configuration Manager is implemented in a custom Microsoft Management Console and is also available as a snap-in that you can add to your own custom consoles. You can start SQL Server Configuration Manager by using one of the following techniques:

- Log on to the database server through a local or remote login, and then start SQL Server Configuration Manager by clicking Start, pointing to

All Programs, Microsoft SQL Server 2012, Configuration Tools, and then selecting SQL Server Configuration Manager. You can also start this tool by clicking Start, typing **sqlservermanager11.msc** in the Search box, and pressing Enter.

■ In SQL Server Management Studio, open the Registered Servers view by pressing Ctrl+Alt+G. Use the Registered Servers toolbar to select the top-level group, and then expand the group nodes by double-clicking them. Right-click the server entry and then select SQL Server Configuration Manager. If your server isn't registered, you need to register it, as discussed in the "Managing Servers" section in Chapter 1, "Managing Your SQL Servers."

When you start SQL Server Configuration Manager, you see the main window, shown in Figure 2-1. You can use SQL Server Configuration Manager to perform several main tasks:

■ Manage the services associated with SQL Server instances.

■ Configure network protocols used by SQL Server instances.

■ Manage the network connectivity configuration.

NOTE On 64-bit computers, you'll find multiple nodes for managing network and client configuration settings. You use the nodes with the suffix (32-bit) to manage 32-bit settings and the other nodes to manage 64-bit settings.

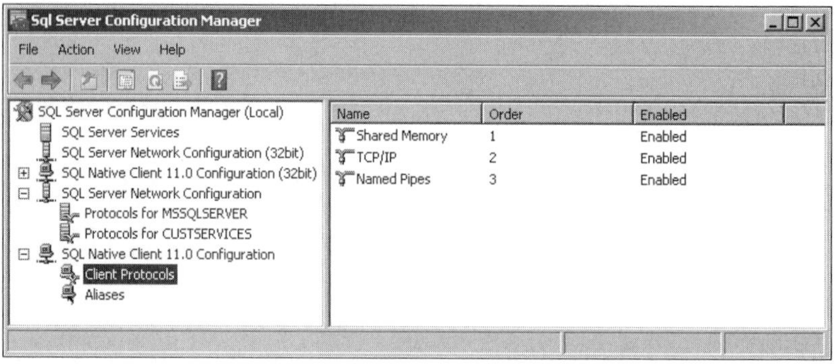

FIGURE 2-1 Clients attempt to use network protocols in a specific order.

The network configuration is set separately for each server instance by using the SQL Server Network Configuration node. The client configuration is set on a per-client basis by using the SQL Native Client Configuration node.

When multiple client protocols are available and configured for use, clients use the protocols in a specified order. The default order is as follows:

1. Shared Memory

2. TCP/IP

3. Named Pipes

NOTE Any system on which you install SQL Server Native Client is a SQL Server client. This can include systems running Windows 7, as well as Windows Server 2008 and Windows Server 2008 R2.

Managing the Connections Configuration

SQL Server installations can be configured to allow local, remote, and dedicated connections. Local connections are used by applications running on the computer that is also running SQL Server. Remote connections are used by clients connecting to the server, by applications running on other servers, and by other servers running SQL Server. Dedicated connections are a special diagnostic feature used by administrators to maintain SQL Server installations when standard connections are not possible (and are managed as a configurable feature rather than as a permissible connection type).

NOTE The default configuration for connections depends on how you have configured service accounts, what components are installed, and other installation options, such as whether you performed an upgrade or a new installation. Typically, a new installation is configured only for local connections. However, if you installed additional components, such as Reporting Services, the configuration usually permits local and remote connections.

Although a configuration for only local connections provides obvious security advantages, you cannot always run SQL Server in this configuration. Often, and more typically, you need to allow incoming connections from remote clients and servers, and in this case, the permitted connection protocols can affect the amount of resources used and the relative security of the server. For remote connections, SQL Server 2012 can use TCP/IP, Named Pipes, or both.

TCP/IP is a widely used protocol suite consisting of Transmission Control Protocol (TCP) and Internet Protocol (IP). SQL Server listens on and communicates over dynamic ports, static ports, or both port types, depending on its configuration. SQL Server 2012 supports both IP version 4 (IPv4) and IP version 6 (IPv6). The IP addresses that SQL Server uses for network communications depend on its configuration as well. TCP/IP includes standards for routing traffic that help to ensure that data packets reach their destination and standards for communications security that help protect sensitive information. This makes TCP/IP ideal for use on both local area networks (LANs) and wide area network (WANs).

Named Pipes is a protocol designed for LANs. With Named Pipes, part of memory is used by one process to pass information to another process so that the output of one process becomes the input of another process. The second process can be local, meaning it is on the same computer as the first process, or it can be remote, meaning it is on a different computer than the first process. Although local named pipes run in kernel mode and are very fast, remote named pipes don't work well on slow networks because named pipes typically generate a lot of message traffic over the network.

Because TCP/IP and Named Pipes require specific and different ports to be open across a firewall, you can limit the server to one protocol or the other to reduce the potential attack surface. Before you change the permissible connection types, however, you should be sure that all clients and applications are configured to use the appropriate network library.

With TCP/IP, SQL Server can communicate using standard IP and the TCP/IP Sockets Net-Library. The default listen port for the default instance is TCP port 1433. The default listen port for named instances is set dynamically unless it is assigned manually by using the SQL Server Configuration Manager. TCP port 1434 is used for client connections. When you use named pipes, SQL Server 2012 uses the Named Pipes Net-Library to communicate over a standard network address: \\.\pipe\sql\query for the default instance and \\.\pipe\MSSQL$*instancename*\sql\query for a named instance. Named pipes require a range of ports to be open for communication across a firewall. With named pipes, the server listens on TCP port 445.

SQL Server 2012 also supports the Shared Memory protocol for local connections. VIA, NWLink, IPX/SPX, and AppleTalk are no longer supported.

Specifying the Shared Memory Network Configuration

The Shared Memory protocol is used only for local connections. If the protocol is enabled, any local client can connect to the server by using this protocol. If you don't want local clients to use the Shared Memory protocol, you can disable it.

You can enable or disable the Shared Memory protocol by completing the following steps:

1. Start SQL Server Configuration Manager. Expand the SQL Server Network Configuration node, and then select the Protocols For entry for the SQL Server instance you want to work with.

2. Right-click Shared Memory, and then do one of the following:
   - Select Enable to enable the protocol to be used.
   - Select Disable to prevent the protocol from being used.

Specifying the Named Pipes Network Configuration

The Named Pipes protocol is used primarily for connections by applications written for early versions of Microsoft Windows. When you enable Named Pipes, SQL Server 2012 uses the Named Pipes Net-Library to communicate over a standard network address: \\.\pipe\sql\query for the default instance and \\.\pipe\MSSQL$*instancename*\sql\query for a named instance. In addition to enabling or disabling the use of Named Pipes, you can configure properties of this protocol to change the named pipe to use.

You can manage the Named Pipes network configuration by completing the following steps:

1. Start SQL Server Configuration Manager. Expand the SQL Server Network Configuration node, and then select the Protocols For entry for a SQL Server instance.

2. Right-click Named Pipes and select Properties.

3. As shown in Figure 2-2, you can now do the following:

   - Use the Enabled list to enable or disable the protocol. Select Yes to allow the protocol to be used, or select No to prevent the protocol from being used.

   - Change the name of the default pipe by typing a new value in the Pipe Name field. (Don't forget to update the client configuration.)

4. Click OK.

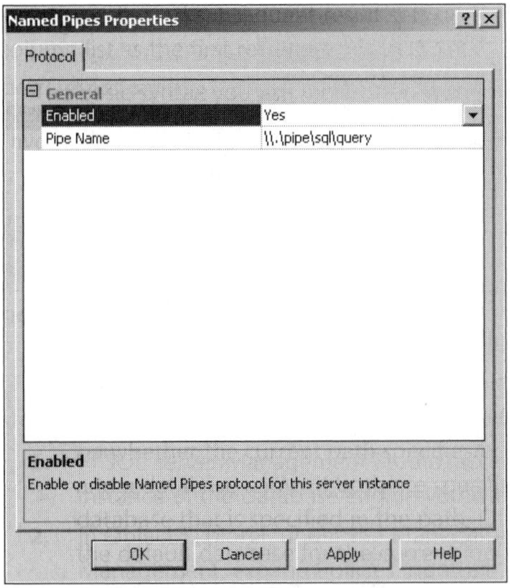

FIGURE 2-2 Configure named pipes for the server instance.

Specifying the TCP/IP Network Configuration

The TCP/IP protocol is the preferred protocol for connections to SQL Server. When you use TCP/IP, SQL Server listens on a specific TCP port and IP address for requests. By default, SQL Server listens on TCP port 1433 on all IP addresses that are configured for its network cards. For security reasons, you might want SQL Server to use a different TCP/IP configuration. If so, you have several options:

- Configure SQL Server to listen on all configured IP addresses and to use the same TCP port configuration across however many IP addresses this includes.

- Configure SQL Server to listen to only specifically enabled IP addresses and then configure each TCP listen port separately for each IP address.

With either configuration approach, you can configure the TCP listen ports manually or dynamically. When you manually assign a TCP listen port, the TCP port is static and changes only if you assign a new value. When you dynamically assign a TCP listen port, the related SQL Server instance dynamically assigns the TCP listen port whenever you start the related service. Because the TCP listen port is dynamically assigned at startup, client applications need a helper service to determine the incoming listen port, and this is where the SQL Server Browser service comes into the picture. When SQL Server instances are using dynamically assigned TCP ports, the SQL Server Browser service checks for incoming connections and directs them to the current port for the related SQL Server instance.

CAUTION You shouldn't use dynamically assigned ports when clients are connecting through a firewall. If you do, clients might experience connection problems whenever the dynamically assigned port changes.

Disabling, Enabling, and Configuring TCP/IP

You can disable or enable and configure TCP/IP by completing the following steps:

1. Start SQL Server Configuration Manager. Expand the SQL Server Network Configuration node, and then select the Protocols For entry for a SQL Server instance.

2. Right-click TCP/IP and select Properties. This displays the TCP/IP Properties dialog box.

3. On the Protocol tab, you can now use the Enabled list to enable or disable the protocol. Select Yes to allow the protocol to be used, or select No to prevent the protocol from being used. If you disabled TCP/IP, click OK and skip the remaining steps.

4. On the Protocol tab (see Figure 2-3), you can configure parameters that control whether and how the SQL Server instance tries to maintain idle TCP/IP connections. Two parameters are used:

    - **Listen All** Controls whether SQL Server listens on all IP addresses that are configured for its network cards. If you set this value to Yes, the settings of the IPAll properties box on the IP Addresses tab apply to all active IP addresses. If you set this value to No, you must configure each IP address separately using the related properties boxes on the IP Addresses tab.

- **Keep Alive** Controls how often SQL Server tries to verify that the computer at the end of a remote connection is still available. By default, SQL Server checks a remote connection after it has been idle for 30,000 milliseconds (30 seconds). In most cases, a value between 30 and 60 seconds will suffice. Depending on how busy the server is and the importance of client activity, you might want to verify and maintain idle connections more frequently, which can ensure that idle connections are not terminated. For example, you could use a smaller value, such as 15,000 or 20,000 milliseconds (15 to 20 seconds), to ensure that idle connections are validated more often.

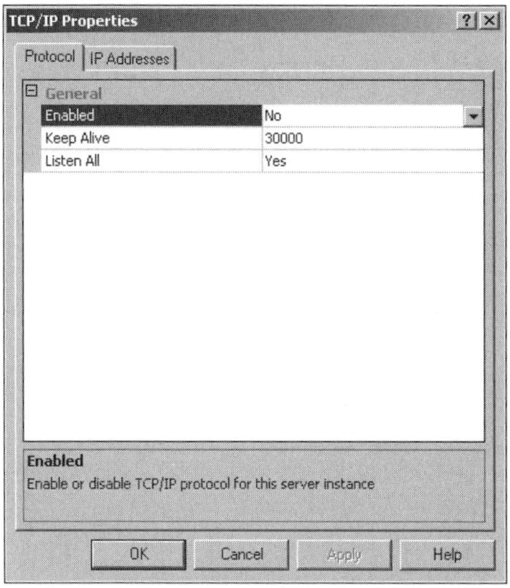

FIGURE 2-3 Configure TCP/IP for the server instance.

5. Click OK.

Using Static TCP/IP Network Configurations

You can configure a SQL Server instance to use a static TCP/IP network configuration by completing the following steps:

1. Start SQL Server Configuration Manager. Expand the SQL Server Network Configuration node, and then select the Protocols For entry for a SQL Server instance.

2. Right-click TCP/IP and then select Properties. On the IP Addresses tab of the TCP/IP Properties dialog box, you should see entries representing the IPv4 and IPv6 addresses configured on the server, as shown in Figure 2-4. Individual IP address entries in numerical order—such as IP1, IP2, IP3, and so on—are for when SQL Server is listening for specific IP addresses. The IPAll entry is used when SQL Server is listening on all IP addresses on the server.

NOTE The IP addresses 127.0.0.1 and ::1 are the local loopback addresses for IPv4 and IPv6, respectively. These addresses are used to listen for connections from local clients.

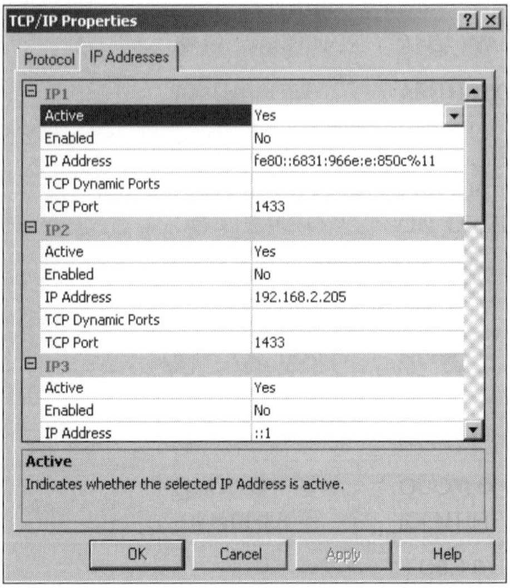

FIGURE 2-4 Configure IP addressing and listening as appropriate.

3. If you want SQL Server to listen on all configured IP addresses on the server, you should do the following:

   a. On the Protocol tab, set Listen All to Yes.

   b. On the IP Addresses tab, scroll down and set a specific TCP listen port for IPAll. The default is 1433. To change the TCP listen port, type the port you want to use in the field provided.

4. If you want to enable listening on specific IP addresses and TCP ports, you should do the following:

   a. On the Protocol tab, set Listen All to No.

   b. On the IP Addresses tab, specify the IP addresses that SQL Server should actively listen on by setting their IP address entries to Active Yes and Enabled Yes. Then type the TCP listen port for each IP address in the fields provided.

   c. On the IP Addresses tab, specify the IP addresses that SQL Server shouldn't actively listen on by setting their IP address entries to Active No and Enabled No.

5. Click OK.

TIP SQL Server can listen to multiple TCP ports on the same IP address. Simply list the ports separated by commas, such as **1433,1533,1534**. Be sure that you don't insert a space between the comma and the values. The TCP Port field is limited to a total of 2,047 characters.

Using Dynamic TCP/IP Network Configurations

You can configure a SQL Server instance to use a dynamic TCP/IP network configuration by completing the following steps:

1. Start SQL Server Configuration Manager. Expand the SQL Server Network Configuration node, and then select the Protocols For entry for a SQL Server instance.

2. Right-click TCP/IP and then select Properties. On the IP Addresses tab of the TCP/IP Properties dialog box, you should see entries representing the IPv4 and IPv6 addresses configured on the server. Individual IP address entries in numerical order—such as IP1, IP2, IP3, and so on—are for when SQL Server is listening for specific IP addresses. The IPAll entry is used when SQL Server is listening on all IP addresses on the server.

   NOTE The IP addresses 127.0.0.1 and ::1 are the local loopback addresses for IPv4 and IPv6, respectively. These addresses are used to listen for connections from local clients.

3. If you want SQL Server to listen to the same dynamic port on all configured IP addresses on the server, you should do the following:

   a. On the Protocol tab, set Listen All to Yes.

   b. On the IP Addresses tab, scroll down and then type **0** (zero) in the TCP Dynamic Ports box.

4. If you want to enable listening on specific IP addresses, you should do the following:

   a. On the Protocol tab, set Listen All to No.

   b. On the IP Addresses tab, specify the IP addresses that SQL Server should actively listen on by setting their IP address entries to Active Yes and Enabled Yes. Then type **0** (zero) in the related TCP Dynamic Ports field.

   c. On the IP Addresses tab, specify the IP addresses that SQL Server should not actively listen on by setting their IP address entries to Active No and Enabled No.

5. Click OK.

Configuring Security for Native Client Configurations

By default, clients do not use Secure Sockets Layer (SSL) or attempt to validate server certificates. You can force protocol encryption, server certificate validation, or both by completing the following steps:

1. Start SQL Server Configuration Manager. Expand SQL Server Network Configuration and SQL Native Client Configuration.

2. Right-click SQL Native Client Configuration, and then select Properties.

3. For Force Protocol Encryption, select Yes to force clients to use SSL, or select No to use unencrypted connections.

4. For Trust Server Certificate, select Yes to force clients to validate server certificates, or select No to skip validation of server certificates.

Configuring the Native Client Protocol Order

Shared Memory is always the preferred local connection protocol. If enabled, Shared Memory is used before other enabled protocols.

You can disable the Shared Memory protocol and change the order of the other protocols by completing the following steps:

1. Start SQL Server Configuration Manager. Expand SQL Native Client Configuration, and then click Client Protocols.

2. Right-click any of the protocols listed, and then select Order. The Client Protocols Properties dialog box opens.

3. In the Client Protocols Properties dialog box, shown in Figure 2-5, you can do the following:

   ■ Change the order of an enabled protocol. First, click the name of the protocol you want to move, and then use the arrow buttons to the right of the Enabled Protocols list to position the protocol where you want it in the list.

   ■ Disable or enable protocols. To disable an enabled protocol, select it, and then click the left arrow button to move the name of the protocol to the Disabled Protocols list. To enable a disabled protocol, select it, and then click the right arrow button to move the name of the protocol to the Enabled Protocols list.

   ■ Enable or disable the Shared Memory protocol. To enable the Shared Memory protocol for local client connections, select Enable Shared Memory Protocol. To disable the Shared Memory protocol for local client connections, clear Enable Shared Memory Protocol.

4. Click OK.

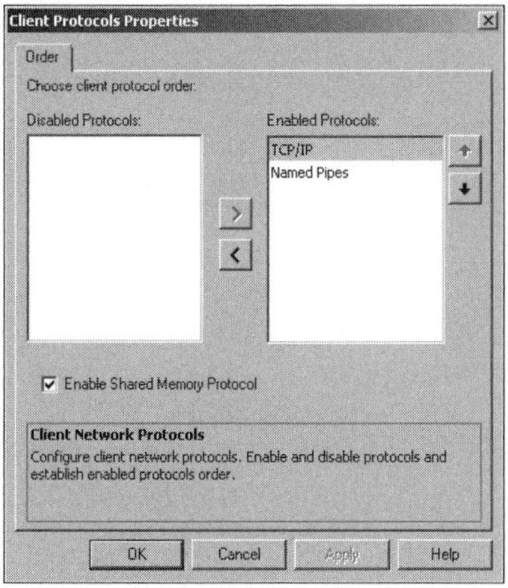

FIGURE 2-5 The Client Protocols Properties dialog box.

Configuring the Shared Memory Native Client Configuration

The Shared Memory protocol is used for local client connections only. You can enable or disable the Shared Memory protocol for clients by completing the following steps:

1. Start SQL Server Configuration Manager. Expand SQL Server Network Configuration and SQL Native Client Configuration, and then click Client Protocols.

2. Right-click Shared Memory and then select Properties.

3. You can now use the Enabled list to enable or disable the protocol. Select Yes to allow the protocol to be used, or select No to prevent the protocol from being used.

Configuring the Named Pipes Native Client Configuration

The Named Pipes protocol is used primarily for connections by applications written for early versions of Windows. The default named pipes are \\.\pipe\sql\ query for the default instance, and \\.\pipe\MSSQL$*instancename*\sql\query for a named instance. The default pipe for clients is set using an alias. The standard alias for clients is sql\query, which refers to the default pipe, such as \\.\pipe\sql\ query or \\.\pipe\MSSQL$*instancename*\sql\query. If you change the default pipe in the server's network configuration, you need to change the default pipe in the client configuration (and for all clients that connect to SQL Server in this way). For example, if SQL Server is using \\.\pipe\sqlserver\app1 as the default pipe, the client must use \sqlserver\app1 as the pipe name.

You can manage the Named Pipes client configuration by completing the following steps:

1. Start SQL Server Configuration Manager. Expand SQL Native Client Configuration, and then click Client Protocols.

2. Right-click Named Pipes, and then select Properties. You can now do the following:

    ■ Use the Enabled list to enable or disable the protocol. Select Yes to allow the protocol to be used, or select No to prevent the protocol from being used.

    ■ Set the default pipe. In the Named Pipes Properties dialog box, enter the default pipe for the client in the field provided, and then click OK.

Configuring the TCP/IP Native Client Configuration

The TCP/IP protocol is the preferred protocol for local or remote connections to SQL Server. When connecting to a default instance of the Database Engine using TCP/IP, the client must know the TCP port value. Thus, if a default instance has been configured to listen on a different port, you must change the client TCP/IP configuration to that port number. When connecting to a named instance of the Database Engine, the client attempts to obtain the port number from the SQL Browser service on the server to which it is connecting. If the SQL Browser service is not running, the TCP port number must be provided in the client configuration or as part of the connection string.

You can configure the TCP/IP client configuration by completing the following steps:

1. Start SQL Server Configuration Manager. Expand SQL Native Client Configuration, and then click Client Protocols.

2. If you want to enable or disable TCP/IP, right-click TCP/IP, and then select Enable or Disable as appropriate.

3. To view TCP/IP connection properties, right-click TCP/IP, and then select Properties.

4. While you are working with the TCP/IP Properties dialog box, you can set the default port by entering the port value for the client in the field provided.

5. You also can configure parameters that control whether and how the client tries to maintain idle TCP/IP connections. Two parameters are used:

    ■ **Keep Alive** Controls when a client first tries to verify that an idle connection is still valid and attempts to maintain the connection. By default, the client checks a connection after it has been idle for 30,000 milliseconds (30 seconds). In most cases, a value between 30 and 60 seconds will suffice. Depending on how busy the server is and the importance of client activity, you might want to verify and maintain idle connections more frequently, which can ensure that idle connections are not terminated. For example, you could use a smaller value, such as 15,000 or 20,000 milliseconds (15 to 20 seconds), to ensure that idle connections are validated more often.

- **Keep Alive Interval** Controls how frequently a client rechecks an idle connection when there is no initial response to the KEEPALIVE transmission. By default, the client retransmits the KEEPALIVE request every 1,000 milliseconds (1 second). If many clients are connecting to a busy server, you might want to lengthen the Keep Alive interval to decrease the number of KEEPALIVE retransmissions.

6. Click OK.

Understanding the Services Configuration

When you install SQL Server on Windows, several services are installed on the server. These services include the following:

- **Distributed Transaction Coordinator** MSDTC coordinates distributed transactions between two or more database servers. The executable file for this service is Msdtc.exe:

  ```
  "C:\Windows\System32\msdtc.exe
  ```

  You cannot configure this service in SQL Server Configuration Manager. Use the Services utility instead.

- **SQL Full-Text Filter Daemon Launcher** The FD Launcher performs document filtering and word breaking for SQL Server full-text search. When multiple instances of SQL Server are installed, you'll see the instance name in parentheses after the service name. The executable file for this service is Fdlauncher.exe, and the service runs under an instance specified in the startup command line, such as (for the default instance, MSSQLSERVER):

  ```
  "C:\Program Files\Microsoft SQL Server\MSSQL11.MSSQLSERVER\MSSQL\
      Binn\fdlauncher.exe" -s MSSQL11.MSSQLSERVER
  ```

- **SQL Server** The SQL Server service is the primary database service. When multiple instances of SQL Server are installed, you'll see the instance name in parentheses after the service name. The executable file for this service is Sqlservr.exe, and the service runs under an instance specified in the startup command line, such as (for the default instance, MSSQLSERVER):

  ```
  "C:\Program Files\Microsoft SQL Server\MSSQL11.MSSQLSERVER\MSSQL\
      Binn\sqlservr.exe" -s MSSQLSERVER
  ```

NOTE Although some components, such as the Database Engine, can be started directly from the command line, services typically are started with the appropriate tool or with NET START. If you start the Database Engine manually, you can set specific startup parameters, as discussed in Chapter 1.

- **SQL Server Agent** The SQL Server Agent is used with scheduling and alerting. For the default database instance, this service is named SQL-ServerAgent. When multiple instances of SQL Server are installed, you'll see the instance name in parentheses after the service name. The executable file for this service is Sqlagent.exe, and the service runs under an instance specified in the startup command line, such as:

```
"C:\Program Files\Microsoft SQL Server\MSSQL11.MSSQLSERVER\MSSQL\
    Binn\SqlAgent.exe" -i MSSQLSERVER
```

- **SQL Server Analysis Services** Analysis Services are used for Online Analytical Processing (OLAP) and data mining. When multiple instances of SQL Server are installed, you'll see the instance name in parentheses after the service name. The executable file for this service is Msmdsrv.exe, and the service runs an initialization file specified by the folder path in the startup command line, such as:

```
"C:\Program Files\Microsoft SQL Server\MSAS11.CUSTDATAW\OLAP\bin\
    msmdsrv.exe" -s "C:\Program Files\Microsoft SQL Server\
    MSAS11.CUSTDATAW\OLAP\Config"
```

The initialization file (Msmdsrv.ini) is defined by using XML and should not be edited directly.

- **SQL Server Browser** The SQL browser (SQLBrowser) provides connection details and information to clients. The executable file for this service is Sqlbrowser.exe, specified with the service startup command line, such as:

```
"C:\Program Files(x86)\Microsoft SQL Server\90\Shared\sqlbrowser.exe"
```

- **SQL Server Integration Services 11.0** MsDtsSrvr provides an enterprise data transformation and integration solution for extracting and transforming data. The executable file for this service is Msdtssrvr.exe, specified with the service startup command line, such as:

```
"C:\Program Files\Microsoft SQL Server\110\DTS\Binn\MsDtsSrvr.exe"
```

- **SQL Server Reporting Services** Reporting Services creates, manages, and delivers reports. For the default database instance, this service is named ReportServer. When multiple instances of SQL Server are installed, you'll see the instance name in parentheses after the service name. The executable file for this service is ReportingServicesService.exe, specified with the service startup command line, such as:

```
"C:\Program Files\Microsoft SQL Server\MSRS11.CUSTDATAW\
    Reporting Services\ReportServer\bin\ReportingServicesService.exe"
```

- **SQL Server VSS Writer** SQLWriter provides the necessary interfaces for backing up and restoring SQL Server by using the Volume Shadow Copy

Service (VSS). The executable file for this service is Sqlwriter.exe, specified with the service startup command line, such as:

```
"C:\Program Files\Microsoft SQL Server\90\Shared\sqlwriter.exe"
```

You cannot configure this service in SQL Server Configuration Manager. Use the Services utility instead.

NOTE In earlier releases, SQL Active Directory Helper service was used to manage integration between SQL Server and Active Directory, performing functions such as registering instances and managing object permissions. The helper service is no longer needed for these functions and is no longer installed. Related system stored procedures now are discontinued as well, including sp_ActiveDirectory_Obj, sp_ActiveDirectory_SCP, and sp_ActiveDirectory_Start.

You should use SQL Server Configuration Manager to view and manage the startup state of SQL Server services. There are file system and registry permissions granted to the service account when managed by using the SQL Server Configuration Manager that are not granted when modifying these entries by using the Services applet. With Windows Server 2008, startup accounts can be domain user accounts, local user accounts, or built-in system accounts. Beginning with Windows Server 2008 Release 2, virtual accounts are used by default and managed service accounts also can be configured.

Virtual accounts are managed local accounts that provide the ability to access resources with a computer identity and credentials. When specifying a virtual account to start a service, you leave the password blank. The service accesses resources using the computer's credentials in the format DomainName\ComputerName$, such as CPANDL\DbServer45$, but they cannot be authenticated to a remote location. Because the computer's credentials are used, no password management is required, and this simplifies administration. Keep in mind that virtual accounts can't be used with SQL Server clusters because the account's security identifier (SID) would be the same on each node of the cluster.

Although virtual accounts are used by default when available, managed service accounts are recommended for when SQL Server needs to access external resources. Managed service accounts are domain user accounts where the account password and the related Service Principal Name (SPN) are managed automatically by a domain controller. As with virtual accounts, you leave the password blank when specifying a managed account to start a service.

A service configured to use a managed service account accesses network resources using credentials in the format DomainName\AccountName$, such as CPANDL\Mssql12$. As the credentials can be authenticated, remote locations can be accessed. Because domain controllers manage the account password, no password management is required, and this simplifies administration while providing additional management options, such as the ability to assign permissions through group membership.

Because accounts used by SQL Server services are granted many privileges and permissions automatically during SQL Server setup, it's best to create any accounts you'll need prior to installing SQL Server. You use Windows PowerShell cmdlets to create and work with managed service accounts. The related cmdlets are only available when you've imported the Active Directory module (using import-module activedirectory). Using managed service accounts is a three-step process:

1. You create the account.
2. You install the account.
3. You configure a service to use the account.

You create a managed service account using New-ADServiceAccount. The basic syntax is as follows:

```
New-ADServiceAccount –DisplayName DisplayName -SamAccountName Name
```

where *DisplayName* is the display name for the account, and *Name* is the pre–Windows 2000 name of the account. For example:

```
New-ADServiceAccount –DisplayName "SQL Agent Account"
-SamAccountName sqlagent
```

The account will have a 240-character, randomly generated password and be created in the Managed Service Account organizational unit (OU). If you need to pass in credentials to create the account, use the –Credential parameter, as shown in this example:

```
$cred = Get-Credential
New-ADServiceAccount –DisplayName "SQL Agent Account"
-SamAccountName pool1 –Credential $cred
```

After you create a managed service account, you can install the account on your database server to make it available. Use Install-ADServiceAccount with the basic syntax as follows:

```
Install-ADServiceAccount -Identity ServiceAccountId
```

ServiceAccountId is the display name or Security Account Manager (SAM) account name of the service account, such as:

```
Install-ADServiceAccount -Identity sqlagent
```

If you need to pass in credentials to create the account, use the –Credential parameter.

Once you've created and installed the managed service account, you should use SQL Server Configuration Manager to configure a service to run with the account. When you manage the service account by using the Configuration Manager, the file share and registry permissions required by SQL Server are handled automatically.

To configure a service to run with the account, follow these steps:

1. Start SQL Server Configuration Manager, and then click SQL Server Services.

2. Right-click the name of the service that you want to work with, and then click Properties.

3. On the Log On tab, select This Account, and then type the name of the managed service account in the format *DomainName\AccountName,* or click Browse to search for the account.

4. Confirm that the password field is blank, and then click OK.

5. Select the name of the service, and then click Start or Restart (as appropriate) to start the service using the managed service account. Confirm that the newly configured account name appears in the Log On As column for the service.

Although managed service accounts are listed in Active Directory Users And Computers, you shouldn't use this management tool to work with managed service accounts. Instead, you should use Get-ADServiceAccount to get information about one or more managed service accounts, Set-ADServiceAccount to set properties on an existing managed service account, and Remove-ADServiceAccount to remove a managed service account from Active Directory Domain Services (AD DS).

Configuring SQL Server Services

Start SQL Server Configuration Manager and click the SQL Server Services node to view the critical SQL Server services configured for all running instances of SQL Server 2012 on the computer you are currently connected to. The services available depend on the components you have installed.

As shown in Figure 2-6, after you select the SQL Server Services node, you see a detailed entry for each service that includes the following information:

- **Name** The common name for the service shown in the user interface
- **State** The status of the service as of the last refresh, such as Running or Stopped
- **Start Mode** The startup state of the service—Automatic, Manual, or Disabled
- **Log On As** The user account under which the service runs
- **Process ID** The identification number of the system process under which the service is running
- **Service Type** The type of SQL Server component to which the service relates, such as Report Server

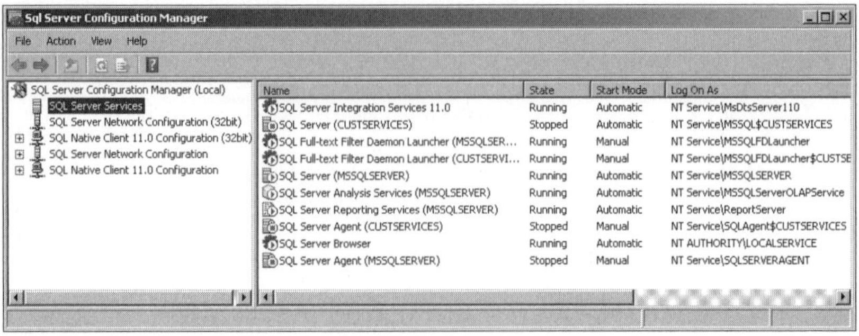

FIGURE 2-6 Examine the service status and configuration.

The Log On As value indicates the type of account being used as follows:

- For services running under local accounts, you see the name of the system account used, such as NT AUTHORITY\LOCALSERVICE for a service running under the Local Service account.

- For services running under domain accounts, you see the domain name followed by the account name, such as CPANDL\SQLEngineering.

- For services running under managed accounts, you see the domain name followed by the account name with a $ suffix, such as CPANDL\SQL-Engineering$.

- For services running under virtual accounts, you see NT SERVICE followed by the service name and the instance name (if applicable), such as NT Service\MSSQLServer for the default instance and NT Service\MSSQLServer$*InstanceName* for a named instance.

Any SQL Server services not being used or not required for your installation should be set to manual startup and stopped if they are running. If you want to prevent a service from running, you should set Start Mode to Disabled. Keep in mind that the SQL Server Browser service provides connection information to client computers. If clients connect to SQL Server remotely, this service is required (in most cases).

When you install SQL Server, SQL Server Setup assigns default access permissions to the user account associated with SQL Server services. Table 2-2 lists the SQL Server services and the default permissions granted. During installation, the user accounts also are assigned access permissions for numerous files and folders used by SQL Server. (Additional permissions that you may want to grant are noted with an asterisk.)

TABLE 2-2 Permissions Assigned Per Service

SERVICE	PERMISSIONS GRANTED
FD Launcher	Log on as a service Bypass traverse checking Adjust memory quotas for a process
SQL Server	Log on as a service Replace a process-level token Bypass traverse checking Adjust memory quotas for a process *Add network write permissions to enable writing to a mail slot with xp_sendmail *Add Act As Part Of The Operating System to allow users who aren't SQL Server administrators to run xp_cmdshell
SQL Server Agent	Log on as a service Replace a process-level token Bypass traverse checking Adjust memory quotas for a process *Grant membership in the Administrators local group to enable autorestart
SQL Server Analysis Services	Log on as a service
SQL Server Browser	Log on as a service
SQL Server Integration Services	Log on as a service Bypass traverse checking Impersonate a client after authentication
SQL Server Reporting Services	Log on as a service

Managing Service State and Start Mode

You can use the Services utility or SQL Server Configuration Manager to manage SQL Server services. With the Services utility, you manage SQL Server services as you would any other service. With SQL Server Configuration Manager, you can manage the service login account, the start mode, and the status. If applicable, you also can manage advanced features such as the dump directory, error reporting, and startup parameters. The advantage that SQL Server Configuration Manager has over the Services utility is that it manages the file share and registry permissions required by SQL Server. Additionally, some advanced options, such as the dump directory, can be configured only by using SQL Server Configuration Manager.

Using SQL Server Configuration Manager, you can stop, start, pause, or restart a server service by completing the following steps:

1. Start SQL Server Configuration Manager, and then select the SQL Server Services node.

2. In the right pane, you see a list of services used by SQL Server and its configured components. You can work with services in several ways:

   - Click the name of the service to select it. Use the Start, Pause, Stop, and Restart buttons on the toolbar to manage the service run state, or click the Properties button to view the service properties.

   - Right-click the service and then use the shortcut menu to manage the service run state, or click Properties to view the service properties.

   - Double-click the service to view the service properties.

You can set a service's start mode by following these steps:

1. Start SQL Server Configuration Manager and then select the SQL Server Services node.

2. In the right pane, right-click a service, and then select Properties from the shortcut menu.

3. On the Service tab of the Properties dialog box, use the Start Mode list to select the start mode, as shown in Figure 2-7. Options include Automatic, Disabled, and Manual.

FIGURE 2-7 Use Service tab options for setting the start mode.

4. Click OK.

Setting the Startup Service Account

SQL Server and its components have specific rights and permissions from the startup service account. These permissions are used whenever the Database Engine or another SQL Server component performs tasks on the local system or across the network. You can configure services to use three different types of built-in accounts: local service, local system, and network service. You also can configure services to use domain accounts.

You can specify a built-in account for a SQL Server service by completing the following steps:

1. Start SQL Server Configuration Manager, and then select the SQL Server Services node.

2. In the right pane, right-click a service to select it, and then select Properties.

3. On the Log On tab of the Properties dialog box, select Built-In Account, and then use the drop-down list to choose the account to use.

4. If the service is running, you must restart the service by clicking Restart. This stops the service and starts it again using the new credentials.

5. Click OK.

You can specify a domain account for a SQL Server service by completing the following steps:

1. Start SQL Server Configuration Manager, and then select the SQL Server Services node.

2. In the right pane, right-click a service to select it, and then select Properties.

3. On the Log On tab of the Properties dialog box, choose the This Account option, as shown in Figure 2-8. Then type the designated account name and password. For domain accounts, specify the domain as part of the account name, such as CPANDL\sqlprimary, where *CPANDL* is the domain name and *sqlprimary* is the account name. For local computer accounts, enter .\followed by the name of the account, such as .\sqlaccount. Click Browse if you want to use the Select User Or Group dialog box to select an account.

4. If the service is running, you must restart the service by clicking Restart. This stops the service and starts it again using the new credentials.

5. Click OK to close the Properties dialog box, and then be sure you've granted the specified domain account the appropriate permissions and privileges. Refer to Table 2-2 earlier in this chapter to determine the groups to which you should add the domain account to ensure that the account has the appropriate access permissions for files and folders used by SQL Server.

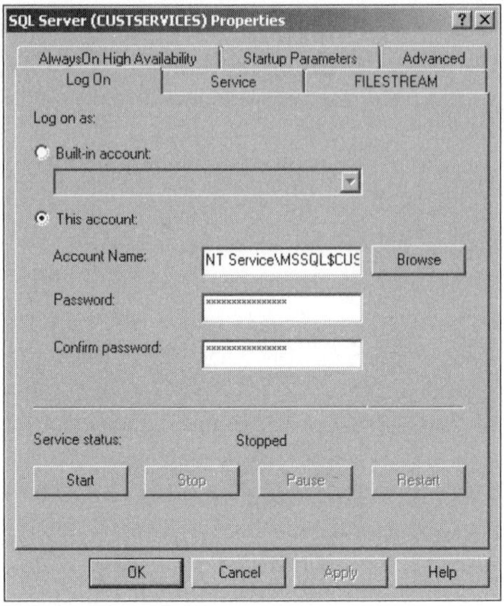

FIGURE 2-8 Set the startup account for a selected service.

Setting Up File Streaming

File streaming allows the SQL Server Database Engine to work with binary large objects (BLOBs) that are stored outside the database. To distinguish standard BLOBs stored in database tables from BLOBs stored outside the database, BLOBS stored outside the database are called FILESTREAM BLOBs. Like standard BLOBs, FILESTREAM BLOBs are specified in the database as varbinary(max) data types and can include any type of unstructured data, from Microsoft Office documents to videos to digital images. Unlike standard BLOBs, FILESTREAM BLOBs do not have a 2-gigabyte (GB) file size limit. You distinguish a FILESTREAM BLOB from a standard BLOB by setting the FILESTREAM attribute on a varbinary(max) column. This tells the Database Engine to store the data for that column on the file system rather than in the database. SQL Server is able to locate the BLOB data because it stores pointers to BLOBs in the database.

Working with File-Stream Data

T-SQL statements can insert, update, query, search, and delete file-stream data. For caching file data while streaming files, the SQL Server Database Engine uses the features of the NTFS file system rather than the SQL Server buffer pool. This helps ensure that memory is available for processing queries and also helps maintain Database Engine performance.

Although you can use an insert operation to prepopulate a FILESTREAM field with a null value, an empty value, or a limited amount of inline data, a large amount of data is streamed more efficiently into a file that uses Win32 interfaces. Here, the Win32 interfaces work within the context of a SQL Server transaction, and you use the Pathname intrinsic function to obtain the logical Universal Naming Convention (UNC) path of the BLOB file on the file system. You then use the OpenSqlFilestream application programming interface (API) to obtain a file handle and operate on the BLOB via the file system by using the following Win32 file streaming interfaces: ReadFile, WriteFile, TransmitFile, SetFilePointer, SetEndOfFile, and FlushFileBuffers. Close the handle by using CloseHandle. Because file operations are transactional, you cannot delete or rename FILESTREAM files through the file system.

When you update a FILESTREAM field, you modify the underlying BLOB data in the file system. When a FILESTREAM field is set to NULL, the BLOB data associated with the field is deleted. To perform partial updates to the data, you cannot use a T-SQL chunked update implemented as UPDATE.Write(). Instead, use a device FS control (FSCTL_SQL_FILESTREAM_FETCH_OLD_CONTENT) to fetch the old content into the file that the opened handle references, which triggers a content copy. When you delete a row or delete or truncate a table that contains FILESTREAM data, you delete the underlying BLOB data in the file system.

FILESTREAM data must be stored in FILESTREAM file groups. A FILESTREAM file group is a special file group that contains file system directories instead of the files themselves. These file system directories are called *data containers* and act as the interface between Database Engine storage and file system storage.

When working with FILESTREAM data, you also should keep in mind the following:

- You can create database snapshots only of standard (non-FILESTREAM) file groups. The FILESTREAM file groups are marked as offline for those snapshot databases. Further, a SELECT statement that is executed on a FILESTREAM table in a snapshot database must not include a FILESTREAM column.

- Log shipping supports file streaming so long as the primary and secondary servers are running SQL Server 2012 or later and have file streaming enabled.

- Database mirroring does not support file streaming. You cannot create a FILESTREAM file group on the principal server and cannot configure database mirroring for a database that contains FILESTREAM file groups.

- Full-text indexing works with a FILESTREAM column in the same way that it does with a varbinary(max) column so long as the FILESTREAM table has a column that contains the file name extension for each FILESTREAM BLOB. The full-text engine indexes the contents of FILESTREAM BLOBs, and whenever a FILESTREAM BLOB is updated, it is re-indexed.

- A varbinary(max) column that has the FILESTREAM attribute enabled at the Publisher can be replicated to a Subscriber with or without the FILESTREAM attribute. You can specify the way in which the column is replicated by using the Article Properties - <Article> dialog box or the @schema_option parameter of sp_addarticle or sp_addmergearticle.

- For failover clustering, FILESTREAM file groups must be put on a shared disk. You also must enable file streaming on each node in the cluster that will host the FILESTREAM instance.

Enabling and Configuring File Streaming

You can enable and configure file streaming by completing the following steps:

1. Start SQL Server Configuration Manager, and then select the SQL Server Services node.

2. In the right pane, right-click the instance of the Database Engine service that you want to configure, and then select Properties.

3. On the FILESTREAM tab of the Properties dialog box, shown in Figure 2-9, you now can use the Enable FILESTREAM For Transact-SQL Access check box to enable or disable file streaming for T-SQL. Select this check box to allow file streaming to be used; clear this check box to prevent file streaming from being allowed. If you disabled file streaming, click OK and skip the remaining steps.

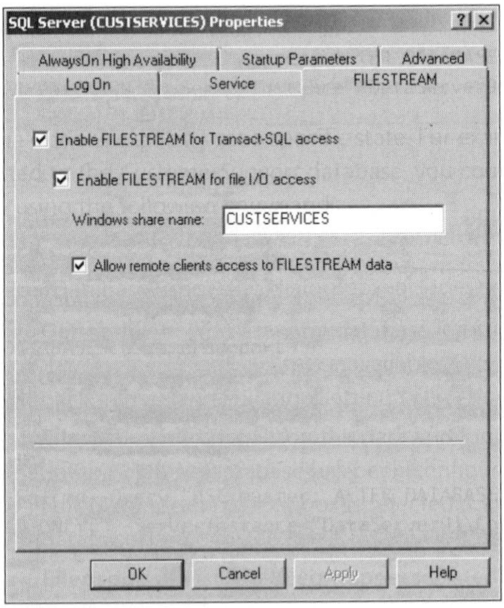

FIGURE 2-9 Configure FILESTREAM data for a Database Engine instance.

4. If you want to enable file I/O streaming access by local clients, select Enable FILESTREAM For File I/O Access, and then specify the name of the Windows share from which files will be streamed. The default share name is MSSQLSERVER, which sets the global root for file streaming as \\?\GLOBALROOT\Device\RsFx0101\<localmachine>\MSSQLSERVER.

5. If you enabled local file streaming and want to enable file I/O streaming access by remote clients, select Allow Remote Clients Access To FILESTREAM Data. Remote file system access to FILESTREAM data is enabled over the Server Message Block (SMB) protocol. If the client is remote, no write operations are cached by the client side, which means that write operations are always sent to the server, where they can be cached if necessary.

6. If you made changes and the service is running, you must restart the service by clicking Restart on the Log On tab. This stops the service and then restarts it using the new settings.

7. Click OK.

Configuring Service Dump Directories, Error Reporting, and Customer Feedback Reporting

You can use advanced service configuration options to configure reporting and error-logging features. When you install SQL Server, you are asked whether you want to enable two types of reports:

- Error reports
- Feature reports (also called Customer Feedback Reporting)

When error reporting is enabled, error reports are generated and sent to Microsoft or a designated corporate error-reporting server whenever fatal errors cause a service to terminate. Error reports help determine the cause of the fatal error so that it can be corrected, and they contain details to identify what caused the error, including the version of SQL Server being used, the operating system and hardware configuration, and data from the memory or files of the process that caused the error.

Error information is also logged in a designated dump directory. The dump directory used depends on the component and its related instance. For example, the dump directory for the default SQL Server instance will be located by default under %ProgramFiles%\Microsoft SQL Server\MSSQL11.MSSQLSERVER\MSSQL\ LOG, and the Reporting Services dump directory will be located by default under %ProgramFiles%\Microsoft SQL Server\MSRS11.CUSTDATAWAREHOUS\Reporting Services\LogFiles.

Customer Feedback Reporting generates reports about component usage that are sent to Microsoft when this feature is configured. These reports help Microsoft understand how components and features are being used.

You can manage reporting and error dumps for each service individually. To do so, complete the following steps:

1. Start SQL Server Configuration Manager, and then select the SQL Server Services node.

2. In the right pane, right-click a service to select it, and then select Properties.

3. Select the Advanced tab in the Properties dialog box. Using the properties boxes shown in Figure 2-10, you now can do the following:

- Use the Dump Directory box to view the current dump directory. To change the dump directory, simply enter the new directory to use. Be sure that the logon account for the selected service has appropriate read and write access to this directory.

- Use the Error Reporting and Customer Feedback Reporting lists to enable or disable reporting as appropriate. Select Yes to enable reporting, or select No to disable reporting.

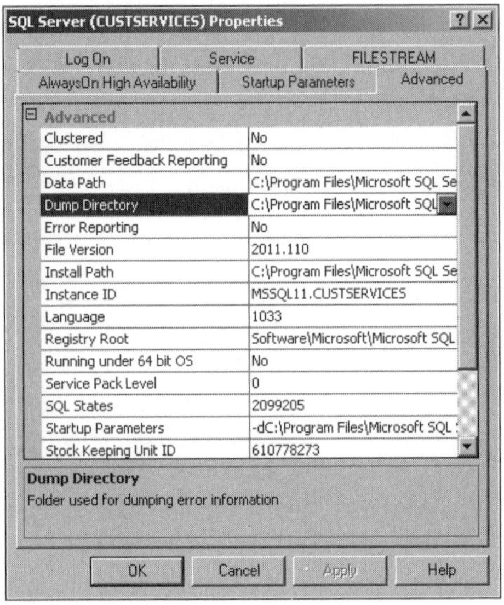

FIGURE 2-10 Set advanced options for a selected service.

4. If you made changes and the service is running, you must restart the service by clicking Restart on the Log On tab. This stops the service and then starts it again using the new settings.

5. Click OK.

PART II

Microsoft SQL Server 2012 Management and Security

Implementing Policy-Based Management

P olicy-Based Management is an extensible and scalable configuration framework that you can use to manage servers, databases, and other objects in your data environments. As an administrator, you need to be very familiar with how Policy-Based Management technology works, and that's exactly what this chapter is about. If you haven't worked with Policy-Based Management technology before, one thing you'll notice immediately is that the technology is fairly advanced and has many features. To help you manage this complex technology, I'll start with an overview of Policy-Based Management and then explore its components.

Introducing Policy-Based Management

Just about every administrative task you perform can be affected by the policy-based framework in some way. The policy-based framework provides the ability to define policies that apply to server instances, databases, and other objects in your data environments. You use these policies to help you control and manage the configuration of data services throughout the enterprise. Through intelligent monitoring and proactive responses, you can prevent changes that deviate from the configurations you specify and want. You also can scale management across multiple servers, which makes enforcing consistent configuration policies easier.

Within the policy-based framework, you use the following objects to configure policy management:

- **Facet**   Defines a management area within the policy-based framework. Each management area has a fixed set of related properties that you can configure. For example, the Backup Device facet has the following properties: BackupDeviceType, Name, PhysicalLocation, and SkipTapeLabel.

- **Condition**   Defines the permitted states for one or more properties of a single facet. For example, you can create a condition called Limit Backup Devices to specify that for the Backup Device facet, BackupDeviceType can be set to hard disk or tape and SkipTapeLabel should always be set to True.

- **Policy**   Contains a single condition that you want to enforce. For example, you can create a policy named Standard Backup Device Policy that assigns the Limit Backup Devices condition.

- **Category**   Contains one or more policies that you want to enforce together. For example, you can create a category named Standard DB Policies that contains all the standard policies that you want to enforce within your Microsoft SQL Server databases.

- **Target**   Defines the servers, databases, or other database objects to which policies are applied. For example, a target set could include all the databases on an instance of SQL Server.

MORE INFO   Put another way, policy-based management is explicit declarative management that you configure using facets, conditions, categories, and targets. *Facets* are fixed lists of things you can set policy on. *Conditions* determine when policy applies. *Categories* group policies together for enforcement. *Targets* determine to which objects policies apply.

You can create and manage policies in several ways. In SQL Server Management Studio, you can create policies from scratch or import existing policy files. The policy creation process includes the following steps:

1. Select a facet that contains the properties you want to configure.
2. Define a condition that specifies the permitted states of the facet.
3. Define a policy that contains the condition and sets one of the evaluation modes listed in Table 3-1.
4. Determine whether an instance of SQL Server is in compliance with the policy, and then take appropriate action.

For scripting, the Microsoft.SqlServer.Management.Dmf namespace contains classes that represent policy-based management objects. You use the root of this namespace, the PolicyStore class, to work with policies. Consider the following example:

```
$comp = get-content c:\data\servers.txt
```

```
$cn = New-Object Microsoft.SqlServer.Management.Sdk.Sfc.SqlStoreConnection
("server='DbServer85';Trusted_Connection=True")

$ps = new-object Microsoft.SQLServer.Management.DMF.PolicyStore($cn)

foreach ($c in $comp) { foreach ($p in $ps.Policies) {
 #Invoke-PolicyEvaluation  }
}
```

Here, you get a list of servers that you want to work with from a text file and then configure a connection to SQL Server. Once you're connected to SQL Server, you access the policy store and work with the policies on each server in your list.

TABLE 3-1 Evaluation Modes for Policy-Based Management

POLICY EVALUATION MODE	DESCRIPTION	EXECUTION TYPE
On Demand	Evaluates the policy only when you directly execute the policy. Also referred to as *ad hoc* policy evaluation.	Manual
On Change: Log Only	Evaluates a policy when a relevant change is made and logs policy violations in the event logs.	Automatic
On Change: Prevent	When nested triggers are enabled, uses data definition language (DDL) triggers to prevent policy violations by detecting changes that violate a policy and rolling them back.	Automatic
On Schedule	Uses SQL Server Agent jobs to evaluate policies periodically. Logs policy violations in the event logs and generates a report.	Automatic

NOTE All facets support the On Demand and On Schedule modes. Facets support the On Change: Log Only mode only if the change of the facet state can be captured by related system events. Facets support the On Change: Prevent mode only if there is transactional support for the DDL statements that change the facet state. Only automatic policies can be enabled or disabled.

Policy categories apply to databases and servers. At the database level, database owners can subscribe a database to a set of policy categories, and those policies govern the database. By default, all databases implicitly subscribe to the default policy category. At the server level, you can apply policy categories to all databases.

You can mark categories as Active or Inactive at the server or database level. Although you can classify policies into different policy categories, a policy can belong only to one policy category.

All objects defined on a SQL Server instance form a target hierarchy. Within a policy, you define a target when you apply filters to the target hierarchy. For example, a target set with a large scope could include all the databases on an instance of SQL Server, while a target set with a small scope could include only the tables and indexes owned by the Sales schema in the Customers database.

The effective policies of a target are those policies that govern the target. For a policy to be effective with regard to a target, the policy must be enabled and the target must be subject to the policy. Within your data services environments, you enforce Policy-Based Management by using configuration servers. A designated configuration server is responsible for monitoring and enforcing policies as assigned. By default, each instance of SQL Server acts as its own configuration server. This means that each SQL Server instance normally handles its own policy monitoring and enforcement.

REAL WORLD   To be notified when messages from automatically executed policies are written to the event logs, you can create alerts to detect these messages and perform necessary actions. The alerts should detect the messages according to their message number. Look for message numbers 34050, 34051, 34052, and 34053. You can configure alerts as discussed in the "Managing Alerts" section in Chapter 10, "Automating and Maintaining SQL Server 2012."

When policies are executed automatically, they execute as a member of the sysadmin role. This allows the policy to write entries to the event logs and raise an alert. When policies are evaluated on demand, they execute in the security context of the current user. To write to the event log, the user must have ALTER TRACE permissions or be a member of the sysadmin fixed server role; otherwise, Windows will not write to the event log and will not fire an alert.

Working with Policy-Based Management

You must be a member of the PolicyAdministratorRole role in the *msdb* database to configure Policy-Based Management settings. This role has complete control of all policies and can create policies and conditions, edit policies and conditions, and enable or disable policies.

When working with policies, keep the following in mind:

- A system administrator or database owner can subscribe a database to a policy or policy group.
- On-demand policy execution occurs in the security context of the user.
- Members of the PolicyAdministratorRole role can create policies that they do not have permission to execute on an ad hoc basis.

- Members of the PolicyAdministratorRole role can enable or disable policies.
- Policies that are in the On Schedule mode use SQL Server Agent jobs that are owned by the sa login.

Although you can manage policies for each instance of SQL Server, you'll likely reuse policies you've defined and then apply them to other instances of SQL Server. With Policy-Based Management, you can apply policies to multiple instances of SQL Server in several ways. As discussed in the "Importing and Exporting Policies" section later in this chapter, you can export the policies you've defined on a particular instance of SQL Server and then import the policies on another instance of SQL Server. During the import process, you can specify whether policies are enabled or disabled and whether to preserve the exported state of the policies.

Being able to export and import policies is useful. However, you don't necessarily need to move policies around to enforce the policies on multiple computers running SQL Server. Instead, you can manage policies by using a central management server. A central management server is a special type of configuration server that is responsible for monitoring and enforcing policy on any instance of SQL Server registered as a subordinate server. As discussed in the "Configuring Central Management Servers" section later in this chapter, you designate central management servers and their subordinates by using SQL Server Management Studio. Because the central management architecture is already an execution environment for Transact-SQL (T-SQL) statements related to policies, you can execute T-SQL statements on multiple instances of SQL Server at the same time from a central management server.

> **REAL WORLD**   Generally, SQL Server does more validation in the graphical user interface (GUI) than in the application programming interface (API). As a result, you may be allowed to create a policy in T-SQL but be restricted from creating the same policy in the GUI. Why? Because SQL Server tries to prevent you from creating policies that might impact performance when working in the GUI, while making it possible for advanced users to be able to work around this.

Because SQL Server stores policy-related data in the *msdb* database, you should back up *msdb* after you change conditions, policies, or categories. Policy history for policies evaluated in the current instance of the Database Engine is maintained in *msdb* system tables. Policy history for policies applied to other instances of the Database Engine or applied to Reporting Services or Analysis Services is not retained.

As summarized in Table 3-2, SQL Server 2012 includes several sets of predefined policies, including those for the Database Engine, Analysis Services, and Reporting Services. By default, the policies are stored as XML files in the following locations, and you must import them into SQL Server:

- Microsoft SQL Server\110\Tools\Policies\DatabaseEngine\1033
- Microsoft SQL Server\110\Tools\Policies\AnalysisServices\1033
- Microsoft SQL Server\110\Tools\Policies\ReportingServices\1033

NOTE On 64-bit computers, policies are located under Program Files (x86) rather than Program Files when you install SQL Server in the default file system location. Surface area configuration is discussed in the "Managing SQL Server Component Feature Access" section in Chapter 2, "Managing SQL Server Services and Clients."

TABLE 3-2 Important Predefined Policies for SQL Server 2012

PREDEFINED POLICY NAME	DESCRIPTION
Asymmetric Key Encryption Algorithm	Checks whether asymmetric keys were created by using 1024-bit or stronger encryption. As a best practice, you should use RSA 1024-bit or stronger encryption to create asymmetric keys for data encryption.
Backup And Data File Location	Checks whether database files are on devices separate from the backup files. As a best practice, you should put the database and backups on separate backup devices. This approach helps safeguard the data in case of device failure and also optimizes the I/O performance for both the production use of the database and the writing of backups.
CmdExec Rights Secured	Checks an instance of SQL Server 2000 to determine whether only members of the sysadmin server role can run CmdExec and ActiveX Script job steps, which is a recommended best practice.
Data And Log File Location	Checks whether data and log files are placed on separate logical drives. As a best practice, placing the files on separate drives allows the I/O activity to occur at the same time for both the data and log files.
Database Auto Close	Checks whether the AUTO_CLOSE option is set to OFF. When AUTO_CLOSE is set to ON, this option can cause performance degradation on frequently accessed databases because of the increased overhead of opening and closing the database after each connection. AUTO_CLOSE also flushes the procedure cache after each connection. As a best practice, you should set the AUTO_CLOSE option to OFF on a database that is accessed frequently.
Database Auto Shrink	Checks whether the AUTO_SHRINK database option is set to OFF. Because frequently shrinking and expanding a database can lead to fragmentation on the storage device, you should set the AUTO_SHRINK database option to OFF in most instances.

PREDEFINED POLICY NAME	DESCRIPTION
Database Collation	Checks whether user-defined databases are defined using a database collation that is the same as the collation for the *master* and *model* databases, which is a recommended best practice. Otherwise, collation conflicts can occur that might prevent code from executing. You can resolve collation conflicts by exporting the data from the user database, importing it into new tables that have the same collation as the *master* and *model* databases, and then rebuilding the system databases to use a collation that matches the user database collation. Or you can modify any stored procedures that join user tables to tables in *tempdb* to create the tables in *tempdb* by using the collation of the user database.
Database Page Status	Checks for user databases that have the database status set to Suspect. The Database Engine marks a database as Suspect when it reads a database page that contains an 824 error. Error 824 indicates that a logical consistency error was detected during a read operation, and it frequently indicates data corruption caused by a faulty I/O subsystem component. Resolve this situation by running DBCC CHECKDB.
Database Page Verification	Checks whether the PAGE_VERIFY database option is set to CHECKSUM. This recommended best practice helps provide a high level of data-file integrity by forcing the Database Engine to calculate a checksum over the contents of the whole page and store the value in the page header when a page is written to disk. When the page is read from disk, the checksum is recomputed and compared to the checksum value that is stored in the page header.
Guest Permissions	Checks whether the Guest user has permission to access a user database. As a best practice, you should revoke the Guest user permission to access non-system databases if it is not required. Although the Guest user cannot be dropped, the Guest user can be disabled by revoking its CONNECT permission. Execute REVOKE CONNECT FROM GUEST within any database other than *master* or *tempdb*.
Last Successful Backup Date	Checks to ensure that a database has recent backups. Scheduling regular backups protects a database against data loss. If there are no recent backups, you should schedule backups by using a database maintenance plan.

PREDEFINED POLICY NAME	DESCRIPTION
Public Not Granted Server Permissions	Checks whether the public server role has server permissions. Every login that is created on the server is a member of the public server role and has server permissions. As a best practice, however, do not grant server permissions directly to the public server role.
Read-Only Database Recovery Model	Checks for read-only user databases that have recovery set to Full. As a best practice, these databases should use the Simple recovery model because they aren't updated regularly.
SQL Server 32-Bit Affinity Mask Overlap	Checks whether the 32-bit instance of SQL Server has one or more processors that are assigned to be used with both the Affinity Mask and the Affinity I/O Mask options. Enabling a CPU with both these options can slow performance by forcing the processor to be overused.
SQL Server 64-Bit Affinity Mask Overlap	Checks whether the 64-bit instance of SQL Server has one or more processors that are assigned to be used with both the Affinity Mask and the Affinity I/O Mask options. Enabling a CPU with both these options can slow performance by forcing the processor to be overused.
SQL Server Affinity Mask	Checks whether the Affinity Mask option is set to 0. This is the default value, which dynamically controls CPU affinity. Using the default value is a recommended best practice.
SQL Server Blocked Process Threshold	Checks the Blocked Process Threshold option and ensures that it is set to 0 (disabled) or to a value higher than or equal to 5 seconds. Setting the Blocked Process Threshold option to a value from 1 through 4 can cause the deadlock monitor to run constantly, and this state is desirable only when you are troubleshooting.
SQL Server Default Trace	Determines whether the Default Trace option is disabled. When this option is enabled, default tracing provides information about configuration and DDL changes to the SQL Server Database Engine.
SQL Server Dynamic Locks	Checks whether the Locks option is set to 0. This is the default value, which dynamically controls locks. Using the default value is a recommended best practice. If the maximum number of locks is reached, batch jobs stop and SQL Server generates "out of locks" errors.

PREDEFINED POLICY NAME	DESCRIPTION
SQL Server I_O Affinity Mask for Non-Enterprise Servers	Checks whether the IO Affinity Mask option is set to 0 for editions of SQL Server other than Enterprise. With this value, SQL Server disk I/O is scheduled to any of the CPUs eligible to process SQL Server threads.
SQL Server Lightweight Pooling	Checks whether the Lightweight Pooling option is set to 0. This is the default value, which prevents SQL Server from using lightweight pooling. Using the default value is a recommended best practice.
SQL Server Login Mode	Checks the login security configuration to ensure Windows authentication is being used. Using Windows authentication is a recommended best practice because this mode uses the Kerberos security protocol, provides support for account lockout, and supports password expiration. For Windows Server 2008, Windows authentication also provides password policy enforcement in terms of complexity validation for strong passwords.
SQL Server Max Degree Of Parallelism	Checks whether the Max Degree Of Parallelism (MAXDOP) option is set to a value greater than 8. Setting this option to a value greater than 8 often causes unwanted resource consumption and performance degradation, so you usually want to reduce the value to 8 or less.
SQL Server Max Worker Threads For SQL Server 2005 And Above	Checks the Max Worker Threads option for potentially incorrect settings. Setting the Max Worker Threads option to a small value might prevent enough threads from servicing incoming client requests in a timely manner. Setting the option to a large value can waste address space because each active thread consumes 512 kilobytes (KB) on 32-bit servers and up to 4 megabytes (MB) on 64-bit servers. For instances of SQL Server 2005 and SQL Server 2012, you should set this option to 0, which allows SQL Server to determine the correct number of active worker threads automatically based on user requests.
SQL Server Network Packet Size	Determines whether the network packet size of any logged-in user is more than 8,060 bytes. As a best practice, the network packet size should not exceed 8,060 bytes. Otherwise, SQL Server performs different memory allocation operations, and this can cause an increase in the virtual address space that is not reserved for the buffer pool.

PREDEFINED POLICY NAME	DESCRIPTION
SQL Server Password Expiration	Checks whether password expiration is enabled for each SQL Server login. As a best practice, you should use ALTER LOGIN to enable password expiration for all SQL Server logins. Additionally, if SQL Server authentication is not required in your environment, you should enable only Windows authentication.
SQL Server Password Policy	Checks whether the Enforce Password policy is enabled for each SQL Server login. As a best practice, you should enable the Enforce Password policy for all the SQL Server logins by using ALTER LOGIN.
SQL Server System Tables Updatable	Checks whether system tables for SQL Server 2000 can be updated. As a best practice, you shouldn't allow updates to system tables.
Surface Area Configuration for Database Engine ...	A set of related policies for determining whether various editions of SQL Server are using default surface area settings. By disabling unneeded features, you can enhance security.
Symmetric Key Encryption For User Databases	Checks whether encryption keys that have a length of less than 128 bytes do not use the RC2 or RC4 encryption algorithm. As a best practice, you should use AES 128 bit or larger to create symmetric keys for data encryption. If AES is not supported by your operating system, you should use 3DES encryption.
Symmetric Key For *master* Database	Checks for user-created symmetric keys in the *master* database.
Symmetric Key For System Databases	Checks for user-created symmetric keys in the *model, msdb,* and *tempdb* databases. As a best practice, you should not create symmetric keys in the system databases.
Trustworthy Database	Checks whether the dbo role for a database is assigned to the sysadmin fixed server role and the database has its trustworthy bit set to ON. As a best practice, you should turn off the trustworthy bit or revoke sysadmin permissions from the dbo database role. Otherwise, a privileged database user can elevate privileges to the sysadmin role and then create and run unsafe assemblies that could compromise the system.

PREDEFINED POLICY NAME	DESCRIPTION
Windows Event Log Cluster Disk Resource Corruption Error	Checks the system event log for EventId 1066. This error can occur when a device is malfunctioning and also as a result of small computer system interface (SCSI) host adapter configuration issues.
Windows Event Log Device Driver Control Error	Checks the system event log for EventId 11. This error can be caused by a corrupt device driver, a hardware problem, faulty cabling, or connectivity issues.
Windows Event Log Device Not Ready Error	Checks the system event log for EventId 15. This error can be caused by SCSI host adapter configuration issues or related problems.
Windows Event Log Disk Defragmentation	Checks the system event log for EventId 55. This error occurs when the Disk Defragmenter tool cannot move a particular data element, and as a result Chkdsk.exe is scheduled to run.
Windows Event Log Failed I_O Request Error	Checks the system event log for EventId 50. This error is caused by a failed I/O request.
Windows Event Log I_O Delay Warning	Checks the event log for error message 833. This message indicates that SQL Server has issued a read or write request from disk and that the request has taken longer than 15 seconds to return. You can troubleshoot this error by examining the system event log for hardware-related error messages. Look also for hardware-specific logs.
Windows Event Log I_O Error During Hard Page Fault Error	Checks the system event log for EventId 51. This error is caused by an error during a hard page fault.
Windows Event Log Read Retry Error	Checks the event log for SQL Server error message 825. This message indicates that SQL Server was unable to read data from the disk on the first try. You need to check the disks, disk controllers, array cards, and disk drivers.
Windows Event Log Storage System I_O Timeout Error	Checks the system event log for EventId 9. This message indicates that an I/O time-out has occurred in the storage system.
Windows Event Log System Failure Error	Checks the system event log for EventId 6008. This event indicates an unexpected system shutdown.

REAL WORLD Guest Permissions policy is meant for non-system databases only. Disabling guest access doesn't apply to *master*, *msdb*, and *tempb* system databases. Some SQL Server features require the guest user to be enabled in the *msdb* database. If guest access is disabled in *msdb*, you may receive error 916 when you try to connect to SQL Server using SQL Server Management Studio or other applications.

Configuring Central Management Servers

By default, each instance of SQL Server is responsible for monitoring and enforcing its own policies. Although this configuration is useful in stand-alone deployments, you often want a more robust solution in the enterprise, and this is where central management servers are useful. Central management servers take over the responsibility of monitoring and enforcing policies from any instance of SQL Server registered as a subordinate server. From a central management server, you also can execute T-SQL statements on multiple instances of SQL Server simultaneously.

You can specify a SQL Server instance that you want to use as a central management server by registering the server in the Registered Servers view. Afterward, you can specify and register the subordinate servers that you will manage via the central management server. Although you must register subordinate servers individually, you can manage subordinate servers collectively by using subordinate server groups.

NOTE Because SQL Server relies on Windows authentication to establish connections to registered servers, you must register all central management servers and subordinate servers by specifying Windows authentication during the registration process. Only members of the ServerGroupAdministratorRole role can manage the central management server. Membership in the ServerGroupReaderRole role is required to connect to a central management server.

Registering Central Management Servers

A central management server cannot be a subordinate server or a member of a subordinate group that it maintains. You can register a central management server by following these steps:

1. In SQL Server Management Studio, use the Registered Servers view to work with central management servers. To use this view, or to display it if it is hidden, press Ctrl+Alt+G.

2. Under the Central Management Servers node, you'll see a list of previously registered central management servers. To register a new server, right-click the Central Management Servers node, and then select Register Central Management Server. This displays the New Server Registration dialog box, shown in Figure 3-1.

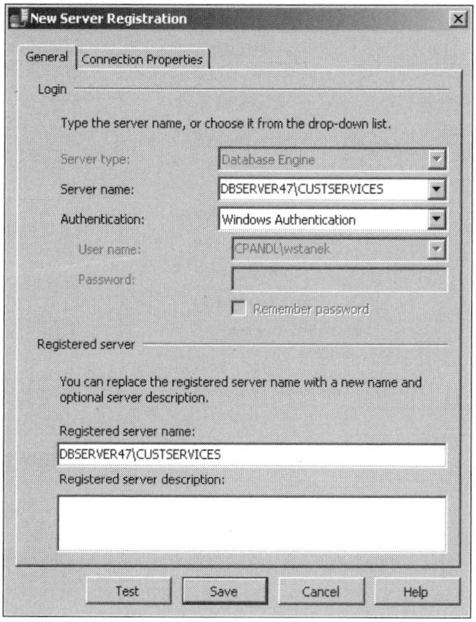

FIGURE 3-1 The New Server Registration dialog box.

3. In the Server Name box, type the fully qualified domain name (FQDN) or host name of the central management server, such as dbsvr23.cpandl.com or DBSvr23.

4. Choose Windows Authentication as the authentication type.

5. The registered server name is filled in for you on the basis of the server name you entered previously. Change the default name only if you want SQL Server Management Studio to use an alternate display name for the server.

6. To test the settings, click Test. If you successfully connect to the server, you will see a prompt confirming this. If the test fails, verify the information you provided, make changes as necessary, and then test the settings again.

7. Click Save.

Registering Subordinate Servers and Groups

After you register a central management server, you can register subordinate servers and create subordinate server groups. While individual subordinate servers don't have to be organized into groups, you can group servers according to their business unit, geographic location, or purpose for easier management.

You create a subordinate server group by completing the following steps:

1. In the Registered Servers view, expand the Central Management Servers node. You'll see a list of previously registered central management servers.

2. Right-click the central management server that will have management responsibility for the subordinate server group, and then select New Server Group.

3. In the New Server Group Properties dialog box, type a name and description for the new group in the boxes provided. Click OK.

You register a subordinate server by following these steps:

1. In the Registered Servers view, expand the Central Management Servers node, and then expand the node for the server that will have management responsibility for the subordinate server.

2. Right-click the server or one of its subordinate groups, and then select New Server Registration.

3. In the Server Name box, type the FQDN or host name of the subordinate server, such as DatabaseServer12.cpandl.com or DatabaseServer12.

4. Choose Windows Authentication as the authentication type.

5. The registered server name is filled in for you on the basis of the previously entered server name. Change the default name only if you want SQL Server Management Studio to use an alternative display name for the server.

6. To test the settings, click Test. If you successfully connect to the server, you will see a prompt confirming this. If the test fails, verify the information you provided, make changes as necessary, and then test the settings again.

7. Click Save.

Moving Subordinate Servers and Server Groups

Sometimes, you need to move a subordinate server or server group to a new location in the central management server hierarchy. You can do this by completing the following steps:

1. In the Registered Servers view, expand the Central Management Servers node and the related server and group nodes as necessary.

2. Right-click the subordinate server or server group that you want to move, point to Tasks, and then select Move To.

3. In the Move Server Registration dialog box, select the node into which you want to place the server or group.

4. Click OK.

The Move To process does not let you move a subordinate server or server group to a different central management server. To move a subordinate server or server group to a different central management server, you need to export the related registration settings and then import them to the new location. The export and import process works like this:

1. In the Registered Servers view, right-click the node with the settings to export, point to Tasks, and then select Export.

2. Click the options (...) button to the right of the Export File box.

3. Use the Save As dialog box to select a save location, type a name for the exported registered servers file, and then click Save.

4. Click OK to close the Export Registered Servers dialog box. If the file exists and you want to replace it with the current settings, click Yes when prompted.

5. Right-click the node where you want to import the settings, point to Tasks, and then select Import.

6. Click the options (...) button to the right of the Import File box.

7. Use the Open dialog box to navigate to the save location, select the exported registered servers file, and then click Open.

8. Click OK to close the Import Registered Servers dialog box. If identical subordinate groups and servers are already registered, you are prompted to replace the existing settings. Click Yes or Yes To All only if you want to overwrite existing settings.

Deleting Subordinate Servers and Server Groups

If you no longer use a server as a subordinate server or no longer want to use a server group, you can remove the entry for the server or server group. Right-click the server or server group, and then select Delete. When prompted to confirm, click Yes. When you delete a server group, SQL Server Management Studio removes the group and all the subordinate server registrations it contains.

Executing Statements Against Multiple Servers

You can query multiple servers at the same time by using central management servers. You can also execute T-SQL statements against local server groups in the Registered Servers view. Keep the following in mind:

- To query all subordinate servers for a central management server, right-click the central management server in the Registered Servers view and select New Query. In the Query Editor, type and execute your T-SQL statements.

- To query every server in a server group, right-click the server group in the Registered Servers view and select New Query. In the Query Editor, type and execute your T-SQL statements.

By default, the results pane combines the query results from all the servers. Because the connections to subordinate servers are executed using Windows authentication in the context of the currently logged-in user, the effective permissions might vary. If a connection cannot be established to one or more servers, those servers are ignored, and results for the other servers are displayed.

The combined results contain the server name but do not contain any login names. If you want, you can modify multiserver results by using the Options dialog box. Click Options on the Tools menu, expand Query Results and SQL Server, and then click Multiserver Results. On the Multiserver Results page, do one or more of the following, and then click OK:

- Configure the Add Login Names To The Results option. Use True to add login names to the results. Use False to remove login names from the results.

- Configure the Add Server Names To The Results option. Use True to add server names to the results. Use False to remove server names from the results.

- Configure the Merge Results option. Use True to merge results in a single results pane. Use False to display results in a separate pane for each server.

Managing Policies Throughout the Enterprise

As discussed previously, you create and manage policies in SQL Server Management Studio. Implementing Policy-Based Management is a multistep process that involves selecting a facet that contains the properties you want to configure, defining a condition that specifies the permitted states of the facet, and defining a policy that contains the condition and sets an evaluation mode. The evaluation mode you set determines whether SQL Server uses automated policy monitoring, reporting, and compliance enforcement.

Importing and Exporting Policies

SQL Server 2012 includes predefined policies for the Database Engine, Analysis Services, and Reporting Services. You can import these predefined policies with their preconfigured conditions if you want to use them with a particular instance of the Database Engine, Analysis Services, or Reporting Services. If you create your own policies, you can export those policies with their conditions to XML files and then import the XML files to another instance of SQL Server.

You can export a policy by completing the following steps:

1. In SQL Server Management Studio, access the Management folder on the instance of the Database Engine you want to work with.

2. In Object Explorer, under the Management node, expand Policy Management and Policies. Right-click a policy, and then click Export Policy. This displays the Export Policy dialog box, shown in Figure 3-2.

FIGURE 3-2 The Export Policy dialog box.

3. Use the options in the Export Policy dialog box to select a save location, and then type the name of the XML file.

4. Click Save. By default, SQL Server preserves the current state of the policy. This state will be set when the policy is imported. Note that any condition associated with the policy is exported as well.

You can import a policy by completing the following steps:

1. In SQL Server Management Studio, access the Management folder on the instance of the Database Engine you want to work with.

2. In Object Explorer, under the Management node, expand Policy Management, right-click Policies, and then click Import Policy.

3. In the Import dialog box, shown in Figure 3-3, click the options (...) button, and then use the Select Policy dialog box to locate the XML file that contains the policy. Select a policy by clicking it, and then click Open. You can select multiple files using Shift+click or Ctrl+click.

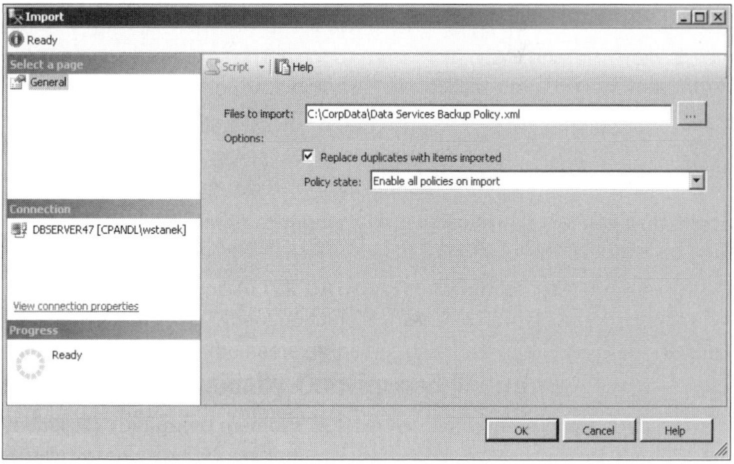

FIGURE 3-3 The Import dialog box.

4. Remember that any condition associated with the policy is imported as well. If identically named policies (and conditions) already exist, the import process will fail with an error stating that the policies exist. To force SQL Server to overwrite existing policies, you must select the Replace Duplicates With Items Imported check box.

5. By default, SQL Server preserves the policy state on import. If a policy was enabled when it was exported, it will be enabled. If a policy was disabled when it was exported, it will be disabled. You can modify this behavior by explicitly setting the state. To enable the policies you are importing, select Enable All Policies On Import in the Policy State list. To disable the policies you are importing, select Disable All Policies On Import.

6. Click OK to begin the import process.

Configuring and Managing Policy Facets

Facets define management areas within the policy-based framework. Each management area has a set of related properties that you can configure by using a particular facet. You can view or modify the current state of any facet properties via the related object.

To view an object's current state and modify this state, follow these steps:

1. In Object Explorer, right-click a server instance, database, or database object, and then click Facets.

2. In the View Facets dialog box, shown in Figure 3-4, use the Facet list to select a facet related to the object. You then see a list of properties that shows the names and values of the facets.

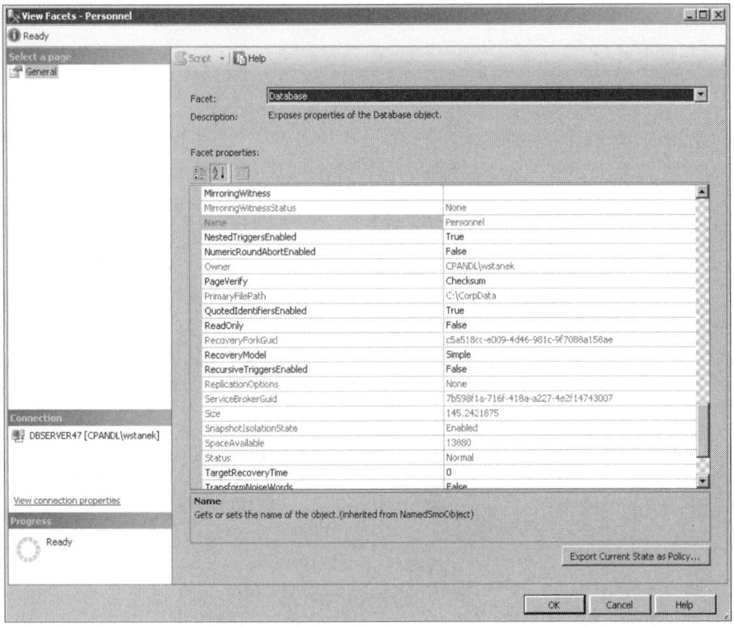

FIGURE 3-4 Modify property values as necessary.

3. Click in the box next to the property to select a property value. If a property appears dimmed, you cannot modify the property value.

4. Click OK.

Exporting an object's current state as policy allows you to use the current configuration of a server instance, database, or other database object to define policies that you want to implement throughout the enterprise. After you export an object's current state as policy, you can save the policy to the Policy Management\Policies node on the local server or to a policy file that you can import on another server.

Exporting an object's current state as policy creates a condition and a policy. To view an object's current state and export this state as policy, follow these steps:

1. In Object Explorer, right-click a server instance, database, or database object, and then click Facets.

2. In the View Facets dialog box, use the Facet list to select a facet related to the object. You then see a list of properties that shows the names and values of the facets.

3. Click Export Current State As Policy to display the Export As Policy dialog box, shown in Figure 3-5.

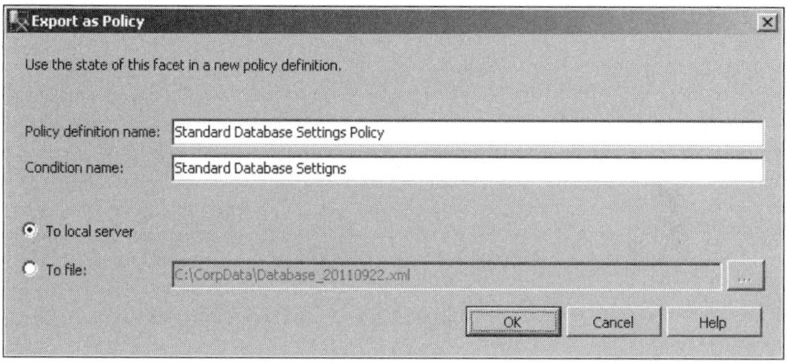

FIGURE 3-5 Export the property settings as a policy.

4. Type a name for the policy, and then type a name for the condition.

5. To save the policy to the Policy Management\Policies node on the local server, select To Local Server, and then click OK to close the Export As Policy dialog box. The related policy and condition are created under the appropriate nodes within Policy Management.

6. To save the policy to a file that you can import on another server, select To File. Click the options (...) button. Use the Export Policy dialog box to select a save location and name for the policy file, and then click Save. Click OK to close the Export As Policy dialog box. Later, you can import the policy using the technique discussed in the "Importing and Exporting Policies" section earlier in this chapter.

Creating and Managing Policy Conditions

Facets represent management areas within SQL Server. Most facets have multiple properties that you can manage or evaluate using conditions. Conditions define the permitted states for properties based on expressed values. Although you can use a single condition in multiple policies, you define conditions for each facet individually.

Defining Conditions Using Properties and Standard Expressions

When you are defining conditions, you join property evaluation expressions by using the And or Or clause to form a logical statement. For example, with the database facet, you might want to establish the condition shown in Figure 3-6. In this example, the evaluation expression specifies the following:

- AutoClose must be True,
- And AutoShrink must be False,
- And PageVerify must be set to either TornPageDetection or Checksum,
- And AutoUpdateStatisticsEnabled must be True,
- And Trustworthy must be True.

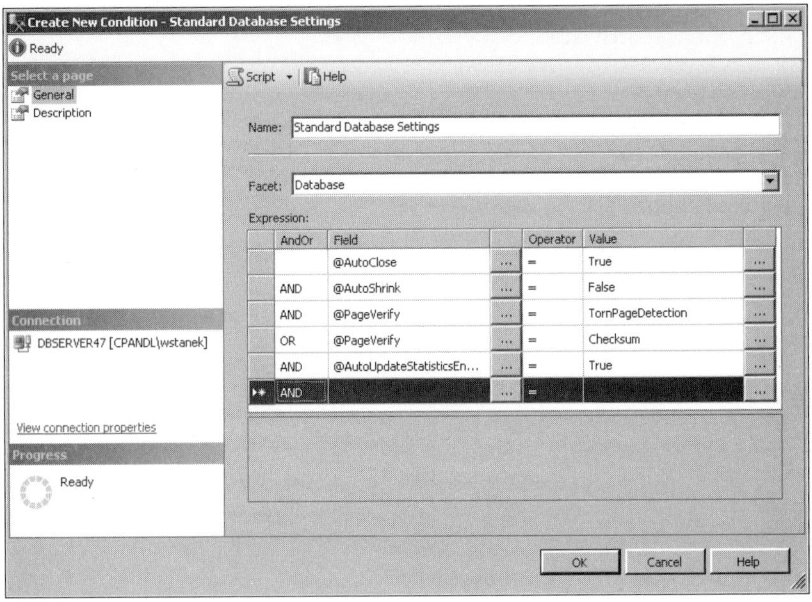

FIGURE 3-6 Define a condition by joining property expressions.

Although the allowed values depend on the property you are configuring, values generally can be numeric, a string, or a fixed list. With properties that are on (true) or off (false), you can set the operator to equals (=) or not equals (!=). When you set a property to equals, the property must equal the specified value. When you set a property to not equals, the property cannot equal the specified value, but it can be set to other permitted values.

With multivalued properties, other operators you can use are as follows:

- **>** Greater than; the property must be greater than the value specified.
- **>=** Greater than or equal to; the property must be greater than or equal to the value specified.

- **<** Less than; the property must be less than the value specified.
- **<=** Less than or equal to; the property must be less than or equal to the value specified.
- **Like** Pattern match, as with the LIKE clause in T-SQL; the property must match a specified pattern. Enclose the Like value in single quotation marks, such as '%computer%' or '[D-Z] arwin'.
- **Not Like** Pattern match, as with the NOT LIKE clause in T-SQL; the property must not match a specified pattern. Enclose the Not Like value in single quotation marks.
- **In** Query or list match, as with the IN clause for T-SQL; the property must match a value in the specified query or list. Enclose the In clause in parentheses, enclose individual values in single quotation marks, and separate values with commas, such as ('Hawaii', 'Idaho', 'Nebraska').
- **Not In** Query or list match, as with the NOT IN clause for T-SQL; the property must not match a value in the specified query or list.

Creating and Modifying Conditions

You can create a condition by completing the following steps:

1. In SQL Server Management Studio, access the Management folder on the instance of the Database Engine you want to work with.

2. In Object Explorer, under the Management node, expand Policy Management, expand Facets, right-click the facet that contains the properties that you want, and then click New Condition.

3. On the General page of the Create New Condition dialog box, type the name of the new condition, such as Standard Database Settings, in the Name box.

4. Confirm that the correct facet is shown in the Facet box, or select a different facet.

5. In the Expression area, construct condition expressions by selecting a facet property in the Field box together with its associated operator and value. When you add multiple expressions, the expressions can be joined by using And or Or.

6. To create complex expressions, press the Shift or Ctrl key, and then click two or more clauses to select a range. Right-click the selected area, and then click Group Clauses. Grouping clauses is like putting parentheses around an expression in a mathematical expression, which forces the clauses to operate as a single unit that is separate from the rest of the condition.

7. Optionally, on the Description page, type a description for the new condition.

8. Click OK to create the condition.

After creating a condition, you can view or modify its settings by completing these steps:

1. In SQL Server Management Studio, access the Management folder on the instance of the Database Engine you want to work with.

2. In Object Explorer, under the Management node, expand Policy Management, expand Conditions, right-click the condition that you want to view or modify, and then select Properties.

3. View the condition settings on the General page. Make changes as necessary, and then click OK.

Although you cannot delete a condition referenced in a policy, you can delete unreferenced conditions. You delete a condition by right-clicking it and then selecting Delete. When prompted to confirm, click OK.

Defining Complex Expressions

Although standard expressions are useful for evaluating conditions, complex expressions give you many more options, including the capability to replace object and schema names at run time. Complex expressions do this by extending the valid syntax for expressions to include a set of predefined functions that can be evaluated on either side of the condition operator. Thus, the standard expression syntax of

```
{property|constant} [operator] {property|constant]
```

becomes

```
{property|constant|function} [operator] {property|constant|function}
```

Available functions allow you to perform many complex tasks. You can add values, count values, or compute averages, and then evaluate the results. You can convert values to strings or concatenate strings and then evaluate the results. You can execute T-SQL queries or WMI Query Language (WQL) scripts and then evaluate the results.

To create a condition that uses complex expressions, complete the following steps:

1. Create a new condition or open an existing condition for editing using the techniques discussed previously.

2. While working with the condition, on the General page, click the options (...) button in the Expression area.

3. In the Advanced Edit dialog box, define your function in the Cell Value box and then click OK.

> **TIP** Available functions and properties are listed under Functions And Properties. Click a property or function to display detailed usage information. Double-click a property to insert it into the cell value area at the current cursor position. Double-click a function to insert its basic syntax into the cell value area at the current cursor position.

Creating and Managing Policies

You use policies to check and optionally enforce conditions. When you create a policy, you can use a condition that you created earlier, or you can create a new condition when you are creating the policy. Although you can use a particular condition in many policies, a policy can contain only a single condition.

When you create a policy, the policy normally is associated with the current instance of the Database Engine. If the current instance is a central management server, the policy can be applied to all subordinate servers. You also can directly create a policy by choosing New from the File menu and then saving the policy to a file. This enables you to create policies when you are not connected to the instance of the Database Engine that you want to work with.

You can create a policy and associate it with a particular instance of the Database Engine by completing the following steps:

1. In SQL Server Management Studio, access the Management folder on the instance of the Database Engine you want to work with.

2. In Object Explorer, under the Management node, expand Policy Management, right-click Policies, and then click New Policy. This displays the Create New Policy dialog box, shown in Figure 3-7.

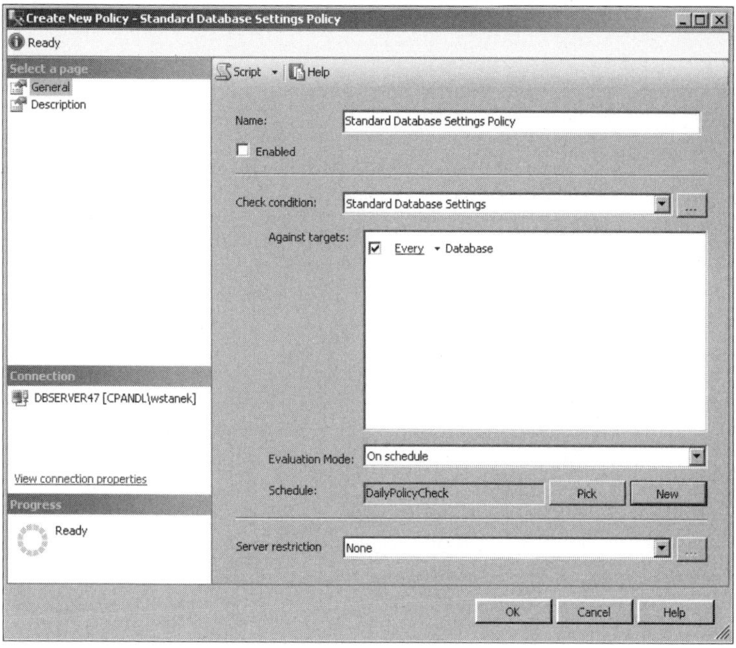

FIGURE 3-7 Create the policy and specify the condition that applies.

3. In the Name box, type the name of the new policy, such as Standard Database Settings Policy.

4. Use the Check Condition list to select one of the existing conditions, or select New Condition. To edit a condition, select the condition, and then click the options (...) button. Make changes as necessary to the condition settings, and then click OK.

5. In the Against Targets box, select one or more target types for this policy. Some conditions and facets can be applied only to certain types of targets. The available target sets appear in the associated box. If no targets appear in this box, the check condition is scoped at the server level. To select a filtering condition for some types of targets, click the Every entry and then select an existing filter condition, or define a condition by selecting New Condition and then specifying the settings for the condition.

6. Use the Evaluation Mode list to select how this policy will behave. Different conditions can have different valid evaluation modes. Available modes can include On Demand, On Change: Prevent, On Change: Log Only, and On Schedule. If you specify a mode other than On Demand, you can enable the policy by selecting the Enabled check box. If you specify On Schedule as the mode, click Pick to select an existing run schedule, or click New to create a new schedule. For more information on creating schedules, see the "Configuring Job Schedules" section in Chapter 10.

7. To limit the policy to a subset of the target types, select a limiting condition in the Server Restriction list, or select New Condition to create a new condition.

8. By default, policies are assigned to the Default category. On the Description page, in the Category box, you can select a different default policy category. (See Figure 3-8.) Otherwise, to create a new category, click New, type a category name, and then click OK.

9. On the Description page, you can type an optional description of the policy. Click OK to create the policy.

REAL WORLD To help administrators understand your policies, you can publish help documents on a website and then refer administrators to the help documentation by using a hyperlink. You can define a help hyperlink by using the Additional Help Hyperlink option on a policy's Description page. Enter the help text for the link in the Text To Display box, and then enter the hyperlink address in the Address box. You can provide a link to a webpage that starts with http:// or https://, or you can provide a mail link that starts with mailto://. After you type a hyperlink, click Test Link to check the validity of the hyperlink. When you are evaluating a server instance, database, or other object for policy compliance, the help text and link are displayed as part of the detailed results.

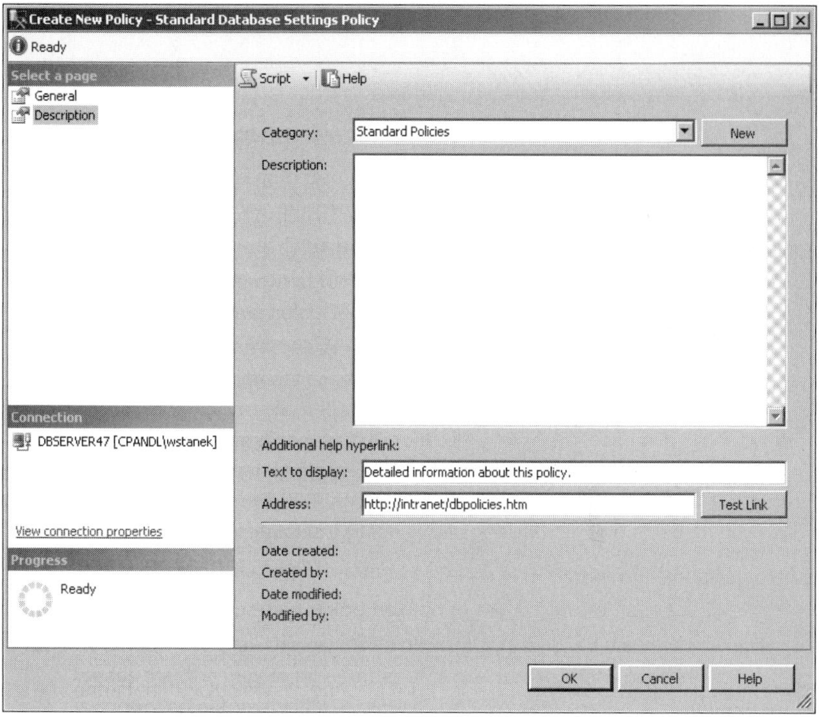

FIGURE 3-8 Assign the policy to a category.

After creating a policy, you can view or modify its settings by completing these steps:

1. In SQL Server Management Studio, access the Management folder on the instance of the Database Engine you want to work with.

2. In Object Explorer, under the Management node, expand Policy Management, expand Policies, right-click the policy that you want to view or modify, and then select Properties.

3. View the policy settings on the General and Description pages. Make changes as necessary. Click OK.

You can manage policies you've created by using the following techniques:

- Delete a policy by right-clicking it and selecting Delete. When prompted to confirm, click OK.
- Disable a policy by right-clicking it and selecting Disable.
- Enable a policy by right-clicking it and selecting Enable.

Managing Policy Categories and Mandating Policies

SQL Server 2012 uses policy categories to help you organize your policies. In a large organization, grouping policies into categories makes policy management easier. You can assign a policy to a category in several ways. By default, any policy you create belongs to the Default category. When you create a policy, you can assign the policy to an available category or to a new category as well. To move a policy to a different policy category, complete the following steps:

1. Right-click the policy that you want to view or modify, and then select Properties.

2. On the Description page, in the Category box, select a different default policy category. Otherwise, to create a new category, click New, type a category name, and then click OK.

3. Click OK to apply the changes.

In addition to helping you organize policies, policy categories help with policy application. Policies within categories are either mandated or not mandated. If a policy is mandated, it means that all databases on the instance of SQL Server must enforce the policy. If a policy is not mandated, it means that you must apply the policy manually as appropriate.

By default, any policy assigned to the Default category is a mandated policy. You can control whether a policy category and its related policies are mandated or not mandated by completing the following steps:

1. In SQL Server Management Studio, access the Management folder on the instance of the Database Engine you want to work with.

2. In Object Explorer, under the Management node, right-click the Policy Management node, and then select Manage Categories.

3. The available categories are listed by name. To create a new policy category, simply click in an empty text box in the Name column and type the category name.

4. In the Manage Policy Categories dialog box, shown in Figure 3-9, select or clear the Mandate Database Subscriptions check box for each category, as appropriate. Click OK.

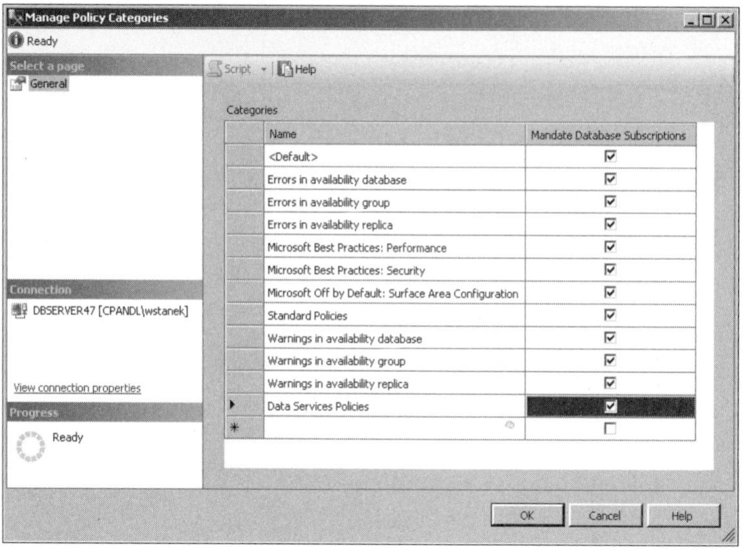

FIGURE 3-9 Specify whether policies within categories are mandated.

You can determine the policies that are applied to a database or other object by completing the following steps:

1. In Object Explorer, right-click a database or database object, point to Policies, and then click Categories.

2. In the Categories dialog box, expand the category entries to determine which policies are being applied. As shown in Figure 3-10, the following information is available:

   - **Name** Shows the name of the policy category.
   - **Subscribed** Indicates whether the selected object has subscribed to the policy category. If the related check box appears dimmed, the policy category is mandated and applies to all databases on the server.
   - **Policy** Shows the policies in the policy category, provided that you've expanded the related category node.
   - **Enabled** Indicates whether the policy is enabled or disabled.
   - **Evaluation Mode** Shows the evaluation mode of the policy.
   - **History** Click the View History link to open the Log File viewer and display the creation and change history for the policy.

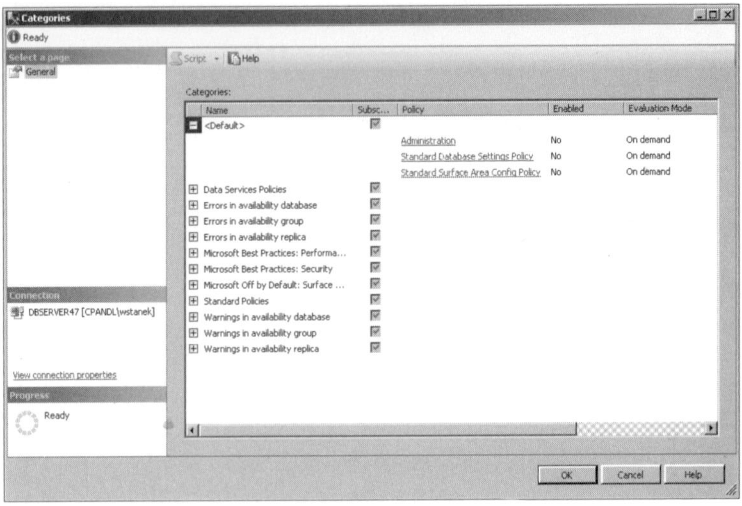

FIGURE 3-10 Determine which policies are being applied.

Evaluating Policies

By using automatically evaluated modes, you can check policy compliance when changes are made or on a regularly scheduled basis. You also can evaluate a policy manually to determine whether a server instance, database, or other object complies with the policy. If you later apply or enforce the policy, you can configure the selected database instance or database object to comply with the policy.

Because the connections to subordinate servers are executed using Windows authentication in the context of the currently logged-on user, the effective permissions might vary. If a connection cannot be established to one or more servers, those servers are ignored, and evaluation against the other servers continues independently.

You can determine whether a particular object complies with a policy by completing the following steps:

1. In Object Explorer, right-click a server instance, database, or database object, point to Policies, and then click Evaluate.

2. The Evaluate Policies dialog box shows only the policies that are appropriate for the object. (See Figure 3-11.) In the Evaluate Policies dialog box, select one or more policies, and then click Evaluate to run the policy in evaluation mode. (The evaluation mode is defined as part of the policy and cannot be changed in the Evaluate Policies dialog box.)

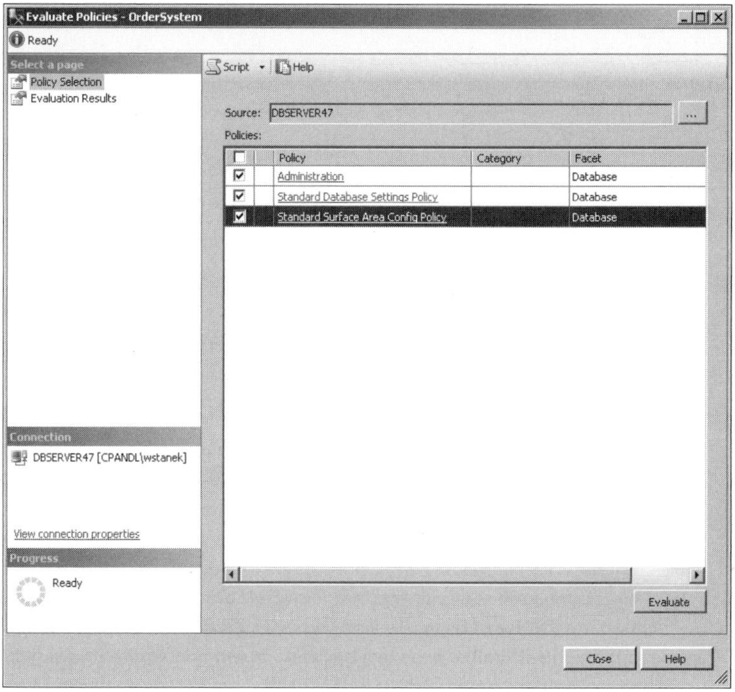

FIGURE 3-11 Evaluate an object against policies to determine compliance.

3. If there are compliance issues, you'll see a red warning icon. You can click the View link that appears in the Details column under Target Details to view the detailed compliance results. As shown in Figure 3-12, the Result column shows whether each property in the joined evaluation expression is in compliance or out of compliance. Expected and actual values are also shown. Note that help text is provided if it was previously defined. Click Close when you finish reviewing the detailed results.

4. In the Evaluate Policies dialog box, clicking Evaluate generates a compliance report for the target set but does not reconfigure SQL Server or enforce compliance. For targets that do not comply with the selected policies and have properties that can be reconfigured by Policy-Based Management, you can enforce policy compliance by selecting the policy or policies to apply on the Evaluation Results page and then clicking Apply.

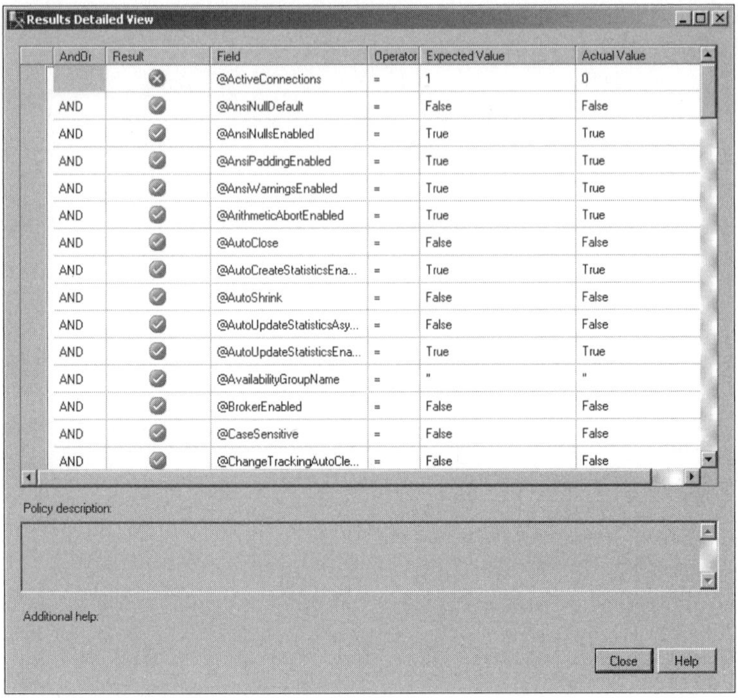

	AndOr	Result	Field	Operator	Expected Value	Actual Value
		❌	@ActiveConnections	=	1	0
	AND	✅	@AnsiNullDefault	=	False	False
	AND	✅	@AnsiNullsEnabled	=	True	True
	AND	✅	@AnsiPaddingEnabled	=	True	True
	AND	✅	@AnsiWarningsEnabled	=	True	True
	AND	✅	@ArithmeticAbortEnabled	=	True	True
	AND	✅	@AutoClose	=	False	False
	AND	✅	@AutoCreateStatisticsEna...	=	True	True
	AND	✅	@AutoShrink	=	False	False
	AND	✅	@AutoUpdateStatisticsAsy...	=	False	False
	AND	✅	@AutoUpdateStatisticsEna...	=	True	True
	AND	✅	@AvailabilityGroupName	=	"	"
	AND	✅	@BrokerEnabled	=	False	False
	AND	✅	@CaseSensitive	=	False	False
	AND	✅	@ChangeTrackingAutoCle...	=	False	False

Policy description:

Additional help:

FIGURE 3-12 Review compliance issues.

5. The first time you try to apply a policy, you'll see a Policy Evaluation Warning dialog box prompting you to confirm the action. Click Yes to proceed. If you don't want to see the warning in the future, select the Do Not Show This Message Again check box before clicking Yes.

6. After you apply a policy, you can review the detailed results by clicking the View link that appears in the Details column under Target Details. If the properties can be reconfigured using Policy-Based Management, the properties will be changed. Click Close when you finish reviewing the detailed results.

7. Optionally, you can export the results to a policy results file for later review. Click Export. Use the Export Results dialog box to select a save location for the results file, type a file name, and then click Save.

You can determine whether the targets of a policy are in compliance by completing the following steps:

1. In Object Explorer, expand Management, Policy Management, and Policies. Right-click a policy, and then click Evaluate.

2. Follow steps 2 through 7 in the previous procedure.

You can determine whether the targets of a policy are in compliance with a schedule by completing the following steps:

1. In Object Explorer, expand Management, Policy Management, and Policies. Right-click a policy, and then click Properties.

2. On the General page, specify On Schedule as the evaluation mode.

3. Click Pick to select an existing run schedule, or click New to create a schedule. Click OK twice to save your changes.

To view the history of compliance checks, right-click the policy and then select View History. In Log File Viewer, expand the available run dates to show additional details. Review the related details in the detailed view by clicking the link provided in the Details column.

Each property in the joined evaluation expression is listed according to whether it is in or out of compliance. If there are compliance issues, you'll see a red warning icon to show properties not in compliance or a green OK icon to show properties in compliance. Expected and actual values are also shown. Note that help text is provided if it was previously defined. Click Close when you finish reviewing the detailed results.

Troubleshooting Policies

In the *msdb* database, you'll find the following views for displaying policy information. These views are owned by the dbo schema:

- syspolicy_conditions
- syspolicy_policies
- syspolicy_policy_execution_history
- syspolicy_policy_execution_history_details
- syspolicy_policy_category_subscriptions
- syspolicy_policy_categories
- syspolicy_system_health_state
- syspolicy_target_sets

SQL Server records compliance issues in the Windows event logs. For scheduled policies, compliance issues are recorded in the SQL Server Agent log as well. To view the history information recorded in the SQL Server Agent logs, right-click the policy and then select View History. Review the related details in the detailed view by clicking the link provided in the Details column. If policies are not enabled or do not affect a target, the failure is not considered an error and is not logged. For more information, see the "Evaluating Policies" section earlier in this chapter.

Remember that compliance checks for scheduled policies occur only during scheduled run times and that on-demand policies run only when you manually execute them. If you have problems with policies set to On Change: Log or On Change: Prevent, be sure that the policies are enabled and that the target you want is not excluded by a filter. You also should ensure the target subscribes to the policy group that contains the policy. As discussed in the "Managing Policy Categories and Mandating Policies" section earlier in this chapter, you can determine the policies that are applied to a database or other object by right-clicking a database or database object, pointing to Policies, and then clicking Categories.

You can determine whether a policy was evaluated by right-clicking the policy and then selecting View History. The policy execution history in the msdb.dbo.syspolicy_policy_execution_history view also provides information about whether a policy was evaluated. You can also determine whether the policy executed for the specific target by checking the policy execution history for the specific target in the msdb.dbo.syspolicy_policy_execution_history_details view. You can determine the execution time for policies by querying the start_date and end_date columns in the msdb.dbo.syspolicy_policy_execution_history view.

For policies that use the On Change: Prevent mode, Service Broker handles the rollback of changes. You should ensure that Service Broker is running and configured properly. If it is, you can check the Service Broker Queue to be sure that it is monitoring for the correct events by using either of the following queries:

T-SQL

```
SELECT * FROM sys.server_event_notifications
WHERE name = N'syspolicy_event_notification';
GO
```

PowerShell

```
Set-Location SQLSERVER:\SQL\DbServer18\OrderSystem
Invoke-Sqlcmd -Query "SELECT * FROM sys.server_event_notifications
WHERE name = N'syspolicy_event_notification';"
```

> **NOTE** In the Windows PowerShell example, you define the working server context by explicitly setting the location. This allows you to invoke SQL commands in this location and is the same as using –ServerInstance "DbServer18\OrderSystem".

Keep in mind that if the nested triggers server configuration option is disabled, On Change: Prevent mode will not work correctly. Policy-Based Management relies on DDL triggers to detect and roll back DDL operations that do not comply with policies that use this evaluation mode. Removing the Policy-Based Management DDL triggers or disabling nested triggers causes this evaluation mode to fail.

Because On Schedule policies rely on SQL Server Agent jobs, you should always check to be sure that SQL Server Agent is running and configured properly. You also should check to ensure that the related SQL Server Agent jobs are enabled and configured properly. Working with SQL Server Agent jobs is discussed in Chapter 10.

If you suspect there is a problem with policy-related jobs, you may be able to use sp_syspolicy_repair_policy_automation to repair the jobs. This stored procedure will attempt to repair triggers and jobs that are associated with On Schedule or On Change policies. Since policies are stored in the *msdb* database, you must run this stored procedure in the context of the *msdb* database, as shown in the following example:

```
EXEC msdb.dbo.sp_syspolicy_repair_policy_automation;
GO
```

CHAPTER 4

Configuring and Tuning Your SQL Servers

- Accessing SQL Server Configuration Data   **112**
- Techniques for Managing SQL Server Configuration Options   **114**
- Configuring SQL Server with Stored Procedures   **123**

Microsoft SQL Server 2012 was designed to adjust to changing workloads dynamically and to self-tune configuration settings. For example, SQL Server can increase or decrease memory usage based on overall system memory requirements. SQL Server also manages memory efficiently, especially when it comes to queries and user connections—and memory is just one of dozens of areas in which configuration settings are adjusted automatically.

Although the SQL Server self-tuning feature works well, there are times when you need to configure SQL Server settings manually. For example, if you are running a large database with special constraints and the database is not performing the way you expect it to, you might want to customize the configuration. You also might need to modify configuration settings for SQL Server accounts, authentication, and auditing. Key tools you use to configure and tune SQL Server include the following:

- **System catalog queries**   Provide a direct way to determine database configuration characteristics and their related settings.
- **Stored procedures**   Let you view and manage configuration settings through stored procedures such as sp_configure.
- **SQL Server Management Studio**   Provides an easy-to-use interface that updates the database and registry settings for you.
- **SQLServr.exe**   Starts SQL Server from the command line. You can use SQLServr.exe to set configuration parameters at startup.

In this chapter, I'll describe the structures available for configuring and tuning SQL Server. I'll start with a look at the SQL Server 2012 system catalog and then continue with a discussion of catalog queries and stored procedures. This discussion provides the essential background for understanding how to configure and tune SQL Server 2012.

Accessing SQL Server Configuration Data

SQL Server 2012 uses an object-based approach to representing servers and databases and all of their configuration characteristics and data contents. At the heart of this object-based structure is the system catalog, which describes the objects in a particular instance of SQL Server along with their attributes. For example, attributes of a database can describe the following:

- The number and names of the tables and views
- The number and names of columns in a table or view
- The column data type, scale, and precision
- The triggers and constraints that are defined on a table
- The indexes and keys that are defined for a table
- The statistics used by the query optimizer for generating query plans

In queries, you can access these attributes and other system catalog information by using the following:

- **Catalog views**   Provide access to metadata stored in a database, which includes database attributes and their values. Catalog views can be used to access all user-available metadata except for metadata related to replication, backup, database maintenance plans, and SQL Server Agent.

- **Compatibility views**   Provide access to many of the system tables included in earlier releases of SQL Server. These views are meant for backward compatibility only and expose the same metadata that is available in SQL Server 2000. They do not expose metadata for new features, such as availability groups, database partitioning, and mirroring.

- **Information Schema views**   Provide access to a subset of metadata stored in a database, which includes database attributes and their values. Information Schema views are based on catalog view definitions in the SQL-92 standard and do not contain metadata specific to SQL Server 2012. Applications that use these views are portable between heterogeneous SQL-92-compliant database systems.

- **ODBC catalog functions**   Provide an interface that Open Database Connectivity (ODBC) drivers can use to return result sets containing system catalog information. The result sets present catalog information in a way that is independent of the structure of the underlying catalog tables.

- **OLE DB schema rowsets**   Provide an IDBSchemaRowset interface that OLE DB providers can use to access system catalog information. The rowsets present catalog information independently from the structure of the underlying catalog tables.

- **System stored procedures and functions**   Provide Transact-SQL (T-SQL) stored procedures and functions that return catalog information.

Catalog views and stored procedures are the recommended methods for accessing a database's metadata, primarily because catalog views present metadata in a format that is independent of any catalog table implementation, which means that the views are not affected by changes in the underlying catalog tables. When you want to configure or manage a server, you typically use stored procedures to help you perform the necessary tasks. Stored procedures provide the functionality to view and manage the configuration of SQL Server and related databases with ease.

Catalog views contain information used by the SQL Server 2012 Database Engine. They provide the most general interface to the catalog metadata and are the most direct way to access and work with this information. All user-available metadata in the system catalog is exposed through catalog views. Catalog views do not contain information about replication, backup, database maintenance plans, or SQL Server Agent.

Like all structures in SQL Server 2012 databases, catalog views follow an object-based hierarchy in which derived objects inherit attributes from base objects. Some catalog views inherit rows from other catalog views. For example, the Tables catalog view inherits all the columns defined in the Objects catalog view. Thus, in addition to columns that are specific to the Tables catalog view itself, the Tables catalog view includes the columns from the Objects catalog view.

You can use system stored procedures to view SQL Server configuration details and to perform general administration. SQL Server 2012 has two main categories of system stored procedures:

- Those meant for administrators
- Those used to implement functionality for database application programming interfaces (APIs)

Of course, you will work with system stored procedures meant for administration and not with those that implement database API functions. System stored procedures are written using T-SQL. Most return a value of 0 to indicate success and a nonzero value to indicate failure. As an example, sp_dboption is a stored procedure for managing the configuration options of SQL Server databases (except for the *master* and *tempdb* databases). When you use sp_dboption to set a database configuration value, a return code of 0 indicates that the option was set as expected. A return code of 1 indicates that the stored procedure failed and the option was not set as expected.

The following example takes the Personnel database offline if there are no current users:

T-SQL

```
USE master;
GO
EXEC sp_dboption "Personnel", "offline", "TRUE";
GO
```

PowerShell

```
Invoke-Sqlcmd -Query "USE master; EXEC sp_dboption 'Personnel',
'offline', 'TRUE';" -ServerInstance "CorpServer17\DataServices"
```

If the stored procedure returns 0, the database was taken offline successfully. A return value of 1 indicates that a problem occurred taking the database offline, and the database is still online. For more information about using stored procedures, see the "Configuring SQL Server with Stored Procedures" section later in this chapter. Note that you can change some options of sp_configure only when Show Advanced Options is set to 1, as in the following examples:

T-SQL

```
exec sp_configure "show advanced options", 1
```

PowerShell

```
Invoke-Sqlcmd -Query "exec sp_configure 'show advanced options', 1"
-ServerInstance "DbServer18\OrderSystem"
```

> **NOTE** When you use Invoke-Sqlcmd, you specify the Database Engine instance with the –ServerInstance parameter in the form –ServerInstance "*ServerName*" for the default instance or –ServerInstance "*ServerName\InstanceName*" for a nondefault instance. For more information on using Invoke-Sqlcmd, see Chapter 1, "Managing Your SQL Servers."

Techniques for Managing SQL Server Configuration Options

You can think of configuration options as a set of rules that define how SQL Server is configured and used. Individual server instances can have different configurations, as can the databases they support, the connections made by applications, and any statements or batch programs that are executed.

Setting Configuration Options

Configuration options can be set for the following:

- **A specific server instance**   Server options are also referred to as *instance-wide* options and are set by executing the sp_configure stored procedure.

- **A specific database** Database options are also referred to as *database-level* options and are set by executing the ALTER DATABASE statement. The database compatibility level can be set by executing the sp_dbcmptlevel stored procedure.

- **A specific connection** Connection options are set by the Microsoft OLE DB Provider for SQL Server or the SQL Server ODBC driver properties and by ANSI SET options when a connection is established.

- **A specific statement or batch** Batch-level options are specified with SET statements. Statement-level options are specified in individual T-SQL statements and affect the remaining T-SQL statements within that batch.

Each of these configuration areas can be thought of as a level in the SQL Server configuration hierarchy. When an option is supported at more than one level, the applicable setting is determined by the following precedence order:

1. A server option
2. A database option
3. A connection (ANSI SET) or batch (SET) option
4. A specific statement (HINT) option

NOTE The stored procedure sp_configure provides the option *user options*, which allows you to change the default values of several SET options. Although *user options* appears to be an instance option, it is a SET option. In previous releases of SQL Server, batch-level options are called *connection-level options*. When you disable multiple active result sets (MARS), batch-level options are considered connection-level options as well.

You use ALTER DATABASE to change settings for a database, sp_configure to change server-level settings, and the SET statement to change settings that affect only the current session. If there are conflicts among configuration options, the options applied later have precedence over options set previously. For example, connection options have precedence over database and server options.

Working with SET Options

Typically, SET options are configured by users within a batch or script and they apply until they are reset or the user's session with the server is terminated. SET options can also be configured within a stored procedure or trigger. In that case, the SET options apply until they are reset inside that stored procedure or trigger, or until control returns to the code that invoked the stored procedure or trigger.

SET options are applied at either parse time or execute time. The parse-time options are QUOTED_IDENTIFIER, PARSEONLY, OFFSETS, and FIPS_FLAGGER. All other SET options are execute-time options. Parse-time options are applied during parsing as they are encountered. Execute-time options are applied during the execution of the code in which they are specified.

Batch statements are parsed in their entirety prior to execution. This means that control flow statements do not affect parse-time settings. In contrast, both control flow and execution affect whether execute-time options are set. Execute-time options are set only if control is changed to a section of the batch containing execute-time options and the related statements are executed without error. If execution fails before an execute-time option is set or during the processing of the statement that sets the option, the option is not set.

When a user connects to a database, some options might be set to ON automatically. These options can be set through user options, server options, or the ODBC and OLE DB connection properties. If the user changes the SET options within a dynamic SQL batch or script, those changes apply only for the duration of that batch or script.

NOTE MARS-enabled connections maintain a list of default SET option values. When a batch or script executes under that connection, the default SET option values are copied to the current request's environment. These values remain in effect unless they are reset within the connection. When the batch or script ends, the execution environment is copied back to the session's default. This ensures that multiple batches executing simultaneously under the same connection run in an isolated SET options environment. However, because the execution environment is copied back to the session default when batch or script execution is complete, the current default environment for a connection depends on the last batch or script that completes execution.

Table 4-1 lists the batch/connection SET options available and indicates the corresponding database and server options supported in SQL Server 2012 as well as the default setting (as applicable). Items with an asterisk provide additional diagnostic information (and are not used for configuration). The SET ANSI_DEFAULTS statement is provided as a shortcut for setting SQL-92 standard options to their default values. The options that reset when this statement is used are as follows: SET ANSI_NULLS, SET CURSOR_CLOSE_ON_COMMIT, SET ANSI_NULL_DFLT_ON, SET IMPLICIT_TRANSACTIONS, SET ANSI_PADDING, SET QUOTED_IDENTIFIER, and SET ANSI_WARNINGS.

NOTE In a future release of SQL Server, SET OFFSETS will be unavailable. Further, ANSI_NULLS, ANSI_PADDING, and CONCAT_NULLS_YIELDS_NULL will always be turned on and you will not be able to turn these settings off. ANSI_NULLS and ANSI_PADDING must be on when you are creating or changing indexes on computer columns or indexed views. The SQL Server Native Client ODBC driver and SQL Server Native Client OLE DB Provider for SQL Server automatically set ANSI_NULLS and ANSI_PADDING to ON when connecting. For connections from DB-Library applications, however, the default for both SET ANSI_NULLS and SET ANSI_PADDING is OFF.

TABLE 4-1 SET Options

SET OPTION	DATABASE OPTION	SERVER OPTION	DEFAULT SETTING
ANSI_DEFAULTS	None	None	N/A
ANSI_NULL_DFLT_OFF ANSI_NULL_DFLT_ON	ANSI_NULL_DEFAULT	user options default	OFF
ANSI_NULLS	ANSI_NULLS	user options default	OFF
ANSI_PADDING	ANSI_PADDING	user options default	ON
ANSI_WARNINGS	ANSI_WARNINGS	user options default	OFF
ARITHABORT	ARITHABORT	user options default	OFF
ARITHIGNORE	None	user options default	OFF
CONCAT_NULL_ YIELDS_NULL	CONCAT_NULL_ YIELDS_NULL	None	OFF
CONTEXT_INFO	None	None	OFF
CURSOR_CLOSE_ ON_COMMIT	CURSOR_CLOSE_ ON_COMMIT	user options default	OFF
DATEFIRST	None	None	7
DATEFORMAT	None	None	mdy
DEADLOCK_PRIORITY	None	None	NORMAL
FIPS_FLAGGER	None	None	OFF
FMTONLY	None	None	OFF
FORCEPLAN	None	None	OFF
IDENTITY_INSERT	None	None	OFF
IMPLICIT_TRANSACTIONS	None	user options default	OFF
LANGUAGE	None	None	us_english
LOCK_TIMEOUT	None	None	No limit
NOCOUNT	None	user options default	OFF

SET OPTION	DATABASE OPTION	SERVER OPTION	DEFAULT SETTING
NOEXEC	None	None	OFF
NUMERIC_ ROUNDABORT	NUMERIC_ ROUNDABORT	None	OFF
OFFSETS	None	None	OFF
PARSEONLY	None	None	OFF
QUERY_GOVERNOR_ COST_LIMIT	None	query governor cost limit	OFF
QUOTED_IDENTIFIER	quoted identifier	user options default	OFF
REMOTE_PROC_ TRANSACTIONS	None	None	OFF
ROWCOUNT	None	None	OFF
SHOWPLAN_ALL*	None	None	OFF
SHOWPLAN_TEXT*	None	None	OFF
SHOWPLAN_XML*	None	None	OFF
STATISTICS IO*	None	None	OFF
STATISTICS PROFILE*	None	None	OFF
STATISTICS TIME*	None	None	OFF
STATISTICS XML*	None	None	OFF
TEXTSIZE	None	None	OFF
TRANSACTION ISOLATION LEVEL	None	None	N/A
XACT_ABORT	None	None	OFF

Working with Server Options

Server options can be set by using the Properties dialog boxes in SQL Server Management Studio or with the sp_configure stored procedure. The difference between these two methods is which options are available to set. Only the most commonly used server configuration options are available through SQL Server Management Studio, but all configuration options are accessible through sp_configure. Table 4-2 lists the server options available and provides the corresponding SET options and database options that are supported in SQL Server 2012, as well as the default setting (as applicable).

NOTE The allow updates option is obsolete. If used, it will cause an error during reconfigure.

TABLE 4-2 Server Options

SERVER OPTION	SET OPTION	DATABASE OPTION	DEFAULT SETTING
allow updates	None	None	0
backup compression default	None	None	0
clr enabled	None	None	0
cross db ownership chaining	None	None	0
default language	None	None	0
filestream access level	None	None	0
max text repl size	None	None	65536
nested triggers	None	None	1
remote access	None	None	1
remote admin connections	None	None	0
remote login timeout	None	None	20
remote proc trans	None	None	0
remote query timeout	None	None	600
server trigger recursion	None	None	1
show advanced options	None	None	0
user options	ANSI_NULL_DFLT_ ON ANSI_NULL_ DFLT_OFF	ANSI_NULL_ DEFAULT	OFF

SERVER OPTION	SET OPTION	DATABASE OPTION	DEFAULT SETTING
ANSI_NULLS	ANSI_NULLS	OFF	
ANSI_PADDING	ANSI_PADDING	ON	
ANSI_WARNINGS	ANSI_WARNINGS	OFF	
ARITHABORT	ARITHABORT	OFF	
ARITHIGNORE	None	OFF	
CURSOR_CLOSE_ON_COMMIT	CURSOR_CLOSE_ON_COMMIT	OFF	
DISABLE_DEF_CNST_CHK	None	OFF	
IMPLICIT_TRANS-ACTIONS	None	OFF	
NOCOUNT	None	OFF	
QUOTED_IDENTIFIER	QUOTED_IDENTIFIER	OFF	

Working with Database Options

Database options are set by executing the ALTER DATABASE statement. In new SQL Server installations, the settings in the *model* and *master* databases are the same. When you create new databases, the default database options for those databases are taken from the *model* database. Whenever you change a database option, the Database Engine recompiles everything in the database cache. Table 4-3 lists the standard database options that are available and provides the corresponding SET and server options supported in SQL Server 2012, as well as the default setting (as applicable).

NOTE Microsoft recommends that ANSI_NULLS and ANSI_PADDING always be set to ON to avoid problems with future versions of SQL Server. Note that AUTO_UPDATE _STATISTICS_ASYNC has no effect unless you set AUTO_UPDATE_STATISTICS to ON.

TABLE 4-3 Database Options

DATABASE OPTION	SET OPTION	SERVER OPTION	DEFAULT SETTING
ANSI_NULL_DEFAULT	ANSI_NULL_DFLT_ON ANSI_NULL_DFLT_OFF	user options default	OFF
ANSI_NULLS	ANSI_NULLS	user options default	OFF

DATABASE OPTION	SET OPTION	SERVER OPTION	DEFAULT SETTING
ANSI_PADDING	ANSI_PADDING	user options default	ON
ANSI_WARNINGS	ANSI_WARNINGS	user options default	OFF
AUTO_CLOSE	None	None	OFF
AUTO_CREATE_STATISTICS	None	None	ON
AUTO_SHRINK	None	None	OFF
AUTO_UPDATE_STATISTICS	None	None	ON
AUTO_UPDATE_STATIS-TICS_ASYNC	None	None	OFF
CONCAT_NULL_YIELDS_NULL	CONCAT_NULL_YIELDS_NULL	None	OFF
CURSOR_CLOSE_ON_COM-MIT	CURSOR_CLOSE_ON_COMMIT	user options default	OFF
CURSOR_DEFAULT	None	None	GLOBAL
MERGE PUBLISH	None	None	FALSE
PUBLISHED	None	None	FALSE
QUOTED_IDENTIFIER	QUOTED_IDENTIFIER	user options default	ON
READ_ONLY	None	None	FALSE
RECOVERY BULK_LOGGED	None	None	FALSE
RECOVERY SIMPLE	None	None	TRUE
RECURSIVE_TRIGGERS	None	None	FALSE
RESTRICTED_USER	None	None	FALSE
SINGLE_USER	None	None	FALSE
SUBSCRIBED	None	None	TRUE
TORN_PAGE_DETECTION	None	None	TRUE

Managing Database Compatibility

By default, when you create a new database in SQL Server 2012, the default compatibility level is 110 (unless the *model* database has a lower compatibility level). When a database is upgraded to SQL Server 2012, pre–SQL Server 2005 databases are upgraded to compatibility level 90. All other databases retain their existing compatibility levels as follows:

- 90 for SQL Server 2005 compatibility level
- 100 for SQL Server2008 compatibility level
- 110 for SQL Server 2012 compatibility level

Although the compatibility level of the *master* database cannot be modified, the compatibility level setting of the *model* database can be changed. This flexibility allows you to create new databases with a non-default compatibility level. To change the compatibility level, you can use the ALTER DATABASE statement.

The ALTER DATABASE statement allows you to set the database compatibility level for a specific database. The ALTER DATABASE statement sets certain database behaviors to be compatible with the specified earlier version of SQL Server. The following example changes the compatibility level of the *Personnel* database to SQL Server 2008:

T-SQL

```
ALTER DATABASE Personnel
SET COMPATIBILITY_LEVEL = 100;
GO
```

PowerShell

```
Invoke-Sqlcmd -Query "ALTER DATABASE Personnel;
SET COMPATIBILITY_LEVEL = 100;" -ServerInstance "DbServer17\Cwhouse"
```

When there are possible conflicts between compatibility (and other) settings, it is important to know which database context is being used. Generally speaking, the current database context is the database defined by the USE statement if the statement is in a batch or script, or it is the database that contains the stored procedure if the statement is in a stored procedure applied to that statement. When a stored procedure is executed from a batch or another stored procedure, it is executed under the option settings of the database in which it is stored. For example, when a stored procedure in the *Support* database calls a stored procedure in the *Personnel* database, the Support procedure is executed under the compatibility level setting of the *Support* database and the Personnel procedure is executed under the compatibility level setting of the *Personnel* database.

Configuring SQL Server with Stored Procedures

You can configure many areas of SQL Server using the SQL Server Properties dialog box, which is discussed in Chapter 1. As you have learned in this chapter, you can also configure SQL Server with stored procedures, such as sp_configure. You execute stored procedures and other queries in SQL Server Management Studio. SQL Server Management Studio has a built-in client tool that sends commands to a SQL Server instance, which in turn parses, compiles, and executes the commands.

The following sections explain how to use SQL Server Management Studio and stored procedures to configure SQL Server. You can find more detailed coverage of SQL Server Management Studio in other chapters.

Using SQL Server Management Studio for Queries

You can start SQL Server Management Studio and access the built-in query client by completing the following steps:

1. Click Start, Programs or All Programs, Microsoft SQL Server 2012, SQL Server Management Studio. Or click Start, type **ssms** in the Search box, and then press Enter.

2. In the Connect To Server dialog box, shown in Figure 4-1, use the Server Type list to select the database component you want to connect to, such as Database Engine.

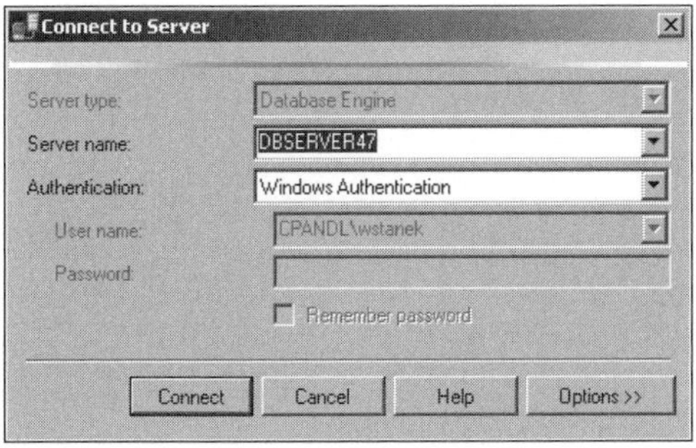

FIGURE 4-1 The Connect To Server dialog box.

3. In the Server Name field, type the name of the server on which SQL Server is running, such as CorpSvr04.

    NOTE You can connect to any server that is visible, as long as remote access is enabled on the server and the server name is resolved. Select the <Browse For More> option in the Server Name drop-down list to look for available servers. You can register the server you want to work with as well. See the "Managing Servers" section in Chapter 1 for details.

4. Use the Authentication list to specify the authentication type as Windows authentication or SQL Server authentication (based on the allowed authentication types when you installed the server). Provide a Windows user name or SQL Server login ID and password as necessary.

- **Windows Authentication** Uses your current domain account and password to establish the database connection. This option works only if Windows authentication is enabled and you have appropriate privileges.

- **SQL Server Authentication** Allows you to specify a SQL Server login ID and password.

5. Click Connect. You connect to the default database (unless you have configured another default previously). To change the database you connect to, click Options prior to clicking Connect, select the Connection Properties tab, and then use the Connect To Database list to select the database you want to connect to.

6. In SQL Server Management Studio, you can connect to the database you previously selected by clicking New Query on the toolbar, and then skip the remaining steps. To connect to a different database, click File, click New, and then select the query type, such as Database Engine Query.

7. In the Connect To Database Engine dialog box, specify the server name or select Browse For More in the drop-down list to search for all computers that are running SQL Server within an Active Directory forest, as well as the different instances running on the SQL Browser service.

8. Specify the authentication technique to use. Click Connect. As before, you connect to the default database (unless you have configured another default previously). To change the database to which you connect, click Options, select the Connection Properties tab, and then use the Connect To Database list to select the database you want to connect to.

If you are working with an active database in SQL Server Management Studio and have already authenticated the connection, you can connect automatically to the currently selected database server instance and use your current authentication information to log on. To do this, right-click the database in Object Explorer view in SQL Server Management Studio, and then select New Query.

Executing Queries and Changing Settings

The query window in SQL Server Management Studio is normally divided into two panes. (See Figure 4-2.) The top pane allows you to enter queries. The lower pane displays results.

If you do not see a separate pane in the lower part of the window, don't worry. It appears automatically when you execute a query. You also can set the pane to open by default by selecting the Show Results Pane option on the Window menu.

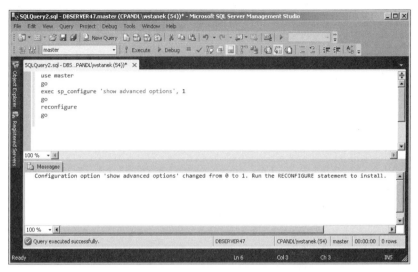

FIGURE 4-2 Executing queries in SQL Server Management Studio.

As you know, you can use sp_configure to view and change SQL Server configuration settings. Two types of configuration settings are available: those that are dynamic and those that are not. In this instance, a dynamic setting is one that you can change without having to stop and restart SQL Server. To execute sp_configure or other types of queries, type a command in the top pane and then click the Execute button on the toolbar (the red exclamation point). You also can execute commands by using these key sequences:

- F5
- Ctrl+E
- Alt+X

NOTE By default, all users have execute permissions on sp_configure so that they can view settings. However, only users with the Alter Settings server-level permission can use sp_configure to change configuration options. By default, only members of the sysadmin and serveradmin fixed server roles have this permission. As with sp_configure, only users with the Alter Settings server-level permission can execute the RECONFIGURE or RECONFIGURE WITH OVERRIDE command.

Whenever you use sp_configure to modify settings, the changes do not take place until you also execute the RECONFIGURE command. You can change some highly risky settings by using only the RECONFIGURE WITH OVERRIDE command. WITH OVERRIDE disables configuration value checking. Although WITH OVERRIDE can be used with any configuration option, it is specifically required to set the recovery interval, min server memory, and max server memory. WITH OVERRIDE also is required when you are setting an option to a value that is not generally recommended.

Additionally, sp_configure settings are divided into two categories: standard and advanced. You can execute standard commands at any time, but you can execute advanced commands only when Show Advanced Options is set to 1. With this setting in effect, you can modify both standard and advanced settings. Follow this procedure to allow modification of advanced settings:

1. In SQL Server Management Studio, type the following:

```
exec sp_configure 'show advanced options', 1
go
reconfigure
go
```

TIP You can disable advanced options later by setting the value to 0.

2. Execute the commands by pressing Ctrl+E.
3. Clear the query window.
4. Now type one sp_configure command for each option you want to change.
5. Type **reconfigure** (or **reconfigure with override**).
6. Type **go**.
7. Execute the commands by pressing Ctrl+E.
8. If you changed any nondynamic settings, stop and restart the server. (See Table 4-4 and Table 4-5 for details.)

Checking and Setting Configuration Parameters

Table 4-4 provides a summary of the standard configuration parameters. The parameters are listed in alphabetical order, with the minimum, maximum, and default values shown. (Several values are given in seconds and denoted as such in the Minimum Value and Maximum Value columns.) The dynamic parameter column tells you whether the setting is dynamic. If you see an "N" in this column, you need to stop and restart the instance of SQL Server to enforce changes. Keep in mind that when you want a server instance to be able to create or attach contained databases, you must enable the use of contained databases by turning on contained database authentication.

TABLE 4-4 Quick Reference Summary for Standard Configuration Parameters

CONFIGURATION OPTION	MINIMUM VALUE	MAXIMUM VALUE	DEFAULT VALUE	DYNAMIC YES/NO
allow updates	0	1	0	Y
backup compression default	0	1	0	Y
clr enabled	0	1	0	Y (except on WOW64 servers)
contained database authentication	0	1	0	Y
cross db ownership chaining	0	1	0	Y
default language	0	9999	0	Y
filestream access level	0	2	0	Y
max text repl size	−1	2147483647	65536	Y
nested triggers	0	1	1	Y
remote access	0	1	1	N
remote admin connections	0	1	0	Y
remote login timeout	0 (s)	2147483647 (s)	20	Y
remote proc trans	0	1	0	Y
remote query timeout	0 (s)	2147483647 (s)	600	Y
server trigger recursion	0	1	1	Y
show advanced options	0	1	0	Y
user options	0	32767	0	Y

Table 4-5 provides a summary of advanced configuration parameters. To view or change these parameters, you have to set the parameter Show Advanced Options to 1. Self-configuring options have an asterisk (*) after their name. (Several values are given in seconds, bytes, and other units of measure, and this is denoted as such in the Minimum Value and Maximum Value columns.) With max worker threads,

1,024 is the maximum recommended for 32-bit operating systems. The default value zero (0) calculates the actual value by using the following formula: 256 + (number of processors − 4) * 8).

NOTE You cannot change some advanced options, although you can view them. Note also that open objects is obsolete and available only for backward compatibility. In SQL Server, the number of open database objects is managed dynamically and limited only by the available memory.

TABLE 4-5 Quick Reference Summary for Advanced Configuration Parameters

CONFIGURATION OPTION	MINIMUM VALUE	MAXIMUM VALUE	DEFAULT VALUE	DYNAMIC YES/NO
ad hoc distributed queries	0	1	0	Y
access check cache bucket count	0	16384	0	Y
access check cache quota	0	2147483647	0	Y
affinity I/O mask	−2147483648	2147483647	0	N
affinity64 I/O mask	−2147483648	2147483647	0	N
affinity mask	−2147483648	2147483647	0	Y
affinity64 mask	−2147483648	2147483647	0	Y
Agent XPs	0	1	0; 1	Y
awe enabled	0	1	0	N
blocked process threshold	0 (s)	86400 (s)	0	Y
c2 audit mode	0	1	0	N
common criteria compliance enabled	0	1	0	N
cost threshold for parallelism	0	32767	5	Y
cursor threshold	−1	2147483647	−1	Y
Database Mail XPs	0	1	0	Y
default full-text language	0	2147483647	1033	Y
default trace enabled	0	1	1	Y
disallow results from triggers	0	1	0	Y
EKM provider enabled	0	1	0	N

CONFIGURATION OPTION	MINIMUM VALUE	MAXIMUM VALUE	DEFAULT VALUE	DYNAMIC YES/NO
fill factor	0 (%)	100 (%)	0	N
ft crawl bandwidth (max)	0	32767	100	Y
ft crawl bandwidth (min)	0	32767	0	Y
ft notify bandwidth (max)	0	32767	100	Y
ft notify bandwidth (min)	0	32767	0	Y
index create memory*	704 (kb)	2147483647 (kb)	0	Y
in-doubt xact resolution	0	2	0	Y
lightweight pooling	0	1	0	N
locks*	5000	2147483647	0	N
max degree of parallelism	0	64; 1024	0	Y
max full-text crawl range	0	256	4	Y
max server memory*	16 (mb)	2147483647 (mb)	2147483647	N
max text repl size	–1 (b)	2147483647 (b)	65536	Y
max worker threads	128	32767	0	N
media retention	0	365	0	N
min memory per query	512 (kb)	2147483647 (kb)	1024	Y
min server memory*	0 (mb)	2147483647 (mb)	0	Y
network packet size	512 (b)	32767 (b)	4096	Y
Ole Automation Procedures	0	1	0	Y
open objects	0	2147483647	0	N
optimize for ad hoc workloads	0	1	0	Y
ph_timeout	1 (s)	3600 (s)	60	Y
precompute rank	0	1	0	Y

CONFIGURATION OPTION	MINIMUM VALUE	MAXIMUM VALUE	DEFAULT VALUE	DYNAMIC YES/NO
priority boost	0	1	0	N
query governor cost limit	0	2147483647	0	Y
query wait	−1	2147483647 (s)	−1	Y
recovery interval*	0 (min)	32767 (min)	0	Y
Replication XPs	0	1	0	Y
scan for startup procs	0	1	0	N
set working set size	0	1	0	N
SMO and DMO XPs	0	1	1	Y
SQL Mail XPs	0	1	0	Y
transform noise words	0	1	0	Y
two digit year cutoff	1753	9999	2049	Y
user connections*	0	32767	0	N
xp_cmdshell	0	1	0	Y

You can view the current settings of all configuration options by executing the following query:

T-SQL
```
exec sp_configure
go
```

PowerShell
```
Invoke-Sqlcmd -Query "exec sp_configure"
-ServerInstance "DataServer91\CorpServices"
```

> **NOTE** Show Advanced Options must be set to 1 to see advanced options.

To view the current setting of a configuration option, execute the following query:

T-SQL
```
exec sp_configure 'optionName'
go
```

PowerShell
```
Invoke-Sqlcmd -Query "exec sp_configure 'optionName'"
```

```
-ServerInstance "DataServer91\CorpServices"
```

where *optionName* is the name of the option you want to examine, such as:

T-SQL

```
exec sp_configure 'max worker threads'
go
```

PowerShell

```
Invoke-Sqlcmd -Query "exec sp_configure 'max worker threads'"
-ServerInstance "DataServer91\CorpServices"
```

To change the value of a setting, execute the following query:

T-SQL

```
exec sp_configure 'optionName', newValue
go
reconfigure with override
go
```

PowerShell

```
Invoke-Sqlcmd -Query "exec sp_configure 'optionName', newValue;
reconfigure with override" -ServerInstance "DataServer91\CorpServices"
```

where *optionName* is the name of the option you want to examine, and *newValue* is the new value for this option, such as:

T-SQL

```
exec sp_configure 'locks', 10000
go
reconfigure
go
```

PowerShell

```
Invoke-Sqlcmd -Query "exec sp_configure 'locks', 10000;
reconfigure " -ServerInstance "DataServer91\CorpServices"
```

> **NOTE** You do not always have to use WITH OVERRIDE. Other than with recovery intervals, minimum server memory, and maximum server memory, WITH OVERRIDE is required only when making ad hoc updates and setting an option to a value that is not generally recommended. Keep in mind that some setting changes are applied only when you restart the SQL Server instance.

Changing Settings with ALTER DATABASE

For SQL Server 2012 and later releases, the ALTER DATABASE statement replaces the sp_dboption stored procedure as the preferred way to change database settings. Although sp_dboption can still be used, it will be removed in a future version of SQL Server. To change database settings, you must be a member of a role granted the ALTER permission on the database or be assigned this permission explicitly. When you execute an ALTER DATABASE statement, a checkpoint occurs in the database for which the option was changed, and this causes the change to take effect immediately. Table 4-6 provides an overview of the database options you can set with ALTER DATABASE.

NOTE With contained databases, you can set options that otherwise would be set at the server level. DEFAULT_FULLTEXT_LANGUAGE sets the default language value for full-text indexed columns. DEFAULT_LANGUAGE sets the default language for all newly created logins. NESTED_TRIGGERS determines whether AFTER triggers cascade and initiate other triggers. TRANSFORM_NOISE_WORDS can be used to suppress error messages related to noise words that cause a Boolean operation on a full-text query to fail. TWO_DIGIT_YEAR_CUTOFF specifies an integer from 1753 to 9999 that represents the cutoff year for interpreting two-digit years as four-digit years.

TABLE 4-6 Quick Reference Summary for Database Options

OPTION	WHEN TRUE OR SET TO VALUE	ACCEPTED VALUES
ALLOW_SNAPSHOT_ ISOLATION	Enables SNAPSHOT transaction isolation, in which statements see a snapshot of data as it exists at the start of the transaction. Here, row versioning is used instead of locking.	ON | OFF
ANSI_NULL_DEFAULT	CREATE TABLE uses SQL-92 rules to determine if a column allows null values.	ON | OFF
ANSI_NULLS	All comparisons to a null value evaluate to UNKNOWN. (When OFF, non-UNICODE values evaluate to TRUE if both values are NULL.)	ON | OFF
ANSI_PADDING	Trailing blanks are inserted into character values, and trailing zeros are inserted into binary values to pad to the length of the column.	ON | OFF
ANSI_WARNINGS	Errors or warnings are issued when conditions such as "divide by zero" occur.	ON | OFF

OPTION	WHEN TRUE OR SET TO VALUE	ACCEPTED VALUES
ARITHABORT	An overflow or divide-by-zero error causes the query or batch to terminate. If the error occurs in a transaction, the transaction is rolled back. (When this option is set to OFF, a warning message is displayed, but execution continues as if no error occurred.)	ON | OFF
AUTO_CLEANUP	Change tracking information is removed automatically after the retention period.	ON | OFF
AUTO_CREATE_STATISTICS	Any missing statistics needed for query optimization are generated automatically.	ON | OFF
AUTO_UPDATE_STATISTICS	Any out-of-date statistics needed for query optimization are generated automatically.	ON | OFF
AUTOCLOSE	After the last user logs off, the database is shut down cleanly and its resources are freed.	ON | OFF
AUTOSHRINK	Automatic periodic shrinking is enabled for the database.	ON | OFF
CHANGE_RETENTION	When change tracking is set to ON, this option sets the retention period for change tracking information.	RetPeriod {DAYS | HOURS | MINUTES}
CHANGE_TRACKING	Turns on and enables change tracking.	ON | OFF
COMPATIBILITY_LEVEL	Sets the database compatibility level.	80 | 90 | 100
CONCAT_NULL_YIELDS_NULL	If either operand in a concatenation operation is NULL, the result is NULL.	ON | OFF
CONTAINMENT	The logins are authenticated by the database, as opposed to being mapped to logins in the master database.	NONE | PARTIAL

OPTION	WHEN TRUE OR SET TO VALUE	ACCEPTED VALUES
CURSOR_CLOSE_ON_COMMIT	Any cursors that are open when a transaction is committed or rolled back are closed. (When this option is set to OFF, cursors remain open when a transaction is committed. Rolling back a transaction closes any cursors except those defined as INSENSITIVE or STATIC.)	ON | OFF
CURSOR_DEFAULT	Cursor declarations default to LOCAL.	LOCAL | GLOBAL
DATE_CORRELATION_OPTIMIZATION	SQL Server maintains correlation statistics between tables in a database that are linked by a foreign key constraint and have datetime columns.	ON | OFF
DB_CHAINING	The database can be the source or target of a cross-database ownership chain. The instance of SQL Server recognizes this setting only when the cross db ownership chaining server option is 0 (OFF). Otherwise, all user databases can participate in cross-database ownership chains, regardless of the value of this option.	ON | OFF
EMERGENCY	Marks the database as read-only, disables logging, and allows access only by members of the sysadmin role.	EMERGENCY
ENCRYPTION	Transparent data encryption is turned on for the database.	ON | OFF
MULTI_USER	Multiple users can access the database.	MULTI_USER
NUMERIC_ROUNDABORT	An error is generated when loss of precision occurs in an expression. (When this option is set to OFF, losses of precision do not generate error messages and the result is rounded to the precision of the column or variable storing the result.)	ON | OFF

OPTION	WHEN TRUE OR SET TO VALUE	ACCEPTED VALUES
OFFLINE	The database is offline. (Otherwise, the database is online.)	OFFLINE
ONLINE	The database is online and available for use.	ONLINE
PAGE_VERIFY	SQL Server can discover damaged database pages.	CHECKSUM | TORN_PAGE_ DETECTION | NONE
PARAMETERIZATION	SQL Server parameterizes all queries in the database.	SIMPLE | FORCED
QUOTED_IDENTIFIER	Double quotation marks can be used to enclose delimited identifiers.	ON | OFF
READ_COMMITTED_ SNAPSHOT	Row versioning is used instead of locking; all statements see a snapshot of data as it exists at the start of the statement, regardless of whether translations use snapshot isolation.	ON | OFF
READ_ONLY	The database is set to read-only (but can be deleted by using the DROP DATABASE statement). The database cannot be in use when this option is set (except for the *master* database).	READ_ONLY
RECOVERY	Causes the recovery model to be reset. SIMPLE allows a checkpoint to truncate the inactive part of the log.	FULL | BULK_ LOGGED | SIMPLE
RECURSIVE_TRIGGERS	Enables recursive firing of triggers. (When this option is set to OFF, it prevents direct recursion but not indirect recursion. To disable indirect recursion, set the nested triggers server option to 0 using sp_configure.)	ON | OFF
RESTRICTED_USER	Only the database owner can use the database.	RESTRICTED_ USER
SINGLE_USER	Only one user at a time can access the database.	SINGLE_USER

OPTION	WHEN TRUE OR SET TO VALUE	ACCEPTED VALUES
TORN_PAGE_DETECTION	Allows incomplete pages to be detected. (This option is being replaced by PAGE_VERIFY.)	ON | OFF
TRUSTWORTHY	Database modules that use impersonation can access resources outside the database.	ON | OFF

Most of the options listed in Table 4-6 accept a value of ON or OFF, which is used to set the state of the option. For example, you can enable transparent data encryption on the *CustomerSupport* database by using the following command:

T-SQL

```
USE master;
GO
ALTER DATABASE CustomerSupport
SET ENCRYPTION ON;
GO
```

PowerShell

```
Invoke-Sqlcmd -Query "USE master; ALTER DATABASE CustomerSupport
SET ENCRYPTION ON;" -ServerInstance "DataServer91\CorpServices"
```

Some options explicitly set a specific state. For example, if no users are currently connected to the *CustomerSupport* database, you could set the database to read-only by using the following command:

T-SQL

```
USE master;
GO
ALTER DATABASE CustomerSupport
SET READ_ONLY;
GO
```

PowerShell

```
Invoke-Sqlcmd -Query "USE master; ALTER DATABASE CustomerSupport
SET READ_ONLY;" -ServerInstance "DataServer91\CorpServices"
```

CHAPTER 5

Tuning and Linking Your SQL Servers

S QL Server Management Studio is the tool of choice for most server and database management tasks. Using SQL Server Management Studio, you can easily access the properties of a registered server and then use the pages and options provided to tune settings. You also can tune your SQL Servers with Transact-SQL (T-SQL) and Windows PowerShell.

Not all tuning tasks are straightforward, however. As networking environments become more and more complex, organizations that have managed with a relative few SQL Servers now need additional ones, or they need to integrate their existing servers with other, heterogeneous data sources. Microsoft SQL Server 2012 provides several features for integrating one SQL Server database with other SQL Server databases or with other data sources. These features include replication, distributed data, and linked servers.

Distributed data includes support for distributed queries, distributed transactions, and remote stored procedure execution. These distributed data features are handled through linked servers, which can be computers running SQL Server or computers running other database server software, such as Oracle Database Enterprise Edition.

NOTE Policy-Based Management settings can affect your ability to configure SQL Server 2012. See Chapter 3, "Implementing Policy-Based Management," for more information.

SQL Server Management Studio Essentials

In Chapter 1, "Managing Your SQL Servers," I discussed techniques for getting started with and using SQL Server Management Studio. Before you can work with a server instance or database, you must connect to it. To save connection information, you can register servers. To organize sets of servers, you can use groups. These server groups can be local groups or groups associated with central management servers. Servers within local groups are independent, but servers within centrally managed groups are not. SQL Server 2012 extends centralized management concepts by introducing SQL Server Utility, utility control points (UCPs), managed instances, and data-tier applications.

Managing the Configuration with SQL Server Management Studio

After you connect to a registered server in SQL Server Management Studio, you can view and manage its configuration properties by using the Server Properties dialog box. To access this dialog box, complete the following steps:

1. Click Start, point to All Programs, Microsoft SQL Server 2012, and then select SQL Server Management Studio.

   TIP With Windows 7 or Windows Server 2008 R2 or later, try this if you'd like a quick and easy way to access SQL Server Management Studio: Click Start, and type **SQL Server Management Studio** into the Search box on the Start menu. Right-click SQL Server Management Studio in the results and then select Pin To Taskbar. Now, whenever you want to access it, simply click the related icon on the taskbar.

2. In the Connect To Server dialog box, use the Server Type list to select the server type you want to connect to, such as Database Engine.

3. In the Server Name box, select or type the name of the server on which SQL Server is running, such as DBServer46.

   NOTE You can connect to any server that is visible, so long as remote access is enabled on the server and the server name is resolved. Select the <Browse For More> option in the Server Name drop-down list to look for available servers. See the "Managing Servers" section in Chapter 1 for details.

4. Use the Authentication list to choose an option for authentication type, either Windows Authentication or SQL Server Authentication (based on the authentication types selected when you installed the server). Provide a SQL Server login ID and password as necessary.

- **Windows Authentication** Uses your current domain account and password to establish the database connection. This authentication type works only if Windows authentication is enabled and you have appropriate privileges.

- **SQL Server Authentication** Allows you to specify a SQL Server login ID and password.

5. Click Connect. You connect to the default instance (unless you have configured another default previously). To change the instance to which you connect, click Options, select the Connection Properties tab, and then use the Connect To Database list to select the instance you want to connect to.

6. In the SQL Server Management Studio Object Explorer view, right-click the server name, and then choose Properties to open the dialog box shown in Figure 5-1.

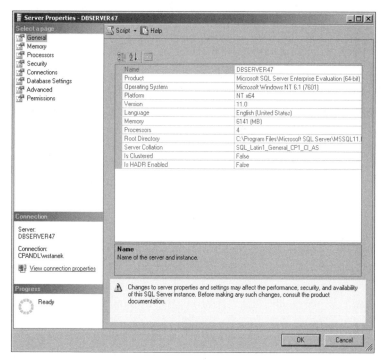

FIGURE 5-1 The General page of the Server Properties dialog box.

Now you can manage common SQL Server configuration settings. For more advanced settings, you need to use a stored procedure, such as sp_configure, as discussed in Chapter 4, "Configuring and Tuning Your SQL Servers."

The Server Properties dialog box has many pages, which are listed at the top of the left pane in Figure 5-1. The rest of the sections in this chapter explain how to use the configuration options provided on these pages. Permissions are discussed in Chapter 7, "Implementing SQL Server 2012 Security."

If you want to view a summary of current settings, run the following query in Query view:

```
USE master
GO
EXEC sp_configure
GO
```

Or use SQL Server PowerShell, as shown in the following example:

```
Invoke-Sqlcmd -Query "USE master; EXEC sp_configure"
-ServerInstance "DataServer91\CorpServices"
```

> **NOTE** Show Advanced Options must be set to 1 to see advanced options, as discussed in Chapter 4.

Determining System and Server Information

General system and server information is available on the General page of the Server Properties dialog box. (See Figure 5-1.) The information on the General page helps you determine the following:

- SQL Server edition
- Operating system version
- SQL Server version
- Platform and chip architecture
- Default language
- Amount of RAM installed on the system
- Number of CPUs
- Root directory location for the selected instance
- Default server collation

You can obtain similar information by using the extended stored procedure xp_msver. Execute the following command:

```
exec xp_msver "ProductName", "ProductVersion", "Language", "Platform",
"WindowsVersion", "PhysicalMemory", "ProcessorCount"
```

TIP You can use Query view to execute the command just shown. Basic techniques for using this utility are covered in the "Configuring SQL Server with Stored Procedures" section in Chapter 4.

You also can use SQL Server PowerShell, as shown in the following example:

```
Invoke-Sqlcmd -Query "exec xp_msver 'ProductName', 'ProductVersion',
'Language', 'Platform', 'WindowsVersion', 'PhysicalMemory',
'ProcessorCount'" -ServerInstance "DataServer91\CorpServices"
```

Configuring Utility Control Points

SQL Server Utility is a central repository for performance data from Database Engine instances. Every instance of SQL Server Utility has a single control point that you must create. A utility control point (UCP) is the central collection point for SQL Server Utility and is used to view performance information collected from managed instances and deployed data-tier applications. You can use this information to help you perform capacity planning and to ensure that resources are not overused.

Your organization can have multiple control points. Each control point can manage instances of SQL Server and data-tier applications. After you enroll an instance in a control point or deploy a data-tier application on a control point, you can monitor resource usage policies on the control point to help determine how the following resources are being used:

- CPU
- Data files
- Log files
- Disks

You use the Utility Explorer view in SQL Server Management Studio to work with control points and managed instances. If this view is not displayed, you can display it by choosing the related option from the View menu.

To configure SQL Server Utility with a control point and managed instances, you need to do the following:

1. Create and then connect to a UCP.
2. Enroll instances of SQL Server with the control point.
3. Optionally, create and register a data-tier application for use with the control point.
4. Establish resource health policies for managed instances and any registered data-tier applications.
5. Grant user rights to view or manage health policies for the instance of SQL Server Utility.

I discuss these procedures in the sections that follow.

Creating a Control Point

Creating a control point creates the related schema, jobs, and policies on the designated instance of SQL Server. It also configures a utility management data warehouse (UMDW) for storing the control point information and enables the control point to collect and store data in the data warehouse.

The control point must be running SQL Server 2012 Developer, Enterprise, or Datacenter Edition. When you are working with one of these editions, you can configured it as your control point by following these steps:

1. On the Getting Started tab of the Utility Explorer view, click Create A Utility Control Point. Alternatively, click Create Utility Control Point on the Utility Explorer toolbar. When the wizard starts, click Next if the Introduction page is displayed.

2. Click Connect. Use the Connect To Server dialog box to specify the instance of SQL Server where you want to create the control point. To create the control point successfully, you must have administrative privileges on this instance, the instance must be running Enterprise Edition or later, and the instance must not already be a control point or enrolled in any other control point. Click Connect to connect to the instance and close the Connect To Server dialog box.

3. Enter a descriptive name for the control point, such as Team Services Control Point. This name is displayed in Utility Explorer.

4. Click Next. Specify a Windows domain account to run the utility collection set. You can use the existing SQL Server Agent service account for this purpose, or you can specify an account to act as the SQL Server Agent proxy account for collection activities. You cannot use a built-in account.

5. When you click Next, the wizard verifies that all conditions for creating the control point have been met. Successful verification allows you to continue. If any part of the verification fails, you need to repeat the creation process.

6. Click Next. Review the summary details to ensure all prerequisites are met. As necessary, correct any warnings or errors. For example, because UCP relies on the SQL Server Agent service, the service must be running on the UCP and configured for automatic startup. If the service isn't configured in this way, you'll see a related error. You'll need to correct the problem and then click Rerun Validation.

7. When you click Next twice, the wizard prepares the instance to act as the control point, creates and initializes the related data warehouse, and then configures and enrolls the control point. Enrolling the control point makes the control point a member of its own managed group. Click Finish.

After you create a control point, you are connected to it automatically in Utility Explorer, as shown in Figure 5-2. When you select the top-level node, Utility Explorer displays a summary view of resource health for managed instances and deployed data-tier applications.

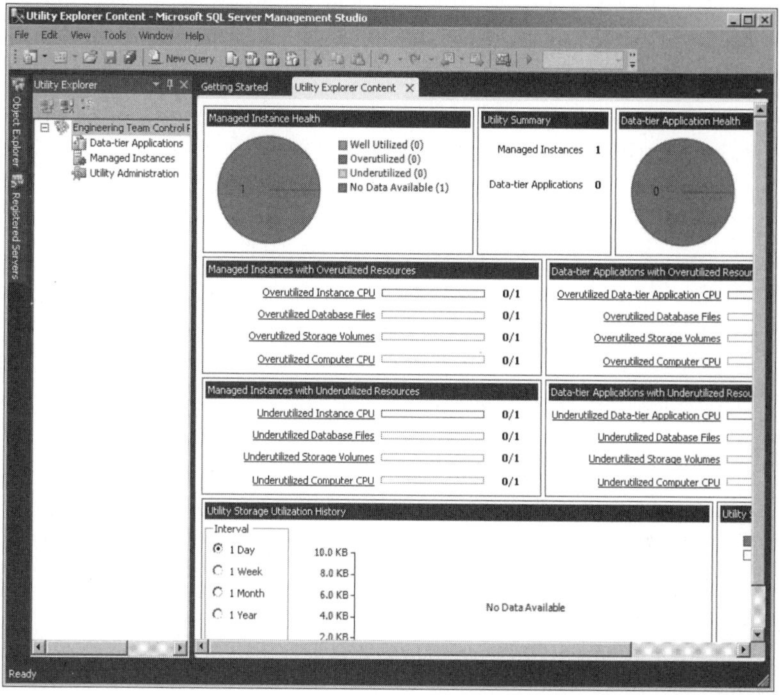

FIGURE 5-2 Utility Explorer with a new control point.

If you want to connect to a different control point, you need to disconnect from the control point you just created by clicking the Disconnect From Utility button on the Utility Explorer toolbar. Then you can connect to a different control point by clicking the Connect To Utility button on the Utility Explorer toolbar and selecting the server hosting the control point that you want to work with in the Connect To Server dialog box.

Enrolling an Instance

Instances of the Database Engine running on SQL Server 2008 R2 or later can be enrolled in a control point. Enrolling an instance with a control point creates a relationship between the control point and the instance, allowing the control point to manage and collect data from the instance. To enroll an instance, follow these steps:

1. On the Getting Started tab of the Utility Explorer view, click Enroll Instances Of SQL Server With A UCP. Alternatively, in the Utility Explorer view, right-click the Managed Instances node and then select Enroll Instance. When the wizard starts, click Next if the Introduction page is displayed.

2. Click Connect. Use the Connect To Server dialog box to specify the instance of SQL Server to enroll. To enroll the instance with the control point successfully, you must have administrative privileges on this instance and the instance must

not already be enrolled with any other control point. Click Connect to connect to the instance and close the Connect To Server dialog box.

3. Click Next. Specify a Windows domain account to run the utility collection set as an administrator on the previously specified instance. You can use the existing SQL Server Agent service account for this purpose, or you can specify an account to act as the SQL Server Agent proxy account for collection activities. You cannot use a built-in account.

4. When you click Next, the wizard verifies that all conditions for enrolling the instance have been met. Successful verification allows you to continue. If any part of the verification fails, you need to repeat the enrollment process.

5. Click Next. Review the summary details. When you click Next again, the wizard enrolls the instance. Click Finish.

After you enroll an instance, the control point's global resource utilization policies are applied and the control point begins to collect and display resource utilization information for the instance.

Deploying Data-Tier Applications

Data-tier applications (DACs) are used to represent all the objects and deployment prerequisites for a database application. Essentially, DACs are containers that include server and database schema objects used by an application, as well as the configuration details and policy requirements. You can extract a DAC from an existing SQL Server database to create a package file containing all related database objects and SQL Server elements. You can then work with and modify the DAC package in Microsoft Visual Studio 2010 or later prior to deploying the application.

Using SQL Server Management Studio, you can extract an application from an instance of SQL Server 2000 or later, and then deploy the DAC to an instance of SQL Server 2008 R2 or later. After you deploy the DAC, you can upgrade the schema to SQL Server 2012 by transferring the source database for the application to a new target database running SQL Server 2012. To do this, you can use SQL Server Integration Services or the bulk copy utility.

To extract a DAC, follow these steps:

1 Install the server and client tools for SQL Server 2012 on the computer running SQL Server. In SQL Server Management Studio, register the instances of SQL Server that you want to work with.

2. In Object Explorer, expand the node for the database instance you want to work with, right-click the user database to extract, click Tasks, and then select Extract A Data-Tier Application. When the wizard starts, click Next if the Introduction page is displayed.

3. Specify a name for the application, an arbitrary application version number, and an optional description. Next, set the file path for the package file. If this

file exists in the specified location and you want to overwrite it, select the Overwrite Existing File check box.

4. When you click Next, the wizard verifies that all conditions for extracting the application have been met. Generally, successful verification means that all the objects in the application are supported and success allows you to continue. If any part of the verification fails, you need to repeat the extraction process.

5. Click Next. Review the summary details. When you click Next again, the wizard builds the package file. Click Finish.

After you build the package file, you can modify it using Visual Studio 2010 or later. To do this, import the package file into a DAC Visual Studio project. When you are ready to test or deploy the application, you can deploy the application to a SQL Server instance by following these steps:

1. In SQL Server Management Studio, connect to a SQL Server 2008 R2 or later instance.

2. In Object Explorer, expand the Management node, right-click the Data-Tier Application node, and then click Deploy Data-Tier Application. When the wizard starts, click Next if the Introduction page is displayed.

3. Click Browse, and then select the .dacpac package file that you want to deploy. Click Next.

4. Specify a name for the DAC and the name of the database to create for hosting the application's database objects.

5. Click Next. Review the summary details. When you click Next again, the wizard creates the new database, the required database schema, and the required logins. Click Finish.

Performing Utility Administration

Control points help you better manage and monitor the resource utilization of enrolled instances and deployed applications. When you connect to a control point using Utility Explorer, you can select the control point node and then click the Utility Explorer Content tab to view resource health and utilization information. As shown in Figure 5-3, the available second-level nodes in the left pane include:

- **Data-Tier Applications** Shows deployed applications by name. For each application, you also can see the application's CPU utilization, the associated server's CPU utilization, file space usage, volume (disk) space usage, the policy type applied, and the associated database instance.

- **Managed Instances** Shows managed instances by name. For each instance, you also can see the instance's CPU utilization, the associated server's CPU utilization, file space usage, volume (disk) space usage, and the policy type applied.

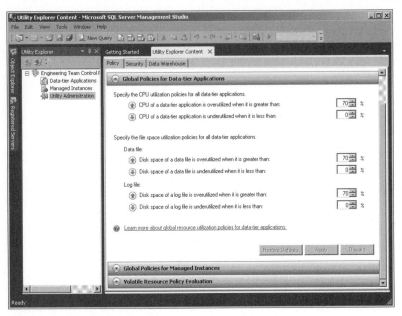

FIGURE 5-3 Utility administration.

- **Utility Administration** Provides access to administration features for policies, security, and the utility's data warehouse. When you select this node, there are three available tabs in the right pane:

  - **Policy** When you are working with the Policy tab, you can set global policies separately for DACs and managed instances. You also can control how policies are evaluated by the control point.

  - **Security** When you are working with the Security tab, you can view logins that have the utility reader role. To add this role to a login, grant the role via the related database instance. To remove this role from a listed login, clear the check box.

  - **Data Warehouse** When you are working with the Data Warehouse tab, you can review details for the control point's data warehouse and configure the data retention period.

Working with Linked Servers and Distributed Data

You can use linked servers to integrate one SQL Server database with other SQL Server databases or with other data sources. Linked servers include support for distributed queries, distributed transactions, and remote stored procedure execution. Linked servers can be computers running SQL Server or computers running other database server software, such as Oracle Database Enterprise Edition.

Before you integrate, you must configure the linked servers you want to use. Linked servers depend on OLE DB providers to communicate with one another. Through OLE DB, you can link instances of SQL Server to other instances of SQL Server as well as to other data sources.

Linked servers allow the execution of distributed queries, distributed transactions, and remote stored procedure calls. Basically, queries and transactions are *distributed* when they make use of two or more database server instances. For example, if a client is connected to one server instance and starts a query that accesses a different server instance, the query is distributed. On the other hand, if the same client queries two different databases on the same server instance, the query is considered a local query and is handled internally.

You can define linked servers that point back to the server on which they are defined. This type of linked server is called a *loopback linked server* because T-SQL statements loop through the SQL Native Client Interface provider and back to the local server. You'll find that loopback linked servers are most useful when you are testing an application that uses distributed queries when only a single instance is physically available on the network.

NOTE You cannot use loopback linked servers in distributed transactions. You'll get an error if you try to execute a distributed query against a loopback linked server from within a distributed transaction. In SQL Server 2012, an INSERT...EXECUTE statement can execute against a loopback linked server when the connection does not have multiple active result sets (MARS) enabled.

Using Distributed Queries

When you execute a distributed query, SQL Server interprets the command and then breaks it down for the destination OLE DB provider by using rowset requests. A *rowset* is a type of database object that enables OLE DB data providers to support data with a tabular format. As their name implies, rowset objects represent a set of rows and columns of data. After creating the rowset objects, the OLE DB provider calls the data source, opens the necessary files, and returns the requested information as rowsets. SQL Server then formats the rowsets as result sets and adds any applicable output parameters.

NOTE With ANSI SQL-92 specifications, the user connections must have the ANSI_NULLS and ANSI_WARNINGS options before they can execute distributed queries. Be sure to configure these options if necessary. For more information, see the "Configuring User and Remote Connections" section earlier in this chapter.

You can create simple distributed queries quickly by making your own rowsets. To do this, you use the OPENROWSET function. When you use this function, you do not need to use linked servers. Also, you can use the OPENROWSET function in place of a table in a query if you pass parameters that identify the OLE DB data source and provider.

You use the OPENROWSET function in the same way that you use virtual tables; simply replace the virtual table reference with an OPENROWSET reference. Sample 5-1 shows the syntax and usage of OPENROWSET.

The BULK rowset provider is similar to the BULK INSERT statement. The data_file parameter is used to specify the data file from which data will be copied into the target table. A format file is required to define the column types in the result set, except when you use SINGLE_BLOB, SINGLE_CLOB, or SINGLE_NCLOB. SINGLE_BLOB returns the contents of the data file as a single-row/single-column rowset of type varbinary(max). SINGLE_CLOB reads the data file as ASCII text and returns the contents of the data file as a single-row/single-column rowset of type varchar(max). SINGLE_NCLOB reads the data file as Unicode text and returns the contents as a single-row/single-column rowset of type nvarchar(max). Both SINGLE_CLOB and SINGLE_NCLOB use the collation of the current database.

SAMPLE 5-1 OPENROWSET Syntax and Usage.

Syntax for SELECT with Table Alias

```
SELECT selection FROM OPENROWSET(rowset_options) AS table_alias
```

Syntax for OPENROWSET

```
OPENROWSET
( { 'provider_name' , { 'datasource' ; 'user_id' ; 'password'
    | 'provider_string' }
      , { [ catalog. ] [ schema. ] object
    | 'query' }
    | BULK 'data_file' ,
        { FORMATFILE = 'format_file_path' [ <bulk_options> ]
        | SINGLE_BLOB | SINGLE_CLOB | SINGLE_NCLOB }
} )

<bulk_options> ::=
    [ , CODEPAGE = { 'ACP' | 'OEM' | 'RAW' | 'code_page' }]
    [ , ERRORFILE = 'file_name' ]
    [ , FIRSTROW = first_row ]
    [ , LASTROW = last_row ]
    [ , MAXERRORS = maximum_errors ]
    [ , ROWS_PER_BATCH = rows_per_batch ]
    [ , ORDER ( { column [ ASC | DESC ] } [ ,...n ] ) [ UNIQUE ]
```

Usage

```
USE pubs
GO
SELECT a.*
FROM OPENROWSET('SQLOLEDB','Pluto';'netUser';'totem12',
'SELECT * FROM pubs.dbo.authors ORDER BY au_lname, au_fname')
AS a
GO
SELECT o.*
```

```
FROM OPENROWSET('Microsoft.Jet.OLEDB.4.0','C:\
customers.mdb';'Admin';'', 'Orders')
AS o
```

When the OPENROWSET BULK option is used with an INSERT statement, you can use standard table hints, such as TABLOCK, as well as the special BULK INSERT table hints IGNORE_CONSTRAINTS, IGNORE_TRIGGERS, KEEPDEFAULTS, and KEEPIDENTITY. When you use the BULK rowset provider with OPENROWSET, you must specify column aliases in the FROM clause or specify column names in the format file. The syntax for the SELECT statement with the table alias then becomes:

```
SELECT selection FROM OPENROWSET(BULK rowset_options) AS
    table_alias[(column1_alias, column2_alias,...)]
```

Simple distributed queries using the OPENROWSET function are useful for infrequent references. For frequent references to OLE DB data sources, use linked servers instead. After you create a linked server (as discussed in the "Adding Linked Servers" section later in this chapter), you can access the linked server by using several different techniques. You can use the EXECUTE statement to execute both commands and stored procedures on a linked server. EXECUTE statements that pass through a command with the AT linked_server_name extension can include data definition language (DDL) and data manipulation language (DML) statements, as well as commands that return more than one result. Sample 5-2 shows the syntax for using EXECUTE in this way.

SAMPLE 5-2 EXECUTE at linked_server Syntax and Usage.

Syntax
```
EXEC [UTE] ( { @string_variable | [ N ] 'command_string' } [ + ...n ]
    [ {, { value | @variable [ OUTPUT ] } } [...n] ] )
    [ AS { LOGIN | USER } = ' name ']
    [ AT linked_server_name ] [;]
```

Usage
```
EXEC ( 'SELECT * FROM william.sales') AT ORADBSVR38;
```

You also can use remote stored procedures that execute against the linked server or distributed queries that access tables in the linked server through SELECT, INSERT, UPDATE, and DELETE statements that reference the linked server using a four-part name. The syntax for a four-part name is as follows:

```
LinkedServerName.DatabaseName.SchemaName.ObjectName
```

In this example, *LinkedServerName* is the name of a previously defined linked server, *DatabaseName* is the name of a database, *SchemaName* is the name of the schema, and *TableName* is the name of a database table, such as:

```
SELECT * FROM ORADBSVR38.Customers.CustomerSchema.Employees
```

Distributed queries can use four-part names only if the OLE DB provider you are using meets certain minimum requirements. The provider must support the

IDBSchemaRowset interface as well as restrictions on name parts. SQL Server uses a period (.) for catalog and schema separators and the double-quotation character for a string literal delimiter, and the provider must support these literals. If the provider provides Unicode string literal prefixes and Unicode string literal suffixes, SQL Server uses these. If the provider does not meet these minimum requirements, you can reference the provider only by using pass-through queries in the OPENDATASOURCE or OPENROWSET function.

Using Distributed Transactions

Distributed transactions are transactions that use distributed queries or remote procedure calls (RPCs). As you might expect, distributed transactions are more involved than distributed queries, primarily because you need a mechanism that ensures that transactions are committed uniformly or rolled back on all the linked servers. For example, if you start a transaction that updates databases on three different server instances, you want to be certain that the transaction is committed when it has completed successfully or that the transaction is rolled back if an error occurs. In this way, you ensure the integrity of the databases involved in the distributed transaction.

In SQL Server, three components are required for distributed transactions to be handled properly:

- **Resource managers**   You must configure resource managers, which are the linked servers used in the distributed transactions. For details about how to configure resource managers, see the "Managing Linked Servers" section later in this chapter.

- **Distributed Transaction Coordinator service**   The Microsoft Distributed Transaction Coordinator (MSDTC) service must be running on all servers that are handling distributed transactions. If it is not, distributed transactions will not work properly.

- **Transaction manager**   The transaction manager coordinates and manages distributed transactions. The transaction manager on SQL Server is the Distributed Transaction Coordinator.

NOTE   Applications other than SQL Server can use the Distributed Transaction Coordinator. If you try to analyze Distributed Transaction Coordinator performance, you should note which applications besides SQL Server are using the Distributed Transaction Coordinator.

Each server instance involved in a distributed transaction is known as a *resource manager*. Resource managers coordinate transactions through a transaction manager such as the Distributed Transaction Coordinator. You can use other transaction managers if they support the X/Open XA specification for distributed transaction processing.

You handle distributed transactions in much the same manner as you handle local transactions. Applications start distributed transactions in several ways:

- Explicitly, by using BEGIN DISTRIBUTED TRANSACTION
- Explicitly, by using the methods or functions available with ODBC, OLE DB, ADO, or the Microsoft .NET Framework to join a distributed transaction started by the application
- Implicitly, by executing a distributed query within a local transaction
- Implicitly, by calling a remote stored procedure within a local transaction (provided that the REMOTE_PROC_TRANSACTIONS option is set to ON)

At the end of the transaction, the application requests that the transaction be either committed or rolled back. To ensure that the transaction is handled properly on all servers, even if problems occur during the transaction, the transaction manager uses a commit process with two phases:

- **Phase 1: The prepare phase** The transaction manager sends a "prepare to commit" request to all the resource managers involved in the transaction. Each resource manager performs any necessary preparatory tasks and then reports its success or failure to the transaction manager. If all the resource managers are ready to commit, the transaction manager broadcasts a commit message and the transaction enters phase 2, the commit phase.

- **Phase 2: The commit phase** The resource managers attempt to commit the transaction. Each resource manager then sends back a success or failure message. If all the resource managers report success, the transaction manager marks the transaction as completed and reports this to the application. If a resource manager fails in either phase, the transaction is rolled back and the failure is reported.

SQL Server applications manage distributed transactions either through T-SQL or through the SQL Server database application programming interface (API). SQL Server itself supports distributed transactions by using the ITransactionLocal (local transactions) and ITransactionJoin (distributed transactions) OLE DB interfaces, as well as the rowset objects discussed previously. If an OLE DB provider does not support ITransactionJoin, only read-only procedures are allowed for that provider. Similarly, the types of queries you can execute on a linked server depend on the OLE DB provider you are using.

With distributed queries and transactions, you can use most DML commands, such as SELECT, INSERT, UPDATE, and DELETE. You cannot, however, use DDL commands, such as CREATE, DROP, or ALTER. If you need to use DDL commands on linked servers, you might want to create stored procedures and then execute these stored procedures remotely when necessary.

Running the Distributed Transaction Coordinator Service

The Distributed Transaction Coordinator service must run on each server that handles distributed transactions. Usually, you should set the service to start automatically when the system starts. This ensures that the distributed transactions are executed as expected. By using SQL Server Configuration Manager, you can control the Distributed Transaction Coordinator service just as you do other SQL Server–related services. For details, see the "Configuring SQL Server Services" section in Chapter 2.

You can view the Distributed Transaction Coordinator service in SQL Server Management Studio by completing the following steps:

1. In SQL Server Management Studio, connect to the server instance you want to use.

2. In the Object Explorer view, expand the Management node. You will see the status of the Distributed Transaction Coordinator service. A green circle with a triangle indicates that the service is running. A red circle with a square indicates that the service is stopped.

Configuring Authentication and Auditing

You configure authentication and auditing options with the Security page of the Server Properties dialog box, as shown in Figure 5-4.

Setting the Authentication Mode

SQL Server security is completely integrated with Windows domain security, allowing for authentication based on user and group memberships as well as standard SQL Server user accounts.

In the Server Properties dialog box, go to the Security page. The Server Authentication options allow you to configure authentication. To use combined authentication, select the SQL Server And Windows Authentication Mode option. Now users in Windows domains can access the server by using a domain account, and other users can be logged on using a SQL Server login ID.

To use domain authentication only, select the Windows Authentication Mode option. Now only users with a domain account can access the server.

> **TIP** If you change the authentication settings, you must restart all SQL Server instance services. With combined authentication, SQL Server first checks to see whether a new login is a SQL Server login. If the login exists, SQL Server uses the password provided to authenticate the user. If the login does not exist, SQL Server uses Windows authentication.

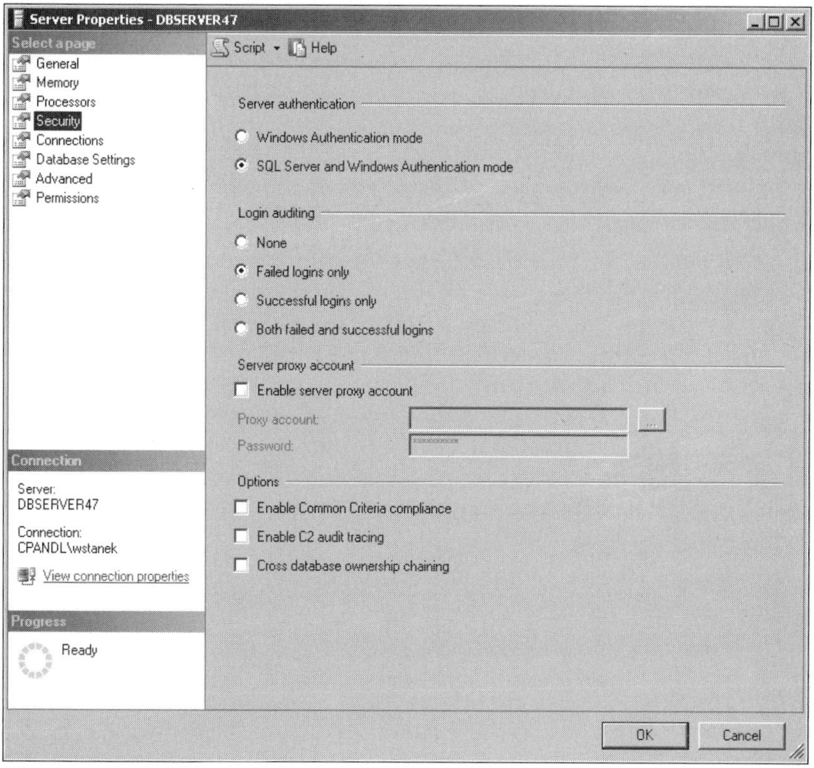

FIGURE 5-4 The Security page options.

Setting the Auditing Level

Auditing allows you to track user access to SQL Server. You can use auditing with both authentication modes as well as with trusted and untrusted connections.

The Login Auditing options on the Security page allow you to configure auditing. When auditing is enabled, user logins are recorded in the Windows application log, the SQL Server error log, or both logs, depending on how you configure logging for SQL Server. The available auditing options include the following:

- **None**   Disables auditing
- **Failed Logins Only**   Audits only failed login attempts (the default setting)
- **Successful Logins Only**   Audits only successful login attempts
- **Both Failed And Successful Logins**   Audits both successful and failed login attempts

To manage the auditing level, complete the following steps:

1. In the Server Properties dialog box, go to the Security page.
2. Select the auditing level you want to use, and then click OK.
3. If you change the auditing settings, you must restart all SQL Server instance services.

Enabling or Disabling C2 Audit Logging

Standards organizations have created many security standards. The Department of Defense (DOD) in the United States created the Trusted Computer System Evaluation Criteria standard as a means of evaluating the security of computer systems. The standard defines the security divisions from D (the lowest) to A (the highest), and it specifies the criteria against which computer systems can be evaluated for each of these classifications. Within divisions C and B are subdivisions known as *classes*. Criteria for classes C2 through A1 require that a user's actions be open to auditing and that there be personnel designated as responsible for audit procedures. C2 audit requirements define specific events and auditable information. B1 and higher classes add further requirements.

On your SQL Server implementation, you can enable C2 audit tracing to meet C2 compliance requirements. When you enable C2 audit tracing, SQL Server audits all logins, logouts, and attempts to access objects, and records them to a file in the \MSSQL\Data directory. If the audit log file reaches its size limit of 200 megabytes (MB), SQL Server creates a new file, closes the old file, and writes all new audit records to the new file. This process continues until the audit data directory fills up or auditing is turned off. You can determine the status of a C2 trace by querying the sys.traces view.

C2 auditing saves a large amount of event information to the audit log file. If the log directory runs out of space, SQL Server shuts itself down. To restart SQL Server after a forced shutdown, you need to use the –f flag to bypass auditing or free up additional disk space for the audit logs.

In the Server Properties dialog box, go to the Security page. You can enable C2 audit logging by selecting the Enable C2 Audit Tracing check box. With sp_configure, the related commands are as follows:

T-SQL
```
exec sp_configure "c2 audit mode", <0 or 1>
GO
RECONFIGURE
GO
```

PowerShell
```
Invoke-Sqlcmd -Query "exec sp_configure 'c2 audit mode', <0 or 1>;
RECONFIGURE;" -ServerInstance "Server\Instance"
```

You use 0 to disable and 1 to enable C2 audit mode.

Enabling or Disabling Common Criteria Compliance

Beginning with SQL Server 2005 Service Pack 2 (SP2), a set of common criteria could be enabled to enhance security and comply with Common Criteria Evaluation Level 4 (EAL4+) security requirements. Common Criteria (CC) is an international security standard meant to be used as the basis for evaluating the security properties of applications and servers. Enabling compliance with these security requirements enforces the following common criteria:

- **Column GRANT should not override table DENY**   Ensures that a table-level DENY takes precedence over a column-level GRANT. Without this criterion, a column-level GRANT takes precedence over a table-level DENY.

- **View login statistics capability**   Ensures that login auditing is enabled so that each time a user logs in to SQL Server, information is made available about the last successful login time, the last unsuccessful login time, and the number of attempts between the last successful and current login times. You can view these statistics by querying the sys.dm_exec_sessions view.

- **Residual Information Protection (RIP) compliance**   Requires previously allocated memory to be overwritten with a known pattern of bits before SQL Server reallocates the memory to a new resource. Although this technique can improve security, overwriting previously allocated memory can slow performance.

In the Server Properties dialog box, go to the Security page. You can enable common criteria compliance by selecting the Enable Common Criteria Compliance check box. With sp_configure, the related commands are:

T-SQL

```
exec sp_configure "common criteria compliance", <0 or 1>
GO
RECONFIGURE
GO
```

PowerShell

```
Invoke-Sqlcmd -Query "exec sp_configure 'common criteria compliance',
<0 or 1>; RECONFIGURE;" -ServerInstance "Server\Instance"
```

You use 0 to disable and 1 to enable common criteria compliance.

Tuning Memory Usage

SQL Server is designed to manage memory dynamically based on needs at any point in time, and it does an excellent job in most cases. Using dynamic memory allocation, SQL Server can request additional memory from the operating system to handle incoming queries, release memory to the operating system for another application you are starting, or reserve memory for possible needs. The default memory settings are the following:

- Configure SQL Server memory dynamically
- Minimum memory allocation set at 0 MB
- Maximum memory allocation set to allow SQL Server to use virtual memory on disk as well as physical RAM
- No memory reserved specifically for SQL Server
- Address Windowing Extensions (AWE) not enabled
- Minimum memory for query execution set at 1,024 kilobytes (KB)

You can change these settings, but you need to be careful about allocating too little or too much memory to SQL Server. Too little memory might prevent SQL Server from handling tasks in a timely manner. Too much memory might cause SQL Server to take essential resources from other applications or the operating system, which might result in excessive paging and cause a drain on overall server performance.

TIP Some statistics can help you allocate memory correctly, such as the number of page faults per second and the cache-hit ratio. Page faults per second can track paging to and from virtual memory. The cache-hit ratio can determine whether data being retrieved is in memory. You will learn more about using these types of statistics in Chapter 12, "SQL Server 2012 Profiling and Monitoring."

This section examines important areas of memory management. The primary method for configuring memory usage is to select options on the Memory page of the Server Properties dialog box, shown in Figure 5-5. You also will learn a better way to configure Windows memory usage for SQL Server.

REAL WORLD If you are running SQL Server 2012 on Windows Server 2003, do not use the Maximize Data Throughput For Network Applications setting. This setting gives priority to applications that perform buffered I/O by caching their I/O pages in file system cache. Using this option might limit the amount of memory available to SQL Server 2012. To view and change this setting, complete the following steps:

1. Access Network Connections in Control Panel.

2. Right-click Local Area Connection, and then select Properties.

3. Select File And Printer Sharing For Microsoft Networks, and then choose Properties.

4. On the Server Optimization tab, choose an appropriate setting other than Maximize Data Throughput For Network Applications.

5. Restart the server to apply the setting change.

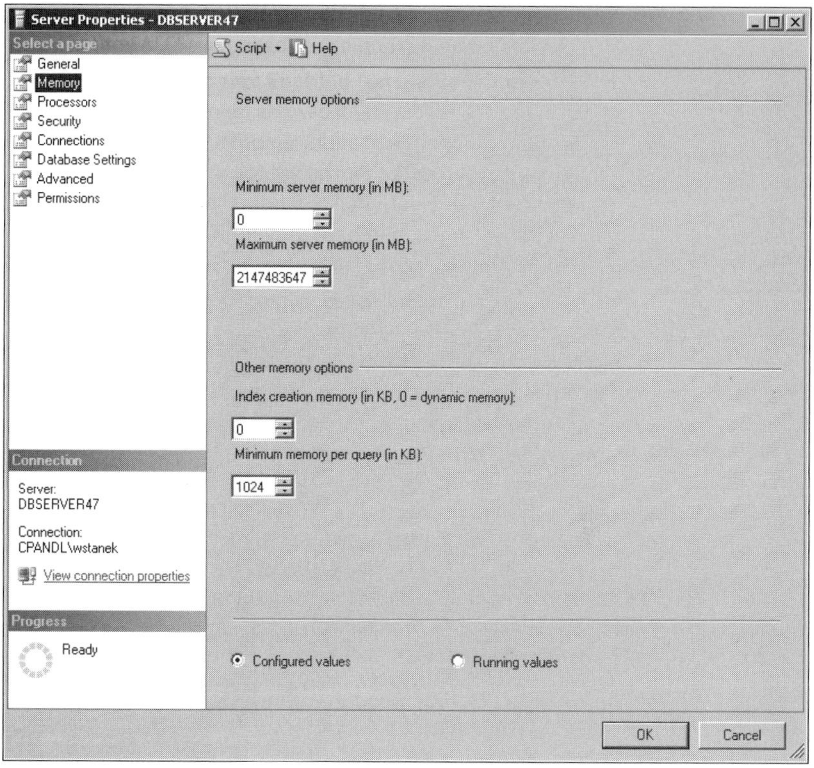

FIGURE 5-5 The Memory page of the Server Properties dialog box.

Working with Dynamically Configured Memory

With dynamically configured memory, SQL Server configures memory usage automatically based on workload and available resources. Total memory usage varies between the minimum and maximum values that you set. The minimum server memory sets the baseline usage for SQL Server, but this memory is not allocated at startup. Memory is allocated as needed based on the database workload. When the minimum server memory threshold is reached, this threshold becomes the baseline, and memory is not released if it will leave SQL Server with less than the minimum server memory threshold.

To use dynamically configured memory, complete the following steps:

1. In the Server Properties dialog box, go to the Memory page.

2. Set the memory usage values to different values in the Minimum Server Memory and Maximum Server Memory boxes, respectively. The recommended maximum value for stand-alone servers is at or near total RAM (physical

memory + virtual memory). However, if multiple instances of SQL Server are running on a computer, you should consider setting the maximum server memory so that the instances are not competing for memory.

3. Click OK.

You can use the stored procedure sp_configure to change the minimum and maximum settings. Use the following commands:

T-SQL

```
exec sp_configure "min server memory", <number of megabytes>
exec sp_configure "max server memory", <number of megabytes>
```

PowerShell

```
Invoke-Sqlcmd -Query "exec sp_configure 'min server memory', <num mb>"
Invoke-Sqlcmd -Query "exec sp_configure 'max server memory', <num mb>"
```

> **BEST PRACTICES** With dynamically configured memory, you usually do not need to set minimum and maximum memory usage values. On a dedicated system running only SQL Server, however, you might achieve smoother operation by setting minimum memory to 8 MB + (24 KB * *NumUsers*), where *NumUsers* is the average number of users simultaneously connected to the server. You also might want to reserve physical memory for SQL Server. SQL Server uses about 8 MB for its code and internal structures. Additional memory is used as follows: 96 bytes for each lock, 2,880 bytes for each open database, and 276 bytes for each open object, which include all tables, views, stored procedures, extended stored procedures, triggers, rules, constraints, and defaults.
>
> You can check the baseline memory usage by using the SQLServer:Memory Manager performance object. Select all counters for monitoring, and use the Report view to examine the memory usage. Pay particular attention to the Total Server Memory counter. See Chapter 12 for more details on monitoring SQL Server performance.

Using Fixed Memory

If you want to override the dynamic memory management features, you can do so by reserving memory specifically for SQL Server. When you reserve physical memory for SQL Server, the operating system does not swap out SQL Server memory pages even if that memory could be allocated to other processes when SQL Server is idle. This means SQL Server has a fixed memory set. On a dedicated system, reserving memory can improve SQL Server performance by cutting down on paging and cache hits. To be sure, however, you should use the Buffer Manager performance object to track buffer cache hits and paging. For more details, see the "Monitoring SQL Server Performance" section in Chapter 12.

To reserve physical memory for SQL Server, complete the following steps:

1. In the Server Properties dialog box, go to the Memory page.

2. Set the Minimum Server Memory and Maximum Server Memory fields to the working set memory size you want to use. Use the same value for both fields.

3. Click OK.

You also can use the stored procedure sp_configure to reserve physical memory. The commands you use to do this are as follows:

T-SQL

```
exec sp_configure "set working set size", 1
go
exec sp_configure "min server memory", <number of megabytes>
go
exec sp_configure "max server memory", <number of megabytes>
go
reconfigure with override
go
```

PowerShell

```
Invoke-Sqlcmd -Query "exec sp_configure 'set working set size', 1;
exec sp_configure 'min server memory', <number of megabytes>;
exec sp_configure 'max server memory', <number of megabytes>;
reconfigure with override;" -ServerInstance "Server\Instance"
```

> **CAUTION** Setting fixed working set memory incorrectly can cause serious performance problems for SQL Server. Use fixed working set memory only in circumstances in which you need to ensure that an exact amount of memory is available for SQL Server.

Enabling AWE Memory Support

Address Windowing Extensions (AWE) memory allows Windows to support up to 64 gigabytes (GB) of physical memory. AWE support is required only on 32-bit operating systems. SQL Server 2012 Enterprise, Standard, and Developer editions include AWE memory support. Analysis Services cannot take advantage of AWE-mapped memory. Additionally, if the available physical memory is less than the user-mode virtual address space, AWE cannot be enabled.

When AWE memory support is enabled, SQL Server 2012 dynamically allocates AWE memory at startup and allocates or deallocates AWE-mapped memory as required within the constraints of the minimum server memory and maximum server memory options. The goal is to balance SQL Server memory use with the overall system requirements. SQL Server always attempts to use AWE-mapped memory, even on computers configured to provide applications with less than 3 GB of user-mode address space.

> **NOTE** The hot-add memory feature requires AWE to be enabled during SQL Server startup. Additionally, note that SQL Server can release AWE-mapped memory dynamically, but the current amount of allocated AWE-mapped memory cannot be swapped out to the page file.

> **TIP** If you enable AWE support, the user or system account under which the instance runs must have the Lock Pages In Memory user privilege. This privilege can be assigned to the account by using Group Policy.

To enable AWE support, complete the following steps:

1. In the Server Properties dialog box, go to the Memory page and select the Use AWE To Allocate Memory option.

2. Consider setting a specific maximum server memory for SQL Server to ensure that other applications have additional memory. For example, you might want to set minimum server memory to 2 GB (2,048 MB) and maximum server memory to 8 GB (8,192 MB) to limit the amount of memory SQL Server 2012 can use.

3. Click OK.

You also can use the stored procedure sp_configure to enable AWE support. The commands you use to do this are as follows:

T-SQL

```
exec sp_configure "awe enabled", 1
reconfigure
go
```

PowerShell

```
Invoke-Sqlcmd -Query "exec sp_configure 'awe enabled', 1; reconfigure"
-ServerInstance "Server\Instance"
```

Optimizing Memory for Indexing

By default, SQL Server 2012 dynamically manages the amount of memory allocated for index creation operations. If additional memory is needed for creating indexes, and the memory is available based on the server memory configuration settings, the server will allocate additional memory for index creation operations. If additional memory is needed but not available, index creation will use the memory already allocated to perform index creation.

Normally, SQL Server self-tuning works very well with this feature. The main exception is in cases in which you use partitioned tables and indexes and have nonaligned partitioned indexes. In these cases, if there is a high degree of parallelism (lots of simultaneous index creation operations), you might encounter problems creating indexes. If this happens, you can allocate a specific amount of index creation memory. For more information, see the "Understanding Table Partitions" section in Chapter 8, "Manipulating Schemas, Tables, and Views"; and the "Creating Partitioned Tables and Indexes" section in Chapter 9, "Using Indexes, Constraints, and Partitions."

To use a specific index creation memory allocation, complete the following steps:

1. In the Server Properties dialog box, go to the Memory page and set a value in the Index Creation Memory box. This value is set in kilobytes.

2. Click OK.

You can also use the stored procedure sp_configure to set the index creation memory size. The related commands are as follows:

T-SQL

```
exec sp_configure "index create memory", <number of kilobytes>
```

PowerShell

```
Invoke-Sqlcmd -Query "exec sp_configure 'index create memory', <num kb>"
-ServerInstance "Server\Instance"
```

> **NOTE** The amount of memory allocated to index creation operations should be at least as large as the minimum memory per query. If it is not, SQL Server will use the amount of memory specified as the minimum memory per query and display a warning about this.

Allocating Memory for Queries

By default, SQL Server allocates a minimum of 1,024 KB of memory for query execution. This memory allocation is guaranteed per user, and you can set it anywhere from 512 KB to 2 GB. If you increase the minimum query size, you can improve the performance of queries that perform processor-intensive operations, such as sorting or hashing. If you set the value too high, however, you can degrade the overall system performance. In light of this, you should adjust the minimum query size only when you are having trouble executing queries quickly.

> **BEST PRACTICES** The default setting of 1,024 KB of RAM works in most cases. However, you might want to consider changing this value if the server operates in an extremely busy environment with lots of simultaneous queries running in separate user connections, or in a relatively slow environment with few (but large or complex) queries. In this case, four factors should determine your decision to adjust the minimum query size:
>
> - The total amount of free memory (when the system is idle and SQL Server is running)
> - The average number of simultaneous queries running in separate user connections
> - The average query size
> - The query response time you hope to achieve

Often a compromise is necessary with these values. You cannot always get an instant response, but you can optimize performance based on available resources.

Use the following equation to get a starting point for the optimization:

FreeMemory / (AvgQuerySize * AvgNumSimulQueries)

For example, if the system has 2,200 MB of free memory, the average query size is 2 MB, and the average number of simultaneous queries is 50, then the optimal value for the query size is 2,200 MB / (2 * 50), or 22 MB. Generally, this value represents the maximum that you should assign given the current environment, and you should lower this value if possible.

To allocate memory for queries, complete the following steps:

1. In the Server Properties dialog box, go to the Memory page and set a value for the Minimum Memory Per Query box. This value is set in kilobytes.

2. Click OK.

You also can use the stored procedure sp_configure to set the minimum query size. The related commands are as follows:

T-SQL

```
exec sp_configure "min memory per query", <number of kilobytes>
```

PowerShell

```
Invoke-Sqlcmd -Query "exec sp_configure 'min memory per query', <num kb>"
-ServerInstance "Server\Instance"
```

Configuring Processors and Parallel Processing

Systems that use multiprocessors can take advantage of the enhancements provided by SQL Server for parallel query execution. You can control how and when processors are used by SQL Server, as well as when queries are processed in parallel.

Optimizing CPU Usage

Multitasking is an important part of the operating system. Often the operating system needs to move threads of execution among different processors. On a system with a light load, moving threads of execution allows the server to improve performance by balancing the workload. On a system with a heavy load, however, the shuffling of threads can reduce performance because processor cache has to be reloaded repeatedly.

SQL Server 2012 supports processor affinity and I/O affinity to optimize how processors are used. Processor affinity assigns processors to specific threads of execution to eliminate processor reloads and reduce thread migration across processors. I/O affinity specifies which processors are eligible to process SQL Server–related disk I/O operations. If you decide to manage affinity manually, you will want some processors to have priority for threading and some processors to have priority for disk I/O, with no overlap between the two. For example, on a 32-processor system running SQL Server 2012 Enterprise Edition, you might want processors 0 through 15 to have processor affinity (which means they manage threads of execution) and processors 16 through 31 to have I/O affinity (which means they manage disk I/O operations).

NOTE There is no specific formula for allocation. You do not need to allocate half of the CPUs to processor affinity and half to I/O affinity. The actual configuration depends on server usage and load.

Affinity settings are configured and optimized automatically when you install SQL Server. If you are trying to optimize performance for a server under a heavy load, you might want to try to optimize the affinity settings. Keep the following guidelines in mind before reconfiguring affinity settings:

- Do not change these settings without careful forethought. You can reduce performance by managing affinity settings incorrectly.

- Do not configure CPU affinity in both the operating system and in SQL Server. Both techniques have the same goal. Use one technique or the other.

- Do not enable the same CPU for both processor and I/O affinity. Each processor can have only one affinity. This means that there are three possible affinity states: processor affinity–enabled, I/O affinity–enabled, or no affinity–enabled.

You can configure processor usage manually by completing the following steps:

1. Start SQL Server Management Studio, and then connect to the server you want to configure.

2. Right-click the server name in the SQL Server Management Studio Object Explorer view, and then choose Properties from the shortcut menu.

3. In the Server Properties dialog box, go to the Processors page, as shown in Figure 5-6.

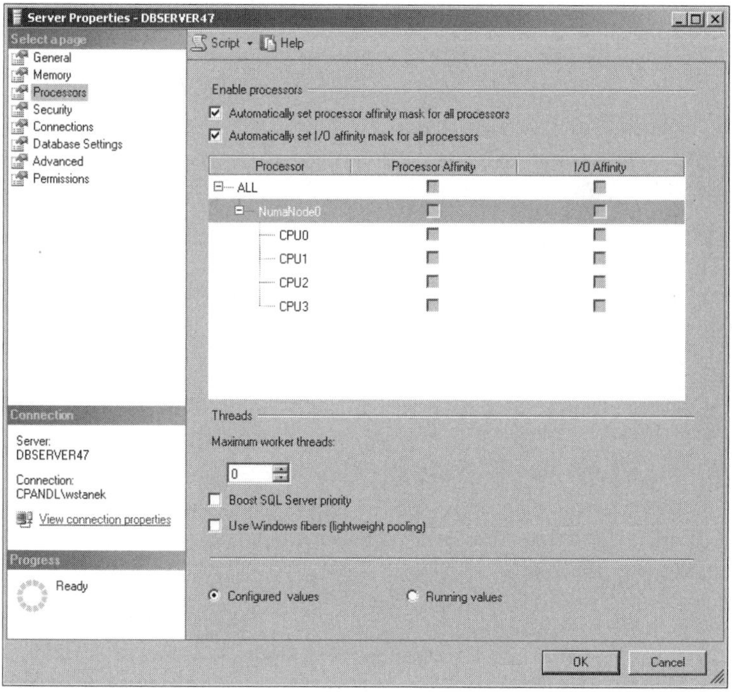

FIGURE 5-6 The Processors page of the Server Properties dialog box.

4. By default, processor affinity is set automatically, and you are unable to change the processor affinity settings. When you clear the Automatically Set Processor Affinity Mask For All Processors check box, the fixed option changes to check boxes that you can select or clear. Use the Processor Affinity check boxes in the Processor list to determine which processors SQL Server uses. Select the check box for processors you want to use, and clear the check box for processors you do not want to use. The first CPU on the system is identified as CPU 0, the second as CPU 1, and so on.

BEST PRACTICES If the system has more processors than SQL Server supports, SQL Server does not use all of them. For example, on an eight-way symmetric multiprocessing (SMP) system, SQL Server Standard Edition can use only four processors. This leaves four processors for other applications and system-level tasks.

You might be tempted to assign SQL Server to the higher-numbered processors (5, 6, 7, and 8), but this is not a good idea. Windows assigns deferred process calls associated with network interface cards (NICs) to the highest-numbered processors. If the system described in the example had two NICs, these calls would be directed to CPU 8 and CPU 7. Be sure to consult the equipment documentation before changing these values.

5. By default, I/O affinity is set automatically, and you are unable to change the I/O affinity settings. When you clear the Automatically Set I/O Affinity Mask For All Processors check box, the fixed option changes to check boxes that you can select or clear. Use the I/O Affinity check boxes in the Processor list to determine which processors SQL Server uses.

6. Click OK. The new settings apply when the SQL Server instance has been stopped and then started again.

You also can use the stored procedure sp_configure to set the affinity mask. The related commands are as follows:

T-SQL
```
exec sp_configure "affinity mask", <integer value>
exec sp_configure "affinity i/o mask", <integer value>
```

PowerShell
```
Invoke-Sqlcmd -Query "exec sp_configure 'affinity mask', <integer value>
exec sp_configure 'affinity i/o mask', <integer value>"
-ServerInstance "Server\Instance"
```

SQL Server interprets the integer value as a bit mask representing the processors you want to use. In this bit mask, CPU 0 is represented by bit 0, CPU 1 with bit 1, and so on. A bit value of 1 tells SQL Server to use the CPU. A bit value of 0 tells SQL Server not to use the CPU. For example, if you want to turn on support for processors 1, 2, and 5, you would have a binary value of

000100110

The corresponding integer value is 38:

32 + 4 + 2 = 38

Setting Parallel Processing

A lot of calculations are required to determine whether parallel processing should be used. Generally, SQL Server processes queries in parallel in the following cases:

- When the number of CPUs is greater than the number of active connections.
- When the estimated cost for the serial execution of a query is higher than the query plan threshold. (The estimated cost refers to the elapsed time in seconds required to execute the query serially.)

Certain types of statements cannot be processed in parallel unless they contain clauses, however. For example, UPDATE, INSERT, and DELETE operations are not normally processed in parallel even if the related query meets the criteria. But if the UPDATE or DELETE statements contain a WHERE clause, or an INSERT statement contains a SELECT clause, WHERE and SELECT can be executed in parallel. Changes are applied serially to the database in these cases.

You can configure parallel processing by completing the following steps:

1. In the Server Properties dialog box, go to the Advanced page.

2. By default, the Max Degree Of Parallelism setting has a value of 0, which means that the maximum number of processors used for parallel processing is controlled automatically. Essentially, SQL Server uses the actual number of available processors, depending on the workload. To limit the number of processors used for parallel processing to a set amount (up to the maximum supported by SQL Server), change the Max Degree Of Parallelism setting to a value greater than 1. A value of 1 tells SQL Server not to use parallel processing.

3. Large, complex queries usually can benefit from parallel execution. However, SQL Server performs parallel processing only when the estimated number of seconds required to run a serial plan for the same query is higher than the value set in the cost threshold for parallelism. Set the cost estimate threshold by using the Cost Threshold For Parallelism box on the Advanced page of the Server Properties dialog box. You can use any value from 0 through 32,767. On a single CPU, the cost threshold is ignored.

4. Click OK. These changes are applied immediately. You do not need to restart the server.

You can use the stored procedure sp_configure to configure parallel processing. The commands are as follows:

T-SQL

```
exec sp_configure "max degree of parallelism", <integer value>
exec sp_configure "cost threshold for parallelism", <integer value>
```

PowerShell

```
Invoke-Sqlcmd -Query "exec sp_configure 'max degree of parallelism',
<integer value> exec sp_configure 'cost threshold for parallelism',
<integer value>" -ServerInstance "Server\Instance"
```

Configuring Threading, Priority, and Fibers

Threads are an important part of a multitasking operating system, and they enable SQL Server to do many things at once. Threads are not processes, however. They are concurrent execution paths that allow applications to use the CPU more effectively.

SQL Server tries to match threads to user connections. When the number of threads that are available is greater than the number of user connections, at least a one-to-one ratio of threads to user connections exists, which allows each user connection to be handled uniquely. When the number of threads available is less than the number of user connections, SQL Server must pool threads; as a result, the same thread might serve multiple user connections, which can reduce performance and response time if additional resources are available and are not being used.

Normally, the operating system handles threads in kernel mode, but it handles applications and user-related tasks in user mode. Switching between modes, such as when the kernel needs to handle a new thread, requires CPU cycles and resources. To allow the application to handle threading directly, you can use fibers. Switching fibers does not require changing modes and therefore can improve performance sometimes.

Another way to improve performance is by increasing the priority of SQL Server threads. Normally, threads have a priority of 1 through 31, and higher-priority threads get more CPU time than lower-priority threads. Higher-priority threads also can preempt lower-priority threads, forcing threads to wait until higher-priority threads finish executing. By increasing thread priority, you can give the threads a higher preference for CPU time and ensure that other threads do not preempt them.

NOTE The complete range for thread priority is 0 through 31. Thread priority 0 is reserved for operating system use.

You configure worker threads, fibers, and thread priority by using the Server Properties dialog box. Go to the Processors page and use these options:

- **Maximum Worker Threads** Sets the maximum number of threads. By default, the value is set to 0, which allows SQL Server to configure the number of worker threads as shown in Table 5-1. However, you can use any value from 10 through 32,767. On a busy server with many user connections, you might want to increase this value. On a slow server with few connections, you might want to decrease this value. Computers with multiple processors can execute one thread per CPU concurrently. Microsoft recommends a maximum setting of 1,024 on 32-bit systems and 2,048 on 64-bit systems.

- **Boost SQL Server Priority** Increases the priority of SQL Server threads. Without boosting, SQL Server threads have a priority of 7 (normal priority). With boosting, SQL Server threads have a priority of 13 (high priority). On a dedicated system running only SQL Server, this option can improve performance. However, if the server runs other applications, the performance of those applications might be degraded.

- **Use Windows Fibers (Lightweight Pooling)** Configures SQL Server to use fibers, which it can handle directly. SQL Server still needs threads to carry out tasks. SQL Server allocates one thread per CPU and then allocates one fiber per concurrent user connection up to the value of Maximum Worker Threads. You must restart the server to apply this option.

REAL WORLD You will want to do exhaustive testing to ensure that there is a net benefit any time you use fibers. Windows Server 2008 R2 and later offer the best support for fibers. Fibers work best when the server has multiple CPUs and a relatively low user-to-CPU ratio. For example, on an installation of Enterprise Edition with 32 CPUs and 250 users, you might see a noticeable performance boost with fibers. But if you have a system with eight CPUs and 5,000 users, you might see performance decrease with fibers.

TABLE 5-1 The Default Maximum Worker Threads Used by SQL Server

NUMBER OF CPUS	32-BIT OPERATING SYSTEM	64-BIT OPERATING SYSTEM
1–4	256	512
5–8	288	576
9–16	352	704
17–32	480	960

You can use sp_configure to set fibers, maximum worker threads, and priority boost by using the following commands:

T-SQL

```
exec sp_configure "lightweight pooling", <0 or 1>
exec sp_configure "max worker threads", <integer value>
exec sp_configure "priority boost", <0 or 1>
```

PowerShell

```
Invoke-Sqlcmd -Query "exec sp_configure 'lightweight pooling', <0 or 1>;
exec sp_configure 'max worker threads', <integer value>;
exec sp_configure 'priority boost", <0 or 1>'"
-ServerInstance "Server\Instance"
```

When setting lightweight pooling (fibers) and priority boost, you use 0 to disable and 1 to enable.

Configuring User and Remote Connections

Requests for data are handled through user connections to client systems. The client opens a connection to SQL Server, makes a request, and waits for a response from SQL Server. When the client is finished with its request, it closes the connection. Other servers and applications also can connect to SQL Server remotely. To configure client connections and remote server connections, you can use the Connections page in the Server Properties dialog box.

Many settings are associated with client and server connections, as you can see in Figure 5-7, which shows the default configuration. This section examines connection settings and cases in which you might want to change these settings.

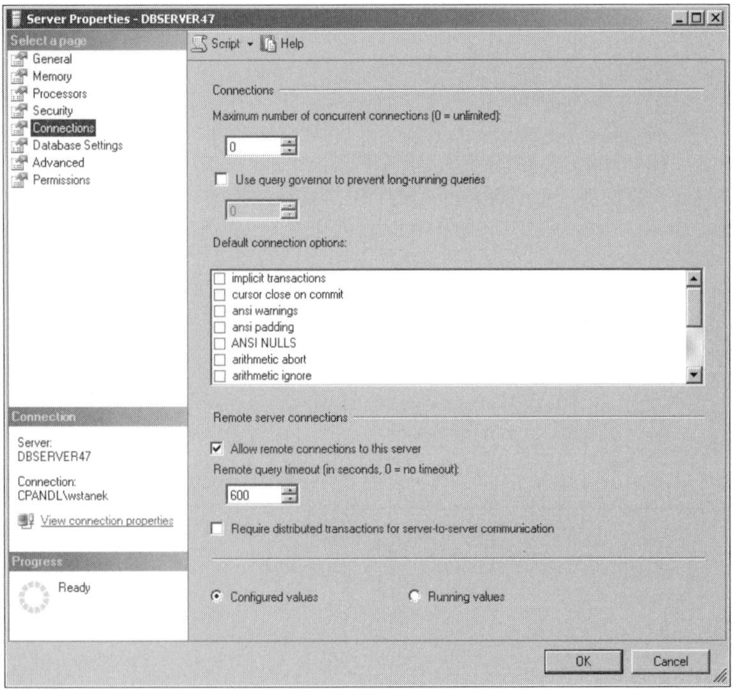

FIGURE 5-7 The default connection settings on the Connections page of the Server Properties dialog box.

Setting Maximum User Connections

On the Connections page, the Maximum Number Of Concurrent Connections box lets you set the maximum number of connections at any one time to SQL Server. You can use a value from 0 through 32,767. By default, the value is set to 0, which means that an unlimited number of connections can be made to SQL Server.

However, the actual number of possible user connections really depends on hardware, application, and other server limitations.

You can determine the number of user connections your system is configured to handle by executing the following command in Query view:

```
select @@max_connections
```

To set the maximum number of user connections, complete the following steps:

1. In the Server Properties dialog box, go to the Connections page.

2. Type a new value in the Maximum Number Of Concurrent Connections box, and then click OK. The new settings apply when the SQL Server instance has been stopped and then started again.

You also can set the maximum number of concurrent connections by using the following command:

```
exec sp_configure "user connections", <integer value>
```

NOTE You should not need to change the value of Maximum Number Of Concurrent Connections. If you do change the setting, be careful. When the server reaches the maximum number of connections, users receive an error message and are not able to connect to the server until another user disconnects and a connection becomes available. The only time you need to set this option is in a situation with a large number of users and you need to limit the number of active connections to ensure that requests for connected users are handled in a timely manner. A better alternative is to add sufficient memory to the system, scale out the database environment to balance the workload, or take both of these steps. If you administer a system with a large number of users, you also should be sure that SQL applications connect and then disconnect promptly when finished to reallocate resources quickly to other users.

Setting Default Connection Options

The Connections page includes a list box labeled Default Connection Options. (See Figure 5-7.) Use the options to set default query-processing options for user connections. Select an option by selecting its check box, and cancel an option by clearing the check box. Any changes you make affect new logins only; current logins are not affected. Furthermore, users can override the defaults by using SET statements, if necessary.

Table 5-2 provides a summary of the connection options, as well as the default state for ODBC and OLE DB (which might be different from the SQL Server default). The table also includes a list of commands you can use with sp_configure, the corresponding value for the configuration bit mask, and the SET commands that can override the default settings in a user session.

TABLE 5-2 Configuring Connection Options

CONNECTION OPTION	WHEN ON	DEFAULT STATE	BIT MASK VALUE	SET COMMAND
Implicit Transactions	Uses transactions implicitly whenever statements are executed.	OFF	2	IMPLICIT_ TRANSACTIONS
Cursor Close On COMMIT	Closes a cursor automatically at the end of a transaction.	OFF	4	CURSOR_ CLOSE_ON_ COMMIT
ANSI Warnings	SQL Server displays null, overflow, and divide-by-zero warnings. Otherwise, no error or NULL might be returned.	OFF	8	ANSI_ WARNINGS
ANSI Padding	Data in fixed-length fields are padded with trailing spaces to fill out the width of the column.	OFF	16	ANSI_PADDING
ANSI Nulls	Comparing anything with NULL gives an unknown result.	OFF	32	ANSI_NULLS
Arithmetic Abort	Causes a query to terminate when an overflow or a divide-by-zero error occurs.	OFF	64	ARITHABORT
Arithmetic Ignore	Returns NULL when an overflow or a divide-by-zero error occurs during a query.	OFF	128	ARITHIGNORE
Quoted Identifier	SQL Server interprets double quotation marks as indicating an identifier rather than as delimiting a string.	OFF	256	QUOTED_IDEN-TIFIER
No Count	Turns off the display of the number of rows returned in a query.	OFF	512	NOCOUNT

CONNECTION OPTION	WHEN ON	DEFAULT STATE	BIT MASK VALUE	SET COMMAND
ANSI Null Default ON	New columns are defined to allow nulls (if you do not allow or disallow nulls explicitly).	OFF	1024	ANSI_NULL_ DFLT_ON
ANSI Null Default OFF	New columns are defined not to allow nulls (if you don't allow or disallow nulls explicitly).	OFF	2048	ANSI_NULL_ DFLT_OFF
Concat Null Yields Null	Returns NULL when concatenating a NULL value within a string.	OFF	4096	CONCAT_NULL_ YIELDS_NULL
Numeric Round Abort	Generates an error when a loss of precision occurs.	OFF	8192	NUMERIC_ ROUNDABORT
Xact Abort	Rolls back a transaction if a T-SQL statement raises a runtime error.	OFF	16384	XACT_ABORT

For sp_configure, the default options are set with the following user options parameter:

```
exec sp_configure "user options", <integer bit mask value>
```

In this case, the bit mask value is the sum of the numeric values for all the options you want to use. Each option has a corresponding SET command as well. When you make a connection, you can use the SET command to override the default setting for the session. For example, if you want to turn on ANSI padding, ANSI nulls, and ANSI warnings, use the bit mask value 56, such as in the following line of code:

```
exec sp_configure "user options", 56
```

In a user session, you can turn these options on or off by using a line of code such as the following:

```
set ansi_padding on set ansi_nulls off
```

Configuring Remote Server Connections

Connections from other servers are handled differently than user connections. You can determine whether servers can connect to this server, how long it takes for remote queries to time out, and whether distributed transactions are used. To configure remote connections, complete these steps:

1. In the Server Properties dialog box, go to the Connections page.

2. To allow servers to connect to this server, select the Allow Remote Connections To This Server option. Remote servers then can log on to the server to execute stored procedures remotely. You must stop and then start the SQL Server instance to apply the change if you select this option.

> **CAUTION** Remote procedure call (RPC) connections are allowed by default. If you change this behavior, remote servers cannot log on to SQL Server. This setting change keeps SQL Server secure from remote server access.

3. By default, queries executed by remote servers time out in 600 seconds. To change this behavior, type a time-out value in the Remote Query Timeout box on the Connections page. Time-out values are set in seconds, and the acceptable range of values is from 0 through 2,147,483,647. A value of 0 means that there is no query time-out for remote server connections.

4. Stored procedures and queries executed on the server can be handled as distributed transactions by using Distributed Transaction Coordinator (DTC). If you want to execute procedures this way, select the Require Distributed Transactions For Server-To-Server Communication check box. If you change this option, you must stop and then start the SQL Server instance.

5. Click OK.

These options can also be set with sp_configure. The related commands are as follows:

```
exec sp_configure "remote access", <0 or 1>
exec sp_configure "remote query timeout", <number of seconds>
exec sp_configure "remote proc trans", <0 or 1>
```

> **NOTE** A value of 0 turns a remote server connection option off, and a value of 1 turns an option on.

Managing Server Settings

You use the Advanced page of the Server Properties dialog box to configure many server settings. As shown in Figure 5-8, you can set the default language, general server behavior, and other options on this page.

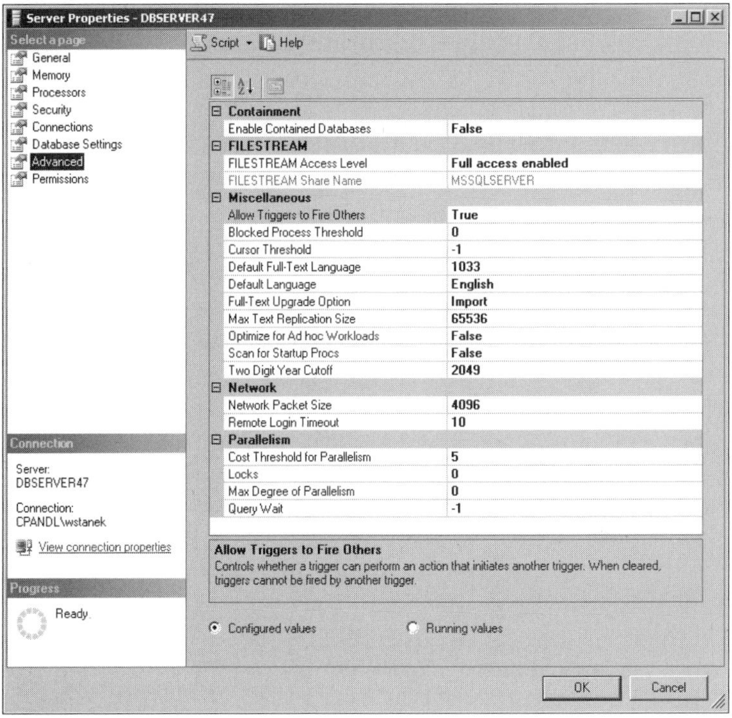

FIGURE 5-8 General server settings options on the Advanced page.

Enabling or Disabling Contained Database Support

When you want a server instance to be able to create or attach contained databases, you must enable the use of contained databases by turning on contained database authentication. User logins for contained databases are authenticated by the database as opposed to being mapped to logins in the master database.

On the Advanced page of the Server Properties dialog box, use the Enable Contained Database list to enable or disable support, and then click OK. With sp_configure, the related commands are as follows:

T-SQL

```
exec sp_configure "contained database authentication", <0 or 1>
```

PowerShell

```
Invoke-Sqlcmd -Query "exec sp_configure
'contained database authentication',<0 or 1>"
-ServerInstance "Server\Instance"
```

Use 0 for disabled or 1 for enabled. Each contained database has its own settings for default full-text language, default language, nested triggers, transforming noise words, and two-digit year cutoff.

Enabling or Disabling File Streaming Support

When file streaming is enabled, the SQL Server Database Engine can work with binary large objects (BLOBs) that are stored outside the database data files. At the server level, you control whether and how file streaming can be used by using the Filestream Access Level setting, which by default is set to Disabled. When file streaming is disabled, BLOB databases cannot be stored on the file system. If you want to enable file streaming, you can do the following on the Advanced page:

- **Enable T-SQL access** Enabling T-SQL access allows you to use T-SQL statements to insert, update, query, search, and delete file-stream data.

- **Enable full access** Enabling full access allows you to use the OpenSqlFilestream API to obtain a file handle and operate on the BLOB via the file system.

On the Advanced page of the Server Properties dialog box, use the Filestream Access Level list to set the access level for file streaming, and then click OK. The first time you enable file streaming, you might need to restart the computer to allow Windows to reconfigure drivers. With sp_configure, the related commands are as follows:

T-SQL
```
exec sp_configure "filestream access level", <0 or 1 or 2>
```

PowerShell
```
Invoke-Sqlcmd -Query "exec sp_configure 'filestream access level',
<0 or 1 or 2>" -ServerInstance "Server\Instance"
```

Use 0 for disabled, 1 for T-SQL access, or 2 for full access. To complete the file-streaming configuration, you must also configure the settings discussed in the "Enabling and Configuring File Streaming" section in Chapter 2.

Setting the Default Language for SQL Server

The default language determines default display formats for dates as well as the names of months and days. All output is in U.S. English unless you are running a localized version of SQL Server. Localized versions of SQL Server are available in French, German, Japanese, Spanish, and other languages. On a localized server, two sets of system messages are available, one in U.S. English and one in the local language. If the default language is set to the local language, SQL Server messages are displayed in the local language. Otherwise, they are displayed in U.S. English.

On the Advanced page of the Server Properties dialog box, use the Default Language list to select the default language, and then click OK. You must stop and then start the SQL Server instance to apply a new default language setting. With sp_configure, the related commands are as follows:

T-SQL

```
exec sp_configure "default language", <language id number>
```

PowerShell

```
Invoke-Sqlcmd -Query "exec sp_configure 'default language',
<language id number>" -ServerInstance "Server\Instance"
```

The language ID number for U.S. English is always 0. The sys.languages system view contains one row for each language present on a server.

Allowing and Disallowing Nested Triggers

By default, SQL Server allows you to nest up to 32 levels of triggers. Nested triggers are useful for executing a series of tasks within a single transaction. For example, an action can initiate a trigger that starts another trigger, which in turn can start another trigger, and so on. Because the trigger is handled within a transaction, a failure at any level causes the entire transaction to roll back, which reverses all changes to the database. As a fail-safe measure, triggers are terminated when the maximum nesting level is exceeded. This protects against an infinite loop.

An option on the Advanced page allows you to configure SQL Server to use nested triggers. To do so, complete the following steps:

1. In the Server Properties dialog box, go to the Advanced page.
2. Set Allow Triggers To Fire Others to True or False as appropriate.
3. Click OK.

With sp_configure, the related commands are as follows:

T-SQL

```
exec sp_configure "nested triggers", <0 or 1>
```

PowerShell

```
Invoke-Sqlcmd -Query "exec sp_configure 'nested triggers', <0 or 1>"
-ServerInstance "Server\Instance"
```

You use 0 to set this option to false and 1 to set it to true.

Controlling Query Execution

The query governor does not allow the execution of any query that has a running time that exceeds a specified query cost. The query cost is the estimated time, in seconds, required to execute a query, and it is estimated prior to execution based on an analysis by the query engine. By default, the query governor is turned off, meaning there is no maximum cost. To activate the query governor, complete the following steps:

1. In the Server Properties dialog box, go to the Connections page.

2. Select the Use Query Governor To Prevent Long-Running Queries option.

3. In the box below the option, type a maximum query cost limit. The valid range is 0 through 2,147,483,647. A value of 0 disables the query governor; any other value sets a maximum query cost limit.

4. Click OK.

With sp_configure, the following command activates the query governor:

```
exec sp_configure "query governor cost limit", <limit>
```

You also can set a per-connection query cost limit by using the following command:

```
set query_governor_cost_limit <limit>
```

NOTE Before you activate the query governor, you should use the Query view to estimate the cost of current queries you are running on the server. This will give you a good idea of a value to use for the maximum query cost. You also can use the Query view to optimize queries.

Configuring Year 2000 Support

SQL Server allows you to insert or modify dates without specifying the century part of the date. However, to be year 2000–compliant, SQL Server interprets two-digit dates within a certain time span. By default, this time span includes the years 1950 through 2049. Using this default setting, all two-digit dates from 50 through 99 are read as years beginning with 19, and all two-digit dates from 00 through 49 are read as years beginning with 20. Thus, SQL Server would interpret a two-digit year of 99 as 1999 and a two-digit year of 02 as 2002.

To maintain backward compatibility, Microsoft recommends that you leave the setting at the default value. However, you can change this value by completing the following steps:

1. In the Server Properties dialog box, go to the Advanced page.

2. Set Two Digit Year Cutoff to a value that is the ending year of the time span you want to use. The valid range for the ending year is 1753 through 9999.

3. Click OK.

NOTE The time span that you select affects all databases on the current server. Also, some older OLE clients support dates only in a range of years from 1931 through 2030. To maintain compatibility with these clients, you might want to use 2030 as the ending year for the time span.

With sp_configure, the related command is the following:

```
exec sp_configure "two digit year cutoff", <ending year>
```

Managing Database Settings

You use the Database Settings page of the Server Properties dialog box to configure server-wide database settings. As shown in Figure 5-9, you can use this page to set index fill, backup and restore options, and recovery intervals for checkpoint execution.

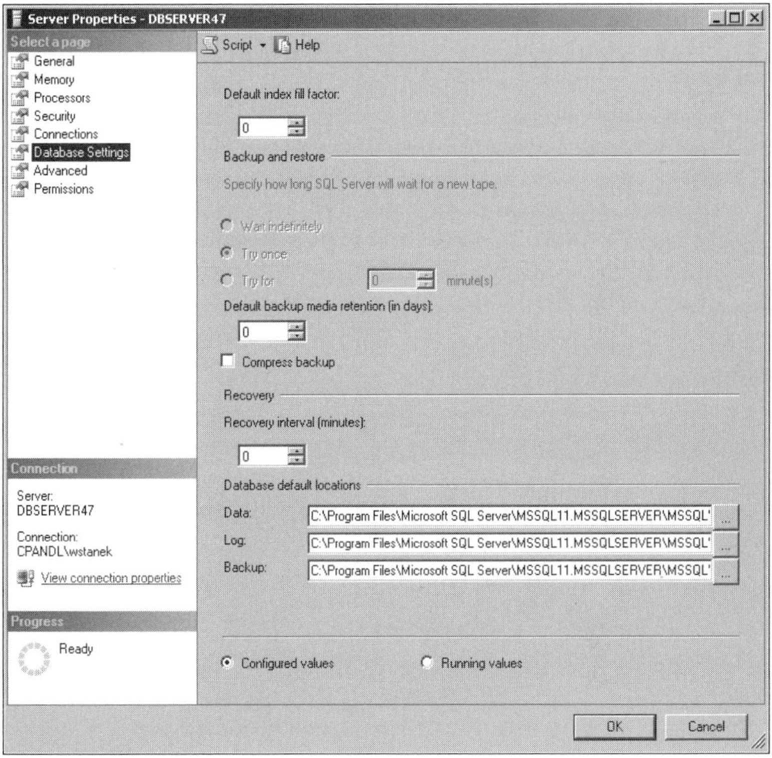

FIGURE 5-9 The Database Settings page of the Server Properties dialog box.

Setting the Index Fill

The default index fill determines how much space SQL Server should reserve when it creates a new index using existing data. Setting the fill factor involves a tradeoff—if you set the fill factor too high, SQL Server slows down when you add data to a table. However, if you set the fill factor too low, read performance can be affected by an amount inversely proportional to the fill factor. For example, a fill factor of 25 percent can degrade read performance by a factor of four (or four times normal), but the setting makes it possible to perform large updates faster initially. Ideally, you should balance the need to make updates quickly with the need to have good read performance, and then select a fill factor that makes sense for your situation.

BEST PRACTICES The fill factor is used only when an index is created; it is not maintained afterward. This allows you to add, delete, or update data in a table without worrying about maintaining a specific fill factor.

The empty space in the data pages can fill up if you make extensive additions or modifications to the data. To redistribute the data, re-create the index and specify a fill factor when you do so. Indexes are discussed more completely in Chapter 9.

By default, the index fill is set to 0, but the valid range is 0 through 100. The setting of 0 is the optimized index fill setting; any other value is an actual fill percentage.

SQL Server handles the optimized setting in much the same way as a fill percentage of 100—SQL Server creates clustered indexes with full data pages and nonclustered indexes with full leaf pages. But the optimized setting of 0 leaves space for growth in the upper level of the index tree, which an index fill setting of 100 does not do. This is the reason why you should use this value only with read-only tables in which you never plan to add data.

If necessary, you can override the default setting when you create indexes, but you have to remember to do this. You also can set a fixed index fill as the default by completing the following steps:

1. In the Server Properties dialog box, go to the Database Settings page.

2. Use the Default Index Fill Factor box to set a fill percentage. A low fill factor provides more room for insertions without requiring page splits, but the index takes up more space. A high fill factor provides less room for insertions that do not require page splits, but the index uses less space.

3. Click OK.

With sp_configure, the related command is the following:

```
exec sp_configure "fill factor (%)", <integer percentage>
```

Configuring Backup and Restore Time-Out Options

You can make SQL Server backups to tape devices. When working with tape devices, you might want to control whether you want to enforce a read/write time-out to wait for a new tape. The options you can use include the following:

- **Wait Indefinitely** SQL Server waits until a new tape is found. If you select this option, however, you will not necessarily receive an error message to let you know that you are having backup problems.

- **Try Once** SQL Server tries once for a response from SQL Server. If there is no response or no tape is available, it quits and typically generates an error.

- **Try For** SQL Server tries to get a response for a specified number of minutes. If there is no response or no tape is available within the wait time, SQL Server quits and usually generates an error.

You set the time-out period by completing the following steps:

1. In the Server Properties dialog box, go to the Database Settings page.
2. To set an indefinite time-out, select the Wait Indefinitely option.
3. To set the backup process to try once and then quit, select the Try Once option.
4. To set the backup process to try for a specified amount of time, select the Try For *n* Minute(s) option, and then enter the time-out period in the box provided.
5. Click OK.

Configuring Backup and Restore Retention Options

As you will learn in Chapter 11, "SQL Server 2012 Backup and Recovery," SQL Server has many features to help you back up and restore data. When you write data to tapes, you can specify the number of days to maintain old files. This value is called the *retention period*, and you set it by completing the following steps:

1. In the Server Properties dialog box, go to the Database Settings page.
2. In the Default Backup Media Retention (In Days) box, enter the number of days you want to maintain old files. The minimum value is 0, which specifies that old files are always overwritten. The valid range is 0 through 365.
3. Click OK.

With sp_configure, the related T-SQL statement to set the retention period for backup files is as follows:

```
exec sp_configure "media retention", <number of days>
```

Flushing the Cache with Checkpoints

Database checkpoints flush all cached data pages to the disk, and these checkpoints are done on a per-database basis. In SQL Server, you control how often checkpoints occur by using the Recovery Interval setting on the Database Settings page. By default, the recovery interval is set to 0, which allows SQL Server to control when checkpoints occur dynamically. This usually means that checkpoints occur about once a minute on active databases. Unless you are experiencing performance problems that are related to checkpoints, you should not change this option.

If you need to set the checkpoint interval manually, you must complete the following steps:

1. In the Server Properties dialog box, go to the Database Settings page.
2. In the Recovery Interval (Minutes) box, enter the checkpoint time in minutes. The valid range is 0 through 32,767, and this is a server-wide setting.
3. Click OK.

With sp_configure, the related command is the following:

```
exec sp_configure "recovery interval", <number of minutes>
```

Compressing the Backup Media

Backup compression reduces the amount of data SQL Server 2012 has to write and the size of your SQL backups. Although using compression can speed up the backup and restore process significantly when working over a network, compression also increases CPU usage. To reduce the impact on SQL Server performance, you can configure backup to run under a user login whose CPU usage is limited by the Resource Governor whenever CPU contention occurs.

To enable backup media compression, complete the following steps:

1. In the Server Properties dialog box, go to the Database Settings page.
2. Select the Compress Backup check box, and then click OK.

With sp_configure, the related command is the following:

```
exec sp_configure "backup compression default", <0 or 1>
```

You use 0 to disable backup compression and 1 to enable it.

Managing Linked Servers

To work properly, distributed queries and transactions depend on linked servers. You configure the linked servers you are using by registering their connection and data source information in SQL Server. Then you can reference the linked server by using a single logical name. If you no longer need to link to a server, you can remove the linked server connection.

Adding Linked Servers

If you want a server to be able to use distributed queries, distributed transactions, or remote command execution, you must configure linked server connections to other servers. For example, if clients that access a server named Zeta make distributed queries to Pluto and Omega, you must configure Pluto and Omega as linked servers on Zeta. If clients that connect to Pluto make distributed queries to Zeta and Omega, you must configure Zeta and Omega as linked servers on Pluto. To add a linked server, complete the following steps:

1. In SQL Server Management Studio, connect to the server instance you want to configure.
2. In the Object Explorer view, expand the Server Objects node.
3. Right-click the Linked Servers entry, and then choose New Linked Server to open the dialog box shown in Figure 5-10.
4. In the Linked Server text box, type the name of the linked server to create.
5. If you are linking to a computer running SQL Server, select the SQL Server option.

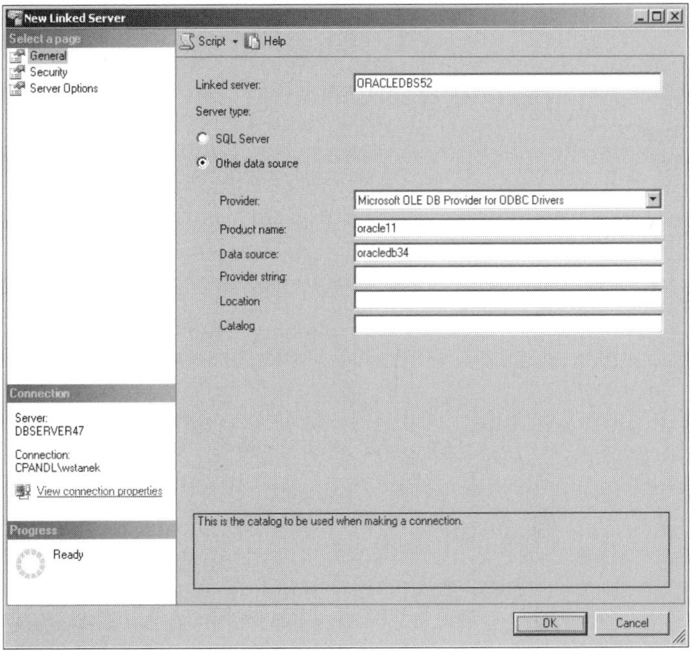

FIGURE 5-10 The New Linked Server dialog box.

6. If you are linking to a different data source, select the Other Data Source option, and then configure the data source by using the text boxes provided. If there is no text box available in the dialog box for a specific option, you cannot configure that option for the selected provider. Provide information in the text boxes as follows:

- **Provider** Select the name of the OLE DB provider to use when communicating with the specified linked server.

- **Product Name** Set the server product name for the OLE DB data source.

- **Data Source** Provide the OLE DB data source, which is used to initialize the OLE DB provider.

- **Provider String** Type a provider-specific connection string that identifies a unique data source.

- **Location** Set the location of the database for the OLE DB provider.

- **Catalog** Indicate the catalog to use when connecting to the OLE DB provider.

REAL WORLD The most commonly used combination of options is provider name and data source. For example, if you are configuring a linked server for a Microsoft Access database or a Microsoft Excel spreadsheet, you would select Microsoft Jet 4.0 OLE DB Provider and then set the data source name. With Oracle, you would select Microsoft OLE DB Provider For Oracle and then set the data source name.

7. In the Select A Page list, select Server Options to configure server-specific settings as follows:

- **Collation Compatible**   Set this option to enable SQL Server to send comparisons on character columns to the provider. Otherwise, SQL Server evaluates comparisons on character columns locally. Set this option only when the linked server has the same collation as the local server.

  NOTE   The Collation Compatible option controls the sort order settings. If you do not select this option, SQL Server uses the local sort order. This affects the order of result sets, and you should note it when you develop SQL Server applications or configure clients that support distributed transactions.

- **Data Access**   Set this option to enable the linked server for distributed query access.

- **RPC**   Set this option to enable remote procedure calls from the linked server.

- **RPC Out**   Set this option to enable RPCs to the linked server.

- **Use Remote Collation**   Set this option to have SQL Server use the collation from the linked server's character columns. If you do not set this option, SQL Server uses the default collation of the local server instance to interpret data from the linked server. Only SQL Server databases take advantage of this option.

- **Collation Name**   Set this option to assign a specific collation for queries and transactions. You must set the Collation Compatible option to False before you can set this option.

- **Connection Timeout**   Use this text box to set the time-out value for connections made to the remote server.

- **Query Timeout**   Use this text box to set the time-out value for queries made to the remote server.

- **Enable Promotion Of Distributed Transactions**   Use this text box to enable calling a remote stored procedure and then automatically starting a distributed transaction and enlisting the transaction with MS DTC. After a distributed transaction has been started, remote stored procedure calls can be made to other instances of SQL Server that have been defined as linked servers. The linked servers are all enlisted in the distributed transaction, and MS DTC ensures that the transaction is completed against each linked server.

8. Click OK to create the linked server. Next, you must configure security settings for the linked server, as discussed in the "Configuring Security for Linked Servers" section later in this chapter.

The corresponding T-SQL command for adding linked servers is sp_addlinkedserver. Use this stored procedure as shown in Sample 5-3.

SAMPLE 5-3 sp_addlinkedserver Syntax and Usage.

Syntax

```
sp_addlinkedserver [@server =] 'server'
    [, [@srvproduct =] 'product_name']
    [, [@provider =] 'provider_name']
    [, [@datasrc =] 'data_source']
    [, [@location =] 'location']
    [, [@provstr =] 'provider_string']
    [, [@catalog =] 'catalog']
```

Usage

```
EXEC sp_addlinkedserver
        @server='ORADBSVR38',
        @srvproduct='Oracle',
        @provider='OraOLEDB.Oracle',
        @datasrc='ORACLE10';
GO
```

Table 5-3 provides a summary of parameter values you can use when configuring various OLE DB providers. The table also shows the sp_addlinkedserver parameter values to use for each OLE DB provider. Because some providers have different configurations, there might be more than one row for a particular data source type.

NOTE When you want to access a mirrored SQL Server database, the connection string must contain the database name to enable failover attempts by the data access provider. You can specify the database name in the @provstr or @catalog parameter. Optionally, the connection string also can provide a failover partner name.

TABLE 5-3 Parameter Values for Configuring OLE DB Providers

REMOTE OLE DB DATA SOURCE	OLE DB PROVIDER	PRODUCT_ NAME	PROVIDER_ NAME	DATA_SOURCE	OTHER
SQL Server	Microsoft OLE DB Provider for SQL Server	SQL Server (default)	—	—	—
SQL Server	SQL Server Native Client 11.0	SQL Server (default)	—	—	—
SQL Server	Microsoft OLE DB Provider for SQL Server	—	SQLNCLI	Network name of SQL Server (for default instance)	Database name optional for catalog field

REMOTE OLE DB DATA SOURCE	OLE DB PROVIDER	PRODUCT_NAME	PROVIDER_NAME	DATA_SOURCE	OTHER
SQL Server	Microsoft OLE DB Provider for SQL Server	—	SQLNCLI	*Servername\ instancename* (for specific instance)	Database name optional for catalog field
Oracle	Microsoft OLE DB Provider for ODBC Drivers	Any	MSDAORA	SQL*Net alias for Oracle database	—
Oracle 8.0 and later	Microsoft OLE DB Provider for ODBC Drivers	Any	OraOLEDB. Oracle	Alias for the Oracle database	—
Access/Jet	Microsoft OLE DB Provider for ODBC Drivers	Any	Microsoft. Jet. OLEDB.4.0	Full path name of Jet database file	—
ODBC data source	Microsoft OLE DB Provider for ODBC Drivers	Any	MSDASQL	System DSN of ODBC data source	—
ODBC data source	Microsoft OLE DB Provider for ODBC	Any	MSDASQL	—	ODBC connection string for *provider_ string*
File system	Microsoft OLE DB Provider for Indexing Service	Any	MSIDXS	Indexing Service catalog name	—
Excel spreadsheet	Microsoft OLE DB Simple Provider	Any	Microsoft. Jet. OLEDB.4.0	Full path name of Excel file	Excel 5.0 for *provider_ string*

Configuring Security for Linked Servers

You use linked server security to control access and to determine how local logins are used. By default, new linked servers are set to have no security context when a user login is not defined. This blocks access to all logins not explicitly mapped to the linked server.

To change the security settings for a linked server, complete the following steps:

1. Start SQL Server Management Studio, and then access the local server that contains the linked server definitions you want to change.

2. In the Object Explorer view, expand the Server Objects node, and then expand the Linked Servers node. Now you should see an entry for each linked server that you created on the currently selected server.

3. Right-click the icon for the linked server you want to configure, and then choose Properties to open the Linked Server Properties dialog box.

4. In the Linked Server Properties dialog box, click the Security page, shown in Figure 5-11.

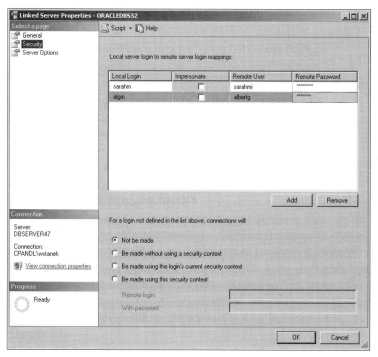

FIGURE 5-11 The Security page of the Linked Server Properties dialog box.

5. Map local logins to remote logins by clicking Add.

6. Configure the following options on a per-login basis:

- **Local Login**   Sets the ID of a local login that can connect to the linked server.

- **Impersonate**   Select this check box to use the local login ID to connect to the linked server. The local login ID must match a login ID on the linked server.

  NOTE If you select the Impersonate check box, you cannot map the local login to a remote login.

- **Remote User**   Sets the remote user to which the local login ID maps on the linked server.

- **Remote Password**   Sets the password for the remote user. If it is not provided, the user might be prompted for a password.

7. Use the options and text boxes in the lower portion of the Security page to set a default security context for all users who do not have a specific login setting for the linked server. These options are used as follows:

- **Not Be Made**   Users without logins are not allowed access to the linked server.

- **Be Made Without Using A Security Context**   Blocks access to all logins not explicitly mapped to the linked server.

- **Be Made Using The Login's Current Security Context**   Logins not explicitly mapped to the linked server use their current login and password to connect to the linked server. Access is denied if the login and password do not exist on the linked server.

- **Be Made Using This Security Context**   Logins not explicitly mapped to the linked server will use the login and password provided in the Remote Login and With Password text boxes.

8. When you finish configuring logins, click OK.

The related T-SQL command for configuring logins is sp_addlinkedsrvlogin. Use this stored procedure as shown in Sample 5-4.

SAMPLE 5-4 sp_addlinkedsrvlogin Syntax and Usage.

Syntax

```
sp_addlinkedsrvlogin [@rmtsrvname =] 'rmtsrvname'
[,[@useself =] 'TRUE' | 'FALSE' | 'NULL']
[,[@locallogin =] 'locallogin']
[,[@rmtuser =] 'rmtuser']
[,[@rmtpassword =] 'rmtpassword']
```

Usage

```
EXEC sp_addlinkedsrvlogin
    @rmtsrvname='ORADBSVR38',
    @useself='false',
    @locallogin=null,
```

```
        @rmtuser='william',
        @rmtpassword='tango98';
GO
```

Setting Server Options for Remote and Linked Servers

You set server options for remote and linked servers using sp_serveroption. Use this stored procedure as shown in Sample 5-5. Key options are summarized in Table 5-4.

SAMPLE 5-5 sp_serveroption Syntax and Usage.

Syntax

```
sp_serveroption [@server =] 'server'
  ,[@optname =] 'option_name'
  ,[@optvalue =] 'option_value' ;
```

Usage

```
EXEC sp_serveroption 'ORADBSVR38', 'rpc out', true;
```

TABLE 5-4 Key Options for sp_serveroption

OPTION NAME	OPTION USAGE/DESCRIPTION
collation compatible	If TRUE, compatible collation is assumed with regard to character set and collation sequence (or sort order), and SQL Server sends comparisons on character columns to the provider. Otherwise, SQL Server always evaluates comparisons on character columns locally.
collation name	Sets the name of the collation used by the remote data source if Use Remote Collation is TRUE and the data source is not a SQL Server data source. The name must be a specific, single collation supported by SQL Server.
connect timeout	Sets the time-out value for connecting to the linked server. Set this option to 0 (zero) to use the sp_configure default.
data access	Set to TRUE to enable a linked server for distributed query access. Set this option to FALSE to disable the linked server for distributed query access.
lazy schema validation	If this option is TRUE, SQL Server skips schema checking of remote tables at the beginning of a query.
query timeout	Sets the time-out value for queries against a linked server. Set this option to 0 (zero) to use the sp_configure default.

OPTION NAME	OPTION USAGE/DESCRIPTION
remote proc transaction promotion	If this option is set to TRUE, calling a remote stored procedure starts a distributed transaction and enlists the transaction with MS DTC. Otherwise, a local transaction will not be promoted to a distributed transaction while calling an RPC on a linked server.
rpc	Set to TRUE to enable RPC from the linked server.
rpc out	Set to TRUE to enable RPC to the linked server.
use remote collation	If this option is set to TRUE, the collation of remote columns is used for SQL Server data sources, and the collation specified in Collation Name is used for non–SQL Server data sources. Otherwise, distributed queries always will use the default collation of the local server, while the collation name and the collation of remote columns are ignored.

Deleting Linked Servers

If you do not need a linked server anymore, you can delete it by completing the following steps:

1. Start SQL Server Management Studio, and then access the local server that contains the linked server definitions you want to delete.

2. In the Object Explorer view, expand the Server Objects node, and then expand the Linked Servers node. Now you should see an entry for each linked server that you created on the currently selected server.

3. Right-click the icon for the linked server you want to remove, and then choose Delete to open the Delete Object dialog box.

4. In the Delete Object dialog box, click OK.

The T-SQL command to drop linked servers is sp_dropserver. The T-SQL command to drop linked server logins is sp_droplinkedsrvlogin. Use these stored procedures as shown in Samples 5-6 and 5-7.

SAMPLE 5-6 sp_dropserver Syntax and Usage.

Syntax

```
sp_dropserver [@server =] 'server'
[, [@droplogins =]{'droplogins' | NULL}]
```

Usage

```
EXEC sp_dropserver 'ORADBSVR38', 'droplogins'
```

SAMPLE 5-7 sp_droplinkedsrvlogin Syntax and Usage.

Syntax

```
sp_droplinkedsrvlogin [@rmtsrvname =] 'rmtsrvname',
[@locallogin =]'locallogin'
```

Usage

```
EXEC sp_droplinkedsrvlogin 'ORADBSVR38', 'william'
```

Troubleshooting Configuration Problems

There are two specific techniques that you can use to resolve SQL Server configuration problems. In this section, you will learn how to recover from a bad configuration and how to rebuild the *master* database.

Recovering from a Bad Configuration

Although SQL Server 2012 has many safeguards that help you avoid configuration settings that keep SQL Server from starting, you might find occasionally that a configuration change prevents SQL Server from starting. If you encounter this situation, you can recover the server instance by completing the following steps:

1. Log on to the affected server locally, or log on remotely through Telnet or Terminal Server. You must log on using a local administrator account or the account used by the database server instance.

2. Make sure that the MSSQLServer or MSSQL$ *instancename* service is stopped. If it is not, stop the service by using one of the following methods:

   - SQL Server Configuration Manager
   - Computer Management
   - Services

   If the instance of SQL Server was installed as a default installation, you can stop the service by using the following command:

   ```
   net stop MSSQLSERVER
   ```

3. From the command prompt, switch to the directory of the associated SQL Server instance (either MSSQL10.MSSQLSERVER\MSSQL\Binn or MSSQL10.InstanceName\MSSQL\Binn). You must be in this directory to use the Sqlservr utility.

4. Start SQL Server from the command line with the following option:

   ```
   sqlservr -s(instancename) -f
   ```

   You must use the −s option to specify the instance of SQL Server if multiple instances of SQL Server are installed. The −f option starts SQL Server in single-user mode with a minimum configuration. This ensures that the bad configuration is not loaded.

5. Wait for the server to start up. SQL Server should write a few pages of output to the screen. Leave the server running.

6. In another command prompt window or Telnet session, start SQLCMD with the user name of a SQL Server account with administrator privileges and password as follows:

```
sqlcmd -U username -P password
```

TIP You must specify the instance to which you are connecting (sqlcmd –U username –P password –S*computername**instancename*) if multiple instances of SQL Server 2012 are installed.

7. If you have accessed SQLCMD properly, you should see the prompt change to >.

8. Reverse the changes made to the configuration by entering commands as you would in SQL Server Management Studio. The main difference is that you follow the commands with GO, as shown in the following example:

```
exec sp_configure "max server memory", 128
go
reconfigure
go
```

9. When you have finished, exit SQLCMD by typing **exit**.

10. From the command line in the window running SQL Server, press Ctrl+C.

11. When prompted, type **Y** for Yes. This stops SQL Server.

12. Restart SQL Server as you normally would. If you have made the appropriate changes, the server should start normally. Otherwise, repeat this procedure.

Changing Collation and Rebuilding the *master* Database

Rebuilding the *master* database restores all system databases to their original contents and attributes. The main reasons for rebuilding the *master* database are as follows:

- To set a new default collation for a database server instance

- To repair a corrupted *master* database when no backup of the *master* database is available

- To repair a corrupted *master* database when the SQL Server instance cannot be started

Run the SQL Server 2012 Setup program again to rebuild the *master* database. If you choose to rebuild the *master* database, keep the following guidelines in mind:

- After you rebuild the *master* database, you should restore the most recent *master*, *model*, and *msdb* databases. If the server was configured for replication, you must restore the most recent *distribution* database. Any data that cannot be restored must be created manually.

- After you rebuild the *master* database, all user databases are detached and unreadable. To recover them, you must re-create all your user databases. You cannot restore the user databases from backup—the restore maintains the information that was set when you created the backup, and you might want instead to move the databases to another server by importing and exporting them using Integration Services and the SQL Server Import And Export Wizard.

- You must reapply any SQL Server updates to bring the *Resource* database up to date. The *Resource* database is updated whenever patches, hot fixes, or service packs are applied to SQL Server.

To rebuild the *master* database, follow these steps:

1. Insert the SQL Server 2012 installation media and then run Setup. In the SQL Server Installation Center, click Maintenance and then click Repair. After Setup checks the support rules, click OK.

2. When the Repair SQL Server 2012 Maintenance Wizard starts, wait for the wizard to validate the setup and then click Next.

3. On the Select Instance page, select the SQL Server instance to repair and then click Next. If there are no blocking processes, click Next again to continue.

4. Click Repair. SQL Server then will rebuild the damaged installation as necessary. When this process is complete, click Next, and then click Finish.

You also can use the following command line to rebuild the *master* database:

```
setup /q /ACTION=REBUILDDATABASE /INSTANCENAME=InstanceName
/SQLSYSADMINACCOUNTS=AccountNames [ /SAPWD=Password ]
[ /SQLCOLLATION=DesiredCollation]
```

where *InstanceName* sets the database instance, *AccountNames* is a space-separated list of users, groups, or both to add to the sysadmin fixed server role, *Password* is the new SA password, and *DesiredCollation* is the collation you want to use, such as:

```
setup /q /ACTION=REBUILDDATABASE /INSTANCENAME=MSSQLSERVER
/SQLSYSADMINACCOUNTS=CPANDL\WilliamS CPANDL\DBADMINS /SAPWD=Quirky345
/SQLCOLLATION= SQL_Latin1_General_CP1_CI_AI
```

Database Administration Essentials

Core database administration involves creating, manipulating, and supporting databases. In Microsoft SQL Server 2012, a database is a collection of data and the objects that represent and interact with that data. Tables, views, stored procedures, triggers, and constraints are typical database objects.

A single database server instance can have up to 32,767 databases, and each database can have more than 2 billion objects. These are theoretical limits, of course, but they demonstrate that SQL Server can handle just about any job. To perform most administration tasks, you must log in to the database using an account that has the sysadmin fixed server role, such as the local sysadmin account (sa). Detailed information about roles and SQL Server security is found in Chapter 7, "Implementing SQL Server 2012 Security."

Database Files and Logs

Each SQL Server database has a transaction log associated with it. A *transaction log* is a history of modifications to the database, and SQL Server uses it to ensure that a database has integrity. All changes to the database are first written to the transaction log and then applied to the database. If the database update is successful, the transaction is completed and recorded as successful. If the database update fails, SQL Server uses the transaction log to restore the database to its original state (which is called *rolling back* the transaction). This two-phase commit process enables SQL Server to restore a database automatically in case of power failure, server outage, or other problems that might occur when you enter a transaction.

SQL Server databases and transaction logs are contained in separate database files. This means that each database always has at least two files associated with it—a data file and a log file. Databases also can have secondary data files. SQL Server uses three types of database files:

- **Primary data files**   Every database has one primary data file. A primary data file stores data and maintains records of other files used in a database. By default, primary data files end with the .mdf extension.

- **Secondary data files**   These files store additional data for a database. Although not all databases have secondary data files, a single database can have multiple secondary data files. By default, these files end with the .ndf extension.

- **Transaction log files**   Every database has at least one transaction log file. This file contains information necessary to restore the database. By default, log files end with the .ldf extension.

> **NOTE**   SQL Server also uses backup devices. Backup devices can be physical devices, such as tape drives, or files that are stored on a local drive or a network share. Additionally, it is important to note that SQL Server data and log files can be stored on either FAT or NTFS partitions, but they cannot be stored on any compressed file system.

> **TIP**   In SQL Server 2012, full-text catalogs are represented logically as virtual objects that refer to groups of full-text indexes rather than as separate database files with physical paths. This is a significant change from SQL Server 2005 and earlier releases.

Database files are specified when you create or modify the database. Because multiple database files are allowed, SQL Server can create databases that span multiple disk drives and that can grow in size as needed. Although the size of a SQL Server database is often measured in gigabytes, with all editions of SQL Server except the Express Edition and the Compact Edition, databases can range in size from 1 megabyte (MB) to a limit of 524,272 terabytes. With the Express Edition and the Compact Edition, databases can have a maximum size of 4 gigabytes (GB).

As you work with databases, keep in mind that SQL Server is designed to expand databases automatically as necessary. This means that the *master, tempdb, msdb,* and other critical databases will not run out of space under normal conditions— provided, of course, that file space is available on the configured drives and that you have not set a maximum database size manually.

System databases are the most important databases on the server. You should never update tables directly in system databases. Instead, use the appropriate management tools or stored procedures to modify the system databases if necessary. The only exception is the *model* database, which you can update with settings and objects. The *model* database is used as a template for a new database when you execute the CREATE DATABASE statement.

Table 6-1 provides a summary of other size and number constraints for SQL Server 2012. These constraints apply to both 32-bit and 64-bit editions unless otherwise noted.

REAL WORLD Wide tables and column sets go hand in hand. To create a table or change a table into a wide table, you add a column set to the table definition. A column set is an untyped XML representation that combines the table's sparse columns into a structured output. Because a column set is not physically stored in the table, a column set is similar to a calculated column. However, while a calculated column is not directly updatable, a column set is.

Wide tables can define up to 30,000 columns by using sparse columns, although the maximum number of nonsparse columns plus computed columns in a wide table remains 1,024 and the maximum row size is 8,019 bytes. In a wide table, most of the data in any particular row should be NULL.

TABLE 6-1 Size and Number Constraints for the Database Engine

DATABASE ENGINE OBJECT	MAXIMUM VALUE
Batch size	65,536 × network packet size; the default is 4 kilobytes (KB).
Bytes in source text of a stored procedure	Lesser of batch size or 250 MB.
Bytes per foreign key	900
Bytes per GROUP BY, ORDER BY	8,060
Bytes per index key	900
Bytes per primary key	900
Bytes per row	8,060 (except for varchar, nvarchar, varbinary, sql_variant, or CLR user-defined type columns).
Bytes per short string column	8,000
Bytes per varchar(max), varbinary(max), xml, text, or image column	$2^{31} - 1$
Characters per ntext or nvarchar(max) column	$2^{30} - 1$

DATABASE ENGINE OBJECT	MAXIMUM VALUE
Clustered indexes per table	1
Columns in GROUP BY, ORDER BY	Limited only by number of bytes.
Columns or expressions in a GROUP BY WITH CUBE or WITH ROLLUP statement	10
Columns per foreign key	16
Columns per index key	16 (15 when you use XML indexes).
Columns per INSERT statement	1,024
Columns per nonwide table	1,024
Columns per primary key	16
Columns per SELECT statement	4,096
Columns per wide table	30,000
Connections per client	Maximum value of configured connections.
Database size	524,272 terabytes.
Databases per instance of SQL Server	32,767
File size (data)	16 terabytes.
File size (log)	2 terabytes.
Filegroups per database	32,767
Files per database	32,767
Foreign key table references per table	Unlimited; recommended maximum is 253 to maintain expected performance levels.
Identifier length (in characters)	128
Instances per computer (no clustering)	50
Instances per computer (with clustering)	25 with shared cluster disk; 50 with Server Message Block (SMB) file shares.
Length of a string containing SQL statements (batch size)	65,536 × network packet size; the default is 4 KB.
Locks per connection	Maximum locks per server.

DATABASE ENGINE OBJECT	MAXIMUM VALUE
Locks per instance of SQL Server	Up to 2,147,483,647 on 32-bit editions for static locks. Otherwise, limited only by memory.
Nested stored procedure levels	32, but limited to 64 databases or two databases with interleaving.
Nested subqueries	32
Nested trigger levels	32
Nonclustered indexes per table	999
Number of distinct expressions in the GROUP BY clause using CUBE, ROLLUP, GROUPING SETS, WITH CUBE, WITH ROLLUP	32
Number of grouping sets generated by operators in the GROUP BY clause	4,096
Parameters per stored procedure	2,100
Parameters per user-defined function	2,100
Partitions per partitioned table or index	15,000
REFERENCES per table	253
Rows per table	Limited by available storage.
Statistics on nonindexed columns	30,000
Tables per database	The sum of the number of all objects in a database cannot exceed 2,147,483,647.
Tables per SELECT statement	Limited only by available resources.
Triggers per table	The sum of the number of all objects in a database cannot exceed 2,147,483,647.
UNIQUE indexes or constraints per table	249 nonclustered and 1 clustered.
User connections	32,767
XML indexes	249

SQL Server 2012 supports row-overflow storage, which enables variable-length columns to be pushed off-row and to exceed the maximum allowed size of 8,060 bytes per row. Row-overflow storage applies only to varchar, nvarchar, varbinary, sql_variant, or Common Language Runtime (CLR) user-defined type columns. It does not apply to varchar(max), nvarchar(max), varbinary(max), text, image, or xml columns, which have a maximum size of $2^{31} - 1$ bytes.

When the Database Engine uses row-overflow storage, it moves the record column with the largest width to another page in the ROW_OVERFLOW_DATA allocation unit while maintaining a 24-byte pointer on the original page. As part of ongoing operations, the Database Engine moves large records to another page dynamically as records are lengthened based on update operations. Update operations that shorten records might cause records to be moved back to the original page in the IN_ROW_ DATA allocation unit. Using the sys.dm_db_index_physical_stats object, you can obtain information about tables or indexes that might contain row-overflow data.

Because records that contain row-overflow data are processed synchronously instead of asynchronously, querying and performing other select operations, such as sorts or joins, slows processing time, and this might have an impact on the server's performance. To reduce the performance impact, consider the frequency with which this overflow data is likely to be queried and the percentage of rows that are likely to overflow. If users or applications are likely to perform frequent queries on many rows of row-overflow data, you should consider normalizing tables so that some columns are moved to another table. You can then make queries against the data using an asynchronous JOIN operation.

NOTE The length of individual columns still must fall within the limit of 8,000 bytes for varchar, nvarchar, varbinary, sql_variant, and CLR user-defined type columns. Only their combined lengths can exceed the 8,060-byte row limit of a table. Note also that the text, ntext, and image data types are deprecated and should not be used for new development.

You can include columns that contain row-overflow data as key or nonkey columns of a nonclustered index. However, the index key of a clustered index cannot contain varchar columns that have existing data in the ROW_OVERFLOW_DATA allocation unit. If a clustered index is created on a varchar column and the existing data is in the IN_ROW_DATA allocation unit, subsequent insert or update actions on the column that would cause the data length to exceed the in-row capacity will fail.

Database Administration Basics

You perform most database administration work through SQL Server Management Studio. You can use SQL Server Management Studio to carry out tasks such as the following:

- Viewing database information
- Checking user and system databases
- Examining database objects

This section examines each of these tasks. Keep in mind that when you've configured Windows PowerShell for remoting and installed the SQL Server management tools on your computer, you can execute commands on remote computers running SQL Server. Invoke-Sqlcmd runs commands remotely when you use the –ServerInstance parameter to specify a remote server instance that you want to work with. Set-Location runs commands locally or remotely based on the SqlServer: provider drive path you use.

Another way to work remotely with servers is to enter a remote session. You can enter an interactive remote session by using Enter-PSSession. Here is an example:

```
enter-pssession -computername dataserver48
```

Here, you use your current credentials to start a remote interactive session with DataServer48. To specify the credentials for the session, use the –Credentials parameter. Related tasks are covered in detail in Chapter 4, "Using Sessions, Jobs, and Remoting," in *Windows PowerShell 2.0 Administrator's Pocket Consultant* (Microsoft Press, 2009).

Viewing Database Information in SQL Server Management Studio

SQL Server organizes information using a top-down hierarchy that starts at the highest level with server groups and then moves down to servers, databases, schemas, and objects. You must work your way down to the database level to view the databases installed on a particular server instance. If you registered a server instance and connected to it previously, you can view its databases by completing the following steps:

1. In SQL Server Management Studio, use the Registered Servers view to select a type of server, such as Database Engine. If you need to expand a server group to see the servers listed in the group, click the plus sign (+) next to the name of the group.

2. In the Registered Servers view, select a server by double-clicking its name in the list. This connects you to the server in the Object Explorer view.

    NOTE If the SQL Server service is stopped, you must restart it before accessing the server. Additionally, if you have not authenticated the server connection and you specify SQL Authentication, you might need to provide a SQL login account and password. You might also need to reestablish a connection with the server. In either case, enter any necessary information, and then click OK or Yes to continue.

3. In the Object Explorer view, click the plus sign (+) next to the server's Databases folder to see a list of the databases available on the server.

4. Right-click the database you want to work with, and then select Properties. This displays the Database Properties dialog box, shown in Figure 6-1.

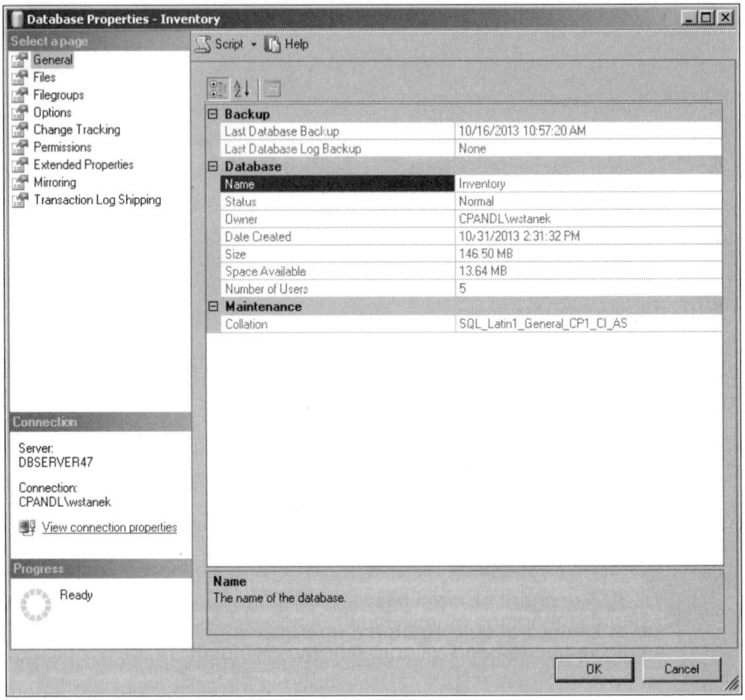

FIGURE 6-1 The General page of the Database Properties dialog box.

The Database Properties dialog box includes several properties pages:

- **General** Provides general database information, such as status, owner, date created, size, and space available. This page also details the last backup date and collation setting.

- **Files** Provides details on the data and log files associated with the database. If the database has been configured for full-text search, the Use Full-Text Indexing check box is selected. Catalog files associated with the database are not listed.

- **Filegroups** Lists the filegroups associated with the database and allows you to add or remove filegroups.

- **Options** Provides controls for viewing and managing standard database options and settings.

- **Change Tracking** Provides controls for viewing and managing change-tracking settings.

- **Permissions** Lists users or roles that have specific permissions allowed or denied in the database. Also allows you to set database permissions for users or roles.
- **Extended Properties** Provides controls for viewing and managing extended database properties.
- **Mirroring** Provides controls for viewing and managing database mirroring settings.
- **Transaction Log Shipping** Details the current log shipping configuration (if any) and allows you to manage log shipping.

Viewing Database Information Using T-SQL

You also can use Transact-SQL (T-SQL) to examine database information. T-SQL is an enhanced version of the standard structured query language that SQL Server uses. In SQL Server Management Studio, access the Query view by right-clicking the name of a server you have connected to already in the Object Explorer view and selecting New Query. Alternatively, click New Query on the main toolbar, select Database Engine Query, and then establish a connection to the Database Engine on a specific server.

After you have accessed the Query view, use the following command, where *dbname* is the name of the database you want to examine, to view database information:

```
sp_helpdb <dbname>
go
```

When you view database information in this way, you get an overview of the database as well as a listing of current data and log files. Table 6-2 summarizes the information available when you view database properties using T-SQL. This data is returned in two result sets. You need to scroll down in the Results pane to see the second result set.

TABLE 6-2 Database Properties Viewable Using T-SQL

COLUMN NAME	DESCRIPTION
compatibility_level	The current compatibility level of the database. The level 110 indicates SQL Server 2012 compatibility.
created	The date the database was created.
db_size	The total size of the database, including all data and log files.
dbid	The unique identifier for the database on the current server.
filegroup	The filegroup associated with the database file. Filegroups allow you to group together sets of database files.

COLUMN NAME	DESCRIPTION
fileid	The unique identifier for the file in the current database.
filename	The full file name and path.
growth	The number of megabytes or percent by which the file grows.
maxsize	The maximum file size. *Unlimited* means there is no limit.
name	The name of the database or file (without a file extension).
owner	The database owner.
size	The current size of a file.
status	The database status.
usage	The way the file is used, such as data only or log only.

Checking System and Sample Databases

A new SQL Server installation includes the system databases listed in Table 6-3. System databases are critical to the proper operation of SQL Server, and an important aspect of the administration process is backing up and maintaining these databases. Sample databases can also be installed, but they are meant only to provide examples and do not need regular maintenance. You can locate and download the examples and sample databases from the Microsoft SQL Server Community Projects & Product Samples website at *www.codeplex.com/ sqlserversamples*. In the Microsoft Product Samples section, you'll find links to samples for the SQL Server components and to the official SQL Server sample databases. If you install the samples, the sample files are installed by default in a component-specific subfolder of C:\Program Files\Microsoft SQL Server\100\ Samples.

TABLE 6-3 Summary of System Databases

DATABASE NAME	DATABASE TYPE	DESCRIPTION
master	System	Maintains information on all databases installed on the server. This database is modified any time you create databases, manage accounts, or change configuration settings. Back up the *master* database regularly.
model	System	Provides a template for all new databases. If you want new databases to have certain objects, properties, or permissions, put these changes in the *model* database. All new databases inherit the changes.

DATABASE NAME	DATABASE TYPE	DESCRIPTION
tempdb	System	Provides a temporary workspace for processing queries and handling other tasks. This database is re-created each time SQL Server is started and is based on the *model* database. However, if you specify a different database size or a different number of files for *tempdb*, those values are used rather than the values specified in the *model* database.
msdb	System	Used by the SQL Server Agent when handling alerts, notifications, and scheduled tasks. You can access all the information in this database by using SQL Server Management Studio options.
distribution	System/Replication	Used by Replication Services when you configure a server as a publisher, distributor, or both. This database is created when you configure replication, but it is not created automatically with a new installation.

Examining Database Objects

The main elements of a SQL Server database are referred to as *objects*. The objects you can associate with a database include the following:

- Certificates
- Constraints
- Defaults
- Indexes
- Keys
- Stored procedures and extended stored procedures
- Tables
- Triggers
- User-defined data types
- User-defined functions
- Views

You also can associate users, roles, rules, and full-text catalogs with databases.

To examine objects within a database, complete the following steps:

1. In SQL Server Management Studio, use the Registered Servers view to select a type of server, such as Database Engine. If you need to expand a server group to see the servers available in the group, click the plus sign (+) next to the name of a group.

2. In the Registered Servers view, select a server by double-clicking its name in the list. This connects you to the server in the Object Explorer view.

NOTE If you have not authenticated the server connection and you specify SQL Authentication, you might need to provide a SQL login account and password. You also might need to reestablish a connection with the server. In either case, enter any necessary information and then click Connect to continue.

3. In the Object Explorer view, work your way down to the database level. Expand the Databases folder, and then expand the entry for a specific database to see a list of nodes for database objects, including the following ones:

- **Database Diagrams** Contains visual diagrams of a database and the information it contains. Use Database Designer to create and manage diagrams.

- **Tables** Contains system and user tables. System tables are used for many purposes, including database mail, database maintenance plans, replication, backup and restore, and log shipping. System tables should not be modified directly.

- **Views** Contains system and user views. Standard views combine data from one or more tables to make working with the data easier. Indexed views have unique clustered indexes to improve query performance. Partitioned views join horizontally partitioned data from tables on one or more servers.

- **Synonyms** Contains synonyms, which are alternate names for schema-scoped objects. Applications can use synonyms to refer to objects in the database abstractly. You can then change the underlying name of the object without having to modify the application programming.

- **Programmability** Contains nodes used to represent most programmable object types and subtypes, including stored procedures, functions, triggers, assemblies, data types, rules, and defaults. This node also contains plan guides.

- **Service Broker** Contains Service Broker–related objects, including message types, contracts, queues, services, routes, and remote service bindings. This node also contains broker priorities.

- **Storage** Contains storage-related objects, including full-text catalogs, partition schemes, and partition functions. This node also contains full-text stoplists.

- **Security** Contains security-related objects, including users, roles, schemas, keys, and certificates. It also contains database audit specifications.

NOTE Database objects are covered in detail in Chapters 8 and 9. For example, you will find more information about views in Chapter 8, "Manipulating Schemas, Tables, and Views."

Plan guides, broker priorities, and full-text stoplists deserve additional discussion. Broker priorities define a priority level and the set of criteria for determining which Service Broker conversations to assign the priority level. Servicer Broker assigns the priority level to any conversation endpoint that uses the same combination of contracts and services that are specified in the conversation priority. Priorities range in value from 1 (low) through 10 (high). The default is 5.

You can create plan guides to help optimize queries that are not performing as expected. In a plan guide, you can specify the T-SQL statement that you want to be optimized and either an OPTION clause that contains the query hints you want to use or a specific query plan you want to use to optimize the query. When the query executes, the query optimizer matches the T-SQL statement to the plan guide and either attaches the OPTION clause to the query at run time or uses the specified query plan.

You can create three types of plan guides:

- **OBJECT plan guide**   Matches queries that execute in the context of T-SQL stored procedures, scalar user-defined functions, multistatement table-valued user-defined functions, and data manipulation language (DML) triggers.

- **SQL plan guide**   Matches queries that parameterize to a specified form, execute in the context of stand-alone T-SQL statements, or execute in batches that are not part of a database object.

- **TEMPLATE plan guide**   Matches stand-alone queries that parameterize to a specified form and override the current PARAMETERIZATION database SET option of a database for a class of queries.

If you've used plan guides with earlier releases of SQL Server, your plan guides remain intact after an upgrade, but they should be validated. You can validate existing plan guides by using the sys.fn_validate_plan_guide function. You also can use SQL Server Profiler to monitor SQL Server for Plan Guide Unsuccessful events, which indicate problems with a plan guide.

The SQL Server Full-Text Engine discards commonly occurring strings, called *stopwords*, that do not help with searches. During index creation, the Full-Text Engine omits stopwords from the full-text index. As a result, full-text queries do not search on stopwords. Stopwords replace SQL Server 2005 noise words.

In SQL Server 2012, you can create and use lists of stopwords. You associate these stoplists with full-text indexes, and then SQL Server applies the list when it builds indexes and applies queries. You create stoplists by uploading the system-supplied stoplist to the database, by creating your own stopwords and lists, or by combining these techniques. The system stoplist includes common stopwords for all supported languages. You can tailor the system-supplied stoplist by adding and removing stopwords.

Creating Databases

SQL Server uses the model database as the prototype for new databases. If you want new databases to have a particular setup, first modify the model database, and then create the new databases. Otherwise, you have to modify the settings of each new database manually.

The easiest way to create a new database is by using SQL Server Management Studio. You also can create databases using T-SQL.

Creating Databases in SQL Server Management Studio

In SQL Server Management Studio, you set database properties with buttons and input boxes and let SQL Server do all the detail work. Create a database with the default options by completing these steps:

1. In SQL Server Management Studio, use the Registered Servers view to select a type of server, such as Database Engine. If you need to expand a server group to see the servers available in a group, click the plus sign (+) next to the name of a group.

2. In the Registered Servers view, select a server by double-clicking its name in the list. This connects you to the server in the Object Explorer view.

3. Right-click the Databases folder, and then select New Database to display the dialog box shown in Figure 6-2.

4. On the General page, type a name for the database in the Database Name box. Although database names can have up to 128 characters, it is a good idea to give a new database a short but descriptive name to make it easier to track.

   NOTE The names of database objects are referred to as *identifiers*. Identifiers can contain from 1 to 128 characters (except for local temporary tables, which can have from 1 to 116 characters), and they must follow the specific naming conventions for the identifier class to which they belong. Generally, if the identifier name uses spaces or if it begins with a number, you must use brackets ([ ]) or double quotation marks (" ") to delimit the name when referencing it in T-SQL commands.

5. Click OK. SQL Server creates the database.

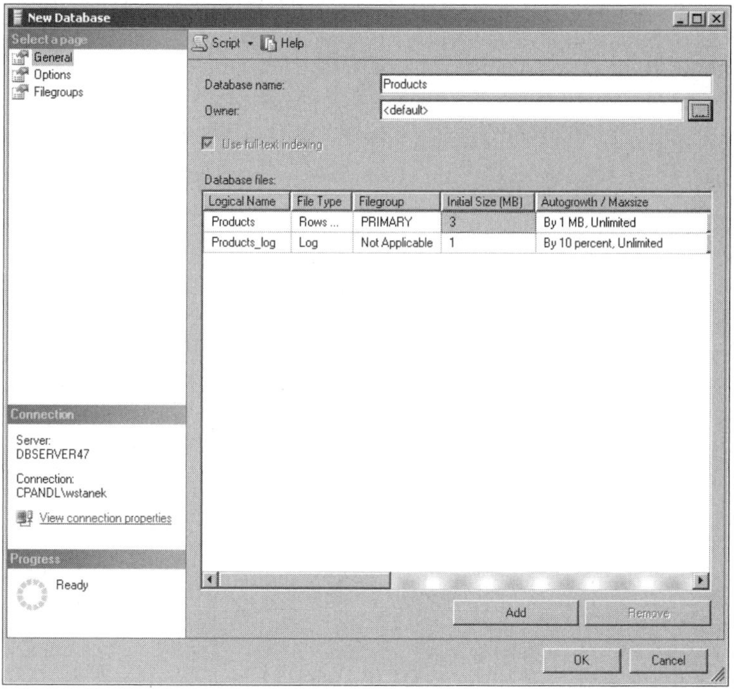

FIGURE 6-2 The New Database dialog box.

To customize the creation process, follow steps 1 through 4 (but not 5) in the previous example, and then continue with these steps:

1. On the General page, set the database owner by clicking the button to the right of the Owner box to display the Select Database Owner dialog box.

2. In the Select Database Owner dialog box, click Browse, and then in the Browse For Objects dialog box, select the check box for the login you want to use as the owner of the database. Click OK twice.

3. By default, SQL Server bases the data file name on the database name. For example, if you use Projects as the database name, the data file is named Projects. You can change the default name by typing a new value.

4. The Filegroup box shows which filegroup the data file belongs to. By default, all files are placed in the primary group. Although the primary data file must be in the primary group, you can create other data files and place them in different filegroups. Filegroups provide options for determining where data is stored and how it is used, as well as how data is backed up and restored.

TIP Filegroups are designed primarily for large databases and advanced administration. If your database might grow fairly large, consider using multiple filegroups. Otherwise, you really do not need to use multiple filegroups.

The primary reason to use filegroups is to improve database response time. You do this by allowing database files to be created across multiple disks, to be accessed by multiple disk controllers, or both. However, in a storage area network (SAN) environment, you might not have control over how logical unit numbers (LUNs) are allocated and therefore might not benefit from this approach.

5. In the Initial Size box, type an initial size for the database in megabytes. Use a size that makes sense for the amount of data that the database will store. By default, new databases have the same size as the *model* database. The size range for databases is 1 MB to many terabytes.

TIP Setting the initial database size to a reasonable value cuts down on the overhead that might be associated with growing the database. Whether you grow the database manually or SQL Server grows it automatically, the database is locked until resizing is complete. This can cause delays in processing queries and handling transactions.

NOTE You cannot shrink a database to a size smaller than it was when you created it. However, you can use the DBCC SHRINKFILE statement to shrink individual data and log files to make them smaller than their original sizes. With DBCC SHRINKFILE, you must shrink each file individually; you cannot shrink the entire database.

6. By default, new databases are set to auto-grow each time a data file needs to be expanded. Click the button to the right of the Autogrowth/Maxsize box to adjust the settings. As Figure 6-3 shows, the Autogrowth feature can be set to grow a database by using a percentage or by an amount in megabytes. You also can restrict the file to a specific maximum size or allow the file to grow as needed indefinitely.

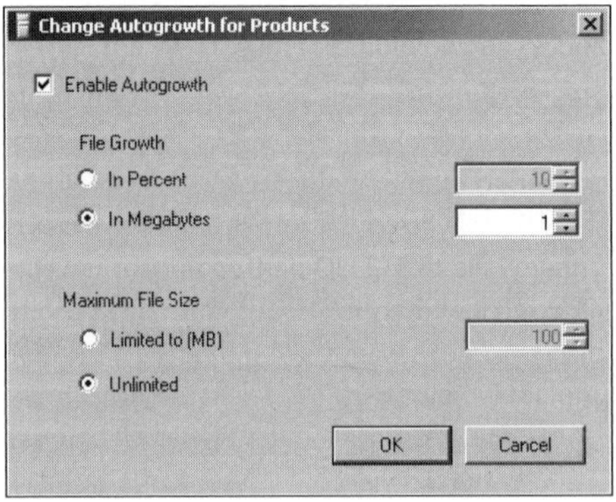

FIGURE 6-3 Configuring the Autogrowth feature.

REAL WORLD The Autogrowth feature helps ensure that databases do not run out of space. When configuring a database, be careful to enable growth by a certain amount, however. Setting a 10 percent growth rate, for example, causes a database that is 250 GB in size to grow by a whopping 25 GB each time a data file needs to be expanded. A server with multiple databases might run out of space as a result of the growth factor. If you set the growth in megabytes, with 1 MB as a minimum growth size, you know exactly how much the database will grow each time the data file expands. However, be careful when growing the database in small increments as this can cause fragmentation over time. You might also want to configure an alert to notify you when the database grows to a certain size. You will learn how to configure an alert in Chapter 10, "Automating and Maintaining SQL Server 2012."

7. In the Path box, type the full path to the data file. The name of the primary data file should end with the .mdf file extension. By default, SQL Server uses the default data location you selected when you installed the server. Click the button to the right of the Path box to find a new path, or you can enter a new path directly.

8. Secondary data files provide an additional location for data. If you want to configure secondary data files, click Add to start on a new line, and then repeat steps 3 through 7. Secondary data file names should end with the .ndf file extension.

9. Transaction logs are listed with the Log file type. After you configure data files, you can configure one or more transaction log files in much the same way that you configure the data files. Type the file name, filegroup, initial size, and path information. Configure Autogrowth and maximum size as necessary. Be sure to name the log files with the .ldf file extension.

NOTE Setting a size for the transaction log can be tricky. You do not want to rob the system of needed space for data, but you do want to avoid a situation in which the transaction logs are resized again and again because a file is locked when it is being expanded. I recommend 2 MB to 3 MB as a minimum for most databases, and 25 percent of total data file size on a moderately active database. Also, placing transaction logs on separate drives from data files will improve database performance.

10. On the Options page, use the Collation list to choose a collation for the database. Windows collation names have two components: a collation designator and a comparison style. The collation designator specifies the alphabet or language whose sorting rules are applied with dictionary sorting and the code page to use when storing non-Unicode character data.

The comparison style specifies additional collation styles as identified by the following abbreviations:

- **100** Linguistic sorting (updated collation to include linguistic sorting for supplementary characters)
- **90** Code-point sorting (updated collation to include code-point sorting)
- **CI** Case insensitive
- **CS** Case sensitive
- **AI** Accent insensitive
- **AS** Accent sensitive
- **KS** Kanatype sensitive
- **WS** Width sensitive
- **BIN** Binary sort order
- **BIN2** Code-point binary sort (for pure code-point comparison collations)

11. Click OK to complete the creation process.

TIP Need to keep objects under a source control system? Configure your settings and then click the Script button on the toolbar before creating the database. This will produce a T-SQL script that reflects all the configuration items you've selected.

After you finish creating a database, you should set options and permissions for that database. You will learn about setting options in the "Setting Database Options in SQL Server Management Studio" section later in this chapter. Setting permissions is covered in Chapter 7.

Creating Databases Using T-SQL

You also can create a database by using the CREATE DATABASE command. This command has options that are similar to those in the Database Properties dialog box. The best way to learn how the command works is by creating databases in SQL Server Management Studio first and then trying to use the CREATE DATABASE command.

The syntax and usage for CREATE DATABASE are shown in Sample 6-1.

SAMPLE 6-1 CREATE DATABASE Command Syntax and Usage.

Syntax

```
CREATE DATABASE database_name
    [ CONTAINMENT = { OFF | PARTIAL }
    [ ON
      [ PRIMARY ] <filespec> [ ,... n ]
      [ , <filegroup> [ ,... n ] ]
      [ LOG ON <filespec> [ ,... n ] ]
    ]
    [ COLLATE collation_name ]
```

```
        [ WITH   <option> [,... n ]
  ]
  [;]


<option> ::=
{ FILESTREAM ( <filestream_option> [,... n ] )
    | DEFAULT_FULLTEXT_LANGUAGE = {
              lcid |  language_name | language_alias }
    | DEFAULT_LANGUAGE = {
              lcid |  language_name | language_alias }
    | NESTED_TRIGGERS = { OFF | ON }
    | TRANSFORM_NOISE_WORDS = { OFF | ON}
    | TWO_DIGIT_YEAR_CUTOFF = <two_digit_year_cutoff>
    | DB_CHAINING { OFF | ON }
    | TRUSTWORTHY { OFF | ON }
}


<filespec>::= {
(NAME = logical_file_name ,
    FILENAME = { 'os_file_name' | 'filestream_path' }
    [ , SIZE = size [ KB | MB | GB | TB ] ]
    [ , MAXSIZE = {  max_size [ KB | MB | GB | TB ] | UNLIMITED } ]
    [ , FILEGROWTH = growth_increment [ KB | MB | GB | TB | % ] ] ) }


<filegroup> ::= {
FILEGROUP  filegroup_name [ CONTAINS FILESTREAM ] [ DEFAULT ]
    <filespec> [ ,... n ]
}
```

Usage

```
USE MASTER
GO
CREATE DATABASE Sample
ON
PRIMARY
( NAME = Sample1,
FILENAME = "c:\data\sampledat1.mdf",
SIZE = 100MB,
MAXSIZE = UNLIMITED,
FILEGROWTH = 10%),
( NAME = Sample2,
FILENAME = "c:\data\sampledat2.ndf",
SIZE = 100MB,
MAXSIZE = UNLIMITED,
FILEGROWTH = 10%)
LOG ON
( NAME = SampleLog1,
FILENAME = "c:\data\samplelog1.ldf",
SIZE = 3MB,
MAXSIZE = UNLIMITED,
FILEGROWTH = 5MB)
GO
```

Altering Databases and Their Options

New databases inherit options from the *model* database. After you create a database, you can modify inherited settings at any time by using SQL Server Management Studio or the ALTER DATABASE statement and other SQL commands. In most SQL Server editions, many standard options can be set to TRUE (ON) or FALSE (OFF) states. Other options accept specific values that specify their configured state, such as GLOBAL or LOCAL.

Setting Database Options in SQL Server Management Studio

To set database options in SQL Server Management Studio, complete the following steps:

1. In SQL Server Management Studio, use the Registered Servers view to select a type of server, such as Database Engine. If you need to expand a server group to see the servers listed in the group, click the plus sign (+) next to the name of a group.

2. In the Registered Servers view, select a server by double-clicking its name in the list. This connects you to the server in the Object Explorer view.

3. Click the plus sign (+) next to the Databases folder. Right-click the name of a database, and then select Properties to display the Database Properties dialog box.

4. In the Database Properties dialog box, select Options in the Select A Page list, as shown in Figure 6-4. Now you can configure options for the database by using the drop-down lists provided. Most options can be turned off using a value of False or turned on using a value of True.

5. Click OK when you finish selecting options. Your changes take effect immediately; you do not need to restart the server.

Modifying Databases Using ALTER DATABASE

SQL Server Management Studio provides one easy way to modify the configuration of a database. Another way to modify a database is to use ALTER DATABASE. You can use the ALTER DATABASE command to perform the following tasks:

- Set database options. You should use the ALTER DATABASE command instead of the sp_dboption stored procedure to do this. The sp_dboption stored procedure is deprecated and will be removed in a future version of SQL Server.

- Add new data and log files to a database. All the files must be placed in the same filegroup.

- Modify properties of data and log files, such as increasing file size, changing the maximum size, or setting file growth rules.

- Add a new filegroup to a database.

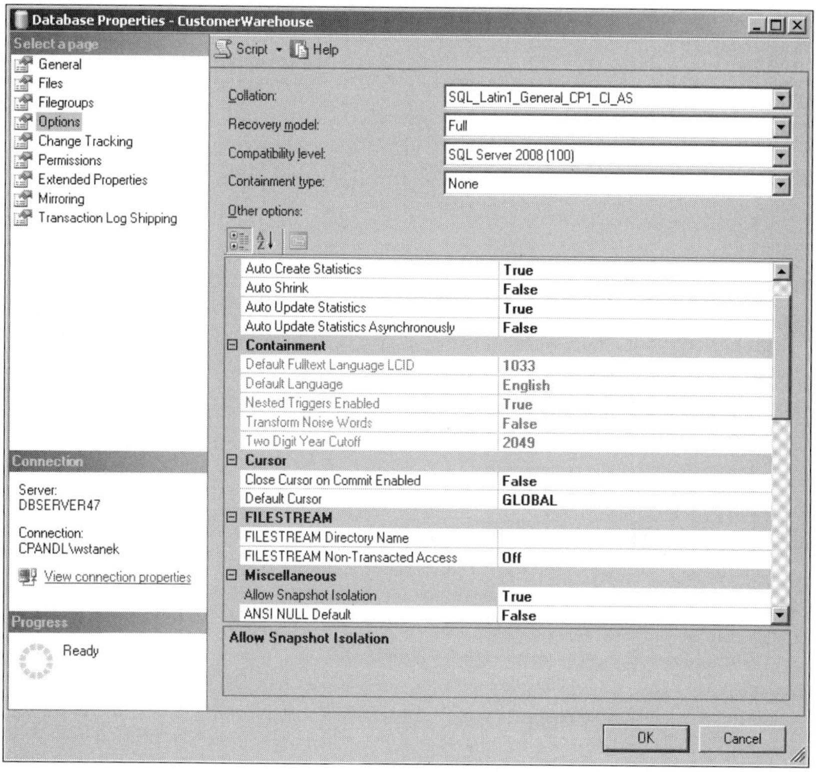

FIGURE 6-4 The Options page of the Database Properties dialog box.

- Modify the properties of an existing filegroup, such as designating whether a filegroup is read-only or read-write and which filegroup is the default.
- Remove files and filegroups from a database. These elements can be removed only when they do not contain data.

The ALTER DATABASE command is designed to make one database change at a time. Its syntax is shown in Sample 6-2. The examples in the listing show how you can use ALTER DATABASE to perform important administrative tasks. You can use the Query view in SQL Server Management Studio or SQLCMD to execute commands. Execute commands with either the Execute Command button or the GO command, respectively.

SAMPLE 6-2 ALTER DATABASE Syntax and Usage.

Syntax

```
ALTER DATABASE { database_name  | CURRENT }
{ <add_or_modify_files>
  | <add_or_modify_filegroups>
  | <set_hadr_options>
```

```
    | <set_database_options>
    | MODIFY NAME = new_database_name
    | COLLATE collation_name }
[;]
<add_or_modify_files>::=
{ ADD FILE <filespec> [ ,...n ] [ TO FILEGROUP { filegroup_name } ]
    | ADD LOG FILE <filespec> [ ,...n ]
    | REMOVE FILE logical_file_name
    | MODIFY FILE <filespec>
}
<filespec>::=
(   NAME = logical_file_name
    [ , NEWNAME = new_logical_name ]
    [ , FILENAME = 'os_file_name' | 'filestream_path']
    [ , SIZE = size [ KB | MB | GB | TB ] ]
    [ , MAXSIZE = { max_size [ KB | MB | GB | TB ] | UNLIMITED } ]
    [ , FILEGROWTH = growth_increment [ KB | MB | | GB | TB | % ] ]
    [ , OFFLINE ]
)
<add_or_modify_filegroups>::=
{   | ADD FILEGROUP filegroup_name
    | REMOVE FILEGROUP filegroup_name
    | MODIFY FILEGROUP filegroup_name
        { <filegroup_updatability_option>
        | DEFAULT
        | NAME = new_filegroup_name
        }
}
<filegroup_updatability_option>::=
{   { READONLY | READWRITE } 
    | { READ_ONLY | READ_WRITE }
}

<set_database_options>::=
    SET {   { <optionspec> [ ,...n ] [ WITH <termination> ] } }

<optionspec>::=
{ <auto_option>   | <change_tracking_option>
    | <containment_option> | <cursor_option> | <database_mirroring_option>
    | <date_correlation_optimization_option> | <db_encryption_option>
    | FILESTREAM ( <FILESTREAM_option> ) | HADR ( <hadr_options> )
    | <db_state_option> | <db_update_option> | <db_user_access_option>
    | <external_access_option> | <parameterization_option> | <recovery_
option>
    | <service_broker_option> | <snapshot_option> | <sql_option>
}

<auto_option> ::=
{ AUTO_CLOSE { ON | OFF }
    | AUTO_CREATE_STATISTICS { ON | OFF }
    | AUTO_SHRINK { ON | OFF }
```

```
  | AUTO_UPDATE_STATISTICS { ON | OFF }
  | AUTO_UPDATE_STATISTICS_ASYNC { ON | OFF }
}

<change_tracking_option> ::=
{ CHANGE_TRACKING {
  = OFF
  | = ON [ <change_tracking_settings> ]
  | <change_tracking_settings>
  }
}
<change_tracking_settings> ::=
  { [ AUTO_CLEANUP = { ON | OFF } [ , ] ]
  [ CHANGE_RETENTION = retention_period { DAYS | HOURS | MINUTES } ] }

<containment_option> ::=
  CONTAINMENT = { NONE | PARTIAL }

<cursor_option> ::=
{ CURSOR_CLOSE_ON_COMMIT { ON | OFF }
  | CURSOR_DEFAULT { LOCAL | GLOBAL }
}
<partner_option> ::=
{ PARTNER { = 'partner_server'
  | FAILOVER  | FORCE_SERVICE_ALLOW_DATA_LOSS
  | OFF | RESUME | SAFETY { FULL | OFF }
  | SUSPEND | TIMEOUT integer
}
<witness_option> ::=
  WITNESS { = 'witness_server' | OFF }
}
<date_correlation_optimization_option> ::=
{ DATE_CORRELATION_OPTIMIZATION { ON | OFF }
}
<db_encryption_option> ::=
  { ENCRYPTION { ON | OFF }
}
<db_state_option> ::=
    { ONLINE | OFFLINE | EMERGENCY }
<db_update_option> ::=
    { READ_ONLY | READ_WRITE }
<db_user_access_option> ::=
    { SINGLE_USER | RESTRICTED_USER | MULTI_USER }
<external_access_option> ::=
{ DB_CHAINING { ON | OFF }
  | TRUSTWORTHY { ON | OFF }
  | DEFAULT_FULLTEXT_LANGUAGE = { <lcid> | <language name> | <language
alias>}
  | DEFAULT_LANGUAGE = { <lcid> | <language name> | <language alias> }
  | NESTED_TRIGGERS = { OFF | ON }
  | TRANSFORM_NOISE_WORDS = { OFF | ON }
```

```
   | TWO_DIGIT_YEAR_CUTOFF = { 1753, ..., 2049, ..., 9999 }
<FILESTREAM_option> ::=
{ NON_TRANSACTED_ACCESS = { OFF | READ_ONLY | FULL }
   | DIRECTORY_NAME = <directory_name>
}
<hadr_options>::=
   { AVAILABILITY GROUP  = group_name | OFF }
   | { SUSPEND | RESUME }
}
<parameterization_option> ::=
{ PARAMETERIZATION { SIMPLE | FORCED }
<recovery_option> ::=
{ RECOVERY { FULL | BULK_LOGGED | SIMPLE }
   | TORN_PAGE_DETECTION { ON | OFF }
   | PAGE_VERIFY { CHECKSUM | TORN_PAGE_DETECTION | NONE }
}
<service_broker_option> ::=
{ ENABLE_BROKER
   | DISABLE_BROKER
   | NEW_BROKER
   | ERROR_BROKER_CONVERSATIONS
   | HONOR_BROKER_PRIORITY { ON | OFF}
}

<snapshot_option> ::=
{ ALLOW_SNAPSHOT_ISOLATION { ON | OFF }
   | READ_COMMITTED_SNAPSHOT {ON | OFF }
}
<sql_option> ::=
{ ANSI_NULL_DEFAULT { ON | OFF }
   | ANSI_NULLS { ON | OFF }
   | ANSI_PADDING { ON | OFF }
   | ANSI_WARNINGS { ON | OFF }
   | ARITHABORT { ON | OFF }
   | COMPATIBILITY_LEVEL = { 90 | 100 | 110 }
   | CONCAT_NULL_YIELDS_NULL { ON | OFF }
   | NUMERIC_ROUNDABORT { ON | OFF }
   | QUOTED_IDENTIFIER { ON | OFF }
   | RECURSIVE_TRIGGERS { ON | OFF }
}
<target_recovery_time_option> ::=
   { TARGET_RECOVERY_TIME = target_recovery_time { SECONDS | MINUTES } }
<termination> ::=
{ ROLLBACK AFTER integer [ SECONDS ]
   | ROLLBACK IMMEDIATE
   | NO_WAIT
}
```

Usage: Adding a File to a Database

```
ALTER DATABASE Customer
ADD FILE
```

```
( NAME = Customerdata2,
    FILENAME = "c:\data\customerdat2.ndf",
    SIZE = 10MB,
    MAXSIZE = 500MB,
    FILEGROWTH = 5MB )
```

Usage: Adding a Filegroup

```
ALTER DATABASE Customer
ADD FILEGROUP Secondary
```

Usage: Adding Files and Placing Them in a Filegroup

```
ALTER DATABASE Customer
ADD FILE
( NAME = Customerdata3,
    FILENAME = "c:\data\customerdat3.ndf",
    SIZE = 10MB,
    MAXSIZE = UNLIMITED,
    FILEGROWTH = 5MB),
( NAME = Customerdata4,
    FILENAME = "c:\data\customerdat4.ndf",
    SIZE = 10MB,
    MAXSIZE = UNLIMITED,
    FILEGROWTH = 5MB)
TO FILEGROUP Secondary
```

Usage: Setting the Default Filegroup

```
ALTER DATABASE Customer
MODIFY FILEGROUP Secondary DEFAULT
```

Usage: Modifying a File

```
ALTER DATABASE Customer
MODIFY FILE
(NAME = Customerdata3,
    SIZE = 20MB)
```

Usage: Removing a File from a Database

```
USE Customer
DBCC SHRINKFILE (Customerdata3, EMPTYFILE)
ALTER DATABASE Customer
REMOVE FILE Customerdata3
```

Usage: Setting the Recovery Model Option

```
ALTER DATABASE Customer
SET RECOVERY FULL
GO
```

Usage: Setting Single User with Rollback of Incomplete Transactions

```
ALTER DATABASE Customer
SET SINGLE_USER
WITH ROLLBACK IMMEDIATE
GO
```

Configuring Automatic Options

SQL Server 2012 has several important features that can be managed automatically. You will find the automatic options on the Options page of the Database Properties dialog box. These options are shown as TRUE when they are set to ON and FALSE when they are set to OFF. In the following list, options in the Database Properties dialog box are shown first, with the related ALTER DATABASE keyword following in parentheses. Automatic options include the following:

- **Auto Close (auto_close)** When this option is set to TRUE, the database closes and resources become available again when the last user connection ends and all database processes are complete. The database reopens automatically when a user connects to the database again. In SQL Server 2012 Express Edition, this option is set to TRUE by default. All other editions set this option to FALSE by default, which can improve database performance because the overhead of opening and closing databases is eliminated. When this option is set to FALSE, the database remains open even if no users are currently using it.

- **Auto Create Statistics (auto_create_statistics)** When this option is set to TRUE (the default), statistics are created by SQL Server automatically for columns used in a WHERE clause and as otherwise needed. These statistics are used to determine the best way to evaluate a query, which in turn can improve query performance.

- **Auto Shrink (auto_shrink)** When this option is set to TRUE, data and log files are reduced in size and compacted automatically. When records are deleted or purged, SQL Server automatically reduces the size of data or log files or both file types. However, log files are reduced in size only when you back up the transaction log or set the Recovery Model to Simple.

run the DBCC SHRINK-DATABASE command periodically or to schedule this task on a recurring basis, as explained in the "Compressing and Shrinking a Database Manually" section later in this chapter.

- **Auto Update Statistics (auto_update_statistics)** When this option is set to TRUE (the default), existing statistics are updated automatically if data in the related tables changes. Otherwise, existing statistics are not updated automatically; you can only update them manually. The UPDATE STATISTICS statement re-enables automatic updating of statistics unless the NORECOMPUTE clause is specified.

- **Auto Update Statistics Asynchronously (auto_update_statistics_async)** When this option is set to TRUE, queries that initiate an automatic update of out-of-date statistics do not wait for the statistics to be updated before compiling. Otherwise, queries that initiate an automatic update of out-of-date statistics wait for the statistics to be updated before compiling.

To manage the automatic features using SQL Server Management Studio, follow these steps:

1. In the Object Explorer view in SQL Server Management Studio, right-click the database you want to configure, and then select Properties from the shortcut menu.

2. In the Database Properties dialog box, select Options in the Select A Page list.

3. Set the individual automatic options to True or False as necessary. Click OK when you finish setting options. Your changes take effect immediately; you do not need to restart the server.

To manage the automatic features using T-SQL, follow these steps:

1. In the Object Explorer view in SQL Server Management Studio, right-click the database you want to configure, and then select New Query from the shortcut menu.

2. In the Query view, type **ALTER DATABASE <*dbname*> SET <*option*> <*option_value*> GO**, where *dbname* is the name of the database you want to examine, *option* is the name of the option to set, and *option_value* is the value for the specified option. The following example shows the commands required to turn on the auto_update_statistics option for the *Personnel* database:

```
ALTER DATABASE Personnel
SET auto_update_statistics ON
GO
```

3. Execute the query by clicking Execute or by pressing F5. If the option is set properly, the command should complete successfully.

Controlling ANSI Compliance at the Database Level

ANSI compliance can be controlled at the database level by using database options. You can find these options listed under the Miscellaneous heading on the Options page of the Database Properties dialog box. The settings for these options are shown as TRUE when they are set to ON and FALSE when they are set to OFF. In the following list, Database Properties dialog box options are listed first, followed by the related ALTER DATABASE keyword in parentheses:

- **ANSI NULL Default (ansi_null_default)**   When this option is set to TRUE, it changes the database default to NULL when no value is specified. You can override this setting by explicitly stating NULL or NOT NULL when you create user-defined data types or column definitions.

- **ANSI NULLS Enabled (ansi_nulls)**   When this option is set to TRUE, any comparison to a null value evaluates to NULL. Otherwise, comparisons of non-Unicode values evaluate to TRUE only when both values are NULL.

- **ANSI Padding Enabled (ansi_padding)**   When this option is set to TRUE, non-null values shorter than the defined column size are padded to fill the length of the column. Values are padded as appropriate for the relevant data type; for example, char columns are padded with trailing blanks, and binary columns are padded with trailing zeroes. When this option is set to FALSE, trailing blanks are trimmed.

- **ANSI Warnings Enabled (ansi_warnings)**   When this option is set to TRUE, SQL Server issues certain warnings that would not be displayed otherwise. For example, if this option is set to TRUE, divide-by-zero errors are displayed. If this option is set to FALSE, these errors are not displayed.

- **Arithmetic Abort Enabled (arithabort)**   When this option is set to TRUE, it terminates a query when an overflow or divide-by-zero error occurs. If the error occurs in a transaction, the transaction is rolled back. When the option is set to FALSE, a warning message might be displayed, but queries and transactions continue as if no error occurred.

- **Concatenate Null Yields Null (concat_null_yields_null)**   When this option is set to TRUE, concatenating a string containing NULL with other strings results in NULL. If this option is set to FALSE, the null value is treated as an empty string.

- **Numeric Round-Abort (numeric_roundabort)**   When this option is set to TRUE, an error is generated when a loss of precision occurs in an expression. When it is set to FALSE, losses of precision do not generate error messages, and the result is rounded to the precision of the column or variable storing the result.

- **Quoted Identifiers Enabled (quoted_identifier)**   When this option is set to TRUE, identifiers must be delimited by double quotation marks ("...") and literals must be delimited by single quotation marks ('...'). All strings that are delimited by double quotation marks are interpreted as object identifiers and do not have to follow the T-SQL rules for identifiers. When this option is set to FALSE, you need to use quoted identifiers only if names contain spaces.

- **Recursive Triggers Enabled (recursive_triggers)** When this option is set to TRUE, a trigger can execute recursively. Triggers can be executed directly or indirectly. If a trigger is direct, a trigger in Table A1 modifies Table A1, which in turn causes the trigger to fire again. If a trigger is indirect, a trigger in Table A1 could modify data in Table A2, which in turn has a trigger that modifies data in Table A1, and this causes the original trigger to fire again. When this option is set to FALSE, only indirect triggers are allowed.

To manage the ANSI compliance features using SQL Server Management Studio, follow these steps:

1. In the Object Explorer view in SQL Server Management Studio, right-click the database you want to configure, and then select Properties from the shortcut menu.

2. In the Database Properties dialog box, select Options in the Select A Page list.

3. Set the ANSI compliance options to True or False as necessary. Click OK when you finish setting these options. Your changes take effect immediately without restarting the server.

To manage the ANSI compliance features using T-SQL, follow these steps:

1. In the Object Explorer view in SQL Server Management Studio, right-click the database you want to configure, and then select New Query from the shortcut menu.

2. In the Query view, type **ALTER DATABASE *<dbname>* SET *<option>* *<option_value>* GO**, where *dbname* is the name of the database you want to examine, *option* is the name of the option to set, and *option_value* is the value for the specified option. The following example shows the commands required to turn on the numeric_roundabort option for the *Personnel* database:

```
ALTER DATABASE Personnel
SET numeric_roundabort ON
GO
```

3. Execute the query by clicking Execute or by pressing F5. If the option is set properly, the command should complete successfully.

Configuring Parameterization

SQL Server can use parameters in T-SQL statements to increase the ability of the relational engine to match new SQL statements with existing, previously compiled execution plans. The PARAMETERIZATION option controls how parameterization works.

When this option is set to SIMPLE, SQL Server parameterizes very few classes of queries and disables forced parameterization. When this option is set to FORCED, any literal value that appears in a SELECT, INSERT, UPDATE, or DELETE statement submitted in any form is converted to a parameter during query compilation. The exceptions are literals that appear in many types of query constructs.

With forced parameterization, individual statements in a batch are always parameterized. After compiling, a parameterized query is executed in the context of the batch in which it was originally submitted. When an execution plan for a query is cached, you can determine whether the query was parameterized by referencing the sql column of the sys.syscacheobjects view. With parameterized queries, the names and data types of parameters come before the text of the submitted batch in this column, such as (@1 tinyint). Only experienced database administrators should use forced parameterization, and they should do so only after determining whether and how this affects performance.

You can override the parameterization behavior for a query and for other queries that are syntactically equivalent but differ only in their parameter values. When SQL Server parameterizes literals, the parameters are converted to the following data types:

- Money type literals parameterize to money.
- Integer literals whose size otherwise would fit within the int data type parameterize to int.
- Large integer literals that are not parts of predicates that involve comparison operators parameterize to numeric data types whose precision is just large enough to support its size and whose scale is 0.
- Large integer literals that are parts of predicates that involve any comparison operator (including <, <=, =, !=, >, >=, !<, !>, <>, ALL, ANY, SOME, BETWEEN, and IN) parameterize to numeric(38,0).
- Fixed-point numeric literals that are not parts of predicates that involve comparison operators parameterize to numeric data types whose precision and scale are just large enough to support its size.
- Fixed-point numeric literals that are parts of predicates that involve comparison operators parameterize to numeric data types whose precision is 38 and whose scale is just large enough to support its size.
- Binary literals parameterize to varbinary(8000) if the literal fits within 8,000 bytes. If it is larger than 8,000 bytes, it is converted to varbinary(max).
- Non-Unicode string literals parameterize to varchar(8000) if the literal fits within 8,000 characters and to varchar(max) if it is larger than 8,000 characters.
- Unicode string literals parameterize to nvarchar(4000) if the literal fits within 4,000 Unicode characters and to nvarchar(max) if the literal is larger than 4,000 characters.
- Floating-point numeric literals parameterize to float(53).

NOTE When arithmetic operators (including +, –, *, /, or %) are used to perform implicit or explicit conversion of int, smallint, tinyint, or bigint constant values to the float, real, decimal, or numeric data types, SQL Server applies different rules of parameterized and nonparameterized values to calculate the type and precision of the expression results.

SQL Server uses simple parameterization by default. When you change the PARAMETERIZATION option from SIMPLE to FORCED, SQL Server flushes all query plans from the plan cache of a database except those that currently are compiling, recompiling, or running. Plans for queries that are actively compiling, recompiling, or running are parameterized the next time they are executed. SQL Server preserves the current setting of the PARAMETERIZATION option when reattaching or restoring a database.

To manage parameterization using SQL Server Management Studio, follow these steps:

1. In the Object Explorer view in SQL Server Management Studio, right-click the database you want to configure, and then select Properties from the shortcut menu.

2. In the Database Properties dialog box, select Options in the Select A Page list.

3. Set the Parameterization option to Simple or Forced as necessary. Click OK when you finish setting this option. Your changes take effect immediately without restarting the server.

To manage parameterization using T-SQL, follow these steps:

1. In the Object Explorer view in SQL Server Management Studio, right-click the database you want to configure, and then select New Query from the shortcut menu.

2. In the Query view, type **ALTER DATABASE <*dbname*> SET PARAMETERIZATION <SIMPLE | FORCED> GO**, where *dbname* is the name of the database you want to examine and the parameterization option is set to a value of SIMPLE or FORCED. The following example shows the commands required to set the parameterization option for the *Personnel* database:

```
ALTER DATABASE Personnel
SET PARAMETERIZATION FORCED
GO
```

3. Execute the query by clicking Execute or by pressing F5. If the option is set properly, the command should complete successfully.

Configuring Cursor Options

Cursors are used with stored procedures, with triggers, and in batch scripts to make the contents of a result set available to other statements. You have limited control over cursor behavior by using the options listed under the Cursor heading on the Options page of the Database Properties dialog box. These options are shown as TRUE when they are set to ON and FALSE when they are set to OFF. In the following list, Database Properties dialog box options are listed first, with the related ALTER DATABASE keyword following in parentheses:

- **Close Cursor On Commit Enabled (cursor_close_on_commit)** When this option is set to TRUE, open cursors are closed automatically when a transaction is committed or rolled back. This behavior is in compliance with SQL-92, but the option is not set to TRUE by default. As a result, cursors remain open across transaction boundaries, and they close only when the related connection is closed or when the cursor is closed explicitly.

  NOTE SQL-92 is the most widely used version of the SQL standard and is sometimes referred to as ANSI SQL.

- **Default Cursor (cursor_default)** When this option is set to LOCAL, cursors are created with local scope unless otherwise specified. As a result, the cursor name is valid only within this scope. When the option is set to GLOBAL, cursors not explicitly set to LOCAL are created with a global scope and can be referenced in any stored procedure, batch, or trigger that the connection executes.

To manage cursor settings by using SQL Server Management Studio, follow these steps:

1. In the Object Explorer view in SQL Server Management Studio, right-click the database you want to configure, and then select Properties from the shortcut menu.

2. In the Database Properties dialog box, select Options in the Select A Page list.

3. Set the Cursor options as necessary. Click OK when you finish setting options. Your changes take effect immediately without restarting the server.

To manage the cursor settings using T-SQL, follow these steps:

1. In the Object Explorer view in SQL Server Management Studio, right-click the database you want to configure, and then select New Query from the shortcut menu.

2. In the Query view, type **ALTER DATABASE <dbname> SET <option> <option_value> GO**, where *dbname* is the name of the database you want to examine, *option* is the name of the option to set, and *option_value* is the value for the specified option. The following example shows the commands required to set cursor_default to GLOBAL for the *Personnel* database:

```
ALTER DATABASE Personnel
SET cursor_default GLOBAL
GO
```

3. Execute the query by clicking Execute or by pressing F5. If the option is set properly, the command should complete successfully.

Controlling User Access and Database State

As you might expect, managing user access and database state is a complex process. In SQL Server Management Studio, you can control the general state of the database, including whether the database is read-only or read-write and who has access to the database.

When a database is set to READ_ONLY, you can read data but not modify it. You use this option to prevent users from changing data and modifying database configuration settings. Several caveats apply when a database is read-only: automatic recovery is skipped at system startup, locking does not take place, and the database will not shrink. The normal mode is READ_WRITE, which allows the database to be read and modified.

When a database is set to SINGLE_USER, only the database owner can access the database. You use this option when you are modifying a database and want to block access to it temporarily. When a database is set to RESTRICTED_USER, only members of the db_owner, dbcreator, or sysadmin roles can use the database, though users with a valid connection might still be able to connect unless you clear the TokenAndPermUserStore cache using DBCC FREESYSTEMCACHE. When a database is set to MULTI_USER, all users with the appropriate permissions to connect to the database are permitted to use it.

To manage the database state using SQL Server Management Studio, follow these steps:

1. In the Object Explorer view in SQL Server Management Studio, right-click the database you want to configure, and then select Properties from the shortcut menu.

2. In the Database Properties dialog box, select Options in the Select A Page list. Now you can manage the database state as follows:

    -   To set the database to the READ_WRITE state, set the Database Read-Only option to False.

    -   To set the database to the READ_ONLY state, set the Database Read-Only option to True.

    -   To allow access only to the database owner, set the Restrict Access option to SINGLE_USER.

    -   To allow access to the members of the db_owner, dbcreator, or sysadmin roles, set the Restrict Access option to RESTRICTED_USER.

    -   To allow all users with the appropriate permissions to connect to the database, set the Restrict Access option to MULTIPLE_USER.

3. Click OK when you finish setting the options. Your changes take effect immediately without restarting the server.

To manage the state settings using T-SQL, follow these steps:

1. In the Object Explorer view in SQL Server Management Studio, right-click the database you want to configure, and then select New Query from the shortcut menu.

2. In the Query view, type **ALTER DATABASE** *<dbname>* **SET** *<keyword>* **GO**, where *dbname* is the name of the database you want to examine, and *keyword* is one of the following states: READ_ONLY, READ_WRITE, SINGLE_ USER, RESTRICTED_USER, or MULTI_USER. The following example shows the commands required to set the *Personnel* database for multiple-user access:

```
ALTER DATABASE Personnel
SET MULTI_USER
GO
```

3. Execute the query by clicking Execute or by pressing F5. If the option is set properly, the command should complete successfully.

Setting Online, Offline, or Emergency Mode

In SQL Server 2012, you can put an individual database online or offline, or you can set an emergency state that allows you to troubleshoot database problems. When this option is set to ONLINE, the database is open and available for use. When it is set to OFFLINE, the database is offline, and you can attach or detach it as necessary. When it is set to EMERGENCY, the database is marked READ_ONLY, logging is disabled, and access is limited to members of the sysadmin fixed server role.

> **NOTE** In SQL Server 2012, the offline or online state of a database file is maintained independently from the state of the database. For a filegroup to be available, all files in the filegroup must be online. If a filegroup is offline, you cannot query the related data using SQL statements. The query optimizer does not consider the filegroup state when selecting a query plan.

To put a database in the online, offline, or emergency state, follow these steps:

1. In the Object Explorer view in SQL Server Management Studio, right-click the database you want to configure, and then select New Query from the shortcut menu.

2. In the Query view, type **ALTER DATABASE** *<dbname>* **SET** *<keyword>* **GO**, where *dbname* is the name of the database you want to examine, and *keyword* is one of the following states: ONLINE, OFFLINE, or EMERGENCY.

The following example shows the commands required to put the *Personnel* database in the emergency state for troubleshooting:

```
ALTER DATABASE Personnel
SET EMERGENCY
GO
```

3. Execute the query by clicking Execute or by pressing F5. If the option is set properly, the command should complete successfully.

Managing Cross-Database Chaining and External Access Options

Ownership chaining is used to determine how multiple objects access each other sequentially. When chaining is allowed, SQL Server compares ownership of a calling object to the owner of the object being called. If both objects have the same owner, the object being called is considered to have the same object permissions as the calling object. In this case, you can achieve a cascade effect if the initial permissions on a view are used when the view needs access to other objects and the owners of these objects are the same.

In some limited circumstances, you might need to configure cross-database ownership chaining between specific databases and across all databases in a single instance. Although this feature is disabled by default, you can enable it by using ALTER DATABASE SET DB_CHAINING ON. When DB_CHAINING is set to TRUE (ON), the database can be the source or target of a cross-database ownership chain. You cannot set DB_CHAINING on the *master*, *model*, or *tempdb* database. You must log in as a member of the sysadmin fixed server role to set this option.

A related option is TRUSTWORTHY. When TRUSTWORTHY is set to TRUE (ON), database modules that use an impersonation context can access resources outside the database. For example, user-defined functions and stored procedures can access resources outside the database. By default, the *master* database has TRUSTWORTHY set to ON. The *model* and *tempdb* databases always have TRUSTWORTHY set to OFF, however, and the value cannot be changed for these databases. If you want to permit another database to access outside resources, you must set TRUSTWORTHY to TRUE (ON). You must be logged in as a member of the sysadmin fixed server role to set this option.

To configure chaining or trustworthiness, follow these steps:

1. In the Object Explorer view in SQL Server Management Studio, right-click the database you want to configure, and then select New Query from the shortcut menu.

2. In the Query view, type **ALTER DATABASE *<dbname>* SET *<option>* *<option_value>* GO**, where *dbname* is the name of the database you want to examine, *option* is the name of the option to set, and *option_value* is the

value for the specified option. The following example shows the commands required to turn on cross-database chaining for the *Personnel* database:

```
ALTER DATABASE Personnel
SET db_chaining ON
GO
```

3. Execute the query by clicking Execute or by pressing F5. If the option is set properly, the command should complete successfully.

Configuring Recovery, Logging, and Disk I/O Error Checking Options

SQL Server 2012 has several options for managing recovery, logging, and I/O error checking. In SQL Server Management Studio, you manage recovery settings by using the Recovery Model and Page Verify settings on the Options page. In T-SQL, you manage these options by using the ALTER DATABASE SET RECOVERY and ALTER DATABASE SET PAGE_VERIFY commands.

Three recovery options are available:

- **FULL**   When recovery is set to FULL, transactions are fully logged and the database can be recovered to the point of failure or to a specific point in time using the transaction logs.

- **BULK_LOGGED**   When recovery is set to BULK_LOGGED (managed in previous versions by using select into/bulk copy), certain SQL commands are not logged in the transaction log. These commands include using SELECT INTO and BULK INSERT with a permanent table, running fast bulk copy, using UPDATETEXT or WRITETEXT without logging, and using a table load. If you set this option and execute any command that bypasses the transaction log, you cannot recover the database from transaction logs and BACKUP LOG commands are prohibited. Instead, use BACKUP DATABASE to back up the entire database, and then later you can back up from the log (provided that you do not run any more commands that bypass the transaction log).

- **SIMPLE**   When recovery is set to SIMPLE (previously managed using trunc.log on chkpt), the transaction log can be truncated automatically. This setting allows the log to be cleared after transactions have been committed. After the transaction log has been cleared, you can perform BACKUP/RESTORE only at the database level (and not with the transaction log).

NOTE   SQL Server supports manual, automatic, indirect, and internal checkpoints. Nonmanual checkpoints occur at various times. A checkpoint is issued for each database when the SQL Server service shuts down normally. Checkpoints do not occur when the SHUTDOWN WITH NOWAIT statement is used. A checkpoint is executed in a single database when a database is changed with sp_dboption. SQL Server also automatically issues a checkpoint on a database as necessary to ensure that the designated recovery interval can be achieved and when the log becomes 70 percent full.

NOTE The transaction log must be large enough to store all active transactions. If it is not, you cannot roll back transactions. In a deployment environment, you should use this option only when you can rely solely on database backups and do not supplement them with transaction log backups. Note also that the tempdb database is always truncated at a checkpoint, regardless of the setting of this option.

Disk I/O errors can cause database corruption problems and are usually the result of power failures or disk hardware failures that occur at the time a page is written to disk. There are three page verification options to help identify incomplete I/O transactions caused by disk I/O errors:

- **CHECKSUM** When PAGE_VERIFY is set to CHECKSUM, checksums are used to find incomplete I/O transactions caused by disk I/O errors. The checksum is computed over the contents of the entire page and stored in the page header when a page is written to disk. When the page is read from disk, the checksum is recomputed and compared to the checksum value stored in the page header. When there are mismatches, error message 824 is reported to both the SQL Server error log and the Windows Event Viewer. Any I/O errors detected by the operating system are logged with error message 823.

- **TORN_PAGE_DETECTION** When PAGE_VERIFY is set to TORN_PAGE_DETECTION, a bit is reversed for each 512-byte sector in an 8-KB database page when the page is written to disk. If a bit is in the wrong state when the page is read later, the page was written incorrectly and a torn page is detected. If SQL Server detects a torn page during a user connection, it sends I/O error message 824, indicating a torn page error, and terminates the user connection. If it detects a torn page during recovery, it marks the database as suspect. In either case, you might want to restore the database from backup and apply any backup transaction logs.

  TIP You can use battery-backed disk caches to ensure that data is successfully written to disk or not written at all. But in this case, do not set torn page detection to TRUE.

- **NONE** When PAGE_VERIFY is set to NONE (OFF), future data page writes will not contain a checksum or torn page bit, and pages will not be verified at read time, even previously written pages that contain a checksum or torn page bit.

  NOTE Early versions of SQL Server used the TORN_PAGE_DETECTION option to help detect I/O errors. This option is still supported, but its use usually is rejected in favor of CHECKSUM. When TORN_PAGE_DETECTION is set to TRUE (ON), SQL Server automatically detects incomplete I/O operations known as torn pages.

SQL Server 2012 also supports supplemental logging, which adds information to the logs for third-party products. You can enable logging of additional information by setting the SUPPLEMENTAL_LOGGING option to TRUE (ON). Using this option adds a lot of information to the logs, however, and can have an impact on overall performance.

Viewing, Changing, and Overriding Database Options

Although SQL Server Management Studio makes setting database options easy, you often will want to use SQL commands to view or change options. To do this, you can use the sp_dboption stored procedure, individual SET commands, or the ALTER DATABASE command. Tasks that you can perform with the sp_dboption and SET commands include the following:

- **Displaying an options list** To display a list of available options, type **EXEC sp_dboption.**

- **Viewing database option settings** To view the current option settings for a database, type **EXEC sp_dboption *<dbname>***, where *dbname* is the name of the database you want to examine, such as EXEC sp_dboption Subs.

- **Enabling database options** To turn on a database option, type **ALTER DATABASE *<dbname>* SET *<option>***, where *dbname* is the name of the database you want to examine and *option* is the name of the option flag to set to the TRUE (ON) state.

- **Setting specific database option values** To set a specific database option value, type **ALTER DATABASE *<dbname>* SET *<option>* *<option_value>***, where *dbname* is the name of the database you want to examine, *option* is the name of the option to set, and *option_value* is the value for the specified option.

- **Overriding database options** Use SET options for individual sessions or database drivers to override default settings. You can also check options by using properties of the Databaseproperty function. See the "Working with SET Options" section in Chapter 4 for more information.

NOTE The sp_dboption stored procedure should not be used to modify the master and tempdb databases. It is supported only for backward compatibility, and it should be used primarily to display database options. Whenever possible, use the ALTER DATABASE command to modify database options instead.

Managing Database and Log Size

With SQL Server 2012, you can manage database and log size automatically or manually. You can use SQL Server Management Studio or T-SQL to configure database and log size. This section looks primarily at configuring these settings through SQL Server Management Studio.

Configuring SQL Server to Manage File Size Automatically

To configure automatic management of database and log size in SQL Server Management Studio, complete the following steps:

1. Start SQL Server Management Studio. In the Object Explorer view, connect to the appropriate server, and then work your way down to the Databases folder.

2. Right-click the database you want to configure, and then select Properties from the shortcut menu.

3. Select Files in the Select A Page list in the Database Properties dialog box. Each data and log file associated with the database is listed under Database Files. For each data and log file, do the following:

   a. Click the button to the right of the file's Autogrowth box to display the Change Autogrowth For dialog box.

   b. Set the file to grow using a percentage or an amount in megabytes, and then either restrict the maximum file growth to a specific size or allow unrestricted file growth.

   c. Click OK.

4. Optionally, access the Options page and set Auto Shrink to True. Auto Shrink compacts and shrinks the database periodically.

5. Click OK. Your changes take effect immediately without restarting the server.

NOTE See the "Creating Databases in SQL Server Management Studio" section earlier in this chapter for tips and advice on sizing databases and transaction logs.

Expanding Databases and Logs Manually

Sometimes you might want to increase the size of a database or log file manually. You can do this by completing the following steps:

1. Start SQL Server Management Studio. In the Object Explorer view, connect to the appropriate server, and then work your way down to the Databases folder.

2. Right-click the database you want to configure, and then select Properties from the shortcut menu.

3. Select Files in the Select A Page list in the Database Properties dialog box. Each data and log file associated with the database is listed under Database Files.

4. To expand a data file, click in the related Initial Size box, and then enter a larger file size.

   You also can create and size a new secondary file for the database. The advantage of using a new file rather than an existing file is that SQL Server does not need to lock what might be an active database file to expand the database.

5. To expand a log file, click in the appropriate Initial Size box, and then enter a larger file size in the text box that becomes available. You can also create and size a new transaction log file.

    TIP With data and log files, the new file size must be larger than the current size. If it is not, you get an error. The reason is that shrinking the database is handled in a different way. See the following section, "Compressing and Shrinking a Database Manually," for more details.

6. Click OK to make the changes. SQL Server locks the database while expanding it, which blocks access.

    TIP You can add files using T-SQL as well. The command you use to do this is ALTER DATABASE. For more information about using this command, see the "Altering Databases and Their Options" section earlier in this chapter.

Compressing and Shrinking a Database Manually

Compressing and shrinking a database is a bit different from expanding it, and in many cases, you want finer control over the process than you get with the Auto Shrink option. Fortunately, you can manage this process manually, and you also can schedule this process on a recurring basis if needed. However, as with auto-growing, don't configure a database to shrink without carefully looking at the performance impact. Not only does shrinking lock the database until the operation is complete, shrinking may trigger auto-grow. You don't want contention between auto-grow and shrink events, and you don't want the database to become overly fragmented from too many auto-grow events.

To compress or shrink all database files (both data and log files) manually in SQL Server Management Studio, complete the following steps:

1. Start SQL Server Management Studio. In the Object Explorer view, connect to the appropriate server, and then work your way down to the Databases folder.

2. Right-click the database you want to configure. Select Tasks from the shortcut menu, choose Shrink, and then choose Database to display the Shrink Database dialog box, shown in Figure 6-5.

3. The Database Size area in the dialog box shows the total amount of space allocated to all database files and the amount of free space. Use this information to decide if you really want to shrink the database.

4. To reorganize data pages and move them to the beginning of the data files, select the Reorganize Files Before Releasing Unused Space check box. This compresses the data pages but does not remove empty data pages.

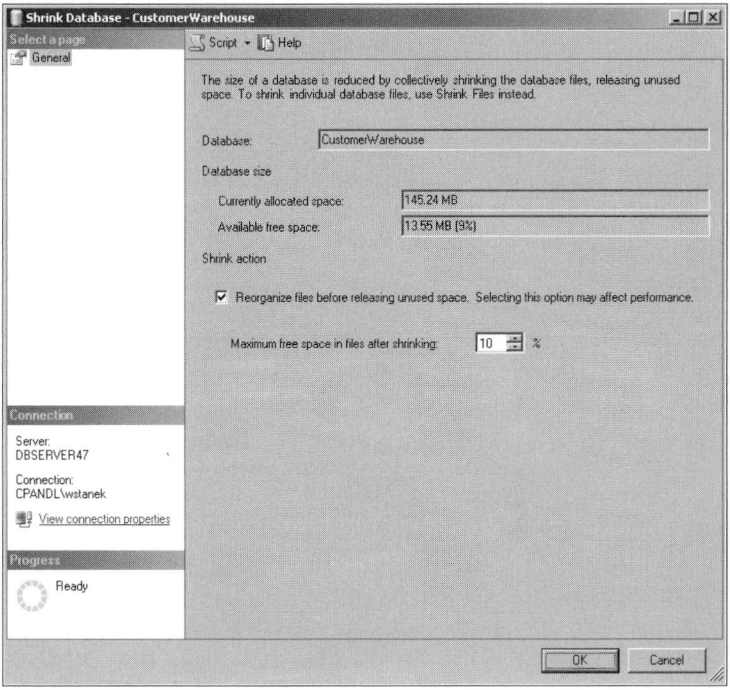

FIGURE 6-5 The Shrink Database dialog box.

NOTE Selecting the Reorganize Files Before Releasing Unused Space option performs the same task accomplished by using DBCC SHRINKDATABASE and specifying the amount of free space that you want in the database after shrinking it. If you clear the check box for this option, the database files are compressed in the same way as when you use DBCC SHRINKDATABASE with TRUNCATEONLY, which means that the file size is reduced without moving any data or reallocating rows to unallocated pages.

NOTE Log files are not reduced in size immediately. Instead, the size is reduced when the transaction log is backed up or the log is truncated, whichever occurs first. Also, you normally cannot shrink a database to a size smaller than the *model* database (which is the database template).

5. In the Maximum Free Space In Files After Shrinking box, set the percentage of free space in the database. To squeeze all the extra space out of the database, use a value of 0 percent, but be aware that the next write operation might cause the database to grow automatically.

6. Click OK to begin. Although other users can be working in the database as it shrinks, you cannot shrink a database while the database is being backed up.

To compress or shrink individual database files manually in SQL Server Management Studio, complete the following steps:

1. Start SQL Server Management Studio. In the Object Explorer view, connect to the appropriate server, and then work your way down to the Databases folder.

2. Right-click the database you want to configure. Select Tasks from the shortcut menu, choose Shrink, and then choose Files to display the Shrink File dialog box, shown in Figure 6-6.

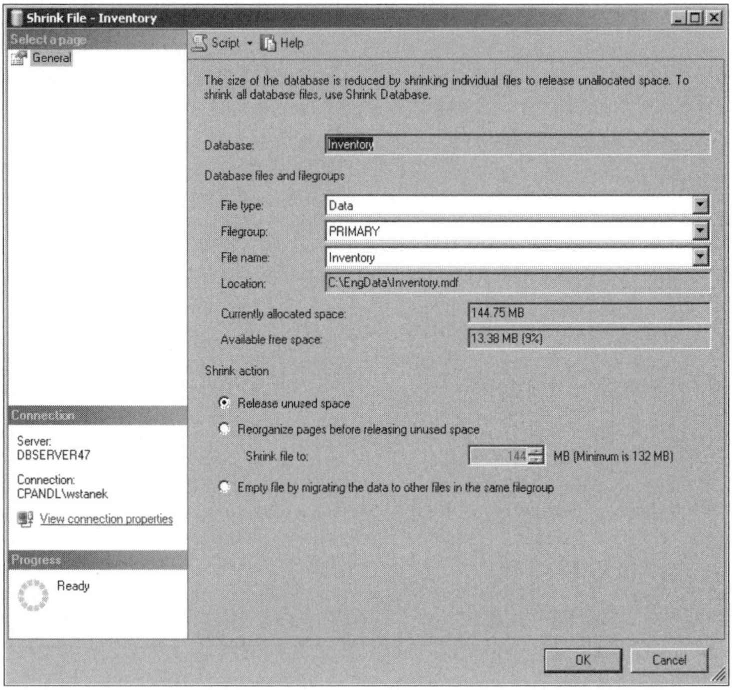

FIGURE 6-6 The Shrink File dialog box.

3. Use the File Type, Filegroup, and File Name lists to select the data or log file that you want to shrink. When you select a specific file, the total amount of space allocated and the amount of free space are shown. Use this information to decide whether you really want to shrink the file.

4. Choose a shrink action as follows:

- **Release Unused Space** Truncates free space from the end of the file. Unused space is released, and the file is reduced in size to the last allocated extent. The file size is reduced without moving any data or reallocating rows to unallocated pages. You can accomplish the same task by using DBCC SHRINKDATABASE with TRUNCATEONLY and specifying the target file.

- **Reorganize Pages Before Releasing Unused Space**   Reorganizes data pages and moves them to the beginning of the data files. This compresses the data pages but does not remove empty data pages. You can accomplish the same task by using DBCC SHRINKDATABASE and specifying the amount of free space that you want in a target file after shrinking it. After you select this option, set the file size by selecting a value in the Shrink File To box. The size cannot be less than the current allocated space or more than the total extents allocated.

- **Empty File By Migrating The Data**   Migrates the data in this file to other files in the same filegroup. This option is equivalent to executing DBCC SHRINKFILE with the EMPTYFILE option, and it allows the file to be dropped later using the ALTER DATABASE command.

5. Click OK. Other users can be working in the database as a file is shrunk.

Another way to shrink a database is to use T-SQL. Two commands are provided, as shown in Sample 6-3.

SAMPLE 6-3 DBCC SHRINKDATABASE and DBCC SHRINKFILE Syntax.

DBCC SHRINKDATABASE Syntax

```
DBCC SHRINKDATABASE ( "database_name" | database_id | 0
    [ ,target_percent ]
    [ , { NOTRUNCATE | TRUNCATEONLY } ] )
[ WITH NO_INFOMSGS ]
```

DBCC SHRINKFILE Syntax

```
DBCC SHRINKFILE (    { " file_name " | file_id }
    { [ , EMPTYFILE]
    | [ [ , target_size ] [ , { NOTRUNCATE | TRUNCATEONLY } ] ]
    } )
[ WITH NO_INFOMSGS ]
```

You use DBCC SHRINKDATABASE to shrink all data files in the database and DBCC SHRINKFILE to shrink a specific data file. By default, these commands also compress the database. You can override this option with TRUNCATEONLY or use NOTRUNCATE to specify that you only want to compress the database. To suppress informational messages, use WITH NO_INFOMSGS.

The following command compresses and then shrinks the *Customer* database to 30 percent free space:

```
DBCC SHRINKDATABASE ( Customer, 30 )
```

The following commands compress and then shrink an individual file in the *Customer* database to 5 MB of free space:

```
USE Customer
DBCC SHRINKFILE ( Customer_Data, 5 )
```

NOTE The DBCC SHRINKFILE command is the only method you can use to shrink individual data and log files to make them smaller than their original size. With DBCC SHRINKFILE, you must shrink each file individually rather than try to shrink the entire database. Additionally, the truncation options for DBCC SHRINKDATABASE and DBCC SHRINKFILE apply only to data files; they are ignored for log files. You cannot truncate transaction logs with these commands.

Manipulating Databases

Other core administration tasks include renaming, dropping, deleting, detaching, and attaching databases. These tasks are examined in this section.

Renaming a Database

Although you cannot rename system databases, you can rename user databases by using either SQL Server Management Studio or the ALTER DATABASE MODIFY NAME statement. With the database in single-user or offline mode, right-click the database name in SQL Server Management Studio and select Rename from the shortcut menu. Then type the database name and press Tab.

To use T-SQL to put the database in single-user mode and change the name, complete the following steps:

1. Ask all users to disconnect from the database. Make sure that all SQL Server Management Studio connections to the database are closed. If necessary, stop the user processes, as explained in Chapter 1, "Managing Your SQL Servers."

2. Access the Query view in SQL Server Management Studio, and then put the database in single-user mode. The following example puts a database called *Customer* in single-user mode:

```
use master
ALTER DATABASE Customer
SET single_user
GO
```

TIP You execute commands in the Query view by clicking Execute or by pressing F5. With SQLCMD, you can execute commands by entering the GO statement.

3. Rename the database by using the ALTER DATABASE statement. In the following example, the *Customer* database is renamed *cust*:

```
ALTER DATABASE Customer
MODIFY NAME = cust
GO
```

4. After you run the SQL commands, set the renamed database back to multiuser mode. The following example sets the *cust* database to multiuser mode:

```
ALTER DATABASE cust
SET multi_user
GO
```

5. Be sure that all commands, applications, and processes that use the old database name point to the new database name. If you do not do this, you will have problems using the database.

Dropping and Deleting a Database

In SQL Server 2012, dropping and deleting a database are the same thing. When you drop a database, you remove the database and its associated files from the server. After you drop a database, it is deleted permanently, and you cannot restore it without using a backup. To delete references to a database without removing the database files, use sp_detach_db, as described later in this section.

You cannot drop system databases, and you cannot drop databases that are currently in use by SQL Server or other users. A database can be dropped regardless of its state. However, any replication or database snapshots on a database must be stopped or dropped before the database can be deleted. Furthermore, if the database is configured for log shipping, you should remove log shipping before dropping the database. Also note that a dropped database can be re-created only by restoring a backup. After you drop a database, you should back up the *master* database.

You can drop a database by completing the following steps:

1. In SQL Server Management Studio, right-click the database you want to drop, and then select Delete to display the Delete Object dialog box.

2. To delete backup and history information from the *msdb* database, select the Delete Backup And Restore History Information For Databases check box.

3. To close existing connections to the database before deleting it, select the Close Existing Connections check box.

   NOTE You cannot drop a database that is being used by SQL Server or by other users. For example, if you are restoring the database or the database is published for replication, you cannot delete it. You also cannot delete the database if there are any active user sessions.

4. Click OK. Optionally, back up the *master* database as explained in Chapter 11, "SQL Server 2012 Backup and Recovery." You back up the *master* database to ensure that the most current system information is stored and that information from the old database will not be restored accidentally with the *master* database.

You also can delete a database with the DROP DATABASE command. The syntax and usage for this command are shown in Sample 6-4.

SAMPLE 6-4 DROP DATABASE Syntax and Usage.

Syntax

```
DROP DATABASE { database_name | database_snapshot_name} [ ,...n ]
```

Usage

```
use master
ALTER DATABASE Customer
SET single_user
GO
DROP DATABASE "Customer"
GO
```

Attaching and Detaching Databases

The attach and detach operations are designed primarily to move database files or disable databases without deleting their files. When you detach a database, you remove references to the server in the *master* database, but you do not delete the related database files. Detached databases are not displayed in SQL Server Management Studio, and they are not accessible to users. If you want to use the database again, you can reattach it. Attaching a database creates a new database that references data stored in existing data and log files.

Before you can detach a database, you must ensure that none of the following conditions is true:

- A database snapshot exists on the database. You must drop all of the database's snapshots before you can detach the database. Snapshots can be deleted, but they cannot be detached or attached.

- The database is being mirrored. You must stop database mirroring and end the mirror session.

- The database is replicated and published. If it is replicated, the database must be unpublished. Before you can detach it, you need to disable publishing by running sp_replicationdboption or sp_removedbreplication.

- The database is suspect. You must put the database into EMERGENCY mode and then detach it.

Usually, attaching a database places it in the same state that it was in when it was detached. However, SQL Server 2012 disables cross-database ownership chaining and sets the TRUSTWORTHY option to OFF when a database is attached. You can re-enable these features if necessary, as discussed in the "Managing Cross-Database Chaining and External Access Options" section earlier in this chapter.

When you attach a database, all primary and secondary data files must be available. If any data file has a different path than it had when the database was first created or last attached, you must specify the file's current path.

Detaching a Database

When you detach a database, you can specify if you want to update the statistics before the database is detached. Updating statistics makes the database easier to use with read-only media; otherwise, you really do not need the update. To update statistics, set the skipchecks flag to FALSE.

Because full-text catalogs are associated with databases in SQL Server 2012, you also can control whether they are maintained or dropped during the detach operation. By default, full-text catalogs are maintained as part of the database. To drop catalogs, set the KeepFullTextIndexFile flag to FALSE.

You detach a database by using sp_detach_db, as shown in Sample 6-5.

SAMPLE 6-5 sp_detach_db Syntax and Usage.

Syntax

```
sp_detach_db [ @dbname= ] "dbname"
    [ , [ @skipchecks= ] "skipchecks" ]
    [ , [ @KeepFulltextIndexFile= ] "KeepFulltextIndexFile" ]
```

Usage

```
exec sp_detach_db "sample", "true"
```

> **TIP** You cannot detach system databases, and you can detach user databases only when they are not in use. Furthermore, before detaching a user database, you might want to close all current connections, put the database in single-user mode, and then run the detach operation.

Using SQL Server Management Studio, you can detach a database by following these steps:

1. With the database in single-user or offline mode, right-click the database name in SQL Server Management Studio, point to Tasks, and select Detach from the shortcut menu.

2. Use the options provided in the Detach Database dialog box to specify whether you want to update statistics, keep full-text catalogs, or both.

3. The Status column displays the current database state as either Ready or Not Ready. If the status is Not Ready, click the link in the Message column to get more information. Otherwise, click OK to detach the database.

Attaching a Database with Multiple Files

When you reattach a database, use the CREATE DATABASE statement with FOR ATTACH. For this statement to work, all primary and secondary data files must be available. If the database has multiple log files, all the log files must be available. The only exception is for a read-write database with a single log file that is currently unavailable. If the database was shut down with no users or open transactions before it was detached, FOR ATTACH automatically rebuilds the log file and updates the primary data file as appropriate. The log file for a read-only database cannot be rebuilt because the primary data file cannot be updated; you must provide the log file or files in the FOR ATTACH clause.

Any full-text catalogs that are part of the database will be attached with the database. To specify a new path to the full-text catalog, you can specify the catalog file by supplying a directory name without a file name.

When you use the CREATE DATABASE statement with FOR ATTACH, you can specify only the primary file name. This file contains pointers to the original locations of all other database files. If the other files have not changed location, you can specify only the primary file name and then let the Database Engine use the primary file to find the rest of the files.

Sample 6-6 shows the code required to attach the database by using the CREATE DATABASE statement with FOR ATTACH.

SAMPLE 6-6 The CREATE DATABASE Statement with FOR ATTACH Syntax and Usage.

Syntax

```
CREATE DATABASE database_name
    ON <filespec> [ ,...n ]
    FOR { ATTACH [ WITH <service_broker_option> ]
        | ATTACH_REBUILD_LOG }
[;]

<filespec> ::=
{
( [ NAME = logical_file_name , ]
    FILENAME = { "os_file_name" | "filestream_path" }
        [ , SIZE = size [ KB | MB | GB | TB ] ]
        [ , MAXSIZE = { max_size [ KB | MB | GB | TB ] | UNLIMITED }]
        [ , FILEGROWTH = growth_increment [ KB | MB | GB | TB | % ] ]
) [ ,...n ]
}
```

Usage

```
CREATE DATABASE Customer
ON (FILENAME = "c:\data\customer_data.mdf")
FOR ATTACH
GO
```

Using SQL Server Management Studio, you can attach a database by following these steps:

1. With the database in single-user or offline mode, right-click the database name in SQL Server Management Studio, point to Tasks, and select Attach from the shortcut menu.

2. In the Attach Databases dialog box, click Add to specify the database to be attached.

3. Use the Locate Database Files dialog box to locate and select the database's .mdf file. Click OK.

4. In the upper panel of the Attach Databases dialog box, note the database name, the Attach As name, and the owner. To attach the database with a different name, enter the name in the Attach As column. To change the owner of the database, click in the Owner column and select a different owner.

5. Click OK to attach the database.

Attaching a Database with Only Data Files

You might not need old transaction logs in a new database. If this is the case, you can restore only data files and let SQL Server create new log files for you. To do this, use the CREATE DATABASE statement with FOR ATTACH_REBUILD_LOG, as shown in Sample 6-7.

SAMPLE 6-7 The CREATE DATABASE Statement with FOR ATTACH_REBUILD_LOG Syntax and Usage.

Syntax

```
CREATE DATABASE database_name
    ON <filespec> [ ,...n ]
    FOR ATTACH_REBUILD_LOG }
[;]

<filespec> ::=
{
[ PRIMARY ]
(
    [ NAME = logical_file_name , ]
    FILENAME = "os_file_name"
        [ , SIZE = size [ KB | MB | GB | TB ] ]
        [ , MAXSIZE = { max_size [ KB | MB | GB | TB ] | UNLIMITED }]
        [ , FILEGROWTH = growth_increment [ KB | MB | % ] ]
) [ ,...n ]
}
```

Usage

```
CREATE DATABASE Customer
ON (FILENAME = "c:\data\customer_data.mdf")
FOR ATTACH_REBUILD_LOG
GO
```

Using SQL Server Management Studio, you can attach a database with only data files by following these steps:

1. With the database in single-user or offline mode, right-click the database name in SQL Server Management Studio, point to Tasks, and select Attach from the shortcut menu.

2. In the Attach Databases dialog box, click Add to specify the database to be attached.

3. Use the Locate Database Files dialog box to locate and select the database's .mdf file. Click OK.

4. In the upper panel of the Attach Databases dialog box, note the database name, the Attach As name, and the owner. To attach the database with a different name, enter the name in the Attach As column. To change the owner of the database, click in the Owner column and select a different owner.

5. In the lower panel of the Attach Databases dialog box, note the data and log files associated with the database. Remove each log file in turn by clicking it in the list to select it and then clicking Remove.

6. When you are ready to continue, click OK to attach the database.

Tips and Techniques

All great administrators know a few tricks to help manage databases more efficiently and keep things running smoothly. Here are a few tips to help you with database administration.

Copying and Moving Databases

All databases except the *model*, *msdb*, and *master* databases can be copied or moved using the Copy Database Wizard. You also can use this wizard to create a copy of a database, to copy or move databases between different instances of SQL Server, and to upgrade databases from SQL Server 2005 or SQL Server 2008 to SQL Server 2012. The Copy Database Wizard uses one of two techniques for copy and move operations:

- **Detach and Attach** This method is the fastest way to copy a database, but it requires the source database to be offline so that it can be detached and then copied and moved. The database is then reattached when the copy/move operation is complete. To use this technique, you must be a member of the sysadmin fixed server role on both the source and destination servers. Also, you should place the database in single-user mode before starting the copy operation to ensure that there are no active sessions. If there are active sessions, the Copy Database Wizard will not execute the move or copy operation.

- **SQL Management Object** This method is slower, but it does not require the source database to be offline. To use this technique, you must be a database owner of the source database and you must have the CREATE DATABASE permission or be a member of the dbcreator fixed server role on the destination database. You do not have to place the database in single-user mode prior to starting the copy/move operation. Active connections are allowed during the operation because the database is never taken offline.

NOTE The copy/move operation preserves full-text catalogs if both the source and destination servers are SQL Server 2012 servers. However, if the source server is a SQL Server 2005 server, the full-text catalogs must be rebuilt and fully populated again after the copy/move operation is complete.

When you move databases between different servers or disk drives, the Copy Database Wizard copies the database to the destination server and verifies that it is online. When you move databases between two instances on the same server, a file system move operation is performed. If you elect to move a database, the Copy Database Wizard deletes the source database automatically after the move is complete. However, the Copy Database Wizard does not delete the source database when you perform a copy operation.

You can copy or move a database by completing the following steps:

1. In SQL Server Management Studio, right-click a database in the Object Explorer view, point to Tasks, and then select Copy Database.

    NOTE To use the detach and attach method, the SQL Server Agent service must be running and the SQL Server Agent job must be running under an Integration Services Proxy account that can access the file system on both the source and destination servers. For this reason, you should be sure that the SQL Server Agent is running on the destination server before you begin. In SQL Server Management Studio, you can start the SQL Server Agent service by right-clicking the related node and then selecting Start.

2. If the Welcome page is displayed when the Copy Database Wizard starts, click Next.

3. On the Select A Source Server page, specify the server that has the database you want to copy or move. Type the Domain Name System (DNS) or host name of the source server, such as SQLSERVER52. (See Figure 6-7.) Alternatively, you can click the button to the right of the Source Server box to browse for available source servers.

4. Windows authentication is used by default, which means that your current login credentials are used to determine if you have appropriate permissions. If you want to use SQL Server authentication, select Use SQL Server Authentication, and then enter your SQL Server user name and password in the text boxes provided. Click Next.

5. On the Select A Destination Server page, specify the server to which you are copying or moving the selected database, and then specify the authentication technique to use. Click Next.

    NOTE SQL Server Agent must be running on the destination server.

6. Select the transfer method—either Use The Detach And Attach Method or Use The SQL Management Object Method. If you choose to detach and attach the database, the source database is reattached automatically by default if failure occurs. To prevent this, clear the If A Failure Occurs, Reattach The Database check box. Click Next.

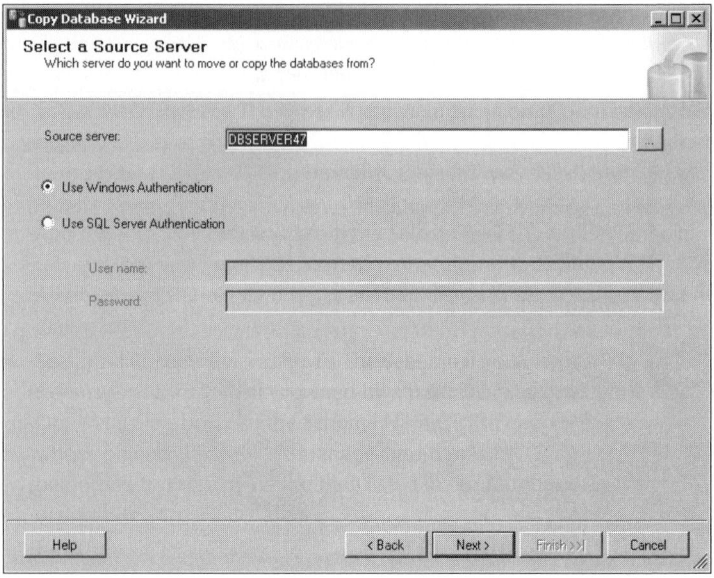

FIGURE 6-7 The Select A Source Server page of the Copy Database Wizard.

7. As shown in Figure 6-8, you now can select the database you want to copy or move. Click Next.

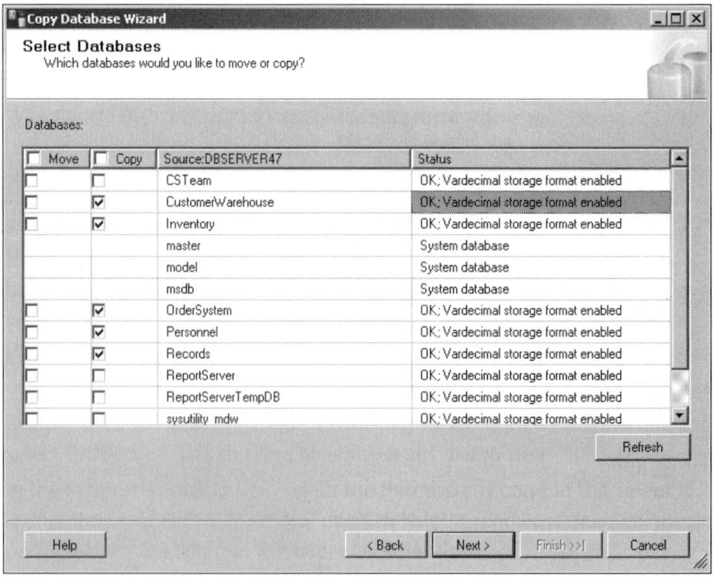

FIGURE 6-8 The Select Databases page of the Copy Database Wizard.

8. Use the Configure Destination Database page shown in Figure 6-9 to define the destination configuration of each database you are copying or moving, one at a time. Pay particular attention to the Source Database and Destination Database boxes. The Source Database box shows the current name of the database on the source. Use the Destination Database box to set the name that will be used on the destination server.

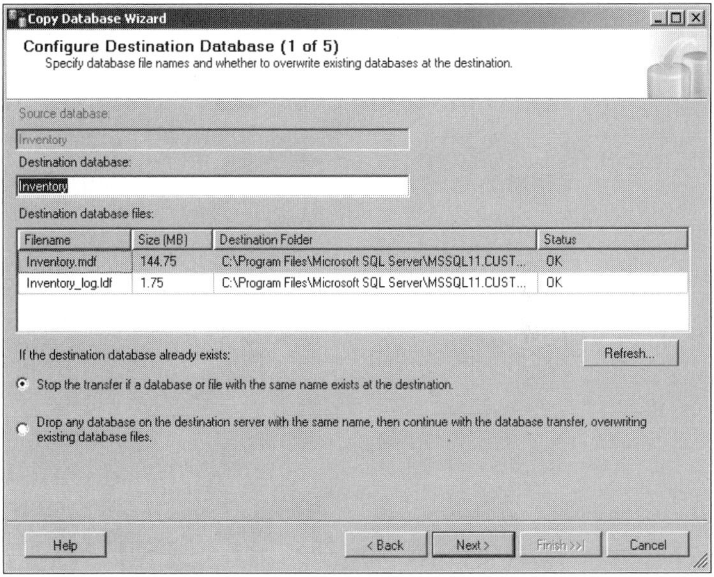

FIGURE 6-9 The Configure Destination Database page of the Copy Database Wizard.

9. Any data and log files associated with the database are shown with their destination file name and folder. You can change the default locations by typing new values. If you are creating a copy of a database on the same source and destination instance, be sure to change the database name and file names.

10. If the destination database already exists, the default option is to stop the transfer. You can drop the existing database and force the transfer by selecting the Drop Any Database option.

11. Click Next. If you are copying or moving multiple databases, you see a Configure Destination Database page for each database. Afterward, you'll be able to select additional objects outside the databases that you want to copy, including stored procedures, SQL Server Agent jobs, user-defined error messages, endpoints, and SQL Server Integration Services (SSIS) packages. Add objects as appropriated and then click Next.

12. On the Configure The Package page, set the package name and logging options you prefer. If you want to save the transfer logs, select the related check box. Click Next.

13. You can run the wizard now or schedule the wizard to run at a later time. To run the wizard immediately and perform the copy/move operations, select Run Immediately. To schedule the wizard to run at a later time, select Schedule, and then click Change Schedule. You then will be able to schedule this task as a new job. See Chapter 10 for details on scheduling.

14. Click Next. Review your choices, and then click Finish. The wizard performs the necessary tasks to prepare and create the copy/move package. If a critical error occurs during these tasks, the operation fails, and you should view the report to determine what error occurred and then resolve it.

Moving Databases

You can use the ALTER DATABASE statement to move any system or user-defined database files except for Resource database files. To move files, you specify the current logical name of the file and the new file path, which includes the new file name. You can move only one file at a time in this manner.

To move data or log files to a new location, follow these steps:

1. Get the logical name of the data and log files associated with the database by typing the following:

```
USE master
SELECT name, physical_name
FROM sys.master_files
WHERE database_id = DB_ID("Personnel");
```

2. Take the database you want to work with offline by typing these commands:

```
ALTER DATABASE Personnel
SET offline
GO
```

3. Move one file at a time to the new location by typing the following:

```
ALTER DATABASE Personnel
MODIFY FILE ( NAME = Personnel_Data, FILENAME =
"C:\Data\Personnel_Data.mdf")
GO
```

4. Repeat the previous step to move other data and log files.

5. Put the database online by typing the following commands:

```
ALTER DATABASE Personnel
SET online
GO
```

You can verify the change or changes by typing this:

```
USE master
SELECT name, physical_name
FROM sys.master_files
WHERE database_id = DB_ID("Personnel");
```

You can move full-text catalogs by their logical name as well. However, when specifying the new catalog location, you specify only new_path rather than new_path/file_name. To move a full-text catalog file to a new location, follow these steps:

1. Take the database you want to work with offline by typing the following:

```
ALTER DATABASE database_name
SET offline
GO
```

2. Move one file at a time to the new location by typing these commands:

```
ALTER DATABASE database_name
MODIFY FILE ( NAME = logical_name, FILENAME = "new_path".
GO
```

3. Repeat step 2 to move other full-text catalog files as necessary.

4. Put the database online by typing the following:

```
ALTER DATABASE database_name
SET online
GO
```

Moving and Resizing *tempdb*

The *tempdb* database contains temporary tables created by users, by SQL Server, or by both. SQL Server 2012 does not store complete transactions for temporary tables in *tempdb*. With temporary tables, SQL Server 2012 stores enough information to roll back a transaction but not enough to redo a transaction.

The *tempdb* database is created each time you start the SQL Server service, which ensures that the database starts clean. As with other databases, the default structure of *tempdb* is based on the *model* database. This means that each time you start SQL Server, a snapshot is taken of the current *model* database and applied to *tempdb*.

By default, the *tempdb* primary data file has a size of 8 MB and is set to grow the database automatically by 10 percent when necessary. On a busy server, this 8 MB can fill up quickly, and as a result, the server might need to expand *tempdb* frequently. Unfortunately, while *tempdb* is expanding SQL Server locks the database.

This can slow down queries and make the server seem unresponsive. Here are some ways you can improve the performance of *tempdb*:

- Expand *tempdb* permanently to accommodate space needs during busy periods. To do this, follow the steps described in the "Expanding Databases and Logs Manually" section earlier in this chapter. Even if the *model* database is smaller, *tempdb* retains this new size.

- By default, *tempdb* is stored in the same location as other data. To resolve any performance issues, you can create a secondary data file for *tempdb* and put this file on its own drive. Or you can move *tempdb* and all its associated files to a new location.

You can move individual *tempdb* files or all *tempdb* files by completing the following steps:

1. Get the logical name of the data and log files associated with *tempdb* by typing the following:

```
USE master
SELECT name, physical_name
FROM sys.master_files
WHERE database_id = DB_ID('tempdb');
GO
```

2. Move each data and log file to a new location one at a time by typing these commands:

```
USE master
GO
ALTER DATABASE tempdb
MODIFY FILE (NAME = logical_name, FILENAME = 'new_path/file_name')
GO
```

3. Repeat step 2 to move other data and log files as necessary.

4. Stop and restart SQL Server.

You can verify the change or changes by typing the following:

```
USE master
SELECT name, physical_name
FROM sys.master_files
WHERE database_id = DB_ID('tempdb');
```

Creating Secondary Data and Log Files

Secondary data and log files can improve the performance of busy databases and can help make large databases easier to manage. You might want to create secondary files to distribute the load over several drives. For example, you could place the primary file on drive D, secondary files on drive E, and transaction logs on drive F.

Another reason you might want to create secondary files is to make restoring a large database easier. For example, if you have a 100-GB database in a single file, you can restore the database only on a drive with 100 GB of space (not including required overhead), which you might not have if a drive fails at 3:00 A.M. on a Sunday. Instead, create several smaller files for the database, such as five 20-GB files, and then you can restore these files to several drives if necessary.

You can create secondary data or log files by completing the following steps:

1. Start SQL Server Management Studio. In the Object Explorer view, connect to the appropriate server, and then work your way down to the Databases folder.

2. Right-click the database you want to manage, and then select Properties to open the Database Properties dialog box.

3. Select the Files page in the Select A Page list in the Database Properties dialog box.

4. On the Files page, click Add to set a secondary data file. Then, in the Database Files area, type a new file name, such as Personnel_Data2 or Personnel_Log2.

5. Set the file type:
   - To create the new file as a data file, select Data under File Type.
   - To create the new file as a log file, select Log under File Type.

6. Set the initial size of the file, click the button to the right of the Autogrowth box, and then set Autogrowth options for the new data or log file.

7. Click the button to the right of the Path box to find a new path, or you can enter a new path directly. The file name is set based on the logical name and file type.

8. Click OK to make the changes.

Preventing Transaction Log Errors

The transaction log is essential to the smooth running of SQL Server. If the log fills up or otherwise fails, SQL Server cannot process most types of queries. To ensure that the transaction log runs smoothly, you might want to use these techniques:

- To reduce the load on the transaction log, use SQL commands that are not logged. This invalidates the transaction logs, as explained in Chapter 10.

- To ensure that the log is cleaned out periodically, set the database Recovery Model to Simple. This invalidates the transaction logs, as explained in Chapter 10.

- To prevent the log from running out of space, do not set a maximum file size, but do increase the frequency of the log backup and watch the amount of free drive space closely.

- To make sure you can recover transactions, increase the permanent size of the log and increase the frequency of the log backup.

Preventing a Filegroup Is Full Error

When you encounter a situation in which writing to a data file is not possible, you will see a Filegroup Is Full error. This error usually occurs when the data file has reached its maximum size or you have run out of file space. To reduce the chances of this error reoccurring, you can use the following techniques:

- Do not set a maximum file size.
- Watch the amount of free drive space closely.
- Remove unused tables, indexes, or objects.

You also might want to schedule data files to be compacted periodically. However, do this only after carefully considering the possible performance impact and subsequent auto-grow operations that can occur. You don't want there to be contention between auto-grow and shrink events, and you don't want the database to become overly fragmented from too many auto-grow events.

Creating a New Database Template

The *model* database is used as the template for all new databases. You can avoid repetitive work by modifying the options and properties of the *model* database; then any new databases created on the server will inherit these options and properties.

Configuring Database Encryption

SQL Server 2012 provides Transparent Data Encryption (TDE) as a database encryption solution. When enabled, TDE performs real-time I/O encryption and decryption of data and log files. TDE relies on a database encryption key (DEK) stored as a certificate in the *master* database or an asymmetric key protected by an encryption module. Encrypting a database with TDE provides physical protection for the data and log files but does not provide encryption across communication channels. You can encrypt communication channels as discussed in the "Configuring Security for Native Client Configurations" section in Chapter 2. Also keep in mind that when you use TDE, FILESTREAM data is not encrypted.

Before you can use TDE, you must create a master key, create or obtain a certificate protected by the master key, and create a DEK and protect it by the certificate. Afterward, you must enable encryption for the database. Sample 6-8 provides the syntax and usage for the related T-SQL commands.

SAMPLE 6-8 Configuring Database Encryption.

Syntax

```
USE master;
GO
CREATE MASTER KEY ENCRYPTION BY PASSWORD = 'Password';
GO
CREATE CERTIFICATE CertificateName WITH SUBJECT =
```

```
                'CertificateSubject'
GO
USE DatabaseName
GO
CREATE DATABASE ENCRYPTION KEY
        WITH ALGORITHM = { AES_128 | AES_192 | AES_256
            | TRIPLE_DES_3KEY }
        ENCRYPTION BY SERVER CERTIFICATE CertificateName
GO
ALTER DATABASE DatabaseName
SET ENCRYPTION ON
GO
```

Usage

```
USE master;
GO
CREATE MASTER KEY ENCRYPTION BY PASSWORD = 'ObyGoxDandy2974728';
GO
CREATE CERTIFICATE PersDBCert WITH SUBJECT = 'Certificate for
        Personnel DB'
GO
USE Personnel
GO
CREATE DATABASE ENCRYPTION KEY WITH ALGORITHM = TRIPLE_DES_3KEY
        ENCRYPTION BY SERVER CERTIFICATE PersDBCert
GO
ALTER DATABASE Personnel
SET ENCRYPTION ON
GO
```

To manage the encryption state of the database by using SQL Server
Management Studio, follow these steps:

1. In the Object Explorer view in SQL Server Management Studio, right-click
   the database you want to configure, and then select Properties from the
   shortcut menu.

2. In the Database Properties dialog box, select Options from the Select A Page
   list. Now you can do the following:

   - Turn on database encryption by setting Encryption Enabled to True.
   - Turn off database encryption by setting Encryption Enabled to False.

3. Click OK when you finish setting the options. Your changes take effect
   immediately without restarting the server.

You can determine the state of database encryption by using the
sys.dm_database_encryption_keys view. Once you enable TDE, all files and
filegroups in the database are encrypted. If any filegroups in a database are
marked READ ONLY, the database encryption operation will fail. With database
mirroring or log shipping, both databases will be encrypted and the log
transactions will be encrypted when sent between the database servers.

When you enable encryption, the Database Engine closes the virtual transaction log and starts the next virtual transaction log to ensure that no clear text is left after the database is set for encryption. The *tempdb* system database is encrypted for similar reasons. Additionally, any new full-text indexes are encrypted when a database is set for encryption.

> **TIP** Once encrypted, data will not compress well. Because of this, Microsoft recommends that you do not use data encryption and backup compression together.

Backup files of encrypted databases also are encrypted by using the DEK. When you restore encrypted backups, the certificate protecting the DEK must be available. Thus, in addition to backing up databases, you must maintain backups of the server certificates to prevent data loss. If you lose a certificate, you will lose your data.

The Database Engine doesn't replicate data automatically from TDE-enabled databases in an encrypted form. You must enable TDE separately if you want to protect the distribution and subscriber databases.

CHAPTER 7

Implementing SQL Server 2012 Security

Microsoft SQL Server 2012 is being used more frequently, both within organizations and for external access to information. Whether employees, contractors, or outside users access your databases, your job as an administrator is to manage that access efficiently. At the server level, you do this by creating logins, configuring login permissions, and assigning roles to logins as appropriate. At the database level, you do this by creating users, configuring user permissions, and assigning database roles to users as appropriate. The permissions and roles you assign determine which actions users can perform, as well as what kinds of data they can access.

Your primary goals in managing security should be the following:

- Balance the user's need for access to data against your need to protect data from unauthorized access.
- Restrict database permissions so that users are less likely to execute harmful commands and procedures (maliciously or accidentally).
- Close off other security holes, such as those that might be caused by ordinary users with membership in administrator-related groups.

Overview of SQL Server 2012 Security

In SQL Server 2012, all objects in a database are located in *schemas*. Each schema is owned by roles rather than by individual users, which allows multiple users to administer database objects. This arrangement resolves an issue in earlier versions of SQL Server in which users could not be dropped from a database without having to reassign the ownership of every object they owned. Now you need to change ownership only for the schema, not for each object.

With regard to overall security for SQL Server 2012, it's important to note several top-level changes. With certificates, the maximum length of private keys you are importing from an external source is 4,096 bits, and you can now specify the private key bits of a certificate using the FROM BINARY option.

On new installations of SQL Server 2012, the service master key and the database master key are encrypted with Advanced Encryption Standard (AES), a newer encryption algorithm than Triple Data Encryption Standard (3DES) used in earlier releases. If you upgraded a server instance to SQL Server 2012, you should use ALTER SERVICE MASTER KEY and ALTER MASTER KEY to regenerate the master keys and upgrade the master keys to AES.

If you have CONTROL SERVER permission on the server instance, you can regenerate the master keys and all the keys they protect using the following commands:

```
ALTER SERVICE MASTER KEY REGENERATE;
GO
USE master
ALTER MASTER KEY REGENERATE WITH ENCRYPTION BY PASSWORD =
'WindowsServerPassword';
GO
```

where *WindowsServerPassword* is a password that meets the Windows password policy requirements of the server. When you execute these commands, the keys are decrypted with the old master key and then encrypted with the new master key.

Working with Security Principals and Securables

SQL Server 2012 makes extensive use of security principals and securables. An entity that can request a server, database, or schema resource is referred to as a *security principal*. An item that can be secured to control access is referred to as a *securable*.

Each security principal has a unique security identifier (SID). Security principals are managed at three levels: Windows, SQL Server, and database. The level at which the security principal is defined sets its scope of influence. Generally, Windows-level and SQL Server-level security principals have an instance-wide scope, and database-level principals have a scope of influence within a specific database.

Table 7-1 lists the security principals at each level. Some security principals, including Windows groups, database roles, and application roles, can include other security principals. These security principals are also referred to as *collections*. Every database user belongs to the public database role. When a user has not been granted or denied specific permissions on a securable, the user inherits the permissions granted to the public role on that securable.

TABLE 7-1 SQL Server Principal Levels and the Included Principals

PRINCIPAL LEVEL	PRINCIPALS INCLUDED
Windows level	Windows domain account
	Windows local account
	Windows group
SQL Server level	Server role
	SQL Server login
	SQL Server login mapped to an asymmetric key
	SQL Server login mapped to a certificate
	SQL Server login mapped to a Windows account
Database level	Database user
	Database user mapped to an asymmetric key
	Database user mapped to a certificate
	Database user mapped to a Windows account
	Application role
	Database role
	Public database role

Security principals can be assigned specific permissions on hierarchical collections of entities referred to as *securables*. As Table 7-2 shows, the three top-level securables are server, database, and schema. Each of these securables contains other securables, which in turn can contain still other securables. These nested hierarchies are referred to as *scopes*. You can also say that the main securable scopes in SQL Server are server, database, and schema.

TABLE 7-2 SQL Server Securable Scopes and the Securables They Contain

SECURABLE SCOPE	SECURABLE CONTAINED
Server	Servers/current instance
	Database
	Endpoint
	Login
	Server role

SECURABLE SCOPE	SECURABLE CONTAINED
Database	Application role
	Assembly
	Asymmetric key
	Certificate
	Contract
	Database role
	Full-text catalog
	Message type
	Remote service binding
	Route
	Schema
	Service
	Symmetric key
	User
Schema	Aggregate
	Constraint
	Function
	Procedure
	Queue
	Statistic
	Synonym
	Table
	Type
	View
	XML schema collection

Understanding Permissions of Securables

Each SQL Server 2012 securable has permissions that can be granted to a security principal. These permissions begin with a keyword or keywords that identify the permission being granted. These keywords are summarized in Table 7-3.

TABLE 7-3 Permission Keywords and How They Work

PERMISSION KEYWORD(S)	PERMISSION GRANTED	PRIMARILY APPLIES TO
ALTER ANY *<Database>*	Grants the ability to create, alter, or drop individual securables for the database. For example, granting a principal ALTER ANY SCHEMA for a database gives the principal the ability to create, alter, or drop any schema in the database.	Database instance
ALTER ANY *<Server>*	Grants the ability to create, alter, or drop individual securables for the server. For example, granting a principal ALTER ANY LOGIN for a server gives that principal the ability to create, alter, and drop any login in that server instance.	Server instance
ALTER	Grants the ability to alter the properties of a particular securable except for ownership. When a principal is granted on a scope, the principal has the ability to alter, create, or drop any securable contained within that scope. For example, granting a principal ALTER permissions on a schema gives that principal the ability to create, alter, and drop objects from the schema.	Stored procedures, Service Broker queues, functions, synonyms, tables, and views
BACKUP/DUMP	Grants permission to back up (dump).	Database instance

PERMISSION KEYWORD(S)	PERMISSION GRANTED	PRIMARILY APPLIES TO
CONTROL	Grants ownership-like capabilities. The principal has all defined permissions on the securable and can grant permissions on the securable as well. When you assign CONTROL permissions, consider the security model's hierarchy. Granting CONTROL at a particular scope implicitly includes CONTROL on all the securables under that scope. For example, CONTROL on a database implies all permissions on the database, including all assemblies and schemas in the database and all objects within all schemas.	Stored procedures, functions, synonyms, Service Broker queues, tables, and views
CREATE <Database Securable>	Grants permission to create the database securable.	Database instance
CREATE <Schema-Contained Securable>	Grants permission to create the schema-contained securable. Remember that ALTER permissions on the schema are needed to create the securable in a particular schema.	Database instance
CREATE <Server Securable>	Grants permission to create the server securable.	Server instance
DELETE	Grants permission to delete the securable.	Synonyms, tables, and views
EXECUTE	Grants permission to execute the securable.	Stored procedures, functions, and synonyms
IMPERSONATE <Login>	Grants the ability to impersonate the login.	
IMPERSONATE <User>	Grants the ability to impersonate the user.	

PERMISSION KEYWORD(S)	PERMISSION GRANTED	PRIMARILY APPLIES TO
INSERT	Grants permission to insert data into the securable.	Synonyms, tables, and views
RECEIVE	Grants permission to receive Service Broker messages.	Service Broker queues
REFERENCES	Grants permission to reference the securable.	Functions, Service Broker queues, tables, and views
RESTORE/ LOAD	Grants permission to restore (load).	
SELECT	Grants permission to view data stored in the securable.	Synonyms, tables, table-valued functions, and views
TAKE OWNERSHIP	Grants the ability to take ownership of the securable.	Stored procedures, functions, synonyms, tables, and views
UPDATE	Grants permission to change data stored in the securable.	Synonyms, tables, and views
VIEW DEFINITION	Grants permission to view the securable definition in the related metadata.	Stored procedures, Service Broker queues, functions, synonyms, tables, and views

Examining Permissions Granted to Securables

SQL Server functions that you will find helpful for examining permissions granted to securables include the following:

- sys.fn_builtin_permissions
- Has_perms_by_name

You will learn more about how these functions are used in the sections that follow.

Examining Built-in Permissions

Each object class from the server scope down has a specific set of grantable permissions. The sys.fn_builtin_permissions function returns a description of the server's built-in permissions hierarchy:

```
sys.fn_builtin_permissions( [ DEFAULT | NULL
    | empty_string | '< securable_class >' ] )

< securable_class >::= APPLICATION ROLE | ASSEMBLY | ASYMMETRIC KEY
    | CERTIFICATE | CONTRACT | DATABASE | ENDPOINT | FULLTEXT CATALOG
    | LOGIN | MESSAGE TYPE | OBJECT | REMOTE SERVICE BINDING | ROLE
    | ROUTE | SCHEMA | SERVER | SERVER ROLE | SERVICE | SYMMETRIC KEY
    | TYPE | USER | XML SCHEMA COLLECTION
```

In the preceding code segment, DEFAULT, NULL, or an empty string returns a complete list of built-in permissions, or you can specify the name of a specific securable class to return all permissions that apply to the class.

The sys.fn_builtin_permissions function is accessible to the public role. You can view the grantable permissions for all objects by using the following query:

```
USE master
GO
SELECT * FROM sys.fn_builtin_permissions(default)
GO
```

If you want to view the grantable permissions for a specific object class, you can use the following query:

```
USE master
GO
SELECT * FROM sys.fn_builtin_permissions('object_class')
GO
```

where object_class is the object class you want to work with. The following example examines the grantable permissions for the LOGIN class:

```
SELECT * FROM sys.fn_builtin_permissions('login')
```

You can also list object classes for which a specific permission has been granted. In the following example, you list object classes that have the SELECT permission:

```
USE master
GO
SELECT * FROM sys.fn_builtin_permissions(DEFAULT)
      WHERE permission_name = 'SELECT';
GO
```

Examining Effective Permissions

The Has_perms_by_name built-in function returns the effective permissions on a securable. Effective permissions include the following:

- Permissions granted directly to the user and not denied
- Permissions implied by a higher-level permission held by the user and not denied
- Permissions granted to a role of which the user is a member and not denied
- Permissions held by a role of which the user is a member and not denied

The Has_perms_by_name function is accessible to the public role. However, you cannot use Has_perms_by_name to check permissions on a linked server. The basic syntax of the Has_perms_by_name function follows:

```
Has_perms_by_name (
                    securable ,
                    securable_class ,
                    permission
                    [, sub-securable ]
                    [, sub-securable_class ]
                    )
```

In the preceding code segment, *securable* sets the name of the securable or NULL if the securable is the server itself. The value of *securable_class* sets the name of the securable class (or NULL if the securable is the server itself), and *permission* is a non-NULL value representing the permission name to be checked. You can use the permission name ANY as a wildcard to determine if the securable has any effective permissions. The optional *sub-securable* and *sub-securable_class* values specify the name of the securable subentity and the class of securable subentity against which the permission is tested. Both of these optional values default to NULL. If the function returns true (1), the securable has the effective permission. If the function returns false (0), the securable does not have the effective permission. A return value of NULL indicates that the query failed.

You can determine if the currently logged-in user has a specific permission on the server by executing the following query:

```
USE master
GO
SELECT has_perms_by_name(null, null, 'permission_name');
GO
```

In this code segment, *permission_name* is the name of the permission to examine.

The following example checks to see if the current user has the ALTER ANY SCHEMA permission:

```
select has_perms_by_name(null, null, 'ALTER ANY SCHEMA');
```

A true (1) or false (0) value is returned to indicate whether the user is granted the permission.

To determine if the current user has any permissions in a specific database, you can execute the following query:

```
USE master
GO
SELECT has_perms_by_name('database_name', 'DATABASE', 'ANY')
GO
```

In this code segment, *database_name* is the name of the database for which you are determining permissions.

The following example determines if the current user has any permissions in the *Personnel* database:

```
SELECT has_perms_by_name('Personnel', 'DATABASE', 'ANY')
```

If the query returns 1, the current user has some permissions for the specific database. You can indicate the current database with the db_name() function, as in:

```
SELECT has_perms_by_name(db_name(),'DATABASE', 'ANY')
```

You can determine the permissions of a specific user by using EXECUTE AS. In the following example, you check to see if EdwardM has any permissions in the *Personnel* database:

```
EXECUTE AS user = 'EdwardM'
GO
SELECT has_perms_by_name('Personnel', 'DATABASE', 'ANY')
GO
REVERT
GO
```

Permissions on schema objects, such as tables and views, can be examined as well. To do this, set the securable to the database name, the securable class to the literal value 'OBJECT', and the permission name to the permission you want to examine. To determine which tables the current user has SELECT permission on in the current database, you use the following query:

```
USE Personnel
GO
SELECT has_perms_by_name(dbname(), 'OBJECT', 'SELECT') as Have_Select,
    * from sys.tables;
GO
```

The current user has SELECT permission on tables with a 1 in the Have_Select column. By specifying the two-part or three-part name, you can examine permissions on a specific table as well. For example, to determine if the current user

has INSERT permission on the Address table in the current database, you use
a two-part name:

```
select has_perms_by_name('Employee.Address', 'OBJECT', 'INSERT')
    as Have_Select, * from sys.tables;
```

or you use a three-part name:

```
select has_perms_by_name('Personnel.Employee.Address', 'OBJECT',
    'INSERT') as Have_Select, * from sys.tables;
```

SQL Server 2012 Authentication Modes

The SQL Server security model has two authentication modes:

- **Windows authentication only** Works best when the database is accessed only within the organization.
- **Mixed security** Works best when outside users need to access the database or when you do not use Windows domains.

You configure these security modes at the server level, and they apply to all databases on the server. Note, however, that each database server instance has a separate security specification. This means that different database server instances can have different security modes.

At the database level, SQL Server also allows you to enable contained database authentication.

Windows Authentication

If you use the Windows authentication mode, you can use the user and group accounts available in the Windows domain for authentication. This lets authenticated users access databases without a separate SQL Server login ID and password. This is beneficial because domain users do not have to keep track of multiple passwords, and if they update their domain password, they will not have to change SQL Server passwords as well. However, users are still subject to all the rules of the Windows security model, and you can use this model to lock accounts, audit logins, and force users to change their passwords periodically.

When you use Windows authentication, SQL Server automatically authenticates users based on their user account names or their group membership. If you have granted the user or the user's group access to a database, the user is granted access to that database automatically. By default, several local accounts are configured to be granted access to SQL Server. These accounts are the local Administrators group account and the local Administrator user account. (Administrator is included because it is a member of the Administrators group by default.) Local accounts are displayed as BUILTIN\<AccountName> or COMPUTERNAME\<AccountName> in SQL Server Management Studio. For example, Administrators is displayed as BUILTIN\Administrators.

REAL WORLD Domain accounts are the best way to manage users who access the database from within the organization. Also, if you assign users to security groups and then configure access for these groups in SQL Server, you cut down on the amount of administration you have to do. For example, if you assign users in the marketing department to a marketing group and then configure this group in SQL Server, you have only one account to manage instead of 10, 20, 50, or more. When employees leave the organization or change departments, you do not have to delete user accounts. When new employees are hired, you do not have to create new accounts, either—you only need to make sure that they are added to the correct security group.

Mixed Security and SQL Server Logins

With mixed security, you use both Windows authentication and SQL Server logins. SQL Server logins are primarily for users outside the company, such as those who might access the database from the Internet or for third-party applications. You can configure applications that access SQL Server from the Internet to use specific accounts automatically or to prompt the user for a SQL Server login ID and password.

With mixed security, SQL Server first determines if the user is connecting using a valid SQL Server login. If the user has a valid login and has the proper password, the user connection is accepted. If the user has a valid login but has an improper password, the user connection is refused. SQL Server checks the Windows account information only if the user does not have a valid login. In this case, SQL Server determines whether the Windows account has permission to connect to the server. If the account has permission, the connection is accepted. Otherwise, the connection is refused.

All SQL Server servers have the built-in sa login and might also have NETWORK SERVICE and SYSTEM logins (depending on the server instance configuration). All databases have built-in SQL Server users known as dbo, guest, INFORMATION_SCHEMA, and sys. The logins and users that are provided for special purposes are discussed in the following section.

Authentication at the Database Level

With contained database authentication, users authenticate in a particular database and do not rely on *master*. These users can have a SQL login with a password stored in the database, or they can be associated with a Windows user or group that's granted access but has no login.

Although users based on logins in the *master* database can be granted access to a contained database, you normally do not want to create a dependency on the server instance. Instead, you rely on contained database users with passwords and authorized Windows principals that are authenticated by the database.

Special-Purpose Logins and Users

You configure access to SQL Server by using server logins. You can configure various levels of access for these logins in the following ways:

- By the roles to which those logins belong
- By permitting access to specific databases
- By allowing or denying object permissions

Just as there are two authentication modes, there are also two kinds of server logins. You create domain logins by using domain accounts, which can be domain or local user accounts, local group accounts, or universal and global domain group accounts. You create SQL Server logins for users by specifying a unique login ID and password. Depending on the way you installed your server instance, several logins may be configured by default, and these can include sa and NT AUTHORITY\SYSTEM.

Startup accounts for various SQL Server services are configured as SQL Server logins. With Windows Server 2008, these startup accounts can be domain user accounts, local user accounts, or built-in system accounts. Beginning with Windows Server 2008 Release 2, services login using virtual accounts by default and you also can configure services to login using managed service accounts. By default, the virtual accounts used by various services impersonate NETWORK SERVICE.

To narrow the scope of access to a specific database, you use database user accounts. Several database users are configured by default, including the dbo user (a special database user), the guest user (a special database user with limited access), the INFORMATION_SCHEMA user, and the sys user.

In this section, you will learn more about these special-purpose logins.

Working with the Administrators Group

The Administrators group is a local Windows group on the database server. This group's members normally include the local Administrator user account and any other users set to administer the system locally. While this group is no longer granted the sysadmin server role by default, local administrators can still access the server instance when in single user mode.

Working with the Administrator User Account

Administrator is a local user account on the server. This account provides administrator privileges on the local system, and you use it primarily when you install a system. If the host computer is part of a Windows domain, the Administrator account usually has domainwide privileges as well. In SQL Server, this account is no longer granted the sysadmin server role by default. However, the Administrator account can still access the server instance when in single user mode.

Working with the sa Login

The sa login is the system administrator's account for SQL Server. With the new integrated and expanded security model, sa is no longer needed, and it is primarily provided for backward compatibility with previous versions of SQL Server. The sa login is granted the sysadmin server role by default.

To prevent unauthorized access to the server, you should set a strong password for this account, and you should also change the password periodically, as you would the password for a Windows account.

BEST PRACTICES Because the sa login is widely known to malicious users, you might want to delete or disable this account if possible. Instead of using the sa login, make system administrators members of the sysadmin server role and have them log on using their own logins. Anyone with the sysadmin server role can then log on and administer the server. If you ever get locked out of the server, you can log on to the server locally by using an account with local administrator privileges and then reset passwords or assign privileges as necessary.

Working with the NT SERVICE and SYSTEM Logins

NETWORK SERVICE and SYSTEM are built-in local accounts on the server. Whether server logins are created for these accounts depends on the server configuration. For example, if you have configured the server as a report server, you will have a login for NT SERVICE/ReportServer. This virtual account will be a member of the special database role RSExecRole on the *master*, *msdb*, *ReportServer*, and *ReportServerTempDB* databases. RSExecRole is used primarily to manage the Report Server schema, and the service account for the server instance will also be a member of this role.

During setup of a server instance on Windows Server 2008 R2, virtual accounts are used with the SQL Server instance, SQL Server Agent, SQL Writer, and other services. For more information on working with virtual accounts, see the "Understanding the Services Configuration" section in Chapter 2, "Managing SQL Server Services and Clients."

Working with the Guest User

The guest user is a special user that you can add to a database to allow anyone with a valid SQL Server login to access the database. Users who access a database with the guest account assume the identity of the guest user and inherit all the privileges and permissions of the guest account. For example, if you configure the domain account GOTEAM to access SQL Server, GOTEAM can access any database with a guest login, and when GOTEAM does so, the person logging in under GOTEAM is granted all the permissions of the guest account. If you were to configure the Windows group DEVGROUP with guest access, you could simplify administration because any user who is a member of the group would be able to access any database as a guest.

By default, the guest user exists in the *model* database and is granted guest permissions. Because *model* is the template for all databases you create, all new databases include the guest account, and this account is granted guest permissions. You can add or delete a guest from all databases except *master* and *tempdb*. Most users access *master* and *tempdb* as guests, and for this reason, you cannot remove the guest account from these databases. This is not a problem, however, because a guest has limited permissions and privileges in *master* and *tempdb*.

Before using the guest user, you should note the following information about the account:

- The guest user is a member of the public server role and inherits the permissions of this role.
- The guest user must exist in a database before anyone can access it as a guest.
- The guest user is used only when a user account has access to SQL Server but does not have access to the database through any other user account.

Working with the dbo User

The database owner, or dbo, is a special type of database user and is granted special privileges. Generally speaking, the user who creates a database is the database owner. The dbo is implicitly granted all permissions on the database and can grant these permissions to other users. Because members of the sysadmin server role are mapped automatically to the special user dbo, logins with the sysadmin role can perform any tasks that a dbo can perform.

Objects created in SQL Server databases also have owners. These owners are referred to as the *database object owners*. Objects created by a member of the sysadmin server role belong to the dbo user automatically. Objects created by users who are not members of the sysadmin server role belong to the user who creates the object and must be qualified with the name of that user when other users reference them. For example, if GOTEAM is a member of the sysadmin server role and creates a table called Sales, Sales belongs to dbo and is qualified as dbo.Sales, or simply Sales. However, if the GOTEAM default schema is the GOTEAM schema and GOTEAM is not a member of the sysadmin server role and creates a table called Sales, Sales belongs to GOTEAM and must be qualified as GOTEAM.Sales.

NOTE Technically, dbo is a special user account, not a special-purpose login. However, you might see it referred to as a *login*. You cannot log in to a server or database as dbo, but you might be the person who created the database or a set of objects in it.

Working with the sys and INFORMATION_SCHEMA Users

All system objects are contained in the schema named sys or the schema named INFORMATION_SCHEMA. These are two special schemas that are created in each database.

The related sys and information schema views provide an internal system view of the metadata for all data objects stored in a database. Do not use INFORMATION_ SCHEMA views to determine the schema of an object. Instead, query the sys.objects catalog view to determine the schema of an object.

The sys and INFORMATION_SCHEMA users own these schemas. Since these users can't be dropped, neither can the schema or objects within that schema.

Permissions

Permissions determine the actions that users can perform on SQL Server or in a database. Permissions are granted according to the login ID, group memberships, and role memberships. Users must have appropriate permissions before they can perform any action that changes database definitions or accesses data. Three types of permissions are used in SQL Server:

- Object permissions
- Statement permissions
- Implicit permissions

Object Permissions

In SQL Server 2012, all object permissions are grantable. You can manage permissions for specific objects, all objects of particular types, and all objects belonging to a specific schema. The objects for which you can manage permissions depend on the scope. At the server level, you can grant object permissions for servers, endpoints, logins, and server roles. You can also manage permissions for the current server instance.

At the database level, you can manage object permissions for application roles, assemblies, asymmetric keys, certificates, database roles, databases, full-text catalogs, functions, schemas, stored procedures, symmetric keys, synonyms, tables, user-defined data types, users, views, and XML schema collections.

You control access to these objects by granting, denying, or revoking the ability to execute particular statements or stored procedures. For example, you can grant a user the right to select information from a table but deny the right to insert, update, or delete information in the table. Table 7-4 provides a summary of object permissions.

TABLE 7-4 Object Permissions

CONFIGURABLE PERMISSIONS	HIGHEST PERMISSION	CONTAINED IN	IMPLIED PERMISSION FROM PARENT
Base Securable: APPLICATION ROLE			
ALTER, CONTROL, VIEW DEFINITION	CONTROL	DATABASE	ALTER ANY APPLICATION ROLE, CONTROL, VIEW DEFINITION
Base Securable: ASSEMBLY			
ALTER, CONTROL, EXECUTE, REFERENCES, TAKE OWNERSHIP, VIEW DEFINITION	CONTROL	DATABASE	ALTER ANY ASSEMBLY, CONTROL, EXE-CUTE, REFERENCES, VIEW DEFINITION
Base Securable: ASYMMETRIC			
ALTER, CONTROL, REFERENCES, TAKE OWNERSHIP, VIEW DEFINITION	CONTROL	DATABASE	ALTER ANY ASYMMETRIC KEY, CONTROL, REFERENCES, VIEW DEFINITION
Base Securable: CERTIFICATE			
ALTER, CONTROL, REFERENCES, TAKE OWNERSHIP, VIEW DEFINITION	CONTROL	DATABASE	ALTER ANY CERTIFICATE, CONTROL, REFERENCES, VIEW DEFINITION
Base Securable: CONTRACT			
ALTER, CONTROL, REFERENCES, TAKE OWNERSHIP, VIEW DEFINITION	CONTROL	DATABASE	ALTER ANY CONTRACT, CONTROL, REFERENCES, VIEW DEFINITION
Base Securable: DATABASE			
ALTER, ALTER ANY APPLICATION ROLE, ALTER ANY ASSEMBLY, ALTER ANY ASYMMETRIC KEY, ALTER ANY CERTIFICATE, ALTER ANY CONTRACT,	ALTER ANY ASSEMBLY, ALTER ANY CERTIFICATE, ALTER ANY CONTRACT,	SERVER	ALTER ANY DATABASE, ALTER ANY EVENT NOTIFICATION,

CONFIGURABLE PERMISSIONS	HIGHEST PERMISSION	CONTAINED IN	IMPLIED PERMISSION FROM PARENT
Base Securable: DATABASE (continued)			
ALTER ANY DATABASE DDL TRIGGER, ALTER ANY DATABASE EVENT NOTIFICATION, ALTER ANY DATASPACE, ALTER ANY FULLTEXT CATALOG, ALTER ANY MESSAGE TYPE, ALTER ANY REMOTE SERVICE BINDING, ALTER ANY ROLE, ALTER ANY ROUTE, ALTER ANY SCHEMA, ALTER ANY SERVICE, ALTER ANY SYMMETRIC KEY, ALTER ANY USER, AUTHENTICATE, BACKUP DATABASE, BACKUP LOG, CHECKPOINT, CONNECT, CONNECT REPLICATION, CONTROL, CREATE AGGREGATE, CREATE ASSEMBLY, CREATE ASYMMETRIC KEY, CREATE CERTIFICATE, CREATE CONTRACT, CREATE DATABASE, CREATE DATABASE DDL EVENT NOTIFICATION, CREATE DEFAULT, CREATE FULLTEXT CATALOG, CREATE FUNCTION, CREATE MESSAGE TYPE, CREATE PROCEDURE, CREATE QUEUE, CREATE REMOTE SERVICE BINDING, CREATE ROLE, CREATE ROUTE, CREATE RULE, CREATE SCHEMA, CREATE SERVICE, CREATE SYMMETRIC KEY, CREATE SYNONYM, CREATE TABLE, CREATE TYPE, CREATE VIEW, CREATE XML SCHEMA COLLECTION, DELETE, EXECUTE INSERT,	ALTER ANY DATABASE EVENT NOTIFICATION, ALTER ANY FULLTEXT CATALOG, ALTER ANY MESSAGE TYPE, ALTER ANY REMOTE SERVICE BINDING, ALTER ANY ROLE, ALTER ANY ROUTE, ALTER ANY SCHEMA, ALTER ANY SERVICE, ALTER ANY SYMMETRIC KEY, CONNECT REPLICATION, CONTROL		ALTER TRACE, AUTHENTICATE SERVER, CONTROL SERVER, CREATE ANY DATABASE, CREATE DDL EVENT NOTIFICATION, EXTERNAL ACCESS, VIEW ANY DEFINITION, VIEW SERVER STATE,

CONFIGURABLE PERMISSIONS	HIGHEST PERMISSION	CONTAINED IN	IMPLIED PERMISSION FROM PARENT
REFERENCES, SELECT, SHOWPLAN, SUBSCRIBE QUERY NOTIFICATIONS, TAKE OWNERSHIP, UPDATE, VIEW DATABASE STATE, VIEW DEFINITION			
Base Securable: ENDPOINT			
ALTER, CONNECT, CONTROL, TAKE OWNERSHIP, VIEW DEFINITION	CONTROL	SERVER	ALTER ANY ENDPOINT, CONTROL SERVER, VIEW ANY DEFINITION
Base Securable: FULLTEXT CATALOG			
ALTER, CONTROL, REFERENCES, TAKE OWNERSHIP, VIEW DEFINITION	CONTROL	DATABASE	ALTER ANY FULLTEXT CATALOG, CONTROL, REFERENCES, VIEW DEFINITION
Base Securable: LOGIN			
ALTER, CONTROL, IMPERSONATE, VIEW DEFINITION	CONTROL	SERVER	ALTER ANY LOGIN, CONTROL SERVER, VIEW ANY DEFINITION
Base Securable: MESSAGE TYPE			
ALTER, CONTROL, REFERENCES, TAKE OWNERSHIP, VIEW DEFINITION	CONTROL	DATABASE	ALTER ANY MESSAGE TYPE, CONTROL, REFERENCES, VIEW DEFINITION
Base Securable: OBJECT			
ALTER, CONTROL, DELETE, EXECUTE, INSERT, REFERENCES, SELECT, TAKE OWNERSHIP, UPDATE,	CONTROL	SCHEMA	ALTER, CONTROL, DELETE, EXECUTE, INSERT, REFERENCES, SELECT,

CONFIGURABLE PERMISSIONS	HIGHEST PERMISSION	CONTAINED IN	IMPLIED PERMISSION FROM PARENT
VIEW CHANGE TRACKING, VIEW DEFINITION			UPDATE, VIEW CHANGE TRACKING, VIEW DEFINITION
Base Securable: REMOTE SERVICE BINDING			
ALTER, CONTROL, TAKE OWNERSHIP, VIEW DEFINITION	CONTROL	DATABASE	ALTER ANY REMOTE SERVICE BINDING, CONTROL, VIEW DEFINITION
Base Securable: ROLE			
ALTER, CONTROL, TAKE OWNERSHIP, VIEW DEFINITION	CONTROL	DATABASE	ALTER ANY ROLE, CONTROL, VIEW DEFINITION
Base Securable: ROUTE			
ALTER, CONTROL, TAKE OWNERSHIP, VIEW DEFINITION	CONTROL	DATABASE	ALTER ANY ROUTE, CONTROL, VIEW DEFINITION
Base Securable: SCHEMA			
ALTER, CONTROL, DELETE, EXECUTE, INSERT, REFERENCES, SELECT, TAKE OWNERSHIP, UPDATE, VIEW CHANGE TRACKING, VIEW DEFINITION	CONTROL	DATABASE	ALTER ANY SCHEMA, CONTROL, DELETE, EXECUTE, INSERT, REFERENCES, SELECT, UPDATE, VIEW CHANGE TRACKING, VIEW DEFINITION
Base Securable: SERVER			
ADMINISTER BULK OPERATIONS, ALTER ANY CONNECTION, ALTER ANY CREDENTIAL, ALTER ANY DATABASE, ALTER ANY ENDPOINT,	CONTROL SERVER, ALTER ANY DATABASE, ALTER ANY EVENT NOTIFICATION,	Not applicable	Not applicable

CONFIGURABLE PERMISSIONS	HIGHEST PERMISSION	CONTAINED IN	IMPLIED PERMISSION FROM PARENT
ALTER ANY EVENT NOTIFICATION, ALTER ANY LINKED SERVER, ALTER ANY LOGIN, ALTER RESOURCES, ALTER SERVER STATE, ALTER SETTINGS, ALTER TRACE, AUTHENTICATE SERVER, CONNECT SQL, CONTROL SERVER, CREATE ANY DATABASE, CREATE DDL EVENT NOTIFICATION, CREATE ENDPOINT, CREATE TRACE EVENT NOTIFICATION, EXTERNAL ACCESS ASSEMBLY, SHUTDOWN, UNSAFE ASSEMBLY, VIEW ANY DATABASE, VIEW ANY DEFINITION, VIEW SERVER STATE	ALTER ANY ENDPOINT, ALTER SERVER STATE		

Base Securable: SERVICE

CONFIGURABLE PERMISSIONS	HIGHEST PERMISSION	CONTAINED IN	IMPLIED PERMISSION FROM PARENT
ALTER, CONTROL, SEND, TAKE OWNERSHIP, VIEW DEFINITION	CONTROL	DATABASE	ALTER ANY SERVICE, CONTROL, VIEW DEFINITION

Base Securable: SYMMETRIC KEY

CONFIGURABLE PERMISSIONS	HIGHEST PERMISSION	CONTAINED IN	IMPLIED PERMISSION FROM PARENT
ALTER, CONTROL, REFERENCES, TAKE OWNERSHIP, VIEW DEFINITION	CONTROL	DATABASE	ALTER ANY SYMMETRIC KEY, CONTROL, REFERENCES, VIEW DEFINITION

Base Securable: TYPE

CONFIGURABLE PERMISSIONS	HIGHEST PERMISSION	CONTAINED IN	IMPLIED PERMISSION FROM PARENT
CONTROL, EXECUTE, REFERENCES, TAKE OWNERSHIP, VIEW DEFINITION	CONTROL	SCHEMA	CONTROL, EXECUTE, REFERENCES, VIEW DEFINITION

CONFIGURABLE PERMISSIONS	HIGHEST PERMISSION	CONTAINED IN	IMPLIED PERMISSION FROM PARENT
Base Securable: USER			
ALTER, CONTROL, IMPERSONATE, VIEW DEFINITION	CONTROL	DATABASE	ALTER ANY USER, CONTROL, VIEW DEFINITION
Base Securable: XML SCHEMA COLLECTI ON			
ALTER, CONTROL, EXECUTE, REFERENCES, TAKE OWNERSHIP, VIEW DEFINITION	CONTROL	SCHEMA	ALTER, CONTROL, EXECUTE, REFERENCES, VIEW DEFINITION

Statement Permissions

Statement permissions control administration actions, such as creating a database or adding objects to a database. Only members of the sysadmin role and database owners can assign statement permissions. By default, normal logins are not granted statement permissions, and you must specifically grant these permissions to logins that are not administrators. For example, if a user needs to be able to create views in a database, you would assign permission to execute CREATE VIEW. Table 7-5 provides a summary of statement permissions that you can grant, deny, or revoke.

TABLE 7-5 Statement Permissions

STATEMENT PERMISSION	DESCRIPTION
CREATE DATABASE	Determines if the login can create databases. The user must be in the *master* database or must be a member of the sysadmin server role.
CREATE DEFAULT	Determines if the user can create a default value for a table column.
CREATE FUNCTION	Determines if the user can create a user-defined function in the database.
CREATE PROCEDURE	Determines if the user can create a stored procedure.
CREATE RULE	Determines if the user can create a table column rule.
CREATE TABLE	Determines if the user can create a table.
CREATE VIEW	Determines if the user can create a view.

STATEMENT PERMISSION	DESCRIPTION
BACKUP DATABASE	Determines if the user can back up the database.
BACKUP LOG	Determines if the user can back up the transaction log.

Implicit Permissions

Only members of predefined system roles or database/database object owners have implied permissions. Implied permissions for a role cannot be changed. You make other accounts members of the role to give the accounts the related implied permissions. For example, members of the sysadmin server role can perform any activity in SQL Server. They can extend databases, kill processes, and so on. Any account that you add to the sysadmin role can perform these tasks as well.

Database and database object owners also have implied permissions. These permissions allow them to perform all activities either with the database, with the object they own, or with both. For example, a user who owns a table can view, add, change, and delete data. That user can also alter the table's definition and control the table's permissions.

Roles

Roles are a lot like Windows security groups—they enable you to assign permissions to a group of users, and they can have built-in permissions (implicit permissions) that cannot be changed. Two types of roles are available:

- **Server roles**   Applied at the server level
- **Database roles**   Applied at the database level

Server Roles

You use server roles to grant server administration capabilities. If you make a login a member of a role, users who use this login can perform any tasks permitted by the role. For example, members of the sysadmin role have the highest level of permissions on SQL Server and can perform any type of task.

You set server roles at the server level, and you predefine them. This means that these permissions affect the entire server and you cannot change the permission set. The following list provides a summary of each server role, from the lowest-level role (bulkadmin) to the highest-level role (sysadmin):

- **bulkadmin**   Designed for domain accounts that need to perform bulk inserts into the database. Members of this role can add members to bulkadmin and can execute the BULK INSERT statement.

- **dbcreator**   Designed for users who need to create, modify, drop, and restore databases. Members of this role can add members to dbcreator and perform these tasks: ALTER DATABASE, CREATE DATABASE, DROP DATABASE, EXTEND DATABASE, RESTORE DATABASE, and RESTORE LOG.
- **diskadmin**   Designed for users who need to manage disk files. Members of this role can add members to diskadmin and can use sp_addumpdevice and sp_dropdevice.
- **processadmin**   Designed for users who need to control SQL Server processes. Members of this role can add members to processadmin and can kill processes.
- **securityadmin**   Designed for users who need to manage logins, create database permissions, and read error logs. Members of this role can add members to securityadmin; grant, deny, and revoke server-level and database-level permissions; reset passwords; and read the error logs. In addition, they can perform these tasks: sp_addlinkedsrvlogin, CREATE LOGIN, ALTER LOGIN, DROP LOGIN, sp_droplinkedsrvlogin, GRANT CONNECT, DENY CONNECT, sp_helplogins, and sp_remoteoption.
- **serveradmin**   Designed for users who need to set serverwide configuration options and shut down the server. Members of this role can add members to serveradmin and can perform these other tasks: DBCC FREEPROCCACHE, RECONFIGURE, SHUTDOWN, sp_configure, sp_fulltext_service, and sp_tableoption.
- **setupadmin**   Designed for users who need to manage linked servers and control startup procedures. Members of this role can add members to setupadmin; add, drop, and configure linked servers; and control startup procedures.
- **sysadmin**   Designed for users who need complete control over SQL Server and installed databases. Members of this role can perform any activity in SQL Server.

Fixed server roles can be mapped to the more granular permissions for SQL Server 2012, as shown in Table 7-6.

TABLE 7-6 Granular Permissions Associated with Fixed Server Roles

FIXED SERVER ROLE	PERMISSIONS GRANTED WITH THIS ROLE
bulkadmin	ADMINISTER BULK OPERATIONS
dbcreator	CREATE DATABASE
diskadmin	ALTER RESOURCES
processadmin	ALTER ANY CONNECTION, ALTER SERVER STATE
securityadmin	ALTER ANY LOGIN
serveradmin	ALTER ANY ENDPOINT, ALTER RESOURCES, ALTER SERVER STATE, ALTER SETTINGS, SHUTDOWN, VIEW SERVER STATE
setupadmin	ALTER ANY LINKED SERVER
sysadmin	CONTROL SERVER

Database Roles

When you want to assign permissions at the database level, you can use database roles. You set database roles on a per-database basis, which means that each database has its own set of roles. SQL Server 2012 supports three types of database roles:

- User-defined (or standard) roles
- User-defined application roles
- Predefined (or fixed) database roles

Standard roles allow you to create roles with unique permissions and privileges. You can use standard roles to group users logically and then assign a single permission to the role rather than having to assign permissions to each user separately. For example, you could create a role called Users that allows users to perform SELECT, INSERT, and UPDATE operations on specific tables in the database but does not allow them to perform any other tasks.

Application roles allow you to create password-protected roles for specific applications. For example, a user could connect through a web-based application called NetReady; this application would activate the role, and the user would then gain the role's permissions and privileges. Standard database roles or other roles cannot be assigned to an application role. Instead, the application role is activated when the application connects to the database.

SQL Server also has predefined database roles. Predefined roles are built in and have permissions that cannot be changed. You use predefined roles to assign database administration privileges, and you can assign a single login to multiple roles. These privileges are summarized in the following list:

- **public** The default role for all database users. Users inherit the permissions and privileges of the public role, and this role provides the minimum permissions and privileges. Any roles that you assign to a user beyond the public role can add permissions and privileges. If you want all database users to have specific permissions, assign the permissions to the public role.
- **db_accessadmin** Designed for users who need to add or remove logins in a database.
- **db_backupoperator** Designed for users who need to back up a database.
- **db_datareader** Designed for users who need to view data in a database. Members of this role can select all data from any user table in the database.
- **db_datawriter** Designed for users who need to add or modify any data in any user table in the database. Members of this role can perform the following tasks on any objects in the selected database: DELETE, INSERT, and UPDATE.
- **db_ddladmin** Designed for users who need to perform tasks related to the data definition language (DDL) for SQL Server. Members of this role can issue any DDL statement except GRANT, REVOKE, or DENY.

- **db_denydatareader** Designed to restrict access to data in a database by login. Members of this role cannot read any data in user tables within a database.
- **db_denydatawriter** Designed to restrict modification permissions in a database by login. Members of this role cannot add, modify, or delete any data in user tables within a database.
- **db_owner** Designed for users who need complete control over all aspects of the database. Members of this role can assign permissions, modify database settings, perform database maintenance, and perform any other administration task on the database, including dropping the database.
- **db_securityadmin** Designed for users who need to manage permissions, object ownership, and roles.
- **dbm_monitor** Designed for users who need to monitor the current status of Database Mirroring.

Fixed database roles can be mapped to the more granular permissions for SQL Server 2012, as shown in Table 7-7.

TABLE 7-7 Granular Permissions Associated with Fixed Database Roles

FIXED DATABASE ROLE	PERMISSIONS GRANTED WITH THIS ROLE
db_accessadmin	ALTER ANY USER, CONNECT WITH GRANT OPTION, CREATE SCHEMA, VIEW ANY DATABASE
db_backupoperator	BACKUP DATABASE, BACKUP LOG, CHECKPOINT, VIEW ANY DATABASE
db_datareader	SELECT, VIEW ANY DATABASE
db_datawriter	DELETE, INSERT, UPDATE, VIEW ANY DATABASE
db_ddladmin	ALTER ANY ASSEMBLY, ALTER ANY ASYMMETRIC KEY, ALTER ANY CERTIFICATE, ALTER ANY CONTRACT, ALTER ANY DATABASE DDL TRIGGER, ALTER ANY DATABASE EVENT NOTIFICATION, ALTER ANY DATASPACE, ALTER ANY FULLTEXT CATALOG, ALTER ANY MESSAGE TYPE, ALTER ANY REMOTE SERVICE BINDING, ALTER ANY ROUTE, ALTER ANY SCHEMA, ALTER ANY SERVICE, ALTER ANY SYMMETRIC KEY, CHECKPOINT, CREATE AGGREGATE, CREATE DEFAULT, CREATE FUNCTION, CREATE PROCEDURE, CREATE QUEUE, CREATE RULE, CREATE SYNONYM, CREATE TABLE, CREATE TYPE, CREATE VIEW, CREATE XML SCHEMA COLLECTION, REFERENCES, VIEW ANY DATABASE
db_denydatareader	Denies SELECT
db_denydatawriter	Denies DELETE, INSERT, UPDATE

FIXED DATABASE ROLE	PERMISSIONS GRANTED WITH THIS ROLE
db_owner	CONTROL WITH GRANT OPTION, VIEW ANY DATABASE
db_securityadmin	ALTER ANY APPLICATION ROLE, ALTER ANY ROLE, CREATE SCHEMA, VIEW DEFINITION, VIEW ANY DATABASE
dbm_monitor	VIEW status of database mirroring, VIEW ANY DATABASE

REAL WORLD The *msdb* database contains a number of special-purpose roles. When users work with SQL Server Integration Services (SSIS), you'll want to assign the db_ssisadmin role to S SIS administrators, the db_ssisoperator role to SSIS operators, and the db_ssisltduser role to limited users. When you use data collectors, you'll want to assign the dc_admin role to DC administrators, the dc_operator role to DC operators, and the dc_proxy role to DC proxy accounts.

Other important special-purpose roles include the PolicyAdministratorRole for administrators who perform configuration and maintenance activities for Policy-Based Management, the ServerGroupAdministratorRole for administrators who manage and work with registered servers, and the ServerGroupReaderRole for those who need to see what server groups are available.

Managing Server Logins

SQL Server can authenticate using Windows logins as well as SQL Server logins. If you have configured the server for mixed security, you can use both authentication types. Otherwise, you can use only Windows logins. You manage logins at the server level.

Viewing and Editing Existing Logins

To view or edit an existing login, follow these steps:

1. Start SQL Server Management Studio. In the Object Explorer view, connect to the appropriate server, and then work your way down to the Security folder.

2. Expand the Security folder at the server level, and then the Logins folder to list the current logins. Right-click a login, and then select Properties to view the properties of the login.

3. The Login Properties dialog box, shown in Figure 7-1, has five pages:

   - **General** Provides an overview of the login configuration, including the authentication mode (which can be changed), the default database and language (which can be changed), and any mapped credentials (which can be added or removed).

   TIP On the General page, reset or change a login's password by entering and confirming the new password in the fields provided. Sysadmins and others with the ALTER ANY LOGIN permission can change a login's password without having to enter the login's old password.

- **Server Roles**   Lists the server roles and allows you to add or remove the login's server roles
- **User Mappings**   Lists databases accessible by the login and allows you to manage, on a per-database basis, the default schema, the user identity for the database, and the assigned database roles
- **Securables**   Shows current object permissions and allows you to manage object permissions for the login
- **Status**   Shows current status of the login, including whether the login is enabled, locked out, or denied permission to connect to the Database Engine

NOTE   In the Connection area of any page, you can click the View Connection Properties link to see detailed information about the user's current connection properties. This information is helpful for troubleshooting connection issues.

4.   When you finish working with the account, click OK.

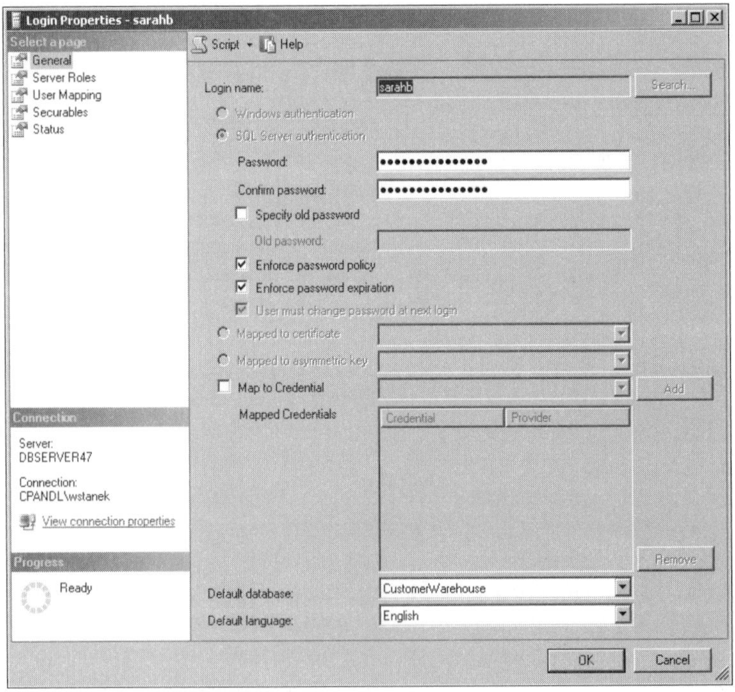

FIGURE 7-1 The Login Properties dialog box.

To view information about a login with Transact-SQL (T-SQL), use sp_helplogins. Sample 7-1 shows the syntax and usage for this command.

SAMPLE 7-1 sp_helplogins Syntax and Usage.

Syntax

```
sp_helplogins [[@LoginNamePattern =] 'login']
```

Usage

```
EXEC sp_helplogins 'goteam'
```

The output provided by sp_helplogins includes the login name, security identifier, default database, and default language. To determine the server roles and Windows groups to which the currently logged-on user either implicitly or expressly belongs, you can execute the following query:

```
USE master
GO
SELECT * FROM sys.login_token;
GO
```

Creating Logins

You create new logins in SQL Server Management Studio by using the Login—New dialog box. If you want to use Windows user or group accounts, you must create these accounts on the local machine or in the Windows domain and then create the related logins. Ask a network administrator to set up the necessary accounts.

To create a login, follow these steps:

1. Start SQL Server Management Studio. In the Object Explorer view, connect to the appropriate server, and then work your way down to the Security folder at the server level.

2. Right-click Logins, and then select New Login to display the Login—New dialog box, shown in Figure 7-2.

3. If you are creating a login for a Windows account, select the Windows Authentication option, and then type the user name in *DOMAIN\username* format, such as CPANDL\georgeh. If you want to search Active Directory for the domain and user information, click Search, and then use the Select User Or Group dialog box to select the user for which you are creating the SQL Server account. Password policy and expiration enforcement are handled by the local Windows password policy automatically.

4. If you want to create a new SQL Server login, select the SQL Server Authentication option. Type the name of the account you want to use, such as Sales or GEORGEH, and then enter and confirm the password for the account. To enforce the local Windows password expiration policy on the SQL Server login, select Enforce Password Policy. If you elect to enforce password policy, you can also elect to enforce password expiration. To do this, select Enforce Password Expiration.

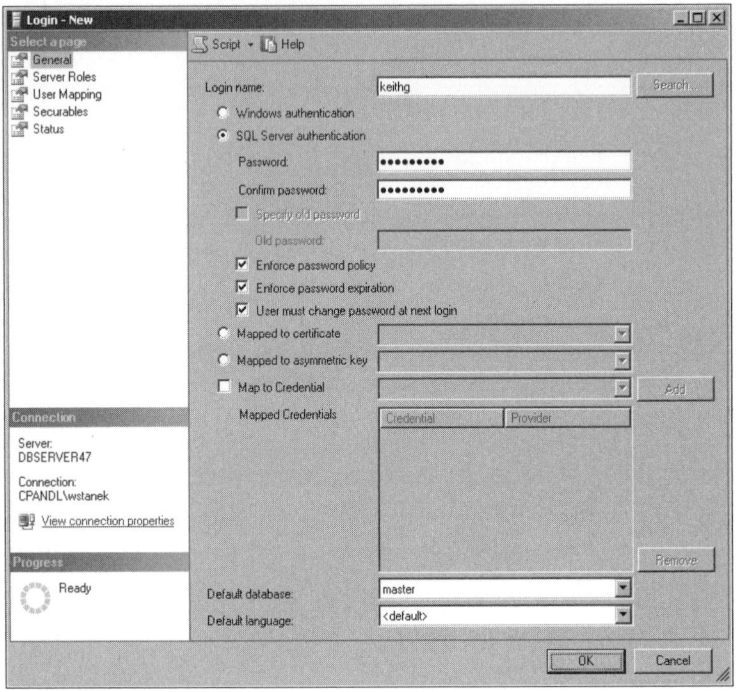

FIGURE 7-2 The Login—New dialog box.

5. Specify the default database and default language for the login. Assigning a default database does not give the login permission to access the database. Instead, this option specifies the database that is used when no database is specified in a command.

6. Click OK to create the login. If you are creating a SQL Server login and an identically named login already exists on the server, you will see an error. Click OK and change the login, or click Cancel if you determine that the new login is not needed.

You have not yet assigned any roles or access permissions. Refer to the "Configuring Server Roles" and "Controlling Database Access and Administration" sections later in this chapter to learn how to configure these options.

You can also create logins with T-SQL. Use CREATE LOGIN as shown in Sample 7-2. To use this statement, you need ALTER ANY LOGIN permission on the server (and if using credentials, you need ALTER ANY CREDENTIAL permission).

SAMPLE 7-2 CREATE LOGIN Syntax and Usage.

Syntax

```
CREATE LOGIN login_name { WITH < option_list1 > | FROM < sources > }
```

```
< sources >::=
    WINDOWS [ WITH DEFAULT_DATABASE = database
    | DEFAULT_LANGUAGE = language [,...] ]
    | CERTIFICATE certificate_name
    | ASYMMETRIC KEY asym_key_name

< option_list1 >::=
    PASSWORD = 'password' [ HASHED ] [ MUST_CHANGE ]
    [ , option_list2 [ ,... ] ]

< option_list2 >::=
    SID = sid
    | DEFAULT_DATABASE = database
    | DEFAULT_LANGUAGE = language
    | CHECK_EXPIRATION = { ON | OFF}
    | CHECK_POLICY = { ON | OFF}
    [ CREDENTIAL = credential_name ]
```

Usage for SQL Logins

```
create login georgeh WITH PASSWORD = 'MZ82$!408765RTM'
```

Usage for SQL Logins Mapped to Credentials

```
create login georgeh WITH PASSWORD = 'MZ82$!408765RTM',
    CREDENTIAL = StanekWR
```

Usage for Logins from a Domain Account

```
CREATE LOGIN [CPANDL\georgeh] FROM WINDOWS;
```

Editing Logins with T-SQL

You can edit logins in SQL Server Management Studio as explained in the "Viewing and Editing Existing Logins" section earlier in this chapter. Editing logins with T-SQL is more work, however, and requires you to use the ALTER LOGIN statement. You need ALTER ANY LOGIN permission to alter logins (and if working with credentials, the ALTER ANY CREDENTIAL permission). When a login is a member of the sysadmin server role, only another member of this role can make the following changes:

- Reset the password without supplying the old password.
- Require a user to change the login password.
- Change the login name.
- Enable or disable the login.
- Change the login credential.
- Force SQL Server to check a password for compliance with Group Policy.
- Force SQL Server to enforce password expiration settings in Group Policy.

Sample 7-3 shows the syntax and usage for ALTER LOGIN.

SAMPLE 7-3 ALTER LOGIN Syntax and Usage.

Syntax

```
ALTER LOGIN login_name
    { ENABLE | DISABLE
    | WITH set_option [ ,... ]
    | ADD CREDENTIAL credential_name | DROP CREDENTIAL credential_name
    }

< set_option >::=
    PASSWORD = 'password' | hashed_password HASHED
    [ OLD_PASSWORD = 'oldpassword' | MUST_CHANGE [UNLOCK] ]
    | DEFAULT_DATABASE = database
    | DEFAULT_LANGUAGE = language
    | NAME = login_name
    | CHECK_POLICY = { ON | OFF }
    | CHECK_EXPIRATION = { ON | OFF }
    | CREDENTIAL = credential_name
    | NO CREDENTIAL
```

Usage for Changing the Login Name

```
ALTER LOGIN georgeh WITH NAME = stanekwr
```

Usage for Changing the Login Password

```
ALTER LOGIN georgeh WITH PASSWORD = '3948wJ698FFF7';
```

Usage for Requiring User to Change Password

```
ALTER LOGIN georgeh MUST_CHANGE
```

Usage for Enforcing Password Policy

```
ALTER LOGIN georgeh CHECK_POLICY=ON
```

Usage for Enforcing Password Expiration

```
ALTER LOGIN georgeh CHECK_EXPIRATION=ON
```

Granting or Denying Server Access

When you create a new login or modify an existing login based on a Windows account, you can grant or deny access to the server's Database Engine explicitly for this login. Explicitly denying access to the server is useful when a particular Windows account should be temporarily restricted from accessing the server.

To grant or deny access for an existing login, complete the following steps:

1. Start SQL Server Management Studio. In the Object Explorer view, connect to the appropriate server, and then work your way down to the Security folder at the server level.

2. Expand the Security folder and the Logins folder to list the current logins. Right-click a login, and then select Properties to view the properties of that login. This opens the Login Properties dialog box (shown previously in Figure 7-1).

3. In the Select A Page list, select Status.

4. To grant access to the server, select the Grant option.

5. To deny access to the server, select the Deny option.

> **NOTE** Denying access to the server does not prevent users from logging in to SQL Server. Instead, it prevents them from using their Windows domain account to log in to SQL Server. Users can still log in if they have a valid SQL Server login ID and password.

6. Click OK.

You can also grant or deny logins with T-SQL. To grant a login for a domain account, use GRANT CONNECT, as shown in Sample 7-4.

> **NOTE** Only members of the sysadmin or securityadmin fixed server role can execute GRANT CONNECT and DENY CONNECT.

SAMPLE 7-4 GRANT CONNECT Syntax and Usage.

Syntax
```
USE [master]
GO
GRANT CONNECT SQL TO 'login'
GO
```

Usage
```
USE [master]
GO
GRANT CONNECT SQL TO 'CPANDL\GEORGEH'
GO
```

To deny access to the server for the account, use DENY CONNECT as shown in Sample 7-5.

SAMPLE 7-5 DENY CONNECT Syntax and Usage.

Syntax
```
USE [master]
GO
DENY CONNECT SQL TO 'login'
GO
```

Usage
```
USE [master]
GO
DENY CONNECT SQL TO 'CPANDL\GEORGEH'
GO
```

Enabling, Disabling, and Unlocking Logins

Similar to Windows accounts, SQL Server logins can be enabled and disabled by administrators. Logins can also become locked based on policy settings and might need to be unlocked. For example, if a login's password expires, the login might become locked.

> **TIP** You can determine whether a login is disabled or locked by selecting the server's Logins node in SQL Server Management Studio. The icon for the login is updated to show the status as locked or disabled.

To enable, disable, or unlock a login, complete the following steps:

1. Start SQL Server Management Studio. In the Object Explorer view, connect to the appropriate server, and then work your way down to the Security folder at the server level.

2. Expand the Security folder and the Logins folder to list the current logins. Right-click a login, and then select Properties to view the properties of that login. This opens the Login Properties dialog box.

3. In the Select A Page list, select Status.

4. You can now do the following:

   - Enable the login by selecting Enabled under Login.
   - Disable the login by selecting Disabled under Login.
   - Unlock the login by clearing the Login Is Locked Out check box.

5. Click OK.

You can also enable, disable, or unlock a login with T-SQL. To grant a login for a domain account, use ALTER LOGIN, as shown in Sample 7-6.

> **NOTE** Only members of the sysadmin or securityadmin fixed server role can execute ALTER LOGIN.

SAMPLE 7-6 Enabling, Disabling, and Unlocking Accounts.

Syntax

```
USE [master]
GO
ALTER LOGIN 'login' DISABLE | ENABLE | UNLOCK
GO
```

Usage for Disabling Logins

```
USE [master]
GO
ALTER LOGIN 'CPANDL\GEORGEH' DISABLE
GO
```

Usage for Enabling Logins

```
USE [master]
GO
```

```
ALTER LOGIN 'CPANDL\GEORGEH' ENABLE
GO
```

Usage for Unlocking Logins

```
USE [master]
GO
ALTER LOGIN 'CPANDL\GEORGEH' UNLOCK
GO
```

Removing Logins

When a user leaves the organization or a login is no longer needed for another reason, you should remove the login from SQL Server. To remove a login, complete the following steps:

1. Start SQL Server Management Studio, and then access the appropriate server.

2. In the server's Security folder, expand the Logins folder.

3. Right-click the login you want to remove, and then select Delete from the shortcut menu.

4. The Delete Object dialog box shows you which account you are deleting. Click OK to remove the account. Remember that you might also need to delete users in each database.

Use DROP LOGIN to delete Windows user and group accounts, as shown in Sample 7-7.

SAMPLE 7-7 DROP LOGIN Syntax and Usage.

Syntax

```
DROP LOGIN 'login'
```

Usage

```
DROP LOGIN 'CPANDL\GEORGEH'
```

Changing Passwords

You manage Windows user and group accounts in the Windows domain or on the local machine. Users can change their own passwords or ask the Windows administrator to reset their passwords, if necessary. For SQL Server logins, you change passwords through SQL Server Management Studio by following these steps:

1. Start SQL Server Management Studio, and then access the appropriate server.

2. In the server's Security folder, expand the Logins folder.

3. Right-click the login you want to change, and then select Properties to display the Login Properties dialog box.

4. Type and then confirm the new password in the boxes provided.

5. Click OK.

To change passwords with T-SQL, you can use ALTER LOGIN, as discussed previously in the "Editing Logins with T-SQL" section earlier in this chapter.

Configuring Server Roles

Server roles set serverwide administrator privileges for SQL Server logins. You can manage server roles by role or by individual logins.

Assigning Roles by Login

To assign or change server roles for a login, follow these steps:

1. Start SQL Server Management Studio. In the Object Explorer view, connect to the appropriate server, and then work your way down to the Security folder at the server level.

2. Expand the Security folder and the Logins folder to list the current logins. Right-click a login, and then select Properties to display the Login Properties dialog box and view the properties of the login.

3. Select the Server Roles page, shown in Figure 7-3.

4. Grant server roles by selecting the check boxes next to the roles you want to use. See the "Server Roles" section earlier in this chapter for more information.

5. When you finish configuring server roles, click OK.

You can also configure server roles with T-SQL. Use ALTER SERVER ROLE to add a login to a server role or to remove a login from a role. You can use it as shown in Sample 7-8.

NOTE To use ALTER SERVER ROLE, you must have ALTER ANY LOGIN permission on the server and membership in the role to which you are adding the new member.

SAMPLE 7-8 ALTER SERVER ROLE Syntax and Usage.

Syntax

```
ALTER SERVER ROLE server_role_name
  { [ ADD MEMBER server_principal ] | [ DROP MEMBER server_principal ]
  | [ WITH NAME = new_server_role_name ] } [ ; ]
```

Usage to Add Member

```
ALTER SERVER ROLE sysadmin ADD MEMBER 'CPANDL\GEORGEH'
```

Usage to Remove Member

```
ALTER SERVER ROLE sysadmin DROP MEMBER 'CPANDL\GEORGEH'
```

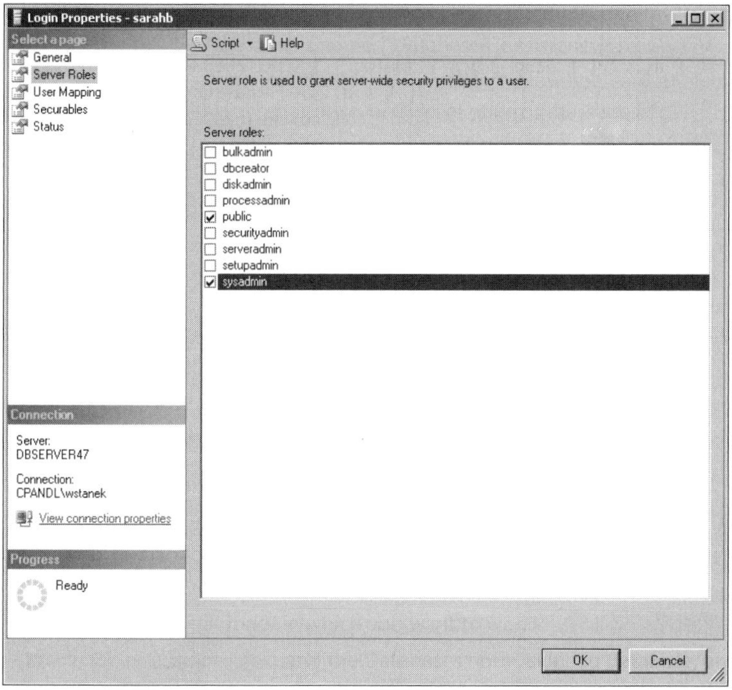

FIGURE 7-3 The Server Roles page of the Login Properties dialog box.

Assigning Roles to Multiple Logins

The easiest way to assign roles to multiple logins is to use the Server Role Properties dialog box. To access this dialog box and configure multiple logins, follow these steps:

1. Start SQL Server Management Studio. In the Object Explorer view, connect to the appropriate server, and then work your way down to the Security folder at the server level.

2. Expand the Server Roles node, right-click the role you want to configure, and then select Properties. This opens the Server Role Properties dialog box, shown in Figure 7-4.

3. To add logins, click Add, and then use the Select Logins dialog box to select the logins to add. You can enter partial names and then click Check Names to expand the name. To search for names, click Browse.

4. To remove a login, select it, and then click Remove.

5. When you finish configuring server roles, click OK.

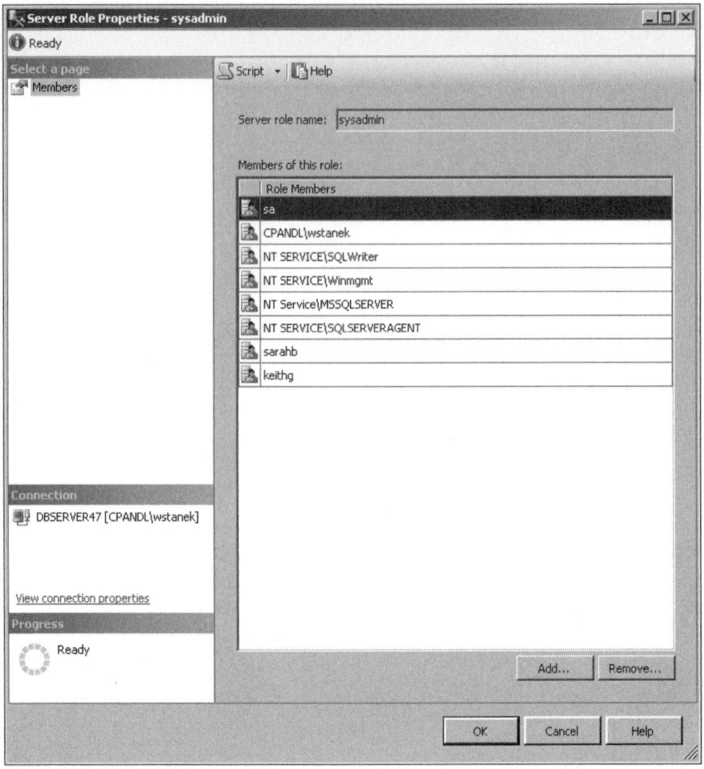

FIGURE 7-4 The Server Role Properties dialog box.

Revoking Access Rights and Roles by Server Login

To revoke access rights or to remove a user from a role in a database, complete the following steps:

1. Start SQL Server Management Studio. In the Object Explorer view, connect to the appropriate server.

2. Expand the server's Security folder, and then expand the related Logins folder.

3. Double-click the login that you want to configure to display the Login Properties dialog box.

4. Select the Server Roles page. Clear the check box next to the server roles that you want to remove from this login.

5. Select the User Mapping page. Clear the check box next to the databases to which this user should not have access. Alternatively, select a database to which access is permitted, and then modify the granted roles by clearing options under Database Role Membership For.

6. When you finish, click OK.

Controlling Database Access and Administration

You control database access and administration with database users and roles. At their most basic, database users are the logins that have the right to access the database and database access roles set administration privileges and other database permissions. However, it is important to remember that SQL Server supports:

- Users based on logins in the *master* database
- Users that authenticate in a contained database
- Users based on Windows principals that have no logins but can authenticate
- Users that cannot authenticate and do not have logins but are granted permissions

Fortunately, all of these various types of users can be created and managed in much the same way.

Viewing and Editing Existing Database Users

To view or edit an existing user, follow these steps:

1. Start SQL Server Management Studio. In the Object Explorer view, connect to the appropriate server, and then expand the Security folder of the database you want to configure.

2. Expand the Users folder at the database level to list the current users. Right-click a user, and then select Properties to view the properties of the user.

3. The Database User Properties dialog box has five pages:

   - **General** Provides an overview of the user configuration, including the user type and login name (which cannot be changed) and the default language and schema of the user (which can be changed).

   TIP On the General page, reset or change a user's password by entering and confirming the new password in the fields provided. Sysadmins and others with the ALTER ANY USER permission can change a user's password without having to enter the user's old password.

   - **Owned Schemas** Lists schemas owned by the user
   - **Membership** Lists database roles the user has been assigned
   - **Securables** Shows current object permissions and allows you to manage object permissions for the user
   - **Extended Properties** Shows any extended properties associated with the user

4. When you finish working with the account, click OK.

To view information about a user with T-SQL, use sp_helpuser. Sample 7-9 shows the syntax and usage for this command.

Syntax

```
sp_helpuser [[@Name_In_Db =] 'account_name']
```

Usage

```
EXEC sp_helpuser 'samg'
```

For standard user accounts, the output provided by sp_helpuser includes the user name, login name, default database, default schema, user ID in the database, and SID, as well as the names of roles to which the user belongs.

Creating Database Users

You create new users in SQL Server Management Studio by using the Database User—New dialog box. If you want to use Windows user or group accounts, you must create these accounts on the local machine or in the Windows domain and then create the related users. Ask a network administrator to set up the necessary accounts.

To create a database user, follow these steps:

1. Start SQL Server Management Studio. In the Object Explorer view, connect to the appropriate server, and then work your way down to the Security folder associated with the database you want to work with.

2. Right-click Users, and then select New User to display the User—New dialog box. Use the User Type list to specify the type of user to create:

    ■ **SQL user with password**   If you want to create a user that authenticates at the database, select SQL User With Password. Type the desired user name, enter and confirm the user's password, and then set the user's default language.

    ■ **SQL user with login**   If you want to create a user based on a login in *master*, select SQL User With Login. Type the desired user name, and then enter the name of the login from *master*. Alternatively, click the Logins options (...) button and then use the Select Login dialog box to find the login to use.

    ■ **SQL user without login**   If you want to create a user that is not based on a login in *master*, select SQL User Without Login and then type the desired user name.

    ■ **User mapped to a certificate**   If you want to create a user mapped to a certificate, select User Mapped To A Certificate. Type the desired user name, click the Certificate Name options (...) button, and then use the Select Certificate dialog box to locate the certificate that you want to use.

    ■ **User mapped to an asymmetric key**   If you want to create a database user mapped to an asymmetric key, select User Mapped To An Asymmetric Key. Type the desired user name, click the Asymmetric Key

Name options (...) button, and then use the Select Asymmetric Key dialog box to locate the asymmetric key that you want to use.

- **Windows user** If you are creating a user for a Windows account, select the Windows User option, and then type the user name in *DOMAIN\username* format, such as CPANDL\georgeh, and the desired login name, such as PennyC.

REAL WORLD The default object is a user or built-in account and default location is the local server. Click the User Name options (...) button, and then use the Select User Or Group dialog box to select the user or group for which you are creating the database user. To use a service account or group, click Object Types, select the appropriate object type, and then click OK. To use an account in a domain, you must click Locations, expand Entire Directory in the Locations dialog box, and then select the Active Directory domain or organizational unit to search.

3. If you want to create a database user based on a login in *master,* select SQL User With Login. Type the user name of the account, such as dbSales or GEORGEH, and then enter the name of the login from *master.* Alternatively, click the Logins options (...) button and then use the Select Login dialog box to find the login to use.

4. As appropriate, set the default schema for the user.

5. Optionally, select Owned Schemas and then specify the schemas owned by the user.

6. Optionally, select Membership and then specify the database roles the user should be a member of.

7. Optionally, select Owned Schemas and then specify the schemas owned by the user.

8. Click OK to create the user. Note that if an identically named user already exists in the database, you will see an error. Click OK, change the user name and try again, or click Cancel if you determine that the new user is not needed.

You can also create users with T-SQL. Use CREATE USER as shown in Sample 7-10.

SAMPLE 7-10 CREATE USER Syntax and Usage.

Syntax

```
CREATE USER [user_name | windows_principal]
    [ { { FOR | FROM }
        { [WITHOUT] LOGIN [login_name | windows_principal]
        | CERTIFICATE certificate_name
        | ASYMMETRIC KEY asym_key_name
        }
    ]
```

```
[ WITH PASSWORD = 'password']
[ WITH DEFAULT_SCHEMA = schema_name ]
[ WITH DEFAULT_LANGUAGE = NONE | language ]
```

Usage for Users Based on Logins in Master

```
create user CPANDL\georgeh FROM LOGIN CPANDL\georgeh
```

Usage for Users That Authenticate at the Database

```
create user CPANDL\georgeh
create user pennyc WITH PASSWORD = 'MZ82$!408765RTM'
```

Usage for Users That Can't Authenticate

```
CREATE USER TestUser WITHOUT LOGIN
CREATE USER TestUser FROM CERTIFICATE TestCert4
CREATE USER TestUser FROM ASYMMETRIC KEY TestKey3
```

Editing Users with T-SQL

You can edit users in SQL Server Management Studio as explained in the "Viewing and Editing Existing Database Users" section earlier in this chapter. Editing users with T-SQL is more work, however, and requires you to use the ALTER USER statement. You need ALTER ANY USER permission to alter users.

Sample 7-11 shows the syntax and usage for ALTER USER. With users authenticated at the database level, you can use ALTER USER to change the user's password as well.

SAMPLE 7-11 ALTER USER Syntax and Usage.

Syntax

```
ALTER USER user_name
    { WITH set_option [ ,... ]  }

< set_option >::=
    PASSWORD = 'password' | [ OLD_PASSWORD = 'oldpassword']
    | DEFAULT_LANGUAGE = { NONE | language }
    | DEFAULT_SCHEMA = { schema_name | NULL }
    | LOGIN = login_name
    | NAME = new_user_name
```

Usage for Changing the User Name

```
ALTER USER juliech WITH NAME = julieh
```

Usage for Changing the User Password

```
ALTER USER georgeh WITH PASSWORD = '3948wJ698FFF7';
```

Removing Users

When a user leaves the organization or a user is no longer needed for another reason, you should remove the user from SQL Server. To remove a user, complete the following steps:

1. Start SQL Server Management Studio, and access the appropriate server, and then work your way down to the Security folder associated with the database you want to work with.
2. In the server's Security folder, expand the Users folder.
3. Right-click the user you want to remove, and then select Delete from the shortcut menu.
4. The Delete Object dialog box shows you which account you are deleting. Click OK to remove the account.

Another way to delete a user is to use DROP USER, as shown in Sample 7-12.

SAMPLE 7-12 DROP USER Syntax and Usage.

Syntax
```
DROP USER 'user'
```

Usage
```
DROP USER 'CPANDL\GEORGEH'
```

Assigning Access and Roles by Login

For individual logins, you can grant access to databases and assign roles by completing the following steps:

1. Start SQL Server Management Studio. In the Object Explorer view, connect to the appropriate server, and then work your way down to the Security folder.
2. Expand the Security folder and the Logins folder to list the current logins. Right-click the login you want to configure, and then select Properties. This opens the Login Properties dialog box.
3. Select the User Mapping page, shown in Figure 7-5.
4. Select the check box for a database for which you want the login to have access. Then, in the Database Role Membership For list, select the check boxes for each role that this login should have on the currently selected database.

   TIP If you select the *msdb* database, as shown in Figure 7-5, you can assign special-purpose roles for SSIS, Policy-Based Management, and server groups.

5. Repeat step 4 for other databases for which the login should have access.
6. When you finish configuring database roles, click OK.

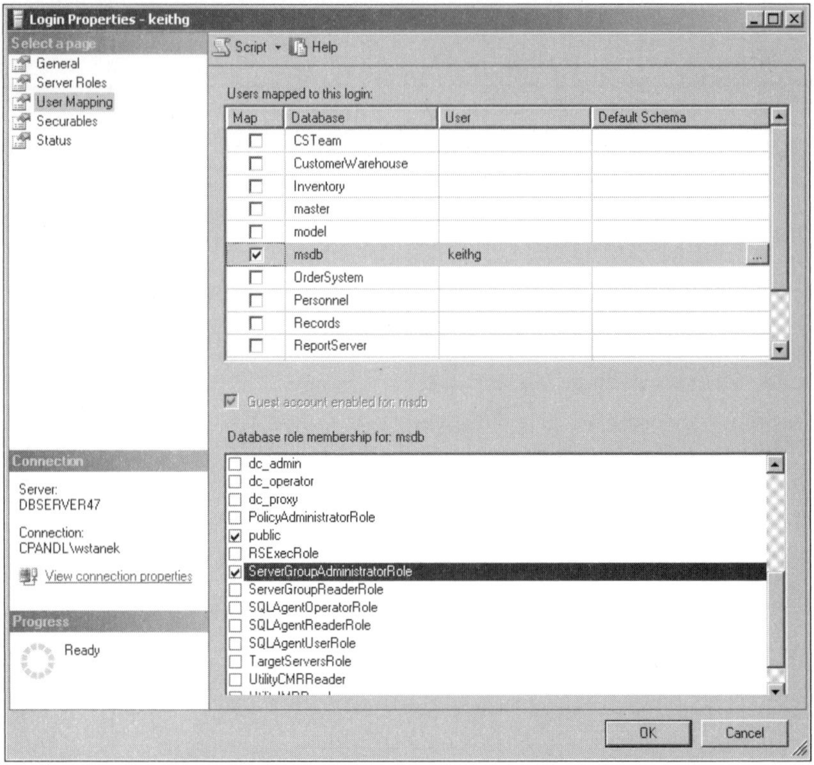

FIGURE 7-5 The User Mapping page of the Login Properties dialog box.

Assigning Roles for Multiple Logins

At the database level, you can assign database roles to multiple logins. To do this, complete the following steps:

1. Start SQL Server Management Studio. In the Object Explorer view, connect to the appropriate server.

2. Expand the Databases folder, and then expand the node for the database you want to configure.

3. Expand the database's Security, Roles, and Database Roles folders. Double-click the role you want to configure. This opens the Database Role Properties dialog box, shown in Figure 7-6.

4. To add role members, click Add to display the Select Database User Or Role dialog box.

5. In the dialog box, enter the name of the user or role to add. Separate names with semicolons. You can enter partial names and then click Check Names to expand the names. To search for names, click Browse.

6. To remove a role member, select a database user or other role, and then click Remove.

7. When you finish configuring database roles, click OK.

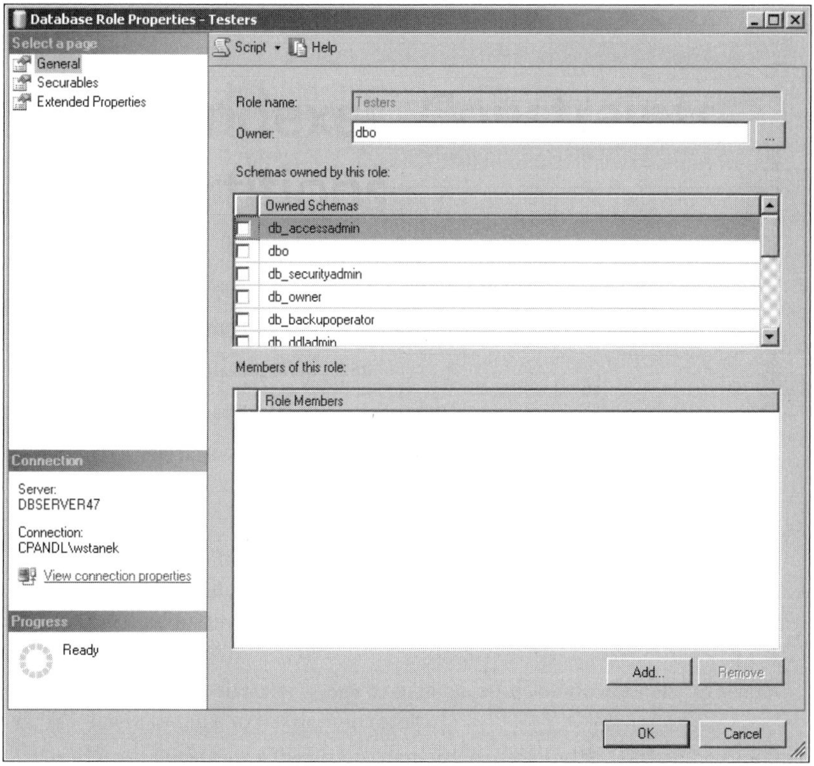

FIGURE 7-6 The Database Role Properties dialog box.

Creating Standard Database Roles

Although predefined roles have a specific set of permissions that you cannot change, you can set permissions for roles you create for a particular database. For example, suppose that a database has three different types of users: standard users who need to view data, managers who need to be able to modify data, and developers who need to be able to modify database objects. In this situation, you can create three roles to handle these user types and then manage only these roles and not the many different user accounts.

To create a standard database role, complete the following steps:

1. Start SQL Server Management Studio. In the Object Explorer view, connect to the appropriate server.

2. Expand the Databases folder, select a database, and then expand the node for it.

3. Expand the database's Security and Roles folders. Right-click Roles, point to New, and then choose New Database Role. This opens the Database Role—New dialog box, shown in Figure 7-7.

4. Type a name for the role in the Role Name box.

    TIP Use a name for the role that is short but descriptive, such as Standard Users, Editors, Testers, or Developers.

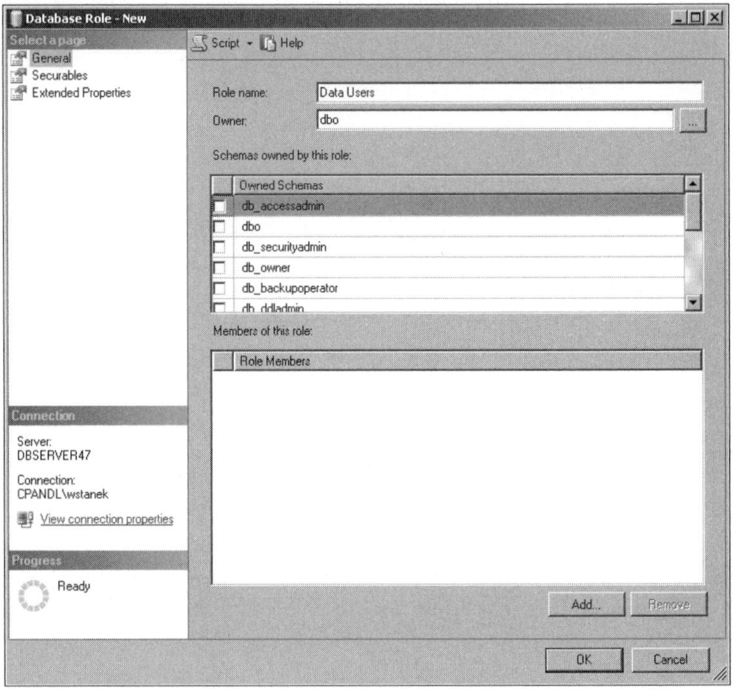

FIGURE 7-7 The Database Role—New dialog box.

5. The default owner of the role is dbo. To set a different owner, click the button to the right of the Owner box to display the Select Database User Or Role dialog box.

6. In the dialog box, enter the name of the users, the roles, or both that should be the owners of this role. Separate names with semicolons. You can enter partial names and then click Check Names to expand the names. To search for names, click Browse.

7. To add role members, click Add to display the Select Database User Or Role dialog box.

8. In the dialog box, enter the names of the users or roles to add. Separate names with semicolons. You can enter partial names and then click Check Names to expand the names. To search for names, click Browse. Click OK.

9. Select Securables in the Select A Page list in the dialog box, and then use the Securables page options to configure database access permissions for this role. For more information about configuring database access permissions, see the "Managing Database Permissions" section later in this chapter.

10. Click OK.

Creating Application Database Roles

Application roles are designed to be used by applications that access the database and do not have logins associated with them. You can configure an application role by completing the following steps:

1. Start SQL Server Management Studio. In the Object Explorer view, connect to the appropriate server.

2. Expand the Databases folder, and then select a database and expand the node for it.

3. Expand the database's Security and Roles folders. Right-click Roles, point to New, and then choose New Application Role. This opens the Application Role—New dialog box, shown in Figure 7-8.

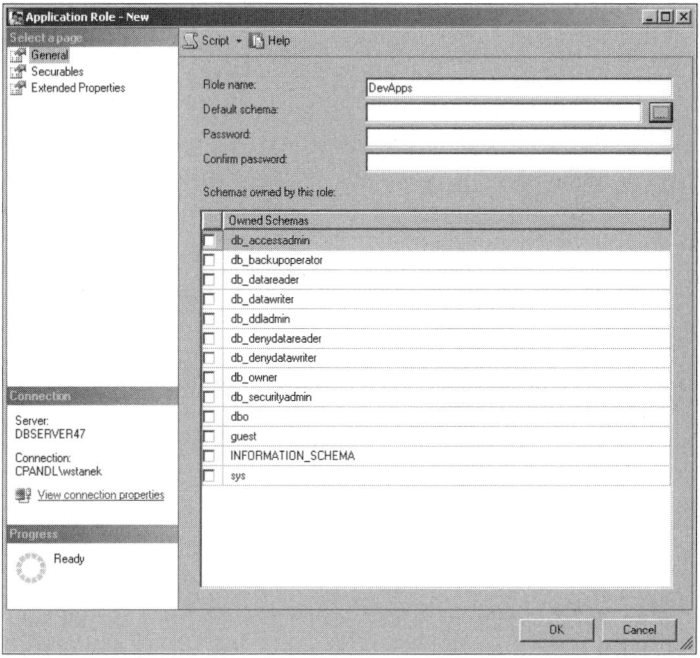

FIGURE 7-8 The Application Role—New dialog box.

4. Type a name for the role in the Role Name box.

5. The default schema for the role is dbo. The default (or base) schema sets the base permissions for the new role. To set a different default schema, click the button to the right of the Default Schema box to display the Locate Schema dialog box.

6. In the dialog box, enter the name of the default schema. You can enter a partial name and then click Check Names to expand the name. To search for a schema to use, click Browse. Click OK.

7. Select Securables in the Select A Page list, and then use the Securables page options to configure database access permissions for this role. For more information about configuring database access permissions, see the "Managing Database Permissions" section later in this chapter.

8. Click OK.

Removing Role Memberships for Database Users

To revoke access rights or to remove a user from a role in a database, complete the following steps:

1. Start SQL Server Management Studio. In the Object Explorer view, connect to the appropriate server.

2. Expand the Databases folder, select a database, and then expand the node for it.

3. Expand the database's Security and Users folders. Double-click the user name. This opens the Database User dialog box.

4. On the General page, clear the check box next to the database roles that this user should not have on the currently selected database.

5. When you finish removing roles for the database user, click OK.

Deleting User-Defined Roles

To delete a user-defined role, complete the following steps:

1. Start SQL Server Management Studio. In the Object Explorer view, connect to the appropriate server.

2. Expand the Databases folder, select a database, and then expand the node for it.

3. Expand the database's Security and Roles folders.

4. If the role that you want to remove is a database role, expand Database Roles. If the role that you want to remove is an application role, expand Application Roles.

5. Select the role you want to delete, and then press the Delete key.

6. The Delete Object dialog box shows you which role you are deleting. Click OK to remove the role.

NOTE User-defined roles cannot be deleted if they have members. First, edit the properties for the role, deleting any currently listed members, and then delete the role.

T-SQL Commands for Managing Access and Roles

SQL Server provides different commands for managing database access and roles. These commands are summarized in Sample 7-13.

SAMPLE 7-13 Commands for Managing Database Access and Roles.

Adding a User to a Database

```
CREATE USER [user_name | windows_principal]
    [ { { FOR | FROM }
        { [WITHOUT] LOGIN [login_name | windows_principal]
        | CERTIFICATE certificate_name
        | ASYMMETRIC KEY asym_key_name
        }
    ]
    [ WITH PASSWORD = 'password']
    [ WITH DEFAULT_SCHEMA = schema_name ]
    [ WITH DEFAULT_LANGUAGE = NONE | language ]
```

Renaming a User or Changing Default Schema

```
ALTER USER user_name
    WITH < set_item > [ ,...n ]

< set_item > ::=
    NAME = new_user_name
    | DEFAULT_SCHEMA = schema_name
```

Changing the User Password

```
ALTER USER user_name WITH PASSWORD = 'password'
```

Removing a User from a Database

```
DROP USER user_name
```

Listing Server Role Members

```
sp_helpsrvrolemember [[@rolename =] 'role']
```

Managing Database Standard Roles

```
CREATE ROLE role_name [ AUTHORIZATION owner_name ]
ALTER ROLE role_name WITH NAME = new_name
DROP ROLE role_name
sp_helprole [[@rolename =] 'role']
```

Managing Database Role Members

```
ALTER SERVER ROLE server_role_name ADD MEMBER server_principal
    [ WITH NAME = new_server_role_name ]
ALTER SERVER ROLE server_role_name DROP MEMBER server_principal
```

```
    [ WITH NAME = new_server_role_name ]
sp_helprolemember [[@rolename =] 'role']
```

Managing Application Roles

```
CREATE APPLICATION ROLE application_role_name
    WITH PASSWORD = 'password' [ , DEFAULT_SCHEMA = schema_name ]

ALTER APPLICATION ROLE application_role_name
        WITH <set_item> [ ,...n ]

<set_item> ::=
    NAME = new_application_role_name
    | PASSWORD = 'password'
    | DEFAULT_SCHEMA = schema_name

DROP APPLICATION ROLE rolename
```

Managing Database Permissions

The database owner, members of sysadmin, and members of securityadmin can assign database permissions. The available permissions include the following:

- **GRANT** Gives permission to perform the related task. With roles, all members of the role inherit the permission.

- **REVOKE** Removes prior GRANT permission but does not explicitly prevent a user or role from performing a task. A user or role can still inherit GRANT permission from another role.

- **DENY** Explicitly denies permission to perform a task and prevents the user or role from inheriting the permission. DENY takes precedence over all other GRANT permissions.

  NOTE DENY is a T-SQL command and is not part of the ANSI SQL-92 standard.

You can grant, deny, and revoke permissions at the database level or the object level. You can also assign permissions by using database roles. For more information, see the "Controlling Database Access and Administration" section earlier in this chapter.

Assigning Database Permissions for Statements

At the database level, you can grant, revoke, or deny permission to execute DDL statements, such as CREATE TABLE or BACKUP DATABASE. These statements are summarized in Table 7-5 earlier in this chapter.

In SQL Server Management Studio, you grant, revoke, or deny database permissions for statements by completing the following steps:

1. Start SQL Server Management Studio. In the Object Explorer view, connect to the appropriate server.

2. Work your way down to the Databases folder by using the entries in the left pane.

3. Select a database, right-click the database name, and then select Properties to display the Database Properties dialog box.

4. In the Select A Page list, select the Permissions page, shown in Figure 7-9.

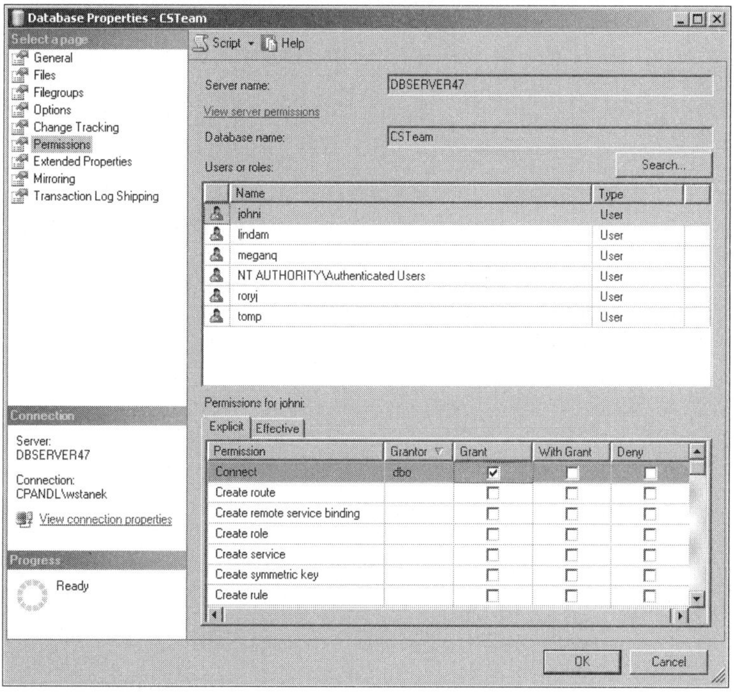

FIGURE 7-9 The Permissions page of the Database Properties dialog box.

5. To assign default permissions for all users, assign permissions to the public role. To add users or roles, click Search, and then use the Select User Or Group dialog box to select the user or role you want to add. To assign permissions for individual users or roles, select the user or role, and then use the Permissions For list to grant or deny permissions as appropriate. Clear both check boxes to revoke a previously granted or denied permission.

6. Click OK to assign the permissions.

With T-SQL, you use the GRANT, REVOKE, and DENY commands to assign permissions. Sample 7-14 shows the syntax and usage for GRANT, Sample 7-15 shows the syntax and usage for REVOKE, and Sample 7-16 shows the syntax and usage for DENY.

SAMPLE 7-14 GRANT Syntax and Usage.

Syntax for Permissions on Servers and Databases

```
GRANT < permission > [ ,...n ]
    TO < principal > [ ,...n ] [ WITH GRANT OPTION ]
    [ AS { SQL_Server_login | database_user
        | database_role | application_role } ]
< permission >::=  ALL [ PRIVILEGES ] | permission_name
    [ ( column [ ,...n ] ) ]
```

Syntax for Permissions on Members of the Object Class

```
GRANT < permission > [ ,...n ] ON [ OBJECT ::]  < securable_name >
    TO < principal > [ ,...n ] [ WITH GRANT OPTION ]
    [ AS { SQL_Server_login | database_user
        | database_role | application_role }
    ]
< permission >::=  ALL [ PRIVILEGES ] | permission_name
    [ ( column [ ,...n ] ) ]
```

Syntax for Permissions on All Other Securables

```
GRANT < permission > [ ,...n ] ON < scope >
    TO < principal > [ ,...n ] [ WITH GRANT OPTION ]
    [ AS { SQL_Server_login | database_user
        | database_role | application_role } ]
< permission >::=  ALL [ PRIVILEGES ] | permission_name
    [ ( column [ ,...n ] ) ]
< scope >::= [ securable_class :: ] securable_name
< securable_class >::= APPLICATION ROLE | ASSEMBLY | ASYMMETRIC KEY
    | CERTIFICATE | CONTRACT | ENDPOINT | FULLTEXT CATALOG
    | LOGIN | MESSAGE TYPE | REMOTE SERVICE BINDING | ROLE
    | ROUTE | SCHEMA | SERVICE | SYMMETRIC KEY | TYPE
    | USER | XML SCHEMA COLLECTION
```

Usage

```
GRANT CREATE DATABASE, CREATE TABLE
TO Users, [CPANDL\Sales]
GRANT SELECT
ON customer..customers
TO public
GRANT INSERT, UPDATE, DELETE
ON customer..customers
TO Devs, Testers
```

SAMPLE 7-15 REVOKE Syntax and Usage.

Syntax for Permissions on Servers and Databases

```
REVOKE [ GRANT OPTION FOR ] < permission > [ ,...n ]
    { TO | FROM } < principal > [ ,...n ] [ CASCADE ]
    [ AS  { SQL_Server_login
        | database_role | application_role } ]
< permission >::=  ALL [ PRIVILEGES ] | permission_name
```

```
    [ ( column [ ,...n ] ) ]
< principal >::= Windows_login | SQL_Server_login
    | SQL_Server_login_mapped_to_certificate
    | SQL_Server_login_mapped_to_asymmetric_key
    | Database_user | Database_role | Application_role
    | Database_user_mapped_to_certificate
    | Database_user_mapped_to_asymmetric_key
```

Syntax for Permissions on Members of the Object Class

```
REVOKE [ GRANT OPTION FOR ] < permission > [ ,...n ]
    ON [ OBJECT ::] < securable_name >
    { TO | FROM } < principal > [ ,...n ] [ CASCADE ]
    [ AS  {  SQL_Server_login | database_user
        | database_role | application_role } ]
< permission >::=  ALL [ PRIVILEGES ] | permission_name
    [ ( column [ ,...n ] ) ]
```

Syntax for Permissions on All Other Securables

```
REVOKE [ GRANT OPTION FOR ] < permission > [ ,...n ] [ ON < scope > ]
    { TO | FROM } < principal > [ ,...n ] [ CASCADE ]
    [ AS  {  SQL_Server_login | database_user
        | database_role | application_role } ]

< permission >::=  ALL [ PRIVILEGES ] | permission_name
    [ ( column [ ,...n ] ) ]
< scope >::= [ < securable_class > :: ] securable_name
< securable_class >::= APPLICATION ROLE | ASSEMBLY | ASYMMETRIC KEY
    | CERTIFICATE | CONTRACT | ENDPOINT | FULLTEXT CATALOG
    | LOGIN | MESSAGE TYPE | REMOTE SERVICE BINDING | ROLE
    | ROUTE | SCHEMA | SERVICE | SYMMETRIC KEY | TYPE
    | USER | XML SCHEMA COLLECTION
```

Usage

```
REVOKE CREATE TABLE, CREATE DEFAULT
FROM Devs, Testers
REVOKE INSERT, UPDATE, DELETE
FROM Users, [CPANDL\Sales]
```

SAMPLE 7-16 DENY Syntax and Usage.

Syntax for Permissions on Servers and Databases

```
DENY < permission > [ ,...n ]
    TO < principal > [ ,...n ] [ CASCADE ]
    [ AS  {  SQL_Server_login | database_user
        | database_role | application_role } ]

< permission >::=  ALL [ PRIVILEGES ] | permission_name
    [ ( column [ ,...n ] ) ]
```

Syntax for Permissions on Members of the Object Class

```
DENY < permission > [ ,...n ] ON [ OBJECT ::] < securable_name >
        TO < principal > [ ,...n ] [ CASCADE ]
    [ AS
        {
                Windows_group | SQL_Server_login | database_user
          | database_role | application_role
        }
    ]
< permission >::=  ALL [ PRIVILEGES ] | permission_name
    [ ( column [ ,...n ] ) ]
< principal >::= Windows_login | SQL_Server_login
    | SQL_Server_login_mapped_to_certificate
    | SQL_Server_login_mapped_to_asymmetric_key
    | Database_user | Database_role | Application_role
    | Database_user_mapped_to_certificate
    | Database_user_mapped_to_asymmetric_key
```

Syntax for Permissions on All Other Securables

```
DENY < permission > [ ,...n ] ON < scope >
    TO < principal > [ ,...n ] [ CASCADE ]
    [ AS { SQL_Server_login | database_user
        | database_role | application_role } ]

< permission >::=  ALL [ PRIVILEGES ] | permission_name
    [ ( column [ ,...n ] ) ]
< scope >::= [ securable_class :: ] securable_name
< securable_class >::= APPLICATION ROLE | ASSEMBLY | ASYMMETRIC KEY
    | CERTIFICATE | CONTRACT | ENDPOINT | FULLTEXT CATALOG
    | LOGIN | MESSAGE TYPE | REMOTE SERVICE BINDING | ROLE
    | ROUTE | SCHEMA | SERVICE | SYMMETRIC KEY | TYPE
    | USER | XML SCHEMA COLLECTION
```

Usage

```
DENY CREATE TABLE
    TO Devs, Testers
DENY INSERT, UPDATE, DELETE
    ON customer..customers
    TO Users, [CPANDL\Sales]
```

Object Permissions by Login

Object permissions apply to tables, views, and stored procedures. Permissions you assign to these objects include SELECT, INSERT, UPDATE, and DELETE. A summary of permitted actions by object is provided in Table 7-4 earlier in this chapter.

In SQL Server Management Studio, you grant, revoke, or deny object permissions by completing the following steps:

1. Start SQL Server Management Studio. In the Object Explorer view, connect to the appropriate server.

2. Work your way down to the Databases folder by using the entries in the left pane.

3. Expand the Databases folder, and then select a database and expand the node for it.

4. Expand the Security and Users folders.

5. Double-click the user you want to configure. This displays the Database User dialog box.

6. In the Select A Page list, select the Securables page, shown in Figure 7-10.

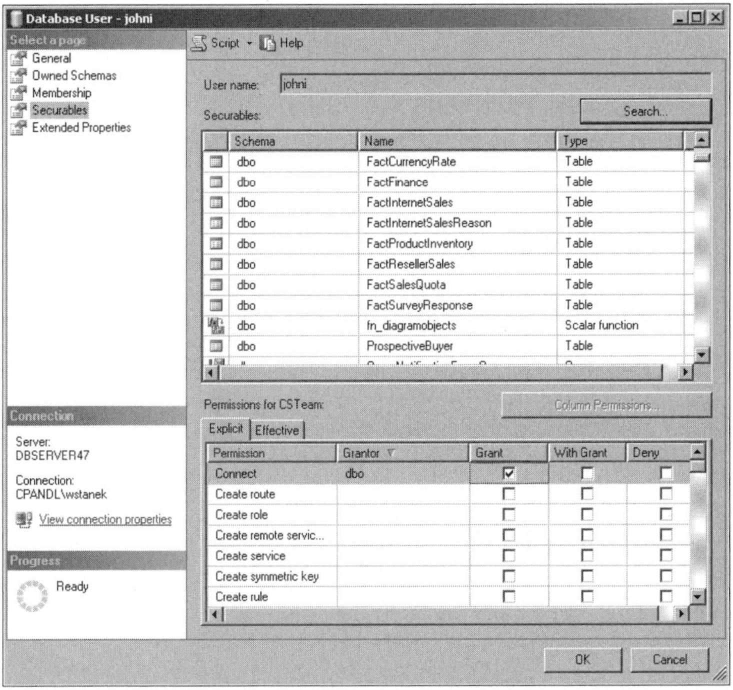

FIGURE 7-10 The Securables page of the Database User dialog box.

7. To assign object permissions, click Search to display the Add Objects dialog box.

8. In the Add Objects dialog box, select the type of objects for which you want to manage permissions:

- Select Specific Objects if you know the name of the objects for which you want to manage permissions. Click OK. In the Select Objects dialog box, click Object Types. Next, in the Select Object Types dialog box, select the types of objects to find, such as Tables And Views, and then click OK. In the Select Objects dialog box, enter the object names. Separate multiple names with a semicolon. You can enter a partial name and then click

Check Names to expand the name. To browse for objects of the selected type, click Browse. When you finish selecting objects, click OK. The selected objects are then listed in the Database User dialog box.

- Select All Objects Of The Types if you want to manage permissions for all objects of a specific type, such as all tables and views, and then click OK. In the Select Objects dialog box, click Object Types. Next, in the Select Object Types dialog box, select the types of objects to find, such as Tables And Views, and then click OK. In the Select Object Types dialog box, select the object types you want to manage, and then click OK. All objects of the selected types are then listed in the Database User dialog box.

- Select All Objects Belonging To The Schema if you want to manage permissions for all objects owned by a particular schema. In the Add Objects dialog box, use the Schema Name list to choose the schema whose objects you want to manage, and then click OK. All objects belonging to the schema are then listed in the Database User dialog box.

9. In the Database User dialog box, you'll see a list of securables that match your criteria. Select a securable in the upper panel to display related permissions in the Permissions For panel. You can now do the following:

- Click the Effective tab to see the effective permissions that a user is granted on a selected securable.

- Click the Explicit tab to set permissions. Grant or deny permissions as appropriate. If you grant a permission and also want the user to be able to grant the permission, select the With Grant option. Clear both check boxes to revoke a previously granted or denied permission.

10. When you finish, click OK to assign the permissions.

Object Permissions for Multiple Logins

You can also assign permissions by object, and in this way assign object permissions for multiple logins. To do this, complete the following steps:

1. In the Object Explorer view, connect to the appropriate server. Work your way down to the Databases folder by using the entries in the left pane.

2. Expand the Databases folder, and then select the folder for the type of objects you want to work with, such as Tables, Views, or Stored Procedures.

3. Double-click the object you want to configure, or right-click the object and select Properties. This displays the Properties dialog box.

4. In the Properties dialog box, select the Permissions page in the Select A Page list, as shown in Figure 7-11. Any users or roles directly assigned permissions on the object are listed in the Users Or Roles list.

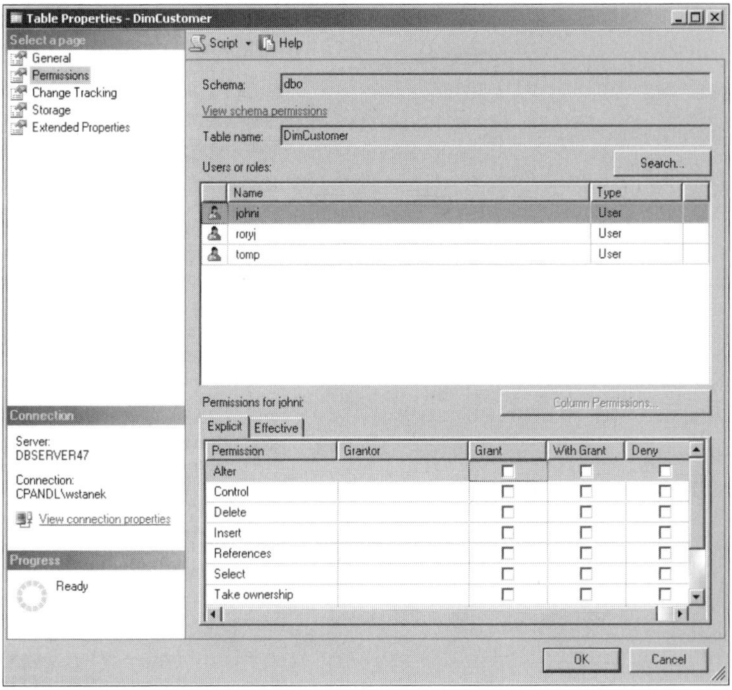

FIGURE 7-11 Permissions for an object.

5. To add specific permissions for users, roles, or both, click Search to open the Select Users Or Roles dialog box. Enter the names of the users or roles to add. Separate names with semicolons. You can enter partial names and then click Check Names to expand the names. To search for names, click Browse.

6. To set permissions for the object, select a user or role in the Users Or Roles list. You can now do the following:

   ■ Click the Effective tab to see the effective permissions for the user or role.

   ■ Click the Explicit tab to set permissions. Grant or deny permissions as appropriate. If you grant a permission and also want the user or role to be able to grant the permission, select the With Grant option. Clear both check boxes to revoke a previously granted or denied permission.

7. When you finish, click OK to assign the permissions.

More information about T-SQL commands for assigning permissions can be found in the "Assigning Database Permissions for Statements" section earlier in this chapter.

PART III

Microsoft SQL Server 2012 Data Management

Manipulating Schemas, Tables, and Views

Objects are the fundamental units of data storage in databases. All data in a database is contained within a Database object. Each Database object contains Schema objects, and those Schema objects contain the tables, indexes, views, and other objects that make up the database. The three basic levels of scoping and ownership are as follows:

- **Database**   Includes all objects defined within a database. This level is owned by a specific user.
- **Schema**   Includes all objects defined within a schema. This level is owned by a database-level security principal.
- **Schema-contained object**   Refers to any individual table, view, or other item that is defined in the database. This level is owned by a specific schema.

When you move databases designed for early versions of Microsoft SQL Server to SQL Server 2012, this model still applies. In these databases, the *dbo* schema is the owner of tables, views, and other related objects, and you can extend the database structure by creating and using other schemas as necessary.

> **NOTE**   Policy-Based Management settings can affect your ability to name objects. For more information, see Chapter 3, "Implementing Policy-Based Management."

Working with Schemas

Schemas are containers of objects and are used to define the namespaces for objects within databases. They are used to simplify management and create object subsets that can be managed collectively. Schemas are separate from users. Users own schemas and always have an associated default schema that the server uses when it resolves unqualified objects in queries. This means that the schema name does not need to be specified when accessing objects in the default schema. To access objects in other schemas, a two-part or three-part identifier is required. A two-part identifier specifies the schema name and the object name in the format *schema_name.object_name*. A three-part identifier specifies the database name, schema name, and object name in the format *database_name.schema_name.object_name*.

SQL Server 2012 allows you to create a database user based on a Microsoft Windows group. You can make that user the owner of a schema, and you can assign that user a default schema. When you create database users based on Windows groups, the rules for determining the default schema are extended. If a user has a default schema, the user's default schema is the first schema that SQL Server searches when it needs to resolve object names. Otherwise, the default schema of a group to which the user belongs is used, and that group is the one with the lowest principal_id.

Security principals are entities that can request SQL Server resources. When you create a principal in a database, SQL Server assigns a unique identifier, the principal_id, as tracked in sys.database_principals. Thus, only Windows groups for which you've created a related database user are considered when determining the default schema. If SQL Server can't determine which default schema to use, the dbo schema is used. The dbo schema also is the default schema of any member of the sysadmin role.

Database synonyms can be used to create alternate names so that a user's default schema contains references to other schemas. For example, if you create a synonym for the *Customers.Contact* table of *dbo.Contact*, any user with *dbo* as the default schema can access the table by using only the table name. Although synonyms can refer to objects in other databases, including remote instances of SQL Server, synonyms are valid only within the scope of the database in which they are defined. This means that each database can have identically named synonyms, and these synonyms can possibly refer to different objects.

Schemas have many benefits. Because users are no longer the direct owners of objects, removing users from a database is a simpler task; you no longer need to rename objects before dropping the user that created them, for example. Multiple users can own a single schema through membership in a role or Windows group, which makes it easier to manage tables, views, and other database-defined objects. Multiple users can share a single default schema, which makes it easier to grant access to shared objects.

Schemas can be used to scope database access by function, role, or purpose, which makes accessing objects contained in a database easier. For example, you can have schemas named for each application that accesses the database. In this way, when users of a particular application access the database, their namespace is set appropriately for the objects they routinely access.

You can work with schemas in Windows PowerShell by running the console locally or by entering a remote session with a database server. Consider the following example:

```
Set-Location
SQLSERVER:\SQL\DbServer18\Default\Databases\OrderSystem
Set-Location schemas
Get-ChildItem | where {$_.Owner eq "DanB"}
```

In this example, you enter a remote session with DbServer18 and then set the working location to the *OrderSystem* database on the default Database Engine instance. After you access the database, you access the schemas within the database and then return a list of all schemas owned by DanB. In the where clause, you can search for any property of the Microsoft.SqlServer.Management.Smo.Schema object, including Id, IsSystemObject, Name, Owner, Parent, State, and Urn.

Creating Schemas

Before you create a table, you should consider the schema name carefully. Schema names can be up to 128 characters. Schema names must begin with an alphabetic character and can also contain underscores (_), "at" symbols (@), pound signs (#), and numerals. Schema names must be unique within each database. Different databases, however, can contain like-named schemas; for example, two different databases each could have an *Employees* schema.

In SQL Server Management Studio, you create a new schema by completing the following steps:

1. In SQL Server Management Studio, connect to the server instance that contains the database in which you want to work.

2. In Object Explorer, expand the Databases node, select a database, and then expand the view to show its resource nodes.

3. Expand the database's Security node, and then right-click the Schemas node. From the shortcut menu, choose New Schema to display the Schema—New dialog box, shown in Figure 8-1.

4. On the General page, specify the name of the schema and set the schema owner. To search for an available database-level security principal to use as the owner, click Search to display the Search Roles And Users dialog box, and then click Browse to open the Browse For Objects dialog box. Select the check box for the user or role to act as the schema owner, and then click OK twice.

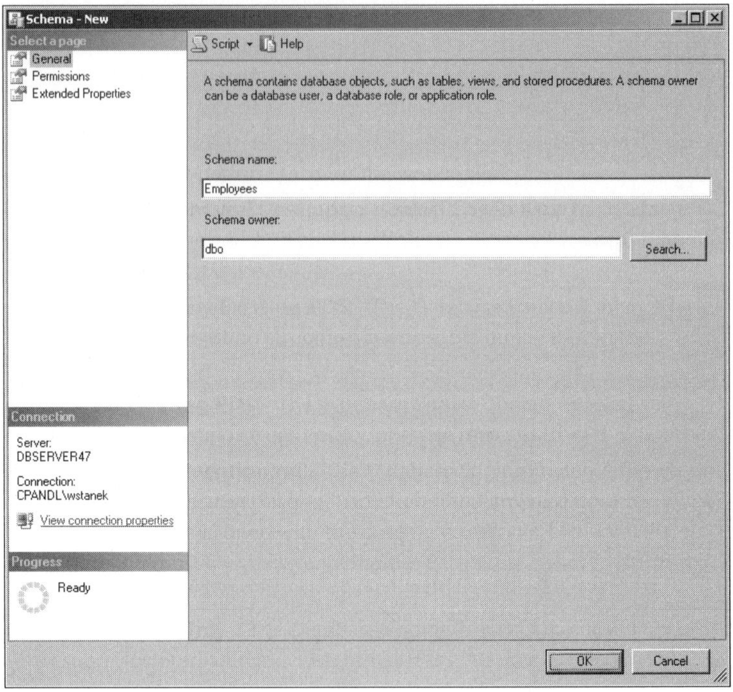

FIGURE 8-1 The Schema—New dialog box.

NOTE The schema owner can be any database-level security principal (database user, database role, or application role). The schema owner can own other schemas. If the schema owner is a role or Windows group, multiple users will own the schema.

Objects created within a schema are owned by the owner of the schema. Although this ownership can be transferred, the schema owner always retains CONTROL permission on objects within the schema.

5. Click OK to create the schema.

The Transact-SQL (T-SQL) command for creating schemas is CREATE SCHEMA. Sample 8-1 shows the syntax and usage for this command. The *schema_element* for the command allows you to use CREATE TABLE, CREATE VIEW, GRANT, REVOKE, and DENY statements to define tables, views, and permissions that should be created and contained within the schema you are defining.

NOTE To specify another user as the owner of the schema being created, you must have IMPERSONATE permission on that user. If a database role is specified as the owner, you must be a member of the role or have ALTER permission on the role.

Syntax

```
CREATE SCHEMA schema_name_clause [ < schema_element > [ , ...n ] ]
< schema_name_clause >::=
    { schema_name | AUTHORIZATION owner_name
    | schema_name AUTHORIZATION owner_name }
< schema_element >::=
    { table_definition | view_definition | grant_statement
    revoke_statement | deny_statement }
```

Usage

```
CREATE SCHEMA Employees AUTHORIZATION DataTeam
```

Modifying Schemas

You might need to change the schema ownership or modify its permissions. You might also want to allow or deny specific permissions on a per-user or per-role basis. After a schema is created, you cannot change the schema name. You must drop the schema and create a new schema with the new name.

In SQL Server Management Studio, you can change the schema owner by completing the following steps:

1. In SQL Server Management Studio, connect to the server instance that contains the database in which you want to work.

2. In Object Explorer, expand the Databases node, select a database, and then expand the view to show its resource nodes.

3. Expand the database's Security node, and then the Schemas node. Right-click the schema you want to work with. From the shortcut menu, choose Properties to display the Schema Properties dialog box.

4. To change the schema owner, click Search on the General page to display the Search Roles And Users dialog box, and then click Browse to open the Browse For Objects dialog box. Select the check box for the user or role you want to assign as the schema owner, and then click OK twice.

You can manage granular permissions for a schema on the Permissions page in the Schema Properties dialog box. Any user or roles that are directly assigned permissions on the object are listed under Users Or Roles. To configure permissions for a user or role, complete the following steps:

1. In the Schema Properties dialog box, select the Permissions page in the Select A Page list.

2. To add specific permissions for users, roles, or both, click Search. This opens the Select Users Or Roles dialog box.

3. In the Select Users Or Roles dialog box, enter the names of the users or roles to add. Separate names with semicolons. You can enter partial names and then click Check Names to expand the names. To search for names, click Browse. When you've selected the users or roles to add, click OK.

4. Select a user or role in the Users Or Roles list. Use the Permissions For list to grant or deny permissions as appropriate. If you grant a permission to a user and also want the user to be able to grant the permission, select the With Grant option. Clear both check boxes to revoke a previously granted or denied permission.

5. When you finish, click OK to assign the permissions.

Moving Objects to a New Schema

As discussed previously, schemas are containers for objects, and there are times when you want to move an object from one container to another. Objects can be moved from one schema to another only within the same database. When you do this, you change the namespace associated with the object, which changes the way that the object is queried and accessed.

Moving an object to a new schema also affects permissions on the object. All permissions on the object are dropped when it is moved to a new schema. If the object owner is set to a specific user or role, that user or role continues to be the owner of the object. If the object owner is set to SCHEMA OWNER, the ownership remains as SCHEMA OWNER, and after the move, the owner of the new schema becomes the owner of the object.

To move objects between schemas, you must have CONTROL permission on the object and ALTER permission on the schema to which you are moving the object. If the object has an EXECUTE AS OWNER specification on it and the owner is set to SCHEMA OWNER, you must also have IMPERSONATE permission on the owner of the target schema.

In SQL Server Management Studio, you can move an object to a new schema by completing the following steps:

1. In SQL Server Management Studio, connect to the server instance that contains the database in which you want to work.

2. In Object Explorer, expand the Databases node, select a database, and then expand the view to show its resource nodes.

3. Right-click the table, view, or other object you want to move. From the shortcut menu, choose View Dependencies. The Object Dependencies dialog box shows the database objects that must be present for this object to function properly and the objects that depend on the selected object. Use this dialog box to understand any dependencies that might be affected by moving the selected object. Click OK.

4. Right-click the table, view, or other object, and then select Design. One of several views displayed in the right pane is the Properties view for the selected object. If this view is not displayed, press F4.

5. Under Identity, click in the Schema list and select a new schema to contain the selected object.

CAUTION All permissions on the object are dropped immediately and irreversibly if you have previously selected the option Don't Warn Me Again, Proceed Every Time. If you see the warning prompt, click Yes to continue moving the object to the designated schema. Click No to cancel the move.

The T-SQL command for moving objects between schemas is ALTER SCHEMA. Sample 8-2 shows the syntax and usage for this command. When you alter a schema, be sure you are using the correct database and are not using the *master* database.

SAMPLE 8-2 ALTER SCHEMA Syntax and Usage.

Syntax

```
ALTER SCHEMA target_schema TRANSFER source_schema.object_to_move
```

Usage

```
ALTER SCHEMA Employees TRANSFER Location.Department
```

Dropping Schemas

If you no longer need a schema, you can drop it, and in this way remove it from the database. To drop a schema, you must have CONTROL permission on the schema. Before dropping a schema, you must first move or drop all the objects that it contains. If you try to delete a schema that contains objects, the drop operation will fail.

In SQL Server Management Studio, you can drop a schema by completing the following steps:

1. In SQL Server Management Studio, connect to the server instance that contains the database in which you want to work.

2. In Object Explorer, expand the Databases node, select a database, and then expand the view to show its resource nodes.

3. Expand the database's Security and Schemas nodes. Right-click the schema you want to drop. From the shortcut menu, choose Delete. This displays the Delete Object dialog box.

4. Click OK to confirm the deletion.

The T-SQL command for deleting schemas is DROP SCHEMA. Sample 8-3 shows the syntax and usage for this command. When you drop a schema, be sure that you are using the correct database and are not using the *master* database.

SAMPLE 8-3 DROP SCHEMA Syntax and Usage.

Syntax

```
DROP SCHEMA schema_name
```

Usage

```
DROP SCHEMA Employees
```

Getting Started with Tables

In SQL Server 2012, the structures of tables and indexes are just as important as the database itself, especially when it comes to performance. Tables are collections of data about a specific entity, such as a customer or an order. To describe the attributes of these entities, you use named columns. For example, to describe the attributes of a customer, you could use these columns: cust_name, cust_address, and cust_phone.

Each instance of data in a table is represented as a single data entry or row. Typically, rows are unique and have unique identifiers called *primary keys* associated with them. However, a primary key is not mandatory in ANSI SQL, and it is not required in SQL Server. The job of a primary key is to set a unique identifier for each row in a table and to allow SQL Server to create a unique index on this key. Indexes are user-defined data structures that provide fast access to data when you search on an indexed column. Indexes are separate from tables, and you can configure them automatically with the Database Engine Tuning Advisor.

TIP Throughout this and other chapters, the focus is on traditional indexes. Traditional indexes, also known as *rowstore indexes,* group and store data for each row and then join all the rows to complete the index. To help meet the needs of very large data warehouses, SQL Server 2012 also supports *columnstore indexes,* which group and store data for each column and then join all the columns to complete the index. Although columnstore indexes can improve performance with common filtering, aggregating, grouping, and star-join queries, they are very different from traditional indexes. For more information, see the "Working with Columnstore Indexes" section in Chapter 9, "Using Indexes, Constraints, and Partitions."

Most tables are related to other tables. For example, a *Customers* table might have a cust_account column that contains a customer's account number. The cust_account column might also appear in tables named *Orders* and *Receivables.* If the cust_account column is the primary key of the *Customers* table, a foreign key relationship can be established between *Customers* and *Orders,* as well as between *Customers* and *Receivables.* The foreign key creates a link between the tables that you can use to preserve referential integrity in the database.

After you have established the link, you cannot delete a row in the *Customers* table if the cust_account identifier is referenced in the *Orders* or *Receivables* table. This feature prevents you from invalidating references to information used in other tables. You first need to delete or change the related references in the *Orders* or *Receivables* tables, or in both tables, before deleting a primary key row in the *Customers* table.

Foreign key relationships allow you to combine data from related tables in queries by matching the foreign key constraint of one table with the primary or unique key in another table. Combining tables in this manner is called a *table join,* and the keys allow SQL Server to optimize the query and quickly find related data.

Table Essentials

Tables are defined as objects in SQL Server databases. Tables consist of columns and rows of data, and each column has a native or user-defined data type. Tables have two units of data storage: data pages and extents. *Data pages* are the fundamental units of data storage. *Extents* are the basic units in which space is allocated to tables and indexes. Data within tables can be organized using partitions.

Understanding Data Pages

For all data types except large-value data types and variable-length columns for which the data exceeds 8 kilobytes (KB), table data is stored in data pages that have a fixed size of 8 KB (8,192 bytes). Each data page has a page header, data rows, and free space that can contain row offsets. The page header uses the first 96 bytes of each page, leaving 8,096 bytes for data and row offsets. Row offsets indicate the logical order of rows on a page, which means that offset 0 refers to the first row in the index, offset 1 refers to the second row, and so on. If a table contains the large object data types varchar(max), nvarchar(max), or varbinary(max), the data might not be stored with the rest of the data for a row. Instead, SQL Server can store a 16-byte pointer to the actual data, which is stored in a collection of 8-KB pages that are not necessarily contiguous. A similar technique is used with variable-length columns in which the data row exceeds 8 KB (except that 24-byte pointers are used).

SQL Server 2012 supports the following types of data pages:

- **Bulk Changed Map (BCM)**   Tracks which extents have been modified by bulk operations since the last log file backup. Each BCM covers 64,000 extents (or approximately 4 GB of data) and has one bit for each extent in the range it covers. If an extent has been changed by a bulk-logged operation, the related bit for the BCM page is set to 1. Otherwise, the bit is set to 0. The backup process uses this bit to scan for extents that have been modified by bulk-logged operations and then includes those extents in the applicable log backup. These data pages speed up logging of bulk copy operations (but only when the database is using the bulk-logged recovery model).

- **Data**   Contains data rows with all data except for nvarchar(max), varchar(max), varbinary(max), and xml data (as well as text, ntext, and image data when *text in row* is set to ON).

- **Differential Changed Map (DCM)**   Tracks which extents have changed since the last database backup. Each DCM covers 64,000 extents (or approximately 4 GB of data) and has one bit for each extent in the range it covers. If an extent is changed since the last backup, the related bit for the DCM page is set to 1. Otherwise, the bit is set to 0. During a differential backup, the backup process uses this bit to scan for extents that have been modified and then includes those extents in the applicable differential backup. These data pages speed up differential backups.

- **Global Allocation Map (GAM)**   Tracks which extents have been allocated by SQL Server. Each GAM covers 64,000 extents (or approximately 4 GB of data) and has one bit for each extent in the range it covers. When this bit is set to 1, the associated extent is not being used (free). When this bit is set to 0, the associated extent is being used, and the bit setting of the Shared Global Allocation Map (SGAM) specifies how. These data pages simplify extent management.

- **Shared Global Allocation Map (SGAM)**   Tracks which extents are being used as mixed extents. Each SGAM covers 64,000 extents (or approximately 4 GB of data) and has one bit for each extent in the range it covers. When this bit is set to 1, the associated extent is being used as a mixed extent and has at least one free page. When this bit is set to 0, the associated extent is not being used as a mixed extent, or it has all its pages allocated. These data pages simplify extent management.

- **Index Allocation Map (IAM)**   Contains information about extents used by a table or index and specifically with one of the following allocation units: IN_ROW_DATA (holds a partition of a heap or index), LOB_DATA (holds large object data types), or ROW_OVERFLOW_DATA (holds variable-length data that exceeds the 8,060-byte row-size limit). Each allocation unit has at least one IAM page for each file on which it has extents. An IAM page covers a 4-GB range in a file, so a file larger than 4 GB would have multiple IAM pages associated with it. IAM pages are located randomly in the database file, with all the IAM pages for a particular allocation unit being linked in a chain.

- **Index**   Contains index entries. Generally, the storage engine reads index pages serially, in key order, using seek.

- **Page Free Space (PFS)**   Tracks whether a page has been allocated and the amount of free space on each page. A PFS has 1 byte for each page. If the page is allocated, the value also indicates whether the page is empty, 1 to 50 percent full, 51 to 80 percent full, 81 to 95 percent full, or 96 to 100 percent full. The Database Engine uses PFS pages to determine which pages in an extent are allocated or free. The relative amount of free space is maintained only for heap and Text/Image pages so that the Database Engine can find a page with free space to hold a newly inserted row. Indexes do not track PFS because index key values determine where a new row is inserted.

- **Text/Image (large object data types)**   Contains text, ntext, image, nvarchar(max), varchar(max), varbinary(max), and xml data, as well as data for variable-length columns in which the data row exceeds 8 KB (varchar, nvarchar, varbinary, sql_variant, and CLR user-defined).

Within data pages, SQL Server stores data in rows. Data rows do not normally span more than one page. The maximum size of a single data row is 8,096 bytes (including any necessary overhead). Effectively, this means that the maximum size of a column is 8,000 bytes, not including large object data types, and that a column can store up to 8,000 ASCII characters or up to 4,000 2-byte Unicode characters. Large object data type values can be up to 2 GB in size, which is too large to be stored in a single data row. With large object data types, data is stored in a collection of 8-KB pages, which might or might not be stored contiguously.

Although collections of pages are ideal for large object data that exceeds 8,096 bytes, this storage mechanism is not ideal when the total data size is 8,096 bytes or less. In this case, you should store the data in a single row. To do this, you must turn off the *large value types out of row* table option by setting its value to zero (0). When this option is turned off, you can place small nvarchar(max), varchar(max), and varbinary(max) values directly in a data row instead of in separate pages. This can reduce the amount of space used to store data and can also reduce the amount of disk I/O needed to retrieve the values.

> **NOTE**   A table that has fixed-length rows always stores the same number of rows on each page. A table with variable-length rows, however, stores as many rows as possible on each page based on the length of the data entered. As you might expect, there is a distinct performance advantage to keeping rows compact and allowing more rows to fit on a page. With more rows per page, you have a better cache-hit ratio and reduce I/O.

> **MORE INFO**   The ntext, text, and image data types are being deprecated in favor of nvarchar(max), varchar(max), and varbinary(max) data types. That said, with text, ntext, and image values, you can store small values directly in a data row instead of in separate pages by turning on the *text in row* option (which also is deprecated).

Understanding Extents

An extent is a set of eight contiguous data pages, which means that extents are allocated in 64-KB blocks and that there are 16 extents per megabyte. SQL Server 2012 has two types of extents:

- **Mixed extents**   With mixed extents, different objects can own pages in the extent. This means that up to eight objects can own a page in the extent.
- **Uniform extents**   With uniform extents, a single object owns all the pages in the extent. This means that only the owning object can use all eight pages in the extent.

When you create a new table or index, SQL Server allocates pages from a mixed extent to the new table or index. The table or index continues to use pages in the mixed extent until it grows to the point at which it uses eight data pages. When this happens, SQL Server changes the table or index to uniform extents. Thereafter, the table or index continues to use uniform extents even if you delete data to get below the eight-page threshold.

Understanding Table Partitions

In SQL Server 2012, tables are contained in one or more partitions, and each partition contains data rows in either a heap or clustered index structure. Partitioning large tables allows you to manage subsets of the table data and can improve response times when working with the table data. To improve read/write performance, you can place partitions into multiple filegroups as well.

By default, tables have only one partition. When a table has multiple partitions, the data is partitioned horizontally so that groups of rows are mapped into individual partitions on the basis of a specific column. For example, you might partition a *Customer_Order* table by purchase date. In this example, you would split the partition on date ranges, and each partition could hold yearly, quarterly, or monthly data.

For a *Customer* table, you might partition by customer ID. You would split the partition on name ranges, and each partition would store customer data that starts with a certain character—such as A, B, C, D, and so on—or a character sequence, such as Aa to Ez, Fa to Jz, Ka to Oz, Pa to Tz, and Ua to Zz.

SQL Server 2012 Enterprise Edition supports on-disk storage compression in both row and page format for tables stored as heaps, tables stored as clustered indexes, nonclustered indexes, and indexed views. You can configure compression of partitioned tables and indexes independently for each partition, regardless of whether partitions are for the same object. This allows different partitions of the same object to use different compression settings. Although enabling compression changes the physical storage format of data, compression does not require application changes. When you plan to use compression, as part of server sizing and capacity planning, you need to consider carefully the additional overhead required to compress and uncompress data. Keep in mind that a large enterprise system is more likely to be I/O-bound than CPU-bound, so here you have to weigh CPU cost against I/O and memory savings.

With partition switching, you can use the T-SQL ALTER TABLE...SWITCH statement to transfer subsets of your data. This statement allows you to assign a table as a partition to an already existing partitioned table, switch a partition from one partitioned table to another, or reassign a partition to form a single table. When you transfer a partition, the Database Engine doesn't move the data; it only changes the metadata about the location of the data.

Working with Tables

SQL Server provides many ways to work with tables. You can create new tables by using the New Table feature in SQL Server Management Studio or the CREATE TABLE command. You can modify existing tables by using the Modify Table feature in SQL Server Management Studio or the ALTER TABLE command. You can also perform other table management functions, including copying, renaming, and deleting tables.

You can work with tables in Windows PowerShell locally or by entering a remote session with a database server. Consider the following example:

```
Set-Location
SQLSERVER:\SQL\DataServer45\Default\Databases\Personnel
Set-Location tables
Get-ChildItem | where {$_.Schema eq "DevPers"}
```

In this example, you enter a remote session with DataServer45 and then set the working location to the *Personnel* database on the default Database Engine instance. After you access the database, you access the tables within the database and then return a list of all tables in the DevPers schema. In the where clause, you can search for any property of the *Microsoft.SqlServer.Management.Smo.Table* object, including AnsiNullsStatus, ChangeTrackingEnabled, Checks, Columns, CreateDate, DataSpaceUsed, DateLastModified, FileGroup, FileStreamFileGroup, FileStreamPartitionScheme, ForeignKeys, FullText Index, HasAfterTrigger, HasClusteredIndex, HasCompressedPartitions, HasDeleteTrigger, HasIndex, HasInsertTrigger, HasInsteadOfTrigger, HasUpdateTrigger, Id, Indexes, IndexSpaceUsed, IsIndexable, IsPartitioned, IsSchemaOwned, MaximumDegreeOfParallelism, Name, Owner, Parent, PartitionScheme, PartitionSchemeParameters, PhysicalPartitions, QuotedIdentifierStatus, Replicated, RowCount, RowCountAsDouble, Schema, State, Statistics, TextFileGroup, TrackColumnsUpdatedEnabled, Triggers, and Urn.

Creating Tables

Before you create a table, you should consider the table name carefully. Table names can be up to 128 characters. Table names must begin with an alphabetic character and can also contain underscores (_), "at" symbols (@), pound signs (#), and numerals. The exception to this rule is temporary tables. Local temporary tables have names that begin with # and are accessible to you only during the current user session. Global temporary tables have names that begin with ## and are accessible to anyone so long as the user session remains connected. Temporary tables are created in the *tempdb* database and are deleted automatically when the user session ends.

Table names must be unique for each schema within a database. Different schemas, however, can contain like-named tables. This means you can create multiple *contacts* tables so long as they are defined in separate schemas. For example, the *Customers*, *Employees*, and *Services* schemas could all have a *contacts* table.

Each table can have up to 1,024 columns. Column names follow the same naming rules as tables and must be unique only on a per-table basis. That is, a specific table can have only one StreetAddress column, but any number of other tables can use this same column name.

In SQL Server Management Studio, you create a new table by completing the following steps:

1. In SQL Server Management Studio, connect to the server instance that contains the database in which you want to work. You must have CREATE TABLE permission in the database and ALTER permission on the schema in which the table is being created.

2. In Object Explorer, expand the Databases node, select a database, and then expand the view to show its resource nodes.

3. To create a new table, right-click the Tables node, and then select New Table from the shortcut menu. Access the Table Designer in SQL Server Management Studio, and you see a window similar to Figure 8-2.

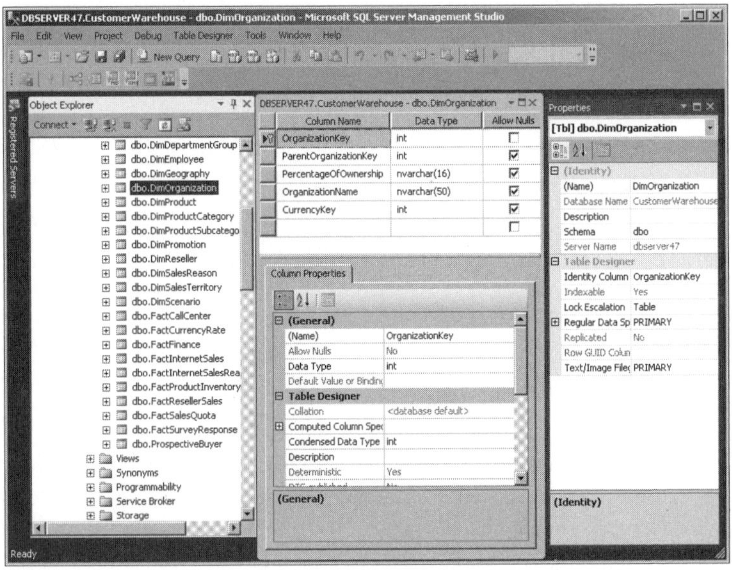

FIGURE 8-2 Create and modify tables in SQL Server Management Studio.

4. Now you can design the table using the views provided, as follows:

   ■ **Active File/Table view**   Provides quick access tabs for switching between open files and a summary. If you select the Table view in the Active File view, you see an overview of the table's columns. Each column is listed with its values for Column Name, Data Type, and Allow Nulls. For fixed-length or variable-length data types, you follow the data type designator with the field length

   ■ **Column Properties view**   When you select a column in the Table view, you can use the Column Properties view to configure the settings for that column. Column properties that appear dimmed are fixed in value and cannot be changed. The values of fixed properties typically depend on the column data type and properties inherited from the *Database* object itself.

- **Table Properties view** Allows you to view and set general table properties, including the table name, description, and schema. You can open this view by pressing F4. Any dimmed properties cannot be changed at the table level and must be managed at the database level.

5. The Table Designer menu also provides options for designing the table. Because the options apply to the selected column in the Table view, you can apply them by selecting a column first and then choosing the appropriate option from the Table Designer menu. The same options are displayed when you right-click a column in the Table view.

As you start creating a table, you should do the following:

- Use the Table Properties view to set the table name, description, and schema. Type the name and description in the boxes provided. Use the drop-down list to select the schema that will contain this table.

- Use the Table Properties view to specify the filegroup (or filegroups) in which the table data will be stored. Regular data and large object data are configured separately.

  - To specify the storage location for regular data, expand the Regular Data Space Specification node, and then use the Filegroup Or Partition Schema Name list to specify the filegroup.

  - To specify the storage location for large object data, use the Text/Image Filegroup list.

- Use the Table view to create and manage columns.

  - Rows in the Table view correspond to columns in the table in which you are working. In Figure 8-2, the columns listed include CustomerID, CustomerType, and AccountNumber.

  - Columns in the Table view correspond to column properties in the table in which you are working. In Figure 8-2, column properties listed include Name, Data Type, and Allow Nulls.

- Use Table Designer menu options to work with a selected column. You can mark the column as the primary key, establish foreign key relationships, check constraints, and more.

- Use the Column Properties view to specify the characteristics for the column you are creating. The characteristics include the following:

  - **Allow Nulls** Shows or determines whether null values are allowed in this column.

  - **Collation** Shows or sets the default collating sequence that SQL Server applies to the column whenever the column values are used to sort rows of a query result.

  - **Data Type** Shows or determines the data type for the column.

- **Default Value Or Binding**   Shows or determines the default value or binding for the column. This value is used whenever a row with a null value for this column is inserted into the database and nulls are not allowed in this column.
- **Description**   Shows or sets a description of the column.
- **Formula**   Shows or sets the formula for a computed column.
- **Identity Increment**   Shows or sets the increment for generating unique identifiers. This property applies only to columns whose Is Identity option is set to Yes.
- **Identity Seed**   Shows or sets the base value for generating unique identifiers. This property applies only to columns whose Is Identity option is set to Yes.
- **Is Identity**   Shows or determines whether the column is used as an identifier column.
- **Is Persisted**   Specifies whether a computed column is persisted.
- **Is Sparse**   Shows or determines whether the column is sparse. Sparse columns are optimized for null values and reduce space requirements for null values while increasing the overhead required to retrieve nonnull values. With filtered indexes on sparse columns, the index size is reduced because only the populated values are indexed, and this can increase index and search efficiency.
- **Length**   Shows or determines the maximum number of characters for values in the column. This property applies only when the column contains fixed-length data type values.
- **Name**   Shows or determines the name of the column.
- **Precision**   Shows or determines the maximum number of digits for values in the column. This property applies only when the column contains numeric or decimal data type values.
- **RowGuid**   Shows or determines whether the column contains globally unique identifiers (GUIDs). This property applies only to columns with the uniqueidentifier data type, and only one uniqueidentifier column can be designated as the RowGuid column.
- **Scale**   Shows or determines the maximum number of digits that can appear to the right of the decimal point for values in the column. This property applies only when the column contains numeric or decimal data type values.
- **Size**   Shows the storage size in bytes for values in the column. This property applies only when the column contains fixed-length data type values.

When you finish creating the table, click Save or press Ctrl+S.

You can create tables with T-SQL using the CREATE TABLE command. Sample 8-4 shows the syntax and usage for this command. Here, you create the *Customers* table under the *Sales* schema. You must have CREATE TABLE permission in the database and ALTER permission on the schema in which the table is being created.

SAMPLE 8-4 CREATE TABLE Syntax and Usage.

Syntax

```
CREATE TABLE [ database_name . [ schema_name ] . | schema_name . ]
              table_name
  ( { <col_def> | <comp_col_def> | <column_set_def> }
  [ <table_constraint> ] [ ,...n ] )
[ AS FileTable ] ( { <column_definition> | <computed_column_definition>
  | <column_set_definition> | [ <table_constraint> ] [ ,... n ] )}
[ ON { part_scheme_name ( part_column_name ) | filegroup
    | "default" } ]
[ TEXTIMAGE_ON { filegroup | "default" } ]
[ FILESTREAM_ON { part_scheme_name | filegroup | "default" } ]
[ WITH ( <table_option> [ ,...n ] ) ] [ ; ]

<col_def> ::=
column_name <data_type>
[ FILESTREAM ] [ COLLATE collation_name ] [ NULL | NOT NULL ]
[ [ CONSTRAINT constraint_name ] DEFAULT constant_expression ]
  | [ IDENTITY [ ( seed ,increment ) ] [ NOT FOR REPLICATION ] ]
[ ROWGUIDCOL ] [ <column_constraint> [ ...n ] ] [ SPARSE ]

<data type> ::=
[ type_schema_name . ] type_name
  [ ( precision [ , scale ] | max
  | [ { CONTENT | DOCUMENT } ] xml_schema_collection ) ]

<column_constraint> ::=
[ CONSTRAINT constraint_name ]
{ { PRIMARY KEY | UNIQUE } [ CLUSTERED | NONCLUSTERED ]
  [ WITH FILLFACTOR = fillfactor
    | WITH ( < index_option > [ , ...n ] ) ]
  [ ON { part_scheme_name ( part_column_name ) | filegroup
    | "default" } ]
  | [ FOREIGN KEY ]
  REFERENCES [ schema_name . ] referenced_table_name
  [ ( ref_column )]
  [ ON DELETE { NO ACTION | CASCADE | SET NULL | SET DEFAULT } ]
  [ ON UPDATE { NO ACTION | CASCADE | SET NULL | SET DEFAULT } ]
  [ NOT FOR REPLICATION ]
  | CHECK [ NOT FOR REPLICATION ] ( logical_expression )
}

<comp_col_def> ::=
column_name AS computed_column_expression
[ PERSISTED [ NOT NULL ] ]
```

```
[ [ CONSTRAINT constraint_name ]
  { PRIMARY KEY | UNIQUE }
  [ CLUSTERED | NONCLUSTERED ] [ WITH FILLFACTOR = fillfactor
    | WITH ( <index_option> [ , ...n ] ) ) ]
  | [ FOREIGN KEY ]
  REFERENCES referenced_table_name [ ( ref_column ) ]
  [ ON DELETE { NO ACTION | CASCADE } ] [ ON UPDATE { NO ACTION } ]
  [ NOT FOR REPLICATION ]
  | CHECK [ NOT FOR REPLICATION ] ( logical_expression )
  [ ON { part_scheme_name ( part_column_name )
    | filegroup | "default" } ]
]

<column_set_def> ::=
column_set_name XML COLUMN_SET FOR ALL_SPARSE_COLUMNS

< table_constraint > ::=
[ CONSTRAINT constraint_name ]
{ { PRIMARY KEY | UNIQUE }
  [ CLUSTERED | NONCLUSTERED ] (column [ ASC | DESC ] [ ,...n ] )
  [ WITH FILLFACTOR = fillfactor |WITH ( <index_option> [ , ...n ] )]
  [ ON { part_scheme_name (part_column_name) | filegroup
    | "default"}]
  | FOREIGN KEY ( column [ ,...n ] )
  REFERENCES referenced_table_name [ ( ref_column [ ,...n ] ) ]
  [ ON DELETE { NO ACTION | CASCADE | SET NULL | SET DEFAULT } ]
  [ ON UPDATE { NO ACTION | CASCADE | SET NULL | SET DEFAULT } ]
  [ NOT FOR REPLICATION ]
  | CHECK [ NOT FOR REPLICATION ] ( logical_expression )
}

<table_option> ::=
{ [DATA_COMPRESSION = { NONE | ROW | PAGE }
  [ ON PARTITIONS ( { <partition_number_expression> | <range> }
    [ , ... n ] ) ]]
  [ FILETABLE_DIRECTORY = <directory_name> ]
  [ FILETABLE_COLLATE_FILENAME = { <collation_name> | database_default } ] ] }

<index_option> ::=
{ PAD_INDEX = { ON | OFF } | FILLFACTOR = fillfactor
  | IGNORE_DUP_KEY = { ON | OFF } | STATISTICS_NORECOMPUTE
    = { ON | OFF}
  | ALLOW_ROW_LOCKS = { ON | OFF} | ALLOW_PAGE_LOCKS = { ON | OFF}
  | DATA_COMPRESSION = { NONE | ROW | PAGE }
  [ ON PARTITIONS ( { <part_number_expression> | <range> }
    [ , ...n ] ) ]
}
<range> ::=
<part_number_expression> TO <part_number_expression>
```

Usage

```
USE OrderSystemDB
CREATE TABLE Sales.Customers
(
    cust_lname varchar(40) NOT NULL,
    cust_fname varchar(20) NOT NULL,
    phone char(12) NOT NULL,
    uid uniqueidentifier NOT NULL
    DEFAULT newid()
)
```

Modifying Existing Tables

When you work with the Table Properties view, you can use the Lock Escalation option to configure lock escalation using the following settings:

- **Auto** With Auto, the Database Engine selects the lock escalation granularity that is appropriate for the table schema. If the table is partitioned, lock escalation is allowed to the heap or B-tree level and the lock will not be escalated later to the table level. This can improve concurrency by reducing lock contention. If the table is not partitioned, the Database Engine uses lock escalation at the table level.

- **Table** With Table, the Database Engine uses lock escalation at the table level regardless of whether the table is partitioned. *Table* is the default value.

- **Disable** With Disable, lock escalation is prevented in most cases, and the Database Engine uses lock escalation only when required. For example, when you are scanning a table that has no clustered index under the serializable isolation level, the Database Engine must use a table lock to protect data integrity.

In SQL Server Management Studio, you modify an existing table by completing the following steps:

1. In SQL Server Management Studio, connect to the server instance that contains the database in which you want to work.

2. In Object Explorer, expand the Databases node, select a database, and then expand the view to show its resource nodes.

3. Expand the Tables node, and then right-click the table you want to modify. From the shortcut menu, choose Design. Then you can access the views for designing tables, which were shown in Figure 8-2 earlier in the chapter.

4. Make any necessary changes to the table, and then click Save or press Ctrl+S. If the changes you make affect multiple tables, you see a prompt showing which tables will be updated and saved in the database. Click Yes to continue and complete the operation.

The T-SQL command for modifying tables is ALTER TABLE. Sample 8-5 shows the syntax and usage for this command. Here, you alter the *Customers* table under the

Sales schema. You must have ALTER TABLE permission. Most of the subset elements are the same as defined for CREATE TABLE. Important exceptions are listed.

SAMPLE 8-5 ALTER TABLE Syntax and Usage.

Syntax

```
ALTER TABLE [ database_name . [ schema_name ] . | schema_name . ]
              table_name
{   ALTER COLUMN column_name
    {
        [ type_schema_name. ] type_name [ ( { precision [ , scale ]
        | max | xml_schema_collection } ) ]
        [ COLLATE collation_name ]
        [ NULL | NOT NULL ] [SPARSE]
    | {ADD | DROP }
        { ROWGUIDCOL | PERSISTED | NOT FOR REPLICATION | SPARSE }
    }
    | [ WITH { CHECK | NOCHECK } ]
    | ADD
    { <column_definition>
    | <computed_column_definition>
    | <table_constraint>
    | <column_set_definition>
    } [ ,...n ]
    | DROP
    {   [ CONSTRAINT ] constraint_name
        [ WITH ( <drop_clustered_constraint_option> [ ,...n ] ) ]
        | COLUMN column_name
    } [ ,...n ]
    | [ WITH { CHECK | NOCHECK } ] { CHECK | NOCHECK } CONSTRAINT
        { ALL | constraint_name [ ,...n ] }
    | { ENABLE | DISABLE } TRIGGER
        { ALL | trigger_name [ ,...n ] }
    | { ENABLE | DISABLE } CHANGE_TRACKING
        [ WITH ( TRACK_COLUMNS_UPDATED = { ON | OFF } ) ]
    | SWITCH [ PARTITION source_partition_number_expression ]
        TO target_table
        [ PARTITION target_partition_number_expression ]
    | SET ( FILESTREAM_ON = { partition_scheme_name | filegroup |
        "default" | "NULL" } )
    | REBUILD
        [ [ WITH ( <rebuild_option> [ ,...n ] ) ]
        | [ PARTITION = partition_number
            [ WITH ( <single_partition_rebuild_option> [ ,...n ] ) ] ]
        ]
    | (<table_option>)
    | (<filetable_option>)
}
[ ; ]
```

```
<drop_clustered_constraint_option> ::=
{ MAXDOP = max_degree_of_parallelism
  | ONLINE = { ON | OFF }
  | MOVE TO { partition_scheme_name ( column_name ) | filegroup
  | "default" }
}

<range> ::=
<partition_number_expression> TO <partition_number_expression>

<rebuild_option> ::=
{ PAD_INDEX = { ON | OFF }
  | FILLFACTOR = fillfactor
  | IGNORE_DUP_KEY = { ON | OFF }
  | STATISTICS_NORECOMPUTE = { ON | OFF }
  | ALLOW_ROW_LOCKS = { ON | OFF }
  | ALLOW_PAGE_LOCKS = { ON | OFF }
  | SORT_IN_TEMPDB = { ON | OFF }
  | ONLINE = { ON | OFF }
  | MAXDOP = max_degree_of_parallelism
  | DATA_COMPRESSION = { NONE | ROW | PAGE}
    [ ON PARTITIONS ( { <partition_number_expression> | <range> }
      [ , ...n ] ) ]
}

<single_partition_rebuild__option> ::=
{ SORT_IN_TEMPDB = { ON | OFF }
  | MAXDOP = max_degree_of_parallelism
  | DATA_COMPRESSION = { NONE | ROW | PAGE} }
}

<table_option> ::=
  { SET ( LOCK_ESCALATION = { AUTO | TABLE | DISABLE } ) }

<filetable_option> ::=
  { [ { ENABLE | DISABLE } FILETABLE_NAMESPACE ]
  [ SET ( FILETABLE_DIRECTORY = directory_name ) ] }
```

Usage

```
USE OrderSystemDB
ALTER TABLE Sales.Customers
ADD uid2 uniqueidentifier NOT NULL DEFAULT newid()
ALTER TABLE Sales.Customers
ALTER COLUMN cust_fname CHAR(10) NOT NULL
ALTER TABLE Sales.Customers
DROP Address2
```

Viewing Table Row and Size Information

In SQL Server Management Studio, you can view table row and size information by completing the following steps:

1. In SQL Server Management Studio, connect to the server instance that contains the database in which you want to work.

2. In Object Explorer, expand the Databases node, select a database, and then expand the view to show its resource nodes.

3. Expand the Tables node, right-click the table you want to examine, and then select Properties from the shortcut menu. This displays the Table Properties dialog box.

Entries under the General section on the Storage page provide details about space used. This information includes the following:

- Data Space shows the amount of space the table uses on disk.
- Index Space shows the size of the table's index space on disk.
- Row Count shows the number of rows in the table.

You can also view row, size, and space statistics for individual tables using the sp_spaceused stored procedure. The following code accesses the *OrderSystemDB* database and then checks the statistics for the *Customers* table under the *Sales* schema:

```
USE OrderSystemDB
GO
EXEC sp_spaceused 'Sales.Customers'
```

Displaying Table Properties and Permissions

In SQL Server Management Studio, you can display table properties and permissions by completing the following steps:

1. In SQL Server Management Studio, connect to the server instance that contains the database in which you want to work.

2. In Object Explorer, expand the Databases node, select a database, and then expand the view to show its resource nodes.

3. Expand the Tables node, right-click the table you want to examine, and then select Properties to display the Table Properties dialog box.

4. Use the General, Permissions, and Extended Properties pages of the dialog box to view the table's properties and permissions.

Displaying Current Values in Tables

In SQL Server Management Studio, you view a table's current data by completing the following steps:

1. In SQL Server Management Studio, connect to the server instance that contains the database in which you want to work.

2. In Object Explorer, expand the Databases node, select a database, and then expand the view to show its resource nodes.

3. Expand the Tables node, right-click the table you want to examine, and then choose Select Top 1000 Rows to display the first 1,000 rows of data contained in the table.

NOTE If you select Edit Top 200 Rows instead, the lower portion of the Query Results pane provides buttons for moving between the rows and a status area. If you select a read-only cell, the status area displays "Cell Is Read Only." If you have modified a cell, the status area displays "Cell Is Modified."

You can also list a table's current data by using the SELECT FROM statement. In the following example, you select from the *Department* table under the *HumanResources* schema in the *Personnel* database:

```
SELECT * FROM [Personnel].[HumanResources].[Department]
```

or

```
SELECT DepartmentID,Name,GroupName,ModifiedDate
  FROM [Personnel].[HumanResources].[Department]
```

Copying Tables

The easiest way to create a copy of a table is to use a T-SQL command. Use SELECT INTO to extract all the rows from an existing table into the new table. The new table must not already exist. The following example copies the *Customers* table under the *Sales* schema to a new table called *CurrCustomers* under the *BizDev* schema:

```
SELECT * INTO BizDev.CurrCustomers FROM Sales.Customers
```

You can also create the new table from a specific subset of columns in the original table. In this case, you specify the names of the columns to copy after the SELECT keyword. Any columns not specified are excluded from the new table. The following example copies specific columns to a new table:

```
SELECT CustName, Address, Telephone, Email INTO BizDev.CurrCustomers
FROM Sales.Customers
```

Renaming and Deleting Tables

In SQL Server Management Studio, the easiest way to rename or delete a table is to complete the following steps:

1. In SQL Server Management Studio, access a database, and then expand the Tables node to list the tables in the database.

2. Right-click the table you want to rename or delete. From the shortcut menu, choose View Dependencies. The Object Dependencies dialog box shows the database objects that must be present for this object to function

properly and the objects that depend on the selected object. Use the information in this dialog box to understand any dependencies that might be affected by renaming or deleting the selected table. Click OK to close the Object Dependencies dialog box.

3. To rename a table, right-click the table, and then choose Rename from the shortcut menu. Now you can type a new name for the table.

4. To delete a table, right-click the table, and then choose Delete to display the Delete Object dialog box. Click OK.

You can also rename tables using the sp_rename stored procedure. You must have ALTER TABLE permission and be a member of the sysadmin or dbcreator fixed server role to rename a table with sp_rename. In the following example, you rename the *Customers* table under the *Sales* schema *CurrCustomers*:

```
EXEC sp_rename 'Sales.Customers', 'CurrCustomers'
```

So long as you have ALTER permission on the schema to which the table belongs or CONTROL permission on the table, you can remove a table from the database by using the DROP TABLE command:

```
DROP TABLE Sales.CurrCustomers
```

If you want to delete the rows in a table but leave its structure intact, you can use DELETE. The following DELETE command deletes all the rows in a table but does not remove the table structure:

```
DELETE Sales.CurrCustomers
```

Because DELETE removes rows one at a time, each row in the table is locked for deletion and the table could still contain empty-page records. SQL Server records a related entry in the transaction log for each deleted row. To use DELETE, you must be a member of the sysadmin fixed server role, a member of the db_datawriter fixed database role, the db_owner, the table owner, or be granted DELETE permission.

TRUNCATE TABLE offers an alternative to DELETE. Like DELETE, TRUNCATE TABLE removes all rows in a table while leaving the table structure intact. Unlike DELETE, TRUNCATE TABLE locks the table and data pages and then deallocates the data pages to remove the table data. Typically, this means that TRUNCATE TABLE is faster and uses fewer resources than DELETE. It also means SQL Server logs only the page deallocations rather than the deletion of each row. To truncate a table, you must be a member of the sysadmin fixed server role, a member of the db_ddladmin fixed database role, the db_owner, or the table owner, or you must be granted ALTER TABLE permission on the table.

NOTE If a table contains an identity column, DELETE retains the identity counter. With TRUNCATE TABLE, the counter for that column is reset to the seed value if it exists, or 1 otherwise.

Adding and Removing Columns in a Table

Using SQL Server Management Studio, you can add or remove columns in a table as discussed in the "Creating Tables" and "Modifying Existing Tables" sections earlier in this chapter. In T-SQL, you modify table columns by using the ALTER TABLE command, which was shown earlier in Sample 8-5.

Adding Columns

The following example adds a unique identifier column to the *Customers* table under the *Sales* schema:

```
USE OrderSystemDB
ALTER TABLE Sales.Customers
ADD uid uniqueidentifier NOT NULL DEFAULT newid()
```

Modifying Columns

To change the characteristics of an existing column, use the ALTER COLUMN command, such as in the following example:

```
USE OrderSystemDB
ALTER TABLE Sales.Customers
ALTER COLUMN cust_fname CHAR(10) NOT NULL
```

Removing Columns

The following example removes the Address2 column from the *Customers* table:

```
USE OrderSystemDB
ALTER TABLE Sales.Customers
DROP COLUMN Address2
```

Scripting Tables

You can re-create and store the SQL commands needed to create tables in a .sql file for later use. To do this, complete the following steps:

1. In SQL Server Management Studio, access a database, and then expand the Tables node to list the tables in the database.
2. Select a table, right-click its name, and then select Script Table As from the shortcut menu.
3. Point to CREATE TO, and then select File to open the Select A File dialog box.
4. In the dialog box, set a folder and file path for the .sql script, and then click Save.

If you open the .sql file, you will find all the T-SQL statements required to re-create the table structure. The actual data in the table is not stored with this procedure, however.

Managing Table Values

In this section, you will learn about the techniques and concepts that you need to work with table values. Whether you want to create a new table or modify an existing one, the techniques and concepts you need to understand are similar.

Using Native Data Types

Native data types are those built into SQL Server and supported directly. All data types have a length value, which is either fixed or variable. The length for a numeric or binary data type is the number of bytes used to store the number. The length for a character data type is the number of characters, and it can be up to two times the length for Unicode data. Most numeric data types also have precision and scale. *Precision* is the total number of digits in a number. *Scale* is the number of digits to the right of the decimal point in a number. For example, the number 8714.235 has a precision of seven and a scale of three.

Table 8-1 summarizes native data types that work with numbers and money. The first column shows the general data type or data type synonym for SQL-92 compatibility. The second column shows the SQL Server data type. The third column shows the valid range. The fourth column shows the amount of storage space used.

REAL WORLD If you store character data in multiple languages, use Unicode data types instead of the non-Unicode data types. SQL Server uses the UTF-16 format to encode Unicode character data. Each character has a unique codepoint, which is a value in the range 0x0000 to 0x10FFFF. Frequently used, or standard, characters have codepoint values that fit into a single 16-bit word. Less frequently used, or supplementary, characters have codepoint values that fit into two 16-bit words. SQL Server 2012 supports supplementary character (SC) collations that can be used with nchar, nvarchar, and sql_variant, such as Latin1_General_100_CI_AS_SC. Level 90 or greater collations can be used in ordering and comparison operations. Level 100 collations support linguistic sorting with supplementary characters. However, supplementary characters are not supported for use in metadata, such as in names of schemas, databases, or objects. With SC collations, surrogate pairs are counted as one character for both the start location and the returned value count.

With nchar and nvarchar, SQL Server 2012 compresses Unicode values that are stored in row-compressed or page-compressed objects, although data stored off-row or in nvarchar(max) columns is not compressed. If you upgrade a database to SQL Server 2012, only new rows that are inserted into row-compressed or page-compressed objects are compressed. Therefore, you must rebuild the object to gain the compression benefits. Where the character is located in the Unicode character set determines the overall compression benefit. English, German, and Hindi characters gain a 50 percent compression benefit, while Turkish, Vietnamese, and Japanese characters gain a 48, 39, or 15 percent benefit, respectively.

TABLE 8-1 Native Data Types for Numbers and Money

SQL-92 NAME—TYPE	SQL SERVER NAME	RANGE—DESCRIPTION	STORAGE SIZE
INTEGERS			
Bit	bit	0, 1, or NULL	1 byte (for each 1-bit to 8-bit column)
Big integer	bigint	-2^{63} through $2^{63} - 1$.	8 bytes
Integer	int	-2^{31} (–2,147,483,648) through $2^{31} - 1$ (2,147,483,647)	4 bytes
small integer	smallint	-2^{15} (–32,768) through $2^{15} - 1$ (32,767)	2 bytes
tiny integer	tinyint	0 through 255	1 byte
MONEY			
Money	money	–922,337,203,685,477.5808 through +922,337,203,685,477.5807	8 bytes
small money	smallmoney	–214,748.3648 through +214,748.3647	4 bytes
DECIMAL			
dec, decimal	decimal	$-10^{38} + 1$ through $10^{38} - 1$	5 to 17 bytes
Numeric	decimal	$-10^{38} + 1$ through $10^{38} - 1$	5 to 17 bytes
APPROXIMATE NUMERIC			
Double precision	float	–1.79E + 308 through 1.79E + 308	4 to 8 bytes
Float	float	–1.79E + 308 through 1.79E + 308. float[(n)] for n = 1 – 53	4 to 8 bytes
Float	real	–1.18E – 38, 0 and –1.18E – 38 through 3.40E + 38. float[(n)] for n = 1 – 24	4 bytes

SQL-92 NAME—TYPE	SQL SERVER NAME	RANGE—DESCRIPTION	STORAGE SIZE
SPATIAL DATA			
	geometry	A variable-length common language runtime (CLR) data type for storing planar (flat-earth) data; represents points, lines, and polygons within a coordinate system	Varies
	geography	A variable-length CLR data type for storing ellipsoidal (round-earth) data; represents geographic objects on an area of the Earth's surface	Varies
OTHER NUMERICS			
Cursor	cursor	A reference to a cursor	Varies
	Hierarchyid, Sql-Hierarchyid	A variable-length CLR data type that logically encodes information about a single node in a hierarchy tree; represents the encoded path from the root of the tree to the node	Varies
Rowversion	rowversion, timestamp	A databasewide unique number that indicates the sequence in which modifications took place in the database (*Rowversion* is a synonym for *timestamp*)	8 bytes
SQL Variant	sql_variant	A special data type that allows a single column to store multiple data types [except text, ntext, sql_variant, image, timestamp, xml, varchar(max), varbinary(max), nvarchar(max), and .NET CLR user-defined types]	Varies
Table	table	A special data type that is used to store a result set temporarily for processing; can be used only to define local variables and as the return type for user-defined functions	Varies

SQL-92 NAME—TYPE	SQL SERVER NAME	RANGE—DESCRIPTION	STORAGE SIZE
Uniqueidentifier	unique-identifier	A globally unique identifier (GUID)	16 bytes
Xml	xml	A special data type that allows you to store XML data; XML markup is defined using standard text characters	Varies

Table 8-2 summarizes native data types for dates, characters, and binary data. Again, the first column shows the general data type or data type synonym for SQL-92 compatibility. The second column shows the SQL Server data type. The third column shows the valid range. The fourth column shows the amount of storage space used.

TABLE 8-2 Native Data Types for Dates, Characters, and Binary Values

SQL-92 NAME—TYPE	SQL SERVER NAME	RANGE—DESCRIPTION	STORAGE SIZE
DATE			
Datetime	datetime	January 1, 1753, through December 31, 9999; accuracy of three-hundredths of a second	Two 4-byte integers
small datetime	smalldatetime	January 1, 1900, through June 6, 2079; accuracy of 1 minute	Two 2-byte integers
Date	date	0001-01-01 through 9999-12-31	3 bytes
Time	time	00:00:00.0000000 through 23:59:59.9999999	3 to 5 bytes
	datetime2	0001-01-01 00:00:00.0000000 through 9999-12-31 23:59:59.9999999	6 to 8 bytes
	datetimeoffset	0001-01-01 00:00:00.0000000 through 9999-12-31 23:59:59.9999999 (in UTC)	8 to 10 bytes
CHARACTER			
Character	char	Fixed-length non-Unicode character data with a maximum length of 8,000 characters	1 byte per character

SQL-92 NAME—TYPE	SQL SERVER NAME	RANGE—DESCRIPTION	STORAGE SIZE
character varying	varchar	Variable-length non-Unicode data with a maximum length of 8,000 characters	1 byte per character
	varchar(max)	Variable-length data to $2^{31} - 1$ (2,147,483,647) characters	1 byte per character + 2-byte pointer
Text	text	Variable-length non-Unicode data with a maximum length of $2^{31} - 1$ (2,147,483,647) characters (deprecated)	1 byte per character
national character	nchar	Fixed-length Unicode data with a maximum length of 4,000 characters	2 bytes per character
national char varying	nvarchar	Variable-length Unicode data with a maximum length of 4,000 characters	2 bytes per character
	nvarchar(max)	Variable-length Unicode data with a maximum length of $2^{31} - 1$ (2,147,483,647) characters	2 bytes per character plus 2-byte pointer
national text	ntext	Variable-length Unicode data with a maximum length of $2^{30} - 1$ (1,073,741,823) characters (deprecated)	2 bytes per character
BINARY			
binary	binary	Fixed-length binary data with a maximum length of 8,000 bytes	Size of data in bytes
binary varying	varbinary	Variable-length binary data with a maximum length of 8,000 bytes	Size of data in bytes

SQL-92 NAME—TYPE	SQL SERVER NAME	RANGE—DESCRIPTION	STORAGE SIZE
	varbinary(max)	Variable-length binary data to $2^{31} - 1$ (2,147,483,647) bytes	Size of data in bytes + 2-byte pointer
Image	image	Variable-length binary data with a maximum length of $2^{31} - 1$ (2,147,483,647) bytes (deprecated)	Size of data in bytes

When you create or modify a table in SQL Server Management Studio, you assign a native data type by clicking in the Data Type column and using the list to select a data type. In T-SQL, you set the data type when you create the table and populate its columns or when you alter a table and add or change columns. Sample 8-6 shows how you can use T-SQL commands to create a table and its columns.

SAMPLE 8-6 Creating a Table and Its Columns.

```
USE OrderSystemDB
CREATE TABLE Sales.Customers
   (CustomerID nchar(5) NOT NULL,
   CompanyName nvarchar(40) NOT NULL,
   ContactName nvarchar(30) NOT NULL,
   ContactTitle nvarchar(30) NOT NULL,
   Address nvarchar(60) NOT NULL,
   City nvarchar(15) NULL,
   Region nvarchar(15) NULL,
   PostalCode nvarchar(5) NULL,
   Country nvarchar(15) NULL,
   Phone nvarchar(24) NULL,
   Fax nvarchar(24) NULL)
```

Using Fixed-Length, Variable-Length, and Max-Length Fields

You can create binary and character data types as fixed-length, variable-length, or max-length fields. When you use fixed-length data types, the column size you specify is reserved in the database and can be written to without manipulating the data in the column. This makes updates to the database quicker than with variable-length fields. When you use variable-length data types, SQL Server squeezes more rows into data pages, if possible. When more rows are included per data page, the process of reading data is usually more efficient, which can translate into improved performance for read operations. When you use max-length data types, SQL Server stores a 2-byte pointer to the actual data in the table's regular data space and stores the actual data in the large object data space. Generally speaking, you should do the following:

- Use fixed-length data types when the size of the data is consistent.
- Use variable-length data types when the size of the data varies.
- Use max-length data types when the size of the data exceeds the fixed-length or variable-length limit.

To gain a better understanding of the performance implications, consider the following scenario: With fixed-length columns of 80, 120, 40, and 500 bytes each, rows would always be written using 750 bytes of storage (740 bytes for data plus 10 bytes of overhead for each row). In this example, 10 rows fit on each data page (8,096/750, without the remainder).

If you use variable-length columns, however, the number of bytes used per row and the number of rows stored per page would vary. For example, assume that the average variable-length row uses 400 bytes. This includes 380 bytes of data and 20 bytes of overhead (12 bytes of overhead for rows that use variable-length data, plus 2 bytes of overhead per variable-length column, thus 4 x 2 + 12 = 20). In this case, 20 rows fit on each data page (8,096/400, without the remainder), which makes data reads more efficient than the fixed-length example.

Using User-Defined Data Types

User-defined data types are special data types that are based on a native data type. You will want to use user-defined data types when two or more tables store the same type of data in a column. These columns must have exactly the same data type, length, and nullability. You can create user-defined data types yourself, or you can let SQL Server do the job. For example, *sysname* is a user-defined data type that is used to reference database object names. The data type is defined as a variable Unicode character type of 128 characters, which is why object names are limited to 128 characters throughout SQL Server. You can apply this concept to ensure that specific data is used exactly as you want it to be used.

Creating User-Defined Data Types

You create user-defined data types at the database level rather than at the table level, which is why user-defined data types are static and immutable (unchangeable). This ensures that no performance penalty is associated with user-defined data types. User-defined data types do have some limitations, however. You cannot declare a default value or check constraint as part of a user-defined data type. You also cannot create a user-defined data type based on another user-defined data type.

> **TIP** When you create user-defined data types in a user-defined database, they apply only to that database. If you want a user-defined data type to apply to multiple databases, define the data type in the *model* database. Then the user-defined data type will exist in all new user-defined databases.

In SQL Server Management Studio, you create a user-defined data type by completing the following steps:

1. In SQL Server Management Studio, connect to the server instance containing the database in which you want to work.

2. In Object Explorer, expand the Databases node, select a database, and then expand the view to show its resource nodes.

3. Expand the Programmability node, right-click Types, point to New, and then select User-Defined Data Type. This opens the New User-Defined Data Type dialog box, shown in Figure 8-3.

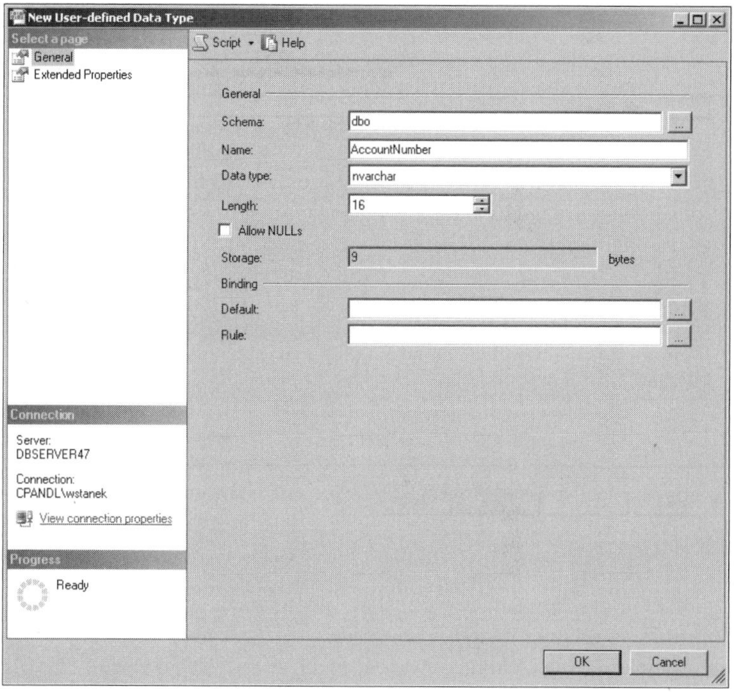

FIGURE 8-3 The New User-Defined Data Type dialog box.

4. The *dbo* schema is the default schema. To place the data type in a different schema, click the button to the right of the Schema box, and then click Browse. Select the schema you want to use, and then click OK twice.

5. Enter a name for the new data type.

6. In the Data Type list, select the data type on which you want to base the user-defined data type.

7. If the data type has a variable length, set the number of bytes or characters for the data type. For fixed-length variables, such as int, you cannot set a length.

8. To allow the data type to accept null values, select Allow Nulls.

9. Optionally, use the Default and Rule lists to select a default value or a rule to bind to the user-defined data type.

10. Click OK. If you open a new table or edit an existing table, you will see the new data type as one of the last entries in the Data Type selection list.

You can create user-defined data types with the CREATE TYPE statement. Sample 8-7 shows the related syntax and usage.

> **NOTE** You create user-defined table types using CREATE TYPE ... AS TABLE. User-defined table types are used with table-valued parameters that allow you to send multiple rows to the server with one call. For more information, see the "Using User-Defined Table Types" section later in this chapter.

SAMPLE 8-7 CREATE TYPE Syntax and Usage for User-Defined Data Types.

Syntax

```
CREATE TYPE [ schema_name. ] type_name
  {  FROM base_type
  [ ( precision [ , scale ] ) ]
  [ NULL | NOT NULL ]
  | EXTERNAL NAME assembly_name [ .class_name ] } [ ; ]
```

Usage

```
USE master
CREATE TYPE USPhoneNumber
FROM char(12) NOT NULL
```

Managing User-Defined Data Types

After you create user-defined data types, you often need to manage their properties. To manage user-defined data types, complete the following steps:

1. In SQL Server Management Studio, connect to the server instance that contains the database in which you want to work.

2. In Object Explorer, expand the Databases node, select a database, and then expand the view to show its resource nodes.

3. Expand Programmability, Types, and User-Defined Data Types to list the current user-defined data types.

4. Right-click the user-defined data type you want to manage, and then select from the following options:

- Properties, to view the data type's properties and set dependencies
- Delete, to delete the data type
- Rename, to rename the data type

5. To see where the data type is used in the database, right-click the user-defined data type, and then select View Dependencies from the shortcut menu.

Allowing and Disallowing Nulls

When you create columns in a table, you can specify whether nulls are allowed. A null means that there is no entry in the column for that row, which is not the same as the value 0 or an empty string. Columns defined with a primary key constraint or identity property cannot allow null values.

If you add a row but do not set a value for a column that allows null values, SQL Server inserts the value NULL—unless a default value is set for the column. When a default value is set for a column and you insert a null value, SQL Server replaces NULL with the default value. Additionally, if the column allows nulls, you can explicitly set a column to null by using the NULL keyword. Do not use quotation marks when setting a null value explicitly.

In SQL Server Management Studio's Table view, you can do the following:

- Allow nulls in a column by selecting the Allow Nulls column property.
- Disallow nulls in a column by clearing the Allow Nulls column property.

For an example of how to allow and disallow nulls with T-SQL, refer to Sample 8-4 earlier in this chapter.

Using Default Values

Null values are useful when you do not know a value or a value is missing. If the use of null values is not allowed according to the design specifications, you can set a default value. A default value is used when no value is set for a column you are inserting into a table. For example, you might want a character-based column to have the value N/A rather than NULL, so you would set the default value as N/A.

Table 8-3 summarizes combinations of default values and nullability that are handled in different ways. The main point to remember is that if you set a default value, the default is used whenever a value is not specified for the column entry. This is true even if you allow nulls.

TABLE 8-3 Default Values and Nullability

COLUMN DEFINITION	NO ENTRY, NO DEFAULT DEFINITION	NO ENTRY, DEFAULT DEFINITION	ENTER A NULL VALUE
Allows null values	Sets NULL	Sets default value	Sets NULL
Disallows null values	Error occurs	Sets default value	Error occurs

Using Sparse Columns

The Database Engine uses the SPARSE keyword in a column definition to optimize the storage of values in that column. When a value in a sparse column is null for any row in the table, the value requires no additional storage space. In this way, sparse columns are optimized for null values and reduce space requirements for null values.

However, sparse columns increase the overhead required to retrieve nonnull values. They also increase the storage space required for fixed-length data types.

Sparse columns are especially appropriate for filtered indexes because sparse columns have many null values. With filtered indexes on sparse columns, the index size is reduced because only the populated values are indexed, and this can increase index and search efficiency. INSERT, UPDATE, and DELETE statements can reference sparse columns by name. You also can view and work with all the sparse columns of a table that are combined into a single XML column called a *column set*.

The text, ntext, timestamp, image, geography, geometry, and any user-defined data types cannot be set as sparse. Although a computed column can contain a sparse column, a computed column cannot be marked as sparse. A sparse column cannot be used as a partition key of a clustered index or heap. However, a sparse column can be used as the partition key of a nonclustered index. Persisted and nonpersisted computed columns that are defined on sparse columns also can be part of a clustered key.

Sparse columns reduce the maximum size of a row from 8,060 bytes to 8,018 bytes. The following also apply to sparse columns:

- Cannot have the FILESTREAM, ROWGUIDCOL, or IDENTITY property
- Cannot have default values or be bound to a rule
- Cannot be part of a clustered index or a unique primary key index
- Cannot be used as the partition key of a clustered index or heap
- Cannot be part of a user-defined table type

In SQL Server Management Studio's Column Properties view, you can do the following:

- Set a column as sparse by setting the option Is Sparse to Yes.
- Set a column as not sparse by setting the option Is Sparse to No.

Using Identities and GUIDs

When you design tables, you often need to think about unique identifiers that can be used as primary keys or can ensure that merged data does not conflict with existing data. Unique identifiers for primary keys might include customer account numbers or Social Security numbers. If a unique identifier is not available, you might want to use the identity property to generate sequential values that are unique for each row in a table. You can also use this unique identifier to generate automatically a customer account number, an order number, or whatever other unique value you need.

Although the identity property provides a local solution for a specific table, it does not guarantee that the value used as an identifier will be unique throughout the database. Other tables in the database might have identity columns with the same values. In most cases, this is not a problem because the identity values are used only within the context of a single table and do not relate to other tables. However, in some situations, you might want to use a value that is unique throughout one or more databases, and if so, GUIDs provide the solution you need.

GUIDs are guaranteed to be unique across all networked computers in the world, which is extremely useful in merge replication. When you are merging data from multiple databases, GUIDs ensure that records are not inadvertently associated with each other. For example, a company's New York, Chicago, and San Francisco offices might have customer account numbers that are unique within those local offices but are not unique at the national level. GUIDs would ensure that account XYZ from New York and account XYZ from Chicago are not merged as the same account.

Identities and GUIDs are not mutually exclusive. Each table can have one identity column and one globally unique identity property. These values are often used together. For example, all clustered indexes in SQL Server should be unique, but they do not have to be unique (although SQL Server adds a 4-byte value to make them unique, if they are not).

In SQL Server Management Studio's Table view, you set identity values for a table by completing the following steps:

1. Create or modify other columns in the table as appropriate, and then start a new column for the identity value.

2. Give the identity column a name, and then select a data type. Identifier columns must use one of the following data types: tinyint, smallint, int, bigint, decimal, or numeric. GUID columns must have a data type of uniqueidentifier.

   TIP When you set the data type for an identifier column, be sure to consider how many rows are in the table, as well as how many rows might be added in the future. A tinyint identifier provides only 256 unique values (0 to 255). A smallint identifier provides 32,768 unique values (0 to 32,767).

3. Clear the Allow Nulls check box for the identity column.

4. To assign a GUID, select the identity column in the Table view. In the Column Properties view, set RowGuid to Yes. A default value of newid is created automatically for you.

   NOTE The newid function is used to generate unique identifier values by combining the identification number of a network card with a unique number from the CPU clock. If a server process generates the identifier, the server's network card identification number is used. If the identifier is returned by application programming interface (API) function calls, the client's network card is used. Network card manufacturers guarantee that no other network card in the next 100 years will have the same number.

5. To assign a unique identity, select the identity column in the Table view, expand Identity Specification in the Column Properties view, and then set Is Identity to Yes.

6. Type a value in the Identity Increment field. This value is the increment that is added to the Identity Seed for each subsequent row. If you leave this field blank, the value 1 is assigned by default.

7. Type a value in the Identity Seed field. This value is assigned to the first row in the table. If you leave this field blank, the value 1 is assigned by default.

8. If you are replicating a database and do not want the column to be replicated, set Is Not For Replication to Yes. Typically, you want to set Is Not For Replication to No to allow the column to be replicated.

NOTE The identity seed and increment values are used to determine the identifier for rows. If you enter a seed value of 100 and an increment of 10, the first row has a value of 100, the second has a value of 110, and so on.

When you create a table in T-SQL, GUIDs are not generated automatically. You must reference the newid function as the default value for the identifier column, as shown in this example:

```
USE OrderSystemDB
CREATE TABLE Sales.Customers
    (cust_lname varchar(40) NOT NULL,
    cust_fname varchar(20) NOT NULL,
    phone char(12) NOT NULL,
    uid uniqueidentifier NOT NULL DEFAULT newid())
```

Also, when you insert a new row into the table, you call newid to generate the GUID, as follows:

```
INSERT INTO Sales.Customers
Values ('Stanek', 'William', '123-555-1212', newid())
```

Using User-Defined Table Types

A user-defined table t ype is a special data type that represents the definition of a table structure. You use user-defined table types when you want to declare table-valued parameters to send multiple rows of data to a T-SQL statement, stored procedure, or function without having to create a temporary table or many parameters.

Understanding User-Defined Table Types

Table-valued parameters are similar to parameter arrays in ODBC and OLE DB, but they are more efficient. A table-valued parameter is scoped to the stored procedure, function, or dynamic T-SQL statement, exactly like other parameters, and has a scope like any other local variable that is created by using a DECLARE statement. You can declare table-valued variables within dynamic T-SQL statements and pass these variables as table-valued parameters to stored procedures and functions. T-SQL passes table-valued parameters to stored procedures or functions by reference to avoid making a copy of the input data.

In many cases, table-valued parameters offer better performance than temporary tables or other techniques that you can use to pass a list of parameters. Table-valued parameters perform well when you are using any of the following:

- Complex server logic to insert fewer than 1,000 rows from formatted data files on the server
- Complex remote client processes to insert any number of rows
- Direct insert with remote client processes to insert fewer than 1,000 rows

However, you are better off using BULK INSERT operations when you are using any of the following:

- Direct inserts from formatted data files on the server to insert any number of rows
- Complex server logic to insert more than 1,000 rows from formatted data files on the server
- Direct inserts of more than 1,000 rows with remote client processes

You create user-defined table types at the database level rather than at the table level. To create and use table-valued parameters, follow these steps:

1. Create a table type by using CREATE TYPE, and then use CREATE TABLE to define the table structure.

2. Create a procedure using CREATE PROCEDURE or a function using CREATE FUNCTION that has a parameter of the table type.

3. Declare a variable of the table type by using DECLARE @local_variable, and then reference the table type.

4. Add rows to the table variable by using an INSERT statement. After the table variable is created and filled, you can pass the variable to a procedure or function. When the procedure or function is out of scope, the table-valued parameter is no longer available. However, the type definition remains until it is dropped.

Table-valued parameters are strongly typed, do not acquire locks for the initial population of data from a client, and do not cause a statement to recompile. They also enable the client to specify sort order and unique keys, and they reduce back-and-forth communications between the client and server. You can obtain information that is associated with table-valued parameters by using the sys.parameters, sys.types, and sys.table_types catalog views.

SQL Server does not maintain statistics on columns of table-valued parameters, and table-valued parameters must be passed as input READONLY parameters to T-SQL routines. You cannot perform data manipulation language (DML) operations such as UPDATE, DELETE, or INSERT on a table-valued parameter in the body of a routine. Additionally, although a table-valued parameter can be in the FROM clause of SELECT INTO or in the INSERT EXEC string of a stored-procedure, you cannot use a table-valued parameter as the target of a SELECT INTO or INSERT EXEC statement.

Creating User-Defined Table Types

In SQL Server Management Studio, you create a user-defined table type by completing the following steps:

1. In SQL Server Management Studio, connect to the server instance containing the database in which you want to work.

2. In Object Explorer, expand the Databases node, select a database, and then expand the view to show its resource nodes.

3. Expand the Programmability node, right-click Types, point to New, and then select User-Defined Table Type. This creates a T-SQL query with the basic structure of the required CREATE TYPE statement.

Sample 8-8 shows how you can use the CREATE TYPE statement to create user-defined table types.

SAMPLE 8-8 Syntax and Usage for Creating User-Defined Table Types.

Syntax

```
CREATE TYPE [ schema_name. ] type_name
{
  AS TABLE ( { <col_def> | <comp_col_def> }
    [ <table_constraint> ] [ ,...n ] )
}
[ ; ]

<col_def> ::=
  column_name <data_type>
  [ COLLATE collation_name ] [ NULL | NOT NULL ]
  [ DEFAULT constant_expression ]
    | [ IDENTITY [ ( seed ,increment ) ] ]
  [ ROWGUIDCOL ] [ <column_constraint> [ ...n ] ]

<data type> ::=
  [ type_schema_name . ] type_name
  [ ( precision [ , scale ] | max |
    [ { CONTENT | DOCUMENT } ] xml_schema_collection ) ]

<column_constraint> ::=
{ { PRIMARY KEY | UNIQUE } [ CLUSTERED | NONCLUSTERED ]
  [ WITH ( <index_option> [ ,...n ] ) ]
  | CHECK ( logical_expression )
}

<comp_col_def> ::=
{ column_name AS computed_column_expression
  [ PERSISTED [ NOT NULL ] ]
  [ { PRIMARY KEY | UNIQUE } [ CLUSTERED | NONCLUSTERED ]
  [ WITH ( <index_option> [ ,...n ] ) ]
  | CHECK ( logical_expression ) ]
}
```

```
<table_constraint> ::=
{ { PRIMARY KEY | UNIQUE }
  [ CLUSTERED | NONCLUSTERED ] ( column [ ASC | DESC ] [ ,...n ] )
  [ WITH ( <index_option> [ ,...n ] ) ]
  | CHECK ( logical_expression )
}

<index_option> ::=
{ IGNORE_DUP_KEY = { ON | OFF } }
```

Usage

```
USE CustomerDB
CREATE TYPE StoreTableType AS TABLE
    ( StoreName VARCHAR(60)
    , StoreNumeric INT )
GO
```

Managing User-Defined Table Types

After you create user-defined table types, you often need to manage their properties. To manage user-defined table types, complete the following steps:

1. In SQL Server Management Studio, connect to the server instance that contains the database in which you want to work.

2. In Object Explorer, expand the Databases node, select a database, and then expand the view to show its resource nodes.

3. Expand Programmability, Types, and User-Defined Table Types to list the current user-defined table types.

4. As with any table, the user-defined table type can have associated columns, keys, constraints, and indexes. Right-click the user-defined table type you want to manage, and then select from the following options:

   - **Properties** To view the table type's properties and set dependencies
   - **Delete** To delete the table type
   - **Rename** To rename the table type

5. To see where the table type is used in the database, right-click the user-defined table type, and then select View Dependencies from the shortcut menu.

Using Views

Views can be thought of as virtual tables because the result sets returned by views have the same general form as a table, with columns and rows, and views can be referenced in queries much like tables. Several types of views can be created. Most views are used to join data from multiple tables so that the data can be accessed in a single result set. For example, you could create a CustOrder view that gets the customer's first name, last name, address, account number, and telephone number from the *Customers* table and the last order details from the *Orders* table, which makes the information more manageable for your company's sales representatives. Views can be created from other views as well, which allows you to extract subsets of data from views and to create supersets that combine data from multiple views. For example, you could create a subset view of the CustOrder view that shows only the customer's first name, last name, and telephone number. You could also create a superset view that combines elements of the CustOrder view, AllCustOrders view, and LastOrder view.

Views can be used to restrict access. Users see only the fields they need to work with, and while granted access to the views, they do not have access to the underlying tables from which the views are created.

Working with Views

To create a view, you use a SELECT statement to select the data in one or more tables and display it as a view. Like tables, views can be partitioned and indexed. A partitioned view joins horizontally partitioned data from a set of base tables from one or more servers. A partitioned view in which all base tables reside in the same database is referred to as a *local partitioned view*. A partitioned view in which one or more base tables reside on one or more remote servers is referred to as a *distributed partitioned view*.

> **TIP** Typically, you use distributed partitioned views rather than local partitioned views because the preferred method for partitioning data locally is through partitioned tables (and local partitioned views are supported only for backward compatibility). Distributed partitioned views are used to create a federation of database servers. A federation is a group of servers that are managed separately, but which cooperate to share the query processing load of a large application or website.

Partitioned views also can be updatable or read-only. Updatable partitioned views are updatable copies of the underlying tables. Read-only partitioned views are read-only copies of the underlying tables. To perform updates on a partitioned view, the partitioning column must be part of the base table's primary key. If this is not possible (or to make read-only partitioned views updatable), you can use INSTEAD OF triggers with a partitioned view. INSTEAD OF triggers execute whenever a user attempts to modify data by using INSERT, UPDATE, or DELETE. Views comprising multiple base tables must use an INSTEAD OF trigger to support inserts, updates, and deletes that reference data in more than one table.

You implement indexed views to improve query performance. The first index created on a view must be a unique clustered index. After the unique clustered index is created, you can create additional nonclustered indexes on the view. A view for which you want to create a unique clustered index must not reference any other views. It can reference only base tables, and those base tables must be in the same database as the view and have the same owner as the view. The view also must be created with the SCHEMABINDING option and is subject to other restrictions as well.

The query processor handles indexed and nonindexed views in different ways. The rows of an indexed view are stored in the database in the same format as a table. If the query optimizer uses an indexed view in a query plan, the indexed view is handled the same way as a base table. With nonindexed views, only the view definition is stored in the database, not the rows of the view. If the query optimizer uses a nonindexed view in an execution plan, only the logic from the view definition is used.

When an SQL statement references a nonindexed view, the parser and query optimizer analyze the source of both the SQL statement and the view and resolve them into a single execution plan. This means that there is not one plan for the SQL statement and a separate plan for the view—there is only one execution plan.

As with tables, views are contained in schemas, and you can assign permissions to views. Typically, you want the base tables and the related views to be in the same schema. It is also important to note that permissions assigned to views are separate from table permissions.

Using Windows PowerShell, you can work with views locally or by entering a remote session with a database server. Consider the following example:

```
Set-Location
SQLSERVER:\SQL\DatabaseServer34\Default\Databases\Inventory
Set-Location views
Get-ChildItem | where {$_.Schema eq "DevPers"}
```

In this example, you enter a remote session with DatabaseServer34 and then set the working location to the *Inventory* database on the default Database Engine instance. After you access the database, you access the view within the database and then return a list of all tables in the *DevPers* schema. In the where clause, you can search for any property of the *Microsoft.SqlServer.Management.Smo.View* object, including AnsiNullsStatus, Columns, CreateDate, DateLastModified, FullText Index, HasAfterTrigger, HasColumnSpecification, HasDeleteTrigger, HasIndex, HasInsertTrigger, HasInsteadOfTrigger, HasUpdateTrigger, Id, Indexes, IsEncrypted, IsIndexable, IsSchemaBound, IsSchemaOwned, Name, Owner, Parent, QuotedIdentifierStatus, ReturnsViewMetaData, Schema, State, Statistics, TextBody, TextHeader, TextMode, Triggers, and Urn.

Creating Views

Views can have up to 1,024 columns. If you understand tables, creating views is a straightforward process. However, there are a few rules to follow. Although the SELECT statement used to create a view can use more than one table and other views, you must have appropriate permissions to select from the referenced objects. The view definition cannot include COMPUTE or COMPUTE BY clauses, an ORDER BY clause (unless there is also a TOP clause), the INTO keyword, the OPTION clause, or a reference to a temporary table or a table variable.

You can create a view in SQL Server Management Studio by completing the following steps:

1. In SQL Server Management Studio, select a database, and then expand the Views node to list the current views in the database. Two types of views are available: system and user. System views provide a summarized report of database information, such as table constraints and table privileges. User views are defined by you or by other database users.

2. To create a new view, right-click the Views node. From the shortcut menu, choose New View to display the Add Table dialog box, shown in Figure 8-4. The Add Table dialog box has tabs that allow you to work with tables, views, functions, and synonyms. If you select Add New Derived Tables from the Query Designer menu and display the dialog box again, you will see a Local Tables tab containing derived tables.

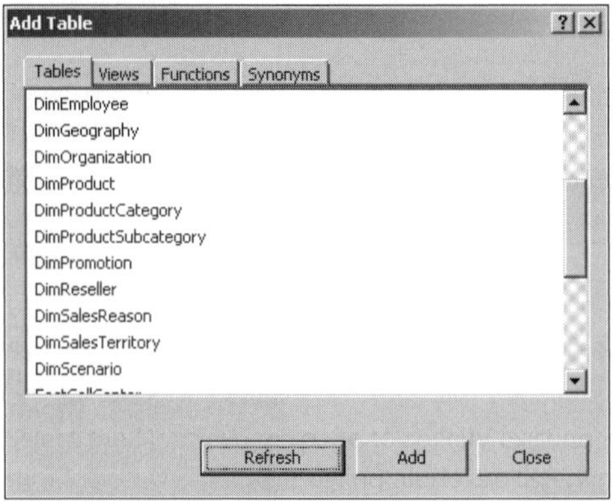

FIGURE 8-4 The Add Table dialog box.

3. In the Add Table dialog box, select a table or other object that contains data you want to add to the view, and then click Add. This displays a view pane for the selected object, which you can use to add columns, fields, and other elements to the view you are creating.

4. When you finish working with the Add Table dialog box, click Close. You can display this dialog box again at any time by selecting Add Table on the Query Designer menu.

5. Use the view panes provided to select the columns and fields to use in the view, as shown in Figure 8-5. Your actions create a SELECT statement that can be used to generate the view.

6. The View Properties pane is not displayed by default. In the right pane, click the tab with the name of the view, and then press F4 to display the View Properties pane.

7. Set the view name, description, and schema. Type the name and description in the fields provided. Use the drop-down list to select the schema that will contain this view.

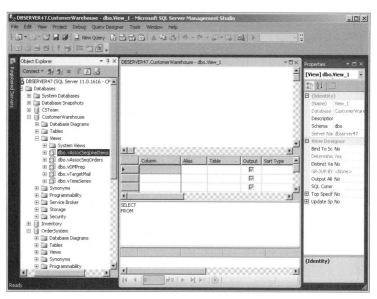

FIGURE 8-5 Select columns and fields to use for a view.

8. You might want to create a dependency within a schema to ensure that any modifications to the underlying structures that the view comprises are not changed without first changing the view. You do this by binding the view to the schema. If you want to bind the view to the schema, set Bind To Schema to Yes.

   NOTE When you bind a view to the schema, views or tables used in the view cannot be dropped unless that view is dropped or changed so that it no longer has schema binding. Furthermore, ALTER TABLE statements executed on tables that participate in views that have schema binding fail when these statements affect the view definition.

9. If you want to ensure that the view shows only distinct rows and filters out duplicate rows, set Distinct Values to Yes.

10. If you want the view to return a partial result set containing the top matches, set Top to Yes, and then define the number of top matches to return as either a fixed maximum or a percentage of the total results.

   ■ To define a fixed maximum, set Expression to the maximum number of results to return and set Percent to No. For example, set Expression to 50 to return the top 50 results.

   ■ To define a percentage of the total results to return, set Expression to the percentage of results to return and set Percent to Yes. For example, set Expression to 10 and Percent to Yes to return the top 10 percent of the result set.

11. If you want to create an updatable view, set Update Using View Rules to Yes. Updatable views cannot be created with distinct values or from top result sets. To make sure that data remains visible through the view after a modification is committed, set Check Option to Yes. Remember, however, that updates performed directly to a view's base tables are not verified against the view even when you select the Check Option.

12. When you finish configuring the view, select Verify SQL Syntax from the Query Designer menu. Correct any errors or issues reported during the verification process before continuing.

13. To retrieve the data from the current definition, press Ctrl+R or select Execute SQL from the Query Designer menu.

14. After you run the view to update it for the latest changes, save the view. Press Ctrl+S or click Save on the toolbar.

You can also create views using the CREATE VIEW statement. You can create a simple view by selecting all the values in a table as follows:

```
CREATE VIEW Sales.CustomView As
SELECT *
FROM Sales.Customers
```

Then you can work directly with the view:

```
SELECT * FROM Sales.CustomView
```

Sample 8-9 shows the full syntax and usage for CREATE VIEW.

SAMPLE 8-9 CREATE VIEW Syntax and Usage.

Syntax

```
CREATE VIEW [ schema_name . ] view_name [ (column [ ,...n ] ) ]
[ WITH <view_attribute> [ ,...n ] ]
AS select_statement
[ WITH CHECK OPTION ] [ ; ]

<view_attribute> ::=
{   [ ENCRYPTION ]
    [ SCHEMABINDING ]
    [ VIEW_METADATA ]      }
```

Usage

```
CREATE VIEW Sales.CustomView As
SELECT cust_id AS Account, cust_lname AS [Last Name],
    cust_fname AS [First Name], state AS Region
FROM Sales.Customers
WHERE (state = 'WA') OR
    (state = 'HI') OR
    (state = 'CA')
```

Modifying Views

You can modify a view in SQL Server Management Studio by completing the following steps:

1. In SQL Server Management Studio, select a database, and then expand the Views node to list the current views in the database.

2. To modify an existing view, right-click the view, and then select Design.

3. If you want to add tables, views, functions, or synonyms, select Add Table from the Query Designer menu.

4. If you want to set view properties, click the tab with the name of the view and then press F4 to display the View Properties pane.

To change an existing view without having to reset its permissions and other properties, use ALTER VIEW. The following example changes the definition of the Sales Custom view used in previous examples:

```
ALTER VIEW Sales.CustomView As
    SELECT cust_id AS Account, cust_lname AS [Customer Last Name],
    cust_fname AS [Customer First Name], state AS Region
    FROM Sales.Customers
    WHERE (state = 'WA') OR
        (state = 'CA')
```

Sample 8-10 shows the full syntax for ALTER VIEW.

SAMPLE 8-10 ALTER VIEW Syntax.

```
ALTER VIEW [ schema_name . ] view_name [ ( column [ ,...n ] ) ]
[ WITH <view_attribute> [ ,...n ] ]
AS select_statement
[ WITH CHECK OPTION ] [ ; ]

<view_attribute> ::=
{   [ ENCRYPTION ]
    [ SCHEMABINDING ]
    [ VIEW_METADATA ]   }
```

Using Updatable Views

SQL Server supports updatable views as well. With an updatable view, you can change the information in the view by using INSERT, UPDATE, and DELETE statements. You can create updatable views if the table columns being modified are not affected by GROUP BY, HAVING, or DISTINCT clauses. Furthermore, an updatable view can be modified only when the columns from one base table are being modified and those columns directly reference the underlying data. This means the data cannot be derived from an aggregate function or computed from an expression that uses other columns.

With updatable views, you usually want to set Check Option to Yes. If you do not set the option, changes to the view might result in rows that are no longer displayed in the view. For example, consider the view created as an example previously. The view included customer information from Washington (WA), Hawaii (HI), and California (CA). If you change a state value to GA, the row would disappear from the view because Georgia-based customers are not displayed in the view.

Managing Views

You can examine view properties, set view permissions, and perform other management tasks, just as you do with tables. To get started managing views, complete the following steps:

1. In SQL Server Management Studio, select a database, and then expand the Views node to list the current views in the database.

2. Select a view, and then right-click it to open a shortcut menu that gives you the following choices to manage the view:

   - **Select Top 1000 Rows**   Displays up to the first 1,000 rows in the result set for the view.

   - **Edit Top 200 Rows**   Displays up to the first 200 rows in the result set for the view and allows you to edit the related values.

   - **Properties**   Examines view properties.

   - **Rename**   Renames the view.

   - **Delete**   Deletes the view.

   - **View Dependencies**   Views objects that depend on the view or objects on which the view depends.

3. To set permissions for a view, right-click the view, and then select Properties. In the View Properties dialog box, select the Permissions page. Now you can manage the permissions for the view.

CHAPTER 9

Using Indexes, Constraints, and Partitions

- Creating and Managing Indexes **362**
- Working with Columnstore Indexes **382**
- Column Constraints and Rules **386**
- Creating Partitioned Tables and Indexes **391**
- Compressing Tables, Indexes, and Partitions **396**

J ust as a fundamental understanding of schemas, tables, and views is essential for success as a database administrator, so is an understanding of indexes, constraints, and partitions. At their most basic, indexes, constraints, and partitions are control elements:

- Indexes provide faster access to data because you do not need to search an entire table to get desired results.

- Constraints control the way column values are used so you can be sure that columns contain acceptable values.

- Partitions allow you to manage subsets of data to improve response times when working with large tables and to make maintenance easier.

The many ins and outs of working with indexes, constraints, and partitions are discussed in this chapter. Keep in mind, though, that many related concepts are introduced in the previous chapter, including partitioning basics, as discussed in the "Understanding Table Partitions" section.

NOTE Policy-Based Management settings can affect your ability to name objects. For more information, see Chapter 3, "Implementing Policy-Based Management."

Creating and Managing Indexes

Indexes help locate and access data. With Microsoft SQL Server 2012, you can create indexes on tables, views, and computed columns. By creating an index on a table, you can search through the data in the table quickly. By creating an index on a view, you can generate a result set of the view that is stored and indexed in the database. By creating an index on a computed column, you can evaluate expressions and index the results (if certain criteria are met).

Indexes are managed separately from tables. You can analyze and implement them automatically using the Database Engine Tuning Advisor. This section examines the techniques you use to work with traditional indexes. Traditional indexes, also known as *rowstore indexes,* group and store data for each row and then join all the rows to complete the index. SQL Server 2012 also supports columnstore indexes, which group and store data for each column and then join all the columns to complete the index. See the "Working with Columnstore Indexes" section later in this chapter to learn how to use columnstore indexes.

Understanding Traditional Indexes

Traditional indexes, like tables, use pages. The structure of index pages is similar to the structure of table data pages. Index pages are 8 KB (8,192 bytes) in size and have a 96-byte header. But unlike data pages, they do not have row offsets. Each index has a corresponding row in the sys.indexes catalog view with an index ID value (index_id) of 1 for clustered indexes or 2 through 250 for nonclustered indexes.

With standard indexes, large object data types (image, ntext, text, varchar(max), nvarchar(max), varbinary(max), and xml) cannot be index key columns, although varchar(max), nvarchar(max), varbinary(max), and xml data types can be included columns. Computed columns that are deterministic can be included, as can computed columns derived from large object data types.

SQL Server maintains indexes using a B-tree structure, which is a basic tree structure consisting of a root node, intermediate-level nodes, and leaf nodes. Because indexes use a tree structure, you can search them quickly and efficiently. Without the tree structure, SQL Server would need to read each table data page in the database in turn, searching for the correct record.

To put this in perspective, consider a simple table in which each data page contains a single row. In this case, if SQL Server searches for data in row 800 and there is no index, SQL Server might have to search 799 other rows before finding the right row. With a tree structure, SQL Server navigates the nodes down the index searching for the row that matches the corresponding index key. In the best-case scenario, in which the index keys have been arranged in a full tree, the number of nodes that need to be searched is proportional to the height of the tree. For example, 27,000 rows might be represented by 30 levels of nodes, and if so, SQL Server would have to navigate a maximum of 15 nodes to find the matching row.

NOTE You might have noticed that I simplified this example to demonstrate the power of indexing. Nevertheless, indexing can improve performance by orders of magnitude, and accessing a database that doesn't use indexing can seem extremely slow. You must be careful, however; indexing the wrong information also can make the database perform slowly, which is why it is so important to select the most referenced or most used column in the table to index.

SQL Server 2012 supports many indexing options:

- Index operations can be performed online, with SQL Server Enterprise Edition and higher, and online indexing depends on the amount of memory allocated for indexing. Online indexing makes it possible for users to access table data and use other indexes on a table while an index is being created, modified, or dropped.

- Columns that are not part of the index key can be included in nonclustered indexes. Including them improves query performance by making all the required data available without the need to access the table data rows. These included columns can exceed the index size limitations of 16 key columns and the maximum key size of 900 bytes.

- Both row-level and page-level index locks are allowed when accessing the index. If you allow row locks, page locks, or both, the Database Engine determines when the locks are used.

- The maximum degree of parallelism can be set using MAXDOP. This controls the number of parallel operations that can occur when you are creating, altering, or dropping an index.

- Indexes can be partitioned on value ranges by using existing partition schemes. When you partition a nonunique, clustered index, the Database Engine adds the partitioning column to the list of clustered index keys if it is not already specified as a key. When you partition a nonunique, nonclustered index, the Database Engine adds the partitioning column as a nonkey (included) column of the index if it is not already specified as such.

SQL Server 2012 supports two main types of indexing:

- Clustered indexes
- Nonclustered indexes

You can create clustered and nonclustered indexes on almost any column. If you want to create indexes on computed columns, you must ensure that the computed column expression always returns the same result for a specific set of inputs. Although you can create an index on any other type of column, you should always select the index column carefully. Selecting the correct column to index improves response time dramatically. Selecting the wrong column to index actually can degrade response time. For more information about which column to index, use the Database Engine Tuning Advisor.

NOTE Exceptions include Common Language Runtime (CLR) user-defined types and very large object data types. With CLR user-defined types, the IComparable interface must be supported to provide a native way to ascertain sort order. Although you cannot create indexes on large object data types, you can and should create primary (and, if you want, secondary) XML indexes on XML data.

SQL Server 2012 also supports several special types of indexing:

- **XML indexes** An XML index is an optimized index for XML data in a table. The first index you create on a column with the xml data type is the primary one. When you create the primary XML index, a clustered index is created for XML data from the clustering key of the user table and an XML node identifier. A primary XML index on an xml column must exist before any secondary XML indexes can be created on the column. Each table can have up to 249 XML indexes. You will learn more about XML indexes in the "Using XML Indexes" section later in this chapter.

- **Filtered indexes** A filtered index is an optimized nonclustered index on a subset of table data. Well-designed filtered indexes reduce index storage costs because you don't need to index full tables. They also improve query performance and execution plan quality because they are smaller than full-table indexes, and they reduce maintenance overhead because they are maintained only when the data in the index is modified. You will learn more about filtered indexes in the "Using Filtered Indexes" section later in this chapter.

- **Spatial indexes** A spatial index is defined on a table column that contains geometric or geographic data. A spatial index on geographic data maps the geographic data to a two-dimensional space. Each table can have up to 249 spatial indexes. You can define spatial indexes only on a table that has a primary key. Primary key metadata cannot be changed while a spatial index is defined on a table, and the maximum number of primary key columns on the table is 15. You can create more than one spatial index on the same spatial column, which might be necessary to index different grid parameters in a single column.

Using Clustered Indexes

A clustered index stores the actual table data pages at the leaf level, and the table data is ordered physically around the key. A table can have only one clustered index, and when this index is created, the following events also occur:

- Table data is rearranged.
- New index pages are created.
- All nonclustered indexes within the database are rebuilt.

As a result, there are many disk I/O operations and extensive use of system and memory resources. If you plan to create a clustered index, be sure you have free space equal to at least 1.5 times the amount of data in the table. The extra free space ensures that you have enough space to complete the operation efficiently.

Normally, you create a clustered index on a primary key. However, you can create a clustered index on any named column, such as cust_lname or cust_id. When you create a clustered index, the values you are indexing should be unique. If the values are not unique, SQL Server appends a 4-byte unique identifier on rows that have duplicates of their primary sort keys.

Using Nonclustered Indexes

In a nonclustered index, pages at the leaf level contain a bookmark that tells SQL Server where to find the data row corresponding to the key in the index. If the table has a clustered index, the bookmark indicates the clustered index key. If the table does not have a clustered index, the bookmark is an actual row locator.

When you create a nonclustered index, SQL Server creates the required index pages but does not rearrange table data. Other indexes for the table are not deleted. Each table can have up to 999 nonclustered indexes.

Using XML Indexes

As mentioned earlier, an XML index is a special type of index for columns of the xml data type. The first XML index you create for a column is the primary. Any other XML indexes on the column are secondaries of the type PATH, VALUE, or PROPERTY.

Before you can create an XML index, you must have a clustered index based on the primary key of the user table, and this key is limited to 15 columns. Two types of XML indexes can be created: primary and secondary. Each xml column in a table can have one primary XML index and one or more secondary XML indexes. However, there must be a primary XML index before a secondary XML index can be created on a column, and you cannot create a primary XML index on a computed xml column.

Also, an XML index can be created only on a single xml column. You cannot create an XML index on a non-xml column, nor can you create a relational index on an xml column. You cannot create an XML index on an xml column in a view, on a table-valued variable with xml columns, or on an xml type variable. Finally, the SET options must be the same as those required for indexed views and computed-column indexes. This means ARITHABORT must be set to ON when an XML index is created and when values in the xml column are being inserted, deleted, or updated.

Using Filtered Indexes

As mentioned earlier, a filtered index is a special type of nonclustered index on a subset of table data. Filtered indexes are useful in several situations. When a table column has only a limited number of relevant values and a query selects only from the relevant values, you can create a filtered index for the relevant data rows. When a table column has multiple categories of data and a query selects only from a particular category or categories, you can create a filtered index for the relevant category or categories.

Filtered indexes are useful when your queries use simple comparison logic in a predicate and the queries are not a replacement for views, which have broader scope and functionality. For example, you could create a filtered index for nonnull data rows using a query that selects only from nonnull values. Or you could create a filtered index for a subset of categories within the data using a query that selects only the categories you need.

> **NOTE** You cannot create filtered indexes on views. You cannot drop, rename, or alter the definition of a table column that is defined in a filtered index expression. You can track dependencies for filtered index expressions by using the sys.sql_expression_ dependencies catalog view.

In some cases, a parameterized query does not contain enough information at compile time for the query optimizer to choose a filtered index. You might be able to rewrite the query to provide the missing information. For example, you could modify the query so that the query results are empty when a parameterized expression is not a subset of the filter predicate.

When creating filtered indexes, you should include only those columns that are required for the query optimizer to choose the filtered index for the query execution plan. The primary key of the table does not need to be included specifically in the filtered index definition. The primary key is included automatically in all nonclustered indexes, including filtered indexes.

When the filtered index expression is equivalent to the query predicate and the query does not return the column in the filtered index expression with the query results, a column in the filtered index expression does not need to be a key or included column in the filtered index definition. When the query predicate uses the column in a comparison that is not equivalent to the filtered index expression, a column in the filtered index expression should be a key or included column in the filtered index definition.

When the comparison operator specified in the filtered index expression results in an implicit or explicit data conversion, an error will occur if the conversion occurs on the left side of a comparison operator. A workaround is to write the filtered index expression with the data conversion operator (CAST or CONVERT) on the right side of the comparison operator. However, this can change the meaning of the conversion.

Determining Which Columns Should Be Indexed

Now that you know how indexes work, you can focus on which columns you should index. Ideally, you should select columns for indexing on the basis of the types of queries executed on the database. SQL Server Profiler can help you determine the types of queries being run. You use SQL Server Profiler to create a trace that contains a good snapshot of activities performed by users on the database.

You can examine this trace manually to see what types of queries are executed, or you can use the trace file as a saved workload file in the Database Engine Tuning Advisor. Regardless of which method you use, keep in mind that the maximum length of all key columns that an index comprises is 900 bytes. This means that the total size in bytes of all columns must be 900 or less. (Columns that are not part of the index key can be included, and these included columns can exceed the index size limitations of 16 key columns and the maximum key size of 900 bytes.) Table 9-1 offers some guidelines about the kinds of tables and columns that can be indexed successfully and those that do not result in useful indexes.

TABLE 9-1 Guidelines for Selecting Tables and Columns to Index

INDEX	DO NOT INDEX
Tables with lots of rows	Tables with few rows
Columns that are often used in queries	Columns that are rarely used in queries
Columns that have a wide range of values and have a high likelihood of rows being selected in a typical query	Columns that have a wide range of values but have a low likelihood of rows being selected in a typical query
Columns used in aggregate functions	Columns that have a large byte size
Columns used in GROUP BY queries	Tables with many modifications but few actual queries
Columns used in ORDER BY queries	
Columns used in table joins	

Table 9-2 provides suggestions for the types of columns that should use clustered or nonclustered indexes.

TABLE 9-2 Guidelines for Using Clustered and Nonclustered Indexes

CONSIDER CLUSTERED INDEX FOR	CONSIDER NONCLUSTERED INDEX FOR
Primary keys that are sequential, such as account or product identifiers	Primary keys that are not sequential identifiers, such as identity columns
Queries that return a range of values by using BETWEEN, >, >=, <, <=, and similar operators	Columns that have lots of distinct values and a clustered index for other columns
Queries that return large result sets	Columns frequently used in search conditions that return exact matches
Columns used in many queries	Queries that return small result sets
Columns with strong selectivity	Columns used in aggregate functions

CONSIDER CLUSTERED INDEX FOR	CONSIDER NONCLUSTERED INDEX FOR
Columns used in ORDER BY or GROUP BY queries	Columns with weak selectivity
Columns used in table joins, typically for foreign keys	Queries that use JOIN or GROUP BY, when there's a clustered index on foreign key columns

Indexing Computed Columns and Views

With SQL Server 2012, you can index computed columns and views as well as tables. Indexes on computed columns and views involve storing results in the database for future reference. With computed columns, the column values are calculated and then used to build the keys stored in the index. With views, the result set is stored by creating a clustered index on the view. In both cases, the stored results are valid only if all connections referring to the results can generate an identical result set, which puts specific restrictions on how you can create indexes on computed columns and views.

You must establish connections referring to the results by using specific SET options, and these options must have the same settings. The options you must set are as follows:

- ANSI_NULLS must be set to ON.
- ANSI_PADDING must be set to ON.
- ANSI_WARNINGS must be set to ON.
- ARITHABORT must be set to ON.
- CONCAT_NULL_YIELDS_NULL must be set to ON.
- QUOTED_IDENTIFIER must be set to ON.
- NUMERIC_ROUNDABORT must be set to OFF.

Furthermore, all operations referencing the view must use the same algorithm to build the view result set, including the following:

- The CREATE INDEX statement that builds the initial result set or is used to calculate the initial keys
- Any subsequent INSERT, UPDATE, or DELETE statements that affect the data used to build the view result set or are used to calculate keys
- All queries for which the query optimizer must determine whether the indexed view is useful

Viewing Index Properties

Both tables and views can have indexes. In SQL Server Management Studio, you can view indexes associated with a table or view by completing the following steps:

1. In SQL Server Management Studio, select a database, and then expand the Tables or Views node as appropriate.

2. Select a table or view, and then expand its node to list the objects it contains.

3. Expand the Indexes node to list the indexes associated with the selected table or view (if any).

4. Right-click an index, and then select Properties to open the Index Properties dialog box, shown in Figure 9-1. This dialog box has several pages that let you view and manage index properties, including the following:

   - **General** Shows general properties, including the index name and type. You can change the index type and add or remove key columns.

   - **Options** Allows you to set options for rebuilding the index, recomputing statistics, using row or page locks, setting the fill factor, and determining the maximum degree of parallelism.

   - **Included Columns** Allows you to view and manage the included columns (with nonclustered indexes).

   - **Storage** Lists the current storage configuration. Allows you to configure filegroups and partition schemes.

   - **Spatial** Lists spatial properties for columns that include geometric or geographic data.

   - **Filter** Lists the filter expression for a filtered index.

   - **Fragmentation** Lists the index fragmentation data, which you can use to determine if you need to reorganize or rebuild the index.

   - **Extended Properties** Lists extended properties. Allows you to add or remove extended properties.

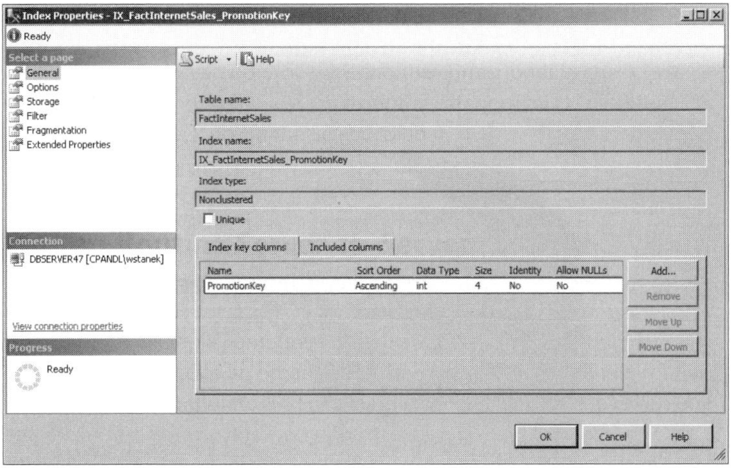

FIGURE 9-1 The Index Properties dialog box.

Using the sp_statistics stored procedure, you can examine the indexes for a specific table or view. To do this, you simply specify the name of the table or view whose indexes you want to examine, as shown in the following example:

```
USE OrderSystemDB
GO
EXEC sp_statistics 'Customers', 'Sales'
```

Creating Indexes

Only the owner of a table or view can create indexes on that table or view. You can create indexes with a design tool in SQL Server Management Studio or with the Transact-SQL (T-SQL) CREATE INDEX statement. To create indexes with the design tool, complete the following steps:

1. In SQL Server Management Studio, connect to the server instance containing the database in which you want to work.

2. In Object Explorer, expand the Databases node, select a database, and then expand it to show the database's resource nodes.

3. Expand the Tables or Views node as appropriate. Right-click the table or view for which you are creating the index, and then select Design from the shortcut menu.

4. On the Table Designer menu, select Indexes/Keys to display the Indexes/Keys dialog box, shown in Figure 9-2.

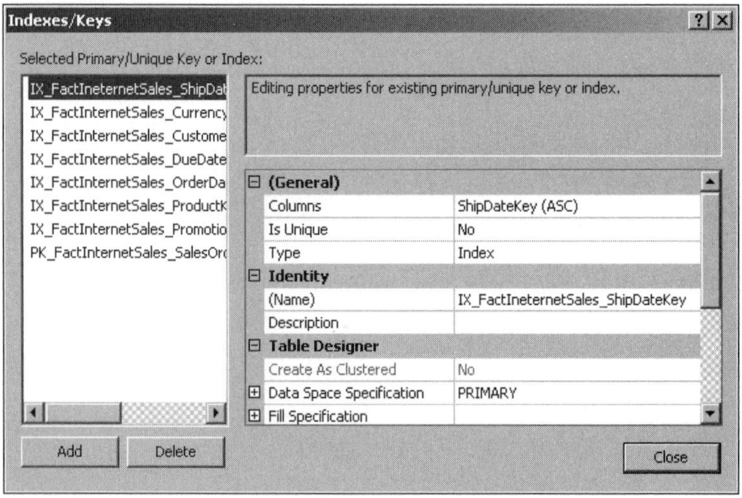

FIGURE 9-2 The Indexes/Keys dialog box.

5. Any current primary/unique keys and indexes are listed in the left pane of the dialog box. You can manage the properties of any of the keys by selecting a key and making the necessary changes. To add an index, click Add.

6. Click in the Columns text box, and then click the button to the right of the Columns box. This displays the Index Columns dialog box, shown in Figure 9-3.

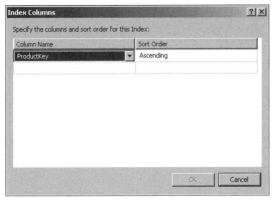

FIGURE 9-3 The Index Columns dialog box.

7. Under Column Name, select the column or columns you want to include in the index. You can select only columns that have valid data types for indexing.

8. Each column can have a separate sort order for the index. By default, the sort order is set to Ascending. You can set the sort order to Descending.

9. When you finish selecting columns to index, click OK to close the Index Columns dialog box.

10. If you want to ensure that data entered into this index is unique, set the option Is Unique to Yes. This ensures the uniqueness of values stored in the index. You cannot set this option for XML indexes.

11. Type should be set to Index by default. Under Identity, use the text boxes provided to enter the index name and description. You can use up to 128 characters for the index name. Ideally, the index name should be short and easy to associate with its purpose, such as [Index for Cust ID].

12. Set the option Create As Clustered to Yes to create a clustered index on the columns selected. Otherwise, a nonclustered index is created. Remember that you can have only one clustered index per table; if the table already has a clustered index, this option is not available.

13. To specify the storage location for the index, expand the Data Space Specification node, and then use the Filegroup Or Partition Schema list to specify the filegroup.

14. To set the fill parameters, expand the Fill Specification node. Set the Fill Factor property to 0 (the default value) to let SQL Server use an optimized fill, as described in the "Setting the Index Fill" section in Chapter 5, "Tuning and Linking Your SQL Servers." Refer to this section as well for information

about setting the Fill Factor property to a different value to set a specific index fill.

15. If you want to ignore duplicate keys, set the option Ignore Duplicate Keys to Yes. When this option is on, any attempt to insert rows that violate the unique index fails with a warning, and the rows are not inserted. Whether this option is set on or off, SQL Server does not allow you to create a unique index on columns that already have duplicate values. Columns that are used in a unique index should be set so that they do not allow nulls. Furthermore, you cannot use the Ignore Duplicate Keys option with XML indexes or indexes created on views.

16. Optionally, turn on automatic statistics updating by setting the option Re-Compute Statistics to Yes. If you set Re-Compute Statistics to No, out-of-date statistics are not recomputed automatically.

17. When you finish configuring the index, click Close. Select File, Save or press Ctrl+S to save the table, which in turn saves the index you created.

18. With nonclustered indexes, you can create filtered indexes by adding the WHERE clause to the CREATE INDEX statement. In SQL Server Management Studio, right-click a nonclustered index, and then select Properties to open the Index Properties dialog box shown previously in Figure 9-1. You can then enter the filter on the Filter page.

Use the T-SQL CREATE INDEX command to create indexes with the syntax shown in Sample 9-1. With a nonclustered index, you can create a filtered index by adding a WHERE clause.

SAMPLE 9-1 CREATE INDEX Syntax.

Syntax Relational Index

```
CREATE [ UNIQUE ] [ CLUSTERED | NONCLUSTERED ] INDEX index_name
    ON <object> ( column [ ASC | DESC ] [ ,...n ] )
    [ INCLUDE ( column_name [ ,...n ] ) ]
    [ WHERE <filter_predicate> ]
    [ WITH ( <relational_index_option> [ ,...n ] ) ]
    [ ON { partition_scheme_name ( column_name )
        | filegroup_name
        | default
        }
    ]
    [ FILESTREAM_ON { filestream_filegroup_name
        | partition_scheme_name | "NULL" } ]
[ ; ]

<object> ::=
{ [ database_name. [ schema_name ] . | schema_name. ]
    table_or_view_name
}
```

```
<relational_index_option> ::=
{ PAD_INDEX = { ON | OFF }
  | FILLFACTOR = fillfactor
  | SORT_IN_TEMPDB = { ON | OFF }
  | IGNORE_DUP_KEY = { ON | OFF }
  | STATISTICS_NORECOMPUTE = { ON | OFF }
  | DROP_EXISTING = { ON | OFF }
  | ONLINE = { ON | OFF }
  | ALLOW_ROW_LOCKS = { ON | OFF }
  | ALLOW_PAGE_LOCKS = { ON | OFF }
  | MAXDOP = max_degree_of_parallelism
  | DATA_COMPRESSION = { NONE | ROW | PAGE}
      [ ON PARTITIONS ( { <partition_number_expression> | <range> }
      [ , ...n ] ) ]
}

<filter_predicate> ::=
    <conjunct> [ AND <conjunct> ]

<conjunct> ::=
    <disjunct> | <comparison>

<disjunct> ::=
        column_name IN (constant ,...)

<comparison> ::=
        column_name <comparison_op> constant

<comparison_op> ::=
    { IS | IS NOT | = | <> | != | > | >= | !> | < | <= | !< }

<range> ::=
<partition_number_expression> TO <partition_number_expression>
```

Syntax XML Index

```
CREATE [ PRIMARY ] XML INDEX index_name
    ON <object> ( xml_column_name )
    [ USING XML INDEX xml_index_name
        [ FOR { VALUE | PATH | PROPERTY } ] ]
    [ WITH ( <xml_index_option> [ ,...n ] ) ]
[ ; ]

<object> ::=
{ [ database_name. [ schema_name ] . | schema_name. ] table_name }

<xml_index_option> ::=
{ PAD_INDEX  = { ON | OFF }
  | FILLFACTOR = fillfactor
  | SORT_IN_TEMPDB = { ON | OFF }
  | IGNORE_DUP_KEY = OFF
  | STATISTICS_NORECOMPUTE = { ON | OFF }
```

```
   | DROP_EXISTING = { ON | OFF }
   | ONLINE = OFF
   | ALLOW_ROW_LOCKS = { ON | OFF }
   | ALLOW_PAGE_LOCKS = { ON | OFF }
   | MAXDOP = max_degree_of_parallelism
}
```

Managing Indexes

After you create an index, you might need to change its properties, rename it, or delete it. You handle these tasks in SQL Server Management Studio by completing the following steps:

1. In SQL Server Management Studio, select a database, and then expand the Tables or Views node as appropriate.

2. Select a table or view and expand its node to list the objects it contains.

3. Expand the Indexes node to list the indexes associated with the selected table or view.

4. Right-click an index. Now you can choose from the following options:

   - Select Properties to view the index properties, including details on space usage and fragmentation.

   - Select Rename to rename an index.

   - Select Rebuild to rebuild the index. In the Rebuild Indexes dialog box, use the Total Fragmentation and Status values to help determine whether or not to proceed. Click OK to proceed with the rebuild. Click Cancel to exit without performing the rebuild. SQL Server 2012 Enterprise Edition and higher perform online index rebuilds and reorganizations. Other editions perform index rebuilds offline and reorganizations online.

   - Select Reorganize to reorganize the index. In the Reorganize Indexes dialog box, check the total fragmentation of the index to determine whether the index needs to be reorganized. By default, both regular data and large object data are reorganized. Clear the Compact Large Object Column Data option if you want to compact only regular index data. Click OK to proceed with the reorganization. Click Cancel to exit without performing the reorganization.

   - Select Delete to drop the index (so long as it is not a primary key or unique constraint).

You can also manage indexes with the T-SQL commands ALTER INDEX and DROP INDEX. You must use these commands cautiously, however, because there are several limitations to them. For example, you cannot drop an index that was created by defining a primary key or unique constraints. Instead, you must drop the constraint with ALTER TABLE. Sample 9-2 shows the syntax for ALTER INDEX, and Sample 9-3 shows the syntax for DROP INDEX.

SAMPLE 9-2 ALTER INDEX Syntax.

```
ALTER INDEX { index_name | ALL }
    ON <object>
    { REBUILD
      [ [PARTITION = ALL]
        [ [ WITH ( <rebuild_index_option> [ ,...n ] ) ]
          | [ PARTITION = partition_number
              [ WITH ( <single_partition_rebuild_index_option>
                       [ ,...n ] )
              ]
          ]
        ]
      ]
    | DISABLE
    | REORGANIZE
        [ PARTITION = partition_number ]
        [ WITH ( LOB_COMPACTION = { ON | OFF } ) ]
    | SET ( <set_index_option> [ ,...n ] )
    }
[ ; ]

<object> ::=
{ [ database_name. [ schema_name ] . | schema_name. ]
      table_or_view_name
}

<rebuild_index_option > ::=
{ PAD_INDEX = { ON | OFF }
  | FILLFACTOR = fillfactor
  | SORT_IN_TEMPDB = { ON | OFF }
  | IGNORE_DUP_KEY = { ON | OFF }
  | STATISTICS_NORECOMPUTE = { ON | OFF }
  | ONLINE = { ON | OFF }
  | ALLOW_ROW_LOCKS = { ON | OFF }
  | ALLOW_PAGE_LOCKS = { ON | OFF }
  | MAXDOP = max_degree_of_parallelism
  | DATA_COMPRESSION = { NONE | ROW | PAGE }
    [ ON PARTITIONS ( { <partition_number_expression> | <range> }
    [ , ...n ] ) ]
}
<range> ::=
{ <partition_number_expression> TO <partition_number_expression>
}

<single_partition_rebuild_index_option> ::=
{ SORT_IN_TEMPDB = { ON | OFF }
  | MAXDOP = max_degree_of_parallelism
```

```
    | DATA_COMPRESSION = { NONE | ROW | PAGE }
}

<set_index_option>::=
{ ALLOW_ROW_LOCKS = { ON | OFF }
  | ALLOW_PAGE_LOCKS = { ON | OFF }
  | IGNORE_DUP_KEY = { ON | OFF }
  | STATISTICS_NORECOMPUTE = { ON | OFF }
}
```

SAMPLE 9-3 DROP INDEX Syntax.

```
DROP INDEX
{ <drop_relational_or_xml_or_spatial_index> [ ,...n ]
| <drop_backward_compatible_index> [ ,...n ]
}

<drop_relational_or_xml_or_spatial_index> ::=
        index_name ON <object>
    [ WITH ( <drop_clustered_index_option> [ ,...n ] ) ]

<drop_backward_compatible_index> ::=
    [ owner_name. ] table_or_view_name.index_name

<object> ::=
{
    [ database_name. [ schema_name ] . | schema_name. ]
        table_or_view_name
}

<drop_clustered_index_option> ::=
{ MAXDOP = max_degree_of_parallelism
  | ONLINE = { ON | OFF }
  | MOVE TO { partition_scheme_name ( column_name )
      | filegroup_name
      | "default" }
    [ FILESTREAM_ON { partition_scheme_name
      | filestream_filegroup_name
      | "default" } ]
}
```

You also can use Windows PowerShell to work with indexes. To do this, you need to access the Indexes collection associated with a particular table or view. Consider the following example:

```
Set-Location SQLSERVER:\SQL\DbServer36\CorpServices\Databases\
  ProdWarehouse
Set-Location tables
$t = Get-ChildItem | where {$_.Name eq "Product"}
foreach ($i in $t.indexes) {$i}
```

In this example, you enter a remote session with DbServer36 and then set the working location to the *ProdWarehouse* database on the CorpServices instance. After you access the database, you access the tables within the database and then return a reference to the Product table. You store this object reference in the *$t* variable. To access each index in the Indexes collection, you use the following foreach clause:

```
foreach ($i in $t.indexes) {$i)
```

This foreach clause iterates through the Indexes collection one index at a time and performs whatever commands are shown between the open and close brackets. Here, by entering $i, you tell Windows PowerShell to print the name of each index. When you work with indexes, you can use any property of the *Microsoft.SqlServer.Management.Smo.Index* object, including BoundingBoxXMax, BoundingBoxXMin, BoundingBoxYMax, BoundingBoxYMin, CellsPerObject, CompactLargeObjects, DisallowPageLocks, DisallowRowLocks, FileGroup, FileStreamFileGroup, FileStreamPartitionScheme, FillFactor, FilterDefinition, HasCompressedPartitions, HasFilter, Id, IgnoreDuplicateKeys, IndexedColumns, IsClustered, IsDisabled, IsFullTextKey, IsIndexOnComputed, IsIndexOnTable, IsPartitioned, IsSpatialIndex, IsSystemNamed, IsUnique, IsXMLIndex, MaximumDegreeOfParallelism, Name, NoAutomaticRecomputation, OnlineIndexOperation, PadIndex, Parent, PartitionScheme, PartitionSchemeParameters, SecondaryXMLIndexType, SortInTempDb, SpaceUsed, SpatialIndexType, State, and Urn.

Using the Database Engine Tuning Advisor

The Database Engine Tuning Advisor is one of the best tools a database administrator can use to facilitate the indexing and optimization processes. But before you start this wizard, you should create a trace containing a representative snapshot of database activity. You will use this snapshot as the workload file in the Database Engine Tuning Advisor. For specific pointers on creating a trace file, see the "Creating and Managing Data Collector Sets" section in Chapter 12, "SQL Server 2012 Profiling and Monitoring."

As a best practice, you should not run the analysis on a production server. Instead, if possible, run the analysis on a restored backup. To use the Database Engine Tuning Advisor, complete the following steps:

1. In SQL Server Management Studio, select Database Engine Tuning Advisor on the Tools menu. Use the Connect To Server dialog box to connect to the server you want to use.

2. The Database Engine Tuning Advisor opens to start a new session, as shown in Figure 9-4. In the Workload panel, type a name for the session, such as Personnel DB Check.

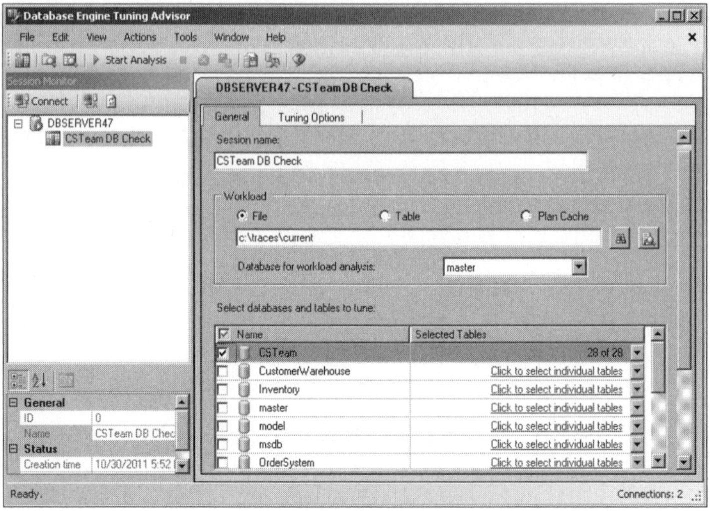

FIGURE 9-4 The Database Engine Tuning Advisor.

Using the Database For Workload Analysis list, select a database to which the Database Engine Tuning Advisor will connect for analyzing the workload:

- If you saved the trace data to a file, select File from the Workload pane, and then click the Browse For A Workload File button (the binoculars icon). Next, use the Select Workload File dialog box to select the trace file you previously created, and then click Open.

- If you saved the trace data to a table, select Table from the Workload pane, and then click the Browse For A Workload Table button (the binoculars icon). Next, use the Select Workload Table dialog box to specify which SQL Server instance to connect to and the source table to use. Because you can't use a trace table to which events are still being written, make sure that tracing has stopped.

- If you want to analyze the top 1,000 events from the current query plan cache, select Plan Cache from the Workload pane.

3. Select the database you want to analyze. You can analyze multiple databases as well as individual tables within specific databases. In most cases, you will want to examine a single database and possibly a subset of tables to reduce the analysis time. Because you are using a trace file, the analysis does not have to be performed on the server where the database or databases you are tuning are located.

4. Select the tables to analyze. If you select a database for tuning, all tables are selected for tuning by default. Click in the appropriate field under Selected Tables to display a list of tables in the selected database. Select the check box for the associated table you want to add, or select the Name check box to add all tables.

5. Select the Tuning Options tab, shown in Figure 9-5. You can limit the tuning time by setting a specific stop time. By default, the stop time is approximately one hour from the time you created the session.

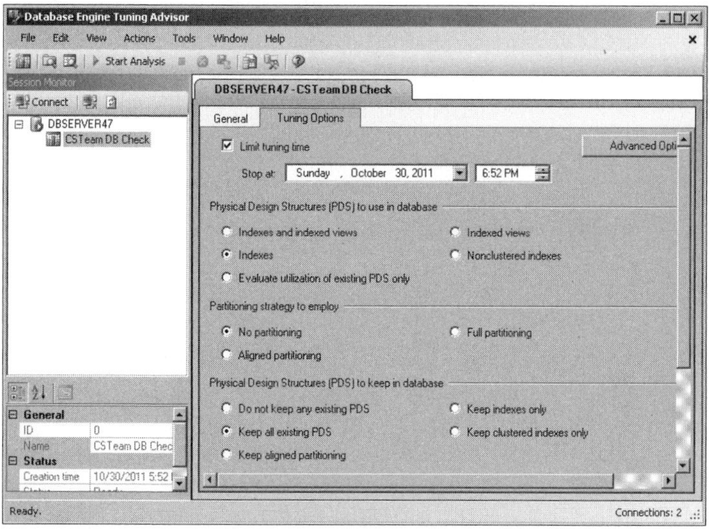

FIGURE 9-5 The Tuning Options tab of the Database Engine Tuning Advisor.

6. Under Physical Design Structures (PDS) To Use In Database, select the type of structures that you want the tuning wizard to recommend, as follows:

- **Indexes And Indexed Views** The Database Engine Tuning Advisor will recommend both clustered and nonclustered indexes, as well as indexed views, to improve performance.

- **Indexes** The Database Engine Tuning Advisor will recommend clustered and nonclustered indexes to improve performance.

- **Indexed Views** The Database Engine Tuning Advisor will recommend only indexed views to improve performance.

- **Nonclustered Indexes** The Database Engine Tuning Advisor will recommend only nonclustered indexes to improve performance.

- **Evaluate Utilization Of Existing PDS Only** The Database Engine Tuning Advisor will not recommend options for improving performance and instead will analyze only the usage of existing structures. This option cannot be used with the Keep All Existing PDS option under Physical Design Structures (PDS) To Keep In Database.

7. Use the following Partitioning Strategy To Employ options to determine whether the Database Engine Tuning Advisor should consider partitioning strategies:

- **No Partitioning** The Database Engine Tuning Advisor will not consider any partitioning strategies.

- **Aligned Partitioning** Newly recommended structures will be partition-aligned to make partitions easy to maintain. This option cannot be used with the Keep Indexes Only option under Physical Design Structures (PDS) To Keep In Database.
- **Full Partitioning** Newly recommended structures will be partitioned to provide the best performance for the workload.

8. Use the following Physical Design Structures (PDS) To Keep In Database options to determine which (if any) existing structures will be considered for removal from the database:

- **Do Not Keep Any Existing PDS** The Database Engine Tuning Advisor will consider all existing structures for possible removal from the database.
- **Keep All Existing PDS** The Database Engine Tuning Advisor will not consider any existing structures for possible removal from the database.
- **Keep Aligned Partitioning** The Database Engine Tuning Advisor will retain existing partition-aligned structures, and any recommended new structures will be aligned with the existing partitioning scheme. (Aligned Partitioning must also be selected as the Partitioning Strategy To Employ option.)
- **Keep Indexes Only** The Database Engine Tuning Advisor will keep existing clustered and nonclustered indexes. All other structures will be considered for possible removal from the database.
- **Keep Clustered Indexes Only** The Database Engine Tuning Advisor will keep existing clustered indexes. All other structures will be considered for possible removal from the database.

TIP If you have selected a strong, representative snapshot of database activity in the trace, you will probably want to select an option other than Keep All Existing PDS and let the Database Engine Tuning Advisor make the appropriate suggestions for you to ensure that existing structures do not conflict with the recommendations the wizard might make.

9. Click the Advanced Options button to set advanced options, as shown in Figure 9-6. The advanced tuning options are as follows:

- **Define Max. Space For Recommendations (MB)** Sets the maximum space that can be used by recommended structures. The default value depends on the database and structures selected.
- **Include Plan Cache Events From All Databases** Sets that you want to include cache entries for all databases.
- **Max. Columns Per Index** Sets the maximum number of columns that can be used in a single index. The default is 1,023, which allows all the columns in a table to be considered.
- **Online Index Recommendations** Sets the type of indexing recommendations. By default, the Database Engine Tuning Advisor

uses recommendations that require the server to be taken offline. Alternatively, you can elect to generate online recommendations when possible or to generate only online recommendations. With SQL Server Enterprise Edition and higher, all the online indexing recommendations can be performed when the server is online.

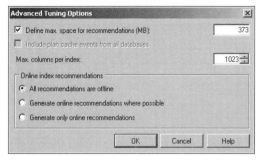

FIGURE 9-6 The Advanced Tuning Options for the Database Engine Tuning Advisor.

10. Click OK to close the Advanced Tuning Options dialog box. When you are ready to proceed, click Start Analysis or press F5. The Database Engine Tuning Advisor begins analyzing your workload file. Progress is shown on the Progress tab. You can click Stop Analysis to stop the analysis at any time.

11. When the analysis is complete, the wizard displays recommendations on the Recommendations tab. The recommendations are listed in two separate panels, Partition Recommendations and Index Recommendations. You can view a tuning summary and tuning reports on the Reports tab of the Database Engine Tuning Advisor. Be sure to note the percentage of estimated improvement you'll gain by making the recommended changes. If the estimated improvement is 0%, this can be an indicator that the trace file might not accurately reflect the database workload.

12. Now you can do the following:

- Select Save Recommendations on the Actions menu to save the recommended changes as a .sql script file. You can review or edit the script by using a text editor and schedule a job to implement the changes later.

- Select Apply Recommendations on the Actions menu to apply the recommendations or schedule the recommendations to be applied later. Under Apply Recommendations, select Apply Now or Schedule For Later as appropriate, and then click OK. If you select Schedule For Later, you can set the run date and time as well.

13. If you choose to apply the changes, the status of each change is displayed in the Applying Recommendations dialog box. The status of each change should be listed as Success. If you see a failure status, read the related error message to determine why the change failed.

Working with Columnstore Indexes

Unlike rowstore indexes, which group and store data for each row and then join all the rows to complete the index, columnstore indexes group and store data for each column and then join all the columns to complete the index. For data warehouses, this approach can improve performance with common filtering, aggregating, grouping and star-join queries.

Using Columnstore Indexes

With columnstore indexes, SQL Server groups and stores data one column at a time and then reads only the columns that are needed for the query. Additionally, SQL Server heavily compresses column data and uses batch processing. Not only can this significantly improve query execution time, it also can significantly reduce memory or processing requirements. How? Less data is read; less data needs processing.

Table 9-3 lists the basic restrictions and data types not supported when using columnstore indexes. The table also indicates when query performance may be slow. Although you cannot create clustered columnstore indexes with the release version of SQL Server 2012, this limitation may be removed in a later service pack or release.

TABLE 9-3 Guidelines for Using Columnstore Indexes

BASIC RESTRICTIONS	UNSUPPORTED DATA TYPES	SLOW WHEN . . .
It cannot act as a primary key or a foreign key.	binary and varbinary	Join conditions include more than one column.
It cannot be a unique index.	CLR types (hierarchyid and spatial types)	Joined tables cannot fit into memory.
It cannot be changed using the ALTER INDEX statement, though it can be disabled and rebuilt.	datetimeoffset with scale greater than 2	Many columns are returned.
It cannot be clustered.	decimal (and numeric) with precision greater than 18 digits	No batch processing occurs because there is no join, filtering, or aggregation.
It cannot be created on a view or indexed view.	ntext, text, and image	Result sets are large because data is not aggregated.
It cannot be created using the INCLUDE keyword.	rowversion (and timestamp)	

BASIC RESTRICTIONS	UNSUPPORTED DATA TYPES	SLOW WHEN . . .
It cannot have more than 1024 columns.	sql_variant	
It cannot include a sparse column or filestream.	uniqueidentifier	
It cannot include the ASC or DESC keyword because sorting is not allowed.	varchar(max) and nvarchar(max)	
It cannot be page-compressed or row-compressed.	xml	

With partitioned tables, columnstore indexes must be partition-aligned with the base table. Because of this, you can create a columnstore index only if the partitioning column is one of the columns in the columnstore index. Unlike rowstore indexes, columnstore indexes don't have key columns and cannot be clustered. Further, tables with columnstore indexes cannot be updated. To update a table with a columnstore index, you must either drop the index, perform the necessary INSERT, UPDATE, MERGE, or DELETE operations, and then rebuild the index; or perform the operations in an empty partition and then use SWITCH partition to add to the table.

Typically, the query optimizer uses columnstore indexes only when it improves performance. A big part of the performance benefits for columnstore indexes comes from compressing the column data and thereby reducing the number of data pages that must be read and processed. Compression works best on character and numeric columns that have many duplicated values.

If the query optimizer uses columnstore indexes on a table where rowstore indexing would have been better, you may find that queries execute slower than expected. Here, you may want to use a query hint that forces the query optimizer to use rowstore indexing or simply drop the columnstore index to revert to rowstore indexing.

If the query optimizer doesn't use columnstore indexes on a table where you think this could improve performance, you temporarily force the use of a columnstore index using the WITH (INDEX) hint. Here, evaluate performance using the hint to determine whether columnstore or rowstore indexes should be used. In the graphical execution plan, the execution mode typically is listed as batch for columnstore indexes and row for rowstore indexes, although batch-mode processing is not always used.

Viewing Columnstore Index Properties

Unlike rowstore indexes, you can create columnstore indexes only on tables. In SQL Server Management Studio, you can view columnstore indexes associated with a table by completing the following steps:

1. In SQL Server Management Studio, select a database, and then expand the Tables or Views node as appropriate.

2. Select a table or view, and then expand its node to list the objects it contains.

3. Expand the Indexes node to list the indexes associated with the selected table or view (if any).

4. Columnstore indexes are listed with the prefix NonClusteredColumnstoreIndex by default. Right-click a columnstore index, and then select Properties to open the Index Properties dialog box, shown in Figure 9-7. This dialog box has several pages that let you view and manage index properties:

   - **General** Shows general properties, including the index name and type. You can change the index type and add or remove key columns.

   - **Options** Allows you to set the maximum degree of parallelism.

   - **Storage** Lists the current storage configuration. Allows you to configure filegroups.

   - **Extended Properties** Lists extended properties. Allows you to add or remove extended properties.

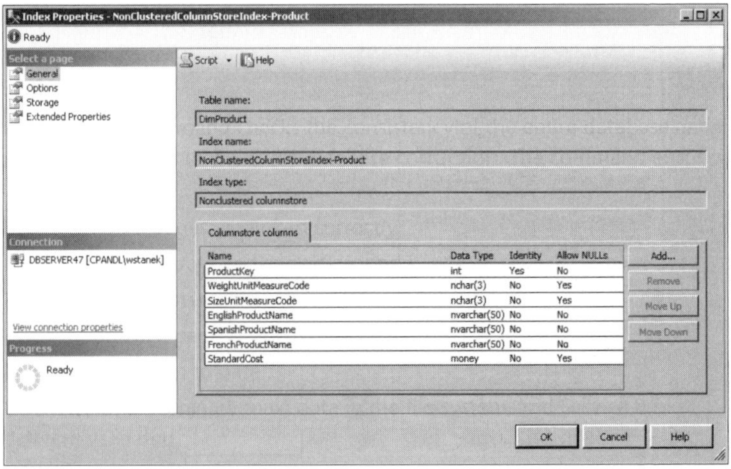

FIGURE 9-7 The Index Properties dialog box.

As with rowstore indexes, you also can examine the indexes for a specific table using the sp_statistics stored procedure.

Creating and Managing Columnstore Indexes

Only the owner of a table can create columnstore indexes on that table. You can create indexes with a design tool in SQL Server Management Studio or with the T-SQL CREATE COLUMNSTORE INDEX statement. To create indexes with the design tool, complete the following steps:

1. In SQL Server Management Studio, connect to the server instance containing the database in which you want to work.

2. In Object Explorer, expand the Databases node, select a database, and then expand it to show the database's resource nodes.

3. Expand the Tables node, and then expand the node for the table you want to work with. Next, right-click Indexes, point to New Index, and then select the appropriate option, such as Non-clustered Columnstore Index.

4. The New Index dialog box has options similar to those in the Index Properties dialog box shown in Figure 9-7. On the General page, type a name for the index or accept the default value.

5. Next, specify the columns to add to the index. To add an index, click Add. Use the Select Columns dialog box to specify the included columns. When you finish selecting columns to index, click OK to close the Select Columns dialog box.

6. To specify the storage location for the index, use the options on the Storage page to specify the desired filegroup.

7. When you finish configuring the index, click OK.

Use the T-SQL CREATE COLUMNSTORE INDEX command to create indexes with the syntax shown in Sample 9-4. After you create a columnstore index, you might need to change its properties, rename it, or delete it. You handle these tasks in SQL Server Management Studio in the same way as you do with rowstore indexes.

SAMPLE 9-4 CREATE COLUMNSTORE INDEX Syntax.

Syntax Relational Index

```
CREATE [NONCLUSTERED ] COLUMNSTORE INDEX index_name
    ON <object> ( column [ ,...n ] )
    [ WITH ( <column_index_option> [ ,...n ] ) ]
    [ ON { partition_scheme_name ( column_name )
        | filegroup_name
        | "default"
        }
    ]
[ ; ]


<object> ::=
{ [ database_name. [ schema_name ] . | schema_name. ]
        table_or_view_name
}
```

```
<column_index_option> ::=
  DROP_EXISTING = { ON | OFF }
  | MAXDOP = max_degree_of_parallelism
}
```

You also can manage columnstore indexes with the T-SQL commands ALTER INDEX and DROP INDEX. You use ALTER INDEX to disable or rebuild the index. If you need to change the index, you must drop it and then re-create it.

Column Constraints and Rules

Column constraints and rules are important aspects of database administration. You use constraints to control the way column values are used, such as whether a value must be unique or whether it must have a specific format. Although you usually apply constraints directly to a specific column, you also can use rules to create constraints that you can apply to multiple tables in a database.

Using Constraints

SQL Server enforces the uniqueness of column values by using unique and primary key constraints. Unique constraints are often used to create secondary keys (for nonclustered indexes) that you can use in conjunction with the primary key. Foreign key constraints identify the relationships between tables and ensure that referential integrity is maintained. Other types of constraints that you might want to use are check constraints and not null constraints. Check constraints restrict the format or range of acceptable values for columns. Not null constraints prevent null values in a column.

Constraints can apply to columns or to entire tables. A column constraint is specified as part of a column definition and applies only to that column. A table constraint is declared independently from a column definition and can apply to several columns in the table. You must use table constraints when you want to include more than one column in a constraint. For example, if a table has three columns in the primary key, you must use a table constraint to include all three columns in the primary key.

Setting Unique Constraints

When you set a unique constraint on a column or columns, SQL Server automatically creates a unique index and then checks for duplicate values. If duplicate key values exist, the index creation operation is cancelled and an error message is displayed. SQL Server also checks the data each time you add data to the table. If the new data contains duplicate keys, the insert or update operation is rolled back and an error message is generated. You can specify that duplicate keys should be ignored by using the IGNORE_DUP_KEY option.

In SQL Server Management Studio, you make a unique index by setting the option Is Unique to Yes when creating the index, as described in the "Creating Indexes" section earlier in this chapter, or by selecting the Unique check box on the General page of the Index Properties dialog box. In T-SQL, you can set the unique constraint when you create the index, as shown in the following example:

```
USE OrderSystemDB
CREATE UNIQUE INDEX [Cust ID Index]
ON Sales.Customers(cust_id)
```

A nonclustered index is created unless a clustered index is specified explicitly, such as in the following code:

```
USE Customer
CREATE UNIQUE CLUSTERED INDEX [Cust ID Index]
ON Sales.Customers(cust_id)
```

Designating Primary Key Constraints

SQL Server allows you to designate any column or group of columns as a primary key, but primary keys are often defined for identity columns. A table can have only one primary key, and because unique values are required, no primary key column can accept null values. Also, when you use multiple columns, the values of all the columns are combined to determine uniqueness.

As for unique constraints, SQL Server creates a unique index for the primary key columns. With primary key constraints, however, the index is created as a clustered index—unless a clustered index already exists on the table or a nonclustered index is specified explicitly.

In SQL Server Management Studio, you set the primary key when designing a new table or modifying an existing table by completing the following steps:

1. Clear the Allow Nulls check box for any columns that will be used in the primary key.

2. Select the column or columns that you want to use as the primary key by pressing Ctrl and clicking the shaded box to the left of the column name.

3. Click Set Primary Key on the toolbar, or select Set Primary Key on the Table Designer menu.

You can also set the primary key when you create or alter tables using T-SQL. Examples are shown in Sample 9-5.

SAMPLE 9-5 Creating a Table and Its Columns with a Primary Key Constraint.

```
USE CUSTOMER
CREATE TABLE Sales.Customers
    (cust_id int NOT NULL,
    cust_lname varchar(40) NOT NULL,
    cust_fname varchar(20) NOT NULL,
    phone char(12) NOT NULL,
    CONSTRAINT PK_Cust PRIMARY KEY (cust_id))
```

```
USE CUSTOMER
ALTER TABLE Sales.Customers
    ADD CONSTRAINT PK_Cust PRIMARY KEY (cust_id)
```

Using Foreign Key Constraints

Foreign key constraints identify the relationships between tables and ensure that referential integrity is maintained. A foreign key in one table points to a candidate key in another table. Foreign keys prevent changes that would leave rows with foreign key values in one table when no candidate keys with that value are included in a related table. You cannot insert a row with a foreign key value if there is no candidate key with that value. The exception is when you insert a null foreign key value.

In the following example, the *Orders* table establishes a foreign key referencing the *Customer* table defined earlier:

```
CREATE TABLE Sales.Orders
    (order_nmbr int,
    order_item varchar(20),
    qty_ordered int,
    cust_id int
        FOREIGN KEY REFERENCES Sales.Customers(cust_id)
        ON DELETE NO ACTION
)
```

The ON DELETE clause defines the actions that are taken if you try to delete a row to which existing foreign keys point. The ON DELETE clause has several options:

- **NO ACTION**   Specifies that the deletion fails with an error and the delete action on the row is rolled back.

- **CASCADE**   Specifies that all rows with foreign keys pointing to the deleted row are to be deleted as well. (CASCADE cannot be used if there is an IN-STEAD OF trigger on the ON DELETE clause.)

- **SET NULL**   Specifies that all values that make up the foreign key are set to NULL if the corresponding row in the parent table is deleted. (Foreign key columns must be nullable.)

- **SET DEFAULT**   Specifies that all the values that make up the foreign key are set to their default values if the corresponding row in the parent table is deleted. (Foreign key columns must have default definitions. If a column is nullable and there is no explicit default, the column is set to NULL.)

You can also set an ON UPDATE clause in T-SQL, as shown in the following example:

```
CREATE TABLE Sales.Orders
    (order_nmbr int,
    order_item varchar(20),
    qty_ordered int,
```

```
cust_id int
    FOREIGN KEY REFERENCES Sales.Customers(cust_id)
    ON UPDATE CASCADE
)
```

The ON UPDATE clause defines the actions that are taken if you try to update a row to which existing foreign keys point. The clause also supports the NO ACTION, CASCADE, SET NULL, and SET DEFAULT options.

Using Check Constraints

Check constraints allow you to control the format or range of values, or both, that are associated with tables and columns. For example, you could use this type of constraint to specify that postal codes must be entered in the format *99999* or that phone numbers must be entered as *9999999999*. Be careful when using check constraints that perform implicit or explicit data type conversion because these types of check constraints might cause partition switching or filtered indexes to fail.

In SQL Server Management Studio, you set check constraints when designing a new table or modifying an existing table by completing the following steps:

1. Select Check Constraints from the Table Designer menu. This displays the Check Constraints dialog box shown in Figure 9-8.

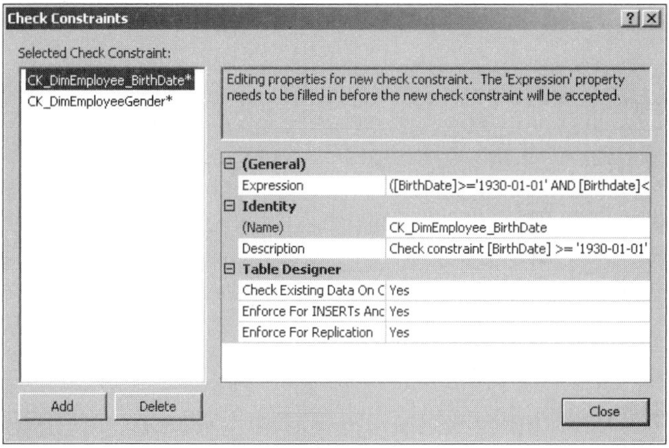

FIGURE 9-8 The Check Constraints dialog box.

2. Now you can do the following:

- **Edit an existing constraint.**   Select it in the Selected Check Constraint list, and then modify the existing constraint expression and definition using the boxes provided.

- **Delete a constraint.**   Select it in the Selected Check Constraint list, and then click Delete. In the Delete Object dialog box, confirm the deletion by clicking OK.

- **Create a new constraint.** Click Add, and then type a name and description of the constraint in the boxes provided. Click the button to the right of the Expression box, enter the check constraint expression, and then click OK.

3. Click Close when you finish working with check constraints.

Check constraint expressions specify permitted characters by using regular expressions as follows:

- Use [0–9] to indicate that any numeral from 0 through 9 is permitted in the designated position. As an example, to format a column to accommodate a nine-digit postal code, you would use the following expression:

```
PostalCode LIKE '[0-9][0-9][0-9][0-9][0-9][0-9][0-9][0-9][0-9]'
```

- Use [a–z] or [A–Z] to indicate that any lowercase letter from *a* through *z* or any uppercase letter from *A* through *Z* is permitted in the designated position. As an example, to format a column to accommodate any five-letter word with the first letter capitalized, you would use the following expression:

```
AccountCode LIKE '[A-Z][a-z][a-z][a-z][a-z]'
```

- Use [a–zA–Z0–9] to indicate that any letter or numeral is permitted in the designated position. As an example, to format a column to accommodate any five-character value, you would use the following expression:

```
CheckCode LIKE '[a-zA-Z0-9][a-zA-Z0-9][a-zA-Z0-9][a-zA-Z0-9]
            [a-zA-Z0-9]'
```

You can also add constraints in T-SQL by using the CREATE TABLE. With ALTER TABLE, you can add, remove, or modify constraints, such as in the following example:

```
USE CUSTOMER
ALTER TABLE Sales.Customers
ADD CONSTRAINT CheckZipFormat
CHECK (([PostalCode] like '[0-9][0-9][0-9][0-9][0-9][0-9][0-9][0-9]
       [0-9]'))
```

Using Not Null Constraints

Not null constraints specify that the column does not accept null values. Normally, you set not null constraints when you create the table. You also can set not null constraints when you alter a table. In SQL Server Management Studio, the Allow Nulls column in the Table view controls the use of this constraint. If the Allow Nulls column is cleared, the related table column does not accept nulls.

Using Rules

A *rule* is a constraint that you can apply to multiple columns or tables. Rules perform the same function as check constraints and are maintained in SQL Server 2012 for compatibility with early versions of SQL Server. Microsoft recommends that you use check constraints rather than rules. Check constraints are more customizable and more concise than rules. For example, although you can apply only one rule to a column, you can apply multiple check constraints to a column.

Rules can be useful in certain situations, however. Constraints are defined within table definitions, whereas rules are independently defined objects and therefore are not limited to only one particular table. Rules are also bound to a table after the table is created, and they are not deleted if the table is deleted. Another advantage of rules is that they can be bound to any user-defined data type.

If you use care when you apply rules, you can still use rules in situations that make them a better choice than constraints. To view existing rules in SQL Server Management Studio, complete the following steps:

1. In SQL Server Management Studio, connect to the server instance that contains the database in which you want to work.

2. In the Object Explorer view, expand the Databases node, and then expand the database to show its resource nodes.

3. Expand the Programmability and Rules nodes. You will see any existing rules listed.

The T-SQL commands for creating and managing rules are CREATE RULE and DROP RULE. You can use CREATE RULE as follows:

```
CREATE RULE CheckZipFormat
AS @value LIKE '[09][09][09][09][09][09][09][09][09]'
```

After you have created a rule, you must activate the rule to use it. You use a special stored procedure called sp_bindrule to bind the rule to a particular table column or user-defined data type. You can also use sp_unbindrule to remove a rule that is bound to a table column or user-defined data type. Use the following syntax when binding and unbinding rules:

```
sp_bindrule <'rule'>, <'object_name'>, [<'futureonly_flag'>]
sp_unbindrule 'object name'
```

Creating Partitioned Tables and Indexes

You create partitioned tables and indexes by using a multistep process that requires the following actions:

1. Creating a partition function to specify how a table or index that uses the function can be partitioned

2. Creating a partition scheme to specify the placement of the partitions within filegroups

3. Creating tables or indexes using the partition scheme

I discuss each of these processes in the sections that follow.

Creating Partition Functions

You use a partition function to specify how a table or index is partitioned. The function maps to a set of partitions. To create a partition function, you specify the number of partitions, the partitioning column, and the range of partition column values for each partition.

Each partition function identifies a single partitioning column. Any data type that is valid for use as an index column can be used as a partitioning column, except timestamp. This means that you cannot specify a column that uses the ntext, text, image, xml, varchar(max), nvarchar(max), varbinary(max), alias, or CLR user-defined types. Computed columns that participate in a partition function must be marked explicitly as PERSISTED.

You create a partition function by using the CREATE PARTITION FUNCTION statement. Sample 9-6 shows the syntax and usage. RANGE LEFT and RANGE RIGHT specify how values are sorted along partition boundaries. The default is RANGE LEFT.

SAMPLE 9-6 CREATE PARTITION FUNCTION Syntax and Usage.

Syntax

```
CREATE PARTITION FUNCTION partition_function_name
    ( input_parameter_type )
AS RANGE [ LEFT | RIGHT ]
FOR VALUES ( [ boundary_value [ ,...n ] ] )
[ ; ]
```

Usage

```
CREATE PARTITION FUNCTION rangePF1 (int)
AS RANGE LEFT FOR VALUES (1, 2000, 4000, 6000);
```

In plain language, RANGE LEFT and RANGE RIGHT tell SQL Server what to do when the current value equals the partition's boundary value. With RANGE LEFT, boundary values are sorted into the respective partition for which they are defined as a boundary. With RANGE RIGHT, the boundary values are sorted into the next higher partition.

In the previous example, the boundary values are 1, 2000, 4000, and 6000 and would be sorted on the left side of the boundary value, as shown in the following table:

	PARTITION 1	PARTITION 2	PARTITION 3	PARTITION 4
Values	value <= 1	value > 1 AND <= 2000	value > 2000 AND <= 4000	value > 6000

If the example were RANGE RIGHT, boundary values would be sorted on the right side of the boundary value, as shown in the following table:

	PARTITION 1	PARTITION 2	PARTITION 3	PARTITION 4
Values	value < 1	value => 1 AND < 2000	value => 2000 AND < 4000	value => 6000

As you can see, when left-ranged, 1, 2000, 4000, and 6000 are sorted into the respective partition for which they are defined as a boundary. When right ranged, 1, 2000, 4000, and 6000 are sorted into the next partition.

Creating Partition Schemes

You use a partition scheme to map the partitions produced by a partition function to a set of filegroups. A partition scheme can use only one partition function. However, a partition function can participate in more than one partition scheme.

When you create a partition scheme, you define the filegroups to which the table partitions are mapped, based on the parameters of the partition function. You must specify enough filegroups to hold the number of partitions, but you can also do the following:

- Map all partitions to the same filegroup.
- Map multiple partitions to the same filegroup.
- Map each partition to a different filegroup.

With NEXT USED, you also can specify additional, unassigned filegroups in case you want to add more partitions later. When you do this, SQL Server marks one of the filegroups with the NEXT USED property, which means that this filegroup will hold the next partition that is added.

You can create a partition scheme using the CREATE PARTITION SCHEME statement. Sample 9-7 shows the syntax and usage.

SAMPLE 9-7 CREATE PARTITION SCHEME Syntax and Usage.

Syntax

```
CREATE PARTITION SCHEME partition_scheme_name
AS PARTITION partition_function_name
[ ALL ] TO ( { file_group_name | [ PRIMARY ] } [ ,...n ] )
[ ; ]
```

Usage

```
CREATE PARTITION SCHEME rangePS1
AS PARTITION rangePF1
TO (filegroup1, filegroup2, filegroup3, filegroup4, filegroup5);
```

Creating Partitions

When you create a table or an index, you can partition it by specifying in the CREATE TABLE or CREATE INDEX statement the partition scheme that the table uses to map the partitions to filegroups and the partitioning column. The partitioning column must match what you've specified in the partition function and in the partition scheme with regard to data type, length, and precision. If the column is computed, you must mark it as PERSISTED.

You can turn a nonpartitioned table into a partitioned table by using one of two techniques:

- Create a partitioned clustered index on the table by using the CREATE INDEX statement. When you do this, SQL Server re-creates the table in a clustered index format. If the table already has a partitioned clustered index applied to it, you can drop the index and rebuild it on a partition scheme by using CREATE INDEX with the DROP EXISTING = ON clause.

- Use the ALTER TABLE...SWITCH statement to switch the data of the table to a range-partitioned table that has only one partition. This partitioned table must already exist before the conversion occurs, and its single partition must be empty.

After you modify the table to create a partitioned table, you can modify the related partition function to add partitions as necessary. You can turn an existing partition table into a nonpartitioned table by modifying the table's partition function so that the table has only one partition. If a table has a partitioned clustered index applied to it, you can obtain the same result by using the CREATE INDEX statement with the DROP EXISTING = ON clause to drop the index and rebuild it as a nonpartitioned index.

With SQL Server Management Studio, you can create partitions after you create a table or index by completing the following steps:

1. In SQL Server Management Studio, select a table and expand its node to list the objects it contains. Expand the Indexes node to list the indexes associated with the selected table.

2. Right-click the table or index that you want to partition, point to Storage, and then select Create Partition. This starts the Create Partition Wizard. If you see the Welcome page, click Next.

3. On the Select A Partitioning Column page, select the one partitioning column that you want to use. Optionally, you can elect to collocate the table to a selected partitioned table, to storage-align indexes with the indexed partitioning column, or both. Click Next.

4. On the Select A Partition Function page, you can type the required definition for a new function or select an existing partition function. Click Next.

5. On the Select A Partition Scheme page, you can type the required definition for a new scheme or select an existing partition scheme. Click Next.

6. On the Map Partitions page, select the partition range as either Left Boundary or Right Boundary. Next, select each filegroup in turn and specify the boundary values. Be sure to enter an additional filegroup in addition to the boundary values.

7. Click Estimate Storage to determine the required space. Click Next.

8. Now you can create a script for adding partitioning, run the script immediately, or schedule a job for partitioning. If you want to create a script, you can set scripting options. If you want to schedule these activities for later, you can click Change Schedule to set the run date and time. Click Next.

9. Review your selections, and then click Finish. If you choose to run a script immediately, the status of each action is displayed on the Create Partition Wizard Progress page. The status of each action should be listed as Success. If you see a failure status, read the related error message to determine why the change failed. You can generate a report by clicking Report and then selecting a report option.

Viewing and Managing Partitions

When you query data or perform updates, there is no difference in the way you reference a partitioned table as opposed to a table that is not partitioned. That said, however, you can focus queries on individual partitions by using the $PARTITION function with the partition function name. This allows you to examine how many rows exist in each partition, access all rows in a subset of partitions, and determine in which partition a row with a particular partition key value currently resides or will reside when inserted.

You can query individual partitions of a partitioned table or index by using $PARTITION. The syntax and usage is shown as Sample 9-8. Here, you determine which partition a particular value would be mapped into.

SAMPLE 9-8 $PARTITION Syntax and Usage.

Syntax

```
[ database_name. ] $PARTITION.partition_function_name(expression)
```

Usage

```
USE CustomerDB;
GO
CREATE PARTITION FUNCTION rangePF1 ( int )
AS RANGE FOR VALUES (100, 2000, 4000, 8000) ;
GO
SELECT $PARTITION.rangePF1 (100) ;
GO
```

Catalog views that contain partitioning information include the following:

■ sys.destination_data_spaces, which gets information about individual partition schemes

- sys.partition_functions, which gets information about individual partition functions

- sys.partition_parameters, which gets information about individual parameters of partition functions

- sys.partition_range_values, which gets information about the boundary values of a partition function

- sys.partition_schemes, which gets information about all the partition schemes in a database

- sys.partitions, which gets partitioning information about a table or index

With SQL Server Management Studio, you can manage existing partitions by completing the following steps:

1. In SQL Server Management Studio, select a table and expand its node to list the objects it contains. Expand the Indexes node to list the indexes associated with the selected table.

2. Right-click the table or index that you want to partition, point to Storage, and then select Manage Partition. This starts the Manage Partition Wizard. If you see the Welcome page, click Next.

3. On the Select A Partition Action page, you can elect to create a staging table for partition switching or manage a sliding-window partition. However, if you are using non-storage-aligned indexes, you cannot switch out or switch in data, which means you can only create a staging table. Click Next.

4. Set the staging table or sliding window options as necessary, and then click Next.

5. Now you can create a script for modifying partitioning, run the script immediately, or schedule a job for modifying partitioning. If you want to create a script, you can set scripting options. If you want to schedule these activities for later, you can click Change Schedule to set the run date and time. Click Next.

6. Review your selections, and then click Finish. If you choose to run a script immediately, the status of each action is displayed on the Manage Partition Wizard Progress page. The status of each action should be listed as Success. If you see a failure status, read the related error message to determine why the change failed. You can generate a report by clicking Report and then selecting a report option.

Compressing Tables, Indexes, and Partitions

SQL Server 2012 Enterprise Edition and higher support on-disk storage compression for tables stored as heaps, tables stored as clustered indexes, nonclustered indexes, and indexed views. Because you can configure the compression of partitioned tables and indexes independently for each partition, different partitions of the same object can use different compression settings.

NOTE You cannot configure page or row compression on columnstore indexes. Columnstore indexes are compressed automatically.

Using Row and Page Compression

The storage engine handles all aspects of compression. In addition to Unicode compression, discussed earlier in the chapter, SQL Server 2012 supports two other types of compression:

- Row compression
- Page compression

Row compression affects the physical storage of data within rows. Most data types are affected in some unique way, but no application changes are required because of these changes. Row compression reduces the metadata overhead associated with records and uses variable-length storage for numeric types and fixed-character strings. For example, if a value can be reduced to 1 byte through compression, storage of the value will use only 1 byte.

When you use page compression with non-leaf-level pages of indexes, the storage engine performs only row compression. When you use page compression with leaf-level pages of tables and indexes, the storage engine uses three different operations to compress the data: row compression, followed by prefix compression, followed by dictionary compression. Typically, with prefix compression, the storage engine finds repeated prefix values for each column, moves the prefixes to a new row immediately following the page header and within the compression information structure, and then changes column values to references to the prefix. Typically, with dictionary compression, the storage engine finds repeated values anywhere on the page and stores them within the compression information structure.

When you create a new table with page compression, the metadata for the table indicates that page compression should be used but no actual compression occurs. As you add data to the first data page, data is row-compressed until you fill the first row. The next row you add initiates page compression using prefix compression and dictionary compression. If page compression has created enough room on the page for an additional row, the storage engine adds the row and the related data is page-compressed, meaning the storage engine applies row, prefix, and dictionary compression. Keep in mind that if the space gained by page compression minus the space that is required for the compression information structure is not significant, the storage engine won't use page compression for a particular page. As you add rows, those rows either fit onto the page or require the storage engine to add a new page. Similar to the first page, the new page is compressed using row compression first, and then as you fill rows, the prefix and dictionary are compressed. (In case of a page split, the new page inherits the compression setting of its source page.)

When you convert an existing table that contains data to page compression, the storage engine rebuilds and reevaluates each page. Rebuilding all the pages causes the storage engine to rebuild the related table, index, or partition.

Compression is not available for system tables. When you compress or uncompress a user table, the storage engine doesn't apply the compression settings to the table's nonclustered indexes automatically. You must configure compression settings for each nonclustered index individually. However, when a clustered index is created on a heap, the clustered index inherits the compression state of the heap unless you specify otherwise.

When you are compressing indexes, leaf-level pages can be compressed with both row and page compression. However, non-leaf-level pages do not receive page compression. Additionally, when the existing data in an index is fragmented, you might be able to reduce the size of the index by rebuilding the index instead of using compression. The fill factor of an index will be applied during an index rebuild, which also could potentially increase the size of the index.

Although the storage engine handles all aspects of compression, the storage engine presents data to most other SQL Server components in an uncompressed state. This means that when a heap is configured for page-level compression, pages receive page-level compression only when data is inserted by using BULK INSERT or INSERT INTO ... WITH (TABLOCK) or a table is rebuilt by executing the ALTER TABLE ... REBUILD statement with the PAGE compression option. Changing the compression setting of a heap requires all nonclustered indexes on the table to be rebuilt so that they have pointers to the new row locations in the heap.

Although compression can allow more rows to be stored on a page, it does not change the maximum row size of a table or an index. You cannot enable a table for compression when the maximum row size plus the compression overhead exceeds the maximum row size of 8,060 bytes. The storage engine checks the row size when the object is initially compressed as well as whenever a row is inserted or modified, and it prevents updates that would not fit on the row when the row is uncompressed. Additionally, with large-value data types and variable-length columns, when the data exceeds 8 KB, data compression is not available for the data that is stored separately.

The disk space requirements for enabling or disabling row or page compression are the same as for creating or rebuilding an index. For partitioned data, you can reduce the space that is required by enabling or disabling compression for one partition at a time. You can determine the compression state of partitions in a partitioned table by querying the data_compression column of the sys.partitions view.

Setting or Changing Compression Settings

With SQL Server Management Studio, you manage compression after you create a table or index by completing the following steps:

1. In SQL Server Management Studio, select a table and expand its node to list the objects it contains. Expand the Indexes node to list the indexes associated with the selected table.

2. Right-click the table or index that you want to compress, point to Storage, and then select Manage Compression. This starts the Data Compression Wizard. If you see the Welcome page, click Next.

3. On the Select Compression Type page, you can configure compression in one of two ways:

   - **Select a partition type for each partition.** Each partition is listed by its partition number, boundary, row count, and current space. Use the Compression Type list for each partition to set the compression level.

   - **Use the same compression type for each partition.** Select the Use Same Compression Type For All Partitions check box, and then use the related drop-down list to set the compression level.

4. Click Calculate to determine the compressed space for the partition or partitions.

5. Now you can create a script for adding compression, run the script immediately, or schedule a job for compressing the partition or partitions. If you want to create a script, you can set scripting options. If you schedule for later, you can click Change Schedule to set the run date and time. Click Next.

6. Review your selections and then click Finish. If you choose to run a script immediately, the status of each change is displayed on the Compression Wizard Progress page. The status of each action should be listed as Success. If you see a failure status, read the related error message to determine why the change failed. You can generate a report by clicking Report and then selecting a report option.

You can compress tables and indexes when you create them using the CREATE TABLE or CREATE INDEX statement. To do this, set the DATA_COMPRESSION clause to the value you want to use. By default, data compression is disabled and set to NONE. If you want tables or indexes to be compressed, you can specify ROW to enable row-level compression or PAGE to enable page-level compression.

You can change the compression state of a table, index, or partition using the ALTER TABLE or ALTER INDEX statement. If you modify a table without specifying a compression state, the existing compression state is preserved.

You can determine how changing the compression state will affect tables and indexes by using the sp_estimate_data_compression_savings stored procedure. To monitor compression statistics for a SQL Server instance, use the Page Compression Attempts/Sec and Pages Compressed/Sec counters of the SQL Server, Access Methods object. To monitor compression statistics for individual partitions, use the sys.dm_db_index_operational_stats function.

Microsoft SQL Server 2012 Optimization, Maintenance, and Recovery

Automating and Maintaining SQL Server 2012

Automation and maintenance go hand in hand. You can automate many routine database administration tasks, most of which have to do with maintenance issues such as backing up databases or running consistency checks. Automation allows you to increase productivity, complete tasks while away from your computer, and more. You can configure the server to monitor processes and user activities, to check for errors, and to alert you when related events occur. If you configure alerts properly, Microsoft SQL Server 2012 can monitor itself, and you can focus on other areas of administration. You can also schedule jobs to automate routine administration tasks. You can configure these jobs to run once or on a recurring basis, such as weekly or on the third Tuesday of every month.

Database Automation and Maintenance

SQL Server 2012 has four main database automation and maintenance components:

- **Database Mail**   Enables email alerts and notifications
- **SQL Server Agent**   Enables self-monitoring by using alerts, operator notifications, and scheduled jobs
- **Database Maintenance Plans**   Enable automated maintenance
- **Log Shipping**   Enables automatic synchronization with standby servers

Typically, when you want to use these automation and maintenance features, you select the following configurations:

1. Configure Database Mail for *msdb* and other databases. The *msdb* database is used by SQL Server Agent for scheduling alerts and jobs and to track operators. When you enable Database Mail, Database Mail objects are created in the *msdb* database. These objects allow *msdb* to act as a mail host server for sending alerts, notifications, and other types of messages.

2. Configure the SQL Server Agent service for your environment. Typically, you want to ensure that the service is started automatically with the operating system, that it uses the correct startup account, and that it has the correct mail profile so that it can be used with Database Mail.

3. Configure SQL Server Agent alerts, jobs, and operators to enable automatic alerts and scheduled jobs. *Alerts* are automatically generated messages that bring an error or issue to the attention of an administrator or other user. *Jobs* are scheduled tasks that run automatically when triggered or at a specific interval. *Operators* are individuals to whom you want to send alerts and notifications.

4. Configure Database Maintenance Plans to automate routine database optimization and maintenance. Even though you can automate many routine tasks, you should regularly review report histories to track maintenance plan execution. Additionally, you might find that occasionally you need to perform some optimization and maintenance tasks manually, and you can do this with database maintenance plans as well.

5. Optionally, configure log shipping to enable other computers running SQL Server to act as standby servers that can be brought online manually in case of primary server failure. Typically, log shipping is used as an alternative to database mirroring, which is discussed in Chapter 11, "SQL Server 2012 Backup and Recovery." However, both features can be configured, enabled, and in use simultaneously on any given SQL Server instance.

Some database maintenance tasks might require exclusive access to SQL Server. In single-user mode, you can connect to an instance using the Query Editor in SQL Server Management Studio. However, Object Explorer might fail because it requires more than one connection for some operations. The best way to manage SQL Server in single-user mode is to execute Transact-SQL (T-SQL) statements by connecting only through the Query Editor in SQL Server Management Studio or by using the Sqlcmd utility.

NOTE You should stop the SQL Server Agent service before connecting to an instance of SQL Server in single-user mode. Otherwise, the SQL Server Agent service uses the connection, and the connection will not be available to you.

You can also use single-user mode to regain access to a server instance as a system administrator. In single-user mode, any member of the computer's local Administrators group can connect to the instance of SQL Server. They do so as a member of the sysadmin fixed server role. This allows you to correct access problems that stem from the sa account becoming disabled or otherwise inaccessible and to work with instances on which there are no valid members of the sysadmin fixed server role.

Databases can also be set to single-user mode. If a database on the current server instance is in single-user mode and there is an active connection to the database, you might not be able to perform a maintenance task. You need to return the database to multiuser mode before continuing. If you cannot obtain access to the database to return it to multiuser mode, you can force the database mode change by following these steps:

1. Log on to the server and open an elevated, administrative command prompt. Use the NET STOP command to stop the SQL Server instance you want to change. For example, if you want to stop the default SQL Server instance, type **net stop mssqlserver**.

2. Use the CD command to change to the Binn directory for the SQL Server instance. For example, type **cd "C:\Program Files\Microsoft SQL Server\ MSSQL11.MSSQLSERVER\MSSQL\Binn"**.

3. Put the server instance in single-user mode by typing **sqlservr –m**.

4. Start a second command prompt, and then open a dedicated administrator connection to SQL Server by typing **sqlcmd –A**. Be sure to provide a user name and password if necessary by using the –U and –P parameters.

5. Perform the necessary maintenance tasks by using Sqlcmd.

6. Set the database in single-user mode back to normal mode by using sp_dboption. For example, if the database is named *cust*, type:

```
USE master
EXEC sp_dboption 'cust', 'single user', 'FALSE';
GO
```

7. At the first command prompt (where SQL Server is running), press Ctrl+C to stop SQL Server. When prompted to confirm, type **Y**.

8. Start the SQL Server instance you are working with by using NET START. For example, if you want to start the default SQL Server instance, type **net start mssqlserver**.

Using Database Mail

Database Mail is an essential part of database automation. You must configure Database Mail so that alerts and other types of messages can be sent to administrators or other users. Database Mail provides SQL Server with the ability to generate and send email messages as a mail client using the Simple Mail Transfer Protocol (SMTP). The Database Mail configuration process performs the following tasks:

- Installs database messaging objects in the *msdb* database
- Configures Database Mail accounts and profiles
- Configures Database Mail security

Database Mail is a full-featured replacement for SQL Mail. Database Mail acts as a mail client and sends its messages to designated SMTP servers. Any SMTP server, including a Microsoft Exchange server, can receive and deliver messages generated by Database Mail.

Performing the Initial Database Mail Configuration

Like most mail clients, Database Mail uses mail profiles and mail accounts to send email messages. The profile defines the mail environment Database Mail uses and can be associated with one or more SMTP mail accounts. Because the mail accounts are used in priority order, you can configure multiple accounts on different mail servers as a safeguard against mail-server failure or network problems that might prevent message delivery. You can then configure the Database Mail profile to use these separate accounts. If mail cannot be delivered to the first account listed in the profile, the second one is tried, and so on.

The mail profile can be public or private. A public profile is available to any user or application for any configured Database Mail host on the current server instance. A private profile is available only to explicitly defined users and applications. If you are configuring Database Mail for SQL Server Agent or a specific application, you usually want to use a private profile. If you are configuring Database Mail for general use, you usually want to use a public profile.

Before you configure Database Mail, you should create the SMTP accounts that Database Mail will use, or have your organization's mail administrator do this. If you are configuring Database Mail for SQL Server Agent, it is a good idea to have the email address and account name reflect this. For example, set the user name as SQL Agent and the email address as sqlagent@yourcompany.com. To configure Database Mail, you need the account user name, email address, and SMTP server name. If the SMTP server requires authentication, and most do, you also need the logon user name and password for the account.

You can use SQL Server Management Studio to configure Database Mail for the first time by completing the following steps:

1. Start SQL Server Management Studio. In the Object Explorer view, connect to the server instance of your choice, and then expand the server's Management folder.

2. Right-click Database Mail, and then select Configure Database Mail. This starts the Database Mail Configuration Wizard. If the Welcome page is displayed, click Next.

3. Accept the default value of Set Up Database Mail By Performing The Following Tasks, and then click Next.

4. When prompted to enable the Database Mail feature, click Yes.

5. On the New Profile page, type the name and description of the mail profile that Database Mail will use, such as Mail Profile For SQL Server Agent. The profile is used to define the mail environment for Database Mail.

6. To specify an SMTP account that the profile will use to send email messages, click Add. This displays the New Database Mail Account dialog box, shown in Figure 10-1.

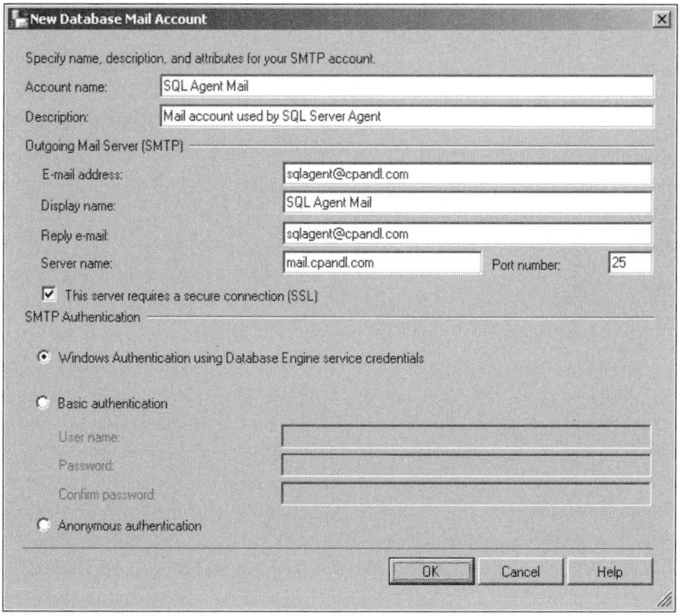

FIGURE 10-1 The New Database Mail Account dialog box.

7. In the Account Name and Description text boxes, enter the name and description of the account you are configuring for use with Database Mail. This information is used only with Database Mail and is shown in SQL Server dialog boxes.

8. In the E-Mail Address box, type the email address of the Database Mail account, such as sqlagent@cpandl.com.

9. In the Display Name box, type the name that will appear in the From field of outgoing messages.

10. In the Reply E-Mail box, type the email address to which replies to Database Mail messages can be sent. For example, if you want administrators to send follow-up information to a lead administrator, you would put the lead administrator's email address in the Reply E-Mail text box.

11. In the Server Name box, type the host name of the mail server, such as smtp. You can also type the fully qualified domain name (FQDN) of the mail server, such as smtp.cpandl.com. Using the full domain name ensures a successful connection when the mail server is in a different domain.

12. By default, most SMTP servers use TCP port 25 for communications. If your SMTP server uses a different TCP port for communications, enter the TCP port number in the field provided. Additionally, select the This Server Requires A Secure Connection (SSL) check box if you've installed a Secure Sockets Layer (SSL) certificate for SQL Server and want to encrypt SMTP communications using SSL.

13. Database Mail needs to log on to the mail server to submit mail for delivery. Select the appropriate option under SMTP Authentication, based on your mail server configuration:

   ■ **Windows Authentication Using Database Engine Service Credentials**   Database Mail logs in to the designated mail server by using the credentials of the SQL Server service (MSSQLService) for the current Database Engine instance.

   ■ **Basic Authentication**   Database Mail logs in to the designated mail server using the user name and password you have provided. Enter a user name for the account. Type and confirm the password for the account in the text boxes provided.

   ■ **Anonymous Authentication**   Database Mail logs in to the designated mail server as an anonymous user. The mail server must be configured to allow anonymous logins (which is not a good security practice).

14. Click OK to close the New Database Mail Account dialog box.

15. Repeat steps 6 through 14 to specify other mail accounts to associate with the Database Mail profile. The account listed first is the account that Database Mail tries to use first. As necessary, use the Move Up and Move Down buttons to set the priority for multiple accounts. Click Next.

16. Database mail supports public and private profiles. A public profile allows any user or role with access to the mail host database (msdb) to send email using that profile. If you are creating a public profile, select the Public check box on the Public Profiles tab.

17. Users or roles can send mail using the default profile without explicitly specifying a profile. If a user or role has no default private profile, the default public profile is used, if configured. To make the public profile the default for all mail host databases and users, set Default Profile to Yes, as shown in Figure 10-2.

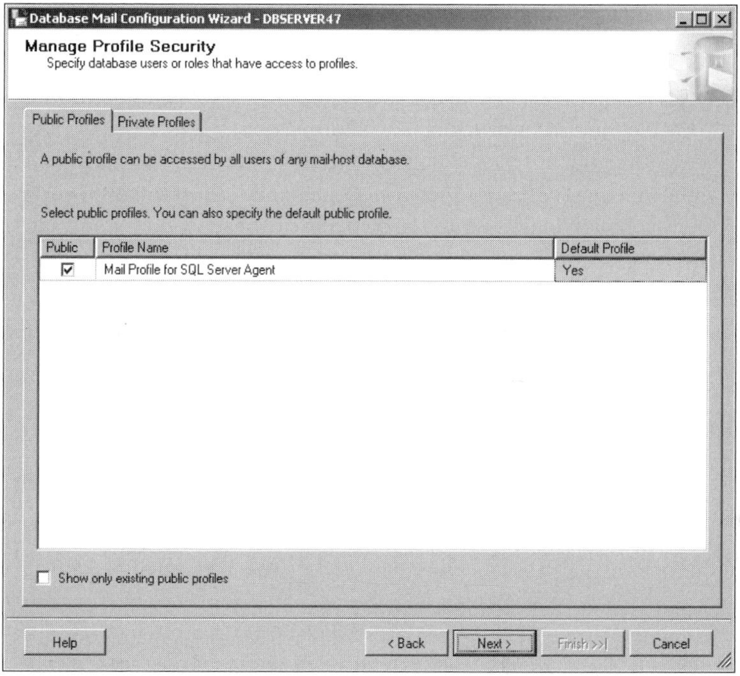

FIGURE 10-2 The Public Profiles tab.

18. If you are creating a private profile, select the Private Profiles tab. Use the User Name list to select a user to which you will grant profile access. The default user is the SQL Server Agent service account. After you select a user in the list, select the Access check box to grant access to the profile, and then repeat this action as necessary to grant access to other users. To make the private profile the default for the selected mail host database and user, set Default Profile to Yes.

19. Click Next. System parameters are used by all database mail hosts configured for a SQL Server instance. Configure the default system parameters by using the following options, and then click Next:

- **Account Retry Attempts** Sets the number of times to retry sending the message. The default is 1. If you have configured multiple accounts, this might be sufficient because it provides for one retry. However, when you are configuring mail for SQL Server Agent, you usually want to set this so that three to five attempts are made to send a message.

- **Account Retry Delay**   Sets the delay (in seconds) between retry attempts. The default is 60 seconds, which is far too long if Database Mail is trying to deliver critical alerts. A retry delay of 20 to 30 seconds might be preferred when you are configuring mail for SQL Server Agent.

- **Maximum File Size**   Sets the maximum size (in bytes) for any generated message, including headers, message text, and included attachments. The default is 1,000,000 bytes (976 KB). When you are configuring mail for SQL Server Agent, this is usually sufficient. If applications generate messages that include graphics or multimedia, however, this might not be sufficient.

- **Prohibited Attachment File Extensions**   Sets the types of files that cannot be sent as attachments by indicating file extensions. To prevent abuse of Database Mail, a more inclusive list would include all file extensions designated as high risk by Attachment Manager in Group Policy, including .ade, .adp, .app, .asp, .bas, .bat, .cer, .chm, .cmd, .com, .cpl, .crt, .csh, .exe, .fxp, .hlp, .hta, .inf, .ins, .isp, .its, .js, .jse, .ksh, .lnk, .mad, .maf, .mag, .mam, .maq, .mar, .mas, .mat, .mau, .mav, .maw, .mda, .mdb, .mde, .mdt, .mdw, .mdz, .msc, .msi, .msp, .mst, .ops, .pcd, .pif, .prf, .prg, .pst, .reg, .scf, .scr, .sct, .shb, .shs, .tmp, .url, .vb, .vbe, .vbs, .vsmacros, .vss, .vst, .vsw, .ws, .wsc, .wsf, and .wsh.

- **Database Mail Executable Minimum Lifetime**   Sets the minimum time for Database Mail to run while generating a message. The lifetime should be set to optimize usage of the Database Mail executable file. You do not want the server to create the related objects in memory and then remove them from memory over and over again. You do want the related objects to be cleared out when they are not needed. The default value of 600 seconds (10 minutes) is generally sufficient.

- **Logging Level**   Determines the level of logging with regard to Database Mail. The default value, Extended, configures Database Mail to perform extended logging of related events. To reduce logging, you can set the level to Normal so that only important events, such as warnings and errors, are logged.

NOTE   The logging level also can be set to Verbose. However, this setting should be used only for troubleshooting Database Mail. When you finish troubleshooting, reset the logging level to Extended or Normal.

20.   Review the setup actions that will be performed, and then click Finish. The Configuring page shows the success or failure of each action. Click the link provided for any error message to see details about the error that occurred, and then take any necessary corrective action. Click Close.

TIP   If you are enabling Database Mail for use with the SQL Server Agent service, you must ensure the service is running and configured for automatic startup. See the "Configuring the SQL Server Agent Service" section later in this chapter for details.

You can check the status of SQL Server Agent in the Object Explorer view in SQL Server Management Studio. If the service is not running, right-click the SQL Server Agent node, and then select Start.

Managing Database Mail Profiles and Accounts

Database Mail can be configured to use one or more mail profiles, and each mail profile can have one or more mail accounts associated with it. Database Mail profiles can be either of the following:

- **Public** Allows any user or role with access to the mail host database (*msdb*) to send email using the profile

- **Private** Allows only explicitly defined users and roles to send email using the profile

Database Mail accounts are used in priority order and are a safeguard against mail server failure or network problems that could prevent message delivery. If mail cannot be delivered to the first account listed in the profile, the second one is tried, and so on.

Users or roles can send mail using the default profile without explicitly specifying a profile. If a user or role has no default private profile, the default public profile is used, if configured. If no profile is specified and there is no private or public default, an error is generated.

To manage profiles and their accounts or to add a profile, follow these steps:

1. Start SQL Server Management Studio. In the Object Explorer view, connect to the server instance of your choice, and then expand the server's Management folder.

2. Right-click Database Mail, and then select Configure Database Mail to display the Database Mail Configuration Wizard. If the Welcome page is displayed, click Next.

3. Select Manage Database Mail Accounts And Profiles, and then click Next.

4. If you have configured multiple Database Mail hosts on this server instance and want to define separate profiles for these Database Mail hosts, select Create A New Profile, click Next, and then follow steps 5 through 13 of the "Performing the Initial Database Mail Configuration" section earlier in this chapter to define the new profile and the accounts associated with this profile.

5. If you want to modify an existing profile or add an account to an existing profile, select View, Change, Or Delete An Existing Profile, and then click Next. Use the Profile Name list to select the profile to manage. You can then add, remove, or prioritize accounts for this profile, as described in steps 6 through 13 of the "Performing the Initial Database Mail Configuration" section of this chapter.

6. Click Next, and then click Finish. The Configuring page shows the success or failure of each action. Click the link provided for any error message to see details about the error that occurred, and then take any necessary corrective action. Click Close.

To set a mail profile as public or private, follow these steps:

1. Start SQL Server Management Studio. In the Object Explorer view, connect to the server instance of your choice, and then expand the server's Management folder.

2. Right-click Database Mail, and then select Configure Database Mail to display the Database Mail Configuration Wizard. If the Welcome page is displayed, click Next.

3. Select Manage Profile Security, and then click Next.

4. The Public Profiles tab shows public profiles. Clear the Public check box if you want to make a profile private. To make a public profile the default for all mail host databases and users, set Default Profile to Yes.

5. The Private Profiles tab shows private profiles that are accessible only to a specific database and user. Use the drop-down lists to select the database and user for which you want to configure a private profile. After selecting a user in the drop-down list, select the Access check box to grant access to the profile, and then repeat this action as necessary to grant access to other users. To make a private profile the default for the selected mail host database and user, set Default Profile to Yes.

6. Click Next, and then click Finish. The Configuring page shows the success or failure of each action. Click the link provided for any error message to see details about the error that occurred, and then take any necessary corrective action. Click Close.

Viewing or Changing Database Mail System Parameters

Database Mail system parameters are set globally for each SQL Server instance. If you want to manage the global system parameters for Database Mail, follow these steps:

1. Start SQL Server Management Studio. In the Object Explorer view, connect to the server instance of your choice, and then expand the server's Management folder.

2. Right-click Database Mail, and then select Configure Database Mail to display the Database Mail Configuration Wizard. If the Welcome page is displayed, click Next.

3. Select View Or Change System Parameters. Click Next.

4. Make changes as appropriate to the system parameters. See the "Performing the Initial Database Mail Configuration" section earlier in this chapter for details about configuring individual parameters.

5. Click Next, and then click Finish. The Configuring page shows the success or failure of each action. Click the link provided for any error message to see details about the error that occurred, and then take any necessary corrective action. Click Close.

Using SQL Server Agent

SQL Server Agent is the driving force behind database automation. It is responsible for processing alerts and running scheduled jobs. When alerts are triggered and when scheduled jobs fail, succeed, or finish, you can notify SQL Server operators. Operator notifications are also processed through SQL Server Agent.

Accessing Alerts, Operators, and Jobs

You can use SQL Server Management Studio to access resources related to SQL Server Agent by completing the following steps:

1. Start SQL Server Management Studio. In the Object Explorer view, connect to the server instance of your choice, and then expand the server's SQL Server Agent folder. (SQL Server Agent must be running to expand the related node.)

2. You should see entries for Alerts, Operators, and Jobs. Select one of these entries in the left pane to display its properties. If the Object Explorer Details window is not displayed automatically, press F7 or choose Object Explorer Details from the View menu.

3. Any jobs or alerts that appear dimmed are configured but not enabled. Double-click an alert, operator, or job entry to access its associated Properties dialog box.

NOTE If you have configured replication on the server, you will see many alerts and jobs that you can configure to make it easier to monitor replication. To start these alerts or jobs, you need to enable them and set the appropriate property settings.

Configuring the SQL Server Agent Service

The SQL Server Agent service executes scheduled jobs, triggers alerts, and performs other automated tasks. Each SQL Server Database Engine instance has its own SQL Server Agent service. You can control the related service (SQLServerAgent or SQLAgent$*instancename*) just as you do the SQL Server service. For SQL Server Agent to work properly, you should configure the SQL Server Agent service to run automatically. The startup account used by the SQL Server Agent service determines access permissions for SQL Server Agent. If the startup account does not have appropriate permissions, SQL Server Agent will not run properly. In most cases, you should use a Microsoft Windows domain account that is a member of the sysadmin role. This ensures that SQL Server Agent can generate alerts, run jobs, and restart services as necessary.

To configure the SQL Server Agent service, complete the following steps:

1. In SQL Server Configuration Manager, select the SQL Server Services node in the left pane to see the related SQL Server services in the right pane.

2. Right-click the SQL Server Agent service for the Database Engine instance you are configuring, and then select Properties.

3. SQL Server Agent can run using a built-in system account or a designated Windows account as follows:

   - Choose Built-In Account to use one of the built-in system accounts as the startup account. The drop-down menu gives you three options: Local System, Local Service, and Network Service. Local System grants access to the local system and certain systemwide privileges, such as Act As Part Of The Operating System. Local Service grants access to the local system as a regular service account. Network Service grants access to the local system and allows SQL Server Agent to access the network, such as when it is necessary to connect to remote systems.

   - Choose This Account to control permissions and privileges using a Windows account. Type the user name and password of a Windows domain account. You can also click Browse to search for an account in the Select User Or Group dialog box.

4. If you changed the service account, you must stop and then restart the service. Do this by right-clicking the SQL Server Agent Service and clicking Restart. If the service is stopped already, click Start instead.

5. On the Service tab, Start Mode should be set to Automatic. If it is not, click in the Start Mode list and select Automatic.

6. Click OK.

Setting the SQL Server Agent Mail Profile

The SQL Server Agent service sends alerts and notifications through email messages. You use Database Mail to do this. When you initially set up Database Mail to send alerts and notifications, you configure one or more databases as mail hosts and define client settings so that users and applications such as SQL Server Agent can send SMTP email messages through your organization's SMTP mail server.

To use Database Mail for SQL Server Agent alerts and notifications, you must do the following:

1. Configure *msdb* as a database mail host.

2. Designate a profile for this database.

3. Grant profile access to the SQL Server Agent service account.

You enable Database Mail for SQL Server Agent and grant access to a profile for sending email by completing the following steps:

1. In the SQL Server Management Studio Management folder, right-click the SQL Server Agent entry, and then select Properties.

2. On the Alert System page, select Enable Mail Profile.

3. Database Mail is the mail system. Use the Mail Profile list to select the Database Mail profile to use for sending email. If you want to test the configuration, click Test.

4. Click OK.

Using SQL Server Agent to Restart Services Automatically

You can configure SQL Server Agent to restart the SQL Server and SQL Server Agent services automatically if they stop unexpectedly. Configuring automatic restart of these services is a good idea because it might keep you from getting paged if the server stops for some reason at 3:00 A.M. on a Tuesday.

To configure automatic service restart, complete the following steps:

1. In the SQL Server Management Studio Management folder, right-click the SQL Server Agent entry, and then select Properties.

2. On the General page, select the Auto Restart SQL Server If It Stops Unexpectedly check box and also select the Auto Restart SQL Server Agent If It Stops Unexpectedly check box.

3. Click OK.

Managing Alerts

Using alerts, you can send email, pager, or Net Send alerts when errors occur or when performance conditions are reached. For example, you can configure an alert to send a message when a Log File Is Full error occurs or when the number of deadlocks per second is more than five. You can also execute a job on an alert event.

Using Default Alerts

Default alerts are configured when you configure features such as replication. The names of alerts configured when you set up replication begin with *Replication:* and include the following:

- **Replication: Agent Success** Tells you that the replication agent was successful
- **Replication: Agent Failure** Tells you that the replication agent failed
- **Replication: Agent Retry** Tells you that the replication agent failed and is retrying
- **Replication: Expired Subscription Dropped** Tells you that an expired subscription was dropped, which means the subscriber will not be updated anymore
- **Replication: Subscriber Has Failed Data Validation** Tells you that data in the subscriber's subscription could not be validated

- **Replication: Subscriber Has Passed Data Validation** Tells you that data in the subscriber's subscription was validated
- **Replication: Subscription Reinitialized After Validation Failure** Tells you that data in the subscriber's subscription was reinitialized with a new snapshot

These replication alerts are disabled by default and do not have operators assigned, either. If you want to use these alerts, you need to enable them and assign operators. Other default alerts for replication are used to issue warnings and are enabled in a standard configuration.

Creating Error Message Alerts

Error message alerts are triggered when SQL Server generates an error message. You can create an error message alert by completing the following steps:

1. In SQL Server Management Studio, access the SQL Server Agent entry on the server running SQL Server Agent.
2. Double-click the SQL Server Agent entry in the left pane to expand it.
3. Right-click Alerts, and then select New Alert from the shortcut menu. This displays the New Alert dialog box, shown in Figure 10-3.

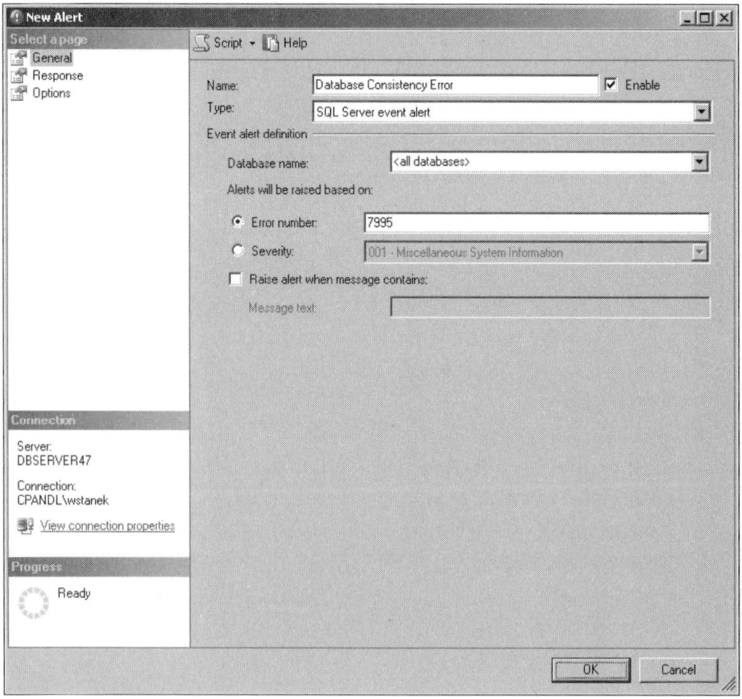

FIGURE 10-3 The New Alert dialog box.

4. Type a short but descriptive name for the alert in the Name text box. In Figure 10-3, the alert is named Database Consistency Error.

5. In the Type list, choose SQL Server Event Alert. Now you can set alerts according to the number or severity level of error messages.

6. Use the Database Name list to choose the database in which the error must occur to trigger the alert. To specify all databases on the server, select the All Databases option.

7. To set alerts by error number, select Error Number, and then type an error number in the related text box. To see all error messages that can be returned by SQL Server, you can query the *master* database by using SELECT * FROM SYS.MESSAGES, as discussed in Chapter 12, "SQL Server 2012 Profiling and Monitoring."

8. To set alerts by severity level, select Severity, and then use the related list to choose a severity level that triggers the alert. You usually want to configure alerts for severity levels 19 through 25 (which are the levels for fatal errors).

9. To restrict alerts to messages containing specific text strings, select the Raise Alert When Message Contains check box, and then type the text to filter for in the Message Text box.

10. Configure the alert response as explained in the next section, "Handling Alert Responses." Click OK to create the alert.

Handling Alert Responses

In response to an alert, you can execute SQL Server jobs, notify operators of the alert, or both. To configure the response to an alert, complete the following steps:

1. In SQL Server Management Studio, access the SQL Server Agent entry on the server running SQL Server Agent.

2. Expand the SQL Server Agent and Alerts folders.

3. Double-click the alert you want to configure, and then select the Response page, as shown in Figure 10-4.

4. To execute a job in response to the alert, select the Execute Job check box.

5. If you want to execute an existing job, use the related jobs list to select it. You can enter the full or partial job name to display matches. To be sure you have the correct job, click View Job to view a job's properties.

6. If you want to create a new job, click New Job, and then configure the job as discussed in the "Scheduling Jobs" section later in this chapter.

7. To notify designated operators of an alert rather than just logging the alert, select the Notify Operators check box.

8. Operators configured to handle alerts and schedule jobs are shown in the Operator List area. The available notification methods depend on how the operator account is configured. You can select the E-Mail, Pager, or Net

Send notification type, or select any two or all three. Click New Operator to configure a new operator, or click View Operator to view the properties of the operator selected in the Operator List area.

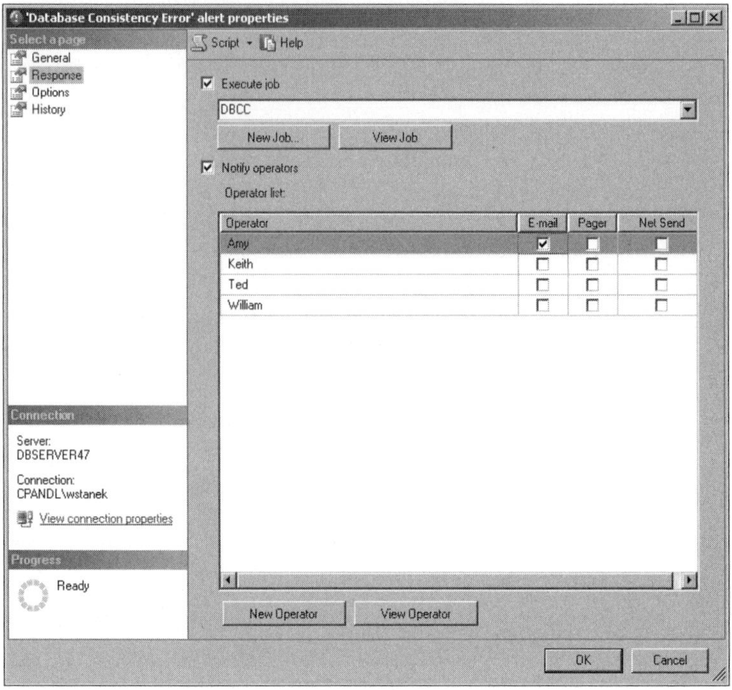

FIGURE 10-4 The Response page of the New Alert dialog box.

9. Select the Options page.

10. Use the Include Alert Error Text In check boxes to specify whether error text should be sent with the notification message. By default, error text is sent only with E-Mail and Net Send notifications.

11. Set an additional message to send to operators by using the Additional Notification Message To Send text box.

12. Set the delay between responses for subsequent alert notifications by using the Delay Between Responses boxes labeled Minutes and Seconds.

   TIP To limit the number of alert responses triggered, you probably want to set a delay response value of five minutes or more.

13. Click OK to complete the configuration.

Deleting, Enabling, and Disabling Alerts

Deleting an alert removes its entry from the alerts list. Because old alerts might be useful to you (or another database administrator) in the future, you might want to disable them instead of deleting them. When an alert is disabled, no alerts are triggered if the related event occurs.

To delete, enable, or disable an alert, complete the following steps:

1. In SQL Server Management Studio, access the SQL Server Agent entry on the server running SQL Server Agent.

2. Expand the SQL Server Agent and Alerts folders.

3. Any alerts that appear dimmed are configured but not enabled. To enable or disable an alert, right-click it, and then select Enable or Disable as appropriate. Click Close.

4. To delete an alert, click it, and then press Delete. In the Delete Object dialog box, click OK to confirm the deletion.

Managing Operators

Operators are special accounts that can be notified when alerts are triggered and when scheduled jobs fail, succeed, or finish. Before operators become available, you need to register them. After you register operators, you can enable or disable them for notifications.

Registering Operators

You register operators by completing the following steps:

1. In SQL Server Management Studio, access the SQL Server Agent entry on the server running SQL Server Agent.

2. Expand the SQL Server Agent folder.

3. Right-click the Operators entry in the left pane, and then choose New Operator to display the New Operator dialog box, shown in Figure 10-5.

4. Type a name for the operator in the Name text box.

5. Specify the E-mail Name, Net Send Address, or Pager E-mail Name (or all three) to notify.

   TIP If you specify a pager account for the operator, you can set a duty schedule for the pager by using the text boxes and check boxes in the Pager On Duty Schedule area. This option is helpful if you have operators who should be notified only during working hours. To set default configuration settings for pagers, access the Alert System page of the SQL Server Agent Properties dialog box.

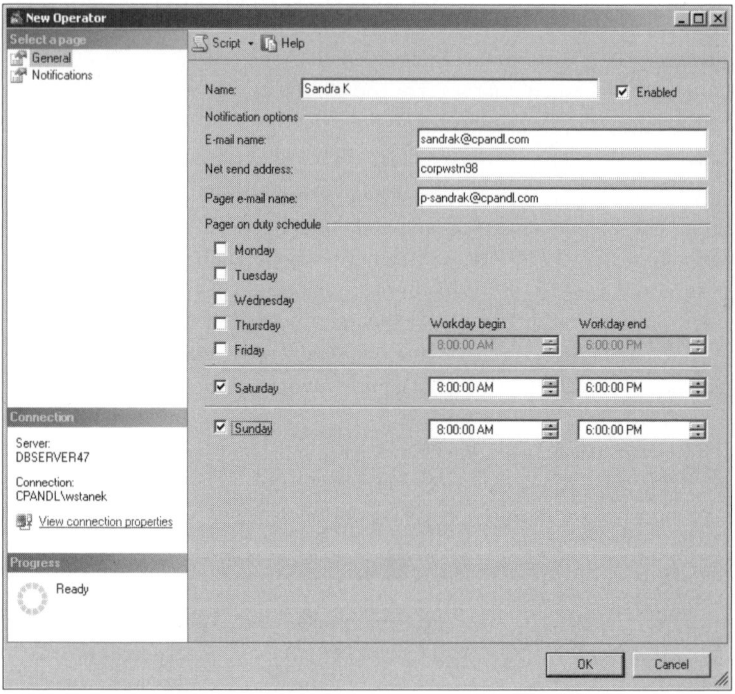

FIGURE 10-5 The New Operator dialog box.

6. Select the Notifications page to specify existing alerts that the operator should receive (if any). Existing alerts are listed in the Alert Name column. If you find an alert that the operator should receive, select the corresponding check box in the E-Mail, Pager, and Net Send columns as appropriate.

7. Click OK to register the operator.

Deleting and Disabling Notification for Operators

When database administrators leave an organization or go on vacation, you might want to delete or disable their associated operator accounts. To do this, complete the following steps:

1. In SQL Server Management Studio, access the SQL Server Agent entry on the server running SQL Server Agent.

2. Expand the SQL Server Agent and Operators folders.

3. To disable an operator, double-click the operator entry in the right pane to display the Operator Properties dialog box. Clear the Enabled check box on the General page, and then click OK.

4. To delete an operator, click its entry in the right pane, and then press Delete. The Delete Object dialog box is displayed.

5. If the operator has been selected to receive alert or job notifications, you will see a Reassign To option in the Delete Object dialog box. To reassign notification duty, select a different operator by using the Reassign To list. You can view or change the properties of this operator by clicking Properties.

6. Click OK to delete the operator.

Configuring a Fail-Safe Operator

When things go wrong with notifications, operators do not get notified and problems might not be corrected in a timely manner. To prevent this, you might want to designate a fail-safe operator. The fail-safe operator is notified in the following situations:

- SQL Server Agent cannot access system tables in the *msdb* database, which is where operator definitions and notification lists are stored.

- All pager notifications to designated operators have failed, or the designated operators are off-duty (as defined in the pager schedule).

NOTE Using the fail-safe operator for pager notification failure might seem strange, but it is a good way to ensure that alerts are handled efficiently. E-mail and Net Send messages almost always reach their destination—but the people involved are not always watching their email or sitting at their computer to receive Net Send messages, so the fail-safe operator is a way to guarantee notification.

To configure a fail-safe operator, complete the following steps:

1. Right-click the SQL Server Agent entry in SQL Server Management Studio, and then select Properties.

2. In the SQL Server Agent Properties dialog box, select the Alert System page.

3. Select the Enable Fail-Safe Operator check box.

4. Use the Operator list to choose an operator to designate as the fail-safe operator. You can reassign the fail-safe duty by selecting a different operator, or you can disable the feature by clearing the Enable Fail-Safe Operator check box.

5. Use the Notify Using check boxes to determine how the fail-safe operator is notified.

6. Click OK.

Scheduling Jobs

Job scheduling is a key part of database automation. You can configure SQL Server jobs to handle almost any database task.

Creating Jobs

You create jobs as a series of steps that contain actions in the sequence in which you want to execute them. When you schedule jobs in conjunction with other SQL Server facilities, such as database backups or data transformation, the necessary commands are configured for you. Normally, these commands are set as step 1, and all you need to do is set a run schedule for the job. You can add extra steps to these jobs and thus perform other tasks. For example, after importing data, you might want to back up the related database. To do this, you schedule the import in the SQL Server Import And Export Wizard and then edit the associated job in SQL Server Management Studio to add another step for backing up the database. By coordinating the two processes, you ensure that the import operation is completed before starting the backup.

Another reason for editing a job created by a different SQL Server facility is to add notifications based on success, failure, and completion of the job. In this way, you can notify operators of certain conditions, and you do not have to search through logs to determine whether the job executed properly.

When you schedule jobs to execute based on alerts, you configure the entire job process from start to finish by performing the following tasks:

- Create a job definition.
- Set steps to execute.
- Configure a job schedule.
- Handle completion, success, and failure notification messages.

Assigning or Changing Job Definitions

Whether you are creating a new job or editing an existing job, the steps for working with job definitions are the same:

1. In SQL Server Management Studio, access the SQL Server Agent entry on the server running SQL Server Agent.
2. Expand the SQL Server Agent and Jobs folders.
3. Existing jobs are shown in the right pane. Double-click a job to access its related Properties dialog box, which is essentially the same as the New Job dialog box shown in Figure 10-6.

    To create a new job, right-click the Jobs entry, and then choose New Job to display the New Job dialog box.
4. In the Name text box, type a descriptive name for the job. The name can be up to 128 characters. (If you change the name of an existing job, the job is displayed with the new name. Any references to the old job name in logs or history files remain the same and are not modified.)
5. Job categories allow you to organize jobs so that they can be searched and differentiated easily. The default category is Uncategorized (Local). Use the Category list to choose a different category for the job.

NOTE Job categories are created and managed through a separate process. To create a new job category or update an existing category, use the techniques described in the "Managing Job Categories" section later in this chapter.

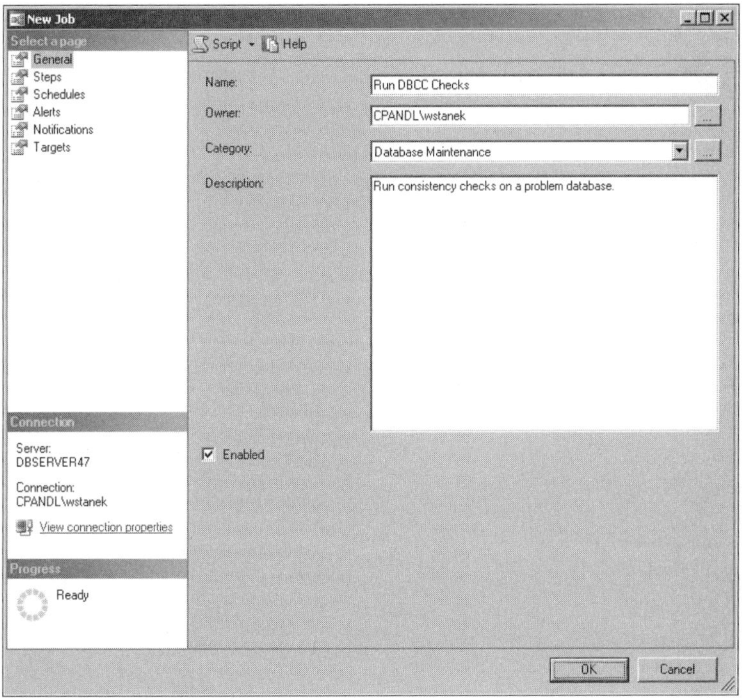

FIGURE 10-6 The General page of the New Job dialog box.

6. By default, the current user owns the job. Administrators can reassign jobs to other users. To do this, use the Owner list. You can use only predefined logins. If the login you want to use is not available, you need to create a login for the account.

7. Type a description of the job in the Description text box. You can use up to 512 characters.

8. If job scheduling across multiple servers is configured, select the Targets page, and then designate the target server. The target server is the server on which the job runs. To run on the currently selected server, select Target Local Server. To run on multiple servers, select Target Multiple Servers, and then choose the target servers.

9. Set Steps, Schedules, and Notifications, as explained in the following sections.

Setting Steps to Execute

Jobs can have one or more steps. SQL Server Agent always attempts to execute the start step, but additional steps can be executed conditionally, such as when the start step succeeds or fails. You work with steps using the Steps page in the New Job dialog box, shown in Figure 10-7. The page displays any existing steps for the job.

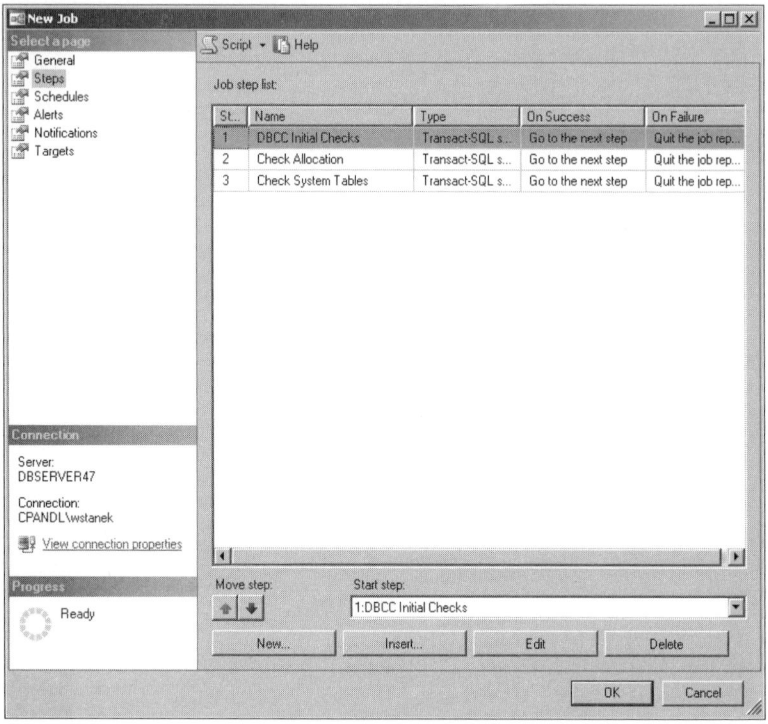

FIGURE 10-7 The Steps page of the New Job dialog box.

You can use the boxes and buttons in this dialog box as follows:

- **New** Creates a new step.
- **Insert** Inserts a step before the currently selected step.
- **Edit** Allows edits to the selected step.
- **Delete** Deletes the selected step.
- **Move Step Up/Down** Changes the order of the selected step.
- **Start Step** Sets which step is executed first. The green flag icon identifies the start step in the step list.

When you create or edit a step, you see a dialog box similar to the one shown in Figure 10-8.

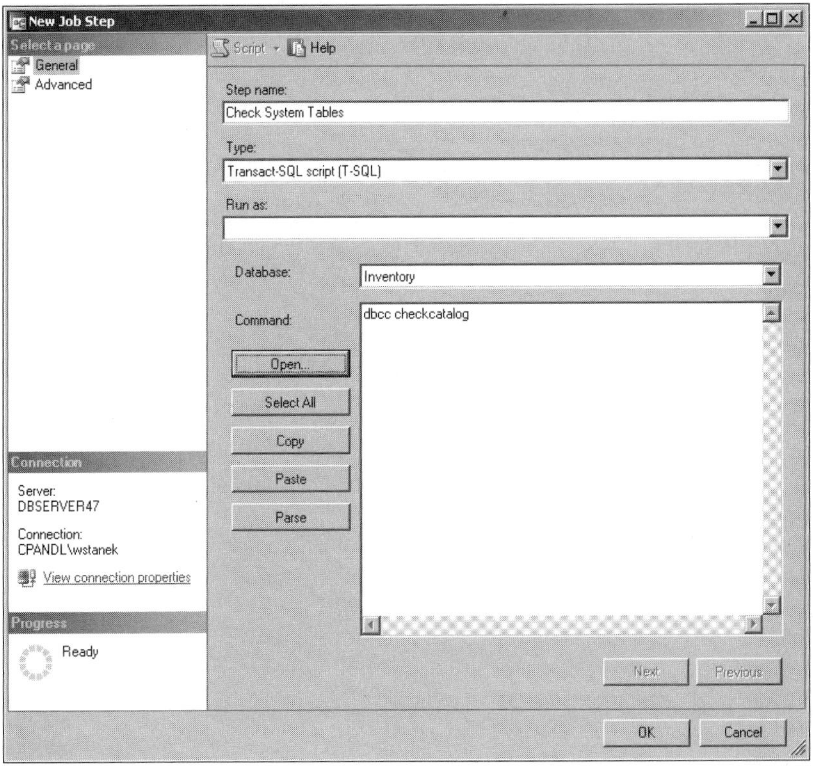

FIGURE 10-8 The New Job Step dialog box.

To configure this dialog box, complete the following steps:

1. Type a short but descriptive name for the step in the Step Name text box.

2. Use the Type list to choose a step type from the following choices:

   ■ **ActiveX Script**   Run ActiveX scripts. You can write ActiveX scripts in VBScript, JScript, or another active scripting language configured for use on the system. Enter script statements directly into the Command area or load the statements from a script file. The entire contents of the script are then stored with this step. Changes made to the script file later are not updated automatically.

   ■ **Operating System (CmdExec)**   Execute operating system commands. Enter the operating system commands on a separate line, being sure that you specify the full path to commands and include any desired command parameters. Commands can run batch scripts, Windows scripts, command-line utilities, or applications.

- **PowerShell**   Run Windows PowerShell scripts. Enter script statements directly into the Command area or load the statements from a script file. The entire contents of the script are then stored with this step. Changes made to the script file later are not updated automatically. Be sure to import the SQLPS module if you want to work with SQL Server.

- **Replication [Agent Name]**   Pass T-SQL commands to designated replication agents. You can script the Distributor, Snapshot, Merge, Queue Reader, and Transaction–Log Reader agents with T-SQL commands. To see examples, refer to the existing jobs that are configured to handle replication, distribution, and subscription processes on the server (if available).

- **SQL Server Analysis Services Command/Query**   Pass commands or queries to SQL Server Analysis Services. Type commands and queries in the Command area or load the commands and queries from an Analysis Server file. To load from a file, click Open, and then select the Analysis Server Command (.xmla) or Analysis Server Query (.mdx) file to use. The entire contents of the file are stored with this step.

- **SQL Server Integration Services Package**   Execute SQL Server Integration Services packages stored on a specific server.

- **Transact-SQL Script (T-SQL)**   Execute T-SQL commands. Type T-SQL commands in the Command area or load the statements from a T-SQL script. To load commands from a script, click Open, and then select the T-SQL script you want to use. The entire contents of the script are then stored with this step.

> **TIP**   Scripts that you change later are not updated automatically. You need to edit the step properties and reload the script file. Additionally, you should not edit existing replication jobs. Instead, modify the replication process as appropriate so that the jobs are re-created as may be necessary.

3. When executing T-SQL commands or scripts, use the Database list to set the database on which the commands are executed.

4. Select the Advanced page, shown in Figure 10-9.

5. Use the On Success Action list to set the action to take when the step succeeds. You can choose from the following options:

   - **Go To The Next Step**   Continues sequential execution of the job
   - **Go To Step ....**   Continues execution of the job at a specified step
   - **Quit The Job Reporting Success**   Halts execution of the job and reports success
   - **Quit The Job Reporting Failure**   Halts execution of the job and reports failure

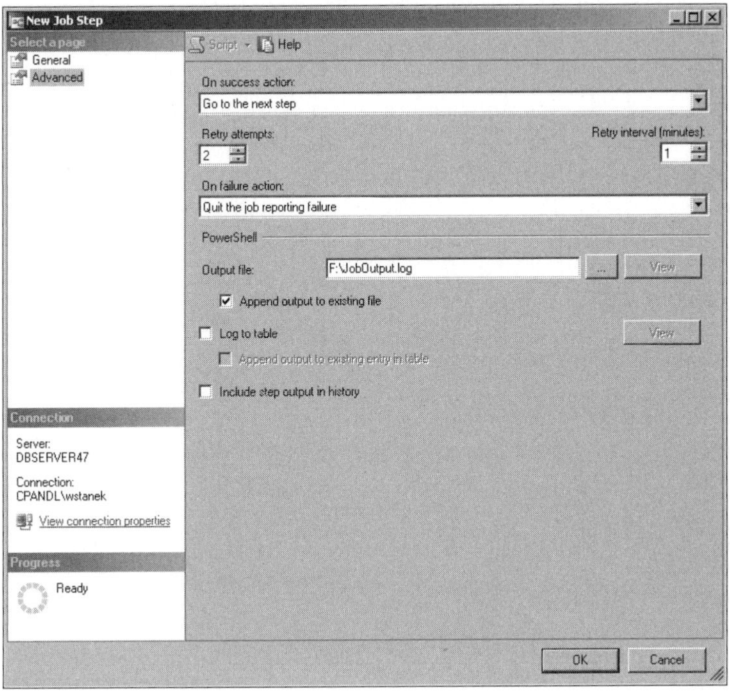

FIGURE 10-9 The Advanced page of the New Job Step dialog box.

6. By default, Retry Attempts is set to 0, and SQL Server Agent does not try to execute steps again. You can change this behavior by setting the number of retry attempts and a retry interval. You do this by using the Retry Attempts and Retry Interval (Minutes) boxes, respectively. The retry interval is the delay in minutes between retries.

7. If the job fails on all retry attempts (if any), the action set in the On Failure Action list is executed. The available options are the same as those for success.

8. Optionally, configure a file for logging output from T-SQL and CmdExec commands. Type the file name and path in the Output File text box, or click the related options button (...) to search for an existing file.

TIP You might want to create a central log file for the output of all jobs or all jobs in a particular category. If you do this, be sure to select the Append Output To Existing File option rather than allow the file to be overwritten. This ensures that the output file does not get overwritten. An alternative is to include the step output in the job history.

9. Click the options button (...) next to the Run As User box to set the login to use when executing commands. By default, commands are run using the current login ID.

10. Click OK to complete the step configuration.

Configuring Job Schedules

You track schedules on the Schedules page of the New Job dialog box, as shown in Figure 10-10. Jobs can have one or more schedules associated with them, and just as you can enable or disable jobs and their individual steps, you can enable or disable individual schedules. This makes the job scheduling process very flexible. For example, you could set one schedule to execute the job on weekdays at 2:00 A.M., another to execute the job every Sunday at 8:00 A.M., and another for execution at 10:00 P.M. only when needed.

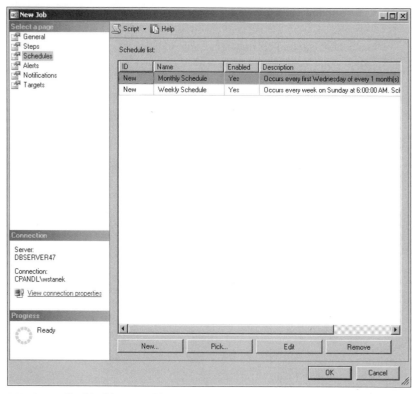

FIGURE 10-10 The Schedules page of the New Job dialog box.

Whether you are creating a new job or editing an existing job, you work with schedules on the Schedules page as follows:

- **Create a new schedule**   Click New to configure a new schedule.
- **Pick a schedule**   Click Pick to select an existing schedule, and then click Edit to view or modify its properties.
- **Edit a schedule**   Select a previously selected schedule, and then click Edit to view or modify its properties.
- **Delete a schedule**   Select a previously selected schedule, and then click Remove to remove the schedule.

You create or edit schedules by completing the following steps:

1. Click New to open the New Job Schedule dialog box, or click Edit to open the Edit Job Schedule dialog box. These dialog boxes are essentially the same except for the title. Figure 10-11 shows the New Job Schedule dialog box.

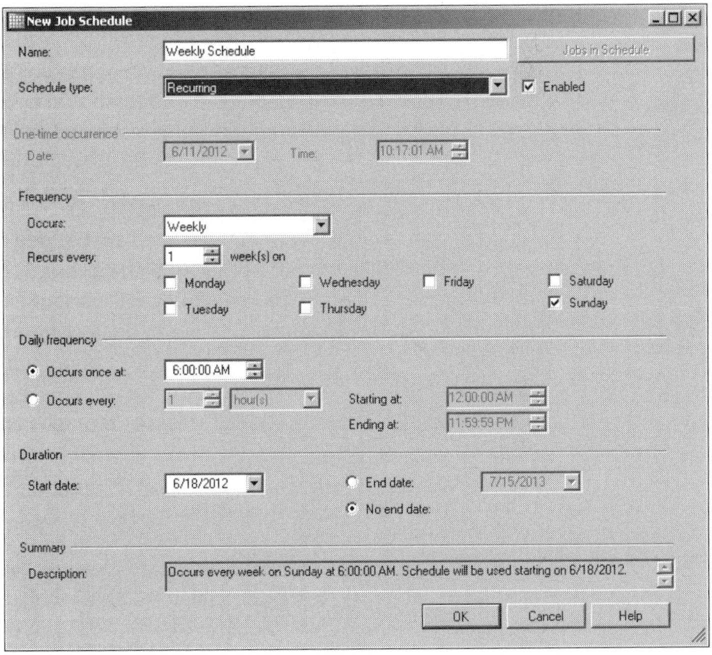

FIGURE 10-11 The New Job Schedule dialog box.

2. Type a name for the schedule, and then select one of the following schedule types:

- **Start Automatically When SQL Server Agent Starts**   Runs the job automatically whenever SQL Server Agent starts.
- **Start Whenever The CPUs Become Idle**   Runs the job whenever the CPU is idle. CPU idle time is specified on the Advanced page of the SQL Server Agent Properties dialog box.

- **One Time**   Runs the job once at the date and time specified in the Date and Time boxes.
- **Recurring**   Runs the job according to the recurring schedule displayed.

3. Recurring jobs are the ones that need the most explanation. You can schedule recurring jobs to run on a daily, weekly, or monthly basis. To run the job on a daily basis, choose Daily from the Occurs list, and then use the Recurs Every box to set the run interval. Daily recurring jobs can run every day, every other day, or every Nth day.

4. To run the job on a weekly basis, choose Weekly from the Occurs list, and then configure the job using these boxes:
   - **Recurs Every Nth Week(s)**   Allows you to run the task every week, every other week, or every Nth week.
   - **Check boxes for days of the week**   Set the day or days of the week on which the task runs, such as on Monday or on Monday, Wednesday, and Friday.

5. To run the job on a monthly basis, choose Monthly from the Occurs list, and then configure the job using these boxes:
   - **Day N Of Every Nth Month**   Sets the day of the month and specifies in which months the job runs. For example, if you select Day 15 of every second month, the job runs on the 15th day of alternating months.
   - **The Nth Day Of Every Nth Month**   Sets the job to run on the Nth occurrence of a day in a given month, such as the second Monday of every month or the third Sunday of every other month.

6. Set the Daily Frequency for the daily, weekly, or monthly job. You can configure jobs to run one or more times on their scheduled run date. To run the job once on a given date, select Occurs Once At and then set a time. To run the job several times on a given date, select Occurs Every and then set a time interval in hours or minutes. Afterward, set a starting and ending time, such as from 7:30 A.M. to 5:30 P.M.

7. By default, schedules begin on the current date and do not have a designated end date. To change this behavior, select the End Date option, and then use the Start Date and End Date boxes to set a new duration for the schedule.

8. Click OK to complete the schedule process.

Handling Job Alerts

Alerts can be generated when jobs are run. You can define and manage job-specific alerts by using the Alerts page of the New Job dialog box. To configure alerts, complete the following steps:

1. Access the Alerts page of the job you want to configure.

2. Any current alerts are listed by name and type. You can take the following actions for an alert:

- Edit an alert by selecting it and clicking Edit.
- Add an alert by clicking Add to display the New Alert dialog box. Use the dialog box features to define the alert as discussed previously.
- Remove an alert by selecting it and clicking Remove.

Handling Notification Messages

Notification messages are generated when a job succeeds, fails, or completes. You can handle these messages in several ways. You can notify operators, log the related event, automatically delete the job, and more. To configure notification, complete the following steps:

1. Access the Notifications page of the job you want to configure. This page is shown in Figure 10-12.

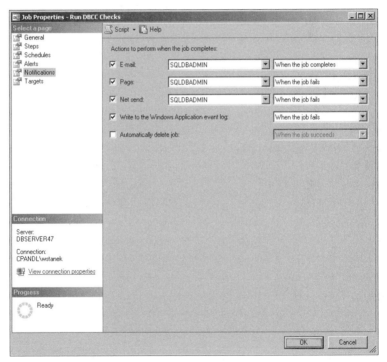

FIGURE 10-12 The Notifications page of the Job Properties dialog box.

2. You can notify operators by using an email message, a page, or a Net Send message. Select the check box for the technique you want to use. Choose an operator to handle the notification, and then choose a notification type. Repeat this process to configure other notification methods.

3. To log a particular type of notification message in the event log, select the Write To The Windows Application Event Log check box, and then select the notification type to log. Usually, you want to log failure, so select When The Job Fails.

4. To delete a job upon notification, select the Automatically Delete Job check box, and then choose the notification type that triggers the deletion.

5. Click OK.

Managing Existing Jobs

In SQL Server Management Studio, you manage jobs with SQL Server Agent. To do that, complete the following steps:

1. In SQL Server Management Studio, access the SQL Server Agent entry on the server running SQL Server Agent.

2. Expand the SQL Server Agent and Jobs folders.

3. Now you can double-click a job entry to access its related Properties dialog box, or right-click a job entry to display a shortcut menu. The following commands are available on the shortcut menu:

   - **Delete**   Deletes the job definition. Before deleting a complex job, you might want to create a script that can be used to re-create the job.

   - **Disable**   Disables the job so that it will not run.

   - **Enable**   Enables the job so that it will run.

   - **Rename**   Allows you to rename the job. Type the new name, and then press Enter or Tab.

   - **Script Job As**   Choose Create To, and then select File to generate a T-SQL script file that you can use to re-create the job.

   - **Start Job At Step**   Starts the selected job if it is not already running.

   - **Stop Job**   Stops the selected job if it is running.

   - **View History**   Displays the Log File Viewer dialog box. This dialog box lets you view summary or detail information about the job execution.

Managing Job Categories

You use job categories to organize jobs into topical folders. When you install SQL Server, default job categories are created automatically. You can add new job categories and change the existing categories at any time.

Working with Job Categories

To create a new job category or update an existing category, complete the following steps:

1. In SQL Server Management Studio, access the SQL Server Agent entry on the server running SQL Server Agent.

2. Expand the SQL Server Agent folder. Right-click Jobs, and then choose Manage Job Categories. This displays the Manage Job Categories dialog box.

3. You can delete a category by selecting it and clicking Delete.

4. You can view the jobs associated with a category by selecting it and clicking View Jobs.

5. To add a category or to change the properties of a category, follow the steps outlined in the following sections, "Creating Job Categories" and "Updating Job Categories."

Creating Job Categories

You can create a new job category by completing the following steps:

1. Access the Manage Job Categories dialog box as explained previously. Click Add to display a Properties dialog box.

2. Type a name for the category in the Name text box, and then select the Show All Jobs check box.

3. All jobs defined on the current server should be listed now. Add a job to the new category by selecting the corresponding check box in the Select column. Remove a job from the new category by clearing the corresponding check box in the Select column.

4. Click OK.

Updating Job Categories

You can update an existing job category by completing the following steps:

1. Access the Manage Job Categories dialog box as explained previously. Click View Jobs to display a New Job Category Properties dialog box.

2. Select the Show All Jobs check box. All jobs defined on the current server should be listed now.

3. Add a job to a new category by selecting the corresponding check box in the Select column. Remove a job from the category by clearing the corresponding check box in the Select column.

4. Click OK.

Automating Routine Server-to-Server Administration Tasks

Any time you deploy multiple computers that run SQL Server or multiple instances of SQL Server within an organization, you need a way to handle routine server-to-server administration tasks. For example, if you have a database on one server, you might need to copy user accounts from one server to another. SQL Server 2012 allows you to automate routine server-to-server administration tasks by using scripts. You can write the scripts to the Query Editor or save them to a file for later use.

The server-to-server administration tasks you can automate include the following:

- Copying user accounts, tables, views, and other objects from one database to another
- Copying alerts, operators, and scheduled jobs from one server to another

The sections that follow explain how you can automate these administration tasks.

Copying User Accounts, Tables, Views, and Other Objects from One Database to Another

Using the Script Wizard, you can generate T-SQL scripts that allow you to re-create the objects contained in a specified database. Scripts can be written to the Query Editor window so that you can run them immediately, or they can be saved to files so that you can run them later. By running a script against a database other than the one from which it was generated, you can create copies of objects in other databases.

Script options summarized in Table 10-1 determine how the copy operation works.

TABLE 10-1 Script Options for the Script Wizard

SCRIPT OPTION	DEFAULT	WHEN TRUE
ANSI Padding	True	Generates statements about ANSI padding.
Append To File	False	Appends the script to an existing file rather than overwriting the file.
Check For Object Existence	False	If the object exists, drops or alters. If the object doesn't exist, creates.
Continue Scripting On Error	False	Continues writing the script if an error occurs.
Convert UDDTs To Base Types	False	Converts user-defined data types (UDDTs) to base types.
Generate Script For Dependent Objects	False	Scripts dependent objects.
Include Descriptive Headers	True	Includes descriptive header comments for each object scripted. (Does not affect how objects are created later; it only sets comments.)

SCRIPT OPTION	DEFAULT	WHEN TRUE
Include System Constraint Names	False	Includes system-generated constraint names to enforce declarative referential integrity.
Include Unsupported Statements	False	Includes statements that are not supported on the specified server instance type.
Schema Qualify Object Names	True	Prefixes object names with the object schema.
Script Bindings	False	Includes options to set binding.
Script Change Tracking	False	Includes the change-tracking information.
Script Check Constraints	True	Checks constraints for each table or view scripted.
Script Collation	False	Writes the collation settings of the object to the script.
Script Data Compression Options	False	Includes the data-compression information.
Script Defaults	True	Scripts the default values for the object.
Script Drop and Create	Script Create	Scripts the CREATE statement for an object; when false, scripts the DROP and CREATE statements.
Script Extended Properties	True	Scripts the extended properties of objects.
Script For Server Version	SQL Server 2012	Creates the script to be compatible with the specified SQL Server version.
Script For The Database Engine Type	Stand-alone Instance	Scripts only features compatible for the specified server instance type. You can specify a stand-alone instance or a SQL Azure database.
Script Foreign Keys	True	Scripts foreign keys for each table or view scripted.
Script Full-Text Indexes	False	Scripts full-text indexes for each table or view scripted.

SCRIPT OPTION	DEFAULT	WHEN TRUE
Script Indexes	False	Scripts indexes for each table or view scripted.
Script Logins	False	Scripts all logins available on the server. Passwords are not scripted.
Script Object-Level Permissions	False	Scripts permissions for the object as per the original database.
Script Primary Keys	True	Scripts primary keys for each table or view scripted.
Script Statistics	Do Not Script Statistics	Controls whether statistics for table or indexed view objects are scripted.
Script Triggers	True	Scripts triggers for each table or view scripted.
Script Unique Keys	True	Scripts unique keys for each table or view scripted.
Script Use Database	True	Sets a USE statement with the name of the original database at the top of the script.
Types Of Data To Script	Schema only	Controls the types of included elements as schema only, schema and data, or data only.

You can create copies of objects by completing the following steps:

1. Start SQL Server Management Studio, and then access the server of your choice.

2. In the Object Explorer view, expand Databases, right-click a database, point to Tasks, and then select Generate Scripts. This starts the Generate And Publish Scripts Wizard. If the Introduction page is displayed, click Next.

3. Select the check boxes for the objects you want to script, and then click Next. Objects you can script include database roles, database triggers, schemas, stored procedures, tables, user-defined functions, users, and views. You can also choose to script the entire database and all database objects.

4. Choose an output option. You can create the script as a file, publish it to a web service such as SQL Azure, copy it to the Clipboard, or send it to a New Query Editor window.

5. Click Advanced. Set the script options summarized in Table 10-1 to determine how the copy operation works, and then click Next. When you publish a

script to a web service, you have a similar (but reduced) set of options, and the default values are different in some instances. You also need to specify a provider and target database.

6. Click Next to review the options, and then click Next again to create the script or publish it to the destination you specified.

7. Review the save or publishing results. If any errors occurred, use the links provided to get more information, correct any problems, and then repeat this entire procedure. Optionally, click Save Report to generate a detailed report. Click Finish.

Copying Alerts, Operators, and Scheduled Jobs from One Server to Another

You use alerts, operators, and scheduled jobs to automate routine administration tasks. If you have already created alerts, operators, and jobs on one server, you can reuse them on another server. To do this, you create a script for the alert, operator, or job you want to copy, and then you run the script against a target server. You need to edit a job's properties to ensure that they make sense for the target server. For example, if you created a set of jobs to check the Support database periodically and then added custom steps to handle various database states, you could copy these jobs to another server and then edit the job properties to apply the tasks to the Customer database on the target server.

You can copy alerts, operators, or jobs from one server to another server by completing the following steps:

1. In SQL Server Management Studio, access the SQL Server Agent entry on the server running SQL Server Agent.

2. Expand the SQL Server Agent folder, and then expand the Alerts, Jobs, or Operators folder as appropriate for the type of object you are copying.

3. Right-click the alert, operator, or job, point to Script...As, Create To, and then select File. In the Save As dialog box, specify the save location and name for the T-SQL script file. Click Save.

4. Use the Object Explorer view to connect to the server on which you want to create the new alert, operator, or job. Right-click the server in the Object Explorer view, and then select New Query.

5. Click Open File or press Ctrl+O. Select the script file you previously created. The script is set to use the *msdb* database because alert, job, and operator objects are stored in that database.

6. Click Execute or press F5 to run the script and create the object in the *msdb* database.

Multiserver Administration

Multiserver administration allows you to use one server to manage alerts and job scheduling for other servers from a central location. You centrally manage alerts through event forwarding. You centrally manage job scheduling by designating master servers and target servers.

Event Forwarding

If you have multiple instances of SQL Server running on multiple systems throughout the network, event forwarding is a time and resource saver. With event forwarding, you can forward application log events to a central server and then process those events on this server. Thus, rather than having to configure alerts on 12 different server instances, you configure event forwarding on 11 servers and have 1 server handle all the incoming events. You can then use the application log's Computer field to determine the system on which the event occurred and take the appropriate corrective actions by using scripts or remote procedure calls.

To configure event forwarding, complete the following steps:

1. In SQL Server Management Studio, access the SQL Server Agent entry on the server running SQL Server Agent.

2. Right-click the SQL Server Agent entry, and then select Properties.

3. Select the Advanced page of the SQL Server Agent Properties dialog box, shown in Figure 10-13.

4. Select the Forward Events To A Different Server check box.

5. Use the Server box to type the name of a registered server that will handle the events. If the server you want to use is not registered, you need to register it and then access the SQL Server Agent Properties dialog box again.

6. Set the type of events to forward by selecting Unhandled Events or All Events. An unhandled event is one that you have not configured alerts for on the current server.

7. In the If Event Has Severity At Or Above list, select the severity threshold for events that are forwarded.

   TIP To reduce network traffic caused by event forwarding, set the severity threshold to a fairly high value. Fatal errors have a severity level of 19 through 25.

8. Click OK.

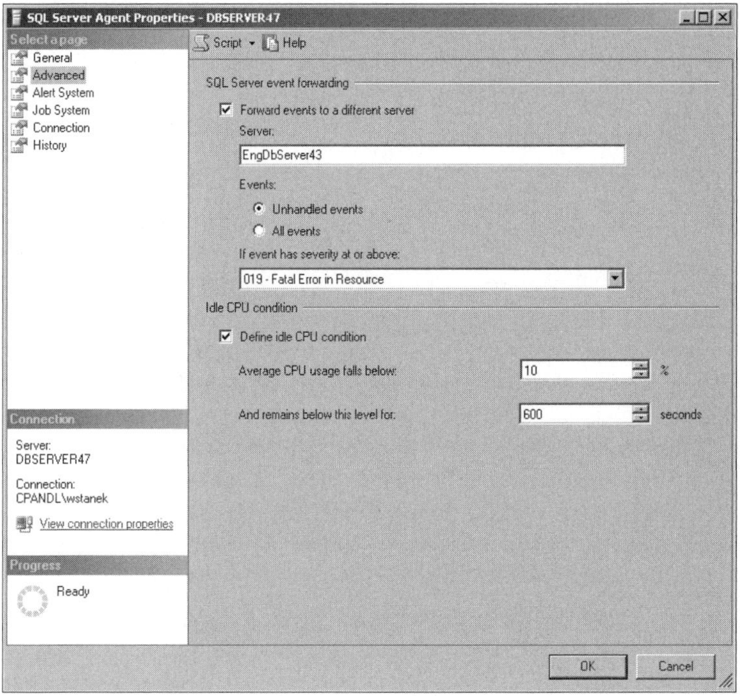

FIGURE 10-13 The Advanced page of the SQL Server Agent Properties dialog box.

Multiserver Job Scheduling

When you want to manage job scheduling centrally, you need to create a master server and one or more target servers. The SQL Server Agent running on the master server can do the following:

- Manage jobs centrally for the target servers. Then you can create jobs on the master server that run on the targets. For details, see the "Assigning or Changing Job Definitions" section earlier in this chapter.

- Download jobs to a target. For details, see the "Managing Existing Jobs" section earlier in this chapter.

Multiserver Scheduling Requirements

For the master/target relationship to work correctly, you must do the following:

- Be sure that the master server and all target servers are running SQL Server 2008 or later.

- Use domain accounts, not local accounts, when configuring the master and targets.
- Be sure that SQL Server Agent is running on the master server and all target servers.

Configuring Master Servers

To create a master server, complete the following steps:

1. In SQL Server Management Studio, access the SQL Server Agent entry on the server running SQL Server Agent.

2. Right-click the SQL Server Agent entry, point to Multi Server Administration, and then select Make This A Master. This starts the Master Server Wizard.

3. If the Welcome page is displayed, click Next.

4. As shown in Figure 10-14, create a special operator to handle multiserver job notifications. This operator, called the Master Server Operator, is created on the master and on all target servers that use this master. Set an email, a pager, and a Net Send address as appropriate. You can change this information later by editing the Master Server Operator properties on the master server. Click Next.

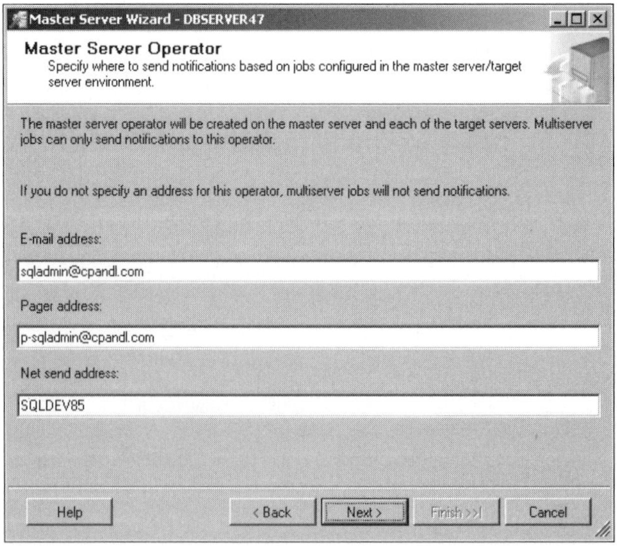

FIGURE 10-14 The Master Server Operator page of the Master Server Wizard.

5. Select the target servers to associate with this master server. If a server is not registered, you can add a connection for it by clicking Add Connection. The process of associating target servers with a master is called *enlisting*. Later, you

can remove the association by right-clicking SQL Server Agent in SQL Server Management Studio, selecting Multi Server Administration, and then selecting Manage Target Servers.

6. When you click Next, the wizard checks to be sure that the versions of SQL Server running on the master and target servers are compatible. If target servers are running different versions of SQL Server, note any compatibility issues listed. Click Close.

7. The target servers use the SQL Server Agent account and Windows security to connect to the master server and download jobs. If appropriate rights aren't assigned to this account, a new login, assigned the appropriate rights, may be needed. By default, a new login is created if needed. If you don't want a new login to be created, clear the Create A New Login check box.

8. Click Next, and then click Finish. The wizard performs the necessary tasks and reports its progress. You will be notified of any errors.

9. Click Close when the configuration is finished.

Configuring Target Servers

You can configure one or more target servers for each master server. You create target servers by completing the following steps:

1. In SQL Server Management Studio, access the SQL Server Agent entry on the server running SQL Server Agent.

2. Right-click the SQL Server Agent entry, point to Multi Server Administration, and then select Make This A Target. This starts the Make TSX Wizard.

3. If the Welcome page is displayed, click Next.

4. Click Pick Server to select a master server for this target server. Use the Connect To Server dialog box to connect to the master server. The master server is the source server from which SQL Server Agent jobs will be downloaded.

5. When you click Next, the wizard checks to be sure that the versions of SQL Server running on the master and target servers are compatible. If target servers are running different versions of SQL Server, note any compatibility issues listed. Click Close.

6. The target server uses the SQL Server Agent account and Windows security to connect to the master server and download jobs. If appropriate rights aren't assigned to this account, a new login, assigned the appropriate rights, may be needed. By default, a new login is created if needed. If you don't want a new login to be created, clear the Create A New Login check box.

7. Click Next, and then click Finish. The wizard performs the necessary tasks and reports its progress. You will be notified of any errors.

8. Click Close when the configuration is finished.

Database Maintenance

Database maintenance involves various tasks. Most of these tasks have been discussed in previous chapters; this section does not go into detail about tasks already covered. Instead, I've provided checklists that you can use as a starting point for your maintenance efforts. The rest of the section explains how to set up maintenance plans and run database consistency checks.

Database Maintenance Checklists

The following checklists provide recommended daily, weekly, and monthly maintenance tasks.

Daily

- Monitor application, server, and agent logs.
- Configure alerts for important errors that are not configured for alert notification.
- Check for performance and error alert messages.
- Monitor job status, particularly jobs that back up databases and perform replication.
- Review the output from jobs in the job history or output file or in both.
- Back up databases and logs (as necessary and if not configured as automatic jobs).

Weekly

- Monitor available disk space on drives.
- Monitor the status of linked, remote, master, and target servers.
- Check the maintenance plan reports and history to determine the status of maintenance plan operations.

Monthly

- Monitor server performance, tweaking performance parameters to improve response time.
- Manage logins and server roles.
- Audit server, database, and object permissions to ensure that only authorized users have access.
- Review alert, job, and operator configurations.

As Needed

- Back up the SQL Server registry data.
- Generate an updated record of configuration information by executing sp_configure.

- Run database integrity checks (and always prior to any full backups).
- Update database statistics. (SQL Server 2012 handles this automatically in most cases.)

Using Maintenance Plans

Maintenance plans provide an automated way to perform essential maintenance tasks. You can run a maintenance plan against a single database or multiple databases running on a designated target server. You can also generate report histories for maintenance plan execution.

You create maintenance plans with the Maintenance Plan Wizard or with the Maintenance Plan Package Designer. Both techniques are similar:

- With the wizard, the wizard's pages guide you through the steps of selecting maintenance tasks to perform, configuring execution history logging, and setting an execution schedule. When you complete the wizard steps, the wizard generates the package that performs the designated maintenance tasks.

- With the package designer, you specify servers, add tasks to perform from a predefined list of maintenance tasks, and configure execution history logging as necessary. After you configure connections to the server on which you want to perform maintenance, you build the maintenance plan by dragging tasks from the Maintenance Plan Tasks toolbox to the design window. The order in which you add tasks sets the order of execution. If a task requires additional input, such as database or server names, double-clicking the task opens a Properties dialog box that lets you specify the information that's needed.

The set of maintenance tasks you can perform is similar whether you are working with the wizard or the designer:

- **Back Up Database** Allows you to specify the source databases and the destination files or tapes and overwrite options for a full, differential, or transaction log backup. In the wizard interface, there are separate task listings for each backup type.

- **Check Database Integrity** Performs internal consistency checks of the data and index pages on the designated databases.

- **Execute SQL Server Agent Job** Allows you to select SQL Server Agent jobs to run as part of the maintenance plan.

- **Execute T-SQL Statement** Allows you to run any T-SQL script as part of the maintenance plan. (Available only in the Maintenance Plan Package Designer.)

- **Clean Up History** Deletes historical data about backup and restore, SQL Server Agent, and maintenance plan operations.

- **Maintenance Cleanup** Deletes files created when executing maintenance plans.

- **Notify Operator**   Sends an email message to a designated SQL Server Agent operator. (Available only in the Maintenance Plan Package Designer.)
- **Rebuild Index**   Rebuilds indexes to improve the performance of index scans and seeks. This task also optimizes the distribution of data and free space on the index pages, allowing for faster future growth.
- **Reorganize Index**   Defragments and compacts clustered and nonclustered indexes on tables and views to improve index-scanning performance.
- **Shrink Database**   Reduces the disk space used by the designated databases by removing empty data and log pages.
- **Update Statistics**   Updates the query optimizer statistics regarding the distribution of data values in the tables. This improves the query optimizer's ability to determine data access strategies, which can ultimately improve query performance.

When you first start working with maintenance plans, you probably want to run the Maintenance Plan Wizard and let the wizard design the necessary package for you. After you have created a package, you can modify it in the Maintenance Plan Package Designer view.

TIP   For most installations, I recommend configuring separate maintenance plans for system and user databases. This approach gives you greater flexibility for determining how and when maintenance operations are performed. For large installations, you might want to have separate maintenance plans for each database so that you can work with different databases on different days or at different times of the day.

Creating Maintenance Plans

You can create a maintenance plan by completing the following steps:

1. In SQL Server Management Studio, access the Management folder on the server where you want to create the maintenance plan. This can be a different server from the one on which the maintenance plan will run.

2. Right-click Maintenance Plans, and then select Maintenance Plan Wizard.

3. If the Welcome page is displayed, click Next. Type a name and description for the maintenance plan, such as Engineering DB Server Maintenance and Backup Plan.

4. By default, maintenance plans run on demand, which means you must start them manually. You also can schedule maintenance plans to run automatically. If you want each maintenance task to have a separate run schedule, select Separate Schedule For Each Task. When you configure each task later, create the necessary schedule by clicking Change, setting a run schedule, and then clicking OK. If you want to use a single run schedule for the entire plan, select Single Schedule For The Entire Plan Or No Schedule, click Change, set a run schedule, and then click OK. Click Next when you are ready to continue.

5. As shown in Figure 10-15, select the check boxes for the maintenance tasks you want to perform, and then click Next. The order in which tasks are listed on the Select Maintenance Task Order page determines the order in which the tasks are executed. Select a task, and then click the Move Up or Move Down button as appropriate to change the task's order. When the tasks are in the run order you want to use, click Next.

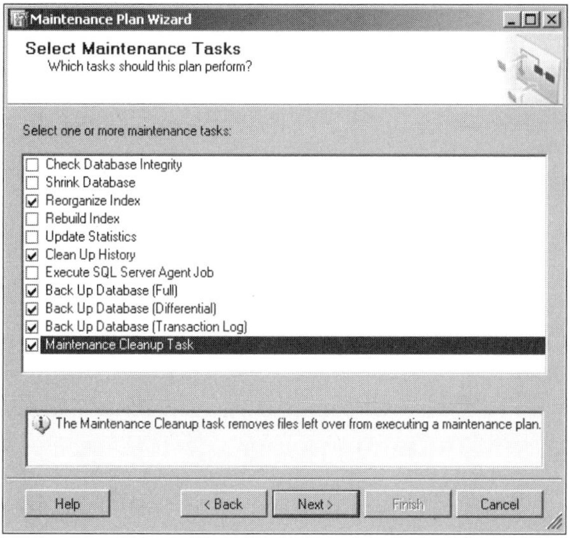

FIGURE 10-15 The Select Maintenance Tasks page of the Maintenance Plan Wizard.

6. Next, for each task that can be applied to one or more databases, you need to choose the database or databases on which the tasks will be performed. Typically, you can perform a task on all databases, all system databases, all user databases, or a combination of one or more individual databases. You might also need to configure individual task parameters. When you finish configuring tasks, click Next. Following are guidelines for each task:

- **Back Up Database** Select the databases for which you want to create a full, differential, or transaction log backup. You can back up to disk or to tape and either append or overwrite existing backup files. Typically, you want to create a backup file for every selected database. With disk-based backups, you can set a specific backup directory and create subdirectories for each database being backed up. You can also set the file extension for the backups. The default extension is .bak. To verify the integrity of backups upon completion, select Verify Backup Integrity.

- **Check Database Integrity** Select the databases on which you want to perform internal consistency checks. By default, both data and index pages are checked. If you want to check only data pages, clear Include Indexes.

- **Execute SQL Server Agent Job**   Select SQL Server Agent jobs to run as part of the maintenance plan. Any available jobs on the server are listed, and you can select the related check box to execute the job whenever the maintenance plan runs.

- **Cleanup History**   Historical data about backup and restore, SQL Server Agent, and maintenance plan operations is stored in the msdb database. When the history cleanup task runs, any historical data that is older than four weeks is deleted on the target server by default. You can modify the type of historical data cleaned up and set the Older Than criteria to different values. For example, you might find that you need to maintain historical data for a full quarter. If so, set Remove Historical Data Older Than to 3 Months.

- **Rebuild Index**   Select the databases on which you want to rebuild indexes. If you select specific databases, you can specify whether all table and view indexes are rebuilt or only a specific table or view index is rebuilt. For example, if you want to rebuild the NWCustomer view in the *Orders* database, click in the Databases list, select These Databases, choose the *Orders* database, and then click OK.

Next, under Object, select View, and then click in the Selection list. Select These Objects, choose dbo.NWCustomers, and then click OK. The affected indexes are dropped and re-created with a new fill factor. You can choose Default Free Space Per Page to re-create indexes with the fill factor that was specified when the indexes were created. Choose Change Free Space Per Page To if you want to specify a new fill factor. The higher the percentage, the more free space is reserved on the index pages and the larger the index grows. Valid values are 0 through 100.

NOTE   Fill factors are discussed in the "Setting the Index Fill" section in Chapter 5, "Tuning and Linking Your SQL Servers." Reorganizing pages changes table indexes and thus invalidates existing statistics. You cannot reorganize data and update statistics in the same plan, and you might want to create separate maintenance plans for handling each of these important tasks.

- **Reorganize Index**   Select the databases you want to defragment and compact. If you select specific databases, you can specify whether all tables and views are reorganized or only a specific table or view is reorganized. For example, if you want to reorganize the Customers table in the *Orders* database, click in the Databases list, select These Databases, choose the *Orders* database, and then click OK. Next, under Object, select Table, and then click in the Selection list. Select These Objects, choose dbo.Customers, and then click OK.

- **Shrink Database**   Select the databases on which you want to reduce disk space by removing empty data and log pages. Use Shrink Database When It Grows Beyond to specify the database size that triggers this task. Free space in a database is removed only when the size of the database file exceeds this value. The default value is 50 MB, which means that if there is more than 50 MB of free space, SQL Server will shrink the database to the size specified. Use Amount Of Free Space To Remain After Shrink to set the amount of unused space that should remain after the database is reduced in size. The value is based on the percentage of the actual data in the database. The default value is 10 percent. Valid values are 0 through 100. Free space can be returned to the operating system or retained for future use by the database.

- **Update Statistics**   Select the databases on which you want to update query optimizer statistics. If you select specific databases, you can specify whether statistics for all tables and views are updated or only a specific table or view is updated. By default, both column and index statistics are updated. You also can specify to update only column or index statistics.

7. Use the Select Report Options page to determine how maintenance plan reports are handled. By default, whenever a maintenance plan runs, a report is generated. The report can be written to a file in any designated folder location, sent by email to a SQL Server Agent operator, or both. Click Next.

8. Review the maintenance plan. Click Finish to complete the process and generate the SQL Server Agent job to handle the designated maintenance tasks. These jobs are labeled according to the name of the maintenance plan. Click Close.

Checking Maintenance Reports and History

Creating a maintenance plan is only the beginning. After you create a plan, you need to check maintenance reports and history periodically. Maintenance reports are stored as text files in a designated directory, sent as email messages to designated SQL Server Agent operators, or both. You can view file-based reports in a standard text editor or word processor. To access maintenance history through SQL Server Management Studio, complete the following steps:

1. In SQL Server Management Studio, access the Management folder on the server of your choice.

2. Right-click Maintenance Plans, and then select View History. This displays the Log File Viewer.

3. Under Select Logs in the left pane, Maintenance Plans should be selected by default. There should also be a log entry for each maintenance plan configured on the server.

4. Choose the maintenance plan or plans for which you want to review a job history.

5. Use the summary in the right pane to review the job history. Click Close when you finish.

Viewing, Editing, Running, and Deleting Maintenance Plans

You can view, edit, run, or delete maintenance plans by completing the following steps:

1. In SQL Server Management Studio, access the Management folder on the server of your choice.

2. Select Maintenance Plans in the left pane. You will see existing maintenance plans in the right pane.

3. Now you can do the following:

    *   View or edit a maintenance plan by double-clicking the maintenance plan entry in the right pane. This opens the plan in the Maintenance Plan Package Designer.

    *   Delete a maintenance plan by selecting its entry and pressing Delete. In the Delete Object dialog box, click OK to confirm the deletion.

    *   Execute the maintenance plan by right-clicking it and selecting Execute.

Checking and Maintaining Database Integrity

When you need to perform database integrity checks, such as before a full backup or after a restore, you can use maintenance plans to handle most of the work. On the rare occasions when you want to perform consistency checks manually, you use the DBCC command. DBCC stands for *database consistency check*. There are many different DBCC commands. The ones you use most often to maintain a database are covered in the following sections.

Using DBCC CHECKDB

The DBCC CHECKDB command checks the consistency of the entire database and is the primary method used to check for database corruption. The command ensures the following:

*   Index and data pages are linked correctly.
*   Indexes are up to date and sorted properly.
*   Pointers are consistent.
*   The data on each page is up to date.
*   Page offsets are up to date.
*   Indexed views, varbinary(max) data in the file system, and Service Broker data are validated.

NOTE When you run DBCC CHECKDB, you do not have to run DBCC CHECKALLOC on the database, DBCC CHECKTABLE on every table and view in the database, or DBCC CHECKCATALOG on database catalogs. DBCC CHECKDB performs similar validation tasks for you.

Sample 10-1 shows the syntax and usage for the DBCC CHECKDB command. When you run the command without a repair option, errors are reported but not corrected. To correct errors, you need to put the database in single-user mode and then set a repair option. After you repair the database, create a backup.

SAMPLE 10-1 DBCC CHECKDB Syntax and Usage.

Syntax

```
DBCC CHECKDB
(    'database_name' | database_id | 0
    [ , NOINDEX | { REPAIR_ALLOW_DATA_LOSS
    | REPAIR_FAST | REPAIR_REBUILD } ] )
    [ WITH {
            [ ALL_ERRORMSGS ]
            [ , ESTIMATEONLY ]
            [ , EXTENDED_LOGICAL_CHECKS ]
            [ , NO_INFOMSGS ]
            [ , TABLOCK ]
            [ , { PHYSICAL_ONLY | DATA_PURITY } ]
    } ]
```

Usage

```
DBCC CHECKDB ('customer', NOINDEX)
DBCC CHECKDB ('customer', REPAIR_REBUILD)
```

The three repair options are REPAIR_FAST, REPAIR_REBUILD, and REPAIR_ALLOW_DATA_LOSS. The REPAIR_FAST option performs minor repairs that do not consume a lot of time and will not result in data loss. The REPAIR_REBUILD option performs comprehensive error checking and correction that requires more time to complete and does not result in data loss (but the database must be in single-user mode). The REPAIR_ALLOW_DATA_LOSS option performs all the actions of REPAIR_REBUILD and adds new tasks that might result in data loss. These tasks include allocating and deallocating rows to correct structural problems and page errors as well as deleting corrupt text objects.

TIP When trying to fix database problems, start with REPAIR_FAST or REPAIR_REBUILD. If these options do not resolve the problem, you might want to try rebuilding non-clustered indexes in the database because this sometimes will repair corruption with data loss. As a last resort, you can try the REPAIR_ALLOW_DATA_LOSS option. Remember that running the REPAIR_ALLOW_DATA_LOSS option might result in an unacceptable loss of important data. To ensure that you can recover the database in its original state, place the DBCC command in a transaction so that you can inspect the results and roll back the transaction if necessary.

Using DBCC CHECKTABLE

To correct problems with individual tables, you can use the DBCC CHECKTABLE command. As shown in Sample 10-2, the syntax and usage for this command are almost the same as for DBCC CHECKDB. The database you want to work with must be selected for use.

SAMPLE 10-2 DBCC CHECKTABLE Syntax and Usage.

Syntax

```
DBCC CHECKTABLE
(   'table_name' | 'view_name'
    [ , NOINDEX | index_id
    | { REPAIR_ALLOW_DATA_LOSS | REPAIR_FAST
    | REPAIR_REBUILD } ] )
    [ WITH {
            [ ALL_ERRORMSGS ]
            [ , ESTIMATEONLY ]
            [ , EXTENDED_LOGICAL_CHECKS ]
            [ , NO_INFOMSGS ]
            [ , TABLOCK ]
            [ , { PHYSICAL_ONLY | DATA_PURITY } ]
    } ]
```

Usage

```
DBCC CHECKTABLE ('receipts')
DBCC CHECKTABLE ('receipts', REPAIR_REBUILD)
```

Using DBCC CHECKALLOC

To check the consistency of database pages, you can use DBCC CHECKALLOC. Again, the syntax for this command is nearly identical to the previous DBCC commands. One item worth noting is that Sample 10-3 shows a NOINDEX option that is maintained only for backward compatibility with previous SQL Server versions. The command always checks the consistency of page indexes.

SAMPLE 10-3 DBCC CHECKALLOC Syntax and Usage.

Syntax

```
DBCC CHECKALLOC
(    [ 'database_name' | database_id | 0 ]
        [ , NOINDEX
    | { REPAIR_ALLOW_DATA_LOSS
    | REPAIR_FAST | REPAIR_REBUILD } ] )
    [ WITH { [ ALL_ERRORMSGS ]
            [ , NO_INFOMSGS ]
            [ , TABLOCK ]
            [ , ESTIMATEONLY ] }
    ]
```

```
DBCC CHECKALLOC ('customer')
DBCC CHECKALLOC ('customer', REPAIR_REBUILD)
```

Using DBCC CHECKCATALOG

Another useful DBCC command is DBCC CHECKCATALOG. You use this command to check the consistency of a database's systems tables. Sample 10-4 shows the syntax and usage of this command.

SAMPLE 10-4 DBCC CHECKCATALOG Syntax and Usage.

Syntax

```
DBCC CHECKCATALOG
[ ( 'database_name' | database_id | 0 ) ]
    [ WITH NO_INFOMSGS ]
```

Usage

```
DBCC CHECKCATALOG ('customer')
```

Using DBCC CHECKIDENT

You use the DBCC CHECKIDENT command to check a table's identity value and set a new identity value. Sample 10-5 shows the syntax and usage of this command.

SAMPLE 10-5 DBCC CHECKIDENT Syntax and Usage.

Syntax

```
DBCC CHECKIDENT
( table_name
    [ , { NORESEED | { RESEED [ ' new_reseed_value ] } } ] )
    [ WITH NO_INFOMSGS]
```

Usage

```
DBCC CHECKIDENT ('customer', NORESEED)
DBCC CHECKIDENT ('customer', RESEED, 50)
```

Using DBCC CHECKFILEGROUP

To check the allocation and structural integrity of all table and index views in a filegroup, you can use the DBCC CHECKFILEGROUP command. Sample 10-6 shows the syntax and usage of this command.

SAMPLE 10-6 DBCC CHECKFILEGROUP Syntax and Usage.

Syntax

```
DBCC CHECKFILEGROUP
[
    [ ( { filegroup | filegroup_id | 0 }
        [ , NOINDEX ] ) ]
    [ WITH {
```

```
      [ ALL_ERRORMSGS | NO_INFOMSGS ]
      [ , TABLOCK ]
      [ , ESTIMATEONLY ] } ] ]
```

Usage

```
USE CUSTOMER
GO
DBCC CHECKFILEGROUP (1, NOINDEX)
GO
```

Using DBCC UPDATEUSAGE

To report and correct pages and row count inaccuracies in catalog views, you can use DBCC UPDATEUSAGE. Sample 10-7 shows the syntax and usage of this command.

SAMPLE 10-7 DBCC UPDATEUSAGE Syntax and Usage.

Syntax

```
DBCC UPDATEUSAGE
    (    { database_name | database_id | 0 }
    [ , { table_name | table_id | view_name | view_id }
    [ , { index_name | index_id } ] ]
        ) [ WITH [ NO_INFOMSGS ] [ , ] [ COUNT_ROWS ]
    ]
```

Usage

```
DBCC UPDATEUSAGE ('CustomerDB')
DBCC UPDATEUSAGE ('CustomerDB', 'Inventory.Item')
```

However, updating usage can be time-consuming, and you might not see any benefit from this because SQL Server 2012 does a good job of intrinsically maintaining row counts and accurately reporting page counts.

SQL Server 2012 Backup and Recovery

Information is the fuel that drives the enterprise, and the most critical information is often stored in databases. Databases are where you find an organization's customer account information, partner directories, product knowledge base, and other important data. To protect an organization's data and to ensure the availability of its databases, you need a solid database backup and recovery plan.

Backing up databases can protect against accidental loss of data, database corruption, hardware failures, and even damage from natural disasters. It is your job as a database administrator to perform backups and store the backups you create in a safe and secure location.

Creating a Backup and Recovery Plan

Creating and implementing a backup and recovery plan is one of your most important duties as a database administrator. Think of database backup as an insurance plan for the future—and for your job. Important data is deleted accidentally all the time. Mission-critical data can become corrupt. Natural disasters can leave your office in ruins. With a solid backup and recovery plan in place, you can recover from any of these situations. Without one, you are left with nothing after a disaster of any kind.

Initial Backup and Recovery Planning

Creating and implementing a backup and recovery plan takes time. You need to figure out which databases need to be backed up, how often the databases should be backed up, and other details. To help you create a plan, consider the following questions:

- **What types of databases are you backing up?** System and user databases often have different backup and recovery needs. For example, the *master* database is essential for all Microsoft SQL Server operations. If the *master* database fails or becomes corrupt, it takes the whole server down with it. But you do not need to back up the *master* database every hour, as you might need to do with a critical user database that handles real-time customer transactions. You need to back up *master* only after you create a database, change configuration values, configure SQL logins, or perform similar activities that make changes to databases on a server.

- **How important is the data in a database?** How you judge the data's importance can help determine when and how you should back it up. Although you might back up a development database weekly, you would probably back up a production database at least daily. The data's importance also drives your decision about the type of backup. To protect the data in a development database, you could make a full backup once a week. For an in-house customer order database that is updated throughout each weekday, you would want to perform full backups twice a week and supplement this with daily differential backups and hourly backups for the transaction logs. You might even set named log marks that allow recovery up to a specific point in the work.

- **How often are changes made to a database?** The frequency of changes can drive your decision about how often a database should be backed up. Because a read-only database does not ordinarily change, it does not need to be backed up regularly. On the other hand, a database that is updated nightly should be backed up after the nightly changes are posted. A database that is updated around the clock should be backed up continually.

- **How quickly do you need to recover the data?** When you create a backup plan, it is important to consider the amount of time it will take to recover lost data. For mission-critical databases, you likely need to get the database online again swiftly; to do this, you might need to alter your backup plan and set a target recovery time. You may even need to look at your drive or storage area network (SAN) configuration to ensure the drives themselves are fast enough and that their redundant array of independent disks (RAID) configuration doesn't add too much overhead.

- **Do you have the equipment to perform backups?** You need backup hardware to perform backups. If you do not have the hardware, you cannot perform backups. To perform timely backups, you might need several backup devices and several sets of backup media. Backup hardware includes optical drives, removable disk drives, and plain old disk drives.

- **Can you compress backups?** SQL Server 2012 Enterprise Edition and higher has support for compressed backups, and any SQL Server 2012 server edition can restore compressed backups. Because a compressed backup is smaller than an uncompressed backup of the same data, SQL Server requires less device I/O, and the backup itself requires less storage space. Typically, this increases backup and restore speed significantly. However, compression and decompression can increase processor overhead significantly, and this could affect server performance adversely. Also, if a database is compressed or encrypted, you may not want to compress backups, as this likely would not reduce the size of the backup much.

- **What is the best time to schedule backups?** You should schedule backups when database usage is as low as possible. Using this approach speeds up the backup process. However, in the real world, you cannot always schedule backups for off-peak hours. This means that you need to plan carefully when important databases are backed up.

- **Do you need to store backups off-site?** Storing copies of backups at an off-site location is essential to the recovery of your systems in the event of a natural disaster. In your off-site storage location, you should also include copies of the software required to restore operations on a new system.

NOTE Availability options, such as log shipping, are not a substitute for backups. Even if you use log shipping, availability groups, or another availability solution, you still need to create backups.

Backing up a database differs from backing up a server or a workstation, primarily because you often need to combine all (or nearly all) of the available techniques to ensure that you can recover a database completely. The basic types of backups you can perform include the following:

- **Full database backups** A full backup of a database includes all objects, system tables, and data. When the backup starts, SQL Server copies everything in the database and also includes portions of the transaction logs that are needed while the backup is in progress. You can use a full backup to recover the complete state of the data in a database at the time the backup operation finishes.

- **Differential backups** Designed to back up data that has changed since the last full backup. Because only changes are stored, this type of backup takes less time, and you can perform it more often. As with full backups, differential backups include portions of the transaction logs that are needed to restore the database when the backup operation finishes.

TIP You can use differential backups only in conjunction with full backups, and you cannot perform differential backups on the *master* database. Do not confuse differential backups with incremental backups. Differential backups record all changes since the last full backup (which means the amount of data that is backed up grows over time). Incremental backups record changes since the most recent full or incremental backup (which means that the size of the data backed up incrementally is usually much smaller than a full backup).

- **Transaction log backups** Transaction logs are serial records of all database modifications and are used during recovery operations to commit completed transactions and to roll back uncompleted transactions. When you back up a transaction log, the backup stores the changes that have occurred since the last transaction log backup and then truncates the log, which clears out transactions that have been committed or canceled. Unlike full and differential backups, transaction log backups record the state of the transaction log at the time the backup operation starts (not when it ends).

- **File and filegroup backups** These backups allow you to back up database files and filegroups rather than an entire database. This type of backup is useful if you are dealing with a large database and want to save time by backing up individual files rather than the entire database. Many factors affect file and filegroup backups. When you use file and filegroup backups, you must back up the transaction log as well. Because of this dependency, you cannot use this backup technique if Truncate Log On Checkpoint is enabled. Furthermore, if objects in the database span multiple files or filegroups, you must back up all the related files and filegroups at the same time.

REAL WORLD When you create full-text indexes, you can specify the filegroup in which an index should be created. If you don't specify a filegroup, the index becomes part of the primary filegroup for the database. However, you might want to store full-text indexes in secondary filegroups because doing so can give you additional recovery options. You can view the filegroup ID of the filegroup that contains a full-text index by selecting the data_space_id column of the sys.fulltext_indexes view.

If the filegroup that contains the full-text index is brought online after the filegroup that contains the table data, users might experience problems with full-text queries. Specifically, full-text queries will fail because the index is not available. When change tracking is enabled, user data manipulation language (DML) statements will fail until the index filegroup is available. Any status functions that ordinarily access the full-text index fail as well. As soon as you bring both the full-text index filegroup and the table data filegroup online, full-text index queries will succeed, and all other full-text operations will be restored.

TIP With databases that have one or more read-only filegroups, you might want to include contingencies for partial backups and partial differential backups in your planning. With a partial backup, you back up all the data in the primary filegroup and every read/write filegroup automatically. Partial backups, however, do not include read-only filegroups automatically. SQL Server includes read-only filegroups only when you explicitly specify them. With a partial differential backup, you back up only the data extents that were modified since the most recent partial backup of the same set of filegroups.

SQL Server 2012 uses recovery models to help you plan backups. The types of databases you are backing up and the types of backups you perform drive the choices for recovery models. Three recovery models are available:

- **Simple** The simple recovery model is designed for databases that need to be recovered to the point of the last backup. The backup strategy with this model should consist of full and differential backups. You cannot perform transaction log backups when the simple recovery model is enabled. SQL Server 2012 turns on the Truncate Log On Checkpoint option, which clears out inactive entries in the transaction log on checkpoint. Because this model clears out transaction logs, it is ideal for most system databases.

- **Full** The full recovery model is designed for databases that need to be recovered to the point of failure or to a specific point in time. When you use this model, all operations are logged, including bulk operations and bulk loading of data. The backup strategy with this model should include full, differential, and transaction log backups or full and transaction log backups only.

- **Bulk-logged** The bulk-logged recovery model reduces log space usage but retains most of the flexibility of the full recovery model. With this model, bulk operations and bulk loads are minimally logged and cannot be controlled on a per-operation basis. You need to redo bulk operations and bulk loads manually if the database fails before you perform a full or differential backup. The backup strategy with this model should include full, differential, and transaction log backups or full and transaction log backups only.

Each database can have a different recovery model. By default, the *master*, *msdb*, and *tempdb* databases use the simple recovery model, and the *model* database uses the full recovery model. The *model* database is the template database for all new databases, so if you change a default setting, all new databases for the database server instance use the new default model. You set the recovery model by completing the following steps:

1. Start SQL Server Management Studio. In the Object Explorer view, connect to the appropriate server.

2. If you plan to switch from bulk-logged recovery to simple recovery, perform a transaction log backup prior to making the change, and then change your backup strategy so that you no longer perform transaction log backups.

3. Expand the Databases folder. If you are configuring recovery for a system database, expand the System Databases folder as well.

4. Right-click the database you want to change, and then choose Properties. This displays the Database Properties dialog box.

5. Use the Recovery Model list on the Options page to change the recovery model, and then click OK.

6. If you switch from simple recovery to full recovery or bulk-logged recovery, add transaction log backups to your backup strategy for the database.

You can restore suspect pages in databases as well. The SQL Server Database Engine marks a data page as suspect in the suspect_pages table in *msdb* if it encounters an error while trying to read the page during a query, DBCC CHECKDB operation, or backup operation. Operating system cyclical redundancy check (CRC) errors, bad checksum, and torn pages are the most common reasons pages are marked as suspect.

The suspect_pages table contains one row per suspect page, up to a limit of 1,000 rows. Entries for pages with errors have an event type of 1 , 2, or 3. Entries for pages that have been restored, repaired, or deallocated have an event type of 4, 5, or 7. Knowing this, you can selectively view pages with errors using the following T-SQL statements:

```
SELECT * FROM msdb..suspect_pages
WHERE (event_type = 1 OR event_type = 2 OR event_type = 3);
GO
```

SQL Server Management Studio allows you to check database pages for corruption, and selectively restore corrupt pages from a database backup and subsequent log backups. To restore pages, the database should be using the full recovery model as a best practice. You must start with a full, file, or filegroup backup and have an unbroken chain of log backups that you are applying to bring the page up to date with the current log file. You cannot restore pages in read-only filegroups.

The Database Engine deletes rows from the suspect_pages table as may be necessary when you use ALTER DATABASE, REMOVE FILE, or DROP DATABASE. If you use, RESTORE or DBCC CHECKDB REPAIR_ALLOW_DATA_LOSS, the Database Engine updates the suspect_pages table to indicate related deallocated, repaired, or restored actions.

AlwaysOn Availability Groups can now be used to group databases for high availability. To support Availability Groups, a server instance must reside on a node in a failover cluster that hosts the availability group, the feature must be enabled, and the server instance must be a database mirroring endpoint. Although Availability Groups do not depend on shared storage, each SQL Server failover cluster instance hosting data replicas does require shared storage. However, unlike traditional mirroring, you can back up replicas in Availability Groups.

SQL Server 2012 includes several features that allow you to create standby servers. The following are the three general types of standby servers:

- **Hot standby server**   A server that is updated and comes online automatically if a primary server or database fails
- **Warm standby server**   A server that is updated automatically but which must be brought online manually if a primary server or database fails
- **Cold standby server**   A server that is updated and must be brought online manually if a primary server or database fails

Database mirroring, log shipping, and database copies allow you to create standby servers. You use database mirroring to establish a hot standby server, called a *mirror server*, on which the database is brought up to date continuously and to which failover can occur automatically if the primary database fails. You use log shipping to establish a warm standby server, called a *secondary server*. On a secondary server, the database is updated automatically from log backups, but you must bring the server online manually if the primary database fails. You create a copy of a database to establish a cold standby server. On a cold standby server, the database is updated manually, and you must bring the server online manually if the primary database fails.

Planning for Mirroring and Mirrored Database Backups

Mirroring allows you to create hot standby servers. You can mirror any database except for *master*, *msdb*, *temp*, and *model*. You can configure and enable mirroring by using the Mirroring page in the Database Properties dialog box. Mirroring requires up to three servers: a principal server, a mirror server, and an optional witness server.

Backups are not used with mirrored databases in the same way that they are with other databases. When mirroring is configured, backups of a principal database are used to initialize the mirror database on the mirror server. As part of the mirror-creation process, you can back up and restore individual files and filegroups. However, you must restore all files and filegroups before you begin mirroring. If you want to work only with a subset of a database and its objects, use replication instead.

When mirroring databases, remember the following information:

- While database mirroring is active, you cannot back up or restore the mirror database.
- Although you can back up the principal database, you cannot use BACKUP LOG WITH NORECOVERY.
- You cannot restore the principal database (that is what mirroring is for). The mirror will correct itself after failover.

Planning for Backups of Replicated Databases

Databases that are replicated present a special problem for backup and restoration planning, primarily because the traditional database architecture is extended to include three server roles (which all have related databases):

- **Publisher**   A server that makes data available for replication, tracks changes to data, and maintains other information about source databases. Each publisher has a *publication* database.

- **Distributor**   A server that distributes replicated data and stores the *distribution* database. Each distributor has a *distribution* database.

- **Subscriber**   A destination server for replication. Subscriber databases store the replicated data, receive updates, and in some cases can also make changes to data. Each subscriber has a *subscription* database.

As you do with other system databases, you should back up the *publication*, *distribution*, and *subscription* databases regularly. On the publisher, distributor, and all subscriber servers, you should back up the *master* and *msdb* system databases at the same time as you back up the replication databases. When you restore the *publication* database, you should also restore the *master* and *msdb* databases on the publisher server. When you restore the *distribution* database, you should also restore the *master* and *msdb* databases on the distributor server. When you restore the *subscription* database, you should also restore the *master* and *msdb* databases on the subscriber server. Restoring *master* and *msdb* is required to ensure that replication configuration, settings, and related replication metadata are consistent with the publication, distribution, or subscription database that you are restoring.

Subscription database backups should be no older than the shortest retention period of all publications to which the subscriber subscribes. If the shortest retention period is 10 days, the backup you plan to restore should be no older than 10 days. To ensure successful recovery of a *subscription* database, subscribers should synchronize with the publisher before the *subscription* database is backed up. They should also synchronize after the *subscription* database is restored. Synchronizing prior to backup helps ensure that if a subscriber is restored from backup, the subscription is still within the publication retention period.

You can restore replicated databases to the same server and database from which the backup was created or to another server or database. If you restore a backup of a replicated database to another server or database, replication settings are not preserved, and you need to re-create all publications and subscriptions after backups are restored, except in the case of a replicated server that also has log shipping configured. If you combine log shipping with replication, you can restore a replicated database to a standby server, and the replication settings are preserved.

With merge replication, any replication-related changes should be captured in the log backups. If you do not perform log backups, the *publication* database should be backed up whenever a setting relevant to replication is changed. After restoring the *publication* database from a backup, you should synchronize the *publication* database with a *subscription* database or reinitialize all subscriptions to the publications in the *publication* database. You can synchronize the *publication* database or reinitialize subscriptions. Be sure to check the identity ranges in tables that contain IDENTITY columns after restoring a database.

> **NOTE** In merge replication, the distribution database has a limited role. It does not store any data used in change tracking, and it does not provide temporary storage of merge replication changes to be forwarded to *subscription* databases (as it does in transactional replication).

With transactional replication, you set the Sync With Backup option on the *distribution* and *publication* databases for the following reasons:

- Turn this option on for the *distribution* database to ensure that transactions in the log of the *publication* database will not be truncated until they have been backed up at the *distribution* database. This allows the *distribution* database to be restored to the last backup, and any missing transactions then can be delivered from the *publication* database to the *distribution* database while replication continues unaffected. Although this has no effect on replication latency, it can delay the truncation of the log on the *publication* database until the corresponding transactions in the *distribution* database have been backed up.

- Turn this option on for the *publication* database if your application can tolerate additional latency to be sure that transactions are not delivered to the *distribution* database until they are backed up at the *publication* database. This allows you to restore the last *publication* database backup at the publisher without any possibility of the *distribution* database having transactions that the restored *publication* database does not have. Latency and throughput are affected because transactions cannot be delivered to the *distribution* database until they have been backed up at the publisher.

Planning for Backups of Very Large Databases

If you need to develop a plan to back up and restore very large databases, you might want to take advantage of parallel backup and restore. The parallel backup and restore process allows SQL Server to use multiple threads to read and write data. This means SQL Server can read data from and write data to multiple data sources. The backup and restore process uses parallel I/O in different ways:

- Backing up uses one thread per disk device to read data from a database when the database has files on several disk devices.

- A restore operation uses one thread per disk device as it initializes a database that it is creating for the restore process if the database is defined with files on several disks.

- Both backup and restore operations use one thread per backup device when a backup set is stored on multiple backup devices.

As you can see from this information, to take advantage of parallel I/O, you must implement your backup strategy so that databases do the following:

- Use multiple disk drives for storing data
- Use multiple backup devices for backing up and restoring data

After you determine the backup operations to use on each database and how often you want to back up each database, you can select backup devices and media that meet these requirements. Backup devices and media are covered later in this chapter.

Planning for Backup Compression

Backup compression is disabled by default. You can set a global default with compression on or off on a per-instance basis by completing the following steps:

1. Start SQL Server Management Studio. In the Object Explorer view, connect to the appropriate server.

2. Right-click the server entry, and then select Properties. This displays the Server Properties dialog box.

3. On the Database Settings page, select the Compress Backup check box to turn on backup compression. Clear the Compress Backup check box to turn off backup compression. Click OK.

Using Transact-SQL (T-SQL), you can set the global default for compression by using the server configuration option Backup Compression Default for the sp_configure stored procedure. As shown in the following example, use a value of 1 to turn compression on:

```
EXEC sp_configure 'backup compression default', '1'
GO
RECONFIGURE WITH OVERRIDE
GO
```

You can override the global default when you create or schedule database backups. However, the global setting is extremely important because the server-level setting for compression determines whether the data that SQL Server sends is compressed when you use log shipping and database mirroring. Specifically, you must enable backup compression at the server level to enable log backup compression for log shipping and database mirroring.

You can calculate the compression ratio of a database backup by dividing the original backup size by the compressed backup size. You can obtain both values from the backupset column in the *msdb* database, as shown in the following example:

```
SELECT backup_size/compressed_backup_size FROM msdb..backupset
```

The compression ratio of a compressed backup depends on the type of data you have compressed. For example, although you can compress encrypted data, encrypted data has a significantly lower compression ratio than unencrypted data.

Additionally, if the database itself is already compressed, compressing the backup won't necessarily reduce the backup size.

In a standard configuration, backup compression—whether used for database backups, log shipping, or log mirroring—can increase processor utilization significantly, and this can have an impact on SQL Server performance. To reduce the performance impact for long-running database backups, you can compress backups by using a user session for which the Resource Governor has limited CPU utilization.

Selecting Backup Devices and Media

Many solutions are available for backing up data. Some are fast and expensive. Others are slow but very reliable. The backup solution that is right for your organization depends on many factors, including the following:

- **Capacity** This refers to the amount of data that you need to back up on a routine basis. Can the backup hardware support the required load given your time and resource constraints?
- **Reliability** The reliability of the backup hardware and media determines how useful the backups that you create are when you need them to restore lost data. Can you afford to sacrifice reliability to meet budget or time needs?
- **Extensibility** The extensibility of the backup solution refers to its ability to expand beyond its original capacity. Will this solution meet your needs as your organization grows?
- **Speed** Consider the speed with which data can be backed up and recovered. Can you afford to sacrifice speed to reduce costs?
- **Cost** The cost of backup solution choices affects your decision. Does the solution fit within your budget?

Capacity, reliability, extensibility, speed, and cost are the main issues that influence your choice of a backup plan. If you determine the relative value of these issues to your organization, you will be able to select an appropriate backup solution for your situation. Some of the most commonly used backup solutions include the following hardware and media:

- **Tape drives** Tape drives are the most common backup devices. Tape drives use magnetic tape cartridges to store data. Magnetic tapes are relatively inexpensive, but they are not highly reliable. Tapes can break or stretch. They can also lose information over time. The average capacity of tape cartridges ranges from 24 gigabytes (GB) to 160 GB. Compared with other backup solutions, tape drives are fairly slow. Their biggest advantage is their lower cost.
- **Digital Audio Tape (DAT) drives** DAT drives are quickly replacing standard tape drives as the preferred type of backup device. Many DAT formats are available. The most commonly used format is Digital Linear Tape (DLT) or Super DLT (SDLT). With SDLT 320 and 600, tapes have a capacity of either 160 GB or 300 GB uncompressed (320 GB or 600 GB compressed).

If you work for a large organization, you might want to look at Linear Tape Open (LTO). LTO-3, LTO-4, and LTO-5 tapes have uncompressed capacity of 400 GB, 800 GB, and 1500 GB, respectively (and compressed capacity of twice that).

TIP To perform faster backup and recovery operations, you can use multiple backup devices with SQL Server. For example, if it normally takes four hours to perform a full backup or restoration of a database, you can cut the backup and restoration time in half by using two backup devices; with four backup devices, you could back up fully or restore the database in an hour.

- **Autoloader tape systems** Autoloader tape systems (tape library systems) use a magazine of tapes to create extended backup volumes capable of meeting an enterprise's high-capacity needs. With an autoloader system, tapes within the magazine are changed automatically as needed during the backup or recovery process. Most autoloader tape systems use DAT tapes formatted for DLT, SDLT, or LTO. Typical DLT drives can record up to 45 GB per hour, and you can improve that speed by purchasing a tape library system with multiple drives. In this way, you can record on multiple tapes simultaneously. In contrast, most SDLT and LTO drives record over 100 GB per hour, and by using multiple drives in a system you can record hundreds of gigabytes per hour. An example enterprise solution uses 16 LTO drives to achieve data transfer rates of more than 13.8 terabytes (TB) per hour and can store up to 500 tapes, for a total storage capacity of more than 800 TB.

- **Removable disk drives** Removable disks, such as external USB drives or eSATA drives, are increasingly being used as backup devices. Removable disks offer good speed and ease of use for a single drive or single system backup. However, disk drives and removable disks tend to be more expensive than standard tape or tape library systems.

- **Disk drives** Disk drives provide the fastest way to back up and restore files. Using disk drives, you can often accomplish in minutes what takes hours with a tape drive. So when business needs mandate a speedy recovery, nothing beats a disk drive. The cost of disk drives, however, might be higher compared to tape library systems.

- **Disk-based backup systems** Disk-based backup systems provide complete backup and restore solutions by using large arrays of disks to achieve high performance. High reliability can be achieved when you use RAID to build in redundancy and fault tolerance. Typical disk-based backup systems use virtual library technology so that Microsoft Windows sees them as autoloader tape library systems. This makes them easier to work with. An example enterprise solution has 128 virtual drives and 16 virtual libraries per node for total storage of up to 7.5 TB per node. When fully scaled, this enterprise solution can store up to 640 TB and transfer up to 17.2 TB per hour.

Selecting a backup device is an important step in implementing a backup and recovery plan, but it is not the only step. You also need to purchase the tapes, the disks, or both that will allow you to implement your backup and recovery plan. The number of tapes, disks, or drives you need depends on the following factors:

- How much data you will be backing up
- How often you will be backing up the data
- How long you need to keep additional data sets

Typically, you implement backups by using a rotation schedule with two or more sets of tapes, disks, or files on a drive. Having more than one set of media allows you to increase media longevity by reducing media usage, and at the same time, it reduces the number of actual tapes, disks, or files you need to ensure that you have data available when necessary.

BEST PRACTICES   For important databases, I recommend using four media sets. Use two sets in regular rotation. Use the third set for the first rotation cycle at the beginning of each month, and use the fourth set for the first rotation cycle of each quarter. This technique allows you to recover the database in a wide variety of situations.

Using Backup Strategies

Table 11-1 lists backup strategies you might want to use. As you can see, these strategies are based on the type of database as well as the type of data. When planning a backup strategy, remember the following:

- The *master* database stores important information about the structure of other databases, including the database size. Whenever database information or structure changes, *master* might be updated without your knowing about it. For example, the size of most databases changes automatically, and when this happens, *master* is updated. Because of this, often the best backup strategy for *master* is to schedule backups every other day and to rotate through several backup sets so that you can go back to several different versions of *master* if necessary.

- You can use transaction logs to recover databases up to the point of failure and up to a point of work, which can be handy for recovering distributed transactions across servers. To recover a database to a point of work, you must insert named log marks into the transaction log by using BEGIN TRANSACTION WITH MARK. You can then recover to a mark in the log by using RESTORE LOG WITH STOPATMARK or RESTORE LOG WITH STOPBEFOREMARK.

TABLE 11-1 Backup Strategies for System and User Databasest

DATABASE TYPE	DETAILS	STRATEGY
User	Recovery up to the minute	Run full backups twice a week if possible. Use nightly differential backups, and back up the recovery transaction log every 10 minutes during business hours. Do not use Truncate Log On Checkpoint, because this will make recovering some transactions impossible. To improve backup/restore speed, use multiple backup devices whenever possible.
	Recovery up to a point of work	Run full backups twice a week if possible. Use nightly differential backups, and back up the recovery transaction log every 10 minutes during business hours. Do not use Truncate Log On Checkpoint. Use named transactions to insert named marks into the transaction logs. To improve backup/restore speed, use multiple backup devices whenever possible.
	Recovery up to the hour	Run full backups twice a week if possible. Use nightly differential backups, and back up the recovery transaction log every 60 minutes during business hours. Do not use Truncate Log On Checkpoint. To improve backup/restore speed, use multiple backup devices whenever possible.
	Recovery of daily changes	Run full backups at least once a week. Use nightly differential backups, and back up the changes transaction log as necessary to manage log size and the backup window during business hours. Do not use Truncate Log On Checkpoint.
	Read-only	Schedule a full backup of the database every 30 to 60 days, and supplement this with an additional full backup whenever the database is modified.

DATABASE TYPE	DETAILS	STRATEGY
System	*distribution*	Available when you configure replication and the server is acting as a distributor. Schedule full backups after snapshots. With transactional replication, schedule regular log backups.
	master	Run full backups immediately after creating or removing databases, changing the size of a database, adding or removing logins, or modifying server configuration settings. Do not forget to maintain several backup sets for *master*.
	model	Treat like a read-only database.
	msdb	If you schedule jobs through the SQL Server Agent, back up this database regularly because this is where the job schedule and history are maintained and backup history is stored.
	publication	Available when you configure replication and the server is acting as a publisher. If you do not perform log backups, the *publication* database should be backed up whenever a setting relevant to replication is changed.
	subscription	Available when you configure replication and the server is acting as a subscriber. *Subscription* database backups should be no older than the shortest retention period of all publications to which the subscriber subscribes.
	tempdb	Normally does not need to be backed up. This database is re-created each time you start SQL Server.

Don't confuse the need for recovery up to the minute or to a point of work with setting a recovery interval or a target recovery time for these reasons:

- A recovery interval sets the maximum number of minutes per database that a server instance needs to recover databases, based on estimates made by the server instance without considering the cost of random I/O during REDO.
- A target recovery time defines a maximum time for the recovery of a specific database, based on the cost of random I/O during REDO and overriding the default recovery interval.

Whenever a SQL Server instance starts, it recovers each database, rolling back transactions that did not commit and rolling forward transactions that did commit but whose changes were not yet written to disk when the server instance was stopped. The server instance's recovery interval sets an upper limit on the time it should take to recover each database.

SQL Server issues automatic checkpoints to meet the desired time limits by estimating the number of data modifications it can roll forward in the recovery interval. Thus, the frequency of automatic checkpoints depends on the number of outstanding writes and whether there is increasing write latency.

You manage recovery time using the recovery interval option of sp_configure. The normal range for the recovery interval is from 1 to 60 minutes, though you can override this limit. By default, the recovery interval is set to 0, which means the interval is configured automatically by SQL Server. For active databases, automatic configuration means recovery should take less than one minute and a checkpoint should occur approximately every minute.

NOTE With the simple recovery model, automatic checkpoints occur when a log becomes 70 percent full, and this normally results in the log getting truncated. With the full and bulk-logged recovery models, automatic checkpoints do not cause a log to be truncated (once a log backup chain is established).

When you need more precise control over the recovery time of a database, you can set a target recovery time, which is configured in seconds or minutes using the SET TARGET_RECOVERY_TIME option of the ALTER DATABASE statement. With target recovery times, SQL Server issues indirect checkpoints in the background to try to ensure that the recovery window you've set can be achieved. For active databases, indirect checkpoints continually write dirty pages to disk in the background, which reduces I/O spiking while possibly increasing the total write load for the server instance.

Creating a Backup Device

Earlier versions of SQL Server required you to configure backup devices before you could back up databases. With SQL Server 2012, you do not need to define backup devices explicitly. Nevertheless, backup devices do provide an easy way to ensure that you create backups that have the same file name and location time after time. By using consistent names and locations, you can manage the backup and recovery processes more easily.

To create a backup device using SQL Server Management Studio, complete the following steps:

1. Start SQL Server Management Studio. In the Object Explorer view, connect to the appropriate server.

2. Expand the server's Server Objects folder.

3. Right-click Backup Devices, and then choose New Backup Device to open the Backup Device dialog box shown in Figure 11-1.

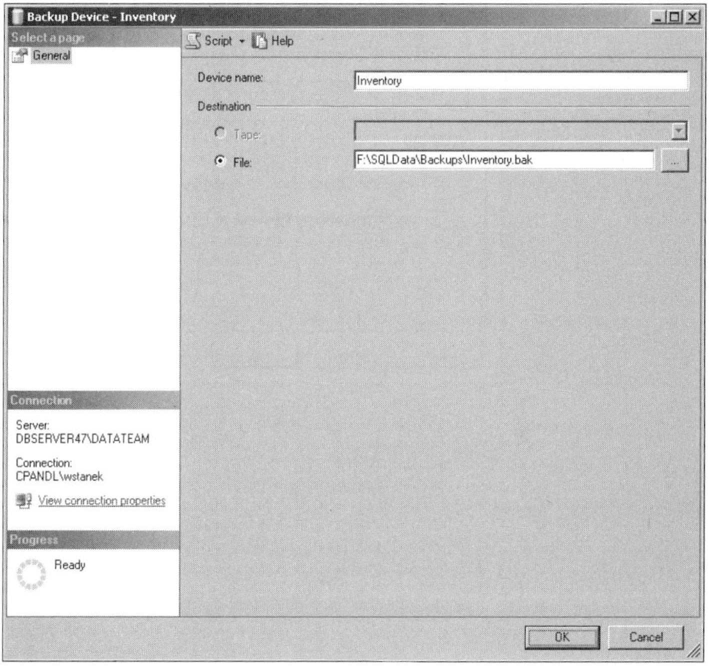

FIGURE 11-1 The Backup Device dialog box.

4. In the Device Name box, type the name of the logical backup device. Use a short but descriptive name, such as Customer Device or Master Device.

5. If you installed a tape drive and want to back up to the tape drive, select the Tape option, and then use the related drop-down list to select the target drive.

6. If you are backing up to a file, select the File option, and then type the full path to the backup file you want to associate with this device, such as F:\SQLData\Backups\Personnel.bak.

7. Click OK. SQL Server will attempt to verify the backup file location. If there is a problem, you will see a prompt notifying you of any issues.

With T-SQL, you can create backup devices by using sp_addumpdevice. Sample 11-1 shows the syntax and usage for this command, which uses many different arguments, including device_type, logical_name, physical_name, controller_type, and device_status. The device_type argument is the type of device you are using—disk or tape. The logical_name argument is the name of the backup device. The physical_name argument is the full path to the backup file, and controller_type is 2 for a disk or 5 for a tape. The device_status argument is either noskip, to read ANSI tape headers, or skip, to skip ANSI tape headers.

SAMPLE 11-1 sp_addumpdevice Syntax and Usage.

Syntax

```
sp_addumpdevice [@devtype =]'device_type',
    [@logicalname =] 'logical_name',
    [@physicalname =] 'physical_name'
    [, {
        [@cntrltype =] controller_type |
        [@devstatus =] 'device_status' }
    ]
```

Usage

```
EXEC sp_addumpdevice 'disk', 'Customer', 'c:\mssql\backup\cust.bak'
EXEC sp_addumpdevice 'disk', 'Customer on Backup Server',
    '\\omega\backups\cust.bak'
EXEC sp_addumpdevice 'tape', 'Customer on Tape', '\\.\tape0'
```

Performing Backups

Backups are an essential part of database administration. They are so important that SQL Server provides multiple backup procedures and several ways to create backups—all designed to help you manage database backup and recovery easily and effectively. In this section, you will learn about standard backup procedures and the T-SQL backup process. The final component in a successful backup strategy involves database maintenance plans, which you learned about in Chapter 10, "Automating and Maintaining SQL Server 2012."

Creating Backups in SQL Server Management Studio

In SQL Server Management Studio, you can start the backup process by right-clicking the database you want to back up, pointing to Tasks, and then selecting Back Up. I will focus on how you use the Back Up Database dialog box to perform backups in the following situations:

- When you want to create a new backup set
- When you want to add to an existing backup set

Creating a New Backup Set

Whenever you back up a database for the first time or start a new rotation on an existing backup set, follow these steps to create the backup:

1. Start SQL Server Management Studio. In the Object Explorer view, connect to the appropriate server.

2. Expand the Databases folder. Right-click the database you want to back up, point to Tasks, and then select Back Up. This opens the Back Up Database dialog box, shown in Figure 11-2.

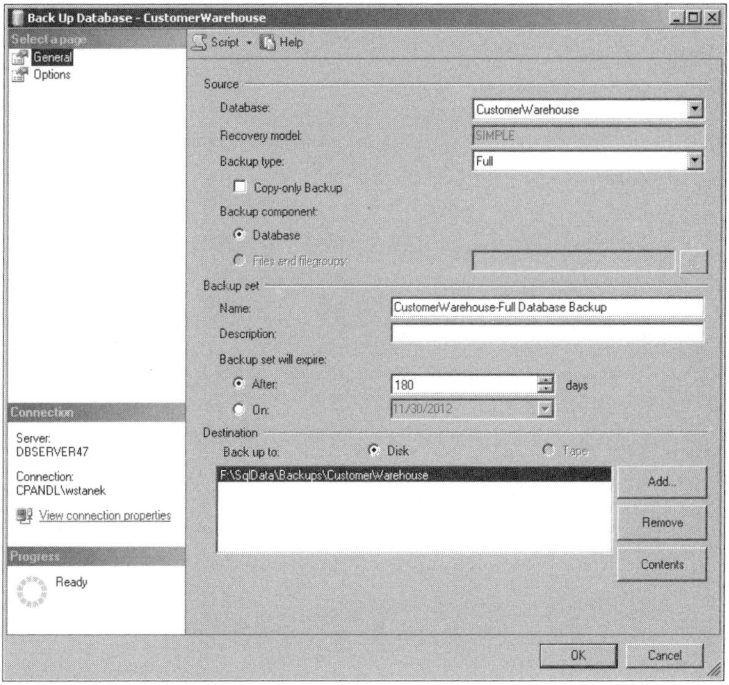

FIGURE 11-2 The Back Up Database dialog box.

3. The database you want to back up should be selected from the Database list in the dialog box. The current recovery model for this database is also shown, but it is dimmed because the recovery model cannot be changed. You cannot create transaction log backups when the recovery model is set to Simple.

4. Because this is a new backup set, select the type of backup you want to perform. Typically, for a first backup, you want to perform a full backup. You can add to the backup set later by using other types of backups.

5. You can back up the entire database or a subset of its files and filegroups. By default, Backup Component is set to Database to create a database backup. If you want to create a file and filegroup backup, select the Files And Filegroups option. The Select Files And Filegroups dialog box opens, and you can select the check boxes for the files and filegroups you want to back up. Click OK after making your selections.

   NOTE The only available backup option for the *master* database is Full. That is because you can only run full backups on *master*.

6. In the Backup Set area, use the Name text box to enter a name for the backup set you are creating. Use an ordinary, nontechnical name that will help you tell at a glance what the backup contains. For example, name the

first backup set for the Customer database Customer Backup Set 1. Then you can add the full, differential, and transaction log backups for this rotation to the set.

7. In the Description box, type a description of the backup, such as "Set 1 contains the weekly full, daily differential, and hourly transaction log backups. This is the full backup for the week."

8. Use the Backup Set Will Expire options to set an expiration interval or date. This allows the backup to overwrite the media after a specified period or date.

9. If a backup set exists and is listed in the Destination area, select it and click Remove.

10. Click Add to display the Select Backup Destination dialog box, shown in Figure 11-3. To use a new file as the backup destination, select the File Name option, and then type the full path to the backup file, such as E:\Data\Backups\Cust.bak or \\Omega\Backups\Cust.bak. To use a backup device, select the Backup Device option, and then choose the backup destination using the drop-down list. Click OK when you are ready to continue.

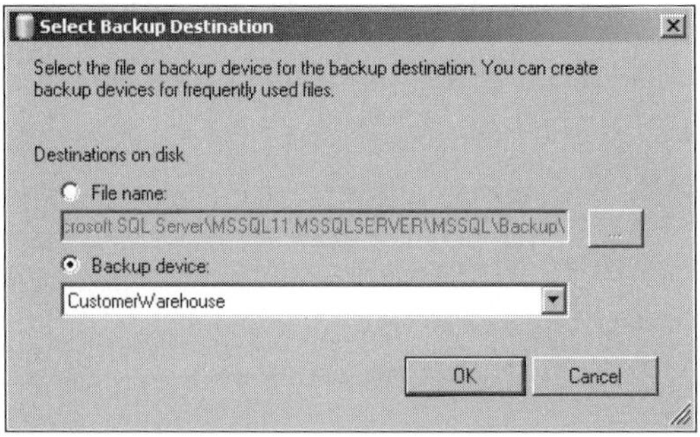

FIGURE 11-3 The Select Backup Destination dialog box.

11. To set additional options for the backup, select the Options page. You use the available options as follows:

- **Back Up To The Existing Media Set** Select this option if you are using an existing media set. You can specify whether to append to the existing backup set or overwrite all existing backup sets.

- **Check Media Set Name And Backup Set Expiration** Use this option to ensure that you are writing to the correct tape set and that the tape expiration date has not been reached. If you select this option, enter the media set name that should be verified.

- **Back Up To A New Media Set, And Erase All Existing Backup Sets** Select this option if you want to create a new media set and erase all existing media sets. Then enter the media set name and an optional description.

- **Verify Backup When Finished** Choose this option to verify the entire backup and check for errors. Generally, it is a very good idea to verify your backups.
- **Perform Checksum Before Writing To Media** Use this option to check the data you are backing up prior to writing it. Selecting this option is the same as using the CHECKSUM or NOCHECKSUM options with the BACKUP statement. If you perform a checksum, you can also specify to continue on checksum error using the CONTINUE_AFTER_ERROR option.
- **Continue On Error** Select this option to continue a backup after encountering one or more errors. If you do not select this option, SQL Server cancels the backup upon encountering an error.
- **Truncate The Transaction Log** Select this option to clean out entries that are no longer needed after the backup. These entries are for transactions that have been committed or rolled back. (This option is set by default for transaction log backups.)
- **Back Up The Tail Of The Log** Use this option to back up the active transaction log (those transactions that have not been completed and are at the tail of the log). When you use the full or bulk-logged recovery model, you must back up the active transaction log before you can restore the database with SQL Server Management Studio.

TIP You usually want to perform one last log backup before you try to restore a corrupt database. When you do, you should clear this option and perform the log backup without truncation. This option is the same as running BACKUP LOG NO_TRUNCATE.

- **Unload The Tape After Backup** Select this option to eject the tape after the backup. Optionally, you also can elect to rewind the tape before unloading. Both options are valid only with tape devices.
- **Set Backup Compression** Use these settings to set the compression option. You can use the server-level default setting or explicitly turn compression on or off.

12. Click OK to start the backup. If you opted to verify the data, the verification process starts immediately after the backup ends.

Adding to an Existing Backup Set

When you want to add to an existing backup set, complete the following steps:

1. Start SQL Server Management Studio. In the Object Explorer view, connect to the appropriate server.
2. Expand the Databases folder. Right-click the database you want to back up, point to Tasks, and then select Back Up to open the Back Up Database dialog box, shown previously in Figure 11-2.

3. The database you want to back up should be selected from the Database list.

4. Select the type of backup you want to perform: Full, Differential, or Transaction Log. Typically, when you are adding to an existing set, you do so using a differential or transaction log backup. You cannot create transaction log backups when the recovery model is set to Simple.

5. You can back up the entire database or a subset of its files and filegroups. By default, Backup Component is set to Database to create a database backup. If you want to create a file and filegroup backup, select the Files And Filegroups option. The Select Files And Filegroups dialog box is then displayed. Select the check boxes for the files and filegroups to back up, and then click OK.

6. In the Backup Set area, use the Name box to enter a name for the backup you are creating. In the Description box, type a description of the backup, such as "Daily differential backup."

7. Use the Backup Set Will Expire options to set an expiration interval or date. This allows the backup to overwrite the media after a specified period or date.

8. A backup set should be listed in the Destination area. If so, click Contents to see the current contents of this backup set. If a backup set is not listed, click Add to display the Select Backup Destination dialog box, and then specify the location of the existing backup. Click OK when you are ready to continue.

9. Select the Options page. Because you are adding more data to the existing backup set, the options Backup To The Existing Media Set and Append To The Existing Backup Set should be selected.

REAL WORLD Because compressed and uncompressed backups cannot coexist in a media set, be sure to set the same compression option. Whether you back up data to a tape or disk drive, you should use the tape rotation technique. Create multiple sets, and then write to these sets on a rotating basis. With a disk drive, for example, you could create these backup files on different network drives and use them as follows:

- \\omega\data1drive\backups\cust_set1.bak   Used in weeks 1, 3, 5, and so on for full and differential backups of the *Customer* database

- \\omega\data2drive\backups\cust_set2.bak   Used in weeks 2, 4, 6, and so on for full and differential backups of the *Customer* database

- \\omega\data3drive\backups\cust_set3.bak   Used in the first week of the month for full backups of the *Customer* database

- \\omega\data4drive\backups\cust_set4.bak   Used in the first week of the quarter for full backups of the *Customer* database

Do not forget that each time you start a new rotation on a media set, you should overwrite the existing media. For example, you should append all backups in week 1. Then, when starting the next rotation in week 3, you should overwrite the existing media for the first backup and append the remaining backups for the week.

10. For transaction log backups, you usually want to select the Truncate The Transaction Log check box. This ensures that inactive entries are cleared out of the transaction log after a backup.

11. Click OK to start the backup. If you opted to verify the data, the verify process starts immediately after the backup ends.

Using Striped Backups with Multiple Devices

Through a process called *parallel striped backups*, SQL Server can perform backups to multiple backup devices simultaneously. As you can imagine, writing multiple backup files at the same time can speed up backup operations dramatically. The key to achieving this speed, however, is having physically separate devices, such as three different tape devices or three different drives that you are using for the backup. You cannot write parallel backups to a single tape device, and you cannot write parallel backups to the same drive.

Multiple devices used in a backup operation are referred to as a *media set*. SQL Server allows you to use from 2 to 32 devices to form a media set. These devices must be of the same type. For example, you cannot create a striped backup with one backup tape device and one backup drive device.

The two main operations involved in parallel striped backups are creating a new media set and adding to an existing media set.

Creating a New Media Set

To create a new media set using multiple devices, complete the following steps:

1. Select the server you want to use, and then create each of the backup devices you need in the media set, as described in the "Creating a Backup Device" section earlier in this chapter.

2. Right-click the database you want to back up, point to Tasks, and then select Back Up to display the Back Up Database dialog box.

3. Follow the procedure outlined in the "Creating a New Backup Set" section earlier in this chapter. Repeat step 10 in that procedure for each backup device you want to use in the media set.

Adding to an Existing Media Set

To add to an existing media set, complete the following steps:

1. Right-click the database you want to back up, point to Tasks, and then select Back Up to display the Back Up Database dialog box.

2. Follow the procedure outlined in the "Adding to an Existing Backup Set" section earlier in this chapter. The only difference is that in step 8 of that procedure, you should see a list of all the backup devices used in the media set. If you do not, you need to add them one by one using the Add button and the related Select Backup Destination dialog box.

Using T-SQL Backup

An alternative to using the backup procedures in SQL Server Management Studio is to use the T-SQL BACKUP statement. You use BACKUP DATABASE to back up databases and BACKUP LOG to back up transaction logs.

> **BEST PRACTICES** If you back up databases using T-SQL, you lose one of the biggest benefits of SQL Server—the automated recovery process. With automated recovery, you do not have to worry about which backup to apply in which situation, which command flags to use, and so on. Furthermore, because you can schedule automated and unattended backups, you do not need to run backups manually through SQL Server as often as in the past. I recommend using the SQL Server Management Studio backup and restore process whenever possible.

BACKUP DATABASE has dual syntax. Sample 11-2 shows the syntax and usage for full and differential backups. A full backup is the default operation.

SAMPLE 11-2 BACKUP DATABASE Syntax and Usage for Full and Differential Backups.

Syntax

```
BACKUP DATABASE { database_name | @database_name_var }
TO < backup_device > [ ,...n ]
[ [ MIRROR TO < backup_device > [ ,...n ] ] [ ...next-mirror ] ]
[ WITH
    [ BLOCKSIZE = { blocksize | @blocksize_variable } ]
    [ [ , ] { CHECKSUM | NO_CHECKSUM } ]
    [ [ , ] { COMPRESSION | NO_COMPRESSION } ]
    [ [ , ] { STOP_ON_ERROR | CONTINUE_AFTER_ERROR } ]
    [ [ , ] DESCRIPTION = { 'text' | @text_variable } ]
    [ [ , ] DIFFERENTIAL ]
    [ [ , ] NAME = { backup_set_name | @backup_set_name_var } ]
    [ [ , ] PASSWORD = { password | @password_variable } ]
    [ [ , ] EXPIREDATE = { date | @date_var }
        | RETAINDAYS = { days | @days_var } ]
    [ [ , ] { FORMAT | NOFORMAT } ]
    [ [ , ] { INIT | NOINIT } ]
    [ [ , ] { SKIP | NOSKIP } ]
    [ [ , ] MEDIADESCRIPTION = { 'text' | @text_variable } ]
    [ [ , ] MEDIANAME = { media_name | @media_name_variable } ]
    [ [ , ] MEDIAPASSWORD = { mediapassword |
        @mediapassword_variable } ]
    [ [ , ] { NOREWIND | REWIND } ]
    [ [ , ] { NOUNLOAD | UNLOAD } ]
    [ [ , ] BUFFERCOUNT = { buffercount | @buffercount_variable }
        | MAXTRANSFERSIZE = { maxtransfersize |
        @maxtransfersize_variable }]
    [ [ , ] RESTART ]
    [ [ , ] STATS [ = percentage ] ]
    [ [ , ] COPY_ONLY ]
]
```

```
<backup_device> ::=
{
  { logical_backup_device_name | @logical_backup_device_name_var }
    |
    { DISK | TAPE } = { 'physical_backup_device_name' |
      @physical_backup_device_name_var }
}
```

Usage

```
USE master
EXEC sp_addumpdevice 'disk', 'Customer Backup Set 1',
    'f:\data\backup\Cust2.dat'
BACKUP DATABASE 'Customer' TO 'Customer Backup Set 1'
```

Sample 11-3 shows the BACKUP DATABASE syntax for file and filegroup backups.

SAMPLE 11-3 BACKUP DATABASE Syntax and Usage for File or Filegroup Backups.

Syntax

```
BACKUP DATABASE { database_name | @database_name_var }
    <file_or_filegroup> [ ,...f ]
TO <backup_device> [ ,...n ]
[ [ MIRROR TO <backup_device> [ ,...n ] ] [ ...next-mirror ] ]
[ WITH
    [ BLOCKSIZE = { blocksize | @blocksize_variable } ]
    [ [ , ] { CHECKSUM | NO_CHECKSUM } ]
    [ [ , ] { COMPRESSION | NO_COMPRESSION } ]
    [ [ , ] { STOP_ON_ERROR | CONTINUE_AFTER_ERROR } ]
    [ [ , ] DESCRIPTION = { 'text' | @text_variable } ]
    [ [ , ] DIFFERENTIAL ]
    [ [ , ] NAME = { backup_set_name | @backup_set_name_var } ]
    [ [ , ] PASSWORD = { password | @password_variable } ]
    [ [ , ] EXPIREDATE = { date | @date_var }
        | RETAINDAYS = { days | @days_var } ]
    [ [ , ] { FORMAT | NOFORMAT } ]
    [ [ , ] { INIT | NOINIT } ]
    [ [ , ] { NOSKIP | SKIP } ]
    [ [ , ] MEDIADESCRIPTION = { 'text' | @text_variable } ]
    [ [ , ] MEDIANAME = { media_name | @media_name_variable } ]
    [ [ , ] MEDIAPASSWORD = { mediapassword |
        @mediapassword_variable } ]
    [ [ , ] { NOREWIND | REWIND } ]
    [ [ , ] { NOUNLOAD | UNLOAD } ]
    [ [ , ] BUFFERCOUNT = { buffercount | @buffercount_variable }
        | MAXTRANSFERSIZE = { maxtransfersize |
        @maxtransfersize_variable }]
    [ [ , ] RESTART ]
    [ [ , ] STATS [ = percentage ] ]
    [ [ , ] COPY_ONLY ]
]
```

```
<file_or_filegroup> :: =
    { FILE = { logical_file_name | @logical_file_name_var }
    |
    FILEGROUP = { logical_filegroup_name |
      @logical_filegroup_name_var }
    | READ_WRITE_FILEGROUPS }
<backup_device> ::=
{
  { logical_backup_device_name | @logical_backup_device_name_var }
    |
    { DISK | TAPE } = { 'physical_backup_device_name' |
      @physical_backup_device_name_var }
}
```

Usage

```
USE master
EXEC sp_addumpdevice 'disk',  'Customer Backup Set 1',
    'f:\data\backup\Cust2.dat'
BACKUP DATABASE Customer
    FILE = 'Customer_data',
    FILEGROUP = 'Primary',
    FILE = 'Customer_data2',
    FILEGROUP = 'Secondary'
    TO 'Customer Backup Set 1'
```

Sample 11-4 shows the syntax for BACKUP LOG. By default, this command truncates the log after the backup.

SAMPLE 11-4 BACKUP LOG Syntax and Usage.

Syntax for Backing Up the Log

```
BACKUP LOG { database_name | @database_name_var }
{
    TO <backup_device> [ ,...n ]
[ [ MIRROR TO <backup_device> [ ,...n ] ] [ ...next-mirror ] ]
    [ WITH
    [ BLOCKSIZE = { blocksize | @blocksize_variable } ]
    [ [ , ] { CHECKSUM | NO_CHECKSUM } ]
    [ [ , ] { COMPRESSION | NO_COMPRESSION } ]
    [ [ , ] { STOP_ON_ERROR | CONTINUE_AFTER_ERROR } ]
    [ [ , ] DESCRIPTION = { 'text' | @text_variable } ]
    [ [ , ] EXPIREDATE = { date | @date_var }
        | RETAINDAYS = { days | @days_var } ]
    [ [ , ] PASSWORD = { password | @password_variable } ]
    [ [ , ] { FORMAT | NOFORMAT } ]
    [ [ , ] { INIT | NOINIT } ]
    [ [ , ] { NOSKIP | SKIP } ]
    [ [ , ] MEDIADESCRIPTION = { 'text' | @text_variable } ]
    [ [ , ] MEDIANAME = { media_name | @media_name_variable } ]
    [ [ , ] MEDIAPASSWORD = { mediapassword |
        @mediapassword_variable } ]
```

```
[ [ , ] NAME = { backup_set_name | @backup_set_name_var } ]
[ [ , ] NO_TRUNCATE ]
[ [ , ] { NORECOVERY | STANDBY = undo_file_name } ]
[ [ , ] { NOREWIND | REWIND } ]
[ [ , ] { NOUNLOAD | UNLOAD } ]
[ [ , ] BUFFERCOUNT = { buffercount | @buffercount_variable }
    | MAXTRANSFERSIZE = { maxtransfersize |
    @maxtransfersize_variable }]
[ [ , ] RESTART ]
[ [ , ] STATS [ = percentage ] ]
[ [ , ] COPY_ONLY ]
]
}
<backup_device> ::=
{
  { logical_backup_device_name | @logical_backup_device_name_var }
    |
    { DISK | TAPE } = { 'physical_backup_device_name' |
      @physical_backup_device_name_var }
}
```

Syntax for Truncating the Log

```
BACKUP LOG { database_name | @database_name_var }
{
    [ WITH
        { NO_LOG | TRUNCATE_ONLY } ]
}
```

Usage

```
USE master
EXEC sp_addumpdevice 'disk', 'Customer_log1',
    'f:\data\backup\Cust_log.dat'
BACKUP LOG Customer
    TO Customer_log1
```

Performing Transaction Log Backups

Transaction logs are essential to the timely recovery of SQL Server databases. Unlike database backups, which can be full or differential, transaction log backups are usually incremental. This means that each transaction log backup has a record of transactions only within a certain time frame. Transaction logs are always applied in sequence—with the completion time of the last full or differential backup marking the beginning of a transaction log sequence.

Consequently, to restore a database, you must apply each transaction log in sequence up to the point of failure. For example, if you run a full backup at 1:00 P.M. and the database fails at 1:46 P.M., you should restore the last full backup and then apply each transaction log backup created after the last full backup, such as the backups at 1:15 P.M., 1:30 P.M., and 1:45 P.M. As you can see, without the incremental transaction log backups, you would lose all the transactions that took place after the 1:00 P.M. full backup.

You perform transaction log backups as you do any other backup. Still, there are a few details that you should know before beginning this kind of backup, and the following sections cover these details.

Options and Commands That Invalidate Log Sequences

Although the normal backup process for transaction logs is fairly straightforward, SQL Server has some tricky features involving the option flags that you can set for the backup, the database, or both. The following database options prevent you from using a transaction log sequence to recover a database:

- **Truncate Log On Checkpoint**   Clears out inactive entries in the transaction log on checkpoint, which means you cannot use the log for recovery.
- **Using Non-Logged Operations**   Commands that bypass the log invalidate a log backup sequence.
- **ALTER DATABASE**   Adding or deleting files with ALTER DATABASE invalidates a backup sequence.

> **TIP**   As mentioned previously, the completion time of the last full or differential backup marks the beginning of a transaction log sequence. If you use any of the previous commands and invalidate a log sequence, perform a full or differential backup to start a new sequence.

Log Truncation Options

When you back up transaction logs, you have several options that determine how the backups are made. With SQL Server Backup in SQL Server Management Studio, you can use the Truncate The Transaction Log option. Setting this option clears out committed transactions from the log after a log backup. The BACKUP LOG command normally clears out committed or aborted transactions after a log backup as well. However, you can override this behavior with the following options:

- **TRUNCATE_ONLY**   Removes inactive entries from the log without creating a backup. This option invalidates the log sequence.
- **NO_LOG**   Same as TRUNCATE_ONLY, but this option does not log the BACKUP LOG command in the transaction log. This option is designed for a situation in which the transaction log or its home drive is full and you must truncate the log without writing to the log device.
- **NO_TRUNCATE**   Writes all the transaction log entries from the last backup to the point of failure. Use this option when the database is corrupt and you are about to restore it.

> **TIP**   After you use TRUNCATE_ONLY or NO_LOG, always perform a full or differential backup. This revalidates the log sequence. Additionally, because you can grow logs automatically, you should rarely encounter a situation in which you need to truncate the log without logging. The log can run out of space only if you set a maximum size or the drive or drives that the log uses run out of space.

Restoring a Database

Occasional database corruption, hardware failure, and natural disasters do happen, and as a database administrator, you need to be able to restore a database if any of these events occur. Even if you are a pro at backup and restore procedures, keep in mind that restoring a database is different from restoring an operating system or recovering other types of applications. The mix of full, differential, and transaction log backups ensures that you can get up-to-the-minute recovery of a database, but it complicates the recovery process.

In the following section, you will find tips and advice on troubleshooting database corruption. After that, you will find step-by-step procedures for restoring a database in various situations, including the following:

- Restoring a database using backups created in SQL Server Management Studio
- Restoring a file or filegroup
- Restoring a database to a different location
- Restoring a database using T-SQL

NOTE   You cannot restore SQL Server 2012 backups using an earlier version of SQL Server. In SQL Server 2012, you cannot restore system database backups that were created by using SQL Server 2000 or SQL Server 2005. You can, however, restore user database backups in SQL Server 2012 that were created by using SQL Server 2000, SQL Server 2005, or SQL Server 2012. After you restore a SQL Server 2005 or SQL Server 2000 database to SQL Server 2012, the database becomes available immediately and is then automatically upgraded to SQL Server 2012 while preserving database compatibility.

Database Corruption and Problem Resolution

All the knowledge you have accumulated as a database administrator is most important in one defining moment: the moment when you attempt to restore a database. The techniques you use to restore a database depend on the backup options you used and the state of the database. As you know, the backup techniques available are full, differential, transaction log, and file/filegroups. What you might not know is how to restore a database by combining these techniques.

Table 11-2 lists some recovery strategies for corrupted databases. These strategies show how to recover a database with various combinations of the available backup operations. If you use SQL Server Management Studio for backup and restore operations, these procedures are performed for you automatically in most cases. The actual step-by-step process is covered later in this chapter.

TABLE 11-2 Recovery Strategies for Databases

BACKUP TYPE	RESTORE PROCESS
Full backups only	Restore the database using the last full backup.
Full and differential backups	Restore the last full backup with NORECOVERY, and then restore the last differential backup with RECOVERY.
Full and transaction log backups	Back up the current transaction log with NO_TRUNCATE. Restore the last full backup with NORECOVERY. Apply log backups from that time forward in sequence using NORECOVERY. Apply the last differential backup with the RECOVERY option.
Full, differential, and transaction log backups	Back up the current transaction log with NO_TRUNCATE. Restore the last full backup with NORECOVERY, then transaction log backups, and then the last differential backup with NORECOVERY. Apply log backups from that time forward in sequence using NORECOVERY. Apply the last backup using the RECOVERY option.

Now you know how to restore a database in theory. But before you begin actually restoring a database, you should be sure that the database is really corrupt and cannot be recovered by other means. To troubleshoot database problems and potential corruption, complete the following steps:

1. Start with the SQL Server logs. See what types of error messages are in the logs, paying particular attention to errors that occur during database startup. Also, look at user-related errors. If you find errors, you can look up the error numbers in SQL Server Books Online or the Microsoft Online Support website (*search.support.microsoft.com*). You access the server logs through the Management folder in SQL Server Management Studio, as discussed in Chapter 12, "SQL Server 2012 Profiling and Monitoring."

2. Check the state of the database. Every time you start SQL Server, it goes through a recovery process on each database. If the recovery process has problems, the mode or state of the database might be abnormal. To check the mode or state, use the Status, Updateability, and UserAccess properties of the databasepropertyex function.

Status returns the current state, which will be one of the following:

- **Online** The database is online (but not necessarily open and fully recovered).
- **Emergency** The database is in emergency mode, which allows a suspect database to be used.
- **Offline** The database was taken offline.
- **Recovering** The database is going through the recovery process.

- **Restoring**   The database is being restored.
- **Suspect**   The database is suspect, which means that it is possibly corrupted.

Updateability returns READ_ONLY to indicate that data can be read but not modified, or READ_WRITE to indicate that data can be read and modified. UserAccess returns the current mode, including:

- **Single_User**   The database is in single-user mode, and only one db_owner, dbcreator, or sysadmin user can access it at a time.
- **Restricted_User**   The database is in restricted-access mode, and only members of db_owner, dbcreator, and sysadmin roles can access it.
- **Multi_User**   The database is in multi-user mode, and all users who have appropriate permissions can access it.

3. If possible, try to use the DBCC command to further troubleshoot or repair the database. DBCC is covered in Chapter 10.

4. If these procedures indicate that you have a corrupt database that cannot be repaired, restore the database from backup.

You can use the databasepropertyex function as shown in Sample 11-5.

SAMPLE 11-5 The databasepropertyex Function Syntax and Usage.

Syntax

```
databasepropertyex('database','property')
```

Usage

```
select databasepropertyex('Customer','Status')
```

You can restore suspect pages in databases using the Restore Page dialog box or the RESTORE DATABASE statement. To initiate a page restore, follow these steps:

1. Start SQL Server Management Studio. In the Object Explorer view, connect to the appropriate server.

2. Expand the Databases folder. Right-click the database you want to work with, point to Tasks, point to Restore, and then click Page. This opens the Restore Page dialog box.

3. Ensure that the correct database is selected in the Database box and then click Check Database Pages to identify corrupted pages.

4. SQL Server Management Studio adds the appropriate suspect pages to the Pages grid automatically and lists available backup sets in the Backup Sets grid. You can add pages by clicking Add, and then entering the File ID and Page ID of the pages to be restored. You can remove pages by selecting them and clicking Remove. You can verify that the backups are readable and complete by using Verify.

5. Click OK to restore the selected pages.

Restoring a Database from a Normal Backup

SQL Server Management Studio tracks all the backups you create for each database; when you need to restore a database, SQL Server Management Studio automatically configures the restore. You can restore a database by using the default settings or by fine-tuning the restore operation as necessary.

To restore a database, complete the following steps:

1. If you are using transaction logs and the database is still running, you should back up the current transaction log with NO_TRUNCATE. If you are using the SQL Server Backup dialog box, this means that you should select Back Up The Tail Of The Log on the Options page of the Back Up Database dialog box when performing the transaction log backup.

2. In SQL Server Management Studio, connect to the appropriate server in the Object Explorer view.

3. Expand the Databases folder. Right-click the database you want to restore. On the shortcut menu, point to Tasks, select Restore, and then select Database. This opens the Restore Database dialog box, shown in Figure 11-4.

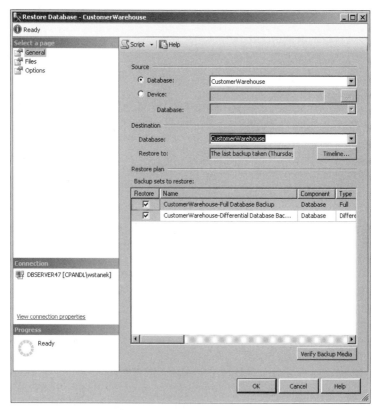

FIGURE 11-4 The Restore Database dialog box.

4. By default, the database you previously selected is listed as the source and destination database. Use the Source options to specify the source and location of the backup sets to restore. Only databases that have backup history in the *msdb* are listed.

   NOTE Restoring a database from a tape device or other backup device is different from a normal backup. This is primarily because you have to work with backup media (tapes) that might contain multiple backups, as well as multiple backup media sets (tape sets). If you are restoring from a device or the database you want to work with isn't on the Database list, select Device, and then click the related properties (...) button. Then you can use the Specify Backup Devices dialog box to specify the backup media and its location for the restore operation. You can add multiple locations and view the contents of additional backup sets as well. When you are finished, click OK to close the dialog box and then use the Device, Database list to select the database you are restoring.

5. If you are restoring a database to its original location, leave the database in the Destination panel's Database list as it is. If you want to restore the database to an alternate location, select a different database to use as the destination or type the name of a new database for the restore operation.

   NOTE This option is provided to allow you to restore a database to a different location, as described in the "Restoring a Database to a Different Location" section later in this chapter. All databases on the server except *master* and *tempdb* are included in the drop-down list as possible values.

6. By default, the database is restored to the most recent possible point in time. If multiple backups are available, you might be able to select a point in time for the restore. For example, if you know that GOTEAM accidentally deleted the Accounts table at 12:16 P.M., you could restore the database to a point just prior to this transaction, such as 12:15 P.M. To use the point-in-time option, click the Timeline button. In the Point In Time Restore dialog box, choose the option Specific Date And Time, select a date and time using the text boxes provided, and then click OK.

7. Use the Backup Sets To Restore grid to select the backup sets to restore. By default, the last full set (including the last full backup, differential backups since the last full backup, and transaction log backups since the last full backup) should be selected. The selected backups can also represent the most current backup set (according to a recovery plan) that meets the point-in-time recovery requirements. Click Verify Backup Media to verify the backup media before you start the restore.

   REAL WORLD Normally, you want to start with the last complete backup set. However, if you know that the last backup set is bad or contains transactions that you do not want to apply, such as a massive table deletion, go back to a previous backup set by selecting a different full backup and its related differential and transaction log backups as the starting point.

8. The Backup Sets to Restore grid provides a backup history for the selected database. You can use the information in the history as follows:

- **Restore**   Allows you to select which backup sets to restore. Default selections are based on the first backup to restore, and they go forward in time through differential and transaction log backups. You should rarely need to change the default selections.
- **Name**   Indicates the name of the backup set.
- **Component**   Shows the backed-up component as Database, File, or a blank entry. A blank entry indicates a transaction log backup.
- **Type**   Indicates the type of backup performed as Full, Differential, or Transaction Log.
- **Server**   Shows the Database Engine instance that performed the backup.
- **Database**   Displays the name of the database backed up.
- **Position**   Shows the position of the backup set in the volume.
- **First LSN**   For log backups, this is the log sequence number (LSN) of the first transaction in the backup set, which helps with ordering transaction logs for the restore operation.
- **Last LSN**   For log backups, this is the LSN of the last transaction in the backup set, which helps with ordering transaction logs for the restore operation.
- **Checkpoint LSN**   For log backups, this is the LSN of the most recent checkpoint at the time the backup was created, which helps with ordering transaction logs for the restore operation.
- **Full LSN**   The LSN of the most recent full database backup.
- **Start Date**   Displays a date and time stamp that indicates when the backup operation started.
- **Finish Date**   Displays a date and time stamp that indicates when the backup operation finished.
- **Size**   Shows the size of the backup.
- **User Name**   Displays the name of the user who performed the backup operation.
- **Expiration**   Indicates the date and time the backup set expires.

9. Optionally, select the Files page to change the restore location for database files.

10. Figure 11-5 shows the Options page. Select the Options page to configure options for the restore operation. You use the restore mode by using one of the following options:

- **Overwrite The Existing Database**   Allows the restore operation to overwrite any existing databases and their related files. (This is the same as using RESTORE with the REPLACE option.)

- **Preserve The Replication Settings** Ensures that any replication settings are preserved when restoring a published database to a server other than the server where the database was originally created. You must select the Leave The Database Ready For Use By Rolling Back Uncommitted Transactions option. (This is the same as using RESTORE with the KEEP_REPLICATION option.)

- **Restrict Access To The Restored Database** Sets the database in restricted-user mode so that only dbo, dbcreator, and sysadmin can access it. (This is the same as using RESTORE with the RESTRICTED_USER option.)

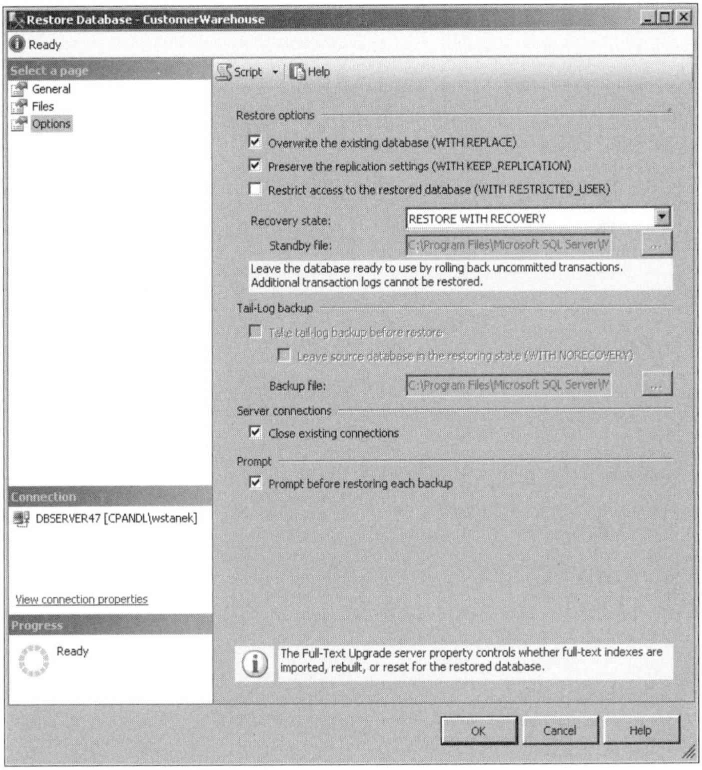

FIGURE 11-5 The Options page of the Restore Database dialog box.

11. Set the recovery state by using one of the following options:

- **RESTORE WITH RECOVERY** Leaves the database in a ready-to-use state. Completes the entire restore process and applies all the selected backups, which can include a full backup, a differential backup, and multiple transaction log backups. All completed transactions are applied, and any uncompleted transactions are rolled back. When the restore process is complete, the database is returned to ready status, and you can use it for normal operations.

- **RESTORE WITH NORECOVERY**   Leaves the database non-operational. This is essentially a manual restore that allows you to go step by step through the backups. SQL Server completes the entire restore process and applies all the selected backups, which can include a full backup, a differential backup, and multiple transaction log backups. When the restore is complete, the database is not returned to ready status, and you cannot use it for normal operations. All transactions have not been processed, and the database is waiting for you to apply additional transaction logs. Apply these transaction logs using this mode, and then for the last transaction log, set the mode to Leave The Database Ready To Use. All completed transactions are then applied, and any uncompleted transactions are rolled back.

- **RESTORE WITH STANDBY**   Leaves the database in read-only mode. This is similar to the Leave The Database Non-Operational option, with some exceptions. When the restore process ends, the database is in read-only mode, and it is ready for additional transaction logs to be applied. With the database in read-only mode, you can check the data and test the database. If necessary, apply additional transaction logs. Then, for the last transaction log, set the mode to Leave The Database Ready To Use. All completed transactions are then applied, and any uncompleted transactions are rolled back.

REAL WORLD   When you use the option RESTORE WITH STANDBY, SQL Server also creates an Undo file, which you can use to undo the restore operation. To commit the restore operations and the final transactions without restoring another transaction log, you could use the following code:

```
RESTORE DATABASE Customer
WITH RECOVERY
```

This commits final transactions (if possible), deletes the Undo file, and puts the database back in operational mode. Although you might want to use WITH RECOVERY at this stage, you probably do not want to use WITH NORECOVERY because you will undo all the changes from the restore and might end up with an empty database.

12. The Take Tail-Log Backup Before Restore option is selected by default as necessary to accommodate a point-in-time recovery. You also can select this option if you want to back up the tail of the log.

13. You can't restore a database when there are active connections. To ensure that existing connections to the database are closed prior to the restore, select Close Existing Connections. This options puts the database in single-user mode prior to initiating the restore and then sets the database to the appropriate mode (based on the selected recovery state) afterward.

14. Prompt Before Restoring Each Backup automatically prompts after completing a successful restore and before starting the next restore. The prompt includes a Cancel button, which is useful to cancel the restore

operation after a particular backup is restored. This is a good option to use when you need to swap tapes for different media sets.

15. When you are ready to start the restore operation, click OK. Stop the restore at any time by clicking Stop (the option appears in the upper-right corner of the dialog box). If an error occurs, you will see a prompt with an error message.

Restoring Files and Filegroups

You can restore files and filegroups from database backups or file backups individually, in combination with each other, or all together. If any changes were made to the files or filegroups, you must also restore all transaction log backups that were created after the files or filegroups were backed up.

Although you can usually recover individual files or filegroups, there are exceptions. If tables and indexes are created that span multiple filegroups, all the related filegroups must be restored together. Do not worry, however, because SQL Server generates an error prior to starting the restore if a required filegroup is missing. Further, if the entire database is corrupt, you must restore all files and filegroups in the database. In both cases, you must also apply transaction log backups created after the file or filegroup backups you are restoring.

To restore files or filegroups, complete the following steps:

1. If you are using transaction logs and the database is still running, you should back up the current transaction log with NO_TRUNCATE. If you are using the SQL Server Backup dialog box, this means that you should select Back Up The Tail Of The Log on the Options page of the Back Up Database dialog box when performing the transaction log backup.

2. In SQL Server Management Studio, connect to the appropriate server in the Object Explorer view.

3. Expand the Databases folder. Right-click the database you want to restore. On the shortcut menu, point to Tasks, select Restore, and then select Files And Filegroups. This opens the Restore Files And Filegroups dialog box.

4. The database currently selected is listed in the To Database box under Destination To Restore. If you are restoring files or filegroups to their original database, this is what you want to use. If you want to restore the files or filegroups to a different database, select the database to use as the destination or type the name of a new database for the restore operation.

   NOTE This option is provided so that you can restore a database to a different location, as described in the next section, "Restoring a Database to a Different Location." All databases on the server except *master* and *tempdb* are listed as possible values.

5. The database currently selected is listed in the From Database list under Source For Restore. If you are restoring files and filegroups for a different database, choose this database instead. Only databases that have backup history in the *msdb* database are listed.

6. The lower portion of the Restore Files And Filegroups dialog box provides a backup history for the files and filegroups in the selected database. You can use the information in the history as follows:

- **Restore** The selected check boxes indicate backup files to restore.

NOTE No default selections are made under Restore; you must choose the files manually.

- **Name** The name of the backup set.
- **File Type** The type of data in the backup. Data that is contained in tables is listed as Rows Data. Binary large object (BLOB) data that is stored in the file system is listed as Filestream Data. Transaction log data is listed as Log.
- **Type** The type of backup performed as Full, Differential, or Transaction Log.
- **Server** The Database Engine instance that performed the backup.
- **File Logical Name** The logical name of the file.
- **Database** The name of the file that was backed up.
- **Start Date** A date and time stamp indicating when the backup operation started.
- **Finish Date** A date and time stamp indicating when the backup operation finished.
- **Size** The size of the backup.
- **User Name** The name of the user who performed the backup operation.

7. Select the backup files you want to restore.

8. Select the Options page to configure options for the restore operation. The available options are similar to those discussed in the "Restoring a Database from a Normal Backup" section earlier in this chapter. Use the Restore Database File As option to change the restore location for database files.

9. When you are ready to start the restore operation, click OK.

Restoring a Database to a Different Location

When you restore a database to a different location, you are essentially copying the database from backups. If you use this procedure to copy a database to a new location on the same computer, you create a copy of the database that can have separate files and a different database name. Restoring a database to a different location is similar to the process discussed previously of restoring files and filegroups. The main differences are as follows:

- On the General page, under Destination, type a new name for the database in the Database box. For example, if you are restoring the Customer database to a new location, name the copy Customer 2 or CustomerCopy.
- When you access the Files page, you must override the default destination paths and enter new destination paths for all the files you are restoring.

Simply click in the Restore As box, and then enter a new file path, or you can click the related properties (...) button to select a new Restore As location.

If you use this procedure to copy a database to a different computer, you can create a working copy of the database on another server. You do not need to create a new database or perform any preliminary work, with one exception—if you want to use backup devices on the destination server, you should set them up beforehand. Also, before you begin the restore, you should be sure that the destination computer is using the same code page, sort order, Unicode collation, and Unicode locale as the source server. If these configuration settings are not identical, you will not be able to run the database on the destination server.

Recovering Missing Data

If you suspect that part of a database is missing or corrupted, you can perform a partial restore to a new location so that you can recover the missing or corrupted data. To do this, use the PARTIAL option with the RESTORE DATABASE statement as discussed in "Using T-SQL Restore Commands" later in this chapter. You can restore partial databases only at the filegroup level. The primary file and filegroup are always restored along with the files that you specify and their corresponding filegroups. Files and filegroups that are not restored are marked as Offline, and you cannot access them.

To carry out the restore and recovery process, complete the following steps:

1. Perform a partial database restore. Give the database a new name and location in the RESTORE DATABASE statement, and use MOVE...TO to move the original database source files to new locations, such as:

```
RESTORE DATABASE new_custdb_partial
    FILEGROUP = 'Customers2'
    FROM DISK='g:\cust.dmp'
    WITH FILE=1,NORECOVERY,PARTIAL,
    MOVE 'cust' TO 'g:\cu2.pri',
    MOVE 'cust_log' TO 'g:\cu2.log',
    MOVE 'cust_data_2' TO 'g:\cu2.dat2'
GO
```

2. Extract any needed data from the partial restore and insert it into the database from which it was deleted.

Creating Standby Servers

The notion of restoring a backup to a different computer can be extended to create a standby backup server that you can bring online if the primary server fails. When you create a standby server, you have two options:

- You can create a cold standby that you synchronize manually.
- You can create a warm standby that SQL Server synchronizes automatically.

Creating a Cold Standby

To create a standby that you synchronize manually, complete the following steps:

1. Install SQL Server on a new server system using an identical configuration. This means that the destination server should use the same code page, sort order, Unicode collation, and Unicode locale as the source server.

2. Copy all the databases on the primary server to this new system by specifying a different restore location in the Restore Database dialog box.

3. Maintain the copies of the databases by periodically applying the transaction log backups from the primary server to the standby server.

4. You might want to leave the standby server in standby mode so that the database is read-only. This allows users to access the database but not make changes.

If one or more databases on the primary server fail for any reason, you can make the corresponding databases on the standby server available to users. However, before you do this, you should synchronize the primary server and the standby server by completing the following steps:

1. On the standby server, apply any transaction log backups created on the primary server that have not been applied yet. You must apply these backups in the proper time sequence.

2. Create a backup of the active transaction log on the primary server, and then apply this backup to the database on the standby server. This ensures up-to-the-minute synchronization. Be sure to recover the database or specify that the database should be put in operational mode after this backup is applied.

   TIP If you need to make the standby server appear to be the primary server, you might need to take the primary server off the network and rename it. Then rename the standby server so that it appears to be the primary one.

3. After you restore the primary server to working condition, any changes to the standby server's databases need to be restored to the primary server. If they are not, those changes are lost when you start using the primary server again.

   NOTE Standby servers are not the same as a SQL Server failover cluster, which is created by using the SQL Server Failover Cluster Wizard and Microsoft Cluster Service. Standby servers store a second copy of a database on their hard disk drives. Virtual servers use a single copy of a database that is accessed from a shared storage device.

Creating a Warm Standby

SQL Server 2012 Enterprise Edition includes a feature called *log shipping*. You can use log shipping to create a standby server that is synchronized automatically with the primary server. To do this, follow these steps:

1. Install SQL Server on a new server system using an identical configuration. This means that the destination server should use the same code page, sort order, Unicode collation, and Unicode locale as the source server.

2. Copy all the databases on the primary server to this new system by specifying a different restore location in the Restore Database dialog box.

3. On the primary server, configure log shipping.

The primary server is referred to as the *source server*. The servers receiving the logs are referred to as *destination servers*. After configuring log shipping, you should periodically check the status of log shipping on the source server and destination servers.

If one or more databases on the primary server fail for any reason, you can make the corresponding databases on the standby server available to users. To do that, follow these steps:

1. Check the status of log shipping on the destination server to be sure that the most recent logs have been applied.

2. Take the primary server off the network and rename it.

3. Rename the standby server so that it appears to be the primary server.

4. Check connections to the new primary server.

After you restore the primary server to working condition, any changes to the standby server's databases need to be restored to the primary server. If they are not, those changes are lost when you start using the primary server again.

Using T-SQL Restore Commands

You can also restore databases using T-SQL. The commands you use are RESTORE DATABASE and RESTORE LOG. You can use RESTORE DATABASE to restore an entire database, specific files and filegroups, or part of a corrupted database. Sample 11-6 shows the syntax and usage for a complete restore. The option WITH RECOVERY is the default mode.

SAMPLE 11-6 RESTORE DATABASE Syntax and Usage for a Complete Restore.

Syntax

```
RESTORE DATABASE { database_name | @database_name_var }
[ FROM <backup_device> [ ,...n ] ]
[ WITH
    [ BUFFERCOUNT = { buffercount | @buffercount_variable } ]
    [ [ , ] { CHECKSUM | NO_CHECKSUM } ]
    [ [ , ] { STOP_ON_ERROR | CONTINUE_AFTER_ERROR } ]
    [ [ , ] MAXTRANSFERSIZE = { maxtransfersize |
        @maxtransfersize_variable }]
    [ [ , ] { CONTINUE_AFTER_ERROR | STOP_ON_ERROR } ]
    [ [ , ] ENABLE_BROKER ]
    [ [ , ] ERROR_BROKER_CONVERSATIONS ]
    [ [ , ] NEW_BROKER ]
    [ [ , ] FILE = { file_number | @file_number } ]
    [ [ , ] PASSWORD = { password | @password_variable } ]
    [ [ , ] KEEP_CDC ]
    [ [ , ] KEEP_REPLICATION ]
```

```
[ [ , ] MEDIANAME = { media_name | @media_name_variable } ]
[ [ , ] MEDIAPASSWORD = { mediapassword |
    @mediapassword_variable } ]
[ [ , ] BLOCKSIZE = { blocksize | @blocksize_variable } ]
[ [ , ] MOVE 'logical_file_name' TO 'operating_system_file_name' ]
    [ ,...n ]
[ [ , ] { RECOVERY | NORECOVERY | STANDBY =
    {standby_file_name | @standby_file_name_var } }
]
[ [ , ] REPLACE ]
[ [ , ] RESTART ]
[ [ , ] RESTRICTED_USER ]
[ [ , ] { REWIND | NOREWIND } ]
[ [ , ] STATS [ =percentage ] ]
[ [ , ] STOPAT = { date_time | @date_time_var } |
    [ , ] STOPATMARK = { 'lsn:lsn_number' } [ AFTER 'datetime' ] |
    [ , ] STOPBEFOREMARK = { 'lsn:lsn_number' } [ AFTER 'datetime' ]
]
[ [ , ] { UNLOAD | NOUNLOAD } ]
]
[;]
<backup_device> ::=
{ { 'logical_backup_device_name' | @logical_backup_device_name_var }
    | { DISK | TAPE } = { 'physical_backup_device_name' |
        @physical_backup_device_name_var } }
```

Usage

```
RESTORE DATABASE Customer
    FROM TAPE = '\\.\tape0'
```

Usage

```
RESTORE DATABASE Customer
    FROM Customer_1
    WITH NORECOVERY,
        MOVE 'CustomerData1' TO 'F:\mssql7\data\NewCust.mdf',
        MOVE 'CustomerLog1' TO 'F:\mssql7\data\NewCust.ldf'
RESTORE LOG Customer
    FROM CustomerLog1
    WITH RECOVERY
```

Using RESTORE DATABASE, you also can restore files and filegroups. Sample 11-7 shows the related syntax and usage.

SAMPLE 11-7 RESTORE DATABASE Syntax and Usage for a File and Filegroup Restore.

Syntax

```
RESTORE DATABASE { database_name | @database_name_var }
    <file_or_filegroup_or_pages> [ ,...f ]
[ FROM <backup_device> [ ,...n ] ]
[ WITH [ RECOVERY | NORECOVERY ]
    [ BUFFERCOUNT = { buffercount | @buffercount_variable } ]
```

```
[ [ , ] { CHECKSUM | NO_CHECKSUM } ]
[ [ , ] { STOP_ON_ERROR | CONTINUE_AFTER_ERROR } ]
[ [ , ] MAXTRANSFERSIZE = { maxtransfersize |
    @maxtransfersize_variable }]
[ [ , ] { CONTINUE_AFTER_ERROR | STOP_ON_ERROR } ]
[ [ , ] FILE = { file_number | @file_number } ]
[ [ , ] PASSWORD = { password | @password_variable } ]
[ [ , ] MEDIANAME = { media_name | @media_name_variable } ]
[ [ , ] MEDIAPASSWORD = { mediapassword |
    @mediapassword_variable }]
[ [ , ] BLOCKSIZE = { blocksize | @blocksize_variable } ]
[ [ , ] MOVE 'logical_file_name' TO 'operating_system_file_name' ]
    [ ,...n ]
[ [ , ] RECOVERY | NORECOVERY ]
[ [ , ] REPLACE ]
[ [ , ] RESTART ]
[ [ , ] RESTRICTED_USER ]
[ [ , ] { REWIND | NOREWIND } ]
[ [ , ] STATS [ =percentage ] ]
[ [ , ] { UNLOAD | NOUNLOAD } ]
]
[;]
<backup_device> ::=
{ { logical_backup_device_name|
      @logical_backup_device_name_var }
  | { DISK | TAPE } = { 'physical_backup_device_name' |
      @physical_backup_device_name_var } }
<file_or_filegroup_or_pages> ::=
{ FILE = { logical_file_name | @logical_file_name_var }
  | FILEGROUP = { logical_filegroup_name |
      @logical_filegroup_name_var } }
  | PAGE = 'file:page [ ,...p ]'  }
```

Usage

```
RESTORE DATABASE Customer
    FILE = 'Customerdata_1',
    FILE = 'Customerdata_2',
    FILEGROUP = 'Primary'
    FROM Customer_1
    WITH NORECOVERY
RESTORE LOG Customer
    FROM CustomerLog1
```

Sample 11-8 shows the syntax for performing a partial restore. This command creates a new database that is based on a partial copy of the backup data. When you use this procedure, database_name represents the new name for the database, and the MOVE...TO command is used to move the original database source files to new locations.

SAMPLE 11-8 RESTORE DATABASE Syntax and Usage for a Partial Restore.

Syntax

```
RESTORE DATABASE { database_name | @database_name_var }
        <files_or_filegroups>
[ FROM <backup_device> [ ,...n ] ]
[ WITH PARTIAL
    [ BUFFERCOUNT = { buffercount | @buffercount_variable } ]
    [ [ , ] { CHECKSUM | NO_CHECKSUM } ]
    [ [ , ]  { STOP_ON_ERROR | CONTINUE_AFTER_ERROR } ]
    [ [ , ] MAXTRANSFERSIZE = { maxtransfersize |
        @maxtransfersize_variable }]
    [ [ , ] { CONTINUE_AFTER_ERROR | STOP_ON_ERROR } ]
    [ [ , ] FILE = { file_number | @file_number } ]
    [ [ , ] PASSWORD = { password | @password_variable } ]
    [ [ , ] MEDIANAME = { media_name | @media_name_variable } ]
    [ [ , ] MEDIAPASSWORD = { mediapassword |
        @mediapassword_variable } ]
    [ [ , ]  BLOCKSIZE = { blocksize | @blocksize_variable } ]
    [ [ , ] MOVE 'logical_file_name' TO 'operating_system_file_name' ]
        [ ,...n ]
    [ [ , ] NORECOVERY ]
    [ [ , ] REPLACE ]
    [ [ , ] RESTART ]
    [ [ , ] RESTRICTED_USER ]
    [ [ , ] { REWIND | NOREWIND } ]
    [ [ , ] STATS [ =percentage ] ]
    [ [ , ] STOPAT = { date_time | @date_time_var } |
        [ , ] STOPATMARK = { 'lsn:lsn_number' } [ AFTER datetime ] |
        [ , ] STOPBEFOREMARK = { 'lsn:lsn_number' } [ AFTER datetime ]
    ]
    [ [ , ] { UNLOAD | NOUNLOAD } ]
]
[;]
<backup_device> ::=
{ { logical_backup_device_name | @logical_backup_device_name_var }
    | { DISK | TAPE } = { 'physical_backup_device_name' |
        @physical_backup_device_name_var } }

<files_or_filegroups> ::=
    { FILE = { logical_file_name | @logical_file_name_var }
    | FILEGROUP = { logical_filegroup_name |
        @logical_filegroup_name_var }}
    [ ,...f ]
```

Usage

```
RESTORE DATABASE cust_part
    FILEGROUP = 'Customers2'
    FROM DISK = 'g:\cust.dmp'
    WITH FILE = 1,NORECOVERY,PARTIAL,
    MOVE 'cust' TO 'g:\cu2.pri',
```

```
        MOVE 'cust_log' TO 'g:\cu2.log',
        MOVE 'cust_data_2' TO 'g:\cu2.dat2'
GO
RESTORE LOG cust_part
        FROM DISK = 'g:\cust.dmp'
        WITH FILE = 2,RECOVERY
GO
```

Sample 11-9 shows how you can use RESTORE LOG.

SAMPLE 11-9 RESTORE LOG Syntax and Usage.

Syntax

```
RESTORE LOG { database_name | @database_name_var }
        <file_or_filegroup_or_pages> [ ,...f ]
[ FROM <backup_device> [ ,...n ] ]
[ WITH
    [ BUFFERCOUNT = { buffercount | @buffercount_variable } ]
    [ [ , ] { CHECKSUM | NO_CHECKSUM } ]
    [ [ , ]  { STOP_ON_ERROR | CONTINUE_AFTER_ERROR } ]
    [ [ , ] MAXTRANSFERSIZE = { maxtransfersize |
        @maxtransfersize_variable }]
    [ [ , ] { CONTINUE_AFTER_ERROR | STOP_ON_ERROR } ]
    [ [ , ] FILE = { file_number | @file_number } ]
    [ [ , ] PASSWORD = { password | @password_variable } ]
    [ [ , ] KEEP_REPLICATION ]
    [ [ , ] MEDIANAME = { media_name | @media_name_variable } ]
    [ [ , ] MEDIAPASSWORD = { mediapassword |
        @mediapassword_variable } ]
    [ [ , ] BLOCKSIZE = { blocksize | @blocksize_variable } ]
    [ [ , ] MOVE 'logical_file_name' TO 'operating_system_file_name' ]
        [ ,...n ]
    [ [ , ] { RECOVERY | NORECOVERY | STANDBY =
            {standby_file_name | @standby_file_name_var } }
    ]
    [ [ , ] REPLACE ]
    [ [ , ] RESTART ]
    [ [ , ] RESTRICTED_USER ]
    [ [ , ] { REWIND | NOREWIND } ]
    [ [ , ] STATS [ =percentage ] ]
     [ [ , ] STOPAT = { date_time | @date_time_var } |
     [ , ] STOPATMARK = { 'mark_name' | 'lsn:lsn_number' }
            [ AFTER datetime ] |
     [ , ] STOPBEFOREMARK = { 'mark_name' | 'lsn:lsn_number' }
            [ AFTER datetime ]
     ]
    [ [ , ] { UNLOAD | NOUNLOAD } ]
]
[;]
<backup_device> ::=
{ { logical_backup_device_name |
```

```
            @logical_backup_device_name_var }
    | { DISK | TAPE } = { 'physical_backup_device_name' |
            @physical_backup_device_name_var } }
<file_or_filegroup_or_pages> ::=
{  FILE = { logical_file_name | @logical_file_name_var }
    | FILEGROUP = { logical_filegroup_name |
            @logical_filegroup_name_var } }
    | PAGE = 'file:page [ ,...p ]'  }
```

Usage

```
RESTORE DATABASE Customer
    FROM Customer_1, Customer_2
    WITH NORECOVERY
RESTORE LOG Customer
    FROM CustomerLog1
    WITH NORECOVERY
RESTORE LOG Customer
    FROM CustomerLog2
    WITH RECOVERY, STOPAT = 'Dec 21, 2012 4:15 AM'
```

Restoring the *master* Database

The *master* database is the most important one in the SQL Server database management system. This database stores information about all the databases on a server, server configuration, server logins, and other important information. If *master* gets corrupted, operations on the server might grind to a halt, and you have to recover *master* using one of two techniques.

If you can start SQL Server, you can restore *master* from backup by using a process similar to what you would use to restore any other database. To do this, complete the following steps:

1. You can back up *master* only by using a full backup. As a result, no differential or transaction log backups will be available. This means that you might not be able to restore *master* exactly as it was before the failure, and that normally, you should use the recovery state of Leave The Database Ready To Use.

2. When you finish restoring the *master* database, you might need to apply manually any changes made since the last full backup.

3. After you check the server and verify that everything is okay, make a full backup of *master.*

If you cannot start SQL Server and you know that *master* is the cause of the problem, you can restore *master* by completing the following steps:

1. Rebuild the *master* database by running Setup. Use Setup to rebuild, verify, and repair the SQL Server instance and its system databases.

2. After you rebuild *master* and get SQL Server back online, you can restore the last backup of *master* to return the server to its most current state.

3. Because Rebuild Master rebuilds the *msdb* and *model* databases, you might need to restore these databases from backup as well.

4. Re-create any backup devices if necessary.

5. Re-enter logins and other security settings if necessary.

6. Restore replication databases if necessary.

7. Restore or attach user databases if necessary.

8. Restore other server configuration settings if necessary.

As you can see from this step-by-step procedure, restoring *master* can take a lot of time and work, which is why it is so important to back up *master* regularly. When you finish recovering the server, be sure to make a full backup of the *master* database.

SQL Server 2012 Profiling and Monitoring

Monitoring server performance, tracking user activity, and troubleshooting errors are essential parts of database administration, and Microsoft SQL Server has several tools that you can use to perform these tasks. Performance Monitor, the standard Windows Server 2008 tool for monitoring servers, has updated counters for SQL Server. These counters allow you to track many different server resources and activities. SQL Server Profiler, an analysis and profiling tool, allows you to trace server events. Other tools and resources are available as well, such as stored procedures and the SQL Server logs.

Monitoring Server Performance and Activity

Monitoring SQL Server is not something you should do haphazardly. You need to have a plan—a set of goals that you hope to achieve. Let's look at some reasons you might want to monitor SQL Server and the tools you can use to do this.

Reasons to Monitor SQL Server

One of the main reasons you monitor SQL Server performance is to troubleshoot problems. For example, if users are having problems connecting to the server, you will want to monitor the server to find out more about what is causing these problems. Your goal is to track down the problem by using the available monitoring resources and then solve the problem effectively.

Another common reason to monitor SQL Server is to improve server performance. To achieve optimal performance, you need to minimize the time it takes for users to see the results of queries and maximize the total number of queries that the server can handle simultaneously. You do this by using the following techniques:

- Resolve hardware issues that might be causing problems. For example, if disk read/write activity is slower than expected, work on improving disk I/O.

- Monitor memory and CPU usage and take appropriate steps to reduce the load on the server. For example, other processes running on the server might be using memory and CPU resources needed by SQL Server.

- Cut down the network traffic load on the server. With replication, for example, you can configure remote stored procedure execution rather than transmit large data changes individually.

Unfortunately, you often have to make tradeoffs in resource usage. For example, as the number of users accessing SQL Server grows, you might not be able to reduce the network traffic load, but you might be able to improve server performance by optimizing queries or indexing.

Getting Ready to Monitor

Before you start monitoring SQL Server, it is a good idea to establish baseline performance metrics for your server. To do this, you measure server performance at various times and under different load conditions. You can then compare the baseline performance with subsequent performance to determine how SQL Server is performing. Performance metrics that are well above the baseline measurements might indicate areas in which the server needs to be optimized or reconfigured.

After you establish the baseline metrics, prepare a monitoring plan. A comprehensive monitoring plan involves the following steps:

1. Determine which server events should be monitored to help you accomplish your goal.
2. Set filters to preferentially select the amount of information that is collected.
3. Configure monitors and alerts to watch the events.
4. Log the event data so that it can be analyzed.
5. Analyze the event data and replay the data to find a solution.

These procedures will be examined later in this chapter in the "Monitoring SQL Server Performance" section. Although you should develop a monitoring plan in most cases, sometimes you might not want to go through all these steps to monitor SQL Server. For example, if you want to check only current user activity levels, you might not want to use Performance Monitor and instead run the stored procedure sp_who. You can also examine this information in the Activity Monitor window in SQL Server Management Studio.

NOTE The stored procedure sp_who reports on current users and processes. When you execute sp_who, you can pass a login name as an argument. If you do not specify a login name, NULL is passed in this argument, so all logins are returned. If you use the keyword *active* as the login name, you will see only active processes; any processes waiting for the next command from a user will be excluded. Instead of a specific login name, such as sa, you can use the numeric value for a system process ID as well.

Monitoring Tools and Resources

The primary monitoring tools you use are Performance Monitor and SQL Server Profiler. Other resources for monitoring SQL Server include the following:

- **Activity Monitor**   This monitor provides information on current users, processes, and locks, as discussed in the "Managing Server Activity" section in Chapter 1, "Managing Your SQL Servers." To display Activity Monitor, press Ctrl+Alt+A, or click the related button on the Standard toolbar.

- **Control Point**   This monitor provides a central collection point for performance information gathered from managed instances and deployed data-tier applications. For more information, see the "Configuring Utility Control Points" section in Chapter 5, "Tuning and Linking Your SQL Servers." In SQL Server Management Studio, use the Utility Explorer view to work with control points. Select View, and then click Utility Explorer.

- **Database Mirroring Monitor**   This monitor provides information on the status of Database Mirroring and allows you to verify the data flow for each failover partner individually. The status is shown as Synchronizing when the principal database is sending log records to the mirrored instance; Synchronized when the mirrored instance is in sync with the principal database; Suspended when the principal database is available but not sending data to the mirrored instance; Disconnected when the server instance cannot connect to its partner; and Unknown when the monitor is not connected to either mirror partner. To display Database Mirroring Monitor, use the Object Explorer view to access an instance of the Database Engine. Right-click the database to be monitored, select Tasks, and then select Launch Database Mirroring Monitor.

- **Job Activity Monitor**   This monitor provides details on the status of SQL Server Agent jobs. To display Job Activity Monitor, use the Object Explorer view to access an instance of the Database Engine. Expand the server node and the SQL Server Agent node, and then double-click Job Activity Monitor.

- **Replication Monitor**   This monitor provides details on the status of SQL Server replication and allows you to configure replication alerts. To display Replication Monitor, use the Object Explorer view to access an instance of the Database Engine. Right-click the Replication node, and then select Launch Replication Monitor.

- **Event logs**   The information in the event logs allows you to troubleshoot systemwide problems, including SQL Server and SQL Server Agent problems. To access event logs, click Start, click Administrative Tools, and then select Event Viewer.

- **SQL Server Agent logs**   The information in these event logs allows you to view informational, auditing, warning, and error messages that can help you troubleshoot SQL Server Agent problems. To access agent logs, use the Object Explorer view to access an instance of the Database Engine. Expand the server node and the SQL Server Agent node. Under the SQL Server Agent node, expand the Error Logs node, and then double-click the log you want to examine.

- **SQL Server logs**   The information in these event logs allows you to view informational, auditing, warning, and error messages that can help you troubleshoot SQL Server problems. To access the server logs, use the Object Explorer view to access an instance of the Database Engine. Expand the server node and the Management node. Under the Management node, right-click the SQL Server Logs node, point to View, and then select SQL Server Log.

NOTE   SQL Server documentation refers to the SQL Server and SQL Server Agent logs as error logs. In their current implementation, however, the logs are more accurately called *event logs*, which is the terminology used in this chapter. Similar to event logs in Microsoft Windows, these logs in SQL Server contain informational and security messages, as well as error messages. To open both types of logs, right-click the SQL Server Logs node and point to View, and then select SQL Server And Windows Log.

- **DBCC statements**   This set of commands allows you to check SQL Server statistics, trace activity, and check database integrity.

- **sp_helpdb**   This stored procedure displays information about databases.

- **sp_helpindex**   This stored procedure reports information about indexes on a table or view.

- **sp_helpserver**   This stored procedure provides information in SQL Server instances configured for remote access or replication.

- **sp_monitor**   This stored procedure shows key SQL Server usage statistics, such as CPU idle time and CPU usage.

- **sp_spaceused**   This stored procedure shows an estimate of disk space used by a table, indexed view, or Service Broker queue in the current database. (Use DBCC UPDATEUSAGE to correct inaccuracies in space usage reports.)

- **sp_who**   This stored procedure shows a snapshot of current SQL Server users and processes.

- **sys.dm_tran_locks**   This dynamic management view shows information about object locks.

In addition to having the use of log files and Transact-SQL (T-SQL) statements, you will find a set of built-in functions that return system information. Table 12-1 provides a summary of key functions and their usages. The values returned by these functions are cumulative from the time SQL Server was last started.

TABLE 12-1 Built-In Functions for Monitoring SQL Server Performance and Activity

FUNCTION	DESCRIPTION	EXAMPLE
@@connections	Returns the number of connections or attempted connections	select @@connections as 'Total Login Attempts'
@@cpu_busy	Returns CPU processing time in milliseconds for SQL Server activity	select @@cpu_busy as 'CPU Busy', getdate() as 'Since'
@@idle	Returns SQL Server idle time in milliseconds	select @@idle as 'Idle Time', getdate() as 'Since'
@@io_busy	Returns I/O processing time in milliseconds for SQL Server	select @@io_busy as 'IO Time', getdate() as 'Since'
@@pack_received	Returns the number of input packets read from the network by SQL Server	select @@pack_received as 'Packets Received'
@@pack_sent	Returns the number of output packets written to the network by SQL Server	select @@pack_sent as 'Packets Sent'
@@packet_errors	Returns the number of network packet errors for SQL Server connections	select @@packet_errors as 'Packet Errors'
@@timeticks	Returns the number of microseconds per CPU clock tick	select @@timeticks as 'Clock Ticks'
@@total_errors	Returns the number of disk read/write errors encountered by SQL Server	select @@total_errors as 'Total Errors', getdate() as 'Since'
@@total_read	Returns the number of disk reads by SQL Server	select @@total_read as 'Reads', getdate() as 'Since'
@@total_write	Returns the number of disk writes by SQL Server	select @@total_write as 'Writes', getdate() as 'Since'
fn_virtualfilestats	Returns input/output statistics for data and log files	select * from fn_virtualfilestats(null,null)

Working with Replication Monitor

When you've configured replication, you use Replication Monitor to track the status of replication throughout the enterprise. By default, only the currently selected publisher is displayed in the Replication Monitor window, but you can add any publishers that you want to monitor and organize them into publisher groups as necessary.

Starting and Using Replication Monitor

To start Replication Monitor, right-click the Replication folder in the Object Explorer view, and then select Launch Replication Monitor. Replication Monitor uses icons to indicate the general status of replication. If any publication has an error status, the error status is indicated by a red circle around an X at all levels within Replication Monitor.

When you select a publisher in the left pane, the right pane shows the replication details for that publisher. By default, this information is refreshed every five seconds, and it can be refreshed immediately by pressing F5. As Figure 12-1 shows, the publisher view has three tabs:

- **Publications**   Shows individual entries for each configured publication. An icon indicates the type and status of the publication as follows:
  - A purple book icon with a blue circle indicates snapshot replication.
  - A blue book icon with a right-facing green arrow indicates transactional replication.
  - A yellow book icon with a left-facing green arrow and a right-facing blue arrow indicates merge replication.
  - A red circle around an X indicates error status.

  At a glance, you can also see the number of subscriptions to the publication, the number of subscriptions being synchronized, the current average performance for subscribers, and the current worst performance for subscribers.

- **Subscription Watch List**   Shows the status of individual subscriptions by type. Use the first drop-down list to specify the type of subscriptions to display and the second drop-down list to specify whether to display all subscriptions of the specified type or some subset, such as the 25 worst-performing subscriptions. Note the status, such as running, error, and so on; the performance level, such as excellent, good, poor, and so on; and the latency.

- **Agents**   Shows the SQL Server Agent jobs common to all publications on the selected publisher. To determine if there are potential replication problems, note the status, last start time, and duration. There might be a problem with jobs that have a status of Never Started and with jobs that have been running for a long time.

Adding Publishers and Publisher Groups

When you first start Replication Monitor, only the currently selected publisher is displayed in Replication Monitor. You can add publishers that you want to monitor and organize them into publisher groups as necessary.

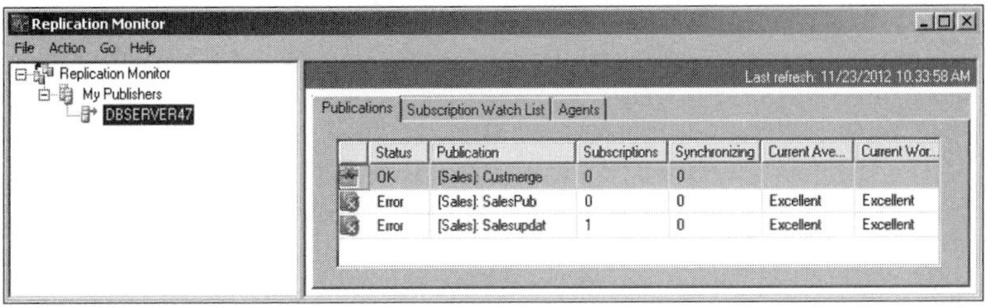

FIGURE 12-1 Replication Monitor.

To start monitoring additional publishers and create publisher groups, follow these steps:

1. Start Replication Monitor. In the left pane, right-click the Replication Monitor node, and then select Add Publisher from the shortcut menu. This displays the Add Publisher dialog box, shown in Figure 12-2.

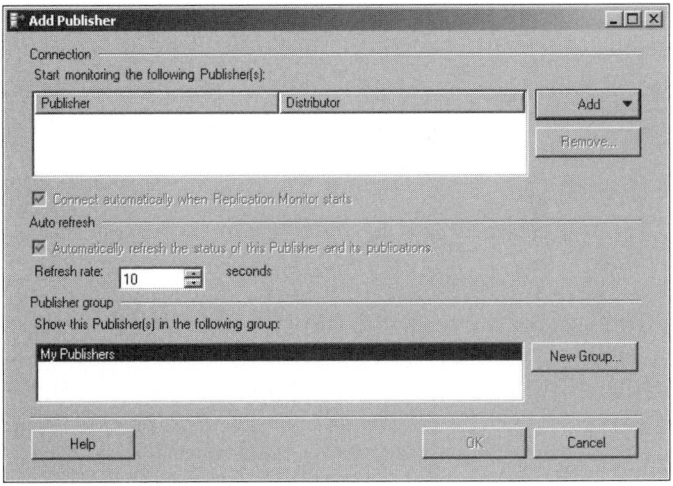

FIGURE 12-2 The Add Publisher dialog box.

2. Click Add, and then do the following:

   ■ Choose Add SQL Server Publisher to configure a connection to a server running SQL Server by using the Connect To Server dialog box. Registered servers are listed in the Server Name list; you can also browse for others. The default authentication is Windows authentication, which uses your current login and password. Click Connect.

- Choose Add Oracle Publisher to configure a connection to an Oracle server by using the Connect To Server dialog box. Registered servers are listed in the Server Name list; you can also browse for others. The default authentication is Oracle Standard authentication, which requires a user login and password. Click Connect.

- Choose Specify A Distributor And Add Its Publishers to configure a connection to a distributor by using the Connect To Server dialog box. Registered servers are listed in the Server Name list; you can also browse for others. The default authentication is Windows authentication, which uses your current login and password. When you click Connect, Replication Monitor connects to the distributor, obtains a list of publishers for the distributor, and then connects to these publishers as well.

NOTE Before you can add an Oracle publisher, you must configure a connection to the Oracle publisher's distributor by choosing Specify A Distributor And Add Its Publishers.

3. Publisher groups make it easier to manage monitoring in complex enterprise environments. Select the publisher group to which to add a publisher or publishers. If you want to create a new group, click New Group, specify the group name, and then click OK. Select the new group under Show This Publisher(s) In The Following Group.

4. Click OK.

Working with the Event Logs

Event logs provide historical information that can help you track down problems with SQL Server. SQL Server writes events to the SQL Server event logs, the SQL Server Agent event logs, and the Windows application log. You can use all three logs to track messages related to SQL Server. However, there are some things you should know about these logs:

- Only the application log provides additional information on all applications running on the server, and only the application log provides features for filtering events based on type. For example, you can filter events so that only error and warning messages are displayed.

- If you start the MSSQLServer or MSSQL$*instancename* service from the command prompt, events are logged to the SQL Server event log and to standard output. No events are recorded in the Windows application log.

- Windows has additional logs that can be helpful when tracking issues. If you are tracking security issues, start with the SQL Server event logs and also examine the Windows security log. If you are having trouble finding the source of a problem that is preventing proper operation of SQL Server, start with the SQL Server logs and also examine the Windows application and system logs.

SQL Server error messages can be cryptic and difficult to read if you do not understand the formatting. Error messages logged by SQL Server can have the following information:

- **An error number that uniquely identifies the error message** System error numbers have one to five digits. System errors are numbered from 1 to 50,000. User-defined errors start at 50,001.

- **A severity level that indicates how critical the message is** Severity levels range from 1 to 25. Messages with a severity level of 0 to 10 are informational messages. Severity levels from 11 to 16 are generated by users, and users can correct them. Severity levels from 17 to 25 indicate software or hardware errors that you should examine.

- **An error state number that indicates the source of the error** Error state numbers have one to three digits and a maximum value of 127. Normally, this points to a specific source or block in the SQL Server code that generated the message.

- **A message that provides a brief description of the error** Read the message to get more information about the error, which will help you in troubleshooting problems.

You might see ODBC and OLE DB return errors from SQL Server that contain similar information as well. The sys.messages catalog view in the *master* database contains a list of error messages and descriptions that can be returned by SQL Server. To see all error messages that can be returned by SQL Server, you can execute the following commands:

T-SQL

```
USE master
GO
SELECT * FROM sys.messages
GO
```

PowerShell Example 1

```
Invoke-Sqlcmd -Query "USE master; SELECT * FROM sys.messages;"
-ServerInstance "DataServer32\TechServices"
```

PowerShell Example 2

```
Set-Location SQLSERVER:\SQL\DataServer32\TechServices
Invoke-Sqlcmd -Query "USE master; SELECT * FROM sys.messages;"
```

Examining the Application Log

The application log contains entries for all database server instances running on the computer, as well as entries for other business applications. You can open the application log in Log File Viewer via SQL Server Management Studio. To do this, under the Management node, right-click the SQL Server Logs node, point to View, and then click SQL Server And Windows Log. Then you can work with SQL Server logs and Windows event logs in the Log File Viewer.

You can work with the application log in Event Viewer by completing the following steps:

1. Click Start, click Administrative Tools, and then choose Event Viewer. This starts Event Viewer.

2. Event Viewer displays logs for the local computer by default. If you want to view logs on a remote computer, right-click the Event Viewer node in the console tree (left pane), and then select Connect To Another Computer to display the Select Computer dialog box. In the dialog box, enter the name of the computer you want to access, and then click OK.

3. In the console tree, expand the Windows Logs node, and then click Application. You should see an application log similar to the one shown in Figure 12-3. Use the information in the Source column to determine which service or database server instance logged a particular event.

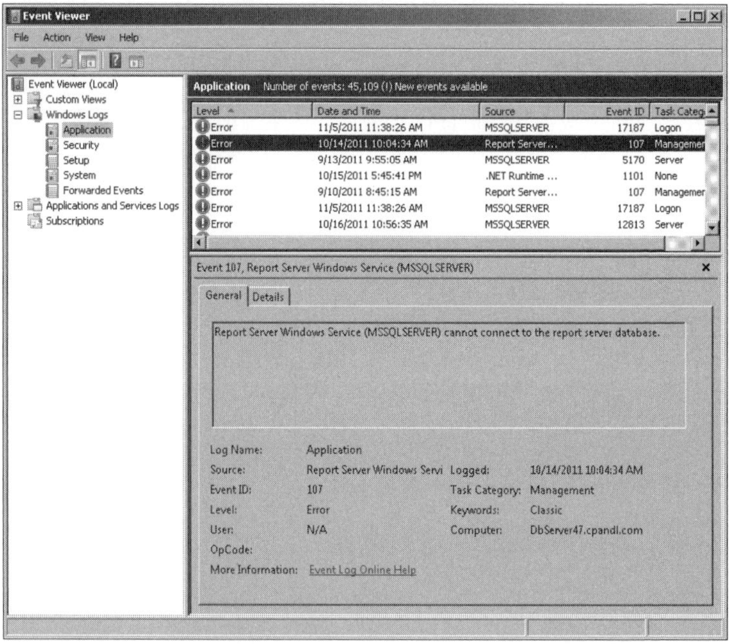

FIGURE 12-3 A Windows application log.

The entries in the main window of Event Viewer provide a quick overview of when, where, and how an event occurred. To obtain detailed information on an event, review the details provided on the General tab in the lower portion of the main window. The event level or keyword precedes the date and time of the event. Event levels include the following:

■ **Information** An informational event that is generally related to a successful action.

- **Audit Success** An event related to the successful execution of an action.
- **Audit Failure** An event related to the failed execution of an action.
- **Warning** A noncritical error that provides a warning. Details for warnings are often useful in preventing future system problems.
- **Error** A noncritical error that you should review.
- **Critical** An error for which there is no recovery.

In addition to the date, time, and event type indicator, the summary and detailed event entries provide the following information:

- **Source** The application, service, or component that logged the event.
- **Event ID** An identifier for the specific event.
- **Task Category** The category of the event, which is sometimes used to describe the related action further.
- **User** The user account that was logged on when the event occurred, if applicable.
- **Computer** The name of the computer on which the event occurred.
- **Description** A text description of the event (provided in detailed entries).
- **Data** Any data or error code output by the event (provided in detailed entries).

Warnings and errors are the two main types of events that you want to examine closely. Whenever one of these types of events occurs and you are unsure of the cause, review the detailed event description. If you want to see only warnings and errors, you can filter the log. To filter a selected log in Windows Server 2008 or Windows Server 2008 R2, complete the following steps:

1. In the actions pane or on the Action menu, choose Filter Current Log.

2. Use the Logged list to select the time frame for including logged events. You can choose to include events from the last hour, the last 12 hours, the last 24 hours, the last 7 days, or the last 30 days.

3. Use the Event Level check boxes to specify the level of events to include. Select the Verbose check box to get additional detail.

4. Use the Event Source list to select event sources to include. If you select specific event sources, all other event sources are excluded.

5. Optionally, use the User and Computer(s) boxes to specify users and computers that should be included. If you do not specify the users and computers to be included, events generated by all users and computers are included.

6. Click OK. You should now see a filtered list of events. Review these events carefully, and take steps to correct any problems that exist. To clear the filter and see all events for the log, click Clear Filter in the actions pane or on the Action menu.

Examining the SQL Server Event Logs

The SQL Server logs record information, warnings, errors, and auditing messages pertaining to SQL Server activity. New logs are created when you start the SQL Server service or when you run the sp_cycle_errorlog stored procedure (which requires sysadmin privileges). When a new log is created, the current log is cycled to the archive. SQL Server maintains up to five archived logs (by default).

You can view the SQL Server event logs in SQL Server Management Studio or through a text editor. In SQL Server Management Studio, you access the event logs by completing the following steps:

1. Start SQL Server Management Studio. In the Object Explorer view, connect to the database server of your choice, and then work your way down to the Management folder.

2. Expand the Management folder, and then double-click the SQL Server Logs entry. The current log is shown with the label *Current*. Archived logs are shown with descriptive labels, such as *Archive #1*.

3. Double-click the log you want to view to open it in Log File Viewer.

4. With Log File Viewer open, you can add other logs to the log file summary by selecting their check boxes, as shown in Figure 12-4.

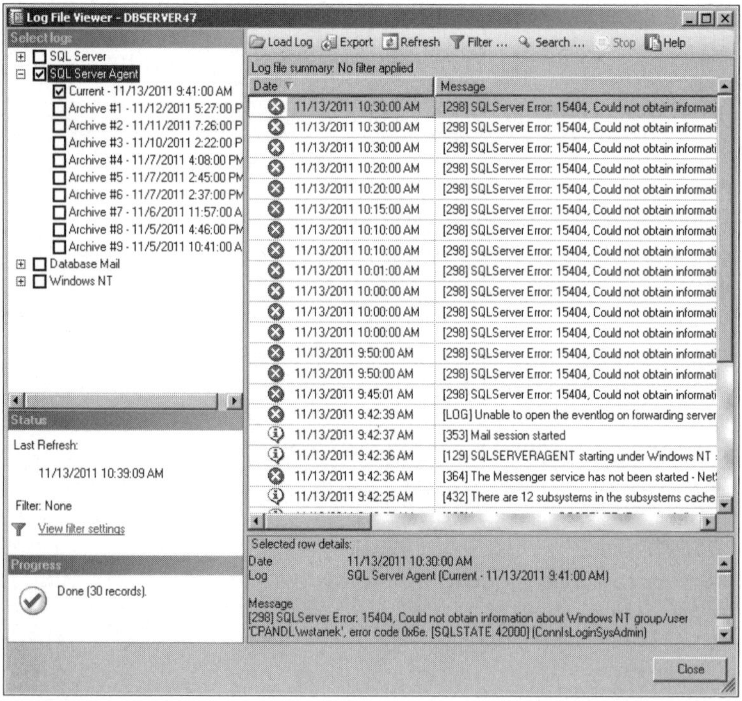

FIGURE 12-4 Log File Viewer.

To access the event logs in a text editor, complete the following steps:

1. Start a text editor, such as Notepad, and then use its Open dialog box to access the SQL Server Log folder, normally located in MSSQL11.MSSQLSERVER\MSSQL\LOG or MSSQL11.*InstanceName*\MSSQL\LOG. Note that by default, permissions for the Log folder are configured so that only the system account, members of the local Administrators group, and SQL Server have access. If you are logged on with an account that has appropriate privileges, you can get permanent Full Control access to the Log folder by clicking Continue when prompted.

2. Open the log you want to examine. The current log file is named ERRORLOG with no file extension. The most recent log backup has the extension .1, the second most recent has the extension .2, and so on. If you are using Notepad or a similar program, you won't see the log files until you specify an appropriate file type, such as All Files (*.*).

To change the number of logs that SQL Server maintains, right-click the SQL Server Logs entry in the Object Explorer view and select Configure. In the Configure SQL Server Error Logs dialog box, select Limit The Number Of Error Log Files, and then set the maximum number of error log files to retain by using the Maximum Number Of Error Log Files combo box. The default number of log files maintained is six: one current log and five archive logs. You can change the number of logs maintained to any value from 6 through 99.

Examining the SQL Server Agent Event Logs

The SQL Server Agent logs record information, warnings, and errors pertaining to SQL Server Agent activity. New logs are created only when you start the SQL Server Agent service. When a new log is created, the current log is cycled to the archive. SQL Server maintains up to five archived agent logs by default.

In SQL Server Management Studio, you access the current SQL Server Agent log by completing the following steps:

1. Start SQL Server Management Studio. In the Object Explorer view, connect to the database server of your choice, and then work your way down to the SQL Server Agent node.

2. Expand the SQL Server Agent node, and then double-click the Error Logs entry. The current log is shown with the label *Current*. Archived logs are labeled *Archive # 1*, and so on.

3. Double-click the log you want to view to open it in Log File Viewer.

4. With Log File Viewer open, you can add other logs to the log file summary by selecting their check boxes.

To access archived SQL Server Agent event logs in a text editor, complete the following steps:

1. Start the text editor, and then use its Open dialog box to access the SQL Server Log folder, which is normally located in MSSQL11.MSSQLSERVER\MSSQL\LOG or MSSQL11.*InstanceName*\MSSQL\LOG.

2. Open the log you want to examine. The name of the current log file is SQLAGENT.OUT. The most recent log backup has the extension .1, the second most recent has the extension .2, and so on.

You can manage the SQL Server Agent logs in several ways. You can force SQL Server Agent to recycle the current log by right-clicking the SQL Server Agent\Error Logs node in the Object Explorer view, selecting Recycle, and then clicking OK. Alternatively, run sp_cycle_agent_errorlog on *msdb* (which requires sysadmin privileges). With either technique, SQL Server closes the current agent log, moves it to an archive log, and starts a new agent log.

You can control the level of logging and set the log file location as well. To do this, complete the following steps:

1. Right-click the SQL Server Agent\Error Logs node in the Object Explorer view, and then select Configure.

2. Use the Error Log File box to set the folder path and file name of the agent log. The default path is MSSQL11.MSSQLSERVER\MSSQL\LOG\SQLAGENT.OUT or MSSQL11.*InstanceName*\MSSQL\LOG\SQLAGENT.OUT. New archive files will also be created in the folder specified as part of the path.

3. Use the Agent Log Level check boxes to control the level of logging for the SQL Server Agent. By default, only error and warning messages are logged. If you want to view informational messages in the logs, select the Information check box as well.

4. Click OK.

Monitoring SQL Server Performance

Performance Monitor is one of the tools of choice for monitoring SQL Server performance. Performance Monitor displays statistics in a graphical format for the set of performance parameters you select. These performance parameters are referred to as *counters*.

When you install SQL Server on a system, Performance Monitor is updated with a set of counters for tracking SQL Server performance parameters. These counters also can be updated when you install services and add-ons for SQL Server. For example, when you configure replication on a server, Replication Monitor is added and made available through SQL Server Management Studio, and Performance Monitor is again updated with a set of objects and counters for tracking replication performance.

Performance Monitor creates a graph depicting the various counters you are tracking. You can configure the update interval for this graph, but it's set to three seconds by default. As you will see when you work with Performance Monitor, the tracking information is most valuable when you record the information in a log file and when you configure alerts to send messages when certain events occur or when certain thresholds are reached, such as when a database log file gets close to running out of free space.

The following sections examine the procedures you use with Performance Monitor.

Choosing Counters to Monitor

Performance Monitor displays information only for counters you are tracking. More than 100 SQL Server counters are available—and if you have configured other SQL Server features, such as replication, you can use even more counters. These counters are organized into object groupings. For example, all lock-related counters are associated with the *SQLServer:Locks* object.

To select which counters you want to monitor, complete the following steps:

1. You can access a stand-alone console by clicking Start, pointing to Administrative Tools, and then clicking Performance Monitor. In Server Manager, you can access this tool as a snap-in under the Diagnostics node. Double-click the Diagnostics node to expand it. Finally, double-click and then select the Performance node.

2. In the Performance console, expand Monitoring Tools, and then select Performance Monitor, as shown in Figure 12-5. Any default counters are shown in the lower portion of the Performance Monitor window. To delete a default counter, click its entry in the Performance Monitor window, and then press the Delete key.

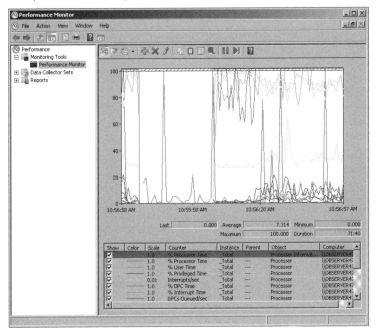

FIGURE 12-5 The Performance Monitor window.

3. The Performance Monitor tool has several views and view types. Be sure that you are viewing current activity by clicking View Current Activity on the toolbar or pressing Ctrl+T. You can switch between the view types (Line, Histogram Bar, and Report) by clicking Change Graph Type or pressing Ctrl+G.

4. To add counters, click the Add button on the toolbar. (Alternatively, press Ctrl+I in Windows Server 2008 or Ctrl+N in Windows Server 2008 R2.) This displays the Add Counters dialog box, shown in Figure 12-6.

> **TIP** The easiest way to learn what you can track is by exploring the objects and counters available in the Add Counters dialog box. Select an object in the Performance Object list, select the Show Description check box, and then scroll through the list of counters for the object.

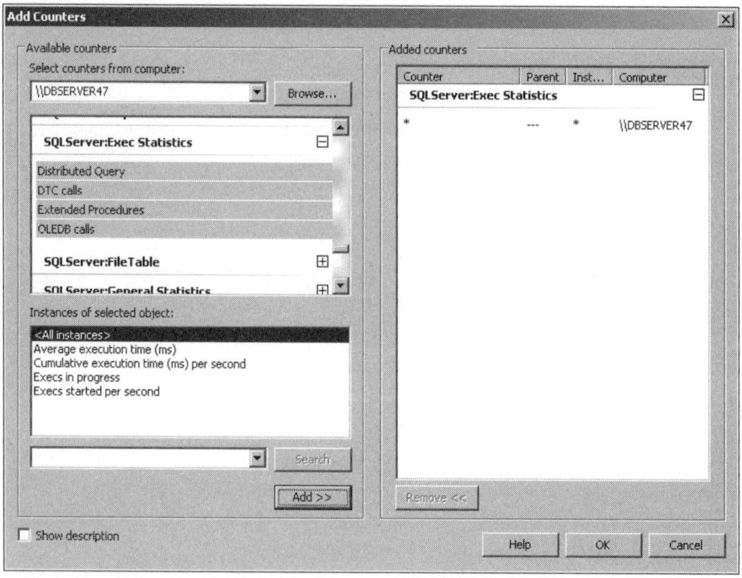

FIGURE 12-6 The Add Counters dialog box.

5. In the Select Counters From Computer list, enter the Universal Naming Convention (UNC) name of the computer running SQL Server that you want to work with, such as \\SQLServer52, or choose Local Computer to work with the local computer.

> **NOTE** You need to be at least a member of the Performance Monitor Users group in the domain or the local computer to perform remote monitoring. When you use performance logging, you need to be at least a member of the Performance Log Users group in the domain or the local computer to work with performance logs on remote computers.

6. In the Available Counters panel, performance objects are listed alphabetically. If you select an object entry by clicking it, all related counters are selected. If you expand an object entry, you can see all the related counters and can then select individual counters by clicking them. For example, you could expand the entry for the *SQLServer:Locks* object and then select the Average Wait Time (ms), Lock Requests/sec, and Lock Timeouts (timeout > 0)/sec counters.

7. When you select an object or any of its counters, you see the related instances. Choose All Instances to select all counter instances for monitoring, or select one or more counter instances to monitor. For example, you could select instances of Application or Database locks.

8. When you've selected an object or a group of counters for an object as well as the object instances, click Add to add the counters to the graph.

9. Repeat steps 5 through 8 to add other performance parameters.

10. Click Close when finished.

TIP Don't try to chart too many counters or counter instances at once. You'll make the display too difficult to read, and you'll use system resources—namely, CPU time and memory—that might affect server responsiveness.

Performance Logging

Data collector sets allow you to specify sets of performance objects and counters that you want to track. After you've created a data collector set, you can easily start or stop monitoring the performance objects and counters included in the set. In a way, this makes data collector sets similar to the performance logs used in earlier releases of Windows. However, data collector sets are much more sophisticated. You can use a single data collector set to generate multiple performance counter and trace logs. You can also perform the following tasks:

- Assign access controls to manage who can access collected data.
- Create multiple run schedules and stop conditions for monitoring.
- Use data managers to control the size of collected data and reporting.
- Generate reports based on collected data.

In the Performance console, you can review currently configured data collector sets and reports under the Data Collector Sets and Reports nodes, respectively. As shown in Figure 12-7, you'll find data sets and reports that are user defined and system defined. User-defined data sets are created by users for general monitoring and performance tuning. System-defined data sets are created by the operating system to aid in automated diagnostics.

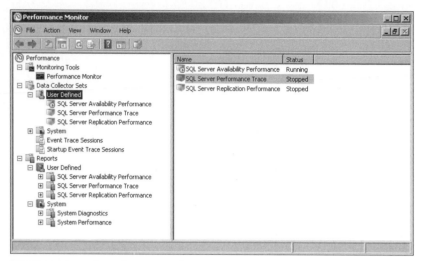

FIGURE 12-7 Access data collector sets and reports.

> **NOTE** Using a management data warehouse, you can create several special-purpose data collector sets automatically and then generate periodic reports to get a better understanding of disk usage, query statistics, and server activity. See the "Configuring a Management Data Warehouse" section later in this chapter for details.

Creating and Managing Data Collector Sets

To view the currently configured data collector sets, access Performance Monitor by selecting the Performance Monitor option on the Administrative Tools menu and then expanding the Data Collector Sets node. You can work with data collectors in a variety of ways:

- You can view currently defined user or system data collector sets by selecting either User Defined or System as appropriate. When you select a data collector set in the left pane, you'll see a list of the related data collectors in the main pane listed by name and type. The Trace type is for data collectors that record performance data whenever related events occur. The Performance Counter type is for data collectors that record data on selected counters when a predetermined interval has elapsed. The Configuration type is for data collectors that record changes to particular registry paths.

- You can view running event traces by selecting Event Trace Sessions. You can then stop a data collector running a trace by right-clicking it and selecting Stop.

- You can view the enabled or disabled status of event traces that are configured to run automatically when you start the computer by selecting Startup Event Trace Sessions. You can start a trace by right-clicking a startup data collector and selecting Start As Event Trace Session. You can delete a startup data collector by right-clicking it and then selecting Delete.

- You can save a data collector as a template that can be used as the basis of other data collectors by right-clicking the data collector and selecting Save Template. In the Save As dialog box, select a directory, type a name for the template, and then click Save. The data collector template is saved as an XML file that can be copied to other systems.

- You can delete a user-defined data collector by right-clicking it and then selecting Delete. If a data collector is running, you need to stop collecting data first and then delete the collector. Deleting a collector deletes the related reports as well.

Collecting Performance Counter Data

Data collectors can be used to record performance data on the selected counters at a specific sample interval. For example, you could sample performance data for the CPU every 15 minutes.

To collect performance counter data, follow these steps:

1. In Performance Monitor, under the Data Collector Sets node, right-click the User-Defined node in the left pane, point to New, and then choose Data Collector Set.

2. In the Create New Data Collector Set Wizard, type a name for the data collector, such as SQL Server Performance Monitor or Replication Performance Monitor.

3. Select the Create Manually option, and then click Next.

4. On the What Type Of Data Do You Want To Include page, the Create Data Logs option is selected by default. Select the Performance Counter check box, and then click Next.

5. On the Which Performance Counters Would You Like To Log page, click Add. This displays the Add Counters dialog box, which you can use as previously discussed to select the performance counters to track. When you finish selecting counters, click OK.

6. On the Which Performance Counters Would You Like To Log page, enter a sample interval and select a time unit in seconds, minutes, hours, days, or weeks. The sample interval specifies when new data is collected. For example, if you sample every 15 minutes, the data log is updated every 15 minutes. Click Next when you are ready to continue.

7. On the Where Would You Like The Data To Be Saved page, type the root path to use for logging collected data. Alternatively, click Browse, and then use the Browse For Folder dialog box to select the logging directory. Click Next when you are ready to continue.

BEST PRACTICES The default location for logging is %SystemRoot%\PerfLogs\Admin. Log files can grow in size very quickly. If you plan to log data for an extended period, be sure to place the log file on a drive with lots of free space. Remember, the more frequently you update the log file, the greater the drive space and CPU resource usage on the system.

8. On the Create The Data Collector Set page, the Run As box lists Default as the user to indicate that the log will run under the privileges and permissions of the default system account. To run the log with the privileges and permissions of another user, click Change. Type the user name and password for the account, and then click OK. User names can be entered in DOMAIN\Username format, such as CPANDL\WilliamS for the WilliamS account in the CPANDL domain.

9. Select the Open Properties For This Data Collector Set option, and then click Finish. This saves the data collector set, closes the wizard, and then opens the related Properties dialog box.

10. By default, logging is configured to start manually. To configure a logging schedule, click the Schedule tab, and then click Add. You can now set the active range, start time, and run days for data collection.

11. By default, logging stops only if you set an expiration date as part of the logging schedule. Using the options on the Stop Condition tab, you can configure the log file to stop manually after a specified period of time, such as seven days, or when the log file is full (if you've set a maximum size limit).

12. Click OK when you finish setting the logging schedule and stop conditions. You can manage the data collector as explained in the "Creating and Managing Data Collector Sets" section earlier in this chapter.

NOTE You can configure Windows to run a scheduled task when data collection stops. You configure tasks to run on the Task tab in the Properties dialog box.

Collecting Performance Trace Data

You can use data collectors to record performance trace data whenever events related to their source providers occur. A source provider is an application or operating system service that has traceable events.

To collect performance trace data, follow these steps:

1. In Performance Monitor, under the Data Collector Sets node, right-click the User-Defined node in the left pane, point to New, and then choose Data Collector Set.

2. In the Create New Data Collector Set Wizard, type a name for the data collector, such as Database Locks Trace or Database Mirroring Trace.

3. Select the Create Manually option, and then click Next.

4. On the What Type Of Data Do You Want To Include page, the Create Data Logs option is selected by default. Select the Event Trace Data check box, and then click Next.

5. On the Which Event Trace Providers Would You Like To Enable page, click Add. Select an event trace provider to track, such as Active Directory Domain Services: Core. By selecting individual properties in the Properties list and

clicking Edit, you can track particular property values rather than all values for the provider. Repeat this process to select other event trace providers to track. Click Next when you are ready to continue.

6. Complete steps 7 through 12 from the previous procedure, "Collecting Performance Counter Data."

Collecting Configuration Data

You can use data collectors to record changes in registry configuration. To collect configuration data, follow these steps:

1. In Performance Monitor, under the Data Collector Sets node, right-click the User-Defined node in the left pane, point to New, and then choose Data Collector Set.

2. In the Create New Data Collector Set Wizard, type a name for the data collector, such as SQL Server Registry or Registry Adapter Info.

3. Select the Create Manually option, and then click Next.

4. On the What Type Of Data Do You Want To Include page, the Create Data Logs option is selected by default. Select the System Configuration Information check box, and then click Next.

5. On the Which Registry Keys Would You Like To Record page, click Add. Type the registry path to track. Repeat this process to add other registry paths. Click Next when you are ready to continue.

6. Complete steps 7 through 12 from the previous procedure, "Collecting Performance Counter Data."

Viewing Data Collector Reports

When you troubleshoot problems, you'll often want to log performance data over an extended period of time and then review the data to analyze the results. For each data collector that has been or is currently active, you'll find related data collector reports. As with data collector sets themselves, data collector reports are organized into two general categories: user-defined and system.

You can view data collector reports in Performance Monitor. Expand the Reports node, and then expand the individual report node for the data collector you want to analyze. Under the data collector's report node, you'll find individual reports for each logging session. A logging session begins when logging starts, and it ends when logging is stopped.

The most recent log is the one with the highest log number. If a data collector is actively logging, you won't be able to view the most recent log. You can stop collecting data by right-clicking a data collector set and selecting Stop. Collected data is shown by default in a graph spanning the start of data collection to the end of data collection.

You can modify the report details by using the following technique:

1. In the monitor pane, press Ctrl+Q or click the Properties button on the toolbar. This displays the Performance Monitor Properties dialog box.

2. Click the Source tab.

3. Specify data sources to analyze. Under Data Source, click Log Files, and then click Add to open the Select Log File dialog box. You can now select additional log files to analyze.

4. Specify the time window that you want to analyze. Click Time Range, and then drag the Total Range bar to specify the appropriate starting and ending times. Drag the left edge to the right to make the start time earlier. Drag the right edge to the left to make the end time later.

5. Click the Data tab. Now you can select counters to view. Select a counter, and then click Remove to remove it from the graph view. Click Add to display the Add Counters dialog box, which you can use to select the counters that you want to analyze.

   NOTE Only counters that you selected for logging are available. If you don't see a counter that you want to work with, you need to modify the data collector properties, restart the logging process, and then check the logs at a later date.

6. Click OK. In the monitor pane, click Change Graph Type to select the type of graphing.

Configuring Performance Counter Alerts

You can configure alerts to notify you when certain events occur or when certain performance thresholds are reached. You can send these alerts as network messages and as events that are logged in the application event log. You can also configure alerts to start application and performance logs.

To configure an alert, follow these steps:

1. In Performance Monitor, under the Data Collector Sets node, right-click the User-Defined node in the left pane, point to New, and then choose Data Collector Set.

2. In the Create New Data Collector Set Wizard, type a name for the data collector, such as DB Application Locks Alert or SQL Server Replication Alert.

3. Select the Create Manually option, and then click Next.

4. On the What Type Of Data Do You Want To Include page, the Create Data Logs option is selected by default. You don't want to use this option or its related check boxes. Instead, select the Performance Counter Alert option, and then click Next.

5. On the Which Performance Counters Would You Like To Monitor page, click Add to display the Add Counters dialog box. This dialog box is identical to the Add Counters dialog box discussed previously. Use the Add Counters dialog box to add counters that trigger the alert. Click OK when you finish.

6. In the Performance Counters panel, select the first counter, and then use the Alert When text box to set the occasion when an alert for this counter is triggered. Alerts can be triggered when the counter is above or below a specific value. Select Above or Below, and then set the trigger value. The unit of measurement is whatever makes sense for the currently selected counter or counters. For example, to create an alert for when processor time is more than 95 percent, you would select Over and then type 95. Repeat this process to configure other counters you've selected.

7. Click Next. Complete steps 8 through 12 from the procedure "Collecting Performance Counter Data" earlier in the chapter.

Configuring a Management Data Warehouse

SQL Server 2012 has a built-in feature called the *management data warehouse*. This feature uses several special-purpose data collector sets to collect disk usage, query statistics, and server activity information automatically. To use this feature, you must configure a data collection host and then set up data collection for SQL Server instances you want to track.

Understanding Management Data Warehouses

When you configure a management data warehouse, you can enable data collection whenever you want to monitor SQL Server performance and then generate reports to review the collected information. When you finish evaluating SQL Server performance, you should free server resources used for collection by disabling data collection.

To enable data collection, you must create a management data warehouse. The warehouse is a database that stores the collected data as well as related report data. By default, the collected data is retained for 14 days, but you can configure a different retention period if desired. As the selected SQL Server instance then will act as a data collection host, you must also ensure that SQL Server Agent is configured properly. SQL Server Agent jobs are used to collected data at periodic intervals on any SQL Server instance for which you've subsequently configured data collection.

Any database you use as a management data warehouse has three special-purpose roles:

- **mdw_reader**   Members of this role are able to access the management data warehouse and read reports.
- **mdw_writer**   Members of this role are able to write and upload data to the management data warehouse. All data collectors must have this role.
- **mdw_admin**   Members of this role have full access and can perform read, write, update, and delete operations in the management data warehouse.

These special-purpose roles are stored in the *msdb* database on the data collection host, and no user is a member of these roles by default. While users who are members of the sysadmin role have full access to data collector views, administrators must be added explicitly to the appropriate role or roles to perform other operations.

Creating the Management Data Warehouse

A management data warehouse stores your data collector information. You can create a management data warehouse by completing the following steps:

1. Start SQL Server Management Studio. In the Object Explorer view, connect to the server you want to use, and then expand the Management folder. If data collection hasn't been configured, you'll see a red down arrow on the Data Collection icon. Right-click Data Collection, and then select Configure Management Data Warehouse.

2. If the Welcome page is displayed, click Next. Select Create Or Upgrade A Management Data Warehouse. Click Next.

3. SQL Server stores the collected data in a database. If you want to use an existing database to store the data, select the database in the list provided. Otherwise, click New and create a database for storing the collected data. Click Next.

4. On the Map Logins And Users page, you can map logins and users to management data warehouse roles. Later, by configuring logins for the *msdb* database, you can modify membership in these roles as discussed in the "Managing Server Logins" section in Chapter 7, "Implementing SQL Server 2012 Security." When you click Next and then click Finish, the wizard sets up the management data warehouse and maps logins and users as necessary. If an error occurs, you need to review the error details, correct the problem, and then repeat this procedure.

Setting Up Data Collection

You can set up data collection by completing the following steps:

1. In SQL Server Management Studio, in the Object Explorer view, expand the Management folder, right-click Data Collection, and then select Configure Management Data Warehouse.

2. If the Welcome page is displayed, click Next. Select Set Up Data Collection, and then click Next.

3. Click the options (...) button to the right of the Server Name box. Connect to the data collection host, and then select the collection database in the list provided.

4. Optionally, set a cache directory that is used to store collected data before it is uploaded to the specified database. If you don't specify a directory, the TEMP directory is used.

5. When you click Next and then click Finish, the wizard starts system collection sets and enables data collection. If an error occurs, you need to review the error details, correct the problem, and then repeat this procedure.

Managing Collection and Generating Reports

When you set up collection, data collection is enabled automatically. You can turn data collection on or off by right-clicking the Data Collection node and selecting Enable Data Collection or Disable Data Collection as appropriate.

In SQL Server Management Studio, in the Object Explorer view, you can generate data collection reports by expanding the Management folder, right-clicking Data Collection, pointing to Reports, pointing to Management Data Warehouse, and then selecting the type of report to generate. You can generate the following reports: Server Activity History, Disk Usage History, or Query Statistics History.

Solving Performance Problems with Profiler

Whether you are trying to track user activity, troubleshoot connection problems, or optimize SQL Server, SQL Server Profiler is one of the best utilities available (at least until we all move to Extended Events, which are replacing SQL Server Profiler and trace stored procedures). Profiler enables you to trace events that occur in SQL Server. Events you can track in Profiler are similar to counters you can monitor in Performance Monitor. They are organized into groups called *event classes*, and you can track one or more events for any of the available event classes. The strengths of Profiler are its advanced features and extensive customization capabilities.

You can record and replay Profiler traces when you want to analyze the data—and this is one area in which Profiler excels. You can use Profiler to do the following:

- Use information to find slow-running queries and then determine what is causing the queries to run slowly.
- Go through statements one step at a time to find the cause of a problem.
- Track a series of statements that cause a particular problem and then replay the trace on a test server to determine the cause.
- Use trace information to determine the cause of deadlocks.
- Monitor user and application activity to discover actions that are using CPU time or queries that are taking a long time to process.

I'll first look at how you can work with Profiler. Then I'll examine how to create and manage traces.

Using Profiler

You can start Profiler in several ways:

- Click Start, type **profiler.exe** in the Search box, and then press Enter.
- On the Start menu, select Microsoft SQL Server 2012, Performance Tools, and then click SQL Server Profiler.
- Select SQL Server Profiler on the Tools menu in SQL Server Management Studio.

Figure 12-8 shows Profiler in the process of running a trace. The columns shown for the trace, such as EventClass, are completely configurable when you set up the trace, allowing you to select or clear columns as necessary. Two columns you want to pay particular attention to are Duration and CPU. The Duration column shows (in milliseconds) how long a particular event has been running. The CPU column shows (in milliseconds) the amount of CPU processing time the event requires.

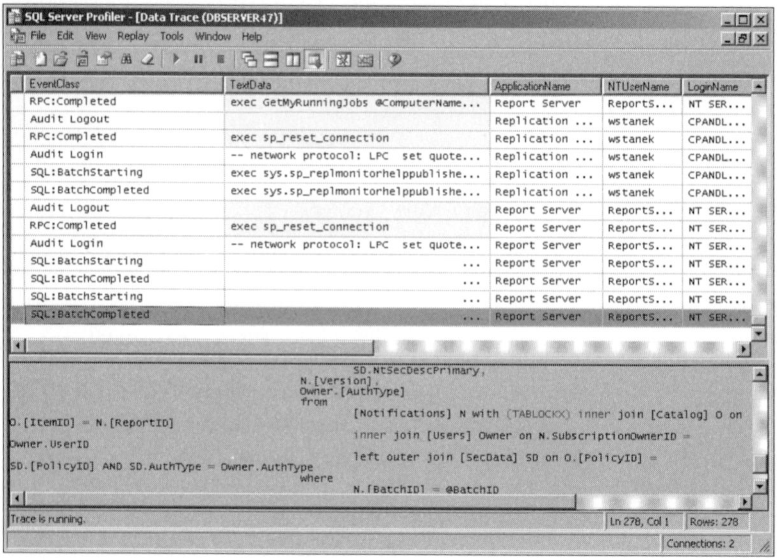

FIGURE 12-8 Using SQL Server Profiler to trace SQL Server events.

Stored procedures provide an alternative to Profiler. Using these stored procedures gives you some options that you do not have with SQL Server Profiler. For example, you can start a trace automatically when SQL Server starts. To create traces with stored procedures, complete the following steps:

1. Create a trace definition using sp_trace_create.
2. Set events to capture using sp_trace_setevent.
3. Set event filters using sp_trace_setfilter.

Creating New Traces

You use traces to record events generated by local and remote SQL Server instances. You run traces in the Profiler window and store them for later analysis.

To start a new trace, complete the following steps:

1. Start SQL Server Profiler, and then click New Trace. Alternatively, select File, New Trace.
2. Use the Connect To Server dialog box to connect to the server you want to trace.

You will see the Trace Properties dialog box, shown in Figure 12-9.

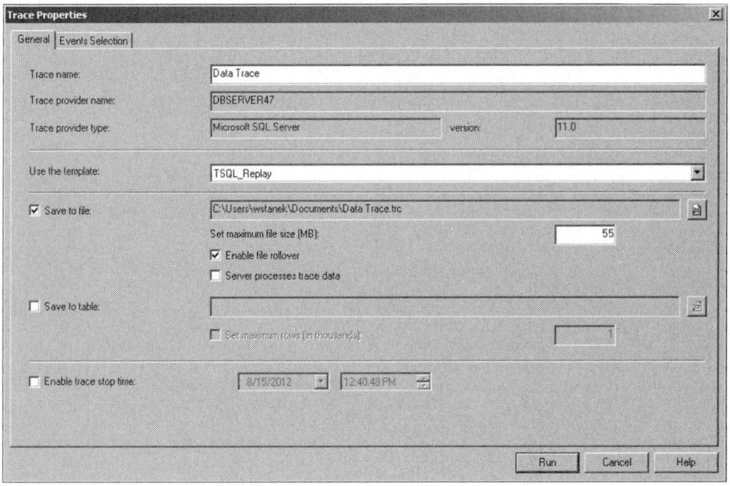

FIGURE 12-9 The Trace Properties dialog box.

3. In the Trace Name text box, type a name for the trace, such as Data Trace or Deadlock Trace For CustomerDB.

4. You can store traces as they are being created by selecting the Save To File or the Save To Table check box, or use both of these options. You can store a running trace later by selecting File, Save As, and then choosing either the Trace File option or the Trace Table option.

BEST PRACTICES There are advantages and disadvantages to using trace files and trace tables. You can use trace files to store traces quickly and efficiently using minimal system resources. Trace tables make it easy to store a trace directly in a table on another server, but you use much more of the system's resources and usually have slower response times. Also, storing a trace saves only the trace data. It does not save the trace definition. To reuse the trace definition, you have to export the trace definition.

5. SQL Server Profiler templates are used to save trace definitions that contain the events, data columns, and filters used in a trace. The Use The Template list lets you to choose a template to use as the basis of the trace. Select the TSQL_Replay template if you want to replay the trace.

NOTE SQL Server Profiler templates end with the .tdf file extension.

6. Click the Events Selection tab, shown in Figure 12-10. The currently selected template determines the events that are selected for tracking by default. The best way to learn the types of events you can trace is to select each event or event class and read its description at the bottom of the Events Selection tab. Move the pointer to a specific column to see details about that data column.

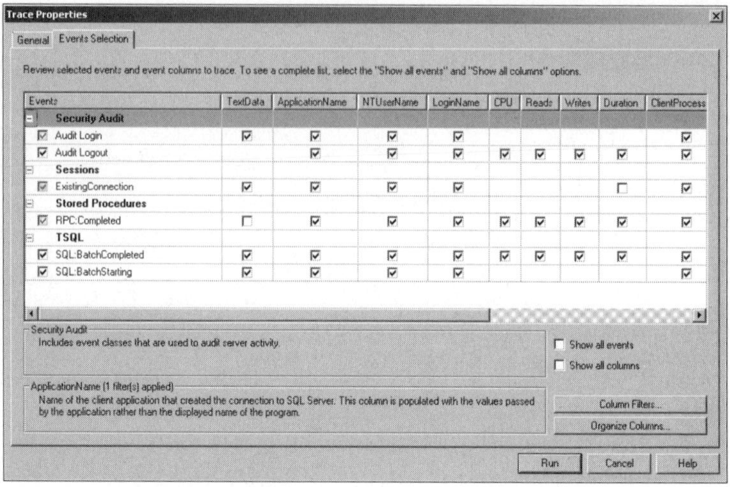

Events	TextData	ApplicationName	NTUserName	LoginName	CPU	Reads	Writes	Duration	ClientProcess
Security Audit									
Audit Login	☑	☑	☑	☑					☑
Audit Logout		☑	☑	☑	☑	☑	☑	☑	☑
Sessions									
ExistingConnection	☑	☑	☑	☑				☐	☑
Stored Procedures									
RPC:Completed	☐	☑	☑	☑	☑	☑	☑	☑	☑
TSQL									
SQL:BatchCompleted	☑	☑	☑	☑	☑	☑	☑	☑	☑
SQL:BatchStarting	☑	☑	☑	☑					☑

Security Audit
Includes event classes that are used to audit server activity.

☐ Show all events
☐ Show all columns

ApplicationName (1 filter(s) applied)
Name of the client application that created the connection to SQL Server. This column is populated with the values passed by the application rather than the displayed name of the program.

Column Filters...
Organize Columns...

[Run] [Cancel] [Help]

FIGURE 12-10 Select events to trace.

7. Only a subset of traceable events and event classes is displayed by default. To see all event classes available, select the Show All Events check box. The event classes that can be traced include Broker, CLR, Cursors, Database, Deprecation, Errors And Warnings, Full Text, Locks, OLEDB, Objects, Performance, Progress Report, Query Notifications, Scale Out Cluster, Scans, Security Audit, Server, Sessions, Stored Procedures, TSQL, Temporary, Transactions, and User Configurable.

8. Only a subset of the traceable data columns is displayed by default. To see all data columns, select the Show All Columns check box.

9. Select event subclasses to add to the trace. If you select a subclass, all data columns for that class are tracked.

10. As necessary, select individual data columns for event subclasses to track specific data columns for an event subclass (versus all data columns for a subclass). At a minimum, you should track the following:

   - Cursors, CursorExecute
   - Cursors, CursorOpen
   - Cursors, CursorPrepare
   - Sessions, ExistingConnection
   - Stored Procedures, RPC:OutputParameter
   - Stored Procedures, RPC:Starting
   - TSQL, Exec Prepared SQL
   - TSQL, Prepare SQL
   - TSQL, SQL:BatchStarting

TIP If you are tracking distributed queries, be sure to add the HostName column that corresponds to the ServerName in the display window. For transactions, be sure to add the TransactionID column. Also, if you plan to replay the trace for troubleshooting, refer to the "Replaying a Trace" section later in this chapter for specific event classes and data columns that you need to select.

11. To focus the trace on specific types of data, you might want to set criteria that exclude certain types of events from being displayed (even though they are still collected). If so, select an event category you want to filter, click the Column Filters button to open the Edit Filter dialog box, and then set filter criteria. For each event category, you can use different filtering criteria. To use the criteria, you click the related plus sign and then enter the appropriate value in the text box provided. When you finish, click OK to close the Edit Filter dialog box. You use the filter criteria as follows:

- **Equals, Not Equal To, Greater Than Or Equal, or Less Than Or Equal** Use these criteria to set the values that trigger the event. Events with values outside the specified range are excluded. For example, with the CPU event category, you can specify that only events using 1,000 milliseconds or more (greater than or equal to) of CPU time are captured. If events use less CPU time than specified, they are excluded.

- **Like or Not Like** Enter strings to include or exclude for this event category. Use the wildcard character (%) to match a series of characters. Use the semicolon (;) to separate multiple strings. For example, you can use the Application Name category to exclude all application names that start with *MS* and *SQL Server* by typing **MS%;SQL Server%**.

12. When you finish configuring the trace, click Run to start the trace.

Working with Traces

Profiler displays information for multiple traces in separate windows that can be cascaded or tiled. Use the buttons on the Profiler toolbar to control your work with traces. Create a new trace by clicking New Trace, and then use the options in the New Trace dialog box to configure the trace. Create a trace template by clicking New Template, setting trace properties, and then clicking Save. Once you have an active trace, you can do the following:

- Start the trace by clicking Start Selected Trace.
- Pause the trace by clicking Pause Selected Trace. You can then use Start Selected Trace to resume the trace at the point at which it was stopped.
- Stop the trace by clicking Stop Selected Trace. If you start the trace again with Start Selected Trace, Profiler displays data again from the beginning of the trace process; new data is appended to the files or tables to which you are capturing data.
- Edit trace properties by clicking Properties.

Use Performance Monitor and SQL Server Profiler together to pinpoint performance issues. By collecting performance data at the same time that you collect trace data, you can play back both captures to see the correlation between various performance issues. For example, you could then correlate specific trace activity to spikes in CPU usage.

Saving a Trace

When you create traces in Profiler, you create trace data and trace definitions. The Profiler window displays trace data, and you can also store it in a file, in a table, or in both. The trace data records a history of events that you are tracking, and you can use this history to replay the events for later analysis. The Trace Properties dialog box displays the trace definition. You can use the trace definition to create a new trace based on the existing trace.

To save trace data, complete the following steps:

1. Access the Profiler window that displays the trace you want to save.
2. Select File, point to Save As, and then select Trace File or Trace Table.
3. Use the Save As dialog box to select a folder location. Type a file name, and then click Save. Trace files end with the .trc extension.

To save a trace definition, complete the following steps:

1. Access the Profiler window that displays the trace with the definition you want to save.
2. Select File, point to Save As, and then select Trace Template.
3. Use the Select Template Name dialog box to select a folder location. Type a file name, and then click OK. Trace templates end with the .tdf extension.

Replaying a Trace

One of the main reasons you create traces is to save them and replay them later. When replaying traces, Profiler can simulate user connections and authentication, which allows you to reproduce the activity recorded in the trace. You can replay traces in different ways to help you troubleshoot different kinds of problems:

- Execute traces step by step to closely monitor each step in the trace.
- Execute traces using the original timeline to simulate user loads.
- Execute traces with a high replay rate to stress-test servers.

As you monitor the trace execution, you can look for problem areas. Then, when you identify the cause of problems you are trying to solve, you can correct them and rerun the original trace definition. If you are still having problems, you need to reanalyze the trace data or look at other areas that might be causing problems. Keep in mind that you might need to specify different events to capture in the subsequent trace.

Requirements for Replaying Traces

Traces that you want to replay must contain a minimum set of events and data columns. If the trace does not contain the necessary elements, you will not be able to replay the trace. The required elements are in addition to any other elements that you want to monitor or display with traces.

> **TIP** If you select the TSQL_Replay template, the required event classes and data classes are enabled for tracing by default. If you select another template, you might need to select the required event classes and data columns manually.

You should capture the following event classes to allow a trace to be replayed and analyzed correctly: Audit Login, Audit Logout, ExistingConnection, RPC Output Parameter, RPC:Completed, RPC:Starting, SQL:BatchCompleted, and SQL:BatchStarting. When you are replaying server-side cursors, you must add CursorClose, CursorExecute, CursorOpen, CursorPrepare, and CursorUnprepare. When you are replaying server-side prepared SQL statements, you must add Exec Prepared SQL and Prepare SQL.

You should capture the following data columns to allow a trace to be replayed and analyzed correctly: ApplicationName, BinaryData, ClientProcessID, DatabaseID, DatabaseName, EndTime, Error, EventClass, EventSequence, HostName, IsSystem, LoginName, NTDomainName, NTUserName, ServerName, SPID, StartTime, and TextData.

Replaying Traces on a Different Server

You can replay a trace on a server other than the server originally traced. When you replay a trace on another server, this server is called the *target system*. To replay traces on the target, you should ensure that all logins contained in the trace meet the following criteria:

- They are created on the target system and are in the same database as the source system.
- They have the same permissions they had originally.
- They have the same passwords they had originally.
- They are set to use a default database that matches the database on the source system.

If these settings are not the same, you will see errors, but the replay operation will continue. Also, database IDs on the target system must be the same as those on the source system. The easiest way to set up databases on the target is to complete the following steps:

1. Back up the *master* database on the source and any user databases used in the trace.
2. Restore the databases on the target as explained in the "Restoring a Database to a Different Location" section in Chapter 11, "SQL Server 2012 Backup and Recovery."

Replaying and Analyzing a Trace

Replaying a trace allows you to analyze problems. To begin, start Profiler, and then select the Open Trace File or Open Trace Table option, as appropriate for the type of trace you want to replay. After you select the trace to replay, the trace is then loaded into the Profiler window. Events and commands recorded in the trace are summarized in the Profiler window, as shown in Figure 12-11. You can select an entry to see an expanded list of commands executed.

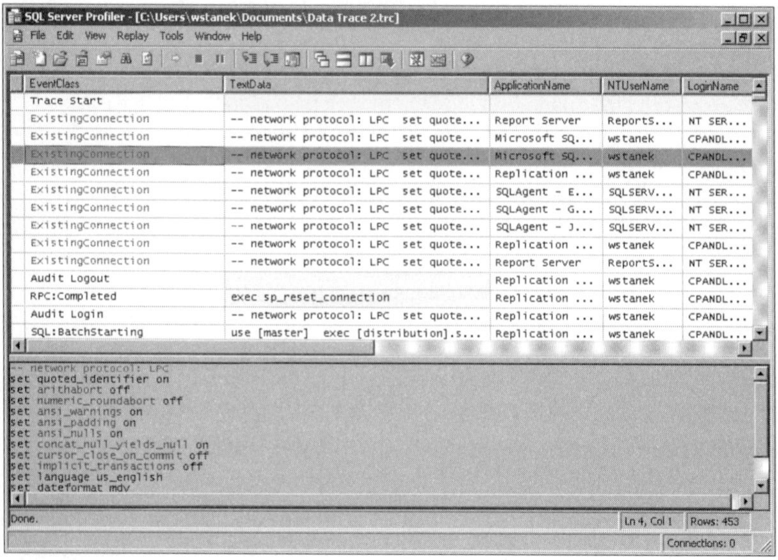

FIGURE 12-11 The Profiler window.

As Figure 12-11 also shows, the toolbar in the replay window differs from the standard toolbar. The buttons provide just about everything that you need to debug traces, including the following:

- **Start Replay**   Starts executing the trace
- **Pause Replay**   Pauses execution of the trace
- **Stop Replay**   Stops execution of the trace
- **Execute One Step**   Allows you to move through the trace one step at a time
- **Run To Cursor**   Allows you to move through the trace using cursor sets
- **Toggle Breakpoint**   Allows you to set breakpoints for the trace execution

When you start the replay, you need to connect to the server, and then the initial dialog box is displayed to configure replay options. (See Figure 12-12.) You configure the options in the Replay Configuration dialog box to control where and how the playback takes place. Start by setting the destination server for the replay operation. By default, the replay server is set to the current (local) server. Click Change to use a different replay server, and then set the replay options.

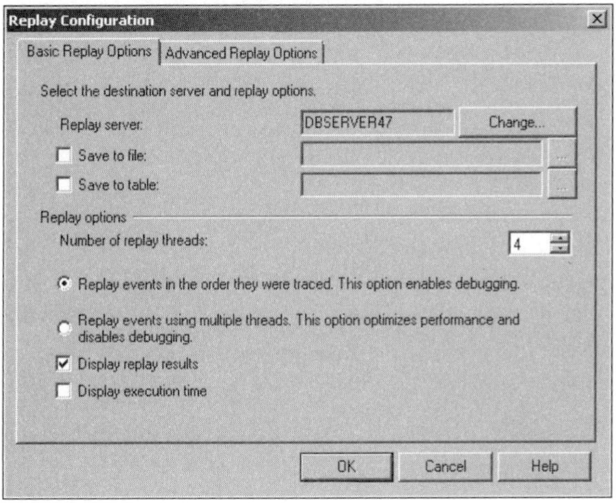

FIGURE 12-12 The Replay Configuration dialog box.

The replay options determine how closely the replay mirrors the original event execution. You can choose from the following options in the dialog box:

- **Replay Events In The Order They Were Traced** Events are started in the order in which they originally started. This enables debugging, but it does not guarantee timing of event execution. Events might be executed sooner than their original start time or after their original start time, depending on current activity levels, the current speed of connections, and other factors.
- **Replay Events Using Multiple Threads** Events are replayed as quickly as they can be processed. No timing is maintained between events. When one event completes, the next event is started. This optimizes performance and disables debugging.

The Display Replay Results check box controls whether the replay results are displayed in the Profiler window. To display results, select this option. To hide results, clear this option.

You can also select an output file to which to save the result of the replay for later viewing. The output file allows you to review the replay just as you would any other trace file.

Index

Index Symbols and Numbers

- (hyphen), 32
$PARTITION function, 395–396
% (wildcard character), 529
.sql file, 337
/ (slash), 32
; (semicolon), 529
< (less than), 97
<= (less than or equal to), 97
> (greater than), 96
>= (greater than or equal to), 96

A

abbreviations, collation style, 210
access
    data, 182
    database
        authentication for, 263–264
        by login, 295–297
        controlling, 291–292
        granting or denying, 284–285
        scoping, 315
    remote
        administration through, 199
        configuring PowerShell for, 23–25
    server, 6, 43
    surface area, 43–49
    user
        authentication for, 263
        controlling, 225
        granting/denying, 284–285
        tracking, 153
access permissions, 66–67, 290, 300
accessing
    alerts, 413
    built-in query client, 123–124
    configuration properties, 138–140
    data, 112
    event logs, 504
    event logs in text editors, 513
    jobs, 413
    maintenance history, 447
    monitoring logs, 504
    Object Explorer views, 5
    operators, 413
    queries, 112
    resources, in SQL Server Agent, 413
accounts
    built-in, 69
    creating, 64–65
    dbo user, 265, 267, 274–275, 302
    domain. See domain accounts
    login, 266
    managed service, 63–65
    startup, 63, 69, 265
    user. See user accounts
    virtual, 63, 66
Active File view, 326
ActiveX scripts, 82, 425
Activity Monitor, 33–34, 41, 503
ad hoc connections, 44, 47
ad hoc policy evaluation, 79–80
ad hoc reports, 49
Add Table dialog
    box, 355–358
adding
    columns, 337
    counters, 516
    linked servers, 180–183
    login names, 92
    logins, to query results, 92
    mail profiles, 411
    media sets, 475
    publisher groups and publishers,
        507–508
    SQL Servers to server groups, 12
    startup parameters, 28–29
    to existing backup sets, 473–475
Address Windowing Extensions (AWE),
        159–160
administration
    database, 198–199, 291–292
    multiserver administration, 438
    Policy-Based Management, 80–81
    remote access, 199
    utility, 145–146
administrator user accounts, 265

About the Author

WILLIAM R. STANEK (*http://www.williamstanek.com/*) has more than 20 years of hands-on experience with advanced programming and development. He is a leading technology expert, an award-winning author, and a pretty-darn-good instructional trainer. Over the years, his practical advice has helped millions of programmers, developers, and network engineers all over the world. His current and forthcoming books include *Windows 7 Pocket Consultant* and *Windows PowerShell 2.0 Pocket Consultant*.

William has been involved in the commercial Internet community since 1991. His core business and technology experience comes from more than 11 years of military service. He has substantial experience in developing server technology, encryption, and Internet solutions. He has written many technical white papers and training courses on a wide variety of topics. He frequently serves as a subject matter expert and consultant.

William has a BS in computer science, magna cum laude, and an MS with distinction in information systems. He is proud to have served in the Persian Gulf War as a combat crew member on an electronic warfare aircraft. He flew on numerous combat missions into Iraq and was awarded nine medals for his wartime service, including one of the United States of America's highest flying honors, the Air Force Distinguished Flying Cross. Currently, he resides in the Pacific Northwest with his wife and children.

William recently rediscovered his love of the great outdoors. When he's not writing, he can be found hiking, biking, backpacking, traveling, or trekking in search of adventure with his family!

Find William on Facebook at *http://www.facebook.com/William.Stanek.Author.* Follow William on Twitter at *http://twitter.com/WilliamStanek.*

About the Technical Reviewer

boB Taylor is a principal premier field engineer at Microsoft. boB's career in IT started more than 39 years ago, programming FORTRAN on punch cards (and he has written assembly language programs on a drum-based computer). He understands the entire development life cycle, having been a line-of-business programmer, a manager and vice president of software engineering, and a director of database technologies. boB started working with SQL Server on version 4.2.1a in the early 1990s. boB holds many industry certifications including Microsoft Certified Architect (2005/2008), Microsoft Certified Master (2005/2008), MCITP, MCSD.NET, MCT, and MCSE. boB has participated in the development of more than 10 different Microsoft Certified Professional certification exams. You can find boB's blog at *http://blogs.msdn.com/boBTaylor*.

The unique spelling of boB's first name comes from the fact that he is a magician (*http://www.majikbybob.com*) and mentalist (*http://www.classicclairvoyant.com*) —the only thing he has done longer than software development.

Windows Server 2008—
Resources for Administrators

**Windows Server® 2008
Administrator's Companion**

Charlie Russel and
Sharon Crawford

ISBN 9780735625051

Your comprehensive, one-volume guide to
deployment, administration, and support. Delve
into core system capabilities and administration
topics, including Active Directory®, security issues,
disaster planning/recovery, interoperability, IIS 7.0,
virtualization, clustering, and performance tuning.

**Windows Server 2008
Administrator's
Pocket Consultant,
Second Edition**

William R. Stanek

ISBN 9780735627116

Portable and precise—with the focused
information you need for administering server
roles, Active Directory, user/group accounts,
rights and permissions, file-system management,
TCP/IP, DHCP, DNS, printers, network performance,
backup, and restoration.

**Windows Server 2008
Resource Kit**

Microsoft MVPs with
Microsoft Windows
Server Team

ISBN 9780735623613

Six volumes! Your definitive resource for deployment
and operations—from the experts who know the
technology best. Get in-depth technical information
on Active Directory, Windows PowerShell® scripting,
advanced administration, networking and network
access protection, security administration, IIS, and
more—plus an essential toolkit of resources on CD.

**Internet Information
Services (IIS) 7.0
Administrator's
Pocket Consultant**

William R. Stanek

ISBN 9780735623644

This pocket-sized guide delivers immediate answers
for administering IIS 7.0. Topics include custom-
izing installation; configuration and XML schema;
application management; user access and security;
Web sites, directories, and content; and performance,
backup, and recovery.

**Windows PowerShell 2.0
Administrator's
Pocket Consultant**

William R. Stanek

ISBN 9780735625952

The practical, portable guide to using cmdlets and
scripts to automate everyday system administration—
including configuring server roles, services, features,
and security settings; managing TCP/IP networking;
monitoring and tuning performance; and other
essential tasks.

ALSO SEE

**Windows PowerShell 2.0
Best Practices**

ISBN 9780735626461

**Windows® Administration
Resource Kit:
Productivity Solutions
for IT Professionals**

ISBN 9780735624313

**Windows Server 2008
Hyper-V™
Resource Kit**

ISBN 9780735625174

**Windows Server 2008
Security Resource Kit**

ISBN 9780735625044

*Microsoft®
Press*

microsoft.com/mspress

Get Certified—Windows Server 2008

Ace your preparation for the skills measured by the Microsoft® certification exams—and on the job. With 2-in-1 *Self-Paced Training Kits*, you get an official exam-prep guide + practice tests. Work at your own pace through lessons and real-world case scenarios that cover the exam objectives. Then, assess your skills using practice tests with multiple testing modes—and get a customized learning plan based on your results.

EXAMS 70-640, 70-642, 70-646

MCITP Self-Paced Training Kit: Windows Server® 2008 Server Administrator Core Requirements

ISBN 9780735625082

EXAMS 70-640, 70-642, 70-643, 70-647

MCITP Self-Paced Training Kit: Windows Server 2008 Enterprise Administrator Core Requirements

ISBN 9780735625723

EXAM 70-640

MCTS Self-Paced Training Kit: Configuring Windows Server 2008 Active Directory®, *Second Edition*

Dan Holme, Nelson Ruest, Danielle Ruest, and Jason Kellington

ISBN 9780735651937

EXAM 70-647

MCITP Self-Paced Training Kit: Windows Server 2008 Enterprise Administrator, *Second Edition*

John Policelli, et al.

ISBN 9780735656659

EXAM 70-642

MCTS Self-Paced Training Kit: Configuring Windows Server 2008 Network Infrastructure, *Second Edition*

Tony Northrup, J.C. Mackin

ISBN 9780735651609

ALSO SEE

Windows Server 2008, Administrator's Pocket Consultant, Second Edition
ISBN 9780735627116

EXAM 70-643

MCTS Self-Paced Training Kit: Configuring Windows Server 2008 Applications Infrastructure, *Second Edition*

J.C. Mackin

ISBN 9780735648784

Windows Server 2008 Administrator's Companion
ISBN 9780735625051

Windows Server 2008 Resource Kit
ISBN 9780735623613

EXAM 70-646

MCITP Self-Paced Training Kit: Windows Server 2008 Server Administrator, *Second Edition*

Orin Thomas, Ian McLean

ISBN 9780735649095

Get Certified—Windows 7

Desktop support technicians and administrators—demonstrate your expertise with Windows 7 by earning a Microsoft® Certification focusing on core technical (MCTS) or professional (MCITP) skills. With our 2-in-1 *Self-Paced Training Kits*, you get a comprehensive, cost-effective way to prepare for the certification exams. Combining official exam-prep guides + practice tests, these kits are designed to maximize the impact of your study time.

EXAM 70-680
MCTS Self-Paced
Training Kit:
Configuring
Windows 7

Ian McLean and Orin Thomas
ISBN 9780735627086

EXAM 70-685
MCITP Self-Paced
Training Kit:
Windows 7
Enterprise Desktop
Support Technician

Tony Northrup and J.C. Mackin
ISBN 9780735627093

EXAM 70-686
MCITP Self-Paced
Training Kit:
Windows 7 Enterprise
Desktop Administrator

Craig Zacker and Orin Thomas
ISBN 9780735627178

Great for on the job

Windows 7
Resource Kit

Mitch Tulloch, Tony Northrup,
Jerry Honeycutt, Ed Wilson,
and the Windows 7 Team
at Microsoft
ISBN 9780735627000

Windows 7
Inside Out,
Deluxe Edition

Ed Bott, Carl Siechert,
Craig Stinson
ISBN 9780735656925

Windows 7
Administrator's
Pocket Consultant

William R. Stanek
ISBN 9780735626997

microsoft.com/mspress

What do you think of this book?

We want to hear from you!

To participate in a brief online survey, please visit:

microsoft.com/learning/booksurvey

Tell us how well this book meets your needs—what works effectively, and what we can do better. Your feedback will help us continually improve our books and learning resources for you.

Thank you in advance for your input!